Venture Capital in Europe

Quantitative Finance Series

Aims and Objectives

- Books based on the work of financial market practitioners and academics
- Presenting cutting-edge research to the professional/practitioner market
- Combining intellectual rigour and practical application
- Covering the interaction between mathematical theory and financial practice
- To improve portfolio performance, risk management and trading book performance
- Covering quantitative techniques

Market

Brokers/Traders; Actuaries; Consultants; Asset Managers; Fund Managers; Regulators; Central Bankers; Treasury Officials; Technical Analysts; and Academics for Masters in Finance and MBA market.

Series Titles

Return Distributions in Finance
Derivative Instruments: theory, valuation, analysis
Managing Downside Risk in Financial Markets: theory, practice & implementation
Economics for Financial Markets
Performance Measurement in Finance: firms, funds and managers
Real R&D Options
Forecasting Volatility in the Financial Markets, Second edition
Advanced Trading Rules, Second edition
Advances in Portfolio Construction and Implementation
Computational Finance
Linear Factor Models in Finance
Initial Public Offerings: an international perspective
Venture Capital in Europe

Series Editor

Dr Stephen Satchell

Dr Satchell is the Reader in Financial Econometrics at Trinity College, Cambridge; Visiting Professor at Birkbeck College, City University Business School and University of Technology, Sydney. He also works in a consultative capacity to many firms, and edits the journal *Derivatives: use, trading and regulations* and the *Journal of Asset Management.*

Venture Capital in Europe

Edited by

Greg N. Gregoriou
Maher Kooli
Roman Kraeussl

ELSEVIER

AMSTERDAM • BOSTON • HEIDELBERG • LONDON • NEW YORK • OXFORD
PARIS • SAN DIEGO • SAN FRANCISCO • SINGAPORE • SYDNEY • TOKYO
Butterworth-Heinemann is an imprint of Elsevier

Butterworth-Heinemann is an imprint of Elsevier
Linacre House, Jordan Hill, Oxford OX2 8DP, UK
30 Corporate Drive, Suite 400, Burlington, MA 01803, USA

First edition 2007

British Library Cataloguing in Publication Data
A catalogue record for this book is available from the British Library

Library of Congress Cataloging-in-Publication Data
A catalogue record for this book is available from the Library of Congress

ISBN–13: 978-0-7506-8259-6
ISBN–10: 0-7506-8259-0

Printed and bound in Great Britain

07 08 09 10 11 10 9 8 7 6 5 4 3 2 1

Contents

Foreword

During the 1980s and 1990s, there was a tremendous boom in the American venture capital industry. The pool of U.S. venture funds – partnerships specializing in early stage equity or equity-linked investments in young or growing firms – has grown from just over US$1 billion in 1980 to about US$160 billion at the end of 2005. Despite the pattern of boom-and-bust that has characterized the sector – the rapid increases in fundraising in the late 1960s, mid-1980s, and late 1990s were followed by precipitous declines in the 1970s, early 1990s, and early 2000s – the American venture industry today is far more developed and mature than it was in earlier decades.

In recent years, this growth has extended outside the U.S.: Israel, India, and China are just three examples of nations that have experienced a dramatic surge in venture investment. In part, the capital has been provided by home-grown groups, but affiliates or branch offices of U.S.-based groups are playing an increasingly important role.

Much of this growth seems to have by-passed Europe. European venture capital funds have long been overshadowed by the funds specializing in buy-outs and other later-stage transactions: not only have the level of such activities been far lower than elsewhere but so have the returns. While there was a brief surge of European venture capital activity in the late 1990s, it proved short-lived and many of the new entrants collapsed early in this decade. Many of the policy initiatives of that era, such as the creation of the pan-European EASDAQ market for young growth companies, have been written off as failures.

The small size and very modest success of the European venture capital industry is troubling because considerable evidence has emerged that venture capitalists play an important role in encouraging innovation. The types of firms that these organizations finance – whether young start-ups hungry for capital or middle-aged firms that need capital to grow – pose numerous problems and uncertainties that discourage other investors.

To be sure, the financing of entrepreneurial firms is a risky business. Uncertainty and informational gaps often characterize these firms, particularly in high-technology industries. These information problems make it difficult to assess these firms, and permit opportunistic behavior by entrepreneurs after the financing is received. To address these information problems, venture investors employ a variety of mechanisms, which seem to be critical in boosting innovation. A considerable body of evidence suggests that the early participation of venture firms – including their guidance, monitoring, shaping of management teams and boards, networking, and credibility – helps innovators successfully nurture start-ups and sustain their success long after their company goes public.

Thus, the state of the European venture capital market is an important public policy issue. This collection of essays will help scholars, investors, and academics better understand the challenges faced by the European venture industry and – hopefully – suggest steps that can address some of these problems.

Josh Lerner
Jacob H. Schiff Professor of Investment Banking
Harvard Business School

Preface

After looking for information on European venture capital we noticed that there was not enough literature in this area and strongly believed an edited book on the subject was warranted. The articles exclusive to this book represent the latest cutting-edge research that examines venture capital in Europe.

Acknowledgments

We would like to thank Karen Maloney, publishing editor at Elsevier, for her support throughout the entire process; and Dennis McGonagle, assistant editor at Elsevier. We would also like to thank the copyeditor, Sue Thomas, as well as the handful of anonymous referees of the selection of papers for inclusion in this book.

About the Editors

Greg N. Gregoriou is Associate Professor of Finance and coordinator of faculty research in the School of Business and Economics at the State University of New York (Plattsburgh). He obtained his Ph.D. (Finance) from the University of Quebec at Montreal, which is part of the joint Doctoral Program in Administration that merges the resources of Montreal's four major universities (McGill, Concordia, and HEC). He is hedge fund editor and editorial board member for the peer-reviewed scientific journal *Derivatives Use, Trading and Regulation* published by Palgrave-MacMillan in London. He has authored over 50 articles on hedge funds and managed futures in various U.S. and U.K. peer-reviewed publications, including the *Journal of Portfolio Management, Journal of Futures Markets, European Journal of Operational Research, Annals of Operations Research, European Journal of Finance, Journal of Asset Management*, and *Journal of Derivatives Accounting*, etc. This is his fourth edited book with Elsevier and his latest book is entitled *Initial Public Offerings: An International Perspective.*

Maher Kooli is Assistant Professor of Finance at the School of Business and Management, University of Quebec in Montreal (UQAM). He holds a Ph.D. in Finance from Laval University (Quebec) and was a postdoctoral researcher in finance at the Center of Interuniversity Research and Analysis on Organisations. Maher also worked as a Senior Research Advisor for la Caisse de Depot et Placement de Quebec (CDP Capital). He has published articles in a wide variety of books and journals including the *Journal of Multinational and Financial Management*, the *Financial Management, The Journal of Private Equity*, the *Canadian Investment Review, Derivatives Use and Trading Regulations, FINECO*, and *Gestion*. He has co-authored a book entitled *Principes de Gestion financiere, Gaëtan Morin edition*. His current research interests include alternative investments, initial public offerings, and mergers and acquisitions.

Roman Kraeussl obtained a first-class honours Masters in Economics with a specialization in Financial Econometrics at the University of Bielefeld, Germany, in 1998. He completed his Ph.D. in Financial Economics on the Role of Credit Rating Agencies in International Financial Markets at Johann Wolfgang Goethe-University, Frankfurt/Main, Germany, in 2002. As the Head of Quantitative Research at Cognitrend GmbH, he was closely involved with the financial industry. Currently he is Assistant Professor of Finance at the Free University of Amsterdam and research fellow with the Centre for Financial Studies, Frankfurt/Main. He is a specialist on venture capital and private equity and has written numerous papers on these topics. Roman is also a Research Fellow at the Center for Financial Studies in Frankfurt/Main.

List of Contributors

Luisa Alemany holds a B.Sc. in Economics and Business Administration from the Complutense University of Madrid, an M.B.A. from Stanford (U.S.A.) and a Ph.D. in Corporate Finance from Complutense University of Madrid. She has gained professional experience in consulting with McKinsey & Co, in finance with Goldman Sachs, and in venture capital with The Carlyle Group. She is currently part of the Finance faculty at ESADE Business School (Barcelona, Spain). Her main research interests are venture capital, valuation of start-ups and companies in general, entrepreneurship, and corporate finance.

Paul U. Ali is an Associate Professor in the Faculty of Law, University of Melbourne and a Visiting Associate Professor in the Faculty of Law, National University of Singapore. Paul was previously a finance lawyer in Sydney. Paul has published several books and journal articles on finance and investment law, including, most recently, *Opportunities in Credit Derivatives and Synthetic Securitisation* (London, 2005) and articles in *Derivatives Use, Trading and Regulation, Journal of Alternative Investments, Journal of Banking Regulation*, and *Journal of International Banking Law and Regulation.*

Ron C. Antonczyk is assistant at the chair of Finance at RWTH Aachen University, Germany's leading Technical University. In 2003 he received his diploma in Business Studies at Humboldt University, Berlin. He has written a textbook on the basics of corporate finance. His research interests include corporate finance and particularly venture capital.

Marina Balboa is Associate Professor of Economics at the University of Alicante, Spain. She has a Ph.D. in Business Administration (Finance) from the University of Alicante. She has published in several international as well as Spanish journals. Her research areas are venture capital, private equity, and corporate finance.

Andreas Bascha joined the German Central Bank in 2002, after he received his Diploma and Ph.D. in Economics from the University of Mannheim and University of Tübingen, in 1996 and 2001, respectively. From 1996 to 2001 he was research and teaching assistant at the University of Bochum and the University of Tübingen. He received a prize from Ernst & Young Stiftung E.V., Stuttgart for his Ph.D. dissertation. His area of specialization is contract theory, and his recent research interests include venture capital, financial intermediation, and banking supervision, especially Basel II. He is currently working in a senior position at the Department of Banking Supervision and Bank Examinations at the German Central Bank, Regional Office in Mainz, Germany.

Véronique Bastin is a Ph.D. student at HEC Management School – University of Liège, Belgium. She has been F.N.R.S. (Belgian National Fund for Scientific Research) Research Fellow at the Research Center for Management of Bio-Industries at the University of Liège. She holds a Masters Degree in Management from the School of Business Administration of the University of Liège. She also studied for one year at Maastricht University, and visited the University of Quebec at Montreal for three months. She is currently finalizing her thesis, which deals with the financial management of biotechnology firms. She has written several papers related to investment and financing policy in the bio-industry and has presented some of them at international finance conferences in Canada and Europe.

Fabio Bertoni is a researcher at the Department of Management, Economics and Industrial Engineering at the Politecnico di Milano. His research activity is in the field of corporate finance. His research interests include venture capital and corporate governance.

Christof Beuselinck is Assistant Professor of Accounting at Tilburg University and research fellow of CENTer. He holds a doctoral degree from Ghent University and was a Marie Curie research fellow at Manchester University. Christof has a specialization in financial reporting of SMEs and VC-backed firms and has written several working papers on the financial reporting characteristics of VC-backed firms, which are currently under review in international peer-reviewed journals.

Robin Boadway is Sir Edward Peacock Professor of Economic Theory at Queen's University and a Fellow of CESifo and the Institute of Intergovernmental Relations. He studied at RMC, Oxford and Queen's and has been a visiting scholar at the Universities of Chicago, Oxford, and Louvain. He has served in the past as President of the Canadian Economics Association and Head of the Department of Economics at Queen's. He has been editor of the *Canadian Journal of Economics* and the *German Economic Review*, and is currently editor of the *Journal of Public Economics*. His research work is in the broad area of public sector economics, with special emphasis on fiscal federalism, tax policy, social policy, and cost–benefit analysis. He has been involved in projects for various organizations including the World Bank, the International Monetary Fund, the Canadian Tax Foundation, the Canadian International Development Agency, the Forum of Federations, the United Nations University, and governments in a number of countries.

Wolfgang Breuer is full professor of Finance at the RWTH Aachen University, Germany's leading Technical University. From October 1995 to February 2000 he was a full Professor of Finance at the University of Bonn. He earned his Ph.D. degree in February 1993 and his postdoctoral degree in July 1995, both at the University of Cologne. After his diploma in 1989 he worked for one year in Frankfurt as a consultant at McKinsey & Co., Inc., before continuing his academic career. Wolfgang Breuer has written about a dozen books, more than 30 articles in books, and numerous peer-reviewed journal articles comprising a great variety of topics in the field of finance. His current research interests focus on portfolio management, international financial management, and corporate finance.

Martin Brixner has been a research assistant at the Center for Entrepreneurial and Financial Studies (CEFS) at the Technische Universität München (TUM), Germany, since 2003. Previously, he graduated at the European Business School – International University

Schloß Reichartshausen (ebs), Oestrich-Winkel, Germany, in business administration. His course of studies comprised semesters at the Sorbonne University, Paris, France, and the San Francisco State University. He majored in finance and business information technology. His research at CEFS focuses on business venture financing, mezzanine financing, and corporate pension schemes.

Hans Bruining is Associate Professor in the Department of Strategy and Business Environment at RSM Erasmus University Rotterdam, The Netherlands. He is senior lecturer in Strategy, Entrepreneurship, and Management Control. His research interests include management buy-outs, strategic renewal, corporate entrepreneurship, corporate governance, private equity, and venture capital. He undertook the first major study of management buy-outs in The Netherlands and received his Ph.D. in 1992 from Erasmus University Rotterdam.

Rachel A. Campbell completed her Ph.D. on Risk Management in International Financial Markets at Erasmus University, Rotterdam in 2001. She currently works at the University of Maastricht as an Assistant Professor of Finance. Her work has been published in a number of leading journals, including the *Journal of International Money and Finance, Journal of Banking and Finance, Financial Analysts Journal, Journal of Portfolio Management, Journal of Risk*, and *Derivatives Weekly*.

Stefano Caselli is associate professor in corporate finance at Bocconi University. He has written many academic papers and books about corporate banking, financing of SMEs, private equity and venture capital, and the new Basle Accord. He is co-editor with Stefano Gatti of the book *Venture Capital: A Euro-System Approach* (Springer, 2003). He is also academic director of Master in International Management CEMS at Bocconi University and Director of the Executive Master in Banking and Finance at SDA Bocconi. He is a member of the board of directors of Enter, the Research Center of Entrepreneurship of Bocconi University.

Massimo G. Colombo is full Professor of Economics of Technical Change at the Department of Economics and Industrial Engineering of the Politecnico di Milano. His main interests cover industrial economics, economics of innovation, and strategic management.

Annalisa Croce is a Ph.D. student in the Doctoral Program in Management, Economics and Industrial Engineering at the Politecnico di Milano. Her scientific activity is mainly in corporate finance. Her areas of research include venture capital and equity valuation.

Stefano Gatti is associate professor in corporate finance at Bocconi University. He has written many academic papers and books about corporate finance, project finance, private equity and venture capital, and company valuation. He is co-editor with Stefano Caselli of the book *Venture Capital: A Euro-System Approach* (Springer, 2003). He is also academic director of the degree in economic and finance at Bocconi University. He is a member of the board of directors of DIR, the research division of SDA Bocconi, and he is a member of the board of directors of the Ph.D. in Finance of Bocconi University.

Michael Halperin is the Director of the Lippincott Library and the Safra Business Research Center of the Wharton School, University of Pennsylvania. He is the author of two books and numerous articles on business research techniques and related authorship on empirical market studies. He is the principal designer of the 'Business FAQ', a knowledge database of business research sources currently being shared by eleven major academic business libraries in the U.S.

Arthur Herst is Professor of Finance at the Open University School of Management (OU). He holds an MA in Business Economics from Erasmus University Rotterdam (EUR). His Ph.D. thesis, titled Lease or Purchase, was published in the U.S. Since 1971 he has had (part-time) functions at the EUR, the OU (doing research and developing material for distance teaching in the fields of finance and investment) and Maastricht University (doing research and responsible for investment and other courses). Since 2002 he has concentrated on the OU, exploring the field of behavioral finance.

Teresa Hogan is a lecturer in Entrepreneurship at Dublin City University, and she recently obtained her Ph.D. from University College Dublin. As well as venture capital, Teresa's research interests include the financing of high-technology enterprises, private capital, high-technology entrepreneurship, academic spin-offs, the Irish software industry, and enterprise education. Teresa has published in finance, entrepreneurship, and management journals, including the *Global Finance Journal, Venture Capital: An International Journal of Entrepreneurial Finance*, and the *International Entrepreneurship and Management Journal.*

Georges Hübner (Ph.D., INSEAD) is the Deloitte Professor of Financial Management at HEC Management School – University of Liège, and is Associate Professor of Finance at Maastricht University. He is also a Research Director at the Luxemburg School of Finance, University of Luxemburg, an Affiliate Professor at EDHEC (Lille/Nice), and an Invited Professor at the Solvay Business School (Brussels). He has taught at the executive and postgraduate levels in several countries in Europe, North America, Africa, and Asia. Georges Hübner has published numerous research articles about credit risk, hedge funds, and derivatives in leading scientific journals and books. He was the recipient of the prestigious 2002 Iddo Sarnat Award for the best paper published in the *Journal of Banking and Finance* in 2001. He is also the inventor of the Generalized Treynor Ratio, a simple performance measure for managed portfolios.

Elaine Hutson holds a Ph.D. in finance from the University of Technology, Sydney, where she worked as a lecturer in finance for 9 years. After submitting her thesis in 1999, she moved to Dublin and is now a lecturer in the School of Banking and Finance at University College Dublin. She has published over 20 articles in a wide variety of books and journals including the *Journal of Empirical Finance*, the *Journal of International Financial Markets, Institutions and Money*, the *International Review of Financial Analysis* and the *Journal of the Asia Pacific Economy*. Elaine's research interests include mergers and acquisitions, the performance, regulation and history of managed funds, international risk management, and asymmetry in financial returns.

Nancy Huyghebaert is Associate Professor of Finance at K.U. Leuven (Belgium), where she obtained her Ph.D. in December 2000. Her work has been published in *Strategic Management Journal, Journal of Corporate Finance, European Financial Management, Journal of Business Finance and Accounting*, and *Tijdschrift voor Economie en Management*. Her current research interests are in corporate finance. She studies the financial structure, the performance, and survival of entrepreneurial firms, with a special interest in the interactions with product-market characteristics. She also examines initial public offerings, privatizations, and mergers and acquisitions.

Anders Isaksson is a Lecturer at the Umeå School of Business and Economics in Umeå, Sweden. His research mainly focuses on small business finance, with a special emphasis on the venture capital process and the relationship between venture capital firms and entrepreneurs. His professional experience includes working as a special advisor on venture capital issues for the Swedish Ministry of Industry, where he acted as a strategic advisor to the minister, representing the government in professional councils and working closely with central authorities. He has published several research papers, textbooks and consultancy reports.

Dieter G. Kaiser is responsible for the institutional research of Benchmark Alternative Strategies in Frankfurt, Germany (since March 2003). He started his professional career in the structured products sector at Dresdner Kleinwort Wasserstein in Frankfurt, Germany. Afterwards he joined Crédit Agricole Asset Management in Frankfurt where he was then responsible for the fund-of-hedge-funds Marketing Support within the Institutional Sales & Marketing division. Dieter G. Kaiser has written several articles on the subject of alternative Investments. He is the author of the German books *Hedge Funds – Demystification of an Investment Class – Structures, Opportunities, Risks* (Gabler, 2004) and *Alternative Investment Strategies – Insights into the Investment Techniques of the Hedge Fund Managers* (Wiley, 2005). He is also co-editor of the *Handbook of Alternative Investments* (Gabler, 2006). Dieter G. Kaiser holds a Diploma in Technical Business Administration from the University of Applied Sciences in Offenburg and a Master of Arts (M.A.) in Banking and Finance from the HfB – Business School of Finance and Management in Frankfurt.

Christoph Kaserer is full professor of financial management at the Munich University of Technology (Technische Universität München, TUM), Germany, and co-director of the Center for Entrepreneurial and Financial Studies (CEFS) at TUM. Since October 2005 he is also dean of TUM business school. He has published research in leading international and German academic journals. Moreover, he is the editor of the *Zeitschrift für Bankrecht und Bankwirtschaft*, a leading German academic journal in the field of finance and law. An active advisor of large private companies and public institutions, he worked as a consultant for the German and the Swiss governments as well as for the European Venture Capital Association (EVCA). Before joining TUM business school, he became full professor of financial management and accounting at Université de Fribourg, Switzerland, in 1999. After graduating in economics at the University of Vienna, Austria, he was appointed research assistant at the department of banking and finance at the University of Würzburg, Germany, where he also earned his qualification as a university lecturer (Habilitation) in 1998.

Andreas Kemmerer is the author of several research articles on the private equity industry. He is currently working on his Ph.D. thesis at the Centre for Financial Studies, University of Frankfurt under the supervision of Professor Wahrenburg. He holds a Master Diploma in Finance from the University of Frankfurt and worked for Haarman & Hemmelrath as an associate in corporate finance and audit. He also had internships at Dresdner and Direct Funding Inc., a mortgage company based in Florida.

Philipp Krohmer completed his masters studies of business administration at the University of Mannheim, Germany, Ècole de Management, Lyon, France and Universidad Autónoma de Barcelona, Spain with a focus on finance and statistics. He is currently finishing his Ph.D. thesis at the Johann Wolfgang Goethe University, Frankfurt/Main, Germany within the research-project 'Venture Capital and the New Markets in Europe', in collaboration with the Center for Financial Studies (CFS). His research and publishing activities focus on performance determinants and investment patterns of closed-end private equity and venture capital funds. He joined CEPRES in 2002 and is as senior consultant responsible for the data center and the initiation and execution of consulting projects. Before joining CEPRES, he worked at HeidelbergCement and Andersen Consulting S.A. (Barcelona).

Rainer Lauterbach is head of the Private Equity department of Harald Quandt Holding. He joined Harald Quandt Holding in the year 2000 after graduation from the Wharton MBA Program. His major in Entrepreneurial Management prepared him well to build a portfolio of venture capital direct investments as CEO of QVentures, an affiliate of Harald Quandt Holding. Parallel to running QVentures, he is responsible for private equity and venture capital fund investments nationally and internationally for Harald Quandt Holding. Before Wharton, he was employed by IBM from 1991 until 1997 in the areas of software and business development in Germany, the U.S. and the U.K. Rainer Lauterbach is enrolled in the external Ph.D. program in Entrepreneurial Finance at the Goethe University in Frankfurt, Germany, with the research focus on risk and performance aspects of venture capital and private equity investments.

Edward J. Lusk is Professor of Accounting at the State University of New York, College of Economics and Business, Plattsburgh, New York, and Emeritus at The Department of Statistics, The Wharton School, The University of Pennsylvania, Philadelphia. As a professor at the Otto-von-Guericke University, Magdeburg Germany, he taught the course 'Venture Capital: The Creation of Tomorrow' in the Master's program for five years.

Tadeusz Lutoborski is a corporate finance advisor and specializes in private equity financing and M&A and is based in Frankfurt. He worked in the finance department for an international consumer goods manufacturer, IT-consulting, and M&A-advisory. He holds a Masters Diploma in Finance from the University of Frankfurt.

Sophie Manigart is full professor of finance and entrepreneurship at Ghent University, Belgium and the Vlerick Leuven-Ghent Management School, and is guest professor at the London Business School. Sophie did part of her doctoral studies at the Wharton School of Business of the University of Pennsylvania and is specialized in the area of entrepreneurial financing. Sophie has published several articles on entrepreneurship and venture capital financing in various journals such as *Journal of Business Venturing, Entrepreneurship,*

Theory and Practice, European Financial Management, Small Business Economics, and *Journal of Private Equity.*

Klaus Mark, Ph.D., works as a consultant at an auditing company in Düsseldorf, Germany, in the division for Corporate Finance and Advisory. He earned his Ph.D. degree in Finance at RWTH Aachen University in June 2005. After his diploma in Political Economics at the University of Bonn he worked for five years as a research analyst at RWTH Aachen University in the Department of Finance. In addition to venture capital his research interests include topics in risk management and the evaluation of firms.

José Martí is Senior Associate Professor of Corporate Finance at the Complutense University of Madrid. He has a Ph.D. in Business Administration (Finance) from the Complutense University of Madrid (1984). He has conducted the yearly surveys on private equity in Spain since the mid-1980s. His research areas are entrepreneurship, venture capital, private equity, and buy-outs.

Robert W. McGee is a professor at the Andreas School of Business, Barry University in Miami, Florida. He has published more than 300 articles and more than 40 books in the areas of accounting, taxation, economics, law, and philosophy. His experience includes consulting with the governments of several former Soviet, East European, and Latin American countries to reform their accounting and economic systems.

Pierre-Armand Michel (MBA, Ph.D., Stern School of Business, New York University) is Professor of Investment Analysis at HEC Management School – University of Liège (Belgium), and Affiliate Professor of Financial Accounting at Solvay Business School – Free University of Brussels. He is also the Academic Director of the Luxembourg School of Finance – University of Luxembourg. He has had the honor of being invited as visiting professor in several universities in Europe, North America, and Africa. Pierre A. Michel has written several books on finance and accounting and has published numerous research articles in leading scientific journals and books about asset valuation, risk estimation, market efficiency, and corporate finance. He is also the President of the Economics and Management Commission of the National Fund of Scientific Research (Belgium). He acts as a consultant on the implementation of value-based management systems, and organizes, directs, and participates in management development programs.

Sheila O'Donohoe (B.Comm, M.B.S., Ph.D.) currently lectures in Finance at the Waterford Institute of Technology, Ireland where she is course director on the M.B.S. in Internationalization. She has lectured in Malaysia and has presented at several Irish and U.K. conferences. Her research interests include the role of venture capital, small firm finance, banking relationships, and mergers and acquisitions.

Andreas Oehler is a Full Professor of Finance at Bamberg University (Germany) and has held a Chair in Management, Business Administration & Finance there since 1994. He received his M.Sc. (Diploma) and his Doctoral degree in Economics, Business Administration & Finance from Mannheim University in 1985 and 1989, and his Postdoctoral degree in Economics & Finance from Hagen University 1994. During his academic career he worked as a senior and managing consultant at Price Waterhouse and other companies.

His major fields of research are empirical, experimental and behavioral finance, risk management, and banking and financial institutions.

Evila Piva is a Ph.D. student in the Doctoral Program in Management, Economics and Industrial Engineering at the Politecnico di Milano. Her scientific activity is mainly in industrial economics and economics of technical change. Her areas of research include academic start-ups, venture capital, and the determinants of the performance of new technology-based firms.

Angela Poech is assistant professor of entrepreneurial finance at Munich University of Technology (Technische Universität München, TUM), Germany, and managing director of the Center for Entrepreneurial and Financial Studies (CEFS). Her educational background is interdisciplinary, as she studied business administration and received her Ph.D. in organizational behavior. During her Ph.D. she worked self-employed in the field of communications and media. Before joining the KfW Endowed Chair in Entrepreneurial Finance she worked for the president of TUM. Her research interest lies in psychological aspects of private equity financing.

Kuntara Pukthuanthong is an Assistant Professor in Finance in the College of Business at San Diego State University. She received a B.A. degree in Economics from Chulalonkorn University, Thailand, an M.B.A. in Finance from Washington University, and a Ph.D. in Finance from the University of California, Irvine. Her research interests are in the area of IPO valuation, entrepreneurial finance, and stock options. She has published or forthcoming papers in the *International Corporate Control and Ownership Journal*, the *Journal of Investment Management*, and the *Journal of Corporate Ownership and Control*.

Marco Rummer is currently affiliated with the Said Business School, Oxford, U.K. as a visiting postdoctoral research fellow and is finishing his Ph.D. in Financial Economics at the University of Bamberg, Germany. He holds an M.Sc. in Economics and Finance from the University of York, U.K., which was funded by the German Academic Exchange Service, and a BA in Management from the Georg-Simon-Ohm Fachhochschule Nuremberg, Germany. His research interests are in empirical and experimental financial markets and corporate finance.

Gregor Schmidt worked as a Corporate Finance Analyst for a German VC firm. After operating in the VC-industry for almost two years, he now works as a Program Consultant at Jet Aviation Management AG in Zurich, Switzerland. He holds two masters degrees: a Master of Commerce in Accounting & Finance and a Diplom Kaufmann in International Management.

Denis Schweizer is a research assistant at the endowed chair of asset management at the European Business School (EBS). His research focus is on the asset allocation of alternative investments. He also works as an academic assistant in the creation of executive educational programs at the EBS Finanzakademie. Additionally he is a speaker for finance programs. He also received a diploma in business administration from the Johann-Wolfgang Goethe University.

Oana Secrieru is an economist at the Bank of Canada. She holds a Ph.D. from Queen's University (Kingston, Ontario) in Canada. Her main research is in the area of public economics, in particular entrepreneurship and venture capital financing. Her other research is in the areas of industrial organization and regulation. She has taught at Queen's University and Central European University.

Melanie Servais is a Commercial Engineer and holds a Masters Degree in Management from the School of Business Administration of the University of Liege. She has been FRFC (National Funds for Collective Research) researcher at the Research Center for Management of Bio-Industries at the University of Liege. Her research has mainly focused on the valuation of the intellectual property of biotechnology companies and the difficulties in finding necessary funds for the unlisted ones.

Dolruedee Thiengtham is a native of Thailand. After completing her undergraduate studies in French at Thammasat University in Bangkok, Thailand, she moved to the U.S. where she received an M.B.A. and MTM (Master of Technology Management) degree from Washington State University in Pullman, Washington. Mrs Thiengtham joined Concordia University in Montreal, Canada, as a staff member in 2002 where she worked in the International Aviation M.B.A. Department and the Office of Dean of the John Molson School of Business. Besides her work she is actively engaged in academic research. She has published articles in the *Canadian Journal of Administrative Sciences* and has articles under review at other peer-reviewed journals. Her research interests are in securities regulation and litigation, aviation finance, and venture capitalism.

Tereza Tykvová graduated from the Charles University of Prague (Economics) in 1997. She went to the University of Saarland, where she attended the postgraduate program 'European Economics' and obtained the title 'Master of Economics – Europe' with a thesis 'Venture Capital in Germany and its Impact on Innovation'. The thesis received the 1999 Prof. Dr. Osthoff Award. Tereza Tykvová was a research assistant at Prof. Keuschnigg's Institute of Public Finance at the University of Saarland. In September 1999 she joined the Centre for European Economic Research (ZEW) in Mannheim. In 2004, she obtained her Ph.D. from the Frankfurt University (supervisor: Prof. Uwe Walz). The topic of her thesis was 'Financing, IPO and Post-IPO Performance with Different Types of Venture Capitalists'. Her fields of interest are venture capital, private equity, and initial public offerings.

Marianne Vigneault is a Professor of Economics at Bishop's University in Canada. She holds a B.A. from Bishop's University, and an M.A. and Ph.D. from Queen's University. She has also taught at Queen's University as a visiting professor. Her research has been in the area of public economics, with particular emphasis on fiscal federalism and tax policies towards entrepreneurs, venture capitalists, and multinational corporations. Professor Vigneault has acted as Chair of the Economics department at Bishop's University and as a consultant and researcher for the Canadian International Development Agency, the World Bank, the federal Department of Finance, and the Institute for the Economy in Transition in Moscow.

Niklas Wagner is assistant professor of finance at Munich University of Technology (Technische Universität München, TUM), Germany, and managing director of the Center for Entrepreneurial and Financial Studies (CEFS). He received a Ph.D. in finance from Augsburg University, Germany, and held postdoctoral visiting appointments at the Haas School of Business, U.C. Berkeley, and at Stanford GSB. Research visits led him to TUM's Center of Mathematical Sciences and to the Department of Applied Economics, University of Cambridge, U.K. His research interests cover the areas of applied financial econometrics, including portfolio optimization, risk management, trading strategies, corporate finance, and applications in behavioral finance. He has published internationally, including papers in the *Journal of Asset Management*, the *Journal of Banking and Finance, Quantitative Finance*, and the *Journal of Empirical Finance*. His industry background is in quantitative asset management.

Mark Wahrenburg holds the chair of bank management at the department of finance, School of Business and Economics at Goethe University Frankfurt, Germany. He is also the dean of the Goethe Business School, Goethe University Frankfurt, which established the Duke Goethe Executive M.B.A. program in cooperation with Duke University's Fuqua School of Business. Furthermore, he is the director of the research program 'Venture Capital and the New Markets in Europe' of the Center for Financial Studies (CFS) and the director of the e-finance lab, both located in Frankfurt/Main.

Thomas Walker is a native of Germany. He received a Ph.D. in Finance and an M.B.A. in Finance and International Business from Washington State University in Pullman, Washington, and a B.Sc. in Wirtschaftsinformatik (Management Information Systems) from the Technical University of Darmstadt, Germany. Dr Walker joined Concordia University in Montreal, Canada, as an Assistant Professor in 2001. Prior to his academic career, he worked for several years in the German consulting and industrial sector at such firms as Mercedes Benz, Utility Consultants International, Lahmeyer International, Telenet, and KPMG Peat Marwick. His research interests are in IPO underpricing, securities regulation and litigation, institutional ownership, insider trading, aviation finance, and venture capitalism.

Uwe Walz has been full Professor of Economics at the University of Frankfurt/Main, Germany since 2002. He received his Ph.D. from the University of Tübingen, Germany in 1992, and teaches at the University of Mannheim, Germany. From 1992 to 1995, he was a postdoctoral fellow of the German Science Foundation and visiting research fellow at the University of California at Berkeley, and at the London School of Economics, U.K. From 1995 to 2002 he was Professor of Economics at the University of Bochum and the University of Tübingen. His area of specialization is industrial organization, and his recent research interests include contract theory, venture capital, (new) capital markets, corporate finance, and economics of network industries. He is Research Program Director for 'Venture Capital and New Markets in Europe' at the Center for Financial Studies, Frankfurt/Main, Research Fellow at the Center for Economic Policy Research (CEPR), London, adjunct to the Stuttgart Institute of Management and Technology (SMIT), and serves as referee for several internationally published journals.

Tom Weidig is a co-author of the first book on managing private equity fund investments. He has written several academic articles on private equity funds, funds of funds, and the impact of the new Basle Accord. His study The Risk Profile of Private Equity has been publicized and endorsed by the European Venture Capital Association, and translated into German and French. He holds a Master of Science in Theoretical Physics from Imperial College London and a Ph.D. from the University of Durham. He was a postdoctoral researcher at the University of Manchester, and a visiting researcher at Trinity College, University of Cambridge. Leaving physics behind, he then worked as a risk analyst in derivatives for the U.S. investment bank Bear Stearns in London. He also worked for the European Investment Fund, researching and modeling private equity funds. He has his own company offering consultancy and expert systems to the industry: http://www.quantexperts.com.

Nina Zieling is a Ph.D. student of Finance at the University Complutense of Madrid. She has a Masters in Finance from the same University and her research focuses on venture capital and private equity.

Part One

European Venture Capital Markets: Recent Developments and Perspectives

1 Venture capital in Europe: Closing the gap to the U.S.

Andreas Oehler, Kuntara Pukthuanthong, Marco Rummer, and Thomas Walker

Abstract

We review recent developments in the European venture capital (VC) markets. For decades, most of the Continent has lagged behind the U.S. in attracting and retaining young entrepreneurs. Despite several government attempts to provide tax incentives and an appropriate infrastructure that would allow young start-up firms to establish themselves, European private and public markets for high-risk companies are still weak. While we document that Europe's VC markets have grown considerably over the past eight years, European VC funds underperform U.S. funds by a significant margin. We explore the reasons behind this underperformance and discuss possible remedies. Our study draws valuable lessons from the U.S. to show how important a flourishing venture capital market is to a country's economic development and how Europe may close the existing gap between the old and the new world.

1.1 Introduction

Although the U.S. venture capital market remains the largest in the world, venture capitalist activity abroad has been growing rapidly in recent years. Accompanying this trend has been an increased interest in the relative performance of venture capital investments around the world and in the reasons behind some of the documented differences (see, for example, Mayer et al., 2004).

Young start-up firms frequently lack sufficient revenue during the first few years of their corporate life and have to look to outside investors for financial support. As noted by Nuechterlein (2000), about two-thirds of the average VC-backed company's total equity is supplied by venture capitalists. Such start-up funding is typically used to develop a prototype and fund marketing and sales. In addition, venture capitalists frequently fund firms during later stages to allow them to grow more quickly than retained earnings alone would allow. If all goes well, the funded firm will reach the point where it can go public, allowing the venture capitalists to realize a return on their investment and exit the firm. Alternatively, venture capitalists can cash out by selling the start-up firm to another company.

In the U.S., both exit strategies are used equally often (Schwienbacher, 2005; Nuechterlein, 2000). In contrast, in Europe – which until recently lacked a liquid, transnational stock market that is at par with the U.S. National Association of Securities Dealers Automated Quotation (NASDAQ) market and which has an underdeveloped equity culture – venture-backed companies are more likely to be acquired by another company or another VC fund than sold to the public through an initial public offering. The lack of appropriate exit venues is frequently viewed as one of the main reasons why the European VC market lags behind that of the U.S. (Bottazzi and Da Rin, 2002).

Our study aims to provide a detailed comparison of the VC markets in Europe and the U.S. and draws important lessons that should be of use for VC fund managers, academics, and regulators alike. In the first part of our study, we analyze venture capital flows both in Europe and the U.S., using a comprehensive sample of venture investments made between 1998 and 2005. We then survey the comparative empirical literature to contrast recent developments in the VC markets both within Europe and between Europe and the U.S. While our results suggest that the European VC markets have caught up with the U.S. in terms of size, the literature notes that large differences still remain. One of the most problematic differences between European and U.S. VC investments is that the former vastly underperform their U.S. counterparts.[1] We identify several factors that may cause these performance differences and examine what European regulators can do to overcome them.

In the second part of our study, we focus our attention on recent developments in the European stock markets. Exiting a VC investment by means of an Initial Public Offering (IPO) is viewed by many VC fund managers as highly desirable. Yet, while regulators across Europe have made numerous attempts to create a financial infrastructure that would make it easier for young high-tech firms to access the equity markets, many of these endeavors have failed.

Finally, in the third part of our study, we discuss various other strategies that regulators can employ to aid entrepreneurial firms and the venture capitalists backing them. If properly implemented, such policies should lead to economic growth and help reduce Europe's high unemployment rates.

1.2 The European and U.S. venture capital markets – a comparison

The venture capital industry started in the U.S. and slowly spread around the globe. As the U.S. VC markets matured, the industry began to emerge in Europe (see Bruton et al., 2005). In the late 1970s, The U.K. and Ireland were among the first European countries to attract venture capitalists. Early VC funds were typically set up as affiliates of U.S. firms and drew heavily on American capital and expertise. Continental Europe followed in the early 1980s, where VC funds were frequently set up by large domestic banks. While the European VC industry closely follows the U.S. model (Manigart, 1994), differences in the institutional environment and in the tax and securities laws governing VC investments have caused the European VC market to develop very differently from that in the U.S.

[1] Cochrane (2005) shows that – after controlling for selection biases using a maximum likelihood estimate – venture capital investments are very similar to traded securities, averaging a log return of approximately 15% per year. Yet, comparable studies in Europe find returns that are frequently below risk-adjusted required rates of return (see, for example, Hege et al., 2006; Engel, 2004).

1.2.1 *Facts and figures*

Table 1.1 provides an overview of the venture capital markets in the 16 largest European economies and the US during the period from 1998 to 2005.[2] In Panel A, we provide information on aggregate VC fund flows in each country.

Panel A provides yearly data of the total VC funds disbursed in a given country per year, measured in US$ million. Panel B divides the VC funds disbursed in a given country by the country's GDP. For better readability, results are displayed in one hundredth of a percent. Data on venture capitalist funding are derived from the Security Data Company's VentureXpert database. GDP data are based on national accounts data provided by the World Bank and the Organisation for Economic Co-operation and Development (OECD).

Consistent with Bottazzi et al. (2004) we observe that during the earlier part of our sample period, the European VC markets were dwarfed by the U.S. market. In 1998, for example, European venture capitalists disbursed approximately US$8 billion, less than half the funds that were disbursed in the U.S. during that year. Fueled by the high-tech boom of the late 1990s (see Mayer et al., 2004) the venture capital markets both in Europe and the U.S. grew rapidly in 1999 and 2000. Yet, while U.S. VC markets experienced a rapid decline in 2001/2002, the European markets remained comparatively strong and actually overtook the U.S. in terms of total funding activity in 2004 and 2005.

To account for differences in the size of each country's economy and thus allow for a better comparison of VC markets across countries, Panel B divides VC fund flows in each country by the country's GDP during that year. The last two rows support the observations we made in Panel A, in that Europe lagged behind the U.S. in the late 1990s but subsequently caught up with the American market.

Interestingly, the figures in Panel B reveal large differences in relative VC market sizes across Europe. Consistent with Bruton et al. (2005), we observe that the U.K. and Ireland have particularly well-developed VC markets, with VC fund flows in some years close to 1% of GDP. In Continental Europe, France and Germany show a well-developed VC market, but also smaller countries such as Belgium and the Netherlands stand out. As Bottazzi and Da Rin (2002) point out, differences in laws, tax regulations, and institutional structures may likely explain some of these differences. The VC market in the Netherlands, for example, flourished earlier than in the rest of Continental Europe because the pension fund industry invested in private equity and because special tax treatment for pension fund contributions created one of the largest pension fund industries in the world (Sormani, 2001). Spinner (2003) notes that other European countries are following suit and are making a series of legislative changes designed to encourage enterprise and jumpstart the venture capital industry. In 2002, for example, Germany overhauled its takeover laws. More recently, tax laws have been introduced that are intended to relax the requirements needed for Benelux countries to create a fiscal unity and allow advantageous tax treatment to apply. At the same time, Italian lawmakers are overhauling financial assistance rules contained in the Italian Code to allow target companies' assets to be used as general security for acquisition finance. The importance of such regulatory changes is emphasized by Cumming et al. (2004).

[2] We also examined fund flows in Eastern Europe. These countries are not included here because their VC markets were either negligible or non-existent throughout our sample period. For important insights on this topic, see Schöfer and Leitinger (2002) who provide recommendations addressed at European regulators to assist the development of a VC industry in these countries.

Table 1.1 The venture capital market in Europe and the U.S.

	1998	1999	2000	2001	2002	2003	2004	2005
Panel A: Total VC Funds Disbursed (in US$ Million)								
Austria	50.1	481.7	155.6	200.8	28.3	64.3	107.7	43.4
Belgium	165.9	531.9	494.0	687.0	825.8	239.6	698.6	649.1
Denmark	15.6	367.1	424.7	270.2	1574.3	547.5	575.5	1231.4
Finland	106.4	92.2	360.1	672.6	615.0	307.1	212.1	368.7
France	436.1	1860.6	5804.0	3186.4	7000.7	4436.9	4189.1	6361.6
Germany	457.7	1472.0	4648.5	2451.9	2985.0	5394.8	10 962.8	8412.3
Greece	0.0	0.0	0.0	65.4	1.6	68.5	0.0	15.1
Ireland	242.0	375.4	587.8	680.9	1298.2	1367.4	800.4	783.4
Italy	151.6	496.0	1367.7	1043.0	670.0	2116.1	1426.1	1637.7
Netherlands	431.5	775.9	1261.0	916.6	636.6	1572.0	922.0	805.8
Norway	3.2	130.0	132.5	298.8	65.3	352.8	137.1	246.9
Portugal	11.0	197.2	47.7	39.3	12.8	0.0	0.0	3.3
Spain	239.9	338.0	480.4	733.1	865.3	1282.6	1038.6	689.1
Sweden	150.8	304.6	1492.9	1540.1	772.1	346.7	570.7	390.6
Switzerland	193.5	297.9	588.3	386.8	393.5	624.9	322.8	564.4
U.K.	5214.0	11 513.2	13 882.8	8264.4	7288.3	6275.6	13 550.5	9911.4
Europe Total	7869.4	19 233.5	31 728.0	21 437.2	25 032.7	24 996.9	35 514.2	32 114.2
U.S.	18 568.0	37 171.7	63 929.8	28 396.8	22 048.4	28 685.0	24 095.4	27 058.7

Panel B: Total VC Funds Disbursed Relative to GDP (in 1/100%)								
Austria	1.35	11.88	8.03	10.41	1.36	2.52	3.69	1.93
Belgium	6.63	21.19	21.63	30.21	33.60	7.88	19.83	18.04
Denmark	0.90	21.20	26.84	17.00	92.01	25.94	23.84	48.39
Finland	8.22	7.21	30.03	55.49	46.59	18.98	11.41	12.68
France	3.00	12.89	43.71	23.78	48.04	24.80	20.47	23.12
Germany	2.13	6.98	24.46	12.96	14.76	22.08	40.00	18.46
Greece	0.00	0.00	0.00	5.57	0.12	3.95	0.00	1.42
Ireland	27.82	39.25	61.90	65.92	107.78	89.88	44.07	66.45
Italy	1.27	4.20	12.73	9.57	5.65	14.41	8.50	9.29
Netherlands	10.97	19.47	34.02	23.86	15.20	30.66	15.92	20.24
Norway	0.21	8.23	7.94	17.60	3.43	15.99	5.48	7.17
Portugal	0.98	17.14	4.48	3.58	1.06	0.00	0.00	0.20
Spain	4.08	5.61	8.27	12.05	12.61	14.56	9.99	5.83
Sweden	6.08	12.11	62.32	70.10	31.95	11.50	16.47	14.00
Switzerland	7.38	11.52	23.91	15.45	14.23	19.42	9.03	9.22
U.K.	36.63	78.85	96.52	57.74	46.57	34.91	63.79	49.04
Europe Average	7.35	17.36	29.17	26.96	29.68	21.09	18.28	19.09
U.S.	21.29	40.35	65.47	28.18	21.13	26.19	20.57	23.43

1.2.2 A review of comparative studies

While our statistics suggest that the European venture capital markets have caught up with the U.S. in terms of size, the extant literature points out that large differences still remain between the two markets.

A detailed comparison between Europe and the U.S. is provided by Schwienbacher (2005) who surveys venture capitalists on both sides of the Atlantic. He finds that European VC investments are not as profitable as those of their U.S. counterparts and attributes the relative underperformance of European VC funds to several factors: (1) European fund managers monitor their portfolio companies much less frequently than their U.S. peers, (2) European VC funds face less liquid markets, both in terms of human capital and in terms of exit strategies that are available to them (forcing them to shop around longer when it comes to replacing key employees or selling shares in one of their ventures), (3) European venture capitalists syndicate less frequently, thus incurring higher risk, and (4) European venture capitalists are much less likely to use convertible securities.

Yet, despite these differences, Schwienbacher also documents that young European and U.S. VC firms are actually quite similar, suggesting that only older and larger VC funds show substantial dissimilarities. As the European VC industry grows and additional funds become established, these factors may ultimately lead to a convergence of both markets.

Schwienbacher's results are not unique. Earlier studies by Cumming and MacIntosh (2003a, 2003b) examine all possible exit routes (not only IPO exits), and find that European venture capitalists have a much harder time exiting their investments (for a comparable U.S. study, see Das et al., 2004). They argue that even the surge in high-tech IPOs in Europe in the late 1990s and the creation of several new stock markets geared to high-tech companies did not alleviate these problems. Other comparative studies between the European and U.S. VC markets include Cumming (2002), Bascha and Walz (2002), and Kaplan et al. (2004). Their results are generally similar.

Engel (2004) notes that European VC firms had to make a large number of write-offs in recent years, suggesting some serious problems and inefficiencies in the European VC markets. Engel cites reports by the European Private Equity and Venture Capital Association (EVCA, 2002, 2001) that list 36.5% of all divestments in Germany in 2001 and 22.1% in 2002 as write-offs, much higher than comparable figures in the U.S.

A more recent study by Hege et al. (2006) provides additional evidence on the performance of European and U.S. venture capitalists. In line with Schwienbacher (2005), they find that U.S. venture capitalists generate significantly higher returns than European VC firms. Their results suggest significant differences in terms of contracting behavior such as staging frequency and syndication that may explain the performance differences. Yet, when they compare U.S. venture funds investing in Europe with their European peers, they find no evidence that would suggest that U.S.-managed funds outperform. Thus, while the U.S. VC market is one of the largest and most successful in the world, they suggest that the U.S. model can not be easily exported or imitated.

While earlier studies by Manigart (1994) and Sapienza et al. (1996) attribute the differences between the venture capital markets to heterogeneous cultural norms, studies by Black and Gilson (1998), Jeng and Wells (2000), and, more recently, Cumming et al. (2006) suggest that capital markets are the primary cause of the discrepancies. In brief, they argue that the presence of a well-developed market for IPOs and a norm of relatively rapid exit by venture capitalists in the U.S. create a vibrant industry that motivates a greater intensity of involvement and a more rapid development of expertise in the

U.S. than, for example, in Germany and other places where public markets for high-risk companies have been comparatively weak. Thus, while their view includes an element of institutional forces (that is, norms of implicit expectations of venture capitalist exit), they focus on the impact of capital markets on differences in industry structure and behavior (see Bruton et al., 2002). In the following section we explore capital market differences in more detail and examine recent developments in Europe that were intended to close the existing gap between the two markets.

1.2.3 European small-company stock markets

Many European countries provide venture capitalists with insufficient exit mechanisms, thus limiting their willingness to pursue certain investments. As a result, young start-up firms may not be able to raise the funds they need, which may ultimately hamper economic growth and job creation in that country (Botazzi and Da Rin, 2002). One of the main reasons for the lack of exit venues lies in the illiquidity of local stock markets. Even though European countries such as Belgium, France, Germany, Italy, the Netherlands and the U.K. have exchanges that are specifically aimed at small and medium start-up companies, entrepreneurs in these countries face some significant financing obstacles (Nuechterlein, 2000). First, unlike in the U.S., institutional investors in Europe tend to concentrate their investments in larger capitalization stocks. Moreover, most European countries prohibit pension funds from investing in VC funds, thus limiting the amount of capital that these VC funds can raise and infuse into start-ups (Hardouvelis et al., 2006). Another problem arises from the fact that many European small-company exchanges are not independent, that is, they are frequently under the same management as the countries' primary markets. With two or more exchanges under their control, managers tend to promote the larger, more prominent exchange (Nuechterlein, 2000). In contrast, the NASDAQ market in the U.S. is independent from both the NYSE and AMEX, resulting in fair competition for new listings among the exchanges. As a result of these differences, venture capitalists in Europe are much more likely to exit their investment through a third-party acquisition than through an initial public offering – the preferred exit venue in the U.S.

To remedy some of these problems, Europe created the EURO Neuer Markt (EURO.NM), a transnational stock exchange specifically aimed at young start-up firms. To overcome the lack of liquidity that most start-ups experienced in their respective home countries, the EURO.NM allowed for cross-border trading in the small company markets of Belgium, France, Germany, the Netherlands, and Italy. The EURO.NM was quite successful. By early 2000, the exchange had attracted over 150 listings with a combined market capitalization of more than US$30 billion (see Nuechterlein, 2000). The member markets share trading and disclosure rules, access to all EURO.NM markets through cross-membership of financial intermediaries, a common infrastructure for the dissemination of market information, and joint marketing agreements to promote companies internationally.

Another attempt by European stock markets to establish a transnational stock market was the European Association of Securities Dealers Automated Quotation (EASDAQ) market, which was created in September 1996, the same year as the EURO.NM, and organized across 14 countries in Europe with headquarters in Brussels. The purpose of the EASDAQ was to provide a broader range of financial resources for start-ups than the typical stock market in Europe. Yet, in contrast to the EURO.NM, the EASDAQ grew with lackluster speed. Within three years of its organization, only 49 firms listed on the exchange with a total market capitalization of US$21 billion. Eventually, in mid 2001, the EASDAQ was acquired by the NASDAQ and has since become NASDAQ Europe. The companies listed on the EASDAQ (now NASDAQ Europe) are generally larger and face tougher listing and disclosure requirements. In addition, the exchange maintains a fast-track trading link with the NASDAQ, which appeals to institutional investors (Nuechterlein, 2000).

Another noteworthy development is the creation of the Neuer Markt by the Frankfurt Stock Exchange in 1997. The market was off to a great start and soon played a dominant role in Europe in terms of issue activity. For example, in both 1999 and 2000 more than 130 firms went public on this stock market segment, even though it had the most rigid listing requirements within the different segments of the Frankfurt Stock Exchange. Yet, after the stock market bubble burst, IPO activity in Germany soon came to a complete standstill, with not a single IPO in 2003. As a result, the Frankfurt Stock Exchange closed the Neuer Markt and established a new stock market segment with new listing requirements. In late 2005 the Frankfurt Stock Exchange founded the Entry Standard, which aims to be a market for small and medium-sized companies with few listing requirements. This stock market segment is modeled on the AIM Market in London, which was very successful even during the market downturn in 2003 and 2004 and also aims to be a market for small and medium-sized companies with few listing requirements.

1.3 Economic effects and government intervention

A flourishing VC industry has been shown to have a positive influence on a country's economic growth and its domestic job market. Nuechterlein (2000), for example, notes that venture-backed companies have historically created a disproportionate number of new jobs – many of them well-paid and highly skilled – and are a key source of research and development spending. When comparing the job markets in the U.S. and Europe, Sener (2006) finds that despite large companies cutting jobs on both continents, the U.S. economy has benefited from a significant number of new business formations, with Europe trailing far behind. This is supported by Shi et al. (2006) who show that between 1995 and 2002, 2300 U.S. companies went public in the U.S., compared with less than 1100 in Europe. As a result, many governments have become increasingly interested in promoting a healthy VC market. Yet, the European and American VC markets have undergone distinct developments in recent years that were not always crowned by success. We discuss the recent developments in both regions, paying particular attention to the question what actions governments can take to promote funding for new ventures.

1.3.1 Governmental promotion of the venture capital industry

Direct government support

There are various ways in which a government can support entrepreneurs and/or the VC industry. One possibility is to provide direct financial support to start-up firms. The U.S. government, for example, designed a program, the Overseas Private Investment

Corporation (OPIC), under which it offers loan guarantees, small business loans, project finance, and political risk insurance for U.S. companies undertaking projects abroad. To be approved for funding, applicants typically have to show that their projects will not only develop and expand business operations in certain emerging markets but also that they have the potential to create U.S. jobs and accelerate U.S. exports (see Madeo, 1994).

Besides financing large overseas projects, the agency has a special program under which it provides financing support for U.S. small and medium-sized enterprises (SMEs). While it is still comparatively small, the program continues to grow. In 2005, for example, OPIC committed US$343.2 million in financing to 52 SME projects, compared with $240.2 million for 49 projects in 2004.[3]

In addition, several U.S. states enacted legislation allowing the creation of Certified Capital Companies (CAPCOs). These VC funds have to invest at least 60% of their capital in private in-state companies for the purpose of stimulating economic growth in regions that have traditionally not received much venture capital. In contrast to private VC firms, which are mainly funded by institutional investors and pension funds, CAPCOs are financed by insurance companies, which are given tax credits as an incentive to become limited partners (see Nuechterlein, 2000). To date, CAPCO legislation has been adopted in five states, including Louisiana, Missouri, Florida, New York, and Wisconsin and is under consideration in eight other states (see Barkley et al., 2001; Rubin and Stankiewicz, 2005).

Tax incentives

High tax rates can be a serious impediment for economic growth. Thus, by reducing taxes, governments can provide a crucial catalyst for the formation and ultimate success of young start-up firms. Nuechterlein (2000) and Gompers and Lerner (2001) provide a good example for the effect of tax reductions, showing that VC financing and new business registrations increased significantly in the U.S. following a decrease in the capital gains tax rate from 49% to 28% in 1978, and to 20% in 1981. In contrast to the U.S., most European countries tax capital gains at rates of 60% or more, hindering the formation and expansion of new ventures.

Another way in which the government can support entrepreneurs relates to the tax treatment of stock options. Many start-up firms – especially those in the high-tech sector – are short on cash during their early years, yet they need to offer competitive salary packages to attract and retain talented employees. To draw employees from larger, more established firms, start-up firms frequently use stock options that require no cash outlay when they are issued but may result in significant payoffs in later years if the company's stock performs well. As noted by Gompers and Lerner (2001), the U.S. tax code makes stock options considerably more attractive than they are in Europe. Specifically, U.S. stock option holders are taxed on their profits when they sell the underlying stock. Stock options in most European countries, on the other hand, are taxed as regular income at the time they are granted (Nuechterlein, 2000). As a result of these differences, European start-ups face a tough time when competing with larger firms in the European labor market, and confront an even tougher challenge if they try to attract talented personnel from the U.S.

[3] Overseas Private Investment Corporation, *OPIC News* – February 2006, Vol. 8 No. 2, page 1.

Adequate infrastructure

Besides providing young start-up firms with a well-developed infrastructure in the form of a reliable and efficient transportation, utility, and communications system, governments can make various other infrastructure investments to spur entrepreneurial development. Following our earlier discussion, establishing a liquid stock market that allows venture capitalists to exit their investments is viewed as one important step a country can take. In addition, it is important to understand that a growing number of businesses are founded with no assets other than their intellectual property rights (Nuechterlein, 2000). The success of many of these businesses depends on a fast and efficient patent and copyright system and the adequate enforcement of the laws governing intellectual property rights. While the European copyright system is widely viewed as one of the most efficient systems in the world, the patent process costs about US$150 000, compared with US$20 000 in the U.S. (see Singer and Stauder, 2003; Nuechterlein, 2000).

Bankruptcy laws

Governments should not only create appropriate exit channels for VC firms but also provide for effective liquidating strategies in case an investment does not perform as planned. While both the U.S. and Europe have well-developed bankruptcy legislation, there are some significant differences that make European bankruptcy laws considerably stricter than comparable U.S. laws.

In Europe, managers can face severe sanctions if they delay a bankruptcy filing past a certain point (see White, 1996). In France, for example, managers can be held personally liable for the firm's debts if they don't file for bankruptcy within 15 days of the firm becoming insolvent. Bankruptcy laws in the U.S., on the other hand, do not impose any penalties for filing delays.

Another difference relates to the question of who initiates the bankruptcy. Voluntary bankruptcy filings are almost always initiated by a company's managers, while involuntary bankruptcies are typically initiated by outside creditors. In the U.S., involuntary bankruptcy is discouraged, as three or more creditors have to file the required petition together. In contrast, under most European laws, any party – including managers, members of boards of directors, workers' representatives, and the bankruptcy court itself (see White, 1996) – is encouraged to initiate an involuntary bankruptcy filing. From the entrepreneur's perspective, it is thus much riskier to operate a business in Europe than it is in the U.S.

Finally, when a European firm files for bankruptcy, courts will appoint an outside party to take a position in the firm, which severely limits the control the existing manager has in the bankruptcy process. In the U.S., the procedure is similar if a firm chooses to liquidate, that is, if it files for Chapter 7 bankruptcy protection. If a firm chooses to restructure, however, it may file for Chapter 11 bankruptcy protection, which allows the existing manager to remain in control. Taken together, U.S. entrepreneurs generally have a better opportunity to restructure their firms (and re-emerge from bankruptcy) than their European peers who lose most of their influence once bankruptcy proceedings have been initiated.

From an entrepreneur's personal perspective, there are large incentives for incorporating in the U.S. as well. A U.S. entrepreneur who manages a company that eventually goes bankrupt is quite frequently viewed as experienced and entrusted to start another firm.

European (and also Asian) entrepreneurs, on the other hand, typically suffer detrimental reputational losses if they have to file for bankruptcy or, as Nuechterlein (2000) puts it, '[in Europe] bankruptcy carries a stigma that frequently destroys an entrepreneur's future.'

Local support

Besides the role that the federal government plays in enhancing entrepreneurial development, support on a local level is also crucial. Such support is generally more developed in the U.S. than it is in Europe. The U.S Small Business Administration (SBA), for example, administers the Small Business Development Center Program, which consists of more than 1100 local offices that provide current and prospective entrepreneurs with management assistance.

SBA centers are allocated throughout the U.S. to provide assistance not only in major urban centers but also in remote regions. In addition, they provide various customized programs to help economically and socially disadvantaged groups such as women, veterans, and the disabled start their own firms.[4] Furthermore, the SBA created the Angel Capital Electronic Network (ACE-Net, recently renamed to Active Capital), an online system that brings together entrepreneurs looking for private investment, and investors who seek investment opportunities. The system allows entrepreneurs to post their business plans on-line for as little as US$450 and to register up to US$5 million in securities for sale per year (see Leach and Melicher, 2006).

Litigation risk

Although the U.S. is, in many respects, one of the best locations for an entrepreneur to start a business, it does have its drawbacks. High wages, high health care costs, and expensive corporate real estate may be one detriment. In addition, entrepreneurs frequently view the high risk of being sued as a major problem. Damage awards or settlements in product liability or employment discrimination suits – to name a few – are often significantly larger in the U.S. when compared with Europe; and, while companies can insure themselves against some of these risks, they do bear the costs indirectly in the form of higher insurance premiums.

Potential problems

While we outlined various ways in which governments can support entrepreneurial development, it is important to understand that none of the prescribed changes are easy to implement. Changing the tax code or bankruptcy laws, for example, is certainly a time-consuming and difficult process. Similarly, with most of Eastern Europe having been under communist rule for more than four decades, it may take some time to instill an entrepreneurial spirit in its people.

Finally, with often large amounts of money at stake, corruption and the resulting misuse and misallocation of funds can become a serious problem. While the U.S. and most European countries are arguably less affected by this issue, the extant academic literature sees corruption as a serious impediment for economic growth in many developing

[4] See also the SBA's website at http://www.sba.gov/sbdc/aboutus.html.

countries. Thus, even if governments adopt strategies aimed at supporting entrepreneurs, corruption can result in the selective granting of tax incentives, the misallocation of government grants, and a variety of related problems.

1.4 Conclusion

Despite various attempts by European governments to provide proper incentives and an adequate infrastructure to help attract and retain young entrepreneurs on the Continent, they have lagged behind the U.S. in doing so. Sure, there are cultural differences between Europe and North America. While a majority of the North American population has its roots in Europe, the pioneer spirit of the early settlers and the belief that with hard work and the proper attitude one can achieve everything (become a 'self-made man') are still ingrained in the average American and foster a strong entrepreneurial spirit. Yet, while cultural differences such as these may be hard to overcome, governments have considerable leverage in influencing the economic environment that may ultimately determine the success or failure of a young entrepreneur.

An expensive and complicated patent system is only one of the hurdles an entrepreneur faces in Europe. Yet, an efficient system to protect intellectual property rights is now more important than ever as we move into the digital age. The lack of adequate exits for venture capitalists is another problem faced by Europe. While several European exchanges have established trenches for high-risk firms in the past, many of them have failed. Many market participants blame corporate scandals for the downfall of the EURO.NM and similar markets across the continent. Yet, the U.S. has had its fair share of scandals as well, but its main exchange for young start-up firms, the NASDAQ, has survived. Rather than establishing short-lived trenches for high-risk firms that can be closed when things go wrong, Europe may be better off if it had an exchange such as the NASDAQ that is independent of other exchanges and has the ability to promote itself without stepping on the toes of larger exchanges behind it.

Finally, the retention of highly qualified employees remains a problem in Europe. As managerial compensation in the U.S. far outweighs European salaries and bonus packages, Europe experiences an out flux of management talent to the U.S. Changing the tax treatment of stock option packages to equal that of the U.S. may at least be one step governments can take to close the salary gap and help retain qualified managers on the Continent.

Both the U.K. and the U.S. have seen dramatic increases in the funds raised and invested in private equity and venture capital over the last 15 years.[5] McGovern (2006) noted that, after a low point in 2003, commitments to venture capital and private equity investments are increasing again. Because of the increased interest in this asset class during the last years, the size of the deals is increasing significantly. As the private equity industry in the U.S. and Europe matures, there is likely to be further interest in emerging markets in the future, particularly Asia.[6]

Furthermore, a maturing industry should lead to the adoption of reporting standards, which would enable investors to compare the performance of different firms. A first

[5] See Myners (2001) for a detailed discussion of the development of institutional investment in the U.K.

[6] For a detailed discussion of global trends in private equity investments see PricewaterhouseCoopers (2005).

attempt has been proposed by the EVCA, which recently published a first set of industry standards that provide, among other things, guidelines for valuation, reporting and corporate governance.

References

Barkley, L., Markley, D. and Rubin, J. (2001). Certified Capital Companies (CAPCOs): Strengths and Shortcomings of the Latest Wave in State-Assisted Venture Capital Programs. *Economic Development Quarterly*, 15(4):350–366.

Bascha, A. and Walz, U. (2001). Convertible Securities and Optimal Exit Decisions in Venture Capital Finance. *Journal of Corporate Finance*, 7(3):285–306.

Black, B. and Gilson, R. (1998). Venture Capital and the Structure of Capital Markets: Banks versus Stock Markets. *Journal of Financial Economics*, 47(3):243–277.

Bottazzi, L. and Da Rin, M. (2002). Venture Capital in Europe and the Financing of Innovative Companies. *Economic Policy*, 17(34):229–270.

Bottazzi, L., Da Rin, M. and Hellmann, T. (2004). The Changing Face of the European Venture Capital Industry: Facts and Analysis. *Journal of Private Equity*, 7(2): 26–44.

Bruton, G., Fried, V. and Manigart, S. (2005). Institutional Influences on the Worldwide Expansion of Venture Capital. *Entrepreneurship Theory and Practice*, 29(6):737–760.

Bruton, G., Manigart, S., Fried, V. and Sapienza, H. (2002). Venture Capitalists in Asia: A comparison with the U.S. and Europe. Working Paper, Vlerick Leuven Gent Management School, Belgium.

Cochrane, J. (2005). The Risk and Return of Venture Capital. *Journal of Financial Economics*, 75(1):3–52.

Coopers & Lybrand (1997). *Economic Impact of Venture Capital*. 1. Available at http://www.pwc.com/extweb/pwcpublications.nsf/docid/3B46A6CD12E9F2B78525713B0068528B

Coopers & Lybrand (1998). *The Economic Impact of Venture Capital in Europe*. Available at http://www.pwc.com/extweb/pwcpublications.nsf/docid/3B46A6CD12E9F2B78525713B0068528B

Cumming, D. (2002). Contracts and Exits in Venture Capital Finance. Working Paper, Rensselaer Polytechnic Institute.

Cumming, D. and MacIntosh, J. (2003a). Venture Capital Exits in Canada and the United States. *University of Toronto Law Journal*, 53:101–200.

Cumming, D. and MacIntosh, J. (2003b). A Cross-Country Comparison of Full and Partial Venture Capital Exits. *Journal of Banking and Finance*, 27(3):511–548.

Cumming, D., Fleming, G. and Schwienbacher, A. (2004). Legality and Venture Capital Exits. *Journal of Corporate Finance*, 12(2):214–245.

Cumming, D., Schmidt, D. and Walz, U. (2006). Legality and Venture Governance Around the World. Working Paper, Rensselaer Polytechnic Institute and Goethe University, Frankfurt.

Das, S., Jagannathan, M. and Sarin, A. (2004). The Private Equity Discount: An Empirical Examination of the Exit of Venture Backed Companies. *Journal of Investment Management*, 1:152–177.

Engel, D. (2004). The Performance of Venture-Backed Firms: The Effect of Venture Capital Company Characteristics. *Industry and Innovation*, 11(3):249–263.

European Private Equity and Venture Capital Association (EVCA) (2001). *A Survey of Private Equity and Venture Capital in Europe, Yearbook 2001*. Zaventem, Belgium.

European Private Equity and Venture Capital Association (EVCA) (2002). *Fund of Funds in Europe Survey 2002*. Zaventem, Belgium.

Gompers, P. and Lerner, J. (2001). The Venture Capital Revolution. *Journal of Economic Perspectives*, 15(2):145–168.

Hardouvelis, A., Malliaropulos, D. and Priestley, R. (2006). EMU and European Stock Market Integration. *Journal of Business*, 79(1):365–392.

Hege, U., Palomino, F. and Schwienbacher, A. (2006). Venture Capital Performance in Europe and the United States: A Comparative Analysis. RICAFE Working Paper No. 001, HEC Paris and University of Amsterdam.

Jeng, L. and Wells, P. (2000). The Determinants of Venture Capital Funding: Evidence across Countries. *Journal of Corporate Finance*, 6(3):241–289.

Kaplan, S., Martel, F. and Strömberg, P. (2004). How Do Legal Differences and Learning Affect Financial Contracts? Working Paper, University of Chicago.

Leach, J. and Melicher, R. (2006). *Entrepreneurial Finance*. Thomson South-Western Publishing, Mason OH.

Lynch, P. (1996). The Upsizing of America. *Wall Street Journal*, 20 September.

Madeo, D. (1994). Clinton Administration Policy Ties Economic Aid to Foreign Policy Goals. *Law and Policy in International Business*, 25(1):1215–1221.

Manigart, S. (1994). The Founding Rate of Venture Capital Firms in Three European Countries (1970–1990). *Journal of Business Venturing*, 9(6):525–541.

Mayer, C., Schoors, K. and Yafeh, Y. (2004). Sources of Funds and Investment Activities of Venture Capital Funds: Evidence from Germany, Israel, Japan and the UK. *Journal of Corporate Finance*, 11(3):586–608.

McGovern, J. (2006). An Overview of Private Equity: Evolution of the Asset Class, Rationale and Considerations for Investing and Keys to Success. Working Paper, PIonline.

Myners, P. (2001). *Institutional Investment in the United Kingdom: A Review*. HM Treasury, London.

Nuechterlein, J. (2000). *International Venture Capital: The Role of Start-Up Financing in the United States, Europe, and Asia*. Council on Foreign Relations, New York.

Overseas Private Investment Corporation (2006) *OPIC News*, 8(2): 1. February 2006.

PricewaterhouseCoopers (2005). *Global Private Equity Report*.

Rubin, J. and Stankiewicz, G. (2005). The new markets tax credit program: a midcourse assessment. *Community Development Investment Review*, 1(1):1–12.

Sapienza, H.J., Manigart, S. and Vermeir, W. (1996). Venture Capital Governance and Value Added in Four Countries. *Journal of Business Venturing*, 11(6):439–469.

Schöfer, P. and Leitinger, R. (2002). Framework for Venture Capital in the Accession Countries to the European Union. Working Paper, Cap Gemini Ernst & Young Consulting and Raiffeisen Zentralbank Österreich AG.

Schwienbacher, A. (2005). An Empirical Analysis of Venture Capital Exits in Europe and the United States. Working Paper, University of Amsterdam.

Sener, F. (2006). Labor Market Rigidities and R&D-based Growth in the Global Economy. *Journal of Economic Dynamics & Control*, 30(5):769–805.

Shi, C., Pukthuanthong, K. and Walker, T. (2006). Disclosure Regulation and IPO Underpricing: An International Analysis. Working Paper, University of California at Irvine.

Singer, M. and Stauder, D. (2003). *The European Patent Convention – A Commentary*. Sweet & Maxwell, London, U.K.

Sormani, A. (2001). The Netherlands: Worldwide Appeal. *European Venture Capital Journal*, 23:1–13.

Spinner, M. (2003). European Adventure. *Financial World*, 53:62–68.

White, M. (1996). The Costs of Corporate Bankruptcy: A U.S.-European Comparison. In Bhandari, J. and Weiss, L. (eds), *Corporate Bankruptcy: Economic and Legal Perspectives*. Cambridge University Press, Cambridge.

2 Public venture capital across Europe: A 15-year perspective

Christof Beuselinck and Sophie Manigart

Abstract

We study the galvanizing role that national EU governments play in the development of local venture capital (VC) markets in ten European countries for the period 1989 to 2003. Results show that the amount of public VC funds invested is of a relatively high importance for some European countries, and varies significantly over country-years. Further, public VC investments primarily flow to early stage deals, whereas private VC does not favor this investment segment. Moreover, we document that whereas private VC investments follow trends in business cycles and exit alternatives, public VC is unrelated to these features.

2.1 Introduction

The venture capital industry has become an important player in the development of enterprises worldwide. It is important for growth-oriented companies 'which generally lack the size, assets and/or operating history to obtain financing from traditional sources, like banks and public capital markets' (National Venture Capital Association (NVCA), 2005). The European VC market has long been underdeveloped compared with its U.S. counterpart, but its economic importance increased dramatically during the last two decades of the previous millennium. From the Lisbon Council in spring 2000 until the end of 2004, over €140 billion of equity capital was invested in 40 000 companies in the European Union, thereby indirectly nurturing employment for over 6.5 million people (EVCA, 2005).[1] Because of its contribution to economic growth, job creation and technological progress, national governments all over the world have embraced the private equity (PE) and VC industry as an essential driver of economic growth and renewal.

Anecdotal evidence as well as academic studies document that access to finance is one of the crucial aspects of fostering innovative entrepreneurship (Jeng and Wells, 2000; Gompers and Lerner, 1999; OECD, 1997). Innovative firms with high growth ambitions typically have a great need for cash, because heavy investments in research and development are not matched with early revenues. Private VC investors partly resolve this

[1] The Lisbon agenda is a commitment by European leaders, formalized at the Lisbon 2000 Spring EU Council, to develop Europe into the most competitive knowledge-based economy by 2010. Fostering and supporting small and medium-sized enterprises by means of sufficient (equity) capital providence is essential in this Lisbon strategy.

demand for funding by providing equity capital to firms that cannot access traditional financing sources such as internal financing, bank debt, or other types of debt (Berger and Udell, 1998). However, the demand for (equity) financing is typically not entirely met by the private VC segment and public authorities therefore often take decisions in an attempt to close this 'equity gap' (Mason and Harrison, 1997). At a European level, the European Investment Fund was set up in the late 1990s to invest in European early stage investment funds (European Commission Report, 2003). However, national and regional governments all across the EU have implemented various policy measures to address the small-firm equity gap since the 1980s. Governments either improve the institutional environment by the establishment of favorable tax schemes for both SMEs and investors, or they also directly impact the early stage investment sector, for example by setting up guarantee schemes, by subsidizing business angel networks, and by direct funding through the creation of fully or partially government-funded VC firms.

The current study focuses on the latter of these support mechanisms and examines the evolution of public money invested in the VC and PE industry (henceforth: public VC) in ten European countries over a 15-year time period, being 1989–2003. We dynamically analyze public VC over a time period with macro-economic downfalls and periods of credit shortage, as well as economic upswings. Consequently, this study provides estimates of the drivers of direct government involvement in local VC markets and thereby supplements the small number of studies dedicated to this issue in the academic literature to date.

Results show that public VC investments are relatively important in some countries, while they are almost non-existent in other countries. When expressed as a proportion of a country's GDP, Belgium and the Scandinavian countries (Finland, Norway, and Sweden) have the highest proportion of public VC investments over the entire 15-year period. The largest EU economies such as Germany, France, Italy, and the United Kingdom invested only minor amounts via public VC investments into the sector. Public VC investments further vary significantly within a single country over the period of analysis. Over all countries combined, public VC accounted for as much as 11% to 15% of total VC investments during the mid-1990s and gradually declined to 4.3% in 2003.

Further, early stage and high-tech VC investments are higher in countries where public VC investments are proportionally more important. This suggests that government funds contribute to the VC segment that suffers most of the equity-financing gap. Whereas private VC investments are highest during economic boom cycles (Acs and Audretsch, 1994) and are positively related to the strength of the IPO market (Jeng and Wells, 2000) we do not find such evidence for public VC investments. This implies that public VC programs are less dependent on economic cycles than private VC investments, providing a stabilizing factor in this cyclical industry.

2.2 Public versus private VC

Numerous academic studies highlight the importance of a healthy VC industry. For instance, Kortum and Lerner (2000) document that VC funding contributed significantly to industrial innovations. The U.S. National Venture Capital Association (NVCA, 2005) reports that VC-backed companies contribute to 10.1 million jobs and comprise 1.8 trillion (10%) of total US industry sales. The European Private Equity and Venture

Capital Association (EVCA, 2003) reports that European VC-backed companies generate significantly higher growth rates in sales, research spending, exports and job creation than comparable non-VC backed companies.

As a result, it is not hard to understand why policymakers are proponents of private equity (PE) in general, and venture capital in particular. Recent action plans have been undertaken to foster entrepreneurship and to facilitate the access to finance for SMEs in the EU (see, for instance, EC Report, 2003 and 1998). In these actions plans, VC is stressed as an essential component to alleviate the financing problems that restrict young, high-tech firms in doing and expanding their business. The EU Commission encourages joint attempts across the EU to improve the institutional environment, thus indirectly promoting the VC industry. Such measures include (1) tax law reviews, (2) allowing institutional investors such as pension funds or insurance companies to invest a fraction of their assets in the VC or PE industry, (3) government-backed guarantee schemes, or (4) the creation of efficient and integrated pan-European trading platforms for high-potential companies.

Indirect measures do not always have the desired effect, however. For example, Holtz-Eakin (2000) shows that inducing preferential tax treatments for SMEs does not solve the equity gap. In addition to providing a stimulating environment for venture capital, European governments therefore directly invest in the VC industry. Despite its importance, there is only limited research on the impact of active government involvement in the VC market. Lerner (1999) studies the U.S. Small Business Innovation Research (SBIR) program between 1983 and 1997. He shows that awardees of this program benefit substantially: they not only grow faster than matched non-awardees but are also able to attract more private VC. Mason and Harrison (1997) document that public effort to invest in early stage firms is essential in the provision of sufficient capital to small, start-up and early stage businesses in Europe.

Jeng and Wells (2000) study determinants of VC funding in a cross-country study of 21 countries (among which 13 EU countries). One of the determinants in their analysis is direct public investment in the VC industry, next to other determinants such as IPO activity, labor market rigidities, and accounting standards. They find that the inflow of public money into the VC industry is less sensitive to changes in the IPO market and conclude that public money especially supports investments in sectors where IPOs are less common. Leleux and Surlemont (2003) study the interaction between public VC funding and private VC funding. Contrary to their crowding-out hypothesis, they find that the availability of public money does not have a negative effect on the availability of private money. On the contrary, public VC funding causes greater amounts of money to be invested in the industry as a whole. They further show that public VC investors do not have a bias, favoring industries that need a lot of employees, nor do public VC firms syndicate their investments less than private VC firms. Both studies thus show that public VC investments can have a positive effect on the VC market as a whole.

2.3 Hypotheses

National authorities can either actively intervene in the economy and business sector or rely on market mechanisms to level out the inefficiencies. We expect that public authorities intervene in the VC market especially when the private sector is not active or is underdeveloped. We therefore expect a negative relation between public VC and private VC investments. This leads to:

> H1: High public VC investments occur in countries and in periods of time where private VC investments are low.

Consistent with earlier studies (Aernoudt, 1999; Mason and Harrisson, 1997) and with the action plans proposed in EU guidelines on fostering entrepreneurial growth (e.g. EC Report, 1998), we expect that government intervention is especially targeted at those segments of the market where the perceived market failure is the greatest. Information asymmetries may deter private VC funds from investing. Information asymmetries are especially high in the seed or start-up segment and in the high-technology segment. High levels of public investments will therefore result in higher levels of seed or start-up investments and of investments in high-tech sectors, leading to:

> H2a: High levels of public VC investments stimulate high levels of seed/start-up VC investments.
> H2b: High levels of public VC investments stimulate high levels of high-tech VC investments.

There is worldwide evidence that investor sentiment is highly correlated with economic cycles and stock market returns. This explains the phenomenon of mergers and acquisitions and IPO waves, and sudden drops or rises in stock prices (Ritter, 1991). This co-movement pattern is likely to be observed in the VC industry too (Acs and Audretsch, 1994). We therefore expect that economic cycles drive the level of private VC investments. Periods of economic growth and prosperity are expected to correspond with high levels of private VC investments whereas periods of economic downturn might result in a substantial reduction in private VC funds. However, provided that national authorities try to close the equity gap and their investment pattern is not dictated by business cycles or return opportunities, we expect public VC investments to be unrelated to macroclimate and stock market returns. This leads to:

> H3: Public VC investments, contrary to private VC investments, are unrelated to macroeconomic business cycles.

2.4 Data

The goal of the present study is to examine the above-stated hypotheses and to provide evidence on the importance of public VC investments in ten European countries over a 15-year time period (1989–2003) and to understand changes in public funding. Data on public VC investments come from the annual statistics of EVCA. Given the unavailability of data on public investment in some European countries (such as Denmark, Germany, Greece, Luxemburg, and Portugal), our study is restricted to ten EU countries for which data are available over the period 1989–2003. These countries are (in alphabetical order) Belgium, Finland, France, Ireland, Italy, Norway, the Netherlands, Spain, Sweden, and the U.K.

We focus on VC as an investment in seed, early stage and expansion companies, as it is estimated that the equity gap is most important for these types of companies. Public VC investments are therefore typically restricted to these investment stages (Mason and

Harrison, 1997). This restriction also allows comparisons of U.S. and EU figures, as VC is defined as early stage equity capital for unquoted companies in the U.S. Our definition is also consistent with other studies on international VC investments (Jeng and Wells, 2000). Hence, we do not include equity capital provided for management buy-outs and buy-ins, nor replacement capital (EVCA, 2005: Glossary).

The yearly EVCA statistics show the amount invested in the VC industry in a particular country, the proportion of public VC investments, the proportion of seed and early stage investments and of high-tech investments in the total VC industry. Country-level macroeconomic data come from the OECD Economic Outlook and include (1) GDP, (2) real GDP growth and (3) output gap.[2] Stock market variables are retrieved from Thomson Financials and include (1) number of listed firms on the main national exchanges, (2) number of newly listed firms less delistings per year, and (3) yearly stock return of a country's market index.

2.5 The evolution of public VC in Europe

In this section, we discuss the evolution of VC investments in the ten European countries of our study. Figure 2.1 shows the time trend for the total VC investments in the ten EU countries. For illustrative purposes, Figure 2.1 also shows the time trend in total PE investments (i.e. VC capital defined as above, plus buy-out and replacement capital). Figure 2.1 shows that VC investments were at low and fairly stable levels until the mid-1990s (never above €2.5 billion) and then sharply increased to almost €15 billion at the

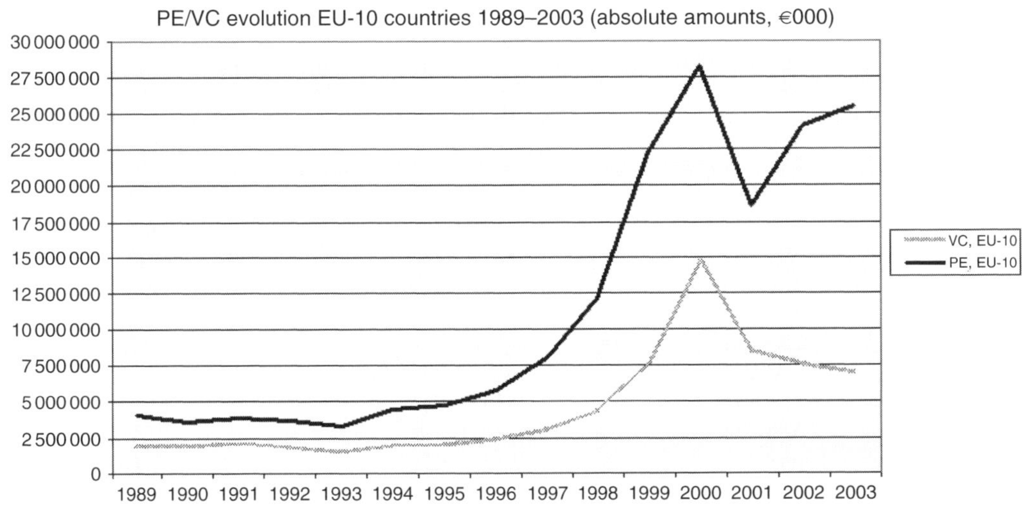

Figure 2.1 Evolution of yearly venture capital (gray line) and private equity (black line) investments (1989–2003, absolute amounts, €000)

[2] The output gap is the percentage of GDP that a country is above/below its optimal GDP, given a non-accelerating inflation rate and unemployment (NAIRU) situation.

end of the millennium. VC and PE investments sharply fell after the tech bubble correction to levels just above €7.5 billion in 2001, further decreasing in 2002 and 2003.

When comparing VC investments with total PE investments, a parallel trend is observed until 2000. However, after the sharp decline in 2001, total PE investments rise substantially again in 2002 and 2003, in contrast with VC investments. This suggests that it is important to consider the VC and PE industry separately, rather than jointly. The dynamics of the two segments do no longer follow similar patterns.

Table 2.1 reports the amount and proportion of public investments in the VC industry in the ten countries of our study. On average, governments invested almost €350 million per year in the ten countries of the study. There is a substantial variation over time, however. While the yearly amount invested was at most €280 million in the first half of the 1990s, it increased to more than €700 million per year in 1999 and 2000. Thereafter, the amount invested by public authorities steadily declined to a level of €300 000 in 2003.

Over all countries and years combined, public investments represent 9.0% of the total investments in the VC industry. There is substantial variation in this proportion over time, but it does not match the pattern of the total amount invested. Public investments were 11% to 12% of total VC investments in the early 1990s and they attained an all-time high of 14.2% in 1995. 1995 is a turning point, as it initiated a steady decrease in the proportion of public investment in the VC industry to an all-time low of only 4.3% in 2003. This shows that although public VC investments were relatively important in funding the VC industry in the first half of the 1990s, its significance reduced substantially thereafter, despite the fact that the total amount invested by public authorities continued to rise until 2000. This shows that the private sector has become much more active since the second half of the 1990s.

Table 2.2 reports yearly public VC investments for each of the ten EU countries in absolute amounts (Panel A) and as a proportion as the country's GDP (Panel B,

Table 2.1 Public VC investments and total VC investments

Year	Public VC investments	Total VC investments	Proportion of public VC to total VC (%)
1989	143 876	1960.268	7.3
1990	238 721	1905.202	12.5
1991	225 939	2159.187	10.5
1992	126 693	1876.209	6.8
1993	139 511	1523.643	9.2
1994	224 391	1987.716	11.3
1995	282 663	1992.745	14.2
1996	269 535	2387.915	11.3
1997	398 756	3096.208	12.9
1998	334 923	4387.459	7.6
1999	712 031	7777.333	9.2
2000	716 169	14 670.923	4.9
2001	628 922	8552.683	7.4
2002	455 232	7575.218	6.0
2003	299 847	7017.690	4.3
Average	346 481	4591.360	9.0

Table 2.2 Public VC investments in ten EU countries

Panel A: Public VC investments in 10 EU countries expressed in 1000 EUR

Year	Belgium	Finland	France	Ireland	Italy	NL	Norway	Spain	Sweden	U.K.
1989	39 886	5158	6083	3919	0	25 962	0	31 849	4099	24 931
1990	44 747	6104	11 074	6606	41 559	23 810	0	19 778	64 000	19 053
1991	62 646	13 817	11 801	2853	31 192	26 282	3011	38 497	19 359	14 489
1992	n/a	9530	9896	0	56 385	28 740	0	4049	701	15 401
1993	44 013	15 814	6435	0	14 356	29 897	14 440	0	1109	11 452
1994	44 608	18 413	11 645	0	53 904	2348	36 535	0	0	34 144
1995	38 981	12 948	13 240	2168	110 665	2622	63 333	0	0	13 111
1996	73 670	20 477	11 267	968	74 222	2837	47 258	0	133	11 507
1997	115 694	39 255	8318	2053	79 352	3668	51 077	0	57 542	7298
1998	118 802	25 445	0	2725	74 547	5340	19 826	24 715	0	13 825
1999	243 931	39 516	18 064	42 002	105 726	4680	0	65 048	128 917	20 649
2000	279 551	30 612	102 313	1276	124 096	79 438	1553	32 649	49 067	13 614
2001	199 908	44 584	40 694	1413	27 305	30 673	98 515	27 321	152 071	4437
2002	174 928	30 542	72 293	1729	56 428	21 520	30 065	59 318	2560	3847
2003	25 159	34 733	351	1187	51 939	87	24 814	158 253	1321	0
Average	107 609	23 130	21 565	4593	60 112	31 947	26 028	30 765	32 059	13 851
Average 1989–1996	49 793	12 783	10 180	2064	47 785	26 512	20 572	11 772	11 175	18 011
Average 1997–2003	165 425	34 955	34 576	7484	74 199	38 158	32 264	52 472	55 925	9096

(*Continued*)

Table 2.2 Continued

Panel B: Public VC investments across 10 EU countries as proportion of GDP – expressed as per MIL

Year	Belgium	Finland	France	Ireland	Italy	NL	Norway	Spain	Sweden	U.K.
1989	0.252	0.061	0.006	0.115	0.000	0.109	0.000	0.111	0.023	0.032
1990	0.266	0.069	0.011	0.180	0.061	0.094	0.000	0.062	0.338	0.025
1991	0.356	0.163	0.011	0.075	0.042	0.098	0.031	0.110	0.094	0.017
1992	n/a	0.115	0.009	0.000	0.072	0.103	0.000	0.011	0.003	0.019
1993	0.231	0.189	0.006	0.000	0.018	0.105	0.145	0.000	0.007	0.014
1994	0.222	0.207	0.010	0.000	0.063	0.077	0.351	0.000	0.000	0.039
1995	0.187	0.134	0.011	0.041	0.120	0.083	0.560	0.000	0.000	0.015
1996	0.350	0.206	0.009	0.017	0.076	0.085	0.377	0.000	0.001	0.012
1997	0.523	0.364	0.007	0.030	0.077	0.104	0.369	0.000	0.265	0.006
1998	0.517	0.217	0.000	0.035	0.070	0.144	0.147	0.046	0.000	0.011
1999	1.023	0.327	0.013	0.464	0.095	0.118	0.000	0.112	0.553	0.014
2000	1.111	0.234	0.071	0.012	0.106	0.189	0.009	0.052	0.198	0.009
2001	0.772	0.326	0.027	0.012	0.022	0.069	0.515	0.040	0.625	0.003
2002	0.654	0.217	0.047	0.013	0.045	0.046	0.149	0.081	0.010	0.002
2003	0.092	0.241	0.000	0.009	0.040	0.000	0.133	0.203	0.005	0.000
Average	0.468	0.205	0.016	0.067	0.060	0.095	0.186	0.055	0.141	0.015
Average 1989–1996	0.266	0.143	0.009	0.053	0.056	0.094	0.183	0.037	0.058	0.022
Average 1997–2003	0.670	0.275	0.024	0.082	0.065	0.096	0.189	0.076	0.236	0.006

Panel C: Average VC (total) as per MIL of GDP, and High-Tech and Seed & Start-up VC investments as a proportion of total VC investments

Variable	Belgium	Finland	France	Ireland	Italy	NL	Norway	Spain	Sweden	U.K.
Average VC investment per million of GDP	0.816	0.766	0.694	0.711	0.445	1.304	0.816	0.574	0.955	1.320
Average percentage high-tech	41.45%	41.40%	26.93%	47.11%	16.06%	27.80%	38.26%	14.54%	30.36%	22.54%
Average percentage seed & start-up	22.70%	30.86%	9.50%	16.67%	9.96%	12.43%	17.69%	14.45%	8.58%	4.74%

expressed as per MIL). Absolute public VC investment reaches fairly high values in several European countries while it is (almost) zero in other countries; there is significant variation over country-years. Belgium has the highest average amount of public VC investment to GDP (0.47 per MIL of GDP) and is followed by the Scandinavian cluster (Finland 0.21 per MIL of GDP, Norway 0.19 per MIL of GDP, and Sweden 0.14 per MIL of GDP). Public authorities of the largest EU economies such as France, Italy, and the U.K. invested only comparatively minor amounts in the VC sector (respectively 0.01, 0.02, and 0.06 per million).

We then compare the average public VC investments with (1) total VC investments over time across countries, (2) the proportion of high-tech VC investments, and (3) the proportion of seed and start-up VC to total VC investments (Table 2.2, Panel C). Total VC investments are highest in the U.K. (1.32 per MIL of GDP), in the Netherlands (1.30 per MIL), and Sweden (0.96 per MIL). The lowest levels of VC investments as a proportion of GDP are observed in Italy (0.45 per MIL), followed by Spain (0.57 per MIL), and France (0.69 per MIL). The level of public VC investments is thus not perfectly related to the level of total VC investments in a country. Interestingly, average proportional investments in high-tech and seed or start-up companies are highest for countries where public VC investment is high (Belgium, Finland, Sweden, and Norway). Ireland is a notable exception where low public VC investment levels coincide with high proportions of high-tech and seed and start-up investments.[3]

2.6 Multivariate analyses

Table 2.3 reports Pearson correlations between the variables of interest for all country-years. Public VC investments are unrelated to private VC investments but, significantly, positively correlated with high-tech VC investments (0.31, $p < 0.01$) and seed and start-up VC investments (0.38, $p < 0.01$). Interestingly, public VC is negatively related to new listings on the stock market (−0.27, $p < 0.01$), suggesting that governments support VC where there are few exit alternatives. However, public VC investments are unrelated to the (current and lagged values of) macro-economic situation and stock market returns.

Table 2.3 Pearson correlation between variables

		(1)	(2)	(3)	(4)	(5)	(6)	(7)
Public VC (%GDP)	(1)	1	–	–	–	–	–	
Private VC (%GDP)	(2)	0.02	1	–	–	–	–	–
% High Tech	(3)	0.31^{**}	0.25^{**}	1	–	–	–	–
% Seed/Start-Up	(4)	0.38^{**}	0.05	0.46^{**}	1	–	–	–
Growth GDP	(5)	0.08	0.13	0.28^{**}	0.05	1	–	–
Outputgap	(6)	0.08	0.38^{**}	0.22^{**}	0.13	0.34^{**}	1	–
Stock Market Return	(7)	−0.01	-0.14^{+}	−0.04	0.02	0.07	-0.33^{**}	1
Net new Stock Listings	(8)	-0.27^{**}	0.36^{**}	-0.19^{*}	-0.35^{**}	−0.12	0.10	−0.07

$^{+}0.05 < p < 0.1$; $^{*}0.01 < p < 0.05$; $^{**}p < 0.01$

[3] Note that during the period of our study, Ireland underwent structural corporate tax changes in an attempt to grow the economy, which probably resulted in less interest in public VC as a support mechanism.

For private VC investments, however, we observe quite a different relationship with the variables of interest. While high levels of private VC investments also correspond to high proportions of high-tech investments (0.25, $p < 0.01$), they are unrelated to the proportion of seed and start-up investments. Furthermore, private VC investments are significantly positively related to the output gap (0.38, $p < 0.01$), suggesting that economic cycles have contemporaneous effects on private investments in the VC sector. Finally, we find that private VC investments are significantly positively related to the size of the national stock market (0.36, $p < 0.01$) suggesting that non-public investments are more likely in countries with higher stock market exit alternatives.

We corroborate our results further by running multivariate tests. The sample is composed of 15 observation years (from 1989 until 2003) across ten different EU countries. This set-up calls for panel data regressions, as these overcome problems of biased and inconsistent parameters in cross-sectional time-series models (Baltagi, 2001). We run two regression models, specified as follows:

$$
\begin{aligned}
VC_{public(it)} &= \alpha_{it} + \beta_{1it} VC_{private(it)} + \beta_{2it} HT\%_{it} + \beta_{3it} SS\%_{it} \\
&\quad + \beta_{4it} nr(listings)_{it} + \beta_{5t} outputgap_t + \varepsilon_{it} \qquad (2.1) \\
VC_{private(it)} &= \alpha_{it} + \beta_{1it} HT\% + \beta_{2it} SS\%_{it} + \beta_{3it} return_{it} \\
&\quad + \beta_{4it} nr(listings)_{it} + \beta_{5t} outputgap_t + \varepsilon_{it} \qquad (2.2)
\end{aligned}
$$

Panel regression (1) (eq. 2.1) models public VC investments (as a percentage of GDP) as a function of private VC investments (as a percentage of GDP) ($VC_{private}$), high-tech VC investments as percentage of total VC investments (HT%), seed and start-up VC investments as percentage of total VC investments (SS%), net number of new listings on the stock market (nr(listings)), and output gap.[4] Panel regression (2) (eq. 2.2) models private VC investments – excluding public funds – as a function of high-tech (HT%) and seed and start-up VC investments (SS%), stock market return (return), number of new listings (nr(listings)), and output gap. We ran additional panel regressions (not reported) with lagged macro and stock market variables but results remain unchanged.

The first column in Table 2.4 reports the results of panel regression (1). Public VC investments are unrelated to the level of private VC investments, which rejects our hypothesis that public VC would offset low levels of purely private VC, and vice versa. We did sensitivity analyses and included lagged values of private VC as a percentage of GDP as a driver of direct public investments in the VC industry. This allows for governments to react to what happened in the past. The results remain unchanged: the amount invested by public authorities in the VC industry is not related to the amount invested by the private sector in the previous years. Hypothesis 1 is thus not supported.

We do find support for hypothesis 2a, but not for hypothesis 2b. Increases in public VC correspond with higher seed and start-up investments (0.33; $t = 2.19$), but no such relation is observed for high-tech VC investments. Further, we find mixed support for hypothesis 3. Public VC investments are higher in times of economic growth (0.01; $t = 1.87$) but are unrelated to the net number of new listings on the stock market. Previous findings again hold when using lagged variables.

[4] For ease of interpretation, the variables HT%, SS%, return and output gap have been divided by 1000 in the two models. This has to be taken into account when interpreting the coefficients.

Table 2.4 Panel estimation models

	Model 1 public VC (% GDP)		Model 2 private VC (% GDP)	
	coefficient	*t*-value sign.	coefficient	*t*-value sign.
Constant	0.000	1.97+	0.001	3.02**
VC private	0.014	0.54	–	–
HT%	−0.010	−0.17	−0.010	−0.04
SS%	0.329	2.19*	−0.061	−0.13
Nr(listings)	0.001	−0.88	0.002	2.53*
Outputgap	0.011	1.87+	0.042	2.23*
Return	–		−0.070	−0.39
R squared	0.108		0.088	

+ $0.05 < p < 0.1$; * $0.01 < p < 0.05$; ** $p < 0.01$

The second model (second column of Table 2.4) shows that investments by private parties in the VC industry are unrelated to high-tech and seed and start-up investments. Both coefficients are low and insignificant. This confirms the univariate findings and is consistent with the idea that private investors favor later stage, non-tech deals. A higher inflow of VC by private parties does not lead to more investments in high-tech companies or in seed and early stage companies. Further, both a favorable macro-economic environment (0.04; $t = 2.23$) and more new listings on stock markets (0.002; $t = 2.53$) positively affect the investments by private parties in the VC industry. Stock returns (both current and lagged), surprisingly, are unrelated to total private VC investments. Also here, results hold when using lagged independent variables.

2.7 Conclusion

The aim of this chapter was to understand patterns of direct public investment in the VC industry in ten European countries over a 15-year time period. We have shown that there is a substantial variation in the degree to which governments are involved in the VC industry. Government is almost completely absent in some countries such as Ireland, France, and the U.K., while it plays an important role as investor in the VC industry in Belgium and in the Nordic countries (Sweden, Norway, and Finland). Public VC investments were higher in the second half of the observation period compared with the first half, in all countries (except in the U.K.). As of 1995, however, the proportion of public VC to total VC decreased steadily.

Multivariate analyses show that direct public investments in the VC industry are not related to the overall economic climate, and are negatively related to the attractiveness of stock markets. Private investments, on the other hand, are significantly and positively related to the overall economic climate and to the attractiveness of stock markets (measured by the number of net new listings). This provides evidence that public investments are less opportunistically driven by the economic climate, and therefore create a stabilizing effect on the VC industry as a whole.

Moreover, more public investments in the VC industry lead to proportionally more investment in seed and start-up companies, while this is not the case for private VC investments. Seed and start-up companies are extremely risky and surrounded with high levels of uncertainty; here information opacity and information asymmetries may deter VC funds (Aernoudt, 1999; Berger and Udell, 1998). These companies are therefore most likely to be affected by the small-firm equity gap. Our results therefore suggest that public investments in the VC industry have a desirable effect, namely they stimulate investments in a category of companies that potentially have the most problems in finding financing from private sources. This supports the findings of Leleux and Surlemont (2003) that public investments play a complementary role to private investments in the VC industry, rather than crowding out the private sector.

Governments can strengthen the VC industry in several ways. They can indirectly stimulate VC by improving the economic conditions, strengthening stock markets, providing strong minority shareholder protection, investing in research and innovation, or by promoting entrepreneurship. They can also directly impact the VC industry by installing favorable tax treatments for investors in the VC industry, by reducing the risk for VC funds (for example by providing state guarantees), or by reducing transaction costs (for example by sponsoring junior VC professionals). Despite the array of indirect measures at their disposal, European governments nevertheless often choose to directly intervene in the VC market. Although this study is one of the first addressing a relatively long time horizon of 15 years in a European content, more research is still needed to understand the trade-off between direct and indirect interventions, and the efficiency of both approaches. We therefore call for additional studies on these features, to better understand differences in public VC investment behavior across countries and over time.

References

Acs, Z. and Audretsch, B. (1994). New Firm Start-Ups, Technology and Macro-Economic Fluctuations. *Small Business Economics*, 6(6):439–449.

Aernoudt, R. (1999). European Policy towards Venture Capital: Myth or Reality? *Venture Capital: An International Journal of Entrepreneurial Finance*, 1(1):47–58.

Baltagi, B.H. (2001). *Econometric Analysis of Panel Data*. John Wiley and Sons, Chichester.

Berger, A.N. and Udell, G.F. (1998). The Economics Of Small Business Finance: The Roles of Private Equity and Debt Markets In The Financial Growth Cycle. *Journal of Banking and Finance*, 22(6–8):613–673.

European Commission Report (1998). *Fostering Entrepreneurship in Europe: Priorities for the Future*. Com(98) 222 final.

European Commission Report (2003). *Access to Finance for Small and Medium-Sized Enterprises*. Com(2003) 713 final.

European Venture Capital and Private Equity Association (EVCA) (2003). *Yearbook*. http://www.evca.com

European Venture Capital and Private Equity Association (EVCA) (2005). *Yearbook*. http://www.evca.com

Gompers, P.A. and Lerner, J. (1999). *The Venture Capital Cycle*. MIT Press, Cambridge, MA.

Holtz-Eakin, D. (2000). Public Policy Towards Entrepreneurship. *Small Business Economics*, 15(4):283–291.

Jeng, L.A. and Wells, P.C. (2000). The Determinants of Venture Capital Funding: Evidence across Countries. *Journal of Corporate Finance*, 6(2):241–289.

Kortum, S. and Lerner, J. (2000). Assessing the Contribution of Venture Capital to Innovation. *RAND Journal of Economics*, 31(4):674–692.

Leleux, B. and Surlemont, B. (2003). Public versus Private Venture Capital: Seeding or Crowding Out? A Pan-European Analysis. *Journal of Business Venturing*, 18(1): 81–104.

Lerner, J. (1999). The Government as Venture Capitalist: The Long-Run Impact of the SBIR Program. *Journal of Business*, 72(3):285–318.

Mason, C.M. and Harrison, R.T. (1997). Business Angel Networks and the Development of the Informal Venture Capital Market in the UK: Is there still a Role for the Public Sector? *Small Business Economics*, 9(2):111–123.

National Venture Capital Association (NVCA) (2005). *Venture Impact: Venture Capital Benefits to the U.S. Economy*. See http://www.nvca.org

Organisation for Economic Cooperation and Development (1997). *Government Venture Capital for Technology-Based Firms*. OECD/GD 97(201):1–34. OECD, Paris. See http://www.oecd.org

Ritter, J.R. (1991). The Long-Run Performance of Initial Public Offerings. *Journal of Finance*, 46(1):3–27.

3 Why venture capital markets are well developed in some countries but comparatively small in others: Evidence from Europe

Kuntara Pukthuanthong, Dolruedee Thiengtham, and Thomas Walker

Abstract

This chapter extends the literature on the relationship between a country's legal system and its financial development. While previous studies have examined firms' access to broader debt and equity sources of external finance, our study focuses specifically on firms' access to venture capital (VC). Venture capital often provides a first stepping stone for young firms and is thus a crucial part of a country's financial development. We employ data on VC financing deals from the Securities Data Company's (SDC) VentureXpert database for the period from 1995 to 2004, which we combine with a series of country-specific factors for the same period. We argue that the origin of a country's legal system affects firms' access to capital. In addition, we hypothesize that an independent judiciary, an adaptable legal system, and effective contract enforcement provide the necessary background for venture capitalists to seek out and finance otherwise risky companies. As an added benefit, our study explores the linkage between venture financing activity and various other country characteristics, helping us address the question why VC markets are well developed in some countries while they are comparatively small in others.

3.1 Introduction

Not every firm has equal access to external financing. Aside from firm-specific factors that may determine how well and how much capital a firm can attract, country-specific factors often play a major role as well. This chapter extends the extant literature that investigates how a country's financial system relates to its legal tradition and economic development by focusing on the VC market in Europe. Using data for approximately 4000 firms in 38 countries around the world, Beck et al. (2005) observe that firms in countries with French legal origin face significantly higher obstacles in accessing external finance than firms in common law countries. In addition, they observe various other countrywide factors that affect a company's access to finance. A potential shortcoming of their dataset, however, is that it is derived from survey data, specifically managers' responses to the World Business Environment Survey (WBES). One problem of working with survey data is that an individual's responses may be subjective and potentially biased. With respect to the WBES survey, this may be particularly problematic as the survey was conducted in 1999, at the height of the 'hot' IPO market in the U.S. and many other countries around the world, when investor optimism and firms' access to finance were arguably better than usual. We aim to overcome this problem by using 'hard' data on venture capitalist financing activity during a ten-year period from January 1995 to December 2004, collected from the Security Data Company's VentureXpert database. The goal of our study is to relate the venture capitalist activity in a given country to various factors describing its economic and legal development and to answer the question whether potential obstacles that firms may face in contracting for external financing are related to linkages running from legal origins to legal traits (see Beck et al., 2005).

3.2 Literature review

There is a substantial body of research that finds a robust relationship between the origin of a country's legal tradition and the operation of its financial system. La Porta et al. (1998), for example, distinguish between commercial and company law that is based on British, French, German, and Scandinavian legal origins and find that these legal origins are important in explaining the creditor and shareholder rights in the respective countries. Similarly, La Porta et al. (1997) and Levine (2003, 1999, 1998) show that cross-country differences in the size of the banking sector and the level of stock market development can be explained by differences in investor protection laws. As Beck et al. (2005) point out, this means that researchers have identified an empirical chain running from legal origin to investor protection laws to financial development.[1]

The legal origins theory states that many aspects of a country's economic state of development are the result of their legal system. The basic thrust of the theory is that common law, as opposed to French civil law, and to a lesser degree German and Scandinavian civil law, is associated with more orientation towards institutions of the market (instead of state interventionism), which is why, according to proponents of the legal origins theory, common law countries tend to be economically more developed (see also Beck et al., 2005).[2] Beck et al. (2003a) summarize the comparative legal literature and note that

[1] Beck et al. (2005, 2003a) provide an excellent review of related studies, pointing out that researchers have also found legal institutions to influence the efficiency with which financial systems allocate capital (Beck and Levine, 2002; Wurgler, 2000), the valuation of firms (Caprio et al., 2003; Claessens et al., 2002; La Porta et al., 2002), the dividend payment policies of corporations (La Porta et al., 2000), the efficiency of equity markets (Morck et al., 2000), and the financial fragility of firms (Johnson et al., 2000). Moreover, Beck et al. (2003b) document a robust connection between legal origin and equity market development as well as property rights protection. Finally, Levine et al. (2000) and Beck et al. (2000b) establish that the component of financial development explained by legal origin explains economic growth.

[2] Common law is also referred to as 'case law' (or 'precedential law') because judges in common law countries tend to base their decisions on prior decisions made by other judges. Judges in civil law countries, on the other hand, generally base their rulings on a strict interpretation of the written codes and laws. Because the weight accorded to judicial precedent is much lower in civil law countries, their legal system tends to be static and inflexible, whereas common law allows the judiciary to dynamically react to new developments.

legal theories emphasize two inter-related channels through which legal origin influences finance.

First, the 'political' channel contends that (a) legal traditions differ in terms of the priority they attach to private property rights versus the rights of the State and (b) the protection of private contracting rights forms the basis of financial development (La Porta et al., 1999). Beck et al. (2003a) note that the English common law evolved in the tumultuous 16th and 17th centuries when Parliament and the English kings battled for control of the country. During those days, the Crown attempted to reassert feudal privileges and sell monopolies to raise revenues. Courts sided with Parliament (composed mostly of wealthy merchants and landowners) and protected private property owners against the Crown. These developments facilitated the ability of private property owners to transact confidently, with positive repercussions on financial development (North and Weingast, 1989). On the other hand, the French and German civil codes, which were developed in the 19th century during the Napoleonic rule in France and Bismarck's rule in Germany, were constructed to solidify State power by placing the 'prince above the law' (Hayek, 1960: 166–167). Because the State dominated the judiciary, legal traditions evolved that focused more on the power of the State and less on the rights of individual investors (Mahoney, 2001). As a result of its promotion of institutions that encourage State power, civil law tradition is believed to have adverse implications on financial development.

Second, the 'adaptability' channel focuses on the flexibility of a legal system in adapting to changing environments. Hayek (1960) points out that legal traditions differ in their ability to evolve with changing conditions. Merryman (1985) extends this line of thought and argues that legal traditions that adapt efficiently to minimize the gap between the contracting needs of the economy and the legal system's capabilities will more effectively foster financial development than more rigid systems. Posner (1973) argues that British common law evolves efficiently as judges respond case-by-case to unforeseen and changing conditions. In addition, Beck et al. (2003a) suggest that since common law grants substantial discretion to judges, inefficient laws are challenged in the courts and, through repeated litigation, efficient rules replace inefficient ones. In reviewing the comparative law literature, they note that legal systems that reject jurisprudence – the law created by judges in the process of solving disputes – and rely instead on changes in statutory law will tend to evolve more inefficiently with negative implications for finance. Beck et al. (2005) note that the Napoleonic doctrine's mistrust of judges and jurisprudence hinders the flexibility of the legal system in countries that follow the French civil code. As a result, financial development is adversely affected in these countries. Yet, not all civil law countries are constrained by a rigid legal system. German and Scandinavian civil law is considered to be much more dynamic as both systems rejected the Napoleonic doctrine and maintained their historical roots in jurisprudence and judicial discretion (Beck et al., 2003a).

It is important to understand that the political and adaptability channels are not mutually exclusive and sometimes make conflicting predictions with respect to a country's financial development. For German civil law countries, for example, the political channel predicts that financial development should be constrained because civil law tradition tends to centralize and intensify state power, making investors more wary, thus restricting the development of free financial systems that is typically observed in common law countries. At the same time, the adaptability channel predicts that German civil law tradition fosters financial development as it is more adaptable to changing environments than the French civil law tradition.

This chapter focuses specifically on a firm's access to venture capital and uses broad cross-country regressions to assess whether legal tradition shapes finance primarily by affecting the power of the State relative to the judiciary or by influencing the adaptability of the law to evolving conditions.

3.3 Data

The data used in this study come from several different sources. We start by identifying all venture capital deals in which funds were provided to European companies between January 1995 and December 2004 in the Securities Data Company's (SDC) VentureXpert database. The VentureXpert database provides detailed information for each venture capital deal, including, for example, the date of each financing round, the amount a company received, and detailed information on the venture capitalists that disbursed the funds.

We combine our dataset with country-level data provided by Demirgüç-Kunt and Maksimovic (1998) and Beck et al. (2005, 2003a). Because their datasets only cover the largest European countries, we eliminate venture capital deals for countries not included in their studies from our dataset. This leaves us with approximately 27 300 venture capital financing rounds provided to more than 12 300 firms in 19 European countries. Table 3.1 provides summary statistics for our dataset.

Our dataset contains a diverse group of countries in terms of venture capitalist (VC) activity. The UK, France and Germany clearly lead Europe with respect to the number of firms that received venture capital funding with approximately 3950, 2500, and 1500 funded firms, respectively. Yet, countries in which fewer than 100 firms received venture capital funding during our sample period (such as Cyprus, Greece, Iceland, and Luxembourg) are also represented. Not surprisingly, the UK, France, and Germany also lead our sample when ranked by the total US$ amount of funds disbursed.[3,4]

With few exceptions, the average size of each financing deal and the average size of the VC syndicate involved in each deal tend to be larger in the larger European economies.[5] Moreover, we observe that in larger economies a bigger proportion of domestic venture capital firms stand behind a given deal. The remainder is usually financed by U.S. venture capitalists and VC firms located in other (typically European) nations. Not surprisingly, our statistics suggest a general trend for larger economies to have more developed venture capital markets than smaller economies.

[3] Note that the VentureXpert database provides information on financing deals in US$ terms. We carry over reported investment amounts directly from their database. This allows us to avoid possible currency conversion issues as well as reporting problems related to the introduction of the Euro during our sample period.

[4] Note that the totals in column 4 of Table 3.1 do not correspond to the figures provided in column 2 and 3 because firms frequently receive more than one financing round.

[5] A notable exception is Luxembourg. Here, few firms received VC funding, but the amounts provided to these firms were considerably higher than in most other countries.

Table 3.1 Summary statistics for our dataset of venture capital deals in 19 European countries between January 1995 and December 2004. The dataset is based on information contained in the Securities Data Company's (SDC) VentureXpert database

Country	No. of Firms Receiving Financing	Average Funds Disbursed Per Financing Round ($000)	Total Funds Disbursed ($Billion)	Average VC Syndicate Size Per Financing Round	Proportion of Domestic VCs Providing Financing	Proportion of US VCs Providing Financing	Proportion of Other VCs Providing Financing
Austria	158	14 014	1.02	1.47	47.7%	24.5%	27.8%
Belgium	318	11 159	3.06	1.77	42.1%	36.3%	21.6%
Cyprus	11	13 243	0.13	1.18	25.0%	41.7%	33.3%
Denmark	298	13 777	3.38	1.49	49.0%	25.9%	25.1%
Finland	590	6974	2.35	1.40	61.6%	26.0%	12.5%
France	2512	16 055	25.37	1.76	52.8%	34.5%	12.7%
Germany	1522	21 242	21.58	1.65	54.8%	25.5%	19.6%
Greece	38	19 453	0.14	1.11	56.8%	35.1%	8.1%
Iceland	22	4430	0.12	1.41	55.9%	32.4%	11.8%
Ireland	276	15 266	4.72	1.82	35.7%	44.1%	20.1%
Italy	440	24 151	6.26	1.42	34.5%	36.6%	28.8%
Luxembourg	47	86 522	3.37	1.61	4.6%	56.9%	38.5%
Netherlands	586	18 797	6.73	1.61	43.3%	37.4%	19.3%
Norway	188	10 428	1.04	1.32	49.6%	36.3%	14.1%
Portugal	193	5112	0.39	1.25	65.3%	26.1%	8.5%
Spain	427	12 909	4.22	1.45	51.6%	27.6%	20.8%
Sweden	575	10 412	4.99	1.64	48.8%	30.2%	21.0%
Switzerland	244	12 758	2.81	1.76	30.7%	35.9%	33.3%
U.K.	3949	17 159	62.24	1.67	58.0%	33.8%	8.1%
Total	12 394	333 861	153.90	n/m*	n/m*	n/m*	n/m*
Average	652	17 572	8.10	1.52	45.7%	34.0%	20.3%

*Not meaningful.

3.3.1 Variable descriptions

Dependent variables

In measuring firms' access to external capital in a given country, we focus our attention on venture capitalist activity. As noted in the introduction, the SDC VentureXpert database provides comprehensive coverage of all venture capital deals during our sample period, making it more objective and arguably more reliable than survey-based data.

In our subsequent analysis, we employ three alternative measures intended to capture venture capitalist activity and the overall size of the venture capital market in a given country. Our first measure, VC_DEALS, represents a log ratio of the average number of venture capital deals in a given country divided by the country's average GDP during our sample period. Specifically, we calculate $\ln(\overline{N_i})/\ln(\overline{GDP_i})$, where $\overline{N_i}$ is the average yearly number of VC deals in country i during our sample period and $\overline{GDP_i}$ is the average GDP of that country. We employ GDP information from yearly country statistics provided by the International Monetary Fund (IMF). By using the number of deals relative to a country's GDP rather than the number of deals itself we adjust for the different size of each country's economy. Our second measure, VC_FIRMS, is calculated in a similar fashion, but considers the number of firms that receive VC financing rather than the number of VC deals. The measures differ because firms frequently receive more than one financing round.

Finally, we define VC_AMT, calculated as the log ratio of the average amount of venture capital funds disbursed in a given country per year, again divided by the country's average GDP during our sample period.[6]

Independent variables

We relate venture capitalist activity to several different measures of legal tradition, judiciary independence, judicial adaptability, and enforcement. In addition, we investigate how our measures relate to other proxies for financial and economic development that are used in the extant literature. Most of our independent variables are based on data provided by Beck et al. (2003a) who themselves collect data from various different sources (see their study for detailed information about each variable). Table 3.2 provides information on some of the key variables used in our subsequent analysis.

To address the question of whether legal origin affects the relative size of the venture capital market in a given country, we distinguish between the four legal origins that are prevalent in our sample, that is, British common law, as well as French, German, and Scandinavian civil code.

To examine the relative importance of the political and adaptability channels, we further introduce two sets of variables. The first variable set is intended to measure the independence of the judiciary from the State, while the second set proxies for the dynamism and flexibility of a country's legal system. In line with the existing literature, we expect independent judiciaries and adaptable legal systems to be positively related with the development of the venture capital market in a given country.

[6] In unreported robustness tests, we also employed venture capital measures that are divided by a country's total stock market capitalization rather than its GDP. Our results are qualitatively and quantitatively robust using either variable definition.

Table 3.2 Country characteristics. Information is provided on a series of variables that describe the origin of a country's legal system, the independence of the judiciary from the State, the adaptability of the legal system, the level of financial development, and other factors of interest. The variables are derived from Demirgüç-Kunt and Maksimovic (1998) and Beck et al. (2005, 2003a)

Country	Legal Origin[a]	Indicators of the Political Channel		Indicators of the Adaptability Channel		Financial Development Indicators			Additional Variables of Interests	
		Tenure of Supreme Court Judges[b]	Supreme Court Power[c]	Case Law[d]	Legal Justification[e]	Private Credit[f]	Stock Market Development[g]	Property Rights[h]	Enforcement[i]	Government subsidies[j]
	LEG_OR	SC_TEN	SC_POW	CAS_LAW	LEG_JUST	PRIV_CR	MCAP	PR_RIG	ENF	GVT_SUBS
Austria	GE	2	0	0	1	0.92	0.11	5	9.80	1.3
Belgium	FR	n/a*	n/a*	0	0.33	0.53	0.34	5	9.74	3.5
Cyprus	UK	n/a*	n/a*	n/a*	0.67	1.05	0.19	3	6.74	n/a*
Denmark	SC	2	1	1	0	0.40	0.31	5	9.66	n/a*
Finland	SC	2	1	1	0.67	0.83	0.22	5	9.57	3.0
France	FR	2	0	0	1	0.91	0.30	4	9.09	2.4
Germany	GE	2	0	1	1	0.96	0.22	5	9.50	2.0
Greece	FR	2	0	0	1	0.32	0.13	4	6.41	n/a*
Iceland	SC	2	1	1	1	0.44	0.09	5	9.63	n/a*
Ireland	UK	2	1	1	0.33	0.68	0.27	5	8.38	n/a*
Italy	FR	2	0	0	1	0.53	0.15	4	8.75	2.9
Luxembourg	FR	n/a*	n/a*	n/a*	0.67	0.33	1.25	5	10.00	n/a*
Netherlands	FR	2	1	0	0.67	1.49	0.56	5	9.68	2.6
Norway	SC	2	1	1	0.67	0.94	0.22	5	9.85	5.9
Portugal	FR	2	0	1	1	0.44	0.13	4	8.63	n/a*
Spain	FR	2	1	0	1	0.75	0.25	4	8.10	2.4
Sweden	SC	2	0	1	0.33	1.34	0.50	4	9.79	4.8

(Continued)

Table 3.2 Continued

Country	Legal Origin[a]	Indicators of the Political Channel		Indicators of the Adaptability Channel		Financial Development Indicators			Additional Variables of Interests	
		Tenure of Supreme Court Judges[b]	Supreme Court Power[c]	Case Law[d]	Legal Justification[e]	Private Credit[f]	Stock Market Development[g]	Property Rights[h]	Enforcement[i]	Government subsidies[j]
	LEG_OR	SC_TEN	SC_POW	CAS_LAW	LEG_JUST	PRIV_CR	MCAP	PR_RIG	ENF	GVT_SUBS
Switzerland	GE	1	1	1	0.67	2.07	0.91	5	9.99	1.4
UK	UK	n/a*	n/a*	1	0.33	1.12	1.03	5	9.10	1.5

[a] Legal Origin (LEG_OR) indicates whether a country's legal system is based on British common law (UK) or the French (FR), German (GE), or Scandinavian (SC) civil code.

[b] Tenure of Supreme Court Judges (SC_TEN) indicates the length of tenure of Supreme Court Judges (0, less than six years; 1, more than six years but not lifelong; 2, lifelong).

[c] Supreme Court Power (SC_POW) is a dummy variable that takes on a value of 1 if Supreme Court Judges have lifelong tenure and jurisdiction over administrative cases, and 0 otherwise.

[d] Case Law (CAS_LAW) is a dummy variable that equals 1 if judges base their decision on case law and 0 otherwise.

[e] Legal Justification (LEG_JUST) indicates whether judgments have to be based on statutory law rather than on principles of equity.

[f] Private Credit (PRIV_CR) represents credit by deposit money banks and other financial institutions to the private sector as a share of GDP.

[g] Stock Market Development (MCAP) measures the total market capitalization of all shares listed on a country's stock exchanges as a share of GDP.

[h] Property Rights (PR_RIG) reflects the degree to which government protects and enforces laws that protect private property.

[i] Enforcement (ENF) is an indicator of the effectiveness of the legal system in enforcing contracts.

[j] Government Subsidies (GVT_SUBS) represents grants on the current account by the public authorities to private and public enterprises as a percentage of GDP.

The property rights variable takes on values from 1 to 5, with 5 representing the strongest property rights protection.

* Not available.

Judiciary independence proxies

To measure the influence of the political channels on venture capitalist activity, we employ two indicators of the power of the judiciary relative to the executive arm of government based on Beck et al. (2003a) and La Porta et al. (2004). Our first variable, the Tenure of Supreme Court Judges (SC_TEN) ranges from 0 to 2. A value of 0 indicates that tenure is for less than six years. If tenure is between six years and lifetime, then the variable is coded as 1. If Supreme Court judges have lifelong tenure, then the variable is coded as 2. The longer the tenure of a Supreme Court judge, the more independent the judiciary is from the State (see Beck et al., 2003a). Larger values of SC_TEN are hypothesized to have a positive relationship with our dependent variables because – according to the political channel – firms in countries with more independent judiciaries should face lower obstacles in accessing and contracting for external finance.

Our second indicator, Supreme Court Power (SC_POW), takes the Tenure of Supreme Court Judges variable and combines it with a dummy variable that indicates whether the Supreme Court has power over administrative cases. The variable takes on a value of 1 if Supreme Court judges have lifelong tenure and have power over administrative cases. This combination would suggest that the Supreme Court is more independent from the State, and, under the political channel would predict a positive effect on firms' access to external finance.

Legal adaptability proxies

In line with Beck et al. (2003a), we use two variables to examine the influence of the adaptability channel on companies' access to venture capital financing. Case Law (CAS_LAW), originally derived from La Porta et al. (2004), is a dummy variable that indicates whether judicial decisions are a source of law, that is, whether they are based on previous court decisions. According to the adaptability channel, countries in which judicial decisions are a source of law will adapt more easily to changing economic and financial circumstances and therefore have higher levels of financial development. As a result, we hypothesize that countries with case law have more developed venture capital markets than countries that have no case law.

The second variable, Legal Justification (LEG_JUST), originally derived from Djankov et al. (2003), indicates whether judgments have to be based on statutory law rather than on principles of equity. The variable takes on values of 0, 0.33, 0.67, and 1, with higher values indicating that the legal system imposes greater requirements that judgments be based on statutory law. As noted by Beck et al. (2003a), the adaptability channel predicts that higher values of Legal Justification will be associated with lower levels of financial development or – in our case – a less-developed venture capital market.

Related financial development measures

Clearly, there is no single measure that captures the level of financial development in a given country. While our study specifically focuses on the venture capital market, the extant literature has employed various other proxies for financial development. We employ three of these measures to examine possible inter-relations between venture capital market developments on the one hand and alternative measures of financial development on the other.

We use Private Credit (PRIV_CR), a measure of credit by deposit money banks and other financial institutions to the private sector as share of GDP, to proxy for the size of the private lending market in a given country. As noted by Beck et al. (2003a), Private Credit excludes credit to the public sector and cross-claims of one financial intermediary on another. It thus measures the amount of savings that is channeled through debt-issuing financial intermediaries to private borrowers. While King and Levine (1993a, 1993b) and Levine et al. (2000) show a strong connection between measures of banking-sector development and economic growth (predicting a positive relationship between Private Credit and our dependent variables), it is also possible that Private Credit may be a substitute for venture capital financing, thus resulting in a negative relationship between these variables.

We follow Beck et al. (2005) and define a country's Stock Market Development (MCAP) as the total value of equity shares traded on a country's stock exchanges divided by the country's GDP. The variable captures the overall size of the equity market in a given country relative to the size of its economy.

Our third variable, Property Rights (PROP_RIG), is an index of the degree to which the government protects private property and enforces laws that protect private property. The data are obtained from Beck et al. (2003a) who themselves derived them from La Porta et al. (2000) and the Index of Economic Freedom. As noted by Beck et al., Property Rights measures a key input into the efficient operation of financial contracts and the development of formal financial institutions: the degree of protection of private property rights. The Property Rights variable takes on values from 1 to 5, with 5 representing the strongest property rights protection.

Other variables of interest

During our data collection, we came across numerous interesting country characteristics that have been employed in the comparative legal and economic literature but rarely in studies such as this. While we discarded many of them in an effort to concentrate only on those that are hypothesized to be most closely related to financial development, two variables sparked our particular interest in the context of this study. The first variable, Enforcement (ENF), is an indicator of the effectiveness of the legal system in enforcing contracts, as defined by Beck et al. (2000a). We include it in some of our regression models as it adds an interesting new perspective to our study. While the quality of a country's legal system is one important factor that may explain the financial development in a given country, we hypothesize that the actual enforcement of the laws is another important aspect. In other words, we argue that a legal system is only beneficial if it is properly enforced.

Our second variable of interest, Government Subsidies (GVT_SUBS), is based on a study by Demirgüç-Kunt and Maksimovic (1998). The variable measures grants on the current account by the public authorities to private and public enterprises as a percentage of GDP. We hypothesize that government subsidies act as a substitute to venture capital financing. That is, we argue that firms with easy access to government grants have less demand for venture capital. Thus, countries that provide firms with generous subsidies should have a less-developed venture capital market.

3.4 Methodology and results

3.4.1 Correlation analysis

We start our empirical analysis by examining the correlation coefficients between all independent and dependent variables. Our results are presented in Table 3.3.

Our dependent variables are all highly positively correlated, suggesting that they represent good alternatives in measuring venture capitalist activity in a given country. They also display positive, albeit smaller, correlations with other commonly used proxies for financial development, namely Private Credit (PRIV_CR), Stock Market Development (MCAP), and Property Rights (PR_RIG).

While not significant, countries with German and Scandinavian legal origins have positive correlations with VC activity when measured by the number of VC deals (VC_DEALS) or the number of VC-backed firms (VC_FIRMS) during our sample period, which is what we expected. Also it is not surprising that French legal origin displays a negative correlation with VC activity. Interestingly, while the British legal origin dummy is negatively correlated with our VC_DEALS and VC_FIRMS variables (which is somewhat unexpected), our third dependent variable, VC_AMT, shows a positive correlation. This suggests that while there may be fewer venture capital deals in British common law countries, the average size of each deal is considerably larger. Most other correlation coefficients are as expected. As some of them are quite large (>0.7 in absolute terms), we will employ models with various variable perturbations to avoid potential multicollinearity issues in our subsequent regression analysis.

3.4.2 Regression analysis

We perform a series of ordinary least squares (OLS) regressions in which we explore the relationship between the development of a country's venture capital market and various country characteristics that describe the origin of that country's legal system, the independence of the judiciary from the State, the adaptability of the legal system, the level of financial development, and other factors of interest. Our results are given in Table 3.4. For robustness and to avoid potential multicollinearity problems that may arise when including sets of highly correlated regressors in our analysis (see discussion above), we present results for several models containing different regressor combinations.

It is worth noting that the results in Panels A, B and C of Table 3.4 show a high degree of consistency, suggesting that our three dependent variables are all influenced by the same factors. The LEGOR_UK variable is consistently positive and in almost all models significant at the 10% level, suggesting that countries whose legal system is based on British common law tend to have more developed venture capital markets, relative to the excluded Scandinavian legal origin dummy. The French and German legal origin dummies, on the other hand, are insignificant in every model, suggesting that they have little explanatory power with respect to a country's venture capital market development.

In line with the political channel argument, the Tenure of Supreme Court Judges has a significant positive effect in almost all model specifications. Thus, an independent judiciary appears to be a significant contributor for having a strong venture capital market. Interestingly, Supreme Court Power (which combines the Tenure of Supreme Court Judges variable with a dummy variable that indicates that the Supreme Court has power over

Table 3.3 Correlation matrix. Pearson correlation coefficients for all dependent and independent variables used in our subsequent regression analysis are provided

	VC_ DEALS[a]	VC_ FIRMS[b]	VC_ AMT[c]	LEGOR_ UK[d]	LEGOR_ FR[d]	LEGOR_ GE[d]	LEGOR_ SC[d]	SC_ TEN[d]	SC_ POW[d]	CAS_ LAW[d]	LEG_ JUST[d]	PRIV_ CR[d]	M CAP[d]	PR_ RIG[d]	ENF[d]
VC_FIRMS	0.961														
VC_AMT	0.619	0.519													
LEGOR_UK	−0.055	−0.048	0.267												
LEGOR_FR	−0.169	−0.065	−0.152	−0.369											
LEGOR_GE	0.041	0.035	−0.082	−0.188	−0.369										
LEGOR_SC	0.202	0.084	0.017	−0.259	−0.510	−0.259									
SC_TEN	−0.041	0.053	−0.055	0.071	0.218	−0.535	0.189								
SC_POW	0.228	0.010	0.333	0.250	−0.327	−0.200	0.378	−0.250							
CAS_LAW	0.359	0.220	0.324	0.306	−0.757	0.074	0.540	−0.218	0.327						
LEG_JUST	−0.381	−0.303	−0.515	−0.368	0.369	0.267	−0.330	0.074	−0.448	−0.393					
PRIV_CR	0.303	0.292	0.167	0.103	−0.359	0.470	−0.071	−0.703	0.192	0.163	−0.116				
MCAP	0.307	0.247	0.702	0.155	0.034	0.046	−0.205	−0.785	0.317	0.234	−0.376	0.352			
PR_RIG	0.547	0.400	0.410	−0.180	−0.294	0.309	0.224	−0.218	0.600	0.383	−0.308	0.077	0.324		
ENF	0.651	0.524	0.530	−0.428	−0.231	0.295	0.369	−0.252	0.273	0.345	−0.259	0.275	0.369	0.733	
GVT_SUBS	−0.13	−0.132	−0.202	−0.298	−0.031	−0.541	0.767	0.357	0.138	0.220	−0.346	−0.208	−0.298	−0.169	0.221

The dependent variables are defined as follows. In each case, venture capital information is derived from the Security Data Company's (SDC) VentureXpert database, and GDP information is from yearly country statistics provided by the International Monetary Fund (IMF).

[a] VC_DEALS represents a log ratio of the average number of venture capital deals in a given country per year divided by the country's average GDP during our sample period.

[b] VC_FIRMS is a log ratio of the number of firms receiving venture capital financing in a given country per year divided by the country's average GDP during our sample period.

[c] VC_AMT is a log ratio of the average amount of venture capital funds disbursed in a given country per year divided by the country's average GDP during our sample period.

[d] The independent variables are derived from Demirgüç-Kunt and Maksimovic (1998) and Beck et al. (2005, 2003a) and are as defined in Table 3.2.

Table 3.4 OLS regression results. Ordinary least squares (OLS) regressions in which VC market size in a given country is regressed on a series of variables that describe the origin of the country's legal system, the independence of the judiciary from the State, the adaptability of the legal system, the level of financial development, and other factors of interest

	Panel A: Dependent Variable = VC_DEALS[a]				Panel B: Dependent Variable = VC_FIRMS[b]				Panel C: Dependent Variable = VC_AMT[c]			
	Coeff. (*p*-value)	Coeff. (*p*-value)	Coeff. (*p*-value)	Coeff. (*p*-value)	Coeff. (*p*-value)	Coeff. (*p*-value)	Coeff. (*p*-value)	Coeff. (*p*-value)	Coeff. (*p*-value)	Coeff. (*p*-value)	Coeff. (*p*-value)	Coeff. (*p*-value)
Constant	−0.140	0.578	0.551	−0.194	−0.048	0.448	0.538	−0.258	0.530***	0.827**	0.824***	0.542***
	(0.615)	(0.209)	(0.157)	(0.589)	(0.858)	(0.194)	(0.115)	(0.439)	(0.000)	(0.012)	(0.000)	(0.007)
LEGOR_UK[d]	0.113*			0.026	0.085*			0.017*	0.074**			0.038*
	(0.079)			(0.119)	(0.093)			(0.085)	(0.040)			(0.081)
LEGOR_FR[d]	0.058		0.027	−0.005	0.075		0.054	0.036	0.026		0.008	−0.021
	(0.333)		(0.724)	(0.941)	(0.208)		(0.418)	(0.573)	(0.288)		(0.813)	(0.487)
LEGOR_GE[d]	−0.013			0.034	0.001			0.060	−0.001			0.006
	(0.826)			(0.628)	(0.977)			(0.370)	(0.983)			(0.831)
SC_TEN[d]		0.082*		0.283*		0.079*		0.283**		0.030		0.114**
		(0.059)		(0.087)		(0.093)		(0.016)		(0.198)		(0.044)
SC_POW[d]	−0.017	−0.029	0.006		−0.034	−0.031	−0.010		−0.002	−0.016	0.006	
	(0.673)	(0.639)	(0.914)		(0.408)	(0.514)	(0.854)		(0.871)	(0.410)	(0.832)	
CAS_LAW[d]		0.138		0.049		0.121		0.052		0.056		0.003
		(0.300)		(0.444)		(0.241)		(0.385)		(0.188)		(0.901)
LEG_JUST[d]	−0.062**	−0.138**	−0.165**		−0.072**	−0.064*	−0.175**		−0.032**	−0.072**	−0.075**	
	(0.044)	(0.049)	(0.018)		(0.036)	(0.067)	(0.011)		(0.035)	(0.028)	(0.017)	
PRIV_CR[d]			0.182				0.204				0.065	
			(0.253)				(0.148)				(0.357)	
MCAP[d]			0.303*	0.370**			0.272*	0.323**			0.105*	0.165**
			(0.093)	(0.036)			(0.095)	(0.044)			(0.074)	(0.031)

(*Continued*)

Table 3.4 Continued

	Panel A: Dependent Variable = VC_DEALS[a]				Panel B: Dependent Variable = VC_FIRMS[b]				Panel C: Dependent Variable = VC_AMT[c]			
	Coeff. (*p*-value)	Coeff. (*p*-value)	Coeff. (*p*-value)	Coeff. (*p*-value)	Coeff. (*p*-value)	Coeff. (*p*-value)	Coeff. (*p*-value)	Coeff. (*p*-value)	Coeff. (*p*-value)	Coeff. (*p*-value)	Coeff. (*p*-value)	Coeff. (*p*-value)
PR_RIG[d]			−0.003 (0.969)				−0.010 (0.879)				0.002 (0.946)	
ENF[d]	0.073** (0.026)				0.057** (0.047)				0.031** (0.019)			
GVT_SUBS[d]		−0.053* (0.077)				−0.041* (0.080)				−0.016 (0.104)		
Adjusted R^2	58.8%	27.6%	25.4%	45.6%	47.3%	22.0%	20.1%	34.7%	67.1%	46.4%	32.4%	53.7%

VC market size is measured as a log ratio of [a]the average number of venture capital deals (VC_DEALS), [b]the average number of firms receiving venture capital funding (VC_FIRMS), and [c]the average amount of funding provided in a given country (VC_AMT) per year, respectively, all relative to the country's average GDP during our sample period. [d]The independent variables are as defined in Table 3.2. For each regression model, we present variable coefficients with *p*-values in brackets below.

***, **, *indicate statistical significance at the 1%, 5%, and 10% level, respectively.

administrative cases) seems to have little influence. The variable is insignificant in all model specifications and shows no clear direction.

We find support for the adaptability channel argument, but it is again reflected in only one of our regressors. Specifically, while Case Law shows no explanatory power, our second adaptability proxy, Legal Justification, is consistently negative and significant at the 5% level in almost all model specifications. Our results are consistent with Beck et al. (2003a) who observe that higher levels of Legal Justification are negatively related to financial development.

When including other proxies for financial market development in our model, we observe that the Private Credit and Property Rights variables are largely insignificant. Not surprisingly, however, we find the Stock Market Development proxy (MCAP) to be significantly positively related to venture capital market size.

Finally, effective contract enforcement, as captured by the ENF variable, appears to be an important factor that contributes to a strong venture capital market. This is not surprising. The venture capital industry has traditionally been risky and may have to rely more than any other industry on a sufficient legal safety net if things go wrong. Our last variable, Government Subsidies, is negatively related to venture capital market size, although the coefficients are only marginally significant at the 10% level in two out of the three models in which we include the variable. The negative relationship is in line with our expectations, suggesting that government funding may act as a substitute to private funding.

3.5 Conclusion

Whether and how legal traits affect a country's financial development are questions that have been on the minds of scholars, politicians, and practitioners alike for a long time. We add to the extant literature by focusing our attention on the venture capital market in Europe. While our sample size is naturally limited as a result, this narrow focus allows for two things. First, it enables us to use 'hard' data on one sector of the financial markets that is known to be a crucial source of capital for young start-up firms. Second, it allows us to analyze financial market development in a homogeneous group of countries that are less affected by cultural or religious differences than a worldwide country sample would be.

Our results are highly robust to different variable definitions and model specifications and provide empirical support for the notion that legal traits indeed matter when it comes to financial market development. We observe that the British common law system is positively associated with a flourishing venture capital market. Consistent with the line of argument in the political and adaptability channels, we further observe that an independent judiciary and a flexible, dynamic legal system are important contributors to a thriving venture capital market. Not surprisingly, we also find that, relative to GDP, venture capital markets tend to be larger in countries with better developed stock markets and in countries whose legal systems are effective in enforcing contracts. Finally, we identify a possible substitution effect between government subsidies and venture capitalist funding as venture capital markets tend to be less developed in countries whose governments act themselves as fund providers.

References

Beck, T. and Levine, R. (2002). Industry Growth and Capital Allocation: Does Having a Market- or Bank-Based System Matter? *Journal of Financial Economics*, 64(2):147–180.

Beck, T., Demirgüç-Kunt, A. and Levine, R. (2000a). A New Database on the Structure and Development of the Financial Sector. *World Bank Economic Review*, 14(3):597–605.

Beck, T., Levine, R. and Loayza, N. (2000b). Finance and the Sources of Growth. *Journal of Financial Economics*, 58(1):261–300.

Beck, T., Demirgüç-Kunt, A. and Levine, R. (2003a). Law and Finance: Why Does Legal Origin Matter? *Journal of Comparative Economics*, 31(4):653–675.

Beck, T., Demirgüç-Kunt, A. and Levine, R. (2003b). Law, Endowments, and Finance. *Journal of Financial Economics*, 70(2):137–181.

Beck, T., Demirgüç-Kunt, A. and Levine, R. (2005). Law and Firms' Access to Finance. *American Law and Economics Review*, 7(1):211–252.

Caprio, G., Laeven, L. and Levine, R. (2003). Governance and Bank Valuation. Working Paper, The World Bank.

Claessens, S., Djankov, S., Fan, J. and Lang, L. (2002). Disentangling the Incentive and Entrenchment Effects of Large Shareholdings. *Journal of Finance*, 57(6):2741–2771.

Demirgüç-Kunt, A. and Maksimovic, V. (1998). Law, Finance and Firm Growth. *Journal of Finance*, 53(6):2107–2137.

Djankov, S., La Porta, R., Lopez-de-Silanes, F. and Shleifer, A. (2003). Courts. *Quarterly Journal of Economics*, 118(2):453–517.

Hayek, F. (1960). *The Constitution of Liberty*. The University of Chicago Press, Chicago IL.

Johnson, S., Boone, P., Breach, A. and Friedman, E. (2000). Corporate Governance in the Asian Financial Crisis. *Journal of Financial Economics*, 58(1):141–186.

King, R. and Levine, R. (1993a). Finance and Growth: Schumpeter Might Be Right. *Quarterly Journal of Economics*, 108(3):717–737.

King, R. and Levine, R. (1993b). Finance, Entrepreneurship, and Growth: Theory and Evidence. *Journal of Monetary Economics*, 32(3):513–542.

La Porta, R., Lopez-de-Silanes, F., Shleifer, A. and Vishny, R. (1997). Legal Determinants of External Finance. *Journal of Finance*, 52(3):1131–1150.

La Porta, R., Lopez-de-Silanes, F., Shleifer, A. and Vishny, R. (1998). Law and Finance. *Journal of Political Economy*, 106(6):1113–1155.

La Porta, R., Lopez-de-Silanes, F., Shleifer, A. and Vishny, R. (1999). The Quality of Government. *Journal of Law, Economics, and Organization*, 15(1):222–279.

La Porta, R., Lopez-de-Silanes, F., Shleifer, A. and Vishny, R. (2000). Agency Problems and Dividend Policies around the World. *Journal of Finance*, 55(1):1–33.

La Porta, R., Lopez-de-Silanes, F., Shleifer, A. and Vishny, R. (2002). Investor Protection and Corporate Valuation. *Journal of Finance*, 57(3):1147–1170.

La Porta, R., Lopez-de-Silanes, F., Pop-Eleches, C. and Shleifer, A. (2004). Judicial Checks and Balances. *Journal of Political Economy*, 112(2):445–470.

Levine, R. (1998). The Legal Environment, Banks, and Long-run Economic Growth. *Journal of Money, Credit, and Banking*, 30(3):569–613.

Levine, R. (1999). Law, Finance, and Economic Growth. *Journal of Financial Intermediation*, 8(1):8–35.

Levine, R. (2003). Napoleon, Bourses, and Growth: with a Focus on Latin America. In Omar, A. and Cadwell, C. (eds) *Market Augmenting Government: Essays in Honor of Mancur Olson*. University of Michigan Press, Ann Arbor MI.

Levine, R., Loayza, N. and Beck, T. (2000). Financial Intermediation and Growth: Causality and Causes. *Journal of Monetary Economics*, 46(1):31–77.

Mahoney, P. (2001). The Common Law and Economic Growth: Hayek Might be Right. *Journal of Legal Studies*, 30(2):503–525.

Merryman, J. (1985). *The Civil Law Tradition: An Introduction to the Legal Systems of Western Europe and Latin America*. Stanford University Press, Stanford CA.

Morck, R., Yeung, B. and Yu, W. (2000). The Information Content of Stock Markets: Why do Emerging Markets have Synchronous Price Movements? *Journal of Financial Economics*, 58(1): 215–260.

North, D. and Weingast, B. (1989). Constitutions and Commitment: The Evolution of Institutions Governing Public Choice in Seventeenth-Century England. *Journal of Economic History*, 49(4):803–832.

Posner, R. (1973). *Economic Analysis of the Law*. Little-Brown, Boston MA.

Wurgler, J. (2000). Financial Markets and the Allocation of Capital. *Journal of Financial Economics*, 58(1–2):187–214.

4 A survey of the venture capital industry in Central and Eastern Europe

Rachel A. Campbell and Roman Kraeussl

Abstract

This chapter analyzes the integration of the European equity markets and the venture capital (VC) industry of the eight former communist countries in the Central- and East-European (CEE) region, which became EU member states in May 2004. It discusses the current state of the VC industry in the CEE region and compares it with the emerging VC industry in Western Europe and the well-developed VC environment in the United States. First results indicate the importance of an integrated European equity market and the importance of a mature VC industry. Further financial integration may improve exit channels for VC and reallocate talent and human capital. For providing an outlook on the VC industry of these particular countries, a qualitative scenario analysis is conducted. We show that the VC industry is developing quickly but some political-cultural aspects like the heritage of communism will make this process even less rapid than in Western Europe. Not the supply of sufficient VC is the main back holding factor but the demand since there is hardly any entrepreneurial spirit in these former communist countries. We conclude by offering some advice on how to alter this situation.

4.1 Introduction

On 1 May 2004, the European Union experienced an extensive enlargement. Ten new members officially joined, of which eight were formerly Communist countries from Central and Eastern Europe (CEE). These CEE countries are characterized by a large number of enterprises established only relatively recently. To grow and to survive in the strong international competition, such enterprises had to rapidly adopt essential innovative and upgrading processes.

A widespread belief exists that venture capital plays an influential role in bringing innovations to market at a rapid pace. It creates economic growth, jobs, and opportunities for further technological development (see Cochrane, 2001; Gompers and Lerner, 2001). Research by the European Private Equity and Venture Capital Association (EVCA, 2005a) shows that venture-backed businesses grow faster than others, are more profitable and dynamically increase employment.

During recent years, VC has gained considerable economic importance throughout Western European countries. However, in CEE countries young and technology-oriented companies still fail to attract the necessary capital. Several reasons can be postulated as an explanation for this difficult financing process. These are, among others, the early development stage of the national financial markets, the insufficient availability of risk capital, as well as the low availability of financing via listing on a stock exchange. Furthermore, commercial banks fail to provide the necessary capital, as these companies have little corporate history and none or only few assets that may serve as collateral.

Research on VC and small business finance in the CEE countries is also in its early stage. It is therefore the aim of this chapter to deepen the understanding of risk capital markets in CEE countries. For the purposes of this analysis, the CEE region comprises the following countries: Bulgaria, Czech Republic, Estonia, Hungary, Latvia, Lithuania, Poland, Romania, Slovakia, and Slovenia.

This chapter is organized as follows. Section 4.2 gives a short overview of the financial markets of CEE and the future challenges for the financial markets in the CEE countries. Section 4.3 presents the recent experience with private equity and VC funding in the CEE region. Section 4.4 discusses an action plan and gives some policy recommendations. Section 4.5 concludes and offers some suggestions regarding possible improvements in order to create a supporting and encouraging framework for venture capital in the CEE countries.

4.2 The route of transition and the current economic environment

It is now 15 years since the CEE region started its transition towards a market economy. Privatization had the top priority in this process. The challenges were enormous: how to transfer an entire state-owned economy into private hands while at the same time maintaining political stability, economic growth, and social fairness.

In many CEE countries the fundamental institutions of a market-driven economy existed before Communism. This advantage supported the transition process, since it could rely on early historical foundations. Most CEE countries entered the accession process with developed infrastructures and, moreover, with a highly qualified workforce (see Klapper et al., 2002).

Economic reforms, market liberalization, and continued inflows of foreign direct investment (FDI) have triggered economic growth in the CEE countries throughout the last 15 years. Trade barriers were eliminated early, which supported the development of export activities. The process of privatization moved ahead and is now nearly complete. Regulation is consistent and stable and tax levels are highly competitive.

Table 4.1 indicates that growth in the CEE region has accelerated, despite the global slowdown that especially hit growth in the EU. Over the last five years, countries such as Estonia, Hungary, Poland, and Slovenia have achieved growth rates of more than 4% a year. On the other hand, wage costs have remained low at approximately 20% of EU level.

The recent economic development of the CEE region also compares well on other indicators of macro-economic performance. Table 4.1 shows that inflation in many of the CEE countries is already at, or even below, Western European levels. In 2004, only Hungary, Slovakia, Slovenia, and high-inflation-ridden Romania still had inflation rates of above 5%. On average, consumer prices in the CEE countries fell to 4.7% last year. Nonetheless, several of the CEE countries still have substantial current account deficits.

Table 4.1 Economic development of CEE countries, 2001–2004

Country	Population in million	Real GDP growth				Inflation, % average				Current account balances, % of GDP			
	2001	2001	2002	2003	2004	2001	2002	2003	2004	2001	2002	2003	2004
Bulgaria	7.9	4.0	4.0	5.0	5.5	7.5	5.8	3.0	4.1	−6.2	−3.4	−5.5	−4.6
Czech Republic	10.2	3.1	2.0	1.9	3.3	4.7	1.8	1.1	3.0	−5.7	−5.3	−5.8	−5.3
Estonia	1.4	5.0	5.0	4.9	5.2	5.8	4.3	3.6	2.9	−6.1	−10.1	−5.0	−5.1
Hungary	10.2	3.8	3.3	3.6	3.9	9.2	5.3	5.3	4.8	−3.4	−4.1	−4.8	−4.6
Latvia	2.4	7.9	6.1	5.5	6.0	2.5	1.9	3.0	3.0	−9.6	−8.7	−8.5	−7.1
Lithuania	3.5	5.9	5.9	5.3	5.7	1.3	0.3	2.1	2.5	−4.8	−5.4	−5.8	−5.4
Poland	38.6	1.0	1.3	2.6	4.1	5.5	1.9	1.1	2.4	−3.9	−3.5	−3.7	−4.0
Romania	22.4	5.7	4.9	4.9	5.0	34.5	22.5	16.2	11.6	−6.0	−3.4	−4.5	−4.5
Slovakia	5.4	3.3	4.4	4.0	4.2	7.3	3.3	8.8	7.5	−8.6	−8.2	−6.6	−6.3
Slovenia	2.0	3.0	2.9	3.2	3.8	8.4	7.5	5.7	5.0	0.2	1.8	1.9	1.7

Source: IMF (2005).

However, despite this strong economic performance, CEE countries have a significantly lower GDP per capita which equals 25% of the original EU-15 countries. Forecasts by the International Monetary Fund (IMF) (2005) suggest that the growth rate of the CEE region in the coming years will remain twice as high as the average growth rate for the EU-15 region.

The financial systems of these former communist economies have been undergoing a deep transformation since 1989. During this process literally all CEE countries have experienced a severe crisis in their banking systems. This triggered an extensive restructuring of numerous domestic banks, including even some large-scale liquidations.

The European Central Bank (ECB, 2002) notes that the financial systems of the CEE countries supply less equity investments and banking lending than in the Western European countries. The average ratio of domestic bank lending to GDP in the CEE countries is around 40%, whereas the average for the Euro area is 140%. Klapper et al. (2002) argue that SMEs suffer from underdeveloped financial systems.

Since 1999 the European Commission (EC) has been supporting capacity building in the financial markets of the CEE countries through the SME Finance Facility, funded by the Phare and Meda programs. This facility has been managed by the European Bank for Reconstruction and Development (EBRD), the Council of Europe Bank in cooperation with Kreditanstalt für Wiederaufbau (KfW), and by the European Investment Bank (EIB), which have offered credit lines to local banks for SME lending.

During recent years, private equity and VC financing has gained acceptance in the capital markets of the CEE region. With an increasing number of private equity investments and exits completed, awareness of private equity as a financing source has grown among both receivers and providers.

As argued in Section 4.3, the conditions for private equity and venture capital financing in CEE countries continue to develop in a positive way. Many former start-up companies have now become more mature market players. Both foreign and domestic industry investors show an increasing interest in buying CEE companies that received VC financing support.

4.3 Recent developments of VC funding in CEE

The VC industry in CEE is almost 15 years old. It is thus relatively young compared with the VC industries of Western Europe and the U.S., and has developed considerably since its inception. According to figures given by EVCA (2005b), during the past 15 years more than €7 billion of funding has been raised for VC funds dedicated to the CEE countries. Over 900 investments in the region were supported, from which more than 400 exits were achieved. Table A4.1 summarizes 25 successful VC-backed exits in the CEE region in recent years.

The development of VC in CEE is, however, still at a relatively early stage. This implies that many VC funds have not yet completed a full cycle of investments and exits. Therefore, overall returns of the industry may not show the true picture.

Based on data from various EVCA yearbooks, this section analyzes the recent developments in the VC industry of the CEE region. The following vital aspects are examined: fundraising activity, investment activity, investment per sector, type of investment, type of investor, type of exit route, fund management teams, laws and regulations, and the role of public policy.

4.3.1 Fundraising activity

The CEE VC market had a very successful year in 2004. Fundraising for CEE expanded rapidly with a total of €496 million, which shows a 59% increase compared with 2003. Already in 2003 fundraising activity had increased by 28% in all of CEE to an overall value of €312 million, compared with €243 million in 2002. This positive development is mainly due to the EU accession in May 2004 and the favorable development of the global VC market.

Figure 4.1 shows that in the last 12 months a significant increase in volume occurred in Hungary, which tripled its funding, and in Poland, where an exceptional increase occurred of more than 15 times its 2003 value. On the other hand, Figure 4.1 also indicates how fragile VC fundraising can be. The Czech Republic, which saw an increase by 68% to €93.8 million in 2003, faced a drop in its VC fundraising to €4.8 million. In 2003 the Baltic States achieved an exceptional increase of more than 50 times the 2002 value, topping €105 million but this fell in 2004 to €7.2 million.

Historically, institutional investors from Western Europe and North America have been the main sources of capital for CEE private equity funds. Domestic funding sources have not yet contributed much. Looking specifically at 2004, the vast majority of funding across the CEE region was provided by non-domestic investors. Table 4.2 shows that non-domestic European sources were the largest providers of capital to CEE private equity funds, contributing €313 million of the total €496 million raised. Non-European institutions accounted for a further €110 million of funds raised, while local sources contributed the remaining €73 million.

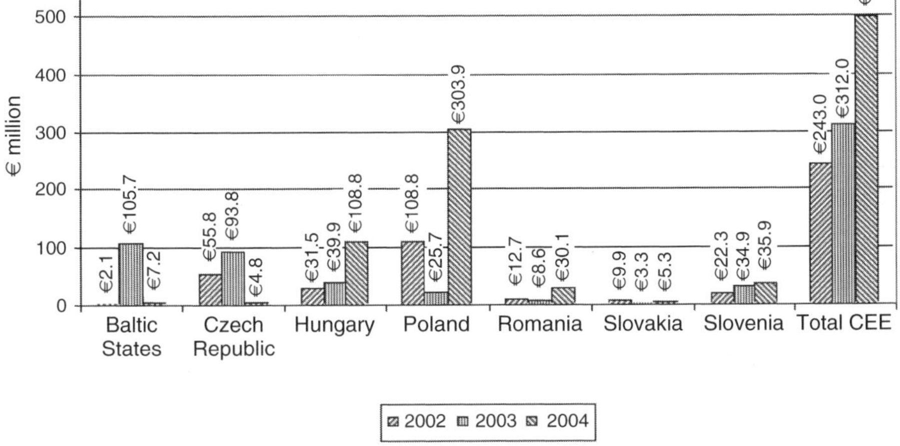

Figure 4.1 Fundraising activity, 2002–2004. *Source*: EVCA (2005b)

Table 4.2 Fundraising activity by region, 2004

€'000	Baltic States	Czech Republic	Hungary	Poland	Romania	Slovakia	Slovenia	Total CEE
Domestic	3426	4839	39 013	407	–	2438	22 724	72 847
Other European	3425	–	69 812	224 438	15 051	531	–	313 257
Non-European	363	–	–	79 036	15 051	2287	13 178	109 915
Total 2004	7214	4839	108 825	303 881	30 102	5256	35 902	496 019

Source: EVCA (2005b).

4.3.2 Investment activity

EVCA (2005b) estimates of total investment activity over the past 15 years indicate that some €5 billion of private equity was invested in more than 900 companies in the CEE region. With respect to the latest data, Figure 4.2 shows that investment levels increased significantly in 2004 with a total of €547 million invested across the CEE region. This is an overall increase of 22% compared with the €448 million invested in 2003. According to EVCA (2005b) figures, total investment for the CEE region was 64% higher in value compared with 2002.

However, the investment trends by country vary. Bulgaria has seen the highest level of investment activity by amount, primarily owing to the completion of two of the largest private equity transactions to date in the CEE region. Many of the private equity fund managers active in the CEE region participated in those transactions. Hungary and Latvia also showed increases in investment by amount, while private equity activity in Poland, the Czech Republic, and Romania decreased compared with 2003.

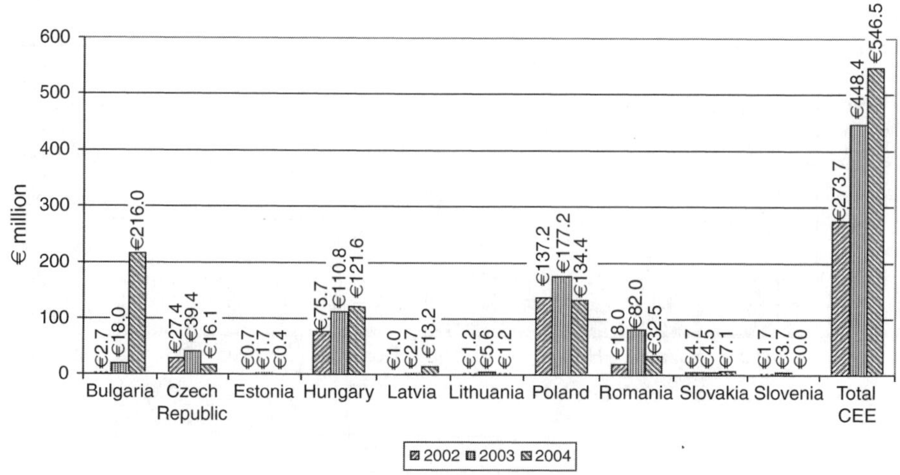

Figure 4.2 Type of investment, 2003–2004. *Source*: EVCA (2005b)

In 2004, total private equity investment in Europe was 0.284% of total European GDP. Since private equity has existed for a shorter period in the CEE region and since debt has become available to support larger transactions only recently, investment levels measured against GDP are below the European average. However, as Table 4.3 shows, the CEE region as a whole managed to increase private equity investments as a percentage of GDP between 2002 and 2004. These figures indicate that there is significant scope for potential growth in investment activity.

4.3.3 Sectoral distribution of investments

The delay in developing VC markets in CEE countries becomes more evident as one compares the sectoral distribution of investments. Table 4.4 shows that most investments in the Czech Republic, Hungary, and Poland target the telecommunication industries and manufacturers of consumer goods and industrial products. Areas such as electronics, biotechnology, medical/health, and industrial automation are more or less neglected. The share of investments in computer-related industries is much lower than the EU-15 average.

4.3.4 Type of investment

In CEE countries the provision of early-stage financing is very low. VC funds are concentrated more on larger deals, excluding the small and risky early-stage ventures. Later-stage investments and buy-outs of larger companies show more attractive returns and lower risk profiles. However, the lack of investment at the seed and early-stage financing stage can become a self-reinforcing downwards cycle. Since few venture capital funds are active in the seed and early stage, the knowledge of how to operate at such stages evaporates. This

Table 4.3 Investments as a percentage of GDP in Central and Eastern Europe, 2002–2004

€'000	Investment as % of GDP 2002	Investment as % of GDP 2003	Investment as % of GDP 2004
Bulgaria	0.016%	0.101%	1.110%
Croatia	0.014%	0.011%	0.015%
Czech Republic	0.037%	0.052%	0.019%
Estonia	0.010%	0.022%	0.004%
Hungary	0.110%	0.154%	0.150%
Latvia	0.011%	0.031%	0.120%
Lithuania	0.008%	0.036%	0.007%
Poland	0.069%	0.098%	0.069%
Romania	0.037%	0.159%	0.055%
Slovakia	0.018%	0.016%	0.021%
Slovenia	0.007%	0.015%	0.000%
Total	0.054%	0.088%	0.096%

Source: EVCA (2005b)

Table 4.4 Sectoral distribution of investments, 2001 (%)

Sectoral Distribution	EU-15	Czech Republic	Hungary	Poland
Agriculture	0.2%	0.0%	0.0%	0.0%
Biotechnology	2.9%	0.0%	0.0%	0.0%
Chemicals and Materials	2.9%	0.0%	0.0%	0.1%
Communications	13.8%	59.5%	48.0%	56.8%
Computer-related	13.3%	4.5%	4.0%	10.1%
Construction	1.8%	0.0%	0.0%	0.0%
Consumer Goods	18.5%	20.5%	0.6%	12.3%
Electronics-related	3.9%	0.0%	0.0%	0.0%
Energy	0.7%	0.0%	0.0%	0.4%
Financial Services	1.8%	0.0%	0.0%	2.9%
Industrial Automation	2.1%	0.0%	0.0%	0.0%
Industrial Products	10.0%	0.9%	24.8%	2.1%
Medical Health-related	7.9%	0.0%	14.4%	2.2%
Other Manufacturing	9.3%	14.6%	0.0%	3.3%
Other Services	5.6%	0.0%	0.9%	6.5%
Transportation	1.2%	0.0%	0.0%	0.0%
Other	4.1%	0.0%	7.3%	3.3%
Total Investment	100.0%	100.0%	100.0%	100.0%

Source: EVCA (2005b)

process does not support future entry. The few remaining seed funds and business angel investors cannot, by themselves, cover the demand of early-stage financing companies for equity investments. This can create an equity gap for early-stage companies across most of the CEE region.

Figure 4.3 shows that, as in 2003, the largest portion of invested VC went into buy-out transactions, followed by expansion capital and replacement capital in 2004. Notably,

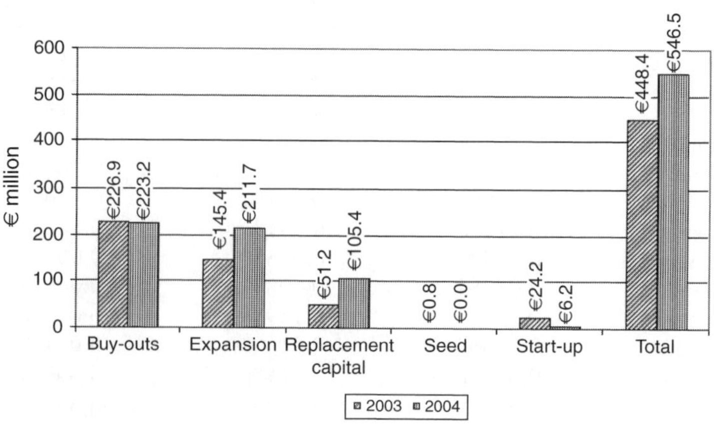

Figure 4.3 Type of investment, 2003–2004. *Source*: EVCA (2005b)

Table 4.5 Type of Investment by CEE Country, 2004

€'000	Baltic States	Bulgaria	Czech Republic	Hungary	Poland	Romania	Slovakia	Slovenia
Seed	–	–	–	–	–	–	–	–
Start-up	706	–	2245	501	–	–	947	1759
Expansion	14 102	3421	13 829	120 561	44 100	7339	6112	2262
Replacement	–	20 684	–	–	59 494	25 204	–	
Buyout	–	191 871	–	500	30 843	–	–	–
Total 2004	14 808	215 976	16 074	121 562	134 437	32 543	7059	4021

Source: EVCA (2005b)

there were no reported seed-stage investments and a significant reduction of start-up investments, which fell from €24.2 million in 2003 to €6.2 million in 2004.

Table 4.5 indicates that all CEE countries have a strong position in expansion finance. Hungary shows an unexpected high level of expansion capital, whereas this kind of investment is not yet available in the Czech Republic. On the other hand, the Czech Republic did at least experience some start-up financing in 2004. Until now, the largest investment in the CEE region was a leveraged buy-out of Bulgarian mobile operator MobilTel, completed in May 2004.

4.3.5 *Type of investor*

Table 4.6 indicates that Poland shows a relatively low dependency on banks in the VC funding process compared with the Czech Republic and Hungary. The importance of pension funds and insurance companies in Poland is, on the other hand, quite high. In this respect, the Czech Republic and Hungary comparably show a very low level. This slightly contradicts the image of a well-developed VC industry.

Table 4.6 Type of investor, 2001 (%)

Type of investor	EU-15	Czech Republic	Hungary	Poland
Academic institutions	0.4%	0.0%	0.0%	0.0%
Banks	21.7%	63.3%	93.3%	32.6%
Capital markets	1.3%	0.0%	0.0%	0.0%
Corporate Investor	10.9%	8.0%	0.0%	0.8%
Fund of funds	11.4%	0.0%	5.1%	7.7%
Government Agencies	5.6%	0.0%	0.0%	8.6%
Insurance Companies	12.9%	0.0%	0.0%	23.1%
Pension Funds	24.2%	0.0%	0.0%	25.7%
Private Individuals	7.4%	26.9%	0.0%	0.7%
Other	4.2%	1.8%	1.6%	0.8%
Total investment	100.0%	100.0%	100.0%	100.0%

Source: EVCA (2005b)

4.3.6 Type of exit route

More than 400 companies have been exited since the VC industry began in CEE countries. Most exits have been completed through trade sales to both international and domestic industry buyers. The Warsaw Stock Exchange particularly has proven to be a viable exit route to the public market for VC-financed companies. Also, exits have been achieved through listings on other domestic and international exchanges, including Prague, the NASDAQ, and the Vienna Stock Exchange.

Table 4.7 focuses on completed exits in 2004 and compares the types and volumes of exits across the CEE region with figures for Europe as a whole. It can be seen that trade sales and sales to management in CEE have a significantly larger share compared with the EU-15.

Figure 4.4 shows measurements with respect to investment cost. It demonstrates that the level of divestment decreased significantly in 2004 compared with 2003, while exit volumes increased by 75% in all CEE countries from 2002 to 2003 with the exception of the Czech Republic.

4.3.7 Fund management teams

Fund management teams in CEE can be separated into two sets. The first set includes regional teams that manage regional funds and typically operate with a network of offices through many countries. The second set is generated by country-focused funds that operate outside the border. Regional teams are usually larger and cover 22 of an estimated total 77 fund management teams active in the CEE countries (see Table 4.8).

4.3.8 Laws and regulations

The volume of private equity investments completed and successfully exited in the CEE region to date underlines the fact that the transformation of the legal systems and regulatory regimes has been supportive. This transformation has been mostly influenced by the

Table 4.7 Type of exit routes in CEE and EU-15, 2004

Exit value at investment cost €'000	Total CEE	Percent of total	Total Europe	Percent of total
Divestment by other means	3613	2.9%	2 478 200	12.7%
Divestment by public market	26 198	21.4%	2 306 318	11.8%
Divestment by trade sale	42 041	34.3%	4 628 477	23.6%
Divestment by write-off	21 310	17.4%	1 904 884	9.7%
Repayment of principal loans	4582	3.7%	4 165 981	21.3%
Sale to another venture capitalist	5826	4.8%	2 555 307	13.1%
Sale to financial institution	4708	3.8%	577 563	3.0%
Sale to management (MBO)	14 283	11.7%	945 748	4.8%
Total 2004	122 561	100.0%	19 562 478	100.0%

Source: EVCA (2005b)

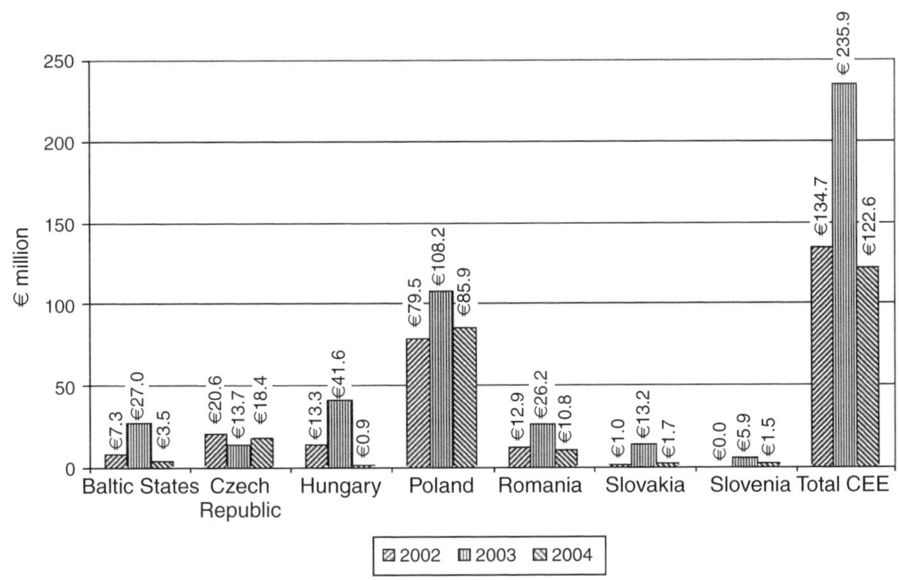

Figure 4.4 Divestments by CEE country, 2002–2004. *Source*: EVCA (2005b)

Table 4.8 Fund management teams, 2004

Country	Number of teams
Czech Republic	7
Hungary	13
Latvia	6
Poland	18
Romania	7
Slovakia	4
Regional	22
Total	77

Source: EVCA (2005b)

need to attract foreign investors. The efforts to join the EU have also been a major force for positive change.

In the CEE countries that joined the EU on 1 May 2004, the process of adopting legal codes to the requirements of the EU is quite advanced. Bulgaria and Romania, who are expected to become EU members in the near future, potentially already in early 2007, are also introducing necessary legislative changes to upgrade their legal and regulatory infrastructures to EU standards.

However, EVCA (2004) reports that the legal and tax environments in the CEE region are not yet as attractive for VC investing as in the EU-15 markets. In the CEE region the slow legal and regulatory processes, inexperienced judiciaries, and complicated bureaucracy are the major drawbacks. It is to be expected that many of these issues will be resolved through time and experience.

4.3.9 *Public policies*

The financial problems of start-ups also require long-term solutions involving the public sector. EU initiatives to overcome problems of SME financing such as the Risk Capital Action Plan (RCAP) and the Financial Services Action Plan (FSAP) are all steps in the right direction and should be further supported.

The introduction of the RCAP pinpointed the need for an appropriate regulatory framework for VC financing. The FSAP was designed in order to speed the establishment of an integrated market by identifying a list of actions that need to be performed.

However, the lack of progress in policy coordination produced isolated and often non-coherent measures. The implementation of the FSAP recommendations has to be done to avoid further European fragmentation.

In addition to EU initiatives, most programs and institutions of CEE countries aim to overcome the equity gap in early-stage SME finance. Table A4.2 gives an overview on various national equity schemes that support SME's access to capital.

4.4 An action plan towards a well-functioning VC market

Despite considerable advances over the last 15 years, CEE risk capital markets are functioning below their potential. This observation is underlined by long-standing market failure in seed and early-stage equity financing. As a result, potential innovations are not fully exploited and, thus, CEE countries lose out on jobs and potential growth (see Iliev, 2006).

Like any other industry, VC markets are subject to the prevailing macro- and micro-economic environment. A number of factors influence the choice of a VC fund manager: the entrepreneurial culture of a particular country, the availability of long-term sources of finance, the quality of the local educational system, the macro-economic policies adopted, and the stock market's role in financing the economy, as well as the local tax and legal environment.

This section proposes a rough outline of an action plan encouraging a well-functioning VC industry in the CEE region. Inspired by the evidence of successful venture capital industries such as in the U.S., one can distinguish between three basic dimensions for successful VC investments: the economic environment, the regulatory environment, and the social/cultural environment.

Removing barriers to allow VC industry to grow and develop across CEE is not equal to lowering regulatory standards. Removing barriers should allow legislation to support entrepreneurship and, thus, strengthen the economic and social base through increased opportunities for job creation, innovation and sustainable growth. Such an environment motivates international investors and VC fund managers to invest in the CEE region.

4.4.1 *Improving the economic environment*

Improving access to finance is an important aspect for fostering entrepreneurship in Europe. However, any public sector action to stimulate investment should focus on the efficiency and long-term sustainability of the VC industry. Such action should aim for programs that work with financial markets and do not crowd-out private investment.

The role of the public sector should primarily be to improve the general conditions of finance and take limited direct action only when market failures require it.

A successful economic framework needs efficient and liquid financial markets and stock exchanges to provide an exit for VC investors. This is not the case for today's fragmented European capital markets. Da Rin et al. (2005) argue that these fragment capital markets do not provide sufficient exit opportunities and hamper the rapid expansion of high-growth firms. VC investors are unable to easily sell their shares, as secondary markets are not sufficiently liquid.

Therefore, the financial industry requires improved conditions for cross-border investments so that VC would contribute to pools of capital available for firms seeking potential investors. NASDAQ in the U.S. is seen as playing a significant role in providing a nation-wide and liquid secondary market.

The setting-up of a (single) pan-European market dedicated to high-growth companies would generate an environment sufficient to attract companies, investors, financial intermediaries, and advisors. This would improve access to capital and liquidity for the best VC-backed companies and thereby would enhance growth prospects for the CEE region.

4.4.2 Improving the regulatory environment

CEE needs a regulatory environment that encourages entrepreneurial activities by providing consistent corporate and tax laws, efficient procedures for the set-up of new companies, and a public administration that sees itself as a service to entrepreneurs rather than a burden. In many CEE countries, the present bankruptcy rules are such that it is very difficult for an entrepreneur who has failed once to start a business again. On the contrary, in the U.S. the 'right to fail' is considered part of the learning process. Whilst protecting the interests of creditors, insolvency and bankruptcy laws should not prevent a second chance.

In order to achieve the scale and liquidity for sustainable operations, investing across European borders would be necessary for VC funds (see Da Rin et al., 2005). However, there is no suitable tax or legal structure for VC funds that is effective across Europe. Also, all European countries do not recognize the principle of tax transparency. This reduces the attractiveness of VC for institutional investors and stands in contrast to well-functioning examples such as in the U.S., where one vehicle can be used throughout the states.

Despite the fact that VC funds become increasingly more pan-European, they still have to structure themselves around 25 national tax regulatory and legal systems. This leads to double taxation, additional levels of intermediary structures, uncertainties and, thus, to increased costs for VC investors that block cross-border VC investments. In order to encourage a positive development of the VC industry, transparent pan-European fund structures need to be supported.

Taxation of VC investments affects their attractiveness. An unfavorable taxation scheme might prevent investments and thus act as a burden on economic growth. A tax environment that encourages risky investments can be favored by low capital gains tax for business angel investments, or by introducing tax breaks for eligible investments. Since tax relief schemes sometimes lead to perverse incentives that distort economic calculations, an alternative for such incentives could be a low capital gains tax rate for long-term investments, whereas shorter investments are taxed at higher rates.

Current administrative costs and legal complexity surrounding European VC investments reduce the overall amounts that an industry is able to attract and invest into growth companies. Only when the tax and legal environments of European countries are effective, can the private equity and venture capital industry contribute to the growth of the European economy.

4.4.3 Promoting a culture of entrepreneurship

The creation of an entrepreneurial spirit is a crucial dimension of a successful environment for well-functioning VC markets. EVCA (2005b) state that in many CEE countries entrepreneurs value their personal control over the company more than the growth possibilities that could be achieved by bringing in outside shareholders. This reduces the number of attractive projects on the demand side of VC finance.

Entrepreneurship education is an essential way to create a greater entrepreneurial attitude amongst young people in the CEE region. Iliev (2006) argues that educational organizations should be encouraged to give students the opportunity to develop entrepreneurial skills through high-quality courses. Especially at technical universities, for example, this could be implemented through the involvement of entrepreneurs in educational programs. Matching scientific potential with entrepreneurial skills will contribute to a better commercialization of research results through spin-offs and more start-ups in knowledge-based sectors.

Furthermore, CEE countries need to create an attractive environment for researchers, enabling interesting research results and a high number of patents. In order to achieve these goals, an intensive cooperation between universities and the economy has to be established.

Finally, as another crucial part of the social/cultural environment, people should be prepared to take risks, both as entrepreneurs and as money investors. A strong equity culture helps the financing of start-up enterprises. The attractiveness of becoming an entrepreneur may also be increased by reducing the stigma linked to business failure.

4.5 Conclusion

Despite considerable advances since the end of the Communist era, the VC industry in CEE countries is functioning below its potential. This reflects on long-standing market failure in seed and early-stage equity financing owing to problems both in the supply of, and in the demand for, risk capital. As a result, potential innovations are not fully exploited and the CEE region loses out on employment and GDP growth.

Based on data from various EVCA yearbooks, this study analyzes the recent developments in the VC industry of the CEE region by focusing on the following: fundraising activity, investment activity, sectoral distribution of investment, type of investment, type of investor, type of exit route, fund management teams, portfolio companies, laws and regulations, and the role of leverage.

In CEE countries young and technology-oriented companies still fail to attract the necessary capital. The reasons for this difficult financing process are the early development stage of financial markets, the low availability of risk capital, as well as the non-suitability of financing via the listing on a single pan-European stock exchange. Furthermore, a pan-European fund structure would avoid inefficiencies such as double taxation and reduce the complexity of operating and managing parallel funds in multiple jurisdictions. In addition, such a workable single structure would reduce costs and time-consuming procedures associated with complicated cross-border vehicles.

This analysis also proposes a rough outline of an action plan encouraging a well-functioning VC industry in the CEE region. Inspired by the evidence of successful venture capital industries such as in the U.S., one can distinguish between three basic dimensions for successful VC investments: the economic environment, the regulatory environment, and the social/cultural environment, necessary for the creation of an entrepreneurial spirit.

Whereas the basis for the economic and legal environment can be established rather quickly, a change in the social environment and the entrepreneurial spirit takes much more time. Nevertheless, much has changed in recent years in CEE. The removal of exchange risks in the near future after the introduction of the Euro will also contribute to further European financial market integration.

To compete effectively in an ever-increasing integrated global economy, CEE countries need to improve their capacity to innovate and foster an entrepreneurial culture. Enterprise and innovation are crucial drivers of progress towards the Lisbon goal of making the European Union 'the most competitive and dynamic knowledge-based economy in the world, capable of sustainable economic growth with more and better jobs and greater social cohesion'.

References

Cochrane, J.H. (2001). *The Risk and Return of Venture Capital.* NBER Working Paper Series, No. 8066.

Da Rin, M., Nicodano, G. and Sembenelli, A. (2005). Public Policy and the Creation of Active Venture Capital Markets. *ECB Working Paper Series*, No. 430, European Central Bank, Frankfurt/Main, January.

European Central Bank (2002). *Financial Sectors in EU Accession Countries.* European Union.

European Commission (2005). *Best Practices of Public Support for Early-Stage Equity Finance.* Final Report of the Expert Group, Directorate-General for Enterprise and Industry, Brussels, September.

European Private Equity and Venture Capital Association (EVCA) (2004). *Central and Eastern European Success Stories.* Special Paper, Zaventeem, Belgium.

European Private Equity and Venture Capital Association (EVCA) (2005a). *Employment Contribution of Private Equity and Venture Capital in Europe.* Research Paper, Zaventeem, Belgium.

European Private Equity and Venture Capital Association (EVCA) (2005b). *Central and Eastern Europe Statistics 2004.* Special Paper, Zaventeem, Belgium.

Gompers, P. and Lerner, J. (2001). The Venture Capital Revolution. *Journal of Economic Perspectives*, 15(2):145–168.

Iliev, I.P. (2006) Barriers to Venture Capital Investment in Innovative SMEs in CEEs – Causes and Policy Implications. In Piech, K. and Radosevic, S. (eds) *Knowledge-Based Economy in Central and East European Countries*, chap. 8. Palgrave Macmillan, Hampshire, UK.

International Monetary Fund (2005) *World Economic Outlook – Globalization and External Imbalances*, World Economic and Financial Surveys, April, Washington, D.C.

Klapper, L., Sarria-Allende, V. and Sulla, V. (2002). *Small and Medium-Size Enterprise Financing in Eastern Europe*. World Bank Policy Research Working Paper, No. 2933, World Bank, Washington D.C., November.

Appendix

Table A4.1 25 Successful VC-backed companies

Name	Activity	Country	Private equity investors	Capital invested	Type of deal	Initial investment	Exit
@Entertainment	Media	Poland	Advent International (lead); Copernicus Capital Partners; Innova Capital	\$66m	Expansion capital	1996	1999
Avonmore Pásztó	Food processing, dairy	Hungary	Euroventures Hungary; Equinox (associated with Advent)	€2.2m	Management buyout	1997	1999
Brewery Holdings	Brewing	Romania	Advent International; Jupiter Asset Management; Oresa Ventures	\$28m	Expansion capital	1996	2000
Cesu Alus	Brewing	Latvia	Norway-Latvia Business Development Fund	\$216 580	Turnaround	1997	1999
ComputerLand	Information technology	Poland	Enterprise Investors	\$4m	Partial buyout/ expansion capital	1994	1997
Czech On Line	Internet and telecommunications	Czech Republic	DBG Eastern Europe	€6.4m	Management buyout	1998	2000
Eldorado	Food retail and wholesale	Poland	Enterprise Investors	\$3.3m	Expansion capital	1999	2003

(*Continued*)

Table A4.1 Continued

Name	Activity	Country	Private equity investors	Capital invested	Type of deal	Initial investment	Exit
Elender Informatika	Internet service provider	Hungary	Advent International; Equinox	$3.2m	Expansion capital	1998	1999
Enigma	Software development	Hungary	Euroventures Hungary; Fast Ventures BV	€1.4m	Start-up	2002	2004
Euronet Worldwide	Financial services, software development	Hungary	Euroventures Hungary; Hungarian-American Enterprise Fund; Innova Capital; Advent International	$8.8m	Expansion capital	1994	Partial and full exits from 1997
GZ Digital Media	Optical disk replication	Czech Republic	Winslow Partners; Patria Asset Management; Croesus	€7.5m	Leveraged buyout	1997	1999 (Patria), 2000 (Croesus), 2002 (Winslow, partial)
HTL Group	Medical instrument manufacturing	Poland	European Renaissance Capital LP	$3m	Expansion capital	1997	2001 (partial)
Hungariocamion	Transportation and logistics	Hungary	DBG Eastern Europe; BA Capital Partners Europe	€13m	Management buyin	1998	2002
Keravit	Refractory ceramics manufacturing	Czech Republic	Czech Venture Partners	€1.25m	Management buyout	1995	2003
Lukas	Financial services	Poland	Enterprise Investors	$15m	Expansion capital	1997	2001
Mineral/ Slezkéizolacní-závody	Construction materials	Czech Republic	Czech Venture Partners	€1.1m	Management buyout	1995	2001
Overseas Express	Transport and logistics	Croatia	Copernicus Capital Partners (via Croatia Capital Partnership)	$1.3m	Expansion capital	2000	2003
Polfa Kutno	Pharmaceutical production	Poland	Enterprise Investors	$14.3m	Buyout/ expansion capital	1995	2003

Semilab	Semiconductor equipment manufacturing	Hungary	Euroventures Hungary; Hungarian-American Enterprise Fund; Venture Capital Hungary	€850 000	Expansion capital	1992	1999
Slovpak	Plastic packaging	Slovakia	Raiffeisen Ost Invest	€1.1m	Management buyout	1998	2002
Spofa Dental	Dental supplies	Czech Republic	Riverside Central Europe Fund	$8.9m (including assumed debt)	Leveraged buyout	1998	2003
Stomil Sanok	Rubber products manufacturing	Poland	Enterprise Investors	$8.7m	Buyout/ expansion capital	1993	2003
Town & City	Outdoor advertising	Poland	Innova Capital	$5m	Expansion capital	1996	1999
Uproar	Internet	Hungary	Euroventures Hungary	$1m	Start-up	1996	1998
Zentiva	Pharmaceuticals	Czech Republic	Warburg Pincus	$125m	Management buyout	1998	2004 (partial)

Source: EVCA (2004), see this publication for more details.

Table A4.2 National equity schemes

Country	Equity scheme	Existence	How funded?	Total funding
Czech Republic	Credit – Program of Support Businesses in Initial Development Stage	Since July 2004	Structural funds, state budget, private funds	€20m for the years 2004–2006
Czech Republic	PROGRESS – Program of Support Businesses in Development Stage	Since January 2005	State budget, private funds	€20m for the years 2005–2006
Latvia	Venture Capital for Small and Medium-Sized Enterprises	Since 1995	Grant from the Norwegian government and Alcatel Telecom Norway	$3m
Hungary	SME Development Fund	Since January 2002	Governmental and commercial banks	€13.6m
Hungary	Equity Fund for Developments in the Field of Information and Telecommunications	Since January 2002	Government	€12.4m
Hungary	Suppliers' Investment Company	Since March 2002	Government	€10m
Hungary	CORVINUS International Investment Co.	Since July 1997	Government, 3 state-owned banks	€40.6m
Poland	National Investment Fund	Since 2005	ERDF, domestic public funds	€27.8
Slovakia	Seed Capital Company	Since 1994	PHARE, state budget	213m Sk

Source: EC (2005).

5 Venture capital in European transition economies: A scoring system

Robert W. McGee

Abstract

Economies that are making the transition from a central planning to a market system are in special need of venture capital (VC) because their infrastructure needs to be rebuilt after decades of neglect, mismanagement, and malinvestment. However, the supply of domestic capital is insufficient to meet their needs. The task of attracting VC is not easy, since they have to compete with more than 160 other countries that are also trying to attract such investment. This chapter examines the special problems that Central and East European transition economies face in trying to attract VC and discusses some of the factors venture capitalists might look at to determine where to invest. Countries are then ranked in terms of investment attractiveness.

5.1 Introduction

Venture capital and foreign direct investment are analogous terms but they are not identical. VC can either be foreign or domestic, whereas FDI is foreign by definition. But the distinctions between the two concepts are more complicated than that.

The Organisation for Economic Co-operation and Development published a benchmark definition of FDI in 1983 and has revised it twice since then. The third was published in 1996 and is 51 pages (OECD, 1996) with the fourth edition now being debated. A briefer definition of FDI is offered by Investorwords.com:

> Direct investments in productive assets by a company incorporated in a foreign country, as opposed to investments in shares of local companies by foreign entities. An important feature of an increasingly globalized economic system. (http://www.investorwords.com)

This same source defines VC as:

> Funds made available for startup firms and small businesses with exceptional growth potential. Managerial and technical expertise are often also provided. Also called risk capital. (http://www.investorwords.com)

Therefore, both the sources of the capital and the targets may be different. FDI comes from foreign investors and may be targeted at either start-up ventures or established enterprises, whereas VC may come from either domestic or foreign investors but is targeted at a start-up enterprise or a small business. There may also be differences in risk premiums where venture capitalists are often willing to take more risk in exchange for higher returns. Those who provide FDI may be looking for above-average returns but may not be willing to take the same amount of risk as a venture capitalist.

However, the two sets of investors also have many things in common. They look at a similar set of factors and attributes before deciding whether, and where, to invest their capital. Basically, they both want above-average returns with a certain amount of safety, although venture capitalists may be more willing to forego safety for higher returns.

A number of studies have examined VC or FDI in transition economies. Wright et al. (1999) analyze the role of VC firms as active investors in Hungary, Poland, and Slovakia and outline the development of the VC markets in each country. Karsai et al. (1998) also analyze the screening and valuation of VC investments in these countries. Aylward (1998) looks at trends in VC finance in developing countries while Schroder (2001) studies the new capital markets in Central and Eastern Europe. Wisniewski (2005) investigates the profit opportunities for venture capitalists in CEE in the decade after the dismantling of communism in Europe whereas Bliss (1999) discusses VC in Poland. Wright et al. (2004) look at the provision of capital to the EU accession countries. Knight (1994) performs a cross-cultural analysis of criteria used by venture capitalists to make investment decisions. Megginson (2004) discusses the possibility of a global VC market, similar to Patricof (1989) a few years earlier. Wright et al. (2005) review and synthesize the disparate literature that has been published on VC in several different disciplines. The European Bank for Reconstruction and Development has published a number of studies on VC in the transition economies of Central and Eastern Europe and has published the results of some VC projects on its website.

Biswas (2002) examines the determinants of FDI for 44 countries and finds that some factors are highly country specific. Chakrabarti (2001) investigates prior studies of the determinants of FDI and concludes that their results conflicted and attempted to determine which variables are strong and which are weak. Lin et al. (2001) investigate the relationship between changes in macro-economic and micro-economic, firm-specific determinants and changes in FDI made by Taiwanese firms. Deichmann et al. (2003) examine the classification of the determinants of FDI in transition economies using 21 socio-economic variables. Bandelj (2002) examines institutional, political, economic, and cultural connections between investors and CEE host countries, and finds the correlations to be highly positive. Kobrin (2005) employs a cross-sectional regression methodology using UNCTAD data to analyze the determinants of liberalization of FDI policies in 116 countries from 1992 to 2001.

5.2 Some factors to consider

Tax rates are one of many factors that venture capitalists look at when trying to determine where to invest. Reaping high profits becomes less attractive if a major portion of those profits is confiscated by high taxes. Protection of property rights is another important factor; nobody wants to invest millions of dollars in a venture that can be expropriated by a government. Likewise, countries that do not have a rule of law that protects property from less than total expropriation or confiscation are not seen as attractive places to invest. The ideal country in which to invest is a place where property rights are strongly protected and after-tax returns are high. Unfortunately, countries that possess both of these attributes are difficult to find. The developed market economies of Western Europe have a strong rule of law but also tend to have high tax rates. Some CEE countries have seen the wisdom of having low tax rates but in many cases their rule of law is still at the development stage.

In addition to political factors there are a number of economic factors to consider. The World Bank has published a series of Enterprise Surveys and Investment Climate Surveys that examine numerous variables. Space does not permit a full listing of these variables for each of the transition economies of CEE, let alone provide a full discussion. However, it will be worthwhile to select one country and list the top ten constraints that entrepreneurs see as being impediments.

Russia is probably the best choice, since it has the largest economy and the largest population of the CEE transition economies. Table 5.1 lists the top ten constraints seen by Russian entrepreneurs as major or very severe obstacles to doing business (World Bank, 2005).

The *Index of Economic Freedom* (IEF) (2006) publishes an annual study that measures economic freedom in more than 160 countries. It looks at 50 variables, subdivided into ten categories. The interactive website also has the capability of subdividing the total sample into geographic regions, of which one is North America and Europe. This subset contains 45 countries, 21 of which are transition economies in CEE. Serbia & Montenegro is not rated. The range of scores is 1 (best) to 5 (worst).

Countries are divided into the following four categories on the basis of scores:

- Free – countries with an overall score of 1.95 or less;
- Mostly Free – countries with an overall score of 2.00 to 2.95;
- Mostly Unfree – countries with an overall score of 3.00 to 3.95;
- Repressed – countries with an overall score of 4.00 or higher.

The following tables examine some of the categories listed by the IEF for this subset of countries. Table 5.2 lists the countries by overall rank.

Table 5.1 Top ten constraints for entrepreneurs: Russian Federation (most severe obstacles listed first)

Rank	
1	Economic and regulatory policy uncertainty
2	Tax administration
3	Macroeconomic instability
4	Tax rates
5	Cost of financing
6	Corruption
7	Skills and education of available workers
8	Access to financing
9	Anticompetitive or informal practices
10	Business licensing and operating permits

Source: http://www.worldbank.org

Table 5.2 Ranking

Country	Overall ranking (out of 161 countries)	Average score for all 50 variables (1 = best; 5 = worst)	Rank within Central & Eastern Europe
Free			
Estonia	7	1.75	1
Mostly Free			
Czech Republic	21	2.10	2
Lithuania	23	2.14	3
Armenia	27	2.26	4
Slovak Republic	34	2.35	5
Slovenia	38	2.41	6
Latvia	39	2.43	7
Hungary	40	2.44	8
Poland	41	2.49	9
Albania	52	2.75	10
Croatia	55	2.78	11
Macedonia	57	2.80	12
Bulgaria	64	2.88	13
Georgia	68	2.98	14
Mostly Unfree			
Bosnia & Herzegovina	74	3.01	15
Moldova	83	3.10	16
Romania	92	3.19	17
Ukraine	99	3.24	18
Russia	122	3.50	19
Repressed			
Belarus	151	4.11	20
Serbia & Montenegro	N/R		

Source: www.heritage.org

The category that is perhaps most relevant for venture capitalists is foreign investment. A country earns a score of 1.0 if barriers to entry are very low. To earn this score, the government has to treat foreign investors on an equal par with domestic investors. The foreign investment code must be transparent and the bureaucracy has to be professional and efficient. There cannot be any restrictions on foreign investments, although exceptions are allowed for restricting investments in sectors that involve national security. There have to be legal guarantees against expropriation of property and there must be provisions for the arbitration of international disputes. Foreign investors have to be able to purchase real estate, while both residents and non-residents must have access to foreign exchange and be able to make international payments, transfers, and capital transactions freely (only Estonia and Armenia fall into this category).

A country receives a score of 2.0 if barriers to foreign investment are low. To earn this score there must be equal treatment for foreign and domestic investment. The foreign investment code must be transparent but the process may face bureaucratic or other informal impediments. There are some general restrictions on foreign investments, or in a few specified sectors such as national security, natural resources or utilities. There must be legal guarantees against expropriation of property and there must be the possibility of international arbitration of disputes. Foreign investors must be able to purchase real estate where both residents and non-residents must face few restrictions on access to foreign exchange or their ability to make international payments, transfers, or capital transactions. The following eight countries fall into this category: Czech Republic, Lithuania, Slovak Republic, Slovenia, Latvia, Hungary, Albania, and Bulgaria.

Countries earn a score of 3.0 if there are moderate barriers to foreign investment. Barriers are considered to be moderate if foreign investment is generally encouraged but foreign investors do not receive equal treatment with domestic investors in all sectors; the foreign investment code is unclear and the investment process faces some bureaucratic impediments or corruption; the country restricts foreign investments through many requirements or in a significant number of sectors; the expropriation of property is very unlikely and the country guarantees compensation when confiscation does occur; foreign investors are restricted in their ability to buy real estate; residents and/or non-residents have restricted access to foreign exchange and have restricted ability to make international payments, transfers, or capital transactions. The following six countries fall into this category: Poland, Croatia, Macedonia, Georgia, Bosnia & Herzegovina, and Romania.

Countries that have high barriers to foreign investment earn a score of 4.0. To earn this score, a country has to permit foreign investment only on a case-by-case basis. The foreign investment code discriminates against foreign investors and foreign investment does not receive equal treatment in all sectors. The investment process is characterized by significant bureaucratic corruption and impediments and foreign investment is restricted in many sectors, with a possibility of expropriation of property. Foreign investors may buy real estate only on a case-by-case basis or only in restricted areas, however, residents and/or non-residents face restrictions on foreign exchanges and the government imposes many controls on international payments, transfers, and capital transactions. Four former Soviet republics – Russia, Ukraine, Moldova, and Belarus – fall into this category.

If a pattern can be seen from these scores it would be that former Soviet republics are the least friendly toward foreign investment, with the exception of Armenia and the three Baltic republics of Estonia, Latvia, and Lithuania, and that former Soviet satellite countries are less unfriendly.

None of the transition economies of CEE earned a score of 5.0. In order to earn this score, there must be very high barriers to foreign investment. Foreign investors must receive unequal treatment. The foreign investment code must be discriminatory, the approval process must be opaque and corruption must be widespread. Foreign investment must be very restricted and few sectors are open to foreign investment. Expropriation of property must have occurred in the recent past. Foreign investors must be unable to purchase real estate. Government must control or prohibit most international payments, transfers, and capital transactions. The only countries in the world that fall into this category are Turkmenistan, Venezuela, Zimbabwe, Burma, Iran, and North Korea.

Table 5.3 shows the scores and rankings for the transition economies in Central and Eastern Europe in the category of foreign investment.

Table 5.3 Barriers to foreign investment

Rank (out of 45 countries in North America & Europe)	Country	Foreign investment score (1 = best; 5 = worst)
Very low		
1	Estonia	1.0
1	Armenia	1.0
Low		
10	Czech Republic	2.0
10	Lithuania	2.0
10	Slovak Republic	2.0
10	Slovenia	2.0
10	Latvia	2.0
10	Hungary	2.0
10	Albania	2.0
10	Bulgaria	2.0
Moderate		
27	Poland	3.0
27	Croatia	3.0
27	Macedonia	3.0
27	Georgia	3.0
27	Bosnia & Herzegovina	3.0
27	Romania	3.0
High		
41	Moldova	4.0
41	Ukraine	4.0
41	Russia	4.0
41	Belarus	4.0
45	Serbia & Montenegro	N/R

Source: http://www.worldbank.org
N/R= not reported.

Another factor venture capitalists consider is regulation. Regulation not only makes it more difficult to do business but it also cuts into the bottom line and increases the cost of doing business. The greater the extent of regulation, the less desirable the country is for investment purposes, all other things being equal. The problem with the transition economies of CEE is that the mentality of the government bureaucracy has not yet let go of the notion that the government should control everything. There is a widespread perception that it will take a generation before substantive change takes place in the minds of the bureaucracy. The generation of communist bureaucrats must pass from the scene, either by death or retirement, before they can be replaced by the younger generation, who did not grow up with the baggage of central planning.

None of the countries in CEE earn the best possible score (1.0). The only European or North American country to earn that score is Denmark. To earn that score, existing regulations have to be straightforward and applied uniformly to all companies. Regulations must not be a burden for business and corruption must be nearly non-existent.

Only two countries – Estonia and Slovenia – earn a score of 2.0. They receive this score because of simple licensing procedures and regulations that are relatively straightforward. Regulations must be applied uniformly most of the time, although sometimes burdensome. Corruption is rare but not non-existent.

Six countries receive a score of 3.0 (moderate) – the Czech Republic, Lithuania, the Slovak Republic, Latvia, Hungary, and Poland. Countries in this category have complicated licensing procedures. Regulations impose substantial burdens on business and regulations may be applied haphazardly. In some cases, regulations are not even published by the government, which makes it difficult for businesses to know what they are expected to comply with. Corruption may exist and poses a minor burden on business.

The category with the largest number of CEE countries (ten) has a score of 4.0 (high). To earn this score a country has highly complicated licensing procedures. Regulations must impose heavy burdens on business, they must be applied haphazardly and they must be unpublished in some instances. Corruption must impose a substantial burden on business. Countries in this category include Armenia, Albania, Croatia, Macedonia, Bulgaria, Georgia, Moldova, Romania, Ukraine, and Russia.

Two countries – Bosnia & Herzegovina and Belarus – earn the highest score (5.0). This score is earned by countries with government-set production quotas and some state planning. Government regulations impede the creation of new businesses, regulations are applied randomly and corruption is widespread.

Table 5.4 displays the scores and rankings.

A third factor of great importance to venture capitalists is labor market rigidity. Ideally, employers should be able to lose employees who are no longer required immediately and at little or no cost. Venture capitalists, indeed all employers, prefer to be able to exercise their right to fire un-needed workers to cut costs. The bloated welfare states of Western Europe place restrictions on this practice. In some cases it is nearly impossible to dismiss employees, even if they are lazy, unproductive, or disruptive. Restrictive labor legislation in these countries prevents employers from exercising their rights to do with their property (business) as they see fit. As a result, labor markets have become rigid. Employers hesitate to hire people they cannot later dismiss if they are not needed.

Such restrictive labor practices increase the cost of doing business and may even push a company into bankruptcy. Thus, venture capitalists prefer not to make investments in countries with restrictive labor practices, all other things being equal. With their accession into the EU, some transition economies are adopting such restrictive labor practices. Some already had such practices under communism and did not lose them during their transition to a market economy. In some cases, restrictive labor practices are one vestige of socialism they have retained. However, some transition economies are better in this area than others.

The World Bank produces statistics on labor practices in transition economies. Table 5.5 shows the difficulty faced by employers in the transition economies of CEE if they try to fire an employee. The scale is from 0 (best) to 100 (worst); 155 countries were included in the survey. The World Bank also calculates average scores for several regions of the world. The CEE countries fall within the Europe & Central Asia region.

Taxation is another factor venture capitalists consider when looking for places to invest. The lower the rate, the better the after-tax return. However, corporate income

Table 5.4 Regulatory burden

Rank (out of 45 countries in North America & Europe)	Country	Regulatory burden score (1 = best; 5 = worst)
Low		
2	Estonia	2.0
2	Slovenia	2.0
Moderate		
13	Czech Republic	3.0
13	Lithuania	3.0
13	Slovak Republic	3.0
13	Latvia	3.0
13	Hungary	3.0
13	Poland	3.0
High		
32	Armenia	4.0
32	Albania	4.0
32	Croatia	4.0
32	Macedonia	4.0
32	Bulgaria	4.0
32	Georgia	4.0
32	Moldova	4.0
32	Romania	4.0
32	Ukraine	4.0
32	Russia	4.0
Very high		
43	Bosnia & Herzegovina	5.0
43	Belarus	5.0
45	Serbia & Montenegro	N/R

N/R= not reported.

tax is not the only tax that corporations pay. They must also pay part of their employees' social security taxes, value-added taxes, and a plethora of other taxes. The total tax burden is not always easy to calculate, especially when some taxes are indirect or hidden.

The World Bank (1996; http://www.worldbank.org) has computed the total taxes a corporation must pay as a percentage of gross profits for 155 countries and this is given in Table 5.6.

5.3 Results

Scores assigned to the *Index of Economic Freedom* (Table 5.2) rankings are as follows: the only country in the Free category (Estonia) received 1 point; countries in the Mostly

Table 5.5 Difficulty of firing workers

Rank		Country	Score (0 = best; 100 = worst)
Central & Eastern Europe (21)	All countries (155)		
Above for Europe and Central Asia			
1	22	Bulgaria	10
2	38	Czech Republic	20
2	38	Albania	20
2	38	Hungary	20
5	60	Russia	30
5	60	Bosnia & Herzegovina	30
7	78	Slovak Republic	40
7	78	Estonia	40
7	78	Macedonia	40
7	78	Poland	40
7	78	Belarus	40
7	78	Lithuania	40
7	78	Serbia & Montenegro	40
Average for Europe & Central Asia 41.5			
Below average			
14	104	Romania	50
14	104	Croatia	50
14	104	Slovenia	50
17	130	Moldova	70
17	130	Latvia	70
17	130	Georgia	70
17	130	Armenia	70
21	146	Ukraine	80

Free category received scores between 2 and 5, depending on their IEF score; countries in the Mostly Unfree category earned scores of between 6 and 8, depending on their IEF; countries in the Repressed category earned a score of 10. Serbia & Montenegro received a score of 10 even though it was not ranked in the IEF. It was not ranked because its economy was so bad that the authors of the IEF considered it to be beyond quantifying.

The Barriers to Foreign Investment (Table 5.3) category received scores as follows: 1 = 2; 2 = 4; 3 = 6; 4 = 8; and 5 = 10. In other words, the IEF scores, which ranged from 1 to 5, were doubled, since the range of the present study is 1 to 10. The IEF scores for the category Regulatory Burden (Table 5.4) were also doubled.

The scores for the category Difficulty of Firing Workers (Table 5.5) were divided by 10, since the scale in that category was to 100. Countries in the Total Tax Payable category (Table 5.6) were assigned scores of between 1 and 5 if they were ranked in the Better Than Average category and scores of between 6 and 10 if they were classified in the Below Average category.

Table 5.6 Total tax payable

Rank		Country	Total tax payable (% of gross profit)
Central & Eastern Europe (21)	All countries (155)		
Better than average			
1	15	Bosnia & Herzegovina	19.7
2	52	Bulgaria	38.6
3	53	Latvia	38.7
4	55	Slovak Republic	39.5
4	55	Estonia	39.5
6	59	Czech Republic	40.1
6	59	Macedonia	40.1
8	61	Russia	40.8
9	64	Lithuania	41.6
10	78	Moldova	44.7
11	84	Serbia & Montenegro	46.3
12	89	Croatia	47.1
13	90	Slovenia	47.1
14	100	Georgia	49.7
Average for Europe and Central Asia 50.2%			
Below average			
15	107	Ukraine	51.0
16	108	Romania	51.1
17	122	Armenia	53.8
18	127	Poland	55.6
19	129	Hungary	56.8
20	144	Albania	71.6
21	150	Belarus	121.8

Source: http://www.worldbank.org

We now assign scores and rankings to the various countries on the basis of the information given above. Lower scores are assigned to the best countries in each of the categories examined and higher scores are assigned to the worst countries. The scores assigned in the various categories are then averaged and the countries ranked.

The 2006 *Index of Economic Freedom* provides a comprehensive approach to the issue. It examines 50 variables, some of them weighted, and ranks countries on the basis of economic freedom. However, while economic freedom may act as a surrogate for desirable investment climate, there is not a complete overlap. Some countries where bribes are commonplace, for example, also provide some superior investment opportunities. The IEF does not consider these possibilities for investment because the goal of that study is different and seeks only to measure economic freedom, which is often, but not always, positively correlated with investment opportunity.

The concluding scores are summarized and ranked in Table 5.7. We find that Belarus has attained the highest average score and Estonia the lowest.

Table 5.7 Combined scores (lowest score is best)

Rank	Country	Table 5.2 Economic Freedom	Table 5.3 Barriers To Foreign Investment	Table 5.4 Regulatory Burden	Table 5.5 Difficulty of Firing Workers	Table 5.6 Total Tax Payable	Average Score
1	Estonia	1	2	4	4	4	3.0
2	Czech Republic	2	4	6	2	5	3.8
3	Hungary	3	4	6	2	6	4.2
3	Lithuania	2	4	6	4	5	4.2
3	Slovak Republic	3	4	6	4	4	4.2
3	Slovenia	3	4	4	5	5	4.2
7	Bulgaria	5	4	8	1	4	4.4
8	Latvia	3	4	6	7	4	4.8
9	Poland	3	6	6	4	6	5.0
10	Albania	4	4	8	2	8	5.2
10	Armenia	3	2	8	7	6	5.2
12	Bosnia & Herzegovina	6	6	10	3	2	5.4
13	Macedonia	5	6	8	4	5	5.6
14	Croatia	5	6	8	5	5	5.8
15	Georgia	5	6	8	7	5	6.2
15	Romania	6	6	8	5	6	6.2
15	Russia	7	8	8	3	5	6.2
18	Moldova	6	8	8	7	5	6.8
19	Ukraine	6	8	8	8	6	7.2
20	Serbia & Montenegro	10	10	10	4	5	7.8
21	Belarus	10	8	10	4	10	8.4

5.4 Conclusion

Any attempt to determine the desirability of investment on the basis of a rigid ranking or a scoring system is problematic at best. There are many cultural, political, and economic factors that need to be considered. Some factors are more important than others. Thus, some kind of weighting of factors is called for. But individuals will have differing opinions about which factors are the most important and which are minor. Thus, even a weighting scheme is highly subjective and not necessarily applicable to any particular investor.

The background and expertise of the individual venture capitalist are also important factors in any decision regarding where to invest. If a venture capitalist wants to invest only in Armenia, since that is where his grandparents are from, the fact that some other countries might be more investor-friendly is irrelevant.

It is impossible to determine where the best investment climates are without taking all these subjective factors into consideration. The present scoring system is an attempt to provide some generic guidelines only, and attempts to answer the question, 'If all other things are equal, where are the best places for a venture capitalist to invest?'. All other things are never equal, of course. Thus, the scoring system discussed in this chapter is only generic, and is subject to adjustment where some variables are more important than others. It is intended to be a mere starting point for discussion.

Another limitation of the present study is that it is restricted to the transition economies of Central and Eastern Europe. Venture capitalists have a choice of over 160 countries in which to invest and the present study examines only 21, a small subset of all investment possibilities. However, if someone wants to invest in Central or Eastern Europe, hopefully this study will provide some guidance, or will at least identify some of the factors that should be considered in the investment decision.

References

Aylward, A. (1998). *Trends in Venture Capital Finance in Developing Countries*. Discussion Paper 36, International Finance Corporation. Washington, DC: World Bank.

Bandelj, N. (2002). Embedded Economies: Social Relations as Determinants of Foreign Direct Investment in Central and Eastern Europe. *Social Forces*, 81(2):411–444.

Biswas, R. (2002). Determinants of Foreign Direct Investment. *Review of Development Economics*, 6(3):492–504.

Bliss, R.T. (1999). A Venture Capital Model for Transitioning Economies. The Case of Poland. *Venture Capital*, 1(3):241–258.

Chakrabarti, A. (2001). The Determinants of Foreign Direct Investment: Sensitivity Analysis of Cross-Country Regressions. *Kyklos*, 54(1):89–114.

Deichmann, J., Eshghi, A., Haughton, D., Sayek, S., Teebagy, N. and Topi, H. (2003). Geography Matters: Kohonen Classification of Determinants of Foreign Direct Investment in Transition Economies. *Journal of Business Strategies*, 20(1): 23–44.

Index of Economic Freedom (2006). Washington, DC and New York: The Heritage Foundation and *The Wall Street Journal*. http://www.heritage.org/research/features/index/

Karsai, J., Wright, M., Dudzinski, Z. and Morovic, J. (1998). Screening and Valuing Venture Capital Investments: Evidence from Hungary, Poland and Slovakia. *Entrepreneurship and Regional Development*, 10:203–224.

Knight, R. (1994). Criteria Used by Venture Capitalists: A Cross Cultural Analysis. *International Small Business Journal*, 13(1):26–37.

Kobrin, S. (2005). The Determinants of Liberalization of FDI Policy in Developing Countries: A Cross-Sectional Analysis, 1992–2001. *Transnational Corporations*, 14(1):67–104.

Lin, Y., Szenberg, M. and Webster, T. (2001). Determinants of Foreign Direct Investment: Taiwan, 1965–1993. *The Journal of Applied Business Research*, 17(2):51–63.

Megginson, W. (2004). Toward a Global Model of Venture Capital? *Accenture Journal of Applied Corporate Finance*, 16(1):7–26.

Organisation for Economic Co-operation and Development (1996). *OECD Benchmark Definition of Foreign Direct Investment, Third Edition*. Paris: OECD.

Patricof, A. (1989). The Internationalisation of Venture Capital. *Journal of Business Venturing*, 17(4): 227–230.

Schroder, M. (ed.) (2001). *The New Capital Markets in Central and Eastern Europe*. New York: Springer.

Wisniewski, P. (2005). *Venture Capital in Central and Eastern Europe: A Decade of Opportunity*. Biggleswade: Spiramus Press.

World Bank (2005). *Investment Climate Surveys: Draft Country Profile. Russian Federation, 2005 Survey*. http://rru.worldbank.org/InvestmentClimate.

Wright, M., Karsai, J., Dudzinski, Z. and Morovic, J. (1999). Transition and Active Investors: Venture Capital in Hungary, Poland and Slovakia. *Post-Communist Economies*, 11(1):27–46.

Wright, M., Kissane, J. and Burrows, A. (2004). Private Equity and the EU Accession Countries of Central and Eastern Europe. *Journal of Private Equity*, 7(3):32–46.

Wright, M., Pruthi, S. and Lockett, A. (2005). International Venture Capital Research: From Cross-Country Comparisons to Crossing Borders. *International Journal of Management Reviews*, 7(3):135–165.

6 Recommendations for the development of a European venture capital regulatory corpus: Lessons from the U.S.

Edward J. Lusk, Gregor Schmidt, and Michael Halperin

Abstract

The essential elementals of the functioning of the IPO markets in the principal countries in the Euro-zone and the U.S. are detailed. The possibilities of strategic behavior in setting the opening price at the IPO launch date from the perspective of the venture capitalist, underwriters, the IPO-firm, and general investors are then examined. Based upon an analysis of 76 IPOs that opened principally on the NASDAQ (73%) and the NYSE (23%) between 1 April 2002 and 31 December 2003, the daily stock price and return information are analyzed to identify the possibility of strategic price setting. The analysis is stratified by three time periods: the first trading day, up to and around the lock-up expiration date, and after. Finally, policy recommendations are offered for the development of the IPO market in the Euro-zone with the eye to avoiding strategic price setting.

6.1 Introduction

The important issue addressed in this research is the need to understand the ways in which a number of factors impact the IPO launch price and its short-term market performance. There are formal factors such as tax law and listing regulations, as well as informal factors such as the underwriting culture that influence the IPO process. Together they frame the environment of diverse wealth-creation possibilities for the participating parties: the IPO firm, the underwriter and investors, and in particular venture capitalists. We offer suggestions intended to guide decision making in the EU regarding the formation of a regulatory corpus, where setting the launch price and subsequent market performance are not materially affected by strategic considerations, thus strengthening the IPO market. In our view, a regulatory corpus must be based on the principle that over time it will create a market where all of the parties involved in the launch of an IPO are able to transparently assess their return/risk trade-off, as one understands it from Markowitz (1952).

Various aspects of this market development principle have been recently considered by the OECD (Baygan, 2004: 5). Of the 19 issues that the OECD considers important to ensure the smooth functioning of venture markets, we identify the following three as key to the development of viable venture markets:

- improve accounting standards and performance benchmarks to reduce opacity of VC funds and protect investors;
- reduce complexity in tax treatment of capital from different sources and types of investments;
- reduce high capital gains tax rates and wealth taxes that can deter VC investments and entrepreneurs.

The OECD highlights Assurance, Transparency, and the Tax System as linchpins for the functioning of markets; they are also essential in the development of a non-strategically determined launch price. In this research, we consider those three attributes, as well as information from an analysis of the market performance of IPOs launched in the U.S. This information may be used as a basis for recommendations to the EU securities study arm, the Committee of European Securities Regulators (CESR), regarding the development of an EU regulatory corpus. To examine these issues and develop the recommendations, we consider first the wealth-creation issues that are involved in the establishment of the final launch price. Then, we look at the IPO's subsequent short-term market performance from our study.

6.2 Wealth creation: the final launch price and its market implications

Problems with Assurance and Transparency often create an environment where moral hazard, information asymmetries, and gaming temptations exist from the perspectives of many of the players in the IPO launch drama. Although the cast of players is indeed large, what ties them together is the final IPO launch price. This simplifies the strategic decision to a choice between underpricing and overpricing. In what follows, for simplicity, assume that bookbuilding is used, and results in a final launch interval that is approved by all of the regulatory special interest groups as: ($P_H > P_f > P_L$); where P_L represents a price lower than the first-day final closing price, P_f, suggesting underpricing, and P_H represents a price higher than P_f, suggesting overpricing. We assume that P_f is the equilibrium price.

6.2.1 Overpricing

Here, the IPO firm wants to generate as much capital as possible – this is the reverse case of the 'money left on the table' scenario; we term it as 'money put in the coffers'. Let us examine the conditions under which this is a benefit to the IPO firm and a detriment to the rest of the launch players. Assume that, as is usually the case, the underwriter buys shares of the IPO firm at the customary spread of 7% (see Chen and Ritter, 2000), and the shares are sold to the institutional subscribers in the underwriter's book starting at P_H. In this case, the IPO firm is the clear winner; this is the worst-case scenario for both the institutional fund managers who just bought overvalued shares, and for the underwriter who just shopped an overpriced issue. It could also be a serious reputation knock for the underwriter and may result in lost future placements. The only case where those who purchased the overpriced shares can benefit is the unlikely situation in which the price continues to slide, to a point where the market believes the stock to be underpriced and this starts a compensating rally.

6.2.2 Underpricing

If the stock is subscribed for and sold at P_L, then it will track upward to P_f, giving increasing first-day returns; there is 'money left on the table', meaning the firm did not receive the amount of money that it could have received. The groups benefiting, at the expense of the IPO firm, are the IPO investors who bought the undervalued shares, and the underwriters who shopped a bargain to their clients. By producing discounts for their institutional clients, the underwriters can take advantage of indirect side payments, which might come in the form of future commission business or investment banking business. It is for just such a practice, known as spinning, that Credit Suisse was fined US$100 million (see Ljungqvist, 2005: 30–31). Figure 6.1 summarizes the interaction of strategic behavior for the principal players in the IPO theatre leading to underpricing, and presents a quadrant graphic for the relationship between the power to influence underpricing and the benefits resulting from it.

6.2.3 Discussion of Figure 6.1

Because underpricing is the 'money left on the table' scenario, the IPO firm has no obvious benefit from underpricing. However, according to Loughran and Ritter (2002: 414), Prospect Theory suggests that the IPO firm may go along with underpricing because they 'will sum the wealth loss from leaving money on the table with the larger wealth gain on the retained shares from a price jump'. From an economic perspective, this assumes that the IPO has shares to issue/re-issue, and that the price jump combines with the shares that could be issued, so that they make up, in NPV terms, the sum forgone. In most cases,

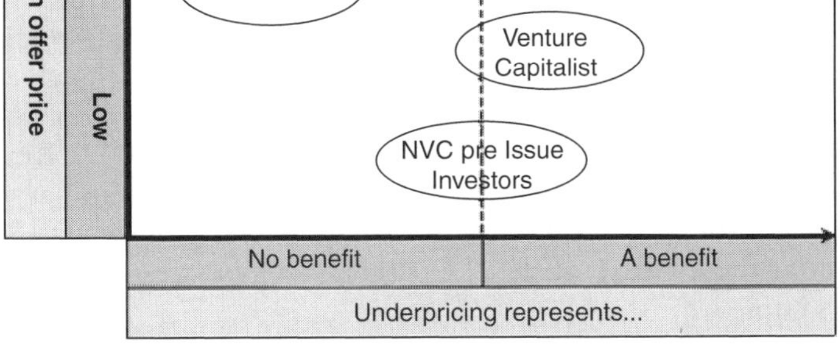

Figure 6.1 Influence on underpricing and wealth consequences.

this scenario seems unlikely (Brealey et al., 2006). On the supply side of the equation, the IPO firm may be able to influence the launch price, if it determines the supply of stocks offered to the market.

According to Aggarwal et al. (2002), the pre-issue IPO shareholders with a short-run orientation may benefit from underpricing if the price run-up in the first day creates a price surge for the shares that they hold. The same benefit can be ascribed to short-run-oriented venture capitalists, who seek an advantageous moment to exit their investments and to redeploy the money into the private equity market, where returns are likely to be higher. However, other, more long-term-oriented, pre-issue investors are likely to be indifferent with respect to underpricing because the momentum effect seems to fade out rather quickly, as we will show in our analysis. In sum, Figure 6.1 traces out the expected main diagonal orientation. Benefit and Influence seem to go hand in hand; essentially because those with the influence, the underwriters, create the circumstances that guarantee the benefit for their clients, the institutional investors. Hence it is not surprising that, according to Hensel (2005), over all of the Standard Industrial Classification (SIC) codes from 1999 to 2005, there has never been a year in the U.S. when the offer-to-open percentage price, on average, has been negative. The underpricing average since the bubble of 2000 has been 5.9%.

Now let us extend the orientations as presented in Figure 6.1, by adding a lock-up period and a tax system, and then examine the actual behavior of IPOs in the U.S. markets so as to formulate recommendations to the EU concerning this aspect of the regulatory corpus.

6.3 A study of strategic price setting from the U.S.

Using VentureXpert, a database of Thomson Venture Economics, 76 companies that went public between 1 April 2002 and 31 December 2003 were identified. The sample consists of 73% NASDAQ and 23% NYSE stocks. VentureXpert classifies IPOs into venture-backed and buy-out-backed. We separate the sample into VC-backed (VC) and non-VC-backed (NVC). Of the 76 companies, 42 were VC and 30 were NVC. Four firms were recorded in both classifications and are therefore excluded when comparing differences between VC and NVC firms. Daily prices and returns were downloaded from the Center for Research in Security Prices (CRSP) database for up to one year after the IPO launch date. That one-year period encompasses four main events: opening, price adjustment at the end of first trading day, subsequent market reaction, and expiration of lock-up period. For both the VC and NVC IPOs, we consider the price and return information for these main events, in both the overpricing and underpricing scenarios.

The empirical evidence regarding strategic price setting, which, given our analysis of Figure 6.1, not surprisingly seems to focus almost exclusively on underpricing (see Ljungqvist, 2005, 1999; Ritter, 2003; Loughran and Ritter, 2002; Ritter and Welch, 2002; Aggarwal et al., 2002; Habib and Ljungqvist, 2001). The summary of these works is that underpricing is the simplest wealth-creation possibility for the IPO launch partners, who usually win at the expense of the IPO firm. Our hypothesis is that underpricing is the case in our sample.

We then examine if and how major parties involved in an IPO are able to strategically exploit a positive relationship for first-day returns. This may depend on subsequent market performance controlling for the length and enforceability of the lock-up period. Finally, we test for excess returns around the lock-up expiration date. Here we define excess returns using the following two benchmarks: (1) the S&P 500 market surrogate index, and (2) the value- and size-adjusted benchmark portfolios (see Ang and Zhang, 2004; Fama and French, 1992). This second benchmark, noted as 2BM, is selected to control for possible market bias introduced by value and size effects. Size is surrogated by market capitalization and value by the ratio of book equity to market equity (B/M ratio). The median NYSE size (50th percentile breakpoint of NYSE) is used to form two equally weighted size portfolios of all NYSE, NASDAQ, and AMEX stocks. Based on value (B/M ratio), three value portfolios are created by using breakpoints at the 30th and 70th NYSE percentiles. This then creates six (Size: Value) groupings that will be matched to our sample for benchmarking purposes: Small: Value, Small: Neutral, Small: Growth, Large: Value, Large: Neutral and Large: Growth.

For tests of statistical significance, we use parametric and non-parametric tests; conservatively, we use the highest *p*-value of the appropriate test for purposes of inference. We then use this information, along with the above-cited literature, as the basis of our recommendations for the Euro-zone regulatory corpus, both in general and also respecting the strategic behavior in determining the launch price.

6.4 Results

This section details the empirical results for the 42 VC and 30 NVC firms, and also examines wealth-creation possibilities. In particular, we test momentum drift and activity around the lock-up period expiration. Finally, we mention the tax aspects that appear to play a role in wealth creation.

6.4.1 *IPO first-day return data*

Table 6.1 presents information on the level of underpricing, the opening/launch IPO price, the number of issued shares and the amount raised at the end of the first day. Consistent with our hypothesis that underpricing is the case in our sample, we observe significant positive average first-day returns for both the VC and NVC firms at a *p*-value less than 0.001, Table 6.1, suggesting that for both groups underpricing overall was the strategy. This reflects the economic reality as we saw it in Figure 6.1, of never passing up a buy-low/sell-high bargain, in particular when you can engineer the bargain using bookbuilding.

Table 6.1 Mean values of the first-day performance for the VC and non-VC backed IPOs

Grouping	N	First-day return	IPO price	Shares traded*	IPO amount*
VC	42	12.94%	$13.10	5.329	$71.155
NVC	30	10.83%	$16.28	13.530	$223.557
All IPOs	76	11.78%	$14.46	8.711	$134.166

* In millions.

There was no statistically significant difference at $p < 0.1$ between the return of the VC (12.94%) and that of the NVC (10.83%) IPOs. This suggests that the underpricing equilibration is the same for both groups. Finally, at a p-value less than 0.001, the NVC IPOs have significantly higher launch prices, more shares issued, and consequently higher IPO proceeds (Table 6.1). This is not unexpected, as Gompers (1996) notes, because VC-backed IPO firms are usually smaller and younger than NVC-backed ones, even though they opened on one of the major exchanges.

6.4.2 Short-term orientation

According to Field and Hanka (2001: 491), the main concern for most venture capitalists is their exit strategy. However, the belief that venture capitalists exit as early as possible is a little simplistic. What they want is to get out at the most advantageous moment considering the taxation system, the return expectations of the IPO stock, and the lock-up period.

6.4.3 Tax and lock-up consideration

To insure the integrity of the market for all investors, without relying on the taxation system to pace out the shares as one conceives of in the dribble scenario, lock-up agreements were invented to create a no-dumping zone/period for the shares controlled by the venture capitalists and related insiders. If the VC firm is taxed as a limited partnership, as it is the case for most firms in our sample, then it is not clear when the shares would be cashed in. That depends on the tax status, the expected trajectory of the prices, and the need for re-deployable cash, relative to the economic alternatives of the individual who gets the share credit from the VC engagement. We hypothesize that if there is a market dip around the lock-up period, it is because just before the lock-up period is to expire, shareholders believe that the holders of the VC shares will likely dump their stock. We suppose that this is the case as a result of the inability of the market to have such tax-status information. Thus, for these organizations, we expect to see a general slide around the lock-up date.

All of the companies in our sample are subject to the same lock-up period of 180 days. Figure 6.2, where the lock-up expiration date is noted as 0, shows the time series of returns, beginning ten days before and ending ten days after the lock-up expiration date. As expected, Figure 6.2 shows a significant drop in returns around the lock-up expiration date for the VC IPOs, while the NVC IPOs did not undergo a dumping adjustment. This probably reflects the known difference in purpose between the two groups. To this extent it is an excellent validity check on the representativeness of the two sample groups.

We tested the effects of VC backing on excess returns before and after the lock-up date (Table 6.2), using the S&P 500, as well as a two-factor value and size benchmark (2BM).

The results around the lock-up are clear. There is a definitive market-price slide for the VC firms and no such slide for the NVC group. Specifically, there is no statistically significant evidence at $p < 0.25$ that the NVC price has changed for the $t \pm 4$ period. For the VC group, there is evidence of a price slide at $p < 0.02$. Further, the difference between the two groups for both time periods is statistically significant at $p < 0.07$, suggesting that the return slide for the VC IPOs is in the expected direction, and is different from that of the NVC firms. The same results obtain for the analysis at the expiration of the

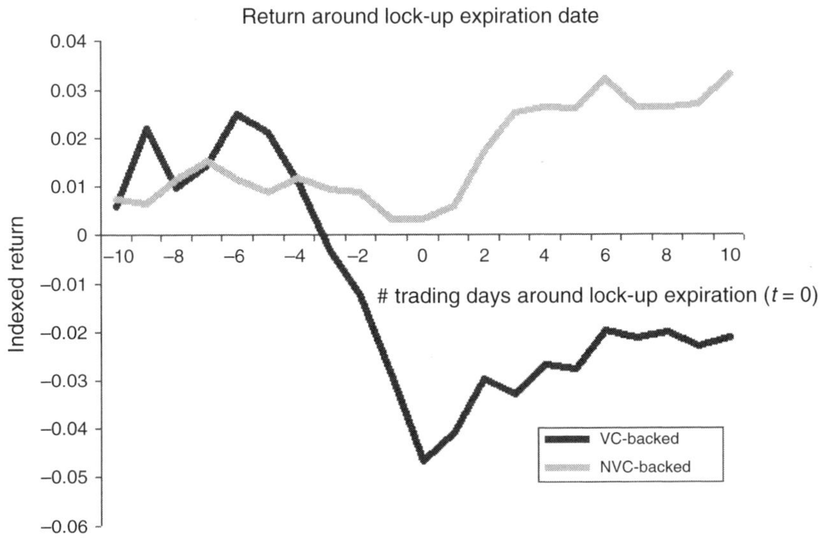

Figure 6.2 Return path around the lock-up.

Table 6.2 Excess returns around lock-up expiration (date t, starting from $t-4$ and ending $t+4$)

	N	Mean (Percentage)
Returns against the S&P 500		
VC	42	−6.43%
NVC	30	0.04%
All IPOs	76	−3.41%
Returns against the 2BM		
VC	42	−5.95%
NVC	30	−0.42%
All IPOs	76	−3.39%

lock-up period, which statistically confirms the graphical results evident from Figure 6.2. For Figure 6.2, also notice that most of the decline happens before the end of the lock-up period, confirming the market-anticipation effect. A pre-event market reaction is also observed by Bradley et al. (2003), who report a similar pattern at the expiration of the quiet period. Consistent with their findings, one can infer that the market acts on rumors, and conjectures that VC investors will likely sell their shares at the end of the lock-up period. For more on the expiration of lock-up periods see also Keasler (2001), Field and Hanka (2001), and Bradley et al. (2000).

6.4.4 Under- and overpricing

Now, let us consider what happens in return over the three time periods by looking at under- and overpricing separately. Consider the information disaggregated for the IPOs into two groups: those IPOs for which there was evidence of underpricing, in that the first-day returns were positive, labeled as 'underpriced', $n = 58$; and a second group labeled as 'overpriced', $n = 18$, in that their first-day returns were negative. Consistent with the literature, we see that the strategic choice seems to have been underpricing, by a margin of more than 3 to 1. This is statistically significant relative to chance at $p < 0.0001$. Now, let us examine the way in which underpricing plays out in the market, to see where the relative economic wealth-creation advantages may lie. This information is presented in Figure 6.3 for the non-stratified, non-controlled analysis of the two categorizations: underpriced and overpriced.

The results that we see in Figure 6.3 are also clear; there is an interesting correlation effect for overpricing, relative to subsequent return. There is a statistically significant positive correlation, $p < 0.1$, between the magnitude of the first-day overpricing differential and the magnitude of the monthly price deterioration. This correlation effect essentially disappears in the fourth month. However, no such effect is evident in the underpriced series. The return path there is stationary as measured by the Fisher's Kappa test, for which the p-value for the null of no autocorrelation structure is $p = 0.94$. Further, we see the same short-term momentum effect for the first three months, during which overpriced IPOs significantly underperform the comparable market index and underpriced IPOs are able to keep pace with the value- and size-indexed performance.

As discussed by Aggarwal et al. (2002), the idea of economic gain by the venture capitalist as a result of underpricing is not borne out, because the return path is stationary rather than momentum-driven. Thus, there is no strategic advantage in terms of return or price subsequent to the post-adjustment price. Therefore, we have clear evidence that IPO firms, as well as (to some lesser extent) the VC firms, which are locked into holding their shares, are losers in the underpricing scenario. Being so locked in, however, could create pressure for a venture capitalist to try to void or avoid lock-up agreements. Field and Hanka (2001: 494) find this effect, especially for venture capitalists engaged in early sales before lock-up expirations, when there is positive price trajectory shortly after the IPO.

Figure 6.3 Returns categorized by under- and overpriced.

6.5 Summary of the U.S. study

The results of our study may be simply summarized as follows.

6.5.1 Clear evidence of underpricing

The wealth-creation possibility from underpricing seems an irresistible temptation. From Figures 6.1 and 6.3, we can intuit who benefits from this strategic behavior. Apparently the group that is involved in shopping the placement has the most to gain and the least to lose relative to the IPO firm. Also, from an economic perspective, it is difficult to believe that Prospect Theory plays any role in the scenarios characterizing our launch group.

6.5.2 Abnormal returns around lock-up expiration

The VC firm backing the IPO also seems to pay in opportunity forgone as the stock takes its predictable drift down around the end of the lock-up period. Hence, possibly resulting from the lack of transparency relative to the taxation considerations, the market seems to expect a prompt exit by the venture capitalist, creating incentives for early sales by that group.

The following recommendations for the EU regulatory corpus are intended to address the above dysfunctional aspects, which seem to characterize venture markets. For our recommendations, we are drawing upon the general information that we presented regarding the development of trading markets, and also on the specifics as we summarized them from our study of the U.S. market.

6.6 Recommendations and conclusion

We concentrate on those aspects that are likely to promote the establishment of non-strategically gamed opening IPO price, as well as to preserve the market integrity subsequent to the launch. Both issues are important as far as the EU regulatory corpus is concerned. Following, we will offer these recommendations and, for each, we also note any Considerations of Special Note (CSN).

Recommendation 1: Assurance and Transparency are the key considerations. The Sarbanes-Oxley Act (SOX) of 2002 in the U.S. may have pushed the right to know beyond reasonable right to privacy and cost to implement limits. One should consider the French law, 2001-420 of 15 May 2001 called the New Economic Regulation (NER) Law (Mossos, 2004). The NER law seems an excellent alternative to the SOX and may well serve as the model for the EU. CSN (1): The *Wall Street Journal* (WSJ) (8 February 2006: Eastern edition (Eed): A16) reports that: 'the Free Enterprise Fund, being represented by Ken Starr, is leading a constitutional challenge arguing that the Public Company Accounting Oversight Board [PCAOB], aptly termed peek-a-boo, established under SOX violates the Appointments Clause of the U.S. Constitution.' Further, the WSJ argues that the substantial costs of meeting SOX transparency requirements may be driving possible IPOs to other jurisdictions. They note: 'A recent London Stock Exchange survey of 80 international companies that went public on its markets found that of those that had contemplated a US listing, 90% decided [Sarbanes-Oxley] made London more attractive.' Also, Kamara et al. (2005) report evidence that, as a result of the current regulatory rigor, small firms seem to be eschewing the public markets. CSN (2): The Fair Fund provision of the SOX is an excellent restitution mechanism and should be a part of the EU regulatory corpus. However, one should find a way to redistribute the collected restitution funds in a timely manner. The vast majority of the restitution funds collected under the aegis of SOX have not been distributed, some for as long as four years.

Recommendation 2: Transparency can be efficiently enhanced by encouraging the various independent evaluations and rating services to provide their specialized stakeholder information as part of the general information of the pre-launch prospectus. CSN: Three organizations with credible track records in developing rating information for a wide range of stakeholder concerns are: INNOVEST (http://www.innovestgroup.com), KLD Research & Analytics, Inc (http://www.kld.com), and the Human Rights Campaign (http://www.hrc.org).

Recommendation 3: In addition to stakeholder information, the IPO prospectus should include information on target prices from the large number of investment rating groups, such as investment banks, servicing the international financial community. These groups are proficient in using audit assurance information, often available for the IPO, in conjunction with the projections and estimations that are often provided as part of the transparency requirements of the securities oversight commission. These target prices can be statistically summarized in the usual manner and be made available to the investing public. CSN: We recommend, for the statistical summary, that a 95% Confidence Interval and the Inter-Quartile Range (IQR) of the collected target prices be presented and clearly explained. These may be usefully employed as a reasonability check of the pre-launch price interval.

Recommendation 4: If the bookbuilding roadshow is used as the way to develop the pre-launch price interval, then the reasonability of this interval should be evaluated using, in addition to the confidence intervals mentioned in Recommendation 3 above, a detailed analysis of the recent history of the launches. CSN (1): Specifically, one may form the following four ratios/multiples for recently launched IPOs: the average of the historical pre-launch price-interval values as a multiple to the book value of the operationally committed long-term assets, net sales, NOPAT, and EPS. These launched IPOs could then be grouped by whether the actual launch resulted in over- or underpricing. This will give two profiles, the multiples of which may be used to evaluate the reasonability of the pre-launch price interval for the IPOs under consideration. CSN (2): These comparative ratio/multiple profiles could be collected by industry, reasonable comparison groups within the industry, or across industries.

Recommendation 5: Because clear gaming issues are inherent in bookbuilding, auctions should be evaluated as a means of eliminating the underpricing bias, which seems inherent to bookbuilding. CSN (1): France and Japan have been using auctions for a number of years. This information should be evaluated (see Derrien and Womack, 2003). CSN (2): The form of the auction, and there are many, probably plays a role in determining the final launch price and should be carefully evaluated. For a discussion of possible issues to be considered, see Brealey et al. (2006) and Hensel (2005).

Recommendation 6: The EU should consider eliminating lock-up periods and search for other ways for shares to enter the market, so as to maintain its smooth functioning. CSN (1): The EU should study the possibility of creating a tax system for capital assets, considering the corporate and individual short- and long-term capital gains rates, as well as special tax considerations for various classes of venture activities and shares. Germany has perhaps the richest menu of possibilities (see OECD, 2004). The goal would be to offer a unified taxation system for capital assets, consistent with and therefore acceptable to the various countries in the EU. CSN (2): Failing this as a possibility, and it will be a daunting task, then the EU should experiment with various dribble systems so as to avoid the dysfunctional market behavior seen around current lock-up dates.

Recommendation 7: The quiet period, used in the U.S. until 2005, is an excellent way to reduce the strategic communication during the sensitive time period around the launch. CSN (1): However, findings by Bradley et al. (2003) point to patterns of abnormal returns at the end of the quiet period, suggesting that an imposed quiet period produces anomalies in the market similar to those created by the lock-up period. CSN (2): Here it is important to assess whether the benefit of having a quiet period can outweigh possible negative effects arising from market anomalies. CSN (3): Such monitoring should be sensitive to the possibilities of exaggerated performance claims and unrealistic downplaying of real advantages. Both can create wealth for various parties.

We did not address other issues critical to the development of a viable venture market, such as the importance of opening up the vast resources of pension funds, and finding a way to iron out the boom or bust IPO roller-coaster. As aspects relating to the above recommendations for the EU regulatory corpus, they should also be studied.

These recommendations for the development of an EU regulatory corpus are based in part upon what we see from the recent market performance of ventures that opened in the U.S. and in part upon the current complicated multinational market configuration of the EU, which is sometimes more European than Union (see Ververka, 2005: 44). Supplementing the OECD's suggestions on assurance, transparency, and taxes, the above-mentioned recommendations provide the first steps for the eventual development of a truly unified EU market system that can survive in the global arena. In this respect, the analysis of the U.S. IPO and venture markets offers a valuable perspective on rules and regulations that might aid in the long-term viability of the European capital markets.

We believe that survival is at issue. The appointment of Barbara C. Mathews, a former senior counsel for the U.S. House Financial Services Committee, to be the European Financial Attaché demonstrates only one of many U.S. influences on the European regularity system (WSJ, 9 February 2006: EEd.: B11). Furthermore the courting of the Euronext NV stock exchange by the NYSE represents another example of how EU capital markets are being challenged in the competition for resources (WSJ, 23 May 2006: EEd.: C1). Therefore, as U.S. hegemony seems to be in evidence both at the policy and market levels, these recommendations can be viewed as the first steps for the EU in the necessary and perhaps overdue process of moving to a simple unified market system. Specifically, these recommendations address the pitfalls as we see them from the U.S. experience and thus over time can offer, in conjunction with the many other issues that need to be addressed, a EU market where (1) IPOs are offered at a fair market price, thus avoiding the systemic gaming that creates side payments to special-interest-groups, and (2) where restrictions on security trading have effectively been eliminated, thus allowing securities a free play in the market. Such characteristics can be important features that over time will enhance the competitive advantage of the EU in the global competition for venture recourses.

Acknowledgments

We wish to thank Mr Nikolay Avramov, Financial Modelling Research Associate, FinAnalytica Inc., Sofia, Bulgaria; Professor Jean-Pierre Chateau, Département Economie, Finance, Group ESC-Rouen, Rouen, France; Mr Guido Heine, Tax Consultant/Controller, IBG Beteiligungsges: Sachsen-Anhalt mbh, Magdeburg, Germany; Professor Dirk Kiesewetter, Chair in Taxation, Faculty of Economics and Management, Otto-von-Guericke University, Magdeburg, Germany; Ms Debra A. Mandel, Managing Director/Partner, Everest Capital Inc., Miami, FL, USA; Ms Zeena Rao, Senior Associate, ICV Capital Partners LLC, NY, U.S.; and Mr. Daniel Wolf, Faculty of Economics and Management, Otto-von-Guericke University, Magdeburg, Germany for their assistance and suggestions. We would also like to thank Ms Ellen Slack of the Lippincott library for her excellent editorial assistance.

References

Aggarwal, R.K., Krigman, L. and Womack, K.L. (2002). Strategic IPO Underpricing, Information Momentum and Lockup Expiration Selling. Working Paper, Amos Tuck School of Business, Dartmouth NH.

Ang, J.S. and Zhang, S. (2004). An Evaluation of Testing Procedures for Long Horizon Event Studies. *Review of Quantitative Finance and Accounting*, 23(3):251–271.

Baygan, G. (2004). *Venture Capital: Trends and Policy Recommendations.* OECD Secretariat, Paris. OECD Papers, 4(10):1–29. Available at SSRN: http://www.oecd.org/sti/micro-policies

Bradley, D.J., Jordan, B.D., Roten, I.C. and Yi, H. (2000). Venture Capital and IPO Lockup Expiration: An Empirical Analysis. *Journal of Financial Research*, 24(3): 465–493.

Bradley, D.J., Jordan, B.D. and Ritter, J.R. (2003). The Quiet Period Goes Out with a Bang. *The Journal of Finance*, 55(1):1–36.

Brealey, R., Myers, S. and Allen, F. (2006). *Corporate Finance. 8th Edition*. New York: McGraw Hill/Irwin.

Chen, H-C. and Ritter, J. (2000). The Seven Percent Solution. *The Journal of Finance*, 55(3):1105–1131.

Derrien, F. and Womack, R. (2003). Auctions vs. Bookbuilding and the Control of Under Pricing in Hot IPO Markets. *Review of Financial Studies*, 16(1):31–61.

Fama, E.F. and French, K.R. (1992). The Cross-Section of Expected Stock Returns. *Journal of Finance*, 47(2):427–465.

Field, L.C. and Hanka, G. (2001). The Expiration of IPO Share Lockups. *The Journal of Finance*, 56(2):471–500.

Gompers, P.A. (1996). Grandstanding in the Venture Capital Industry. *Journal of Financial Economics*, 42(1):133–156.

Habib, A.M. and Ljungqvist, A.P. (2001). Underpricing and Entrepreneurial Wealth Losses in IPOs: Theory and Evidence. *Review of Financial Studies*, 14(2):433–458.

Hensel, N. (2005). Efficiency in IPO Issuance Processes? *Business Economics*, 40(4):55–66.

Kamara, E., Karaca-Mandic, P. and Talley, E. (2005). Going-Private Decisions and the Sarbanes-Oxley Act of 2002: A Cross-Country Analysis. Working Paper, Rand Corporation.

Keasler, T.R. (2001). The Underwriter's Early Lock-up Release: Empirical Evidence. *Journal of Economics and Finance*, 25(2):214–228.

Ljungqvist, A.P. (1999). IPO Underpricing, Wealth Losses and the Curious Role of Venture Capitalists in the Creation of Public Companies. Working Paper, NYU Stern School of Business, New York.

Ljungqvist, A.P. (2005). IPO Underpricing. In Eckbo, B.E. (ed.), *Handbooks in Finance: Empirical Corporate Finance*. New York: Elsevier/North Holland.

Loughran, T. and Ritter, J.R. (2002). Why Don't Issuers Get Upset about Leaving Money on the Table in IPOs? *Review of Financial Studies*, 15(2):413–443.

Markowitz, H. (1952). Portfolio Selection. *Journal of Finance*, 7(1):77–91.

Mossos, E. (2004). Sarbanes-Oxley Goes to Europe: A Comparative Analysis of United States and European Union Corporate Reforms after Enron. *Currents: International Trade Law Journal*, 13:9–22.

Organisation for Economic Co-operation and Development Economic Survey: Germany. (2004). *Developing Risk Capital Markets*. Paris: OECD Secretariat. OECD Papers, Chapter 5:1–6.

Ritter, J.R. (2003). Differences between European and American IPO Markets. *European Financial Management*, 9(4): 421–443.

Ritter, J.R. and Welch, I. (2002). A Review of IPO Activity, Pricing and Allocations. *Journal of Finance*, 57(4):1795–1828.

Veverka, M. (2005). The Plight of the European Startup. *Barron's*, 85(43):44.

Part Two

Evaluation, Exit Strategies, and Theoretical Aspects

7 Productivity growth in Spanish venture-backed firms

Luisa Alemany and José Martí

Abstract

This chapter presents an innovative proposal to analyze the economic impact of venture capital (VC) on investee companies in order to address the issue of causality. We test whether productivity growth rates are better in venture-backed companies than in comparable non-venture-backed ones for a sample of 518 Spanish companies. This approach is superior to the isolated analysis of employment or sales growth since venture-backed companies would benefit from a flow of funds that the non-venture-backed would not obtain. Our findings show that labor productivity gains are statistically higher in the venture group for industry, trade and services sectors. Regarding capital productivity growth, rates are statistically significant in all sectors except for raw materials.

7.1 Introduction

Many discussions take place as to whether venture capital (VC) has a positive effect on the economy, or whether it is only the investors who benefit. Previous research has looked at the economic impact of venture-backed firms in terms of employment, sales, taxes, or investments (Alemany and Martí, 2005; Data Resources Incorporated-Wharton Econometric Forecasting Associates (DRI-WEFA), 2002; Manigart and Van Hyfte, 1999; Amit et al., 1998). These studies show that venture-backed firms grow faster, create more employment, pay more taxes and are more innovative than similar companies financed by other sources of capital.

On the other hand, the issue of productivity is under strong scrutiny in all developed regions as the growth rates of recent years seem to slow down or even decrease. European Union productivity growth is clearly lower than that of the U.S. or Japan, indicating some structural problems that may influence these results. The situation is even worse for countries such as Spain or Italy, that have shown negative productivity growth rates for 2005 (Van Ark et al., 2006).

Regarding the methodology followed in previous studies on the impact of VC, productivity is also important because some argue that there could be a causality effect whereby venture-backed companies outperform the non-venture ones because they are better; or because they are granted additional resources that their non-venture-funded counterparts do not have. The analysis of productivity growth, rather than employment or sales growth, implies that venture-backed companies are able to perform better, even if the new funding is taken into account, showing a better use of their total resources.

The aim of this chapter is to analyze whether venture-backed firms show better productivity growth rates than comparable non-venture-backed ones, controlling for the activity sector in which they operate. The contribution to the literature on the impact of VC is related to the range of analyses currently performed, which are focused on employment, sales or innovation, and to the gains in productivity in investee firms.

The geographical focus of the study is Spain, including investments performed in companies at various stages of development in the period 1995–1999. Based on a sample that includes 93% of the population of venture investments in Spain, we follow their accounts until 2002 and compare productivity growth rates with a control group of non-venture-backed firms, also taking the official reports of the European Commission as a benchmark (O'Mahony and Van Ark, 2003).

Our results show that labor productivity growth is better in venture-backed companies in some sectors, such as industry and trade, whereas capital productivity is significantly better in all sectors except for raw materials. The implication is that policies aimed to improve the VC market may exert a positive impact on the productivity growth rates of the country.

The remainder of the chapter is organized as follows. Section 7.2 begins with a short literature review on productivity that focuses on Europe and, more specifically, on Spain, and then links productivity to the measurement of the economic impact of venture funding. Section 7.3 presents the data and methodology of analysis. It also includes a brief description of the Spanish VC market. The main results are presented in Section 7.4; Section 7.5 concludes, by introducing some implications for future research.

7.2 Literature review and hypotheses

Productivity is a straightforward indicator. It measures the relationship between the output obtained in the production process with the inputs required to generate that output. Productivity measurement is important because its growth means performance improvement, both at the country and at the industry level (Schreyer and Pilat, 2001).

According to Schreyer (2001) there are at least five purposes in measuring productivity. The first is to trace technological change and to understand whether it has an impact on the sectors or enterprises adopting it. The second objective is to determine if the country, sector, or firm under analysis has reached an optimum level of efficiency. Third, as productivity depends on many inputs, some of them more easily observable and measurable than others, it can be used to estimate real cost savings. Fourth, productivity can be used as a benchmark to compare with and to help identify inefficiencies. Finally, at the country level, it is a good indicator of living standards and the stage of development of the economy. Increases in productivity over a period of years mark the beginning of a new era in terms of wealth for the society. Cases such as China and other Asian countries can be cited.

Depending on the objective pursued with the productivity measurement as well as on the amount of data available, there are different productivity ratios. They are generally classified in two groups: labor productivity and capital productivity. The difference lies in the input used in each of them. Regarding the output, gross output and value-added are the two most commonly used.

Additionally, productivity ratios can be classified into single-factor productivity, when there is only one input under consideration, and multifactor productivity when the input is a combination of two or more items.

Productivity growth rates have traditionally been measured at the country or sector level. This was largely because it was almost impossible to obtain data at the firm level. However, in recent years these data have become increasingly accessible, allowing for some interesting studies at the firm level (Aw et al., 1997; Baily et al., 1997, 1996; Tybout, 1996).

Haltiwanger (2000) finds that previous studies at the establishment or firm level show a strong heterogeneity and has questions regarding our understanding of aggregate growth. The author identifies reallocation of outputs and inputs across individual firms and within sectors as one of the key findings. It is interesting to note that there are large differentials in the levels and in the productivity growth rates observed across firms, even in the same sector of activity.

The core finding of Haltiwanger (2000) is that reallocation clearly contributes to aggregate productivity growth. One of the explanations proposed might be that of differences in entrepreneurial and managerial skills. These variables are manifested in differences in job and productivity growth rates among firms.

The Commission of the European Union identified productivity as the key for competitiveness of European companies (Commission of the European Communities, 2002). However, results for Europe during the last few years are worrisome ('Europe' refers to the EU before enlargement, that is, the membership until 30 April 2004). Productivity rates have been declining. While the mean annual productivity growth rate from 1987 to 1995 was 2.1%, it was only 1.4% from 1995 to 2005. The figures were even worse in recent years, when the annual productivity growth rate from 2000 to 2005 was only 1.0%, and in 2005 it dropped to 0.5% (Van Ark et al., 2006).

These results compare negatively with other developed economies such as the U.S. or Japan, which grew 1.8% and 1.9% during 2005, respectively. Rapidly developing countries such as China and India grew 8.4% and 4.4%, respectively, in 2005.

The worst countries in Europe, responsible in part for the low average attained in 2005, are Spain and Italy. Spanish labor productivity was −1.3% in 2005, followed by Italy with −0.9%. Other countries such as the U.K., France, or Germany showed positive growth.

The case of Spain is especially surprising because the country's total working hours keep growing well above the European average. The EU average was 1.1% in 2005; in the list of 15 countries Spain ranks first, with an annual growth of 4.8%. This explains why the Spanish economy grows while productivity is falling. The high rate of immigration, mainly from Latin America and North Africa, adds more resources, helping the economy to grow. However, this influx is mainly in low-skilled jobs and industries, which does not improve productivity (Van Ark, 2006).

In a recent survey (OECD, 2005) some measures that could help to improve Spanish productivity were proposed. Regarding the labor market, although some important reforms took place in 1997, especially with the lowering of severance payments, further reforms are needed to increase market flexibility. Also, some reforms in the education system, in company training, and in the promotion of business research and development are recommended. Finally, the OECD study mentions that the low level of VC investment in early-stage companies is not helping to develop more start-ups. Improvements in the VC market would contribute to increased productivity.

This last remark by the OECD is also highlighted in the last European Innovation Scoreboard (TrendChart, 2006). This study elaborates the Summary Innovation Index for all European countries, based on 26 indicators included in five categories regarding innovation, knowledge, and entrepreneurship. The results classify the European countries into four groups: (1) leading countries; (2) those of average performance; (3) those catching up and (4) those losing ground. Spain is in the last group, ranking 19 in Europe, and with few possibilities of moving up. One of the indicators of the study is the early stage venture capital invested as a percentage of GDP.

The importance given to VC to improve both productivity and innovation is one of the motivations of this study that will add empirical evidence to the OECD recommendations and the use of the venture capital indicator in the Summary Innovation Index.

The economic impact of VC was one of the research issues in the late 1990s (Gompers and Lerner, 2001b). Recently, some papers have found evidence of the effect exerted on innovation, employment, or sales. Hellmann and Puri (2002, 2000), and Alemany and Martí (2005) concentrate on companies located in developed areas. Kortum and Lerner (2000) and Baum and Silverman (2004) analyze high-technology firms. Others follow larger countrywide samples in Belgium (Manigart and Van Hyfte, 1999), Germany (Belke and Schaal, 2004; Engel and Keilbach, 2004; Engel, 2002), or Italy (Bertoni et al., 2005), or even focus on several OECD countries in aggregate terms (Belke et al., 2003).

A common problem related to the analysis of the economic impact of VC is the possibility that venture-backed firms perform better because they were already better prior to the first venture round. Baum and Silverman (2004), Bertoni and Grilli (2005), and Balboa et al. (2006) have already addressed the causality issue.

In a sample of 204 biotechnology start-ups founded in Canada during the period from 1991 to 2000, Baum and Silverman (2004) analyze whether venture capitalists pick winners or build them. They study whether three initial start-up characteristics, such as social capital, intellectual capital, and human capital, influence the financing decision of the venture capitalist and the post-investment performance of investee firms in the same way. Their results are not conclusive. They find that social and intellectual capital show the same effect on the financing decision and the future performance of firms, whilst human capital does not.

Bertoni et al. (2005) analyze whether 537 high-technology Italian companies showing high employment growth have easier access to venture capital. They find only weak evidence for the fact that firms' growth prior to the first VC round leads to a greater likelihood of obtaining access to VC financing.

Balboa et al. (2006) study sales and employment growth in a sample of 250 Spanish venture-backed companies at the expansion stage, invested in between 1993 and 1999. Their results show that sales and employment growth in those companies is not significantly different from that of comparable non-venture-backed companies prior to the investment, while it is different from the moment of investment onwards.

Summarizing, there is sound evidence of the positive economic impact of VC and some initial results suggest that the improved performance of venture-backed companies is indeed driven by the funding and managerial support provided to portfolio companies. Nevertheless, a research question to be addressed is the effect of the funding itself. That is, venture-backed companies obtain additional funding to that provided by other traditional sources which non-venture-backed companies do not get. As a result, the better performance could be linked to the additional funding rather than to the value added by venture capitalists. The analysis of productivity gains in venture-backed and non-venture-backed companies could provide evidence of the better performance of the former, even allowing for their ability to hire more people and increase their assets because of the additional funding received. Therefore, the hypotheses to be tested are:

H1: Labor productivity is higher in VC-funded companies than in non-venture-backed comparable companies.
H2: Capital productivity is higher in VC-funded companies than in non-venture-backed comparable companies.

7.3 Data and methodology

This chapter focuses on the Spanish venture capital market. The first Spanish venture organization began its operations in 1972 (Martí Pellón, 2002). The origins of VC in Spain are related to the need to assist Spain's less-developed regions with the creation and building of a new industrial economy. Regions such as Galicia, Extremadura, or Andalusia had economies mainly based on agriculture, fishing, and mining. The first venture organizations supported entrepreneurs in the industrial sector. This early development contrasts with that of VC in the U.S., which was driven by support to innovations and inventions from top universities (Gompers and Lerner, 2001a). The early venture investors in Spain were funded with government-related capital. The integration of Spain into the EU marked the beginning of a private-sector-led VC market.

Table 7.1 summarizes Spanish VC key figures. Panel A gives fundraising values from 1991 to 2005, and the number of investors. Panel B presents values of total money invested (in nominal terms) and the number of VC-backed companies. It differentiates those companies that were receiving funds for the first time.

The reasons behind the development of VC in Spain have somehow marked the trends followed by investors since. Although in the late 1990s there was a strong increase in investment in technology-based companies, reaching a peak in 2000 with 26% of total funds invested (see Table 7.2), after the internet bubble the investors returned to more traditional sectors. The same applies to the stage of investment, where the expansion stage accounts for over 60% of total investments in most years. It is worth noting the decreasing weight of early stage companies, which is related to the low labor productivity rates observed in some sectors.

The study is based on the investee companies that received venture capital in Spain in the period 1995 to 1999. From the total number of initial investments stated in Table 7.1, we exclude companies belonging to the financial and real estate sectors, and eliminate double counting of syndicated investments, resulting in a total population of 559 companies. We found historical financial and employment data for a sample of 518 firms. Table 7.3 shows the distribution of the population and the sample investee companies by year of the initial investment. The sample has no survival bias since the missing companies include both early failures as well as successful companies that were acquired before the third year after the investment.

The sample is quite heterogeneous, including companies from different sectors of activity and in different stages of development. For the purpose of the analysis, we consider that the sector of activity clearly influences the productivity of a company and therefore

Table 7.1 Venture capital in Spain: supply and demand (1991 to 2005)

Panel A: Supply side

	1991	1992	1993	1994	1995	1996	1997	1998	1999	2000	2001	2002	2003	2004	2005
Funds raised (€million)	124	165	245	120	131	74	414	778	637	2507	1071	860	1118	2111	4042
Capital under management (€million)	822	944	1180	1197	1274	1311	1553	2188	2570	5025	6076	6730	7603	9438	12 814
Number of investors	46	48	54	56	53	52	53	56	58	70	85	94	98	110	124
of which state-owned (Percent)	39	38	39	38	38	38	38	32	31	26	22	21	20	19	18

Panel B: Demand side

	1991	1992	1993	1994	1995	1996	1997	1998	1999	2000	2001	2002	2003	2004	2005
Funds invested (€million)	129	116	97	136	165	213	286	349	717	1310	1241	969	1347	1996	4118
Number of companies affected*	230	220	219	211	199	169	233	223	305	411	393	381	427	402	465
Initial investments	143	107	104	132	118	108	172	162	203	303	249	229	256	240	328

* Including follow-on investments.

Source: Database of Professor Jose Martí Pellón and http://www.webcapitalriesgo.com

Table 7.2 Venture capital investments in technology: Spain 1995–2005

	1995	1996	1997	1998	1999	2000	2001	2002	2003	2004	2005
Funds invested (€ million)	165	213	286	349	717	1310	1241	969	1347	1996	4118
Percent growth	–	28.5	34.6	22.1	105.0	82.8	−5.2	−21.9	38.9	48.2	106.3
Funds in technology (€ million)	–	11	41	90	81	343	216	82	76	181	2153
Percent technology/total	–	5.2	14.3	25.8	11.3	26.2	17.4	8.5	5.7	9.0	52.3
Funds invested by stage (percentage)											
Early stage	12	9.5	8.3	13.8	10.9	16.5	9.8	11	4.9	3.6	2.9
Expansion stage	68.9	78.2	61.2	39.8	55.5	54.3	63.0	61.3	65.5	60.7	15.8
Late stage	19.1	12.3	30.5	46.3	33.7	29.3	27.2	27.6	29.6	35.7	81.4

Source: Database of Professor Jose Martí Pellón and http://www.webcapitalriesgo.com

Table 7.3 Population and sample by year of first venture capital financing (number of companies)

	1995	1996	1997	1998	1999	Total
Population	89	82	114	129	145	559
Sample	82	74	106	122	134	518
Percentage of sample	92.1	90.2	93.0	94.6	92.4	92.7

Table 7.4 Number of companies of the sample by economic activity (1995 to 1999)

Number of companies	1995	1996	1997	1998	1999	Total	% total
Raw materials	4	3	9	8	8	32	6.2
Industry	45	42	58	49	56	250	48.2
Trade	12	5	13	17	14	61	11.8
Services	16	14	17	36	35	118	22.8
Technology	5	10	9	12	21	57	11.0
TOTAL	82	74	106	122	134	518	100

we use this classification. In our sample the dominant sector is industry with almost half of the companies included in this group (see Table 7.4). Companies in the service sector represent 23% and trade and technology account for 11% each. The last group of companies, raw materials, includes only 6% of the sample.

For the 518 companies of the sample we calculate productivity ratios and observe their growth during the period from the time of the first round of venture financing, year 0, to three years later. All figures are first transformed into constant terms, base 2001, following the recommendation of the OECD in Schreyer (2001) and Schreyer and Pilat (2001). We have analyzed two groups of one-factor productivity ratios: labor productivity and capital productivity.

For the labor productivity calculation we compute sales as main output, and number of employees and total personnel costs as inputs. Table 7.5 shows that our sample includes a large proportion of start-ups, 41%, and therefore using value-added as an output measure

Table 7.5 Number of companies in the sample by stage of development (1995 to 1999)

	Early	Growth	Late	Total
Raw materials	19	11	2	32
Industry	90	125	35	250
Trade	22	32	7	61
Services	52	47	19	118
Technology	29	23	5	57
TOTAL	212	238	68	518
Percentage of total	40.9%	45.9%	13.2%	100%

can be misleading; companies that are starting up do not generate positive value-added until they reach their financial equilibrium. As we are working with an average, the negative value-added of early stage companies reduces the group average and the results do not represent the performance of the group. One possible solution is to divide the sample by stage of development and then by sector of activity and year of first round of financing. The problem encountered with this solution is that the groups analyzed are too small to be representative. Table 7.5 presents the number of companies classified by stage and by sector of activity. It can be observed that only within the industrial group could it be satisfactory to perform such an analysis.

Regarding capital productivity, we use sales as the output and total assets as the input. First we calculate the mean ratios for the sample companies classified according to their sector of activity for each year, from year 0 when they first received venture funds, to three years after that date. On average, venture capitalists in Spain divest their stake in their portfolio companies during the fourth year. Then we calculate the average growth rate for the period. In order to test our two hypotheses, the results obtained by sector of activity are compared with those of a control group of similar non-venture-backed companies, matched one by one with our venture-backed sample, to observe significant differences for each productivity ratio.

Table 7.6 shows the labor and capital productivity ratios observed in the sample and in the control group. We can observe differences between the different activity sectors as some of them are more productive than others. The case of technology, for which a higher ratio was expected, especially in labor productivity, is affected by the larger number of start-ups within this group (51% versus 41% for the sample).

7.4 Results

Table 7.7 shows the results of the annual productivity growth rates for the three ratios, between year 0 and year 3.

Regarding the first labor productivity ratio, growth rates of venture- and non-venture-backed companies are statistically different in the Industry (1%), Trade (5%) and Services (5%) sectors, whilst they are not in the Raw materials and Technology sectors. The results found for Raw materials could be related to the geographical situation of those companies, which were mainly located in less-developed areas. Regarding companies in the Technology sector, the results could be linked to the technology bubble bursting or to the early-stage nature of most of them, which could mean that a 3-year period is not long enough to show substantial changes in sales growth.

Turning to the changes in the second labor ratio, sales per personnel costs, no statistical differences are found in any sector. Therefore, this measure does not provide any evidence for the better evolution of venture-backed companies over time. This result could be explained by the fact that after a venture financing round, investee companies have additional resources to hire skilled managers that would help the company grow. It may well be that the limited length of the period analyzed is not long enough to capture the effect of the new management on sales growth.

The final measure is the capital productivity ratio, sales to total assets. Excluding companies in the Raw material sector, venture-backed firms show significantly higher

Table 7.6 Productivity ratios at the time of the first venture capital round

Panel A: Sales/employee (constant Thousands Euro, base 2001)

	Mean			Standard deviation	
	Venture-backed	Non-venture-backed	P-value	Venture-backed	Non-venture-backed
Raw materials	84.1	146.9	0.274 (a)	134.2	211.2
Industry	199.9	119.2	0.157 (a)	136.0	116.1
Trade	184.7	595.8	0.005 (b)	209.1	861.7
Services	158.2	350.7	0.163 (b)	541.6	949.6
Technology	52.7	91.9	0.008 (a)	57.1	60.4
Total	116.8	221.5	–	274.9	565.7

Panel B: Sales/personnel costs (constant Euro, 2001)

	Mean			Standard deviation	
	Venture-backed	Non-venture-backed	P-value	Venture-backed	Non-venture-backed
Raw materials	6.5	12.4	0.171 (b)	6.8	16.6
Industry	12.5	5.8	0.282 (b)	83.2	5.9
Trade	16.3	15.9	0.943 (a)	30.0	16.8
Services	12.2	17.8	0.632 (a)	54.8	82.4
Technology	3.3	4.5	0.224 (a)	3.5	5.3
Total	11.5	9.5	–	64.3	37.5

Panel C: Sales/total assets (constant Euro, 2001)

	Mean			Standard deviation	
	Venture-backed	Non-venture-backed	P-value	Venture-backed	Non-venture-backed
Raw materials	0.34	1.37	0.022 (b)	0.42	2.05
Industry	0.79	1.38	0.000 (b)	0.57	0.82
Trade	1.19	1.91	0.016 (b)	1.22	1.65
Services	0.84	1.65	0.001 (b)	0.98	2.05
Technology	0.72	1.71	0.000 (b)	0.63	1.31
Total	0.82	1.53	–	0.80	1.40

[a] Equal variances assumed (Levene's test).

[b] Equal variances not assumed (Levene's test).

Table 7.7 Productivity ratios annual growth rates from year 0 to year 3 (%)

	Sales/Employee			Sales/Personnel costs			Sales/Total assets		
	Venture-backed CAGR	Control group CAGR	Z (a)	Venture-backed CAGR	Control group CAGR	Z (a)	Venture-backed CAGR	Control group CAGR	Z (a)
Raw materials	90.9	13.8	0.462	32.7	9.6	0.131	18.4	14.0	0.452
Industry	38.6	7.1	−3.158***	15.4	7.4	−0.16	24.1	7.2	−3.164***
Trade	122.8	−1.8	−1649**	13.6	−1.5	−0.139	23.9	−4.8	−2.595***
Services	47.9	−0.9	−2.386**	17.7	−3.6	−0.665	25.2	1.3	−3.014***
Technology	83.2	0.5	−1.414	46.1	0.5	−1.55	29.1	−3.6	−3.208***
Total	59.2	4.1		20.6	3.5		24.7	3.8	

[a] Mann-Whitney non-parametric test.
** Significance level at 5 per cent
*** Significance level at 1 per cent

productivity rates from year 0 to year 3. This finding provides evidence of the value added by venture capitalists to portfolio companies, beyond the comparative advantage of the additional funding which allows the investee companies to increase the firm's assets to fuel sales growth.

7.5 Conclusion

After more than 60 years since the first VC fund was created in the U.S. to help immature companies start up and grow, various studies have addressed the issue of the economic impact of venture capital. The early surveys, conducted since the 1980s by consultancy firms, lacked methodological support. In the 1990s the impact on innovation, employment, and sales has been addressed successfully, providing evidence for the positive impact of venture funding compared with non-venture-backed firms.

Nevertheless, some questions remain regarding the causality of VC funding. Some papers have already addressed the question of whether venture capitalists pick the winners that consequently perform better, or, else, help to build them. Another question is related to the different situations of venture- and non-venture-backed companies, even if they were similar at the time of the first financing round, since capital productivity would attract additional funding whereas sales to asset ratio would not. An innovative proposal to account for that difference is the analysis of productivity changes in both groups of companies, since the individual analysis of employment or sales growth would not be sufficient to show a superior performance of venture-backed companies.

This is the main contribution of this chapter. We analyze labor and capital productivity growth in a representative sample of Spanish venture-backed companies. The case of Spain is relevant because productivity growth rates are currently negative and this might turn into a slowdown in welfare and economic growth in the years to come. Venture capital has been identified as one of the factors that could help improve productivity and innovation.

Our findings show that labor productivity gains are statistically significant in the venture group for the industry, trade, and services sectors if the ratio sales to number of employees is computed. Nevertheless, no differences are found when the ratio sales to personnel costs is calculated for any sector. For capital productivity, growth rates are statistically significant in all sectors except Raw materials.

These results provide further evidence of the positive economic impact of venture funding in countries where productivity growth is a core issue for government authorities. The implication for policy makers is that a positive environment for VC activity would enhance, in the long term, the competitiveness of the economy.

Regarding the questions pending for future research, more analysis is merited on the issue of labor productivity gains in technology venture-backed companies and on the ratio sales to personnel costs. It remains to be analyzed whether a longer time frame would also result in positive, statistically significant results. Finally, this approach should be applied in other countries, such as the U.S., where productivity growth could be an issue since it may be losing its competitive edge.

References

Alemany, L. and Martí, J. (2005). *Unbiased Estimation of Economic Impact of Venture Capital Backed Firms*. European Finance Association 2005 Moscow Meetings Paper SSRN ID 673341: 33.

Amit, R., Brander, J. and Zott, C. (1998). Why Do Venture Capital Firms Exist? Theory and Canadian Evidence. *Journal of Business Venturing*, 13(6):441–466.

Aw, B.Y., Chen, X. and Roberts, M.J. (1997). *Firm-level Evidence on Productivity Differentials, Turnovers, and Exports in Taiwanese Manufacturing*. NEBR Working Paper 6235, Cambridge MA.

Baily, M.N., Bertelsman, E.J. and Haltiwanger, J. (1996). Downsizing and Productivity Growth: Myth or Reality? *Small Business Economics*, 8(4):259–278.

Baily, M.N., Bartelsman, E.J. and Haltiwanger, J. (2001). Labor Productivity: Structural Change and Cyclical Dynamics. *The Review of Economics and Statistics*, 83(3):420–433.

Balboa, M., Martí, J. and Zieling, N. (2006). *Does Venture Capital Really Improve Portfolio Companies' Growth? Evidence from Growth Companies in Continental Europe*. European Financial Management Association Conference Proceedings, Madrid Conference, June 2006.

Baum, J.A.C. and Silverman, B. S. (2004). Picking Winners or Building Them? Alliance, Intellectual, and Human Capital as Selection Criteria in Venture Financing and Performance of Biotechnology Startups. *Journal of Business Venturing*, 19(3):411–436.

Belke, A. and Schaal, A. (2004). Venture Capital Investment and Labor Market Performance: New Empirical Evidence for OECD countries. Institute for the Study of Labor Discussion Paper Series IZA DP No. 1447, University of Hohenheim, Bonn.

Belke, A., Fehn, R. and Foster, N. (2003). Does Venture Capital Investment Spur Employment Growth? CESifo Working Paper 930. Department of Economics, University of Vienna.

Bertoni, F. and Grilli, L. (2005). The Causality Relationship Between External Private Equity Financing and the Growth of New Technology-Based Firms. Working Paper. D. Di Ingegneria Gestionale, Politecnico di Milano.

Bertoni, F., Colombo, M. and Grilli, L. (2005). External Private Equity Financing and the Growth of New Technology Based Firms: The Chicken and Egg Problem Revisited. Working Paper. D. Di Ingegneria Gestionale, Politecnico di Milano.

Commission of the European Communities (2002). *Productivity: The Key to Competitiveness of European Economies and Enterprises*. Communication From the Commission to the Council and the European Parliament. COM (2002) 262 final: 19.

Data Resources Incorporated-Wharton Econometric Forecasting Associates (DRI-WEFA) (2002). *Measuring the Importance of Venture Capital and its Benefits to the United States Economy*. Lexington MA: DRI-WEFA.

Engel, D. (2002). *The Impact of Venture Capital on Firm Growth: An Empirical Investigation*. ZEW Discussion Paper 02-02.

Engel, D. and Keilback, M. (2004). *Firm Level Implications of Early Stage Venture Capital Investment: An Empirical Investigation*. ZEW Discussion Paper 02-02.

Gompers, P. and Lerner, J. (2001a). *The Money of Invention: How Venture Capital Creates New Wealth*. Boston MA: Harvard Business School Press.

Gompers, P. and Lerner, J. (2001b). The Venture Capital Revolution. *Journal of Economic Perspectives*, 15(2):46–168.

Haltiwanger, J. (2000). Aggregate Growth: What Have We Learned from Microeconomic Evidence? OECD Economics Department Working Paper 267:0–26.

Hellmann, T. and Puri, M. (2000). The Interaction Between Product Market and Financing Strategy: The Role of Venture Capital. *The Review of Financial Studies*, 13(4):959–984.

Hellmann, T. and Puri, M. (2002). Venture Capital and the Professionalization of Start-up Firms: Empirical Evidence. *Journal of Finance*, 57(1):169–197.

Kortum, S. and Lerner, J. (2000). Assessing the Contribution of Venture Capital to Innovation. *RAND Journal of Economics*, 31(4):674–692.

Manigart, S. and Van Hyfte, W. (1999). Post-investment Evolution of Belgian Venture Capital Backed Companies: An Empirical Study. *Frontiers of Entrepreneurship Research*. Proceedings of the 19th Annual Entrepreneurship Research Conference. 6 pp.

Martí Pellón, J. (2002). *Oferta y demanda de capital riesgo en España, 2001*. Madrid: Biblioteca Civitas Economía y Empresa.

O'Mahony, M. and Van Ark, B. (2003). *EU Productivity and Competitiveness: An Industry Perspective – Can Europe Resume the Catching-up Process?* Luxembourg: Enterprise Publications – European Commission.

Organisation for Economic Cooperation and Development (2005). *OECD Economic Surveys: Spain, 2005*. OECD.

Schreyer, P. (2001). *Measuring Productivity: Measurement of Aggregate and Industry-Level Productivity Growth*. OECD Manual, 154 pp.

Schreyer, P. and Pilat, D. (2001). Measuring Productivity. *OECD Economic Studies*, 33(2):127–170.

TrendChart (2006). *European Innovation Scoreboard 2005: Comparative Analysis of Innovation Performance*. 46 pp.

Tybout, J.R. (1996). Heterogeneity and Productivity Growth: Assessing the Evidence. In Roberts, M.J. and Tybout, J.R. (eds) *Industrial Evolution in Developing Countries: Micro Patterns of Turnover, Productivity, and Market Structure*. New York: Oxford University Press for the World Bank, 43–72.

Van Ark, B. (2006). *Presentation: Spain's Productivity Performance in International Comparative Perspective*. Madrid, The Conference Board – CEDE, 26 pp.

Van Ark, B., Guillemineau, C. and McGuckin, R.H. (2006). As U.S. Productivity Slows, Emerging Economies Grow Rapidly, but Europe Falls Further Behind. *The Conference Board – Executive Action Series* 176:11.

8 Is the Spanish public sector effective in backing venture capital?

Marina Balboa, José Martí, and Nina Zieling

Abstract

This chapter analyzes the role of private versus public venture capital (VC). Firms backed with public funds are expected to grow at a lower rate since such funds are more oriented to social aims and regional development of depressed areas. Focusing on employment growth and using a sample of venture-backed Spanish firms, results show that only private VC has a significant impact on this variable. This chapter also studies whether this result could be related simply to geographical location, since the bulk of public funds are invested in underdeveloped areas that lack the appropriate networks to foster growth. Results show that while the positive impact of private funds is significant both in developed and underdeveloped areas, this is not the case for public funds. This questions the role played by Spanish public VC and points to the importance of the managerial support that is inherent in private venture capital.

8.1 Introduction

The role played by venture capitalists in investment firms is thought to be important, since they are specialized financial intermediaries (Chan, 1983) that provide a number of non-financial inputs along with their financial contribution (Sapienza et al., 1996; Ehrlich et al., 1994; Sahlman, 1990). Evidence from the literature has shown that the managerial support provided by venture capitalists to their investment firms exercises a positive impact on growth. While most literature has been focused on companies located in the U.S. (National Venture Capital Association (NVCA), 2004; Davila et al., 2003; Hellmann and Puri, 2002, 2000; Kortum and Lerner, 2000) there are some that base their studies on countries such as Belgium (Manigart and Van Hyfte, 1999), Germany (Engel and Keilbach, 2005; Belke and Schaal, 2004; Engel, 2002), Canada (Business Development Bank of Canada, 2000), or several OECD countries (Belke et al., 2003).

Most of the research carried out so far does not analyze the role of venture capital according to the nature of the fund provider. However, there are fundamental differences between private- and public-sector-related funds. While the former are profit-oriented, focusing on investments that provide the highest returns, the latter are aimed at fostering economic growth and innovation in certain areas (Leleux and Surlemont, 2003). Two exceptions to this body of literature are Lerner (1999), who argues that public-sector funding seems to be effective only in regions that already have substantial venture financing, and Wallsten (2001), who points out that, even though public-sector funding has benefits, it is unlikely that it is able to create regional technology clusters.

This raises a question about the role of public VC as a tool for regional development and firm growth. This question has scarcely been addressed in the literature, and the aim of this chapter is to analyze the differential impact of private- versus public-sector-related investors. The study is based in Spain, where support for VC activity from public authorities helped the initial development of the market in the mid-1970s and still has an important role.

The contribution of this chapter is twofold. First, the performance of public VC-backed firms is compared with those receiving private funds and also with those not receiving VC funds at all. Assessing the impact of public funds committed to this activity is vital to justify the existence of specific schemes. Second, the effect of location is identified, since the empirical study is carried out in both developed and less developed regions. This is considered important since the impact of venture capital could differ between these regions because of the networks already established in those more developed.

The remainder of the chapter is organized as follows. Section 8.2 includes a review of the role of VC, considering both the type of investor involved, namely private versus public sector, and the effect of location. Section 8.3 describes the data used in the empirical analysis and contains a descriptive analysis. The methodology applied is shown in Section 8.4. Results are commented on in Section 8.5. Section 8.6 concludes, and contains a discussion on the implications for policy makers and some questions for further research.

8.2 The role of venture capital

Most of the literature analyzes the role of VC on employment growth and innovation of high-tech start-up companies both in the U.S. and Europe. Hellmann and Puri (2002) rely on a sample of over 170 Silicon Valley start-ups and find that VC helps to build up the human resources of investment companies. Davila et al. (2003) also analyze a Silicon Valley dataset with a sample of 494 venture-backed and non-venture-backed technology start-ups, and find that the existence of VC motivates qualified staff to join and stay in the company. Engel (2002) uses a sample of German companies and finds that surviving venture-backed firms have higher employment growth rates compared with surviving non-venture-backed ones; a similar result is found by Engel and Keilbach (2005) for the same market.

Regarding the effect on innovation, Hellmann and Puri (2000) use data on 173 venture-backed and non-venture-backed start-ups located in Silicon Valley and find that the probability of receiving VC is higher for more innovative firms, which again is the same result found in Engel and Keilbach (2005). Hellmann and Puri (2000) also find that VC does have an impact on the time taken to bring a product to market, especially for innovators. In the same sense, Romain and van Pottelsberghe (2004) find that VC contributes to the introduction of new products and processes to the market. Kortum and Lerner (2000) examine the contribution of VC on patented inventions across 20 industries and find that venture funding does have a strong positive impact on innovation.

Some European studies consider several fundamental variables in their analysis. Manigart and Van Hyfte (1999) show evidence of the positive impact of VC on growth of total assets and cash flow when comparing 187 Belgian venture-backed firms with similar non-venture-backed ones. Alemany and Martí (2005), using a sample of 323 venture-backed firms from the three most developed Spanish regions, find evidence of the positive impact of VC on the growth of employment, sales, gross margin, total assets, intangible assets, and corporate taxes paid. Finally, a recent study on the Italian market (AIFI and PriceWaterhouseCoopers, 2006) finds that both VC and private equity have a positive impact on the growth of employment, sales and earnings before interest, taxes, depreciation, and amortization.

8.2.1 Government venture capital

The interest of public authorities in VC as a tool to fuel innovation and/or regional development can be seen in nearly every country. Even in the U.S., where there is a mature VC market, there are public schemes aimed at promoting small business growth. Lerner (1999) examines the impact of the largest public VC initiative in the U.S., namely the Small Business Innovation Research program, finding that the target companies grew significantly faster than a matched set of firms over a ten-year period. Nevertheless, this effect was only significant in areas where there was a major concentration of VC activity. In the same vein Wallsten (2001) finds that although public funding has its benefits, it is not able to create regional technology clusters.

Regarding the European experience, the lack of an adequate environment (Martí and Balboa, 2006) has resulted in a concentration of investments in more established companies, since performance measures have shown poor results in early stage investments but high returns in late stage deals (British Venture Capital Association, 1995; Nederlandse Vereniging van Participatiemaatschappijen, 1993). As a consequence, both the European Commission and national governments have established policy measures as well as direct action schemes to correct this situation (Aernoudt, 1999; OECD, 1997). Manigart and Beuselinck (2001) study the determinants of the flow of government VC funds in a panel of ten European countries. They find that an increase in the number of initial public offerings indicates a favorable VC climate, thus leading to a decrease in the need for direct supply of government funds.

The influx of money from government agencies, however, may distort the correct functioning of the private VC market. Since public sector venture capitalists may operate with different objectives to those of the private ones, they could attract the best projects with subsidized discount rates, leaving only second-best projects to their private counterparts. The result could be a crowding-out effect that would replace private-sector VC with government-funded VC (Wallsten, 2001; Khanna and Sandler, 2000).

Leleux and Surlemont (2003) analyze the role played by public authorities in the venture capital scene in 15 European countries in the period 1990–1996. They find that the intensity of venture capital with public sector backing is high in Europe, with the countries with the largest proportions of public VC being those smallest in size. Their findings, however, do not support the crowding-out hypothesis.

In summary, and as commented above, it seems that private venture capital should outperform public direct investments. In order to test the difference in performance between publicly and privately funded firms, the following hypotheses are proposed, which will be analyzed in the empirical analysis using a sample of Spanish firms at all stages of development and in both high- and low-tech industries.

H1a: Privately venture-backed companies show a significantly higher growth rate than firms with public sector venture backing.
H1b: Companies financed by private sector venture capitalists grow significantly more than similar non-venture-backed companies, but companies financed by public sector venture capitalists do not grow significantly more than similar non-venture-backed companies.

8.2.2 Regional differences in the role of venture capital

The paper by Florida and Kenney (1998) is one of the few focusing on the role of VC in different regions. They find that the existence of well-developed venture capital networks in technology-based regions significantly accelerates the pace of technological innovation and economic development in those regions. In fact, they show that the effect of VC is not important in less developed areas. This result is in line with Wallsten (2001), who, however, focuses his analysis on just early stage high-tech companies. In a more general context than that of venture capital, the results of Audretsch and Keilbach (2004) show that entrepreneurship is positively related to productivity, so that regions with high levels of entrepreneurship capital are those that exhibit significantly higher levels of output and productivity.

One of the possible reasons underlying these results is that companies located in less developed regions face important disadvantages in several aspects, such as the lack of infrastructure, the lack of access to highly skilled human capital, the lack of geographical proximity to multinational companies, or, as Florida and Smith (1993) point out, the lack of access to the sources of later-stage financing. In this sense Davila et al. (2003) find that although the entry of a venture capitalist to a firm sends a positive signal to the human capital market, this is not expected to be enough to compensate for the unattractive location of the firm.

Moreover, it turns out that public direct investments are used mainly to foster regional development (Leleux and Surlemont, 2003), so most of these funds are expected to flow to underdeveloped regions. The opposite is true for private funds, since private investments tend to be concentrated in highly developed regions (Florida and Kenney, 1998). Therefore, if firms in underdeveloped regions underperform compared with those in more developed regions this could be related to the reasons already stated – mainly, that public VC is not as effective as private. The following hypotheses are then proposed:

H2a: Companies financed by private sector venture capitalists located in developed regions grow significantly more than similar non-venture-backed companies in the same region. However, public venture-financed firms in developed regions do not grow significantly more than similar non-venture-backed companies in the same region.
H2b: Companies financed by private sector venture capitalists and located in underdeveloped regions significantly outperform non-venture-backed firms located in the same region. However, companies backed by public sector venture capitalists located in underdeveloped regions do not significantly grow more than non-venture-backed firms located in the same area.

8.3 Data and descriptive analysis

Chapter 7 shows evidence of the effect of venture capital on productivity in Spain, measured by several rates. In this chapter, we analyze quite different issues for this country. Specifically, the focus of this chapter is on testing several hypotheses regarding location and nature of the funds provided, since they play a major role in explaining the impact of this activity. The main reason for this focus is that the managerial support provided by venture capitalists, and which is the main driver of the positive impact that this activity exerts on the economy, is inherent to private funds and not so much to public ones. Similarly, the literature has shown that firms benefiting most from venture funds are those located in developed regions. Therefore, addressing the importance of these factors is relevant in explaining the value-added of venture capital.

The sample analyzed in this chapter expands the one in Chapter 7 and considers the VC investments carried out in Spain between 1993 and 1999, with accounting data until 2002. Out of a population of 735 investments in this period, the sample analyzed excludes: (i) both real estate and financial firms; (ii) companies located in foreign countries, as we are analyzing the role of public versus private VC in Spain; (iii) companies that had merged with others and for which there are no stand-alone data available. These companies belong to the successful segment, because a trade sale is one of the best exits for a venture capitalist; (iv) companies that had gone bankrupt quickly, having never presented their annual accounts to the Commercial Registry and, therefore, data about them are severely lacking.

The final sample analyzed includes 539 VC-backed companies. A control group of 539 non-VC-backed companies, one for each venture-backed firm in the panel, has been created. The criteria used to match firms are: size, age, activity, and geographical location. In this way, the control group is composed of firms that are as similar as possible to those that are venture-backed at the moment of investment.

In order to have complete information for all firms in the sample, two datasets have been used. The first one has been held by Professor José Martí (Universidad Complutense) since 1987 and includes all relevant data regarding venture capital and private equity activity of all funds active in the Spanish market at any moment from 1987 on. The second database, named SABI (Bureau van Dijk and Informa, see http://www.bvdep.com/SABI.html), provides fundamental data on 650 000 Spanish companies over time, including profit and loss accounts, balance sheets and some additional data such as the date of foundation of the company, its status, and its activity presented to the Commercial Registry.

Table 8.1 shows descriptive statistics of all the investments made in the venture-backed companies included in the population and in the sample. Both the number and the volume of investments made have been increasing over time except for the year 1996, as is usual in developing markets such as the Spanish one. It can be observed that the descriptive statistics are very similar in both groups, so the sample is highly representative of the population.

For the purposes of this study, the sample of venture-backed companies has been broken down by geographical location and nature of funds. Regions have been classified according to EU criteria, so that a region is considered as underdeveloped if the per capita GDP is below 75% of the European average over the period of analysis. Table 8.2 shows the number of investments in the sample according to these characteristics on a yearly basis. It can be observed that this number is rather similar in both developed and underdeveloped regions, except for the year 1996, and that it has been increasing over

Table 8.1 Descriptive statistics of investments for the population and the sample

Year	Population				Sample				
	Number	% of Total	Mean[a]	SD[a]	Number	% of Sample	% of Population	Mean[a]	SD[a]
1993	80	10.9%	0.628	1.066	43	8.0%	53.8%	0.664	1.044
1994	98	13.3%	1.094	2.440	57	10.6%	58.2%	1.297	2.682
1995	89	12.1%	1.161	2.331	68	12.6%	76.4%	1.277	2.400
1996	82	11.2%	1.765	4.060	61	11.3%	74.4%	1.715	3.308
1997	114	15.5%	1.716	3.678	96	17.8%	84.2%	1.844	3.896
1998	128	17.4%	2.464	4.500	102	18.9%	79.7%	2.620	4.820
1999	144	19.6%	3.473	7.650	112	20.8%	77.8%	3.794	8.206
Total	**735**	**100.0%**	**1.927**	**4.609**	**539**	**100.0%**	**73.3%**	**2.158**	**4.970**

[a]Mean and SD in €million (based on 2001 prices).

Table 8.2 Number of firms by region and nature of funds, on a yearly basis

	1993	1994	1995	1996	1997	1998	1999
Region							
Developed	22	28	36	20	37	55	59
Underdeveloped	21	29	32	41	59	47	53
Total	**43**	**57**	**68**	**61**	**96**	**102**	**112**
Private Funds							
Developed Region	13	14	19	12	21	39	43
Underdeveloped Region	6	12	10	15	15	16	13
Total	**19**	**26**	**29**	**27**	**36**	**55**	**56**
Public Funds							
Developed Region	9	14	17	8	16	16	16
Underdeveloped Region	15	17	22	26	44	31	40
Total	**24**	**31**	**39**	**34**	**60**	**47**	**56**

time. Regarding the nature of funds, public funds have been increasingly invested in firms located in underdeveloped regions, while the opposite is true for private funds.

Table 8.3 shows that a total of 257 venture-backed companies are located in developed regions and 282 firms in underdeveloped ones. Public funds tend to invest in underdeveloped regions, as noted above. It can also be observed that public funds invest, on average, fewer funds than their private counterparts, both in developed and underdeveloped regions.

Table 8.4 describes VC investments according to several firm characteristics, distinguished by nature of funds. It can be observed that public funds invest more in younger firms than do private ones. However, for both types of funds the amount invested is positively related to the age of the firm, which is usually the case for venture capital. Both

Table 8.3 Descriptive statistics of investments by region and nature of funds

Regions and Nature of Fund	Number	% of Total	Mean[a]	SD[a]
Underdeveloped Regions				
Public Funds	195	69%	0.826	2.158
Private Funds	87	31%	3.101	7.054
Total	**282**	**100%**	**1.528**	**4.422**
Developed Regions				
Public Funds	96	37%	0.935	1.175
Private Funds	161	63%	3.991	6.552
Total	**257**	**100%**	**2.849**	**5.435**
Total Spain	**539**			

[a] Mean and SD in € million (based on 2001 prices).

Table 8.4 Descriptive statistics of investments by age, activity, and number of employees of the venture capital-backed companies according to the nature of funds

	Public sector funds				Private sector funds			
	Number	% of Total	Mean	SD	Number	% of Total	Mean	SD
Age (years)								
<= 5	183	62.9%	0.701	2.056	130	52.4%	3.017	6.342
5–10	36	12.4%	0.652	0.710	49	19.8%	3.156	4.335
10–20	41	14.1%	1.288	2.006	35	14.1%	4.254	7.854
>20	31	10.7%	1.491	1.431	34	13.7%	6.370	9.006
Activity								
Raw materials	25	8.6%	0.889	2.373	9	3.6%	1.460	2.431
Industry	168	57.7%	0.979	2.078	101	40.7%	3.627	5.770
Technology	29	10.0%	0.819	1.047	31	12.5%	3.903	5.675
Services	50	17.2%	0.575	1.616	76	30.6%	4.012	8.311
Trade	19	6.5%	0.613	0.830	31	12.5%	3.451	7.334
Number of employees								
<= 10	85	29.2%	0.270	0.271	44	17.7%	1.045	2.655
11–50	99	34.0%	0.721	1.602	59	23.8%	1.314	3.399
51–100	51	17.5%	1.243	1.886	43	17.3%	2.744	3.259
101–250	16	5.5%	1.277	0.749	39	15.7%	5.208	7.905
251–500	15	5.2%	3.657	5.384	20	8.2%	8.669	7.319
> 500	25	8.6%	0.712	1.040	43	17.3%	6.846	10.600
Total	**873**	**100.0%**	**0.862**	**1.889**	**248**	**100.0%**	**3.679**	**6.731**

Data refer to the year of investment. Mean and SD in € million (based on 2001 prices).

public- and private-sector-backed venture capitalists concentrate on industrial companies, with the service sector being the second category. Finally, around 81% of the firms that receive funds from public sector venture capitalists employ up to 100 people. This figure is around 59% for ones receiving private capital.

8.4 Methodology

In order to study both the effect of the nature of the funds provided and the location, the empirical analysis uses the absolute growth of employment as dependent variable. The growth is calculated in absolute rather than relative terms because, as Baum and Silverman (2004) point out, measuring growth in relative terms would imply a distorting effect on the averages when the changes from one period to another are high enough. Some descriptive statistics of this variable are shown in Table 8.5. The evolution of the mean absolute growth of employment both for venture-backed companies and their comparable group, distinguishing by location and nature of funds, can be observed in Panel A. The *p*-value of the test for the difference in means is reported for each group. It can be observed that while the difference in means is significant both in developed and underdeveloped regions in the case of private funding, it is significant only in underdeveloped regions for public funding.

Panel B shows the mean values of the venture-backed companies distinguished by nature of funds and region. Privately backed firms located in developed regions show a significantly higher growth than those located in underdeveloped regions. In contrast, publicly funded firms do not show significantly different employment growth depending on the region of origin. To sum up, results show that private funding does have an impact on employment growth, both in developed and underdeveloped regions. However, the

Table 8.5 Descriptive statistics of the absolute growth of the number of employees of companies by region and nature of funds

Panel A: Venture-backed versus non-venture-backed firms by region and nature of fund

Type of firm	Developed regions		Underdeveloped regions	
	Mean	Standard Deviation	Mean	Standard Deviation
Private funds				
Venture-backed	76.716	555.959	26.664	140.613
Non-venture-backed	14.629	178.745	0.987	25.190
p-value	*0.0008*		*0.0000*	
Public funds				
Venture-backed	5.422	103.702	7.770	82.965
Non-venture-backed	2.454	11.690	1.174	15.153
p-value	*0.2470*		*0.0046*	

Panel B: Venture capital investments by nature of funds and region

Region	Private funds		Public funds	
	Mean	Standard Deviation	Mean	Standard Deviation
Developed region	76.716	555.959	5.422	103.702
Underdeveloped region	26.664	140.613	7.771	82.965
p-value	*0.0053*		*0.3180*	

impact is greater for firms located in developed areas. On the contrary, for firms receiving public venture funding there is no difference in growth related to geographical area.

The independent variables considered in the analysis include two control variables and one dummy. The first control variable is the growth of total assets, since the growth of employment can be related to the variation in the total assets held by the company. Since growth patterns are also affected by the current economic situation, the second control variable is the growth of Gross Domestic Product (GDP). Finally, the dummy variable introduced differs according to the analysis carried out in particular and is the variable that is used to analyze the effect of nature of funds and location.

The empirical analysis is divided into two parts. In the first analysis, three aspects are analyzed. First, venture-backed firms are compared with the control group to determine the effect of VC as a whole. The dummy variable in this case is 1 if the company is venture-backed and 0 otherwise. Second, companies funded by private sector venture capitalists are compared with their corresponding control group and the same analysis is carried out for the investments of public funds. In the first case, the dummy variable is 1 if the company has received private funds, and in the second case the dummy takes a value of 1 if the company is backed by public sector venture funds. Finally, public and private funds are compared by including a dummy that takes a value of 1 if the company is publicly financed.

In the second analysis the effect of location is introduced. Three aspects are also analyzed. First, venture-backed companies located in underdeveloped regions are compared with those in developed regions. The dummy variable is 1 if the venture-backed company is located in underdeveloped regions and 0 otherwise. Second, private venture investments are compared with their respective control group, both in developed and underdeveloped regions. Finally, the latter analysis is also carried out for public investments. In both cases the analysis will determine whether location matters along with the nature of funds.

The panel data methodology is applied in all cases since the sample refers to the evolution of a company's activity over time. The random effects approach has been used to estimate the models. This is because the variables of interest are the dummies that represent (i) whether the firm has received venture capital; (ii) whether the funds come from public or private sources; (iii) the region in which the firm is located. If a fixed effect approach is employed, these dummies can not be estimated since they take constant values over time.

8.5 Results

Table 8.6 shows the results of public versus private VC investments. The results indicate that, in all cases, employment growth depends on the growth of total assets, as expected. The other control variable, growth of GDP, however, is not significant. The first regression analysis shows that venture capital has a positive effect on employment growth since the dummy variable is highly significant. The same result is found when considering private funds, but not when analyzing public funds. Finally, the comparison between public and private funds yields the same result, since the dummy variable that takes a value of 1 if the firm is backed by public sector funds is negative and significant. Therefore, these results confirm the evidence found in the descriptive analysis, and provide evidence of a significantly positive impact of VC in the case of private capital sources, but not in the case of public funding.

Table 8.6 Employment growth of companies by nature of funds. Regression models

Independent variables	Dependent variable: Employment growth			
	Venture-backed versus non-venture-backed firms – whole sample	Private venture-backed versus non-venture-backed firms	Public venture-backed versus non-venture-backed firms	Public versus private venture-backed firms
Growth in total assets	1.72E-06***	1.54E-06***	2.15E-06***	1.77E-06***
	(1.26E-07)	(1.98E-07)	(9.89E-08)	(1.67E-07)
Gross Domestic Product growth	355.181	774.429	9.816	505.538
	(272.081)	(559.046)	(126.894)	(460.564)
Dummy venture capital/Dummy Public-Private	16.318***	31.010***	2.848	−34.934***
	(5.284)	(11.404)	(2.442)	(9.338)
Constant	−10.334	−22.202	−0.732	18.513
	(11.502)	(23.670)	(5.379)	(19.227)
R^2	0.037	0.031	0.145	0.046
Number of Companies	993	455	538	520
Number of Observations	5239	2420	2819	2815

*** significance level 0.01; ** significance level 0.05; * significance level 0.10. Numbers in parentheses are *p*-values.

The results for public funds may be driven by the fact that such funds could be specialized in investments made in underdeveloped regions, given that their main aim is to foster economic development in those depressed areas. If this is the case, then public VC might just have a significant impact in those areas. In order to analyze the different roles that public and private funds may therefore have, depending on the area in which the investment is made, Table 8.7 shows the results of the second analysis. Results show that the growth of employment is higher for venture-backed companies located in developed areas, although this is just significant at the 10% level. When introducing both the nature of funds and location, results show that for firms located in developed areas, only privately funded firms grow more than those not receiving venture capital. On the contrary, firms located in underdeveloped areas do not grow more than those not receiving VC, whether financed by private or public funds.

8.6 Conclusion

Policy makers around the world are anxious to find tools that may help their regions emulate the success of Silicon Valley and create new centers of innovation and high technology (Wallsten, 2001). Governments in most countries have established programs aimed at developing their economies through the use of venture capital. In the U.S., the federal government launched the Small Business Investment Companies (SBIC) program in 1958. In Europe, the European Investment Fund was established in 1994 as a way

Table 8.7 Employment growth of companies by region and nature of funds. Regression models

Independent variables	Dependent variable: Employment growth				
	Developed versus Underdeveloped Regions	Developed Regions		Underdeveloped Regions	
	Venture-backed firms	Private venture-backed versus non-venture-backed firms	Public venture-backed versus non-venture-backed firms	Private venture-backed versus non-venture-backed firms	Public venture-backed versus non-venture-backed firms
Growth in total assets	1.77E-06***	1.27E-06***	6.32E-07***	6.53E-06***	4.21E-06***
	(1.67E-07)	(2.50E-07)	(1.53E-07)	(2.51E-07)	(1.20E-07)
Gross Domestic Product growth	488.696	1418.405*	444.350*	−504.333*	−272.243**
	(460.633)	(858.827)	(248.735)	(287.777)	(124.609)
Dummy Venture Capital/Dummy Region	−18.094*	37.475**	1.929	3.768	1.262
	(9.383)	(16.659)	(4.790)	(5.737)	(2.398)
Constant	9.749	−42.975	−16.097	20.667*	9.619*
	(19.254)	(35.908)	(10.463)	(12.291)	(5.303)
R^2	0.042	0.022	0.020	0.450	0.408
Number of Companies	520	298	182	157	356
Number of Observations	2815	1559	1000	861	1819

*** significance level 0.01; ** significance level 0.05; * significance level 0.10. Numbers in parentheses are *p*-values.

to provide funds to small and medium-sized enterprises, and the European Union also manages the Seed Capital Action Programme through the allocation of resources of the European Commission. Most European countries have also established specific schemes, such as the Kreditanstalt für Wiederaufbau (KfW) in Germany, the Guarantee Scheme in The Netherlands, the Plan Innovation in France or the UK High Technology Fund in the United Kingdom.

However, the role played by public VC in this activity has yet to be analyzed, since as Manigart et al. (2002) show, receiving VC from the right backer is perhaps more important than receiving venture capital per se. The contribution of this chapter is to analyze whether public sector related funds flowing to this industry are as effective as those from private sources. Also, this analysis is further extended to take into account the location of investment firms, both in developed and underdeveloped regions. The study is based on a highly representative sample of investments made in Spain, which makes this study interesting as Spain is a country where public sector funding played a principal role in the 1980s, sharing this role with private-sector investors since the early 1990s.

Our results provide evidence that firms with private VC backing outperform those with public VC support. Furthermore, the latter do not even outperform similar comparable companies not financed by VC organizations, either in developed or in underdeveloped regions. The results confirm the assumption of Wallsten (2001) and Leleux and Surlemont (2003) that public entities making direct VC investments tend to do so in ways that could be counterproductive. The authors state that public fund managers may not have the experience or adequate incentives to select and support their portfolio companies.

Results also show that venture-backed firms located in developed areas outperform those in underdeveloped regions, in line with the findings of Florida and Kenney (1998). It may be that the limited public VC contribution is not sufficient to drive rapid growth. Even though there is a positive impact, it would be necessary to complement VC support in Spain with heavy investment in infrastructure, education, and research and development to create the necessary environment firms need to grow faster.

The implications of these results for policy makers lead to the adopting of alternative management strategies, such as assigning the allocation of public money to experienced private management teams rather than creating management structures that are neither independent in their activity nor experienced in venture capital investing. Also, government policies should be directed to building the skills of the workforce and potential entrepreneurs (Queen, 2002), since the demand side of the market should be stimulated in order to promote economic growth.

Questions for future research could be related to analyzing the determinants of the impact of public VC and to the possible ways of allocating public money more efficiently. Also, it would be interesting to test the effect of public VC in other countries where government still plays an important role, as in the case of Spain. Another interesting analysis entails the study of schemes that consider cooperation between public and private funds in order to enhance the growth of joint investments.

References

Aernoudt, R. (1999). European Policy Towards Venture Capital: Myth or Reality? *Venture Capital*, 1(1):47–58.

AIFI (Italian Private Equity and Venture Capital Association) and PriceWaterhouse-Coopers (2006). *The Economic Impact of Private Equity and Venture Capital in Italy*. Milan: Associazione Italiana del Private Equity e Venture Capital. http://www.seca.ch/newsletter/pdf-News54/The%20economic%20impact%20of%20private%20equity%20and%20venture%20capital%20in%20italy.pdf

Alemany, L. and Martí, J. (2005). Unbiased Estimation of Economic Impact of Venture Capital Backed Firms. Working Paper, European Finance Association 2005 Meeting. Escuela Superior de Administración y Dirección de Empresas Business School, Barcelona.

Audretsch, D. and Keilbach, M. (2004). Entrepreneurship Capital and Economic Performance. *Regional Studies*, 38(8):949–959.

Baum, J. and Silverman, B. (2004). Picking Winners or Building Them? Alliance, Intellectual, and Human Capital as Selection Criteria in Venture Financing and Performance of Biotechnology Startups. *Journal of Business Venturing*, 19(3):411–436.

Belke, A. and Schaal, A. (2004). *Venture Capital Investment and Labor Market Performance: New Empirical Evidence for OECD Countries.* Institute for the Study of Labor, Discussion Paper Series IZA DP No. 1447, University of Hohenheim, Stuttgart.

Belke, A., Fehn, R. and Foster, N. (2003). Does Venture Capital Investment Spur Employment Growth? CESifo, Working Paper No. 930. University of Hohenheim, Stuttgart.

British Venture Capital Association (1995). *Performance Measurement Survey, 1994.* London: British Venture Capital Association.

Business Development Bank of Canada (2000). *Economic Impact of Venture Capital, Eighth Annual Survey.* Toronto: BCBC.

Chan, Y.S. (1983). On the Positive Role of Financial Intermediation in Allocation of Venture Capital in a Market with Imperfect Information. *Journal of Finance*, 38(5): 1543–1568.

Davila, A., Foster, G. and Gupta, M. (2003). Venture Capital Financing and the Growth of Startup Firms. *Journal of Business Venturing*, 18(6):689–708.

Ehrlich, S.B., De Noble, A.F., Moore, T. and Weaver, R.R. (1994). After the Cash Arrives: A Comparative Study of Venture Capital and Private Investor Involvement in Entrepreneurial Firms. *Journal of Business Venturing*, 9(1):67–82.

Engel, D. (2002). *The Impact of Venture Capital on Firm Growth: An Empirical Investigation.* ZEW, Discussion Paper No. 02. Centre for European Economic Research (ZEW), Mannheim.

Engel, D. and Keilbach, M. (2005). *Firm Level Implications of Early Stage Venture Capital Investment: An Empirical Investigation.* Max-Planck-Gesellschaft, Discussion Paper on Entrepreneurship, Growth and Public Policy No. 2205. Centre for European Economic Research (ZEW), Mannheim.

Florida, R. and Kenney, M. (1998). Venture Capital, High Technology and Regional Development. *Regional Studies*, 22(1):33–48.

Florida, R. and Smith, D.F. (1993). Venture Capital Formation, Investment and Regional Industrialization. *Annals of the Association of American Geographers*, 83(3):434–451.

Hellmann, T. and Puri, M. (2000). The Interaction between Product Market and Financing Strategy: The Role of Venture Capital. *The Review of Financial Studies*, 13(4):959–984.

Hellmann, T. and Puri, M. (2002). Venture Capital and the Professionalization of Start-up Firms: Empirical Evidence. *Journal of Finance*, 57(1):169–197.

Khanna, J. and Sandler, T. (2000). Partners in Giving: The Crowding-Out Effects of U.K. Government Grants. *European Economic Review*, 44(8):1543–1556.

Kortum, S. and Lerner, J. (2000). Assessing the contribution of venture capital to innovation. *RAND Journal of Economics*, 31(4):674–692.

Leleux, B. and Surlemont, B. (2003). Public Versus Private Venture Capital: Seeding or Crowding Out? A Pan-European Analysis. *Journal of Business Venturing*, 18(1):81–104.

Lerner, J. (1999). The Government as Venture Capitalist: The Long-Run Effects of the SBIR Program. *Journal of Business*, 72(3):285–318.

Manigart, S. and Beuselinck, C. (2001). Supply of Venture Capital by European Governments. Ghent University, Working Paper No. 111. University of Ghent, Ghent, Belgium.

Manigart, S. and Van Hyfte, W. (1999). Post-Investment Evolution of Belgian Venture Capital Backed Companies: An Empirical Study. Mimeo. University of Ghent, Ghent.

Manigart, S., Baeyens, K. and Van Hyfte, W. (2002). The Survival of Venture Capital Backed Companies. *Venture Capital*, 4(2):103–124.

Martí, J. and Balboa, M. (2006). A Framework for Self-Regulation in Venture Capital and Private Equity: Evidence in European Markets. *International Journal of Entrepreneurship and Innovation Management*, forthcoming.

National Venture Capital Association (2004). *Venture Impact 2004, Venture Capital Benefits to the U.S. Economy*. Virginia: Global Insight.

Nederlandse Vereniging van Participatiemaatschappijen (1993). *Venture Capital Returns in the Netherlands, First Edition*. The Hague: Nederlandse Vereniging van Participatiemaatschappijen.

Organisation for Economic Cooperation and Development (1997). *Government Venture Capital for Technology-Based Firms*. OECD/GD, 201. Paris.

Queen, M. (2002). Government Policy to Stimulate Equity Finance and Investor Readiness. *Venture Capital*, 4(1):1–5.

Romain, A. and Van Pottelsberghe, B. (2004). *The Economic Impact of Venture Capital*. German Central Bank, Discussion Paper No. 18. Université Libre de Bruxelles, Brussels.

Sahlman, W.A. (1990). The Structure and Governance of Venture-Capital Organizations. *Journal of Financial Economics*, 27(2):473–521.

Sapienza, H., Manigart, S. and Vermeir, W. (1996). Venture Capitalist Governance and Value Added in Four Countries. *Journal of Business Venturing*, 11(6):439–469.

Wallsten, S. (2001). *The Role of Government in Regional Technology Development: The Effects of Public Venture Capital and Science Parks*. Stanford Institute for Economic Policy, Research Discussion Paper No. 00–39. Stanford University, Stanford CA.

9 A review of the venture capital industry in Italy

Fabio Bertoni, Massimo G. Colombo, Annalisa Croce, and Evila Piva

Abstract

This chapter describes the venture capital (VC) industry in Italy. First, we outline the evolution of the industry since the mid-1990s in terms of investments, divestments, and fundraising activity. Second, we provide evidence that New Technology-Based Firms (NTBFs) in Italy benefit significantly from VC investments. Third, we describe the framework of policies supporting VC. The overall picture suggests some interesting observations. Despite the bank-centric nature of the financial system in Italy that slowed down the emergence of the industry, VC is proven to be able to improve dramatically the performance of recipient firms. Nevertheless this does not seem to be sufficient to feed the 'virtuous capital cycle' that usually characterizes the VC industry. We interpret the recent evolution of the industry in Italy as a switch in the demand/supply equilibrium with rational expectations on both sides: on the one hand VC funds do not invest in seed and early stage companies because of the lack of good investment opportunities; on the other, entrepreneurs, being aware of the scarcity of VC support for new firms, refrain from starting new ventures. We conclude by defining those characteristics a VC-related policy should have in order to succeed.

9.1 Introduction

Italy has historically been considered as having a bank-based financial system, with a relatively marginal role played by the Stock Market (Roell, 1996), poor shareholder protection (La Porta et al., 1998), and significant importance of State-owned companies (Faccio and Lang, 2002), even when compared with other countries in continental Europe. During the past decade, an effort to move the system to a more market-based paradigm has been made. Regulatory reforms in 1998 (Consolidated Law of Finance), 2000 (stricter Corporate Governance rules), and 2004 (Reform of the Commercial Law) increased, at least theoretically, shareholder protection. The creation in 1999 of a New Market (Nuovo Mercato) for young high-tech firms with significant growth potential contributed, until the first part of 2001, to the sharp increase in the number of IPOs.[1] The median age of companies going public in Italy, historically much higher than in the rest of Europe or the U.S., decreased and the difference is now insignificant (Dalle Vedove et al., 2005). Even though the effort involved in developing a more market-based financial system has been

[1] For an analysis of the rise and fall of Europe's new stock markets see Giudici and Rosenboom (2004).

significant, its effectiveness has been jeopardized by the concurrence of a series of events that dramatically reduced investor's confidence, such as the burst of the internet bubble and some large corporate scandals.[2] The number of IPOs in 2000 (32, 20 of which on the Nuovo Mercato) was nearly twice the number of IPOs between 2002 and 2004 (18), and the Nuovo Mercato itself was closed in 2005.

The financial literature has clearly highlighted the key role of VC in providing external financing to young technology-based firms (Denis, 2004; Gompers and Lerner, 2004). These firms face significant difficulties in raising equity financing from stock markets and, at the same time, have poor access to bank debt (Carpenter and Petersen, 2002a). Nevertheless, in a bank-based financial system VC faces less favorable conditions than in a market-based one. The lack of a well-functioning stock market makes exit by means of an IPO less viable, thus hindering the development of early stage VC (Jeng and Wells, 2000). Accordingly, Dalle Vedove et al. (2005) show that only 26 venture-backed companies went public in Italy in the ten-year period from 1995 to 2004.

In this chapter we analyze the VC industry in Italy, combining two complementary perspectives. First we describe the 'supply side' (Section 9.2): we outline the current state of the VC industry and illustrate its evolution since the mid-1990s. During this period the VC industry experienced two dramatically different phases. During the first phase, from 1997 to 2001, VC flourished and the volume and number of investments, especially in early stage and high-tech companies, grew steadily. During the second phase, following the burst of the internet bubble, VC firms switched to a more 'cautious' strategy, focusing on later stage Private Equity (PE) investments and buy-outs while early stage investments almost disappeared.

Second, in Section 9.3 we deal with the 'demand side' of the VC industry. Relying on RITA (Research on Entrepreneurship in Advanced Technologies), a unique hand-collected proprietary database, we illustrate the main characteristics and evolution of Italian New Technology-Based Firms (NTBFs) as well as their ability to attract VC financing. It is well recognized in the financial literature (Denis, 2004; Gompers and Lerner, 2004; Carpenter and Petersen, 2002a) that these firms are the main beneficiaries of VC financing. Accordingly the demand for VC is crucially dependent on the behavior of these firms. Interestingly we show that the number of firms founded in the 2001–2003 period is substantially lower than the figure for the 1998–2000 period, confirming that the lack of VC deals is due to a contemporaneous reduction in supply and demand.

In Section 9.4 we study the effect of VC financing on firm's growth and investments. We show that Italian NTBFs benefit significantly from VC investments. The analysis on a representative sample of NTBFs shows that, after obtaining VC financing, firms are less financially constrained and are characterized by a higher growth rate. Interestingly significant differences are found relative to the identity of the investor. Financing from Independent Venture Capital Funds (IVC) has a much stronger effect on firm's performance (such as investments and growth) than financing by Corporate Venture Capital (CVC).

In Section 9.5 we describe the framework of policies supporting VC in Italy. Finally, Section 9.6 concludes with summary remarks.

[2] In the aftermath of the bursting of the high-tech bubble, three major corporate scandals occurred in Italy: Cirio in 2002 (the first corporate bond default in Italy), and Parmalat and Giacomelli in 2003 (corporate fraud). The collapse of the three companies, which operated in mature sectors such as Food and Retail distribution, wiped out more than €3 billion of shareholder and bondholder savings.

9.2 Venture capital in Italy: the supply side

This section describes the Italian PE and VC industry. The section is structured as follows. In Section 9.2.1 we describe operators in the Italian VC industry. We highlight that there is only a small number of operators that specialize in early-stage financing and, accordingly, this segment is highly concentrated. In Section 9.2.2 we describe the evolution of the VC industry from 1998 to 2004. We show that the dismal situation of VC in 2004 is the result of a slowdown after an expansion phase that started in the mid-1990s and ended with the burst of the internet bubble in 2001.

9.2.1 Venture capital and private equity in Italy in 2004

According to the Italian Venture Capital Association (AIFI), in Italy in 2004 there were 97 VC and PE firms, 73 of which have been active during the year.[3] In Table 9.1 VC and PE investors are classified in different categories: Italian closed-end funds, Early stage funds, Pan-European funds, Italian banks and subsidiaries, and Public VC funds.[4] Table 9.1 shows, for each category, the number of investors and the number and amount of investments made in 2004.

A total of 248 VC and PE investments were made during 2004 for a total of €1480 million, corresponding to 0.113% of GDP. The average size of investment is €6.0 million but this figure varies dramatically across different types of investors and stages of investment. In terms of number and amount of investments, the most important category is the Italian closed-end funds, which represent 51% of the total number of firms, 36% of the total number of investments, and 46% of the total invested amount with an average investment size of €7.7 million. Pan-European funds (such as, for instance, Morgan Grenfell Private Equity and the Carlyle Group) are the second most relevant category. Even though they represent only 7% of the number of firms, they account for 23% of total deals and 38% of the total invested amount. Pan-European funds are

Table 9.1 Venture capital and private equity investors in Italy in 2004 by type of investor

	Italian closed-end funds	Early stage funds	Pan-European funds	Italian banks and subsidiaries	Public VC funds	Total
Number of investors	49 (51%)	7 (7%)	19 (20%)	13 (13%)	9 (9%)	97 (100%)
Number of investments	89 (36%)	57 (23%)	49 (20%)	39 (16%)	14 (6%)	248 (100%)
Amount invested	682 (46%)	152 (10%)	564 (38%)	49 (3%)	33 (2%)	1480 (100%)
Average investment	7.7	3.1	9.9	1.3	2.4	6

Source: Elaboration of AIFI data.

[3] A VC firm is considered active if it made at least one investment, disinvestment, or fundraising activity during the year.

[4] Public VC funds include funds from State, Regions and other cooperative investors.

mainly focused on the buy-out segment and mega-deals; accordingly, the average size of investments is the highest: €49.9 million.

Early stage funds that specialize in seed and start-up equity financing, mostly (but not only) in high-tech companies, account for 7% of total investors. Investments made by early stage funds account for 23% of the deals but only 10% of the total invested amount. With €52 million, this barely corresponds to 0.011% of Italian GDP. The average size of investment is €3.1 million.

In recent years Italian banks and their subsidiaries have played a decreasing role within the industry, preferring most often to replace direct investment activity with the institution of Italian SGRs (Società di Gestione del Risparmio).[5] Nevertheless, banks still represent approximately 13% of the total number of investors. They are active in every stage of investments, with a particular focus on replacement and expansion financing. While 16% of the recorded deals are carried out by banks or their subsidiaries, they account for only 3% of the total amount invested in 2004. The average size of investments is, in fact, equal to €1.3 million, a value that is well below the average of €6.0 million. Finally, public VC funds, which represent 9% of the total number of firms, were prevalently active in start-up and expansion investment activity, with the goal of promoting entrepreneurship and fostering the development of some specific areas or industrial sectors. In 2004, investments by these actors represented 6% in number and 2% in terms of amount of total investments. The average investment by public venture capitalists is €2.4 million.

Some interesting considerations derive from the categorization of investments along different stages. In particular, following the classification by EVCA we distinguish four stages: Seed and Start-up, Expansion, Replacement, and Buy-out.

Table 9.2 shows that, in 2004, 50 investments (20% of the total number of investments) were made in 36 seed/start-up companies (17% of the total number of invested companies). The average investment per company is rather small (€0.64 million); consequently seed/start-up investments represent only 2% of the total invested amount. This corresponds to €23 million, which is a negligible fraction of Italian GDP (less than 0.002%). Expansion financing represents 51% of the deals, 53% of the invested companies, and 31% of the total invested amount. The average size of the investment per company, €4.13 million, is substantially higher than for seed and start-up companies.

Table 9.2 Venture capital and private equity investments in Italy in 2004 by stage

	Early stage		Late stage		Total
	Seed/Start-up	**Expansion**	**Replacement**	**Buy-out**	
Number of investments	50 (20%)	126 (51%)	24 (10%)	48 (19%)	248 (100%)
Number of invested companies	36 (17%)	111 (53%)	21 (10%)	40 (19%)	208 (100%)
Amount invested	23 (2%)	458 (31%)	83 (6%)	916 (62%)	1480 (100%)
Average investment	0.64	4.13	3.95	22.9	7.12

Source: Elaboration of AIFI data.

[5] SGRs are legally independent structures that manage closed-end funds. As of today about 50% of them are owned by Italian banks.

The €458 million invested in expansion deals represent 0.035% of GDP. Replacement financing accounts for only 10% in number (both of investments and of invested companies) and 5% of the total invested amount. The average investment per company is €3.95 million. Finally, buy-outs account for 19% in terms of number of investments (and invested companies) but, with €916 million, they represent the largest fraction, namely 62%, of the total invested amount. This latter result is determined by the large average size of buy-out investments compared with other categories: €22.9 million per invested firm.

The comparison between the Italian and the European VC industry yields some interesting considerations. According to EVCA statistics surveying VC in 20 European countries, in 2004 Italy ranked 12th in terms of the ratio of VC and PE investments over GDP, with all other large European economies ranking well above, for example the U.K. (1st), France (3rd) and Germany (7th). On average in 2004, seed and early-stage financing represented 6.4% of total investments in Europe, compared with only 2% in Italy. In other words, the Italian VC industry is small in size (relative to GDP) and focused on later-stage investments.

The small size of the VC and PE industry in Italy also produces a very high industry concentration, particularly in seed and early stage VC investments. According to AIFI data, although 13 VC firms invested in early stage companies in 2004, 67% of the invested amount is due to only three VC firms, and the figure rises to more than 90% for the first five. Hence, the seed/start-up segment is highly concentrated and very few players dominate the market.

9.2.2 Evolution of the venture capital and private equity industry in Italy

In this section we analyze the evolution of the VC and PE industry in Italy in the seven-year period from 1998 to 2004. The Italian VC industry, and in particular the size and relevance of early stage investments, fluctuated significantly in this period. Table 9.3 reports the evolution of the VC and PE industry in terms of number and amount of investments, from 1998 to 2004.

If we examine the overall VC and PE industry without distinguishing early from late stage financing, we observe that from 1998 to 2000 the number of investments increased from 269 to 646 and the amount invested increased from €944 million to €2970 million. After the internet bubble burst, the number of investments decreased gradually to a minimum of 248 in 2004. In contrast the invested amount peaked in 2003, reaching €3071 million. The reason for this apparent conundrum becomes clear when we distinguish between early and later-stage investments. Early stage investments, both in number and amount, increased substantially from 1998 to 2000, when this type of investment represented 52.5% of the deals and 18.2% of the total amount invested (from 34.9% and 10.9%, respectively, in 1998). In 2000 Italian VC firms invested €540 million in seed/start-up deals; this amount equals 0.046% of GDP. Since then, early stage investments have been rapidly declining: the fraction of this category within the total number of deals decreased to 45.4% in 2001, 16.3% in 2002, and then slightly increased to 19.3% in 2003 and 20.2% in 2004. The decrease is even more impressive if we look at the fraction of total investments devoted to seed and start-up stages. This share decreased from 18.2% in 2000 to 13.3% in 2001, but then it fell dramatically to 2.5%, 1.9%, and 1.6% of total investments in 2002, 2003, and 2004. In 2004 the amount of seed/start-up deals represents only 5% of the number of expansion deals and 0.002% of GDP, so it

Table 9.3 Early stage VC investments in Italy from 1998 to 2004

Stage	Investments	1998	1999	2000	2001	2002	2003	2004
Seed and	Number	94 (35%)	153 (39%)	339 (53%)	222 (45%)	49 (16%)	65 (19%)	50 (20%)
start-up	Amount	103 (11%)	147 (8%)	540 (18%)	291 (13%)	65 (3%)	59 (2%)	23 (2%)
Expansion	Number	92 (34%)	124 (32%)	235 (36%)	186 (38%)	137 (46%)	175 (52%)	126 (51%)
	Amount	300 (32%)	356 (20%)	966 (33%)	745 (34%)	806 (31%)	583 (19%)	458 (31%)
Later stages	Number	83 (31%)	113 (29%)	72 (11%)	81 (17%)	115 (38%)	96 (29%)	72 (29%)
	Amount	541 (57%)	1268 (72%)	1464 (49%)	1150 (53%)	1742 (67%)	2429 (79%)	979 (68%)
All stages	Number	269 (100%)	390 (100%)	646 (100%)	489 (100%)	301 (100%)	336 (100%)	248 (100%)
	Amount	944 (100%)	1771 (100%)	2970 (100%)	2186 (100%)	2613 (100%)	3071 (100%)	1460 (100%)

[a] Amount invested is in € million.
Source: Elaboration of AIFI data.

is fair to acknowledge that early-stage financing has presently dried up in Italy. Note also that the average size of seed/start-up investments has been declining almost steadily from €1.59 million in 2000 to €0.46 million in 2004. Expansion investments, on the other hand, exhibit a much more stable dynamic over time. Between 1998 and 2001 expansion investments accounted for a share of the total number of deals between 31.8% (in 1999) and 38% (in 2001) and a share of the total amount invested between 20.1% (in 1999) and 34.1% (in 2001).

Since 2002 the share of expansion deals has been increasing, reaching 52.1% in 2003 (down to 50.8% in 2004). However, this increase did not translate into an increase in the share of the invested amount, which remained quite stable around 30% (with the exception of a decline to 19.2% in 2003). The evolution over time of the average size of deal also differs quite remarkably from that of early stage investments; average deal size ranges between €5.88 million in 2002 and €2.87 million in 1999.

Results in Table 9.3 show that overall the VC and PE industry suffered because of the unstable behavior of financial markets post-2000. Nevertheless, a few years after the internet bubble burst, the industry, taken as a whole, recovered and in 2003 the overall amount invested exceeded that of 2000. What has changed dramatically is its composition, to the detriment of seed and start-up investments which now account for a negligible share of the total invested amount.

9.3 Venture capital in Italy: the demand side

In the previous section we described the evolution and current state of the VC industry in Italy from a supply-side perspective. In this section we analyze the demand side of the industry. More precisely, we focus on Italian NTBFs, since these firms are most likely to benefit from VC financing (Carpenter and Petersen, 2002a, 2002b). For this purpose we rely on data provided by the RITA database, the most comprehensive source of information on Italian NTBFs.

In Section 9.3.1 we illustrate the general characteristics of the RITA dataset and we describe its sampling process. In Section 9.3.2 we present the sectoral distribution of sample firms and their evolution over time. In Section 9.3.3 we report statistics about sample firms' access to external equity financing.

9.3.1 The RITA database

The RITA (Research on Entrepreneurship in Advanced Technology) database was developed at the Department of Management, Economics and Industrial Engineering of Politecnico di Milano. It provides information on a sample of 1974 Italian high-tech start-ups that were founded in 1980 or later, were independent at founding and remained so up to 1 January 2004, and operate in high-tech sectors in both manufacturing and services.

The development of the database had a series of steps. First, Italian firms that complied with the above criteria relating to age and sector of operations were identified. For the construction of the target population a number of sources were used. These included lists provided by national industry associations, on-line and off-line commercial firm directories, and lists of participants in industry trades and expositions. Information provided by the national financial press, specialized magazines, other sectoral studies, and regional Chambers of Commerce was also considered. Altogether, 1974 firms were selected for inclusion in the database. For each firm, a contact person was also identified. Unfortunately, data provided by official national statistics do not allow obtaining a reliable description of the population of Italian NTBFs. Second, a questionnaire was sent to the contact person of the target firms either by fax or by e-mail. The first section of the questionnaire provided detailed information on the human capital characteristics of firms' founders. The second section comprised further questions concerning the characteristics of the firms, including their access to external equity financing and their post-entry performance. Finally, answers to the questionnaire were checked for internal coherence by educated personnel and were compared with published data (basically data provided by firms' annual reports and financial accounts) if they were available. In several cases, phone or face-to-face follow-up interviews were made with firms' owner-managers. This final step was crucial in order to obtain missing data and ensure that data were reliable.

9.3.2 The sectoral distribution of Italian NTBFs

In the RITA database firms have been classified into seven subclasses: aerospace; information and communication technology manufacturing; robotics and automation; biotechnologies, pharmaceuticals and advanced materials; software; internet and telecommunication services; and multimedia content.

Table 9.4 shows the sectoral distribution of sample firms. Most Italian NTBFs operate in internet and telecommunication services (33.0% of the sample), software (27.3%) and ICT manufacturing (21.6%). On the other hand relatively few operate in biotechnologies pharmaceuticals and advanced materials (4.9%), and aerospace (0.8%). Table 9.4 also reports the sectoral distribution of firms funded in the 1998–2000 and 2001–2003 period. It is worth noting that internet and telecommunications services account for more than half the number of NTBFs founded after 1998.

The number of NTBFs founded in the three-year period between 2001 and 2003 (213) is less than half the figure for the three-year period between 1998 and 2000 (444). It should

Table 9.4 Distribution of NTBFs across sectors, and periods of founding

	1980–2003	1998–2000	2001–2003
Aerospace	15 (0.8%)	2 (0.5%)	0 (0.0%)
ICT manufacturing	427 (21.6%)	60 (13.5%)	20 (9.4%)
Robotics and automation	197 (10.0%)	32 (7.2%)	18 (8.5%)
Biotech, pharmaceuticals and advanced materials	96 (4.9%)	17 (3.8%)	4 (1.9%)
Software	539 (27.3%)	83 (18.7%)	43 (20.2%)
Internet and TLC services	652 (33.0%)	238 (53.6%)	127 (59.6%)
Multimedia content sector	48 (2.4%)	12 (2.7%)	1 (0.5%)
Total	1974 (100.0%)	444 (100.0%)	213 (100.0%)

Source: Elaboration of RITA report (2005).

be noted that, because of the sampling procedure, younger NTBFs are more difficult to identify than older ones and this is likely to bias downwards our figures about the number of NTBFs that have been founded in recent years. However, the difference is much higher than could be explained by a mere sampling bias. In other words we observe that, after the burst of the speculative bubble, the demand for VC financing dried up. This suggests that, after 2001, a switch in the demand/supply equilibrium occurred: on the one hand venture capitalists do not invest in seed and start-up because of the inadequate deal-flow; on the other, would-be entrepreneurs, aware that VC support for new firms is scarce, refrain from starting new ventures.

9.3.3 NTBFs' access to external equity financing

In this section we focus on the recourse of Italian NTBFs to external equity financing. Of RITA NTBFs, 12.4% obtained equity financing from external investors.

In Table 9.5 we distinguish three sources of VC financing: Independent Venture Capital funds (IVC), Corporate Venture Capital investors (CVC), and other institutional investors (for instance banks and insurance companies).

Table 9.5 shows that 6.4% and 6.9% of Italian NTBFs obtained IVC and CVC financing, respectively. On the other hand, only 1.5% of firms in the RITA sample obtained external equity financing by investors other than IVC and CVC, such as insurance companies and banks. The sector with the highest intensity of VC financing is Multimedia content (26.9%. resorting to VC). Biotechnologies, pharmaceuticals and advanced materials, and internet and telecommunications services exhibit higher than the average VC financing intensity (18.2% and 15.0%, respectively), with CVC financing prevailing in the former subclass and IVC financing in the latter. VC financing in the ICT manufacturing sector is in line with the average (13.0% obtained VC financing, 7.0% by IVCs and 6.1% by CVCs). Conversely, the percentage of VC-backed firms in automation and robotics and in software is substantially lower than the average.

In general, the first round of IVC and CVC financing occurs in the very early years of a firms' life. In fact, 43.7% and 26.8% of the NTBFs that obtained access to VC were financed for the first time whilst in the seed and start-up stages, respectively.

Table 9.5 Recourse to VC financing in NTBFs by sector and type of investor (%)

Sector	VC	IVC	CVC	Other VC
Aerospace	0.0%	0.0%	0.0%	0.0%
ICT manufacturing	13.0%	7.0%	6.1%	1.7%
Robotics and automation	9.6%	3.8%	5.8%	0.0%
Biotech and Pharma	18.2%	4.5%	9.1%	4.5%
Software	7.5%	2.5%	6.3%	0.6%
Internet and TLC services	15.0%	10.2%	7.8%	1.8%
Multimedia content	26.9%	11.5%	11.5%	3.8%
Total	12.4%	6.4%	6.9%	1.5%

Source: Our elaboration of RITA report (2005).

9.4 The effect of venture capital on NTBF performance

As we highlighted in the above sections, both the supply of and the demand for VC financing have been declining in Italy since 2001. It is thus very interesting, this notwithstanding, to assess whether and to what extent Italian NTBFs benefited from VC financing. Bertoni et al. (2005, 2006) assess the effect of VC on the performance of Italian NTBFs under two complementary perspectives. Bertoni et al. (2006) analyze firm's investment behavior and how it is affected by the presence of VC. Bertoni et al. (2005) study how VC influences firm's growth. In addition, these studies compare two different sources of external capital, namely IVC and CVC, and show that their effects differ markedly. Moreover their results hold even when controlling for the endogenous nature of VC financing. In other words, firms growing more rapidly or having a higher investment rate are more likely both to obtain and to look for VC financing. It is thus important to control for the endogeneity of VC in order to obtain unbiased estimates.[6]

Bertoni et al. (2006) analyze both the level and the cash-flow sensitivity of investments in fixed and intangible assets in a longitudinal hand-collected dataset comprising 378 Italian NTBFs observed between 1994 and 2003. The cash-flow sensitivity of investments, and its changes resulting from external equity financing, is gauged by looking at the effect of three different types of perturbations in the cash-flow pattern: short-run shocks, long-run parallel shifts, and random fluctuations. The authors find that sample NTBFs exhibit a significant investment–cash-flow sensitivity. This result is interpreted as a signal of the existence of binding financial constraints that negatively affect investments of these firms: firms invest more (less) in years in which their cash flow is higher (lower), even when controlling for investment opportunities. Investments by VC-backed firms are not significantly affected by short-run shocks in cash flows: this indicates that VC is generally effective in reducing a firm's financial constraints. However, the effect of VC differs markedly between IVC and CVC. After receiving financing from IVC, a firm's investment rate increases significantly and is nearly independent from both short-run shocks and long-run parallel shifts in cash flows. Results for CVC-backed firms are considerably different: the increase in the investment rate is much lower than that for IVC-backed firms and the dependence on cash flows is still significant, even though to a lesser extent than for non-VC-backed firms. Investments by IVC-backed firms are also less volatile than investments by CVC-backed firms in response to random cash-flow fluctuations.

A similar pattern is highlighted by Bertoni et al. (2005) in their study on firm's growth. The effect of VC financing on firm's growth is substantial: firms increase their growth rate considerably after having received VC financing. Albeit the marginal effect is decreasing over time, it is still significant three years after the first round of VC financing. Again, IVC and CVC exhibit a dramatically different effect. CVC-backed firms are characterized by an increase in the growth rate but the effect is significantly smaller than for IVC-backed firms. The increase in the number of employees resulting from CVC in the first three years after the first round of financing is respectively 13.77%, 9.05%, and 8.45%, while the increase resulting from IVC is respectively 54.81%, 99.67%, and 108.52%.

Altogether these results highlight that even in a bank-based financial system such as exists in Italy, and under quite unfavorable conditions, VC financing plays a key role in

[6] The authors adopt a Generalized Method of Moments to control for the endogeneity of the financial structure of sample firms.

supporting investments and growth of NTBFs. They also indicate that the identity of the investor matters: financing obtained from IVC is associated with superior benefits to the investee firms than other types of VC financing, such as CVC.

9.5 Public policy in support of the venture capital industry

Previous sections have shown that in recent years both the demand and supply of VC in Italy has declined, despite the substantial benefits that investee companies exhibited both in terms of growth and in terms of independence of their investment policy from cash availability. In this situation, there is a desperate need for technology policy measures aimed at favoring simultaneously the demand for and the supply of VC financing to Italian NTBFs. Even so, in Italy there have been very few policy measures directed to the VC industry at national level.

The first serious attempt to revamp the VC industry dates back to 2000, when law 388 (see sections 103 and 106) was voted by Parliament. This law basically establishes a public co-financing scheme for investments in early stage firms (that is, firms that are less than three years old). The Ministry of Productive Activities selects banks and other financial intermediaries eligible to apply for funding and grants to them bridge financing to acquire temporary (that is, less than seven-year) minority participation in the equity of young SMEs. To get access to the subsidy, firms' shares must be newly issued and represent at least 20% of the equity capital. The maximum anticipation is 50% of the total investment for each initiative up to a maximum of €2.06 million. When the stake is sold, the beneficiaries of the anticipation pay back 50% of the capital gain, less a compensation fee composed of a management fee (to cover the costs for the firm's selection and participation management) and a success fee. So far the results of L.388/2000 have been quite unsatisfactory, the reason possibly being a very slow take up. Up to June 2005, only 17 investors had been admitted to the benefits of the law, with three additional ones in the pipeline. Out of a budget of €202 million, which may support an invested amount of up to €404 million, only €3.3 million have been invested in three firms.

Note that at 12.5%, the tax rate that applies to capital gains in Italy is very low. In addition, since 2003 only capital gains realized by individuals are taxed, while those realized by firms are tax exempt. Paradoxically, this discourages risky early stage investments in new technology-based firms, as these latter investments do not enjoy any more favorable tax treatment than later stage investments in more mature industries. In our view, combined with a lack of measures expressly aimed at encouraging the creation of and supporting the development of NTBFs, this is probably one of the key reasons for the current unsatisfactory development of the VC industry in Italy.

A new and recent attempt to revitalize the Italian VC industry is law 311 voted in December 2004 (Legge Finanziaria 2005). This law (sections 1, 222, and 223) establishes the creation of a fund of funds, with a capital of €100 million, aimed at co-financing closed-end funds that invest in innovative SMEs especially in early stages. On the one hand, L.311/2004 generates incentives for private investors by allowing them to enjoy extra benefits from successful investments, but without giving them guarantees for losses. On the other hand, companies eligible for financing are only SMEs with investment projects aimed at introducing ICT-based products and/or process innovations, or located in underdeveloped areas in southern regions. These constraints are likely to reduce substantially the effectiveness of this policy measure.

In recent years, as a result of the reform of Title V of the Constitution, some Italian Regions have designed their own policy schemes in support of the VC industry. These policy measures usually establish regional 'funds of funds' and include a co-investment scheme and/or a guarantee scheme that provides private (co-)investors with a partial shield against loss of the invested capital. Among these measures, an important example is provided by the NEXT Fund established by the Lombardy Region in 2000 and managed by Finlombarda.[7] NEXT Fund is the first Italian closed-end fund of funds which offers its subscribers a guarantee on invested capital. NEXT can invest in VC funds (up to a maximum share of 25%) or directly co-invest in firms (up to a maximum amount of €750 000). Target firms are innovative SMEs in early stage phases that have headquarters and production activities in Lombardy and operate in biotechnology, electronics and other ICT industries, mechanical engineering, chemical, industrial design, ICT, robotics and automation, textile, and environment-related sectors. In September 2004 the fundraising activity was completed and in February 2006 NEXT made the first investment in a university spin-off that operates in the biotech industry.

9.6 Conclusion

The purpose of this chapter has been to illustrate the development of the VC industry in Italy. We have focused both on the supply side of VC and its evolution since the late 1990s, and on the demand side of VC financing from NTBFs. We have also described the policy measures aimed at supporting VC at both national and regional level.

The overall picture illustrated in the chapter suggests some interesting concluding remarks. First, despite the bank-based nature of the financial system slowing down the emergence of the VC industry in Italy, venture capitalists prove to be able to improve dramatically the performance of invested firms. VC-backed firms exhibit significant increases in both growth and investment rates. This suggests that the bundle of financial and non-financial support provided by VC to invested firms effectively increases their performance. Nevertheless, this does not seem to be sufficient to feed the 'virtuous capital cycle' that usually characterizes the VC industry.

We interpret the recent evolution of the industry in Italy as a switch in the demand/supply equilibrium with rational expectations on both sides. On the one hand, VC funds do not invest in seed and early stage companies because of the inadequate deal-flow. On the other hand, would-be entrepreneurs, aware that VC support for new firms is scarce, refrain from starting new ventures.

Unfortunately the policy measures designed since year 2000 have focused exclusively on the VC supply side and, thus, failed to address this coordination problem. Accordingly their effects have been, so far, negligible: after the burst of the high-tech bubble, VC investments shifted to later-stage investments and the early stage segment nearly dried up. In these circumstances, there is a need for policy measures that move the system away from this perverse equilibrium acting on both the demand and supply side of the market.

[7] Finlombarda is a private company created in 1971 by the most important Lombard banks. Its mission is to support regional and local administrations to realize investments and use innovative finance instruments.

Such policies should promote early stage VC investments (for instance, introducing tax relief) and, at the same time, foster the creation of new ventures (for instance, promoting academic start-ups) and facilitate their contact with VC firms (for instance, organizing road-shows for promising new ventures).

References

Bertoni, F., Colombo, M.G. and Grilli, L. (2005). *External Private Equity Financing and the Growth of New Technology Based Firms: What Comes First?* Research in Entrepreneurship and Small Business XIX Conference, November 17–18, Naples, Italy.

Bertoni, F., Croce, A. and Colombo, M.G. (2006). *Firm's Investments and (Corporate) Venture Capital.* European Financial Management Association Annual Meeting, June 28–July 1, Madrid.

Carpenter, R.E. and Petersen, B.C. (2002a). Capital Market Imperfections, High-Tech Investment, and New Equity Financing. *Economic Journal*, 112:F54–F72.

Carpenter, R.E. and Petersen, B.C. (2002b). Is the Growth of Small Firms Constrained by Internal Finance? *The Review of Economics and Statistics*, 84(2):298–309.

Dalle Vedove, F., Giudici, G. and Randone, P.A. (2005). The Evolution of Initial Public Offerings in Italy. BitNotes 14:1–38.

Denis, D.J. (2004). Entrepreneurial Finance: An Overview of the Issues and Evidence. *Journal of Corporate Finance*, 10(5):301–326.

Faccio, M. and Lang, L. (2002). The Ultimate Ownership of Western European Corporations. RITA(2005). Rapporto Sulle Nuove Imprese Italiane Adalta Technologia. Milano: DIG. *Journal of Financial Economics*, 65:365–395.

Giudici, G. and Rosenboom, P. (2004). *The Rise and Fall of Europe's New Stock Markets.* Amsterdam: Elsevier.

Gompers, P. and Lerner, J. (2004). *The Venture Capital Cycle.* Cambridge MA: MIT Press.

Jeng, L.A. and Wells, P.C. (2000). The Determinants of Venture Capital Funding: Evidence across Countries. *Journal of Corporate Finance*, 6(2):241–289.

La Porta, R., Lopez-de-Silanes, F., Shleifer, A. and Vishny, R.W. (1998). Law and Finance. *Journal of Political Economy*, 106(6):113–155.

RITA (2005). Rapporto sulle nuove imprese italiane ad alta tecnologia. Milano: DIG.

Roell, A. (1996). The Decision to Go Public: An Overview. *European Economic Review*, 40(3):1071–1081.

10 Exit strategy and the intensity of exit-directed activities among venture capital-backed entrepreneurs in Sweden

Anders Isaksson

Abstract

The purpose of this chapter is to analyze exit strategies and exit-directed activities among entrepreneurs in venture capital relationships. The study focuses on the effect of the VC organization (independent, public sector, and captive) on strategy and exit-directed activities. The study is based on a questionnaire sent to 282 entrepreneurs in VC-backed companies in Sweden (with a response rate of 54%). The results indicate that firms with a trade sale strategy tend to have a higher degree of exit activities compared with other exit strategies. Furthermore, the type of VC organization involved (especially when comparing private independent venture capitalists with public sector venture capitalists) also affects exit strategies and activities.

10.1 Introduction

The potential for exit from a prospective investment is crucial for a venture capitalist's investment decision. Because the young high-growth firms in which venture capitalists invest rarely pay dividends, it is the exit that enables the venture capitalist to cash-out and generate the capital gains needed to produce sufficient returns and to make new investments. Black and Gilson (1998) highlighted the importance of exit mechanisms (especially active stock markets) for a VC industry. Some of the propositions made by Black and Gilson (1998) were later supported empirically by Cumming et al. (2006).

Three basic questions can be asked about VC exits: why do venture capitalists exit? When do they exit? How do they exit? Basically, venture capital companies exit their investment to get the return from their investments needed for them to survive – or to continue their operations.

When venture capitalists exit is a question that has received some attention in research. The greatest attention has been paid to the pricing and timing of exits in the course of an initial public offering (Neus and Walz, 2005; Brav and Gompers, 1997; Gompers, 1995; Megginson and Weiss, 1991; Barry et al., 1990). In their 'general theory of venture capital exits' Cumming and MacIntosh (2002: 10) attempt to give a general explanation of when venture capitalists exit: 'A VC will exit from an investment when the projected marginal value added (PMVA) resulting from its stewardship efforts, at any given point in time, is less than the projected marginal cost (PMC) of these efforts.' Even though the authors admit that several assumptions behind this theory are unrealistic (for instance it assumes that the investment can be sold for a true value at any given point) it is still a good starting point when trying to understand a venture capitalist's exit strategy. The optimal exit strategy for a venture capitalist should logically be to exit their investments when the cost of the project exceeds the benefits.

Another limitation with the general theory is that it assumes that venture capitalists are in full control of the decision. As Smith (2001) points out, the VC process involves at least two parties, the venture capitalist and the entrepreneur. The optimal exit time for the venture capitalist might not be the optimal time for the entrepreneur. The decision to pursue a certain exit mechanism is, in most cases, endorsed by both the entrepreneur and the venture capitalist. The contractual arrangements surrounding the exit are most often quite general, focusing especially on worst-case scenarios (Isaksson et al., 2004). An example of such contractual arrangements is redemption rights that, after some period of time, give the venture capitalist the right to demand that the entrepreneur buys back the venture capitalist's shares in the firm (Kaplan and Strömberg, 2003). Hence, the decision to pursue an IPO or a trade sale is a decision made by the board of directors of the portfolio company, in which the entrepreneur usually has the majority vote. Therefore, in this chapter, the exit decision is assumed to be the strategy of the entrepreneurial firm (or in other words, the agreed strategy).

The third question, how do VC companies exit their investments, can be answered shortly by describing different exit mechanisms. For instance, Cumming and MacIntosh (2002) outline the following five exit mechanisms: IPO, acquisition, secondary sale, buy-back, and write-offs. These will be explained in more detail later in the chapter. However, the 'how' question can also be extended, leading to what could be called questions about exit-directed activities. These include questions related to how exit issues are handled and the intensity of these activities during the whole VC process. One (of very few) example of research concerning this broader issue is Relander et al. (1994), who identified two patterns of exit activity, one called 'the path sketcher' and the other 'the opportunist.'

A factor that has been suggested to affect the behavior of venture capitalists is their organizational structure (Cumming and MacIntosh, 2002; Van Osnabrugge and Robinson, 2001; Wright and Robbie, 1996). Cumming and MacIntosh (2002) discussed (but did not test) how public sector venture capitalists might behave differently from private-sector venture capitalists (because of statutory constraints, among other things). Wright and Robbie (1996) also suggested that differences in compensation structure (between private and captive venture capitalists) could affect their behavior. Van Osnabrugge and Robinson (2001) investigated how the difference between venture capitalists' source of funds (captives and independent venture capitalists) affected the management styles and investment preferences of these different VC organizations (for instance because of the power of fund providers). Van Osnabrugge and Robinson (2001) also find that venture capital firms' source of funds may have some degree of influence over the operations of a VC firm.

Research on VC exits has been rather limited despite the apparent importance of the issue. A book edited by Bygrave et al. (1994) is one of the first published works that more thoroughly discuss VC exit issues. Included in this book is a chapter by Relander et al., who introduced the concept of exit strategy; the conclusions drawn were, however, based on rather limited case study data. The research by Cumming and MacIntosh on exit mechanism and strategies in the U.S. and Canada is also notable (for instance see Cumming and MacIntosh, 2001, 2002, 2003). There is also a study by Wang and Sim (2001) on exit strategies in Singapore. A working paper by Schwienbacher (2002) on VC exits in Europe and in the U.S. should also be mentioned in this context because it is the only study that looks at exits in Europe on an aggregated level.

Given this background, the purposes of this chapter are the following:

1. To examine empirically the relationship between exit strategies and venture capitalists' organizational form.
2. To examine empirically whether the intensity of exit-directed activities depends on the exit strategy and the venture capitalists' organizational form.

10.2 Research framework

10.2.1 Exit mechanisms

Cumming and MacIntosh (2002) outline the following five exit mechanisms: (1) an IPO, when the portfolio firm's shares are sold after being introduced on an established (public) share market; (2) an acquisition (sometimes referred to as a trade sale), where the whole entrepreneurial firm is sold to another company; (3) a secondary sale, when the VC firm sells their part of the portfolio company's shares only; (4) a buy-back (or buy-out), where either the entrepreneur or the management of the firm buys back the venture capitalist's shares of the company. And, finally, if the project fails, the VC firm's last resort is (5) a reconstruction, liquidation, or bankruptcy of the portfolio company. These mechanisms are discussed below.

In an IPO, the firm sells shares to members of the public for the first time. The VC will typically not sell shares into the public market at the date of the public offering. Rather, securities will be sold into the market over a period of months or even years following the public offering. Alternatively, after the offering the venture capitalist may dispose of investments by making a dividend of entrepreneurial firm shares to the venture funds' owners (subscribers to the fund – investors). According to Cumming and Macintosh (2002) IPOs are the most preferred exit mechanism for highly valued firms. Bienz (2005) also shows that IPOs normally yield higher returns than other exit mechanisms and that this is not because IPOs are more profitable per se but because firms that are exited via this route are of higher quality than the ones exited by other means. One important aspect of IPO exits is the distribution of control after the IPO where exiting via an IPO allows the entrepreneur to retain part of his equity, and thus makes it possible for the entrepreneur to maintain some control over the firm.

An acquisition exit (often referred to as trade sale) is when the venture capitalist exits by selling their interests and those of the entrepreneurs to a third party who purchase the entire venture. One way in which this is accomplished is to structure the transactions as a sale of all the shares of the firm, in return for cash, shares in the buyer, or other assets. The buyers will often be larger, established companies (industrial buyer) that are seeking a foothold in the technology possessed by the selling firm; hence the exit is often referred to as a trade sale. In some instances, the buyer will be another venture capitalist. This will most often be a private equity investor, since they target more mature firms. Petty et al. (1992) highlighted that a problem with trade sales is that they usually result in the entrepreneur losing his or her company (it is sold). This may influence the decision to choose other exit mechanisms, even if a trade sale might be more economically beneficial.

In a secondary sale the venture capitalist may also exit by means of a sale of shares to a third party. This type of exit differs from an acquisition in that only shares belonging to the venture capitalist are sold to the third party. The EVCA (2004) divides sale to another party into three categories: sale to another venture capitalist, sale to a financial institution, or sale to management.

Wang and Sim (2001) analyze the exit strategies of VC-backed companies in Singapore. They highlight the importance of the entrepreneur's retention of ownership and control after the exit and find that firms where ownership and control is important (in their case family-owned firms) experience more IPO exits than do other firms. An explanation for this is that an IPO gives the entrepreneur an option to keep some control, while a trade sale often results in an entrepreneur's total loss of control. Wang and Sim (2001) also find that IPOs are more common in high-technology firms (firms with higher potential).

In a buy-back, the entrepreneur (or a group of insiders) repurchases the shares held by the venture capitalist (buys out the venture capitalist). A buy-back can be seen as a form of secondary sale – as mentioned above a sale to management is grouped together with other forms of secondary sales in EVCA statistics. A buy-back will often involve considerable borrowing to retrieve the venture capitalist's shares (Cumming and MacIntosh, 2002) and thus becomes a leveraged buy-out (LBO) or management buy-out (MBO). In many cases, the buy-back can be an effect of exit clauses (for instance redemption rights) that are written in the initial contract. As insurance for the venture capitalist there can be a clause in the shareholder agreement that forces the founder to buy out the venture capitalist if an IPO or a trade sale has not occurred within a certain time frame (Kaplan and Strömberg, 2003; Cumming, 2002).

Exit by reconstruction, liquidation, or bankruptcy is obviously a worst-case scenario. It occurs when the venture fails and the venture capitalist tries to minimize losses. The investment may be written off or the company forced into bankruptcy and liquidation. Reconstruction is another alternative. This may involve a complete take-over by the venture capitalist, dismissal of the entrepreneur, and engagement of a new management team in the hope of recovering all or part of the investment at a later point. Even if the venture failed there may be something worth recovering, such as assets, technology, or patents. If the venture capitalist continues to hold shares in the non-viable venture, the investment may fall under the category 'living dead'. Living dead investments have not lost the entrepreneurial team and are still functioning, however not at a benefit for the venture capitalist (Ruhnka et al., 1992). Alternatively, the venture is recreated under a new identity and a new team. This most often occurs when there is still trust in the technology, but there is a need for a change of focus.

10.2.2 Exit-directed activities

Relander et al. (1994) discuss exit-directed activities during the different phases of the VC process. In their case studies of European VC firms they find two broad types of exit activities: the 'path sketcher' and the 'opportunist.' Path sketchers are working actively with exit problems during the whole VC investment process to increase the probability of successful exits. They are aware that the majority of successful exits take place through a trade sale. They analyze thoroughly the business and exit possibilities of an investment target and the exit possibilities influence the deal structure. At times, this kind of venture capitalist, together with the entrepreneur, is able to identify potential buyers by name simply by looking at companies that could benefit from the improvements made by the venture (as it overcomes technological design barriers). Opportunists, on the other hand, trust that their management skills and the concept of the investment target will lead to an exit opportunity 'when the time is right.' Before making an investment, these venture capitalists carry out a thorough business analysis (due diligence) and may also map out some exit opportunities, but these have little influence over their investment decision. The targeted exit route for opportunists is an IPO (Relander et al., 1994).

10.2.3 The structure of VC organizations and its effects on venture capitalists' behavior

Venture capital companies can be divided into several different categories based on source of contributed funds or on the ownership structure of the company. The organizational form is divided into three different types: private independent, captive, and public sector VC organizations.

Private independent venture capitalists invest their capital through funds organized as limited partnerships in which the VC firm serves as the general partner. Independent VC is the dominant form of VC organization both in the U.S. (Sahlman, 1990) and in Europe, where 76.8% of total funds raised in 2004 was contributed by independent venture capitalists (EVCA, 2004). This form of VC organization has also become the dominant form in Sweden.

The presence of an external investor may have several implications for the behavior of the venture capitalist. Investors may, for instance, influence investment strategies and time horizons of the venture capitalist (Sahlman, 1990). However, the most important effect is probably the more pronounced need for reputation and track record required by independent venture capitalists in order to attract investors' attention. For instance, Gompers (1995) argues that this may have caused some venture capitalists to go public with companies earlier than is ideal. Furthermore, Schwienbacher (2002) found in his survey of European venture capitalists that there was a widespread belief that successful IPOs would give significant reputation benefits. Thus, independent venture capitalists might pursue an IPO exit strategy, even if a trade sale strategy is more expected and rational.

If the venture capitalist is funded mainly from internal sources by a parent organization it is often labeled a captive VC organization (Jeng and Wells, 2000). A captive venture capitalist is indeed a company that belongs to an established corporation that invests its own resources. The parent organization is often a financial institution, such as a bank or insurance company, but can sometimes be a larger non-financial company. The latter form is called a corporate VC organization. Definitions vary to some extent among researchers and practitioners. For instance, Cumming and MacIntosh (2002) separate the captive firms with regard to their parent company's line of business (corporate industrial and corporate financial). Captive VC organizations (and especially the corporate VC type) can often differ in their strategic objectives from private independent companies, which typically have investment return or financial objectives as their primary goal. Wright and

Robbie (1996) find that captive U.K. firms differ in several dimensions from independent venture capitalists.

Finally, public sector VC organizations are financed and controlled by government institutions (either on a local, regional, or a national level). As will be discussed more in the following section, the degree of government influence might vary. The main implication on exit strategy and activity is suggested to be a result of the statutory constraints under which they operate. Cumming and MacIntosh (2002) compare exits in the U.S. with exits made in Canada. We should note that the Canadian sample contains public sector venture capitalist organizations (and other forms) while the U.S. data come entirely from private VC organizations. Given the presence of public sector venture capitalists, the authors hypothesize that their Canadian sample would show fewer IPOs and acquisitions, and more secondary sales and buy-backs. They note that the statutory constraints of public sector venture capitalists would result in more investments in lower growth firms and hence result in less profitable exits.

Further, Ayayi (2004) points out several problems created by labor-sponsored VC funds (LSVCFs in Canada). A major finding was that tax incentives make LSVCFs irresistible to investors and flood the LSVCFs with more money than they may be able to invest wisely because of their general management and their restrictive regulations. The managers of LSVCFs lacked VC experience and/or experience in the entrepreneurial field. Consequently, they tended neither to be specialized in any particular industry nor able to focus their investment decisions on specific stages of development. The returns of the LSVCFs are also considerable lower than those of their competitors.

10.2.4 The Swedish venture capital market and organizations

Sweden is one of the leading private equity markets in Europe. According to the EVCA's yearly survey for Europe, Sweden comes second behind the U.K. in terms of percentage of GDP (EVCA, 2004). According to the Swedish Private Equity & Venture Capital Association (SVCA, 2006) the Swedish VC market today consists of approximately 80 VC companies that, in total, manage around US$10 billion (numbers translated with an exchange rate of 7.8SEK per US$). Of these funds, around US$4.8 billion are already invested in approximately 1200 portfolio firms; of these, about 1000 firms are located in Sweden (EVCA, 2004). Note that the private equity sector (firms mainly focusing on buy-out investments) are not included in these numbers. Current statistics show that during 2005 a total of 540 investments were made by the actors in the Swedish VC market, with investments amounting to US$560 million (NUTEK, 2006).

The Swedish government has played an active role in developing the Swedish VC market. The approach taken has been one of direct involvement, with institutional solutions such as formal VC companies and state-owned funds. The Swedish government and some commercial banks, for instance, jointly started Sweden's first VC company in 1974. During the 1970s and 1980s the Swedish government (by local, regional, or national bodies) founded around 30 VC firms, most of them with a regional development focus. Private independent VC firms began to establish in the early 1980s. However, government-owned (or controlled) VC firms were still the dominant actors during this time. Since the mid-1990s the private VC market in Sweden has grown tremendously and government funds have been reduced. Of the active VC companies in Sweden, approximately nine can be categorized as public sector VC companies. The degree of government influence shifts from foundations that are set up by the Swedish government for special purposes to regional VC companies owned by regional or local governmental bodies. The public sector VC firms are all managed in a very similar way to private independent VC firms, and often they invest together. It is important to note also that the public sector VC companies in Sweden state that their decisions are independent of government influence. They see themselves as independent actors in the Swedish VC market. There are no VC firms in Sweden that are directly managed by the Swedish government. However, the government can definitely influence these companies indirectly by, for instance, setting goals, appointing managers and the board of directors, and so on.

One notable feature that separates all public sector VC companies from their private counterparts is the existence of higher long-term goals beyond making business profits. Industrifonden, one of the leading public sector VC companies in Sweden, may serve as an example. The fund is a foundation that was set up by the government. In the foundation's charter it states that its all-embracing purpose is to strengthen the renewal and growth of small and medium-sized enterprises in Sweden. By different rules and regulations (including EU regulations) the foundation's frame of operations are limited and directed towards certain areas. In other words, they are forced to operate under statutory constraints. Operationally and tactically Industrifonden acts completely free from government influence; that is, the government cannot decide where and when they should invest. However, the government influence can be quite high on a long-term strategic level.

Another factor that could affect the behavior of public sector VC companies vis-à-vis their private counterparts is the scarcity of incentives for investment managers in public sector VC companies. Sahlman (1990) argues that the venture capitalists' compensation system (salary, bonuses, and profits distribution to partners in the VC firm) plays a critical role in aligning the interests of the venture capitalists and the limited partners. Referring to an industry survey, he finds that the base salary to general partners on average accounted for less than half of the total compensation. Sahlman (1990: 495) concludes, 'The implication is that the venture capitalists have incentives to engage in activities that increase the value of the carried interest.' Even though some Swedish public sector VC companies have bonus systems for their employees, the bonus is very low compared with that observed in the private sector. For instance, the president of the largest public sector VC company in Sweden (Industrifonden) has a base salary that constituted over 94% of his total compensation (according to recent annual reports from Industrifonden).

10.3 Data collection

A questionnaire was sent to 353 CEOs of VC-backed firms in Sweden. The sample was selected depending on what year the investment was made. For each investment year 1998–2001, the original goal was to randomly select 100 active firms. Because not enough investments were made in 2001, the goal of 400 firms in total was not completely met. From the original sample of 353 firms, 71 were excluded (leaving 282 firms) because the respondents indicated they did not currently have any VC invested in their firm (37 firms) or because their address was incorrectly provided and could not be found through other sources (34 firms). The only portfolio firms included in the sample were those considered to meet target group considerations for the survey (that is, firms with an active relationship with a venture capitalist). The questionnaire was sent out in May and June 2002 and was followed up by two reminders. Each contact provided the firms with a new questionnaire and a pre-stamped return envelope. The questionnaire was also introduced by a letter that explained the importance of the research, gave contact information, and an assurance of confidentiality. After two reminders, the final usable sample consisted of 152 firms, corresponding to an effective response rate of 54%.

The median firm in the sample employs 16 persons, has a turnover of approximately 1.6 million SEK, and has a book value of assets close to 16 million SEK. The growth (median values) is 33% in employees, 17% in turnover, and 48% in total assets. To assess the potential non-response bias, the key indicators of the responding and non-responding firms are compared. No statistically significant differences are identified in number of employees, turnover, and total book value of assets.

The measure of exit strategy is based on a question in which the respondents were asked to state what exit mechanism (if any) the venture capitalist and entrepreneur have planned. Four different choice categories were provided: IPO, trade sale, buy-back, and other. For each exit strategy the respondents could state the first and second choice. Their first choice of exit mechanism was considered the preferred exit strategy.

A set of questions was developed to assess the intensity of the exit-directed activities. The questions were, as far as possible, adapted from the previous research on VC exit behavior, primarily from Relander et al. (1994), and Isaksson (1998). The first question asks if there is a clearly defined strategy (if there is something that could be called an exit strategy). Second, is it a living strategy (something they are working with)? And third, does the strategy have an effect on how the firm is managed (is it integrated into the general management strategy)? The goal was to capture the level of activity and the degree of integration of the exit strategy into the firm's general strategy. The questions, number of responses, range, mean values, and standard deviations are presented in Table 10.1.

To assess the overall exit-directed activities, an equally weighted additive index 'Intensity of exit-directed activities' was constructed. The descriptive statistics for the index are also summarized in Table 10.1. The value of Cronbach alpha for this index formed by the three questions is 0.59. This value is below the generally accepted 0.7 (Nunally, 1978). However, given the exploratory nature of this study this value is acceptable, which is also a point raised by Nunally (1978). Furthermore, the five-point Likert scale may have contributed to the rather modest value of alpha (Duhachek et al., 2005).

Table 10.1 Questions assessing the intensity of exit-directed activities (five-point Likert scale 'strongly disagree' to 'strongly agree')

	N	Min	Max	Mean	Standard deviation
We have a clear exit plan	150	1	5	2.59	1.38
Our exit plans have influenced our firm's general strategy	150	1	5	2.38	1.38
We are working purposefully to reach a favorable exit	150	1	5	3.40	1.30
Index "Intensity of exit-directed activities"	150	3	15	8.49	2.99

10.4 Results and discussion

The data contain responses from 152 firms. A total of 70 different VC companies were involved. Table 10.2 gives some descriptive data.

10.4.1 *Exit strategy*

An examination of the exit strategies among the VC-backed entrepreneurs revealed some notable results. The most common exit strategy is trade sale (38% of respondents). Exiting by trade sale has historically been the most common type of exit in Sweden according to EVCA statistics (EVCA, 2004). Given these statistics, it is hardly surprising that trade sales are also the most expected exit strategy. The results are also in line with Scwienbacher (2002) who found that 39% of European VC companies had a strict preference for trade sales. The second most common exit strategy is IPO (28%). This is higher than reported by Scwienbacher (2002) (11% for European venture capitalists).

Surprisingly, there are many entrepreneurs who are unsure of their investor's exit strategy (26% of respondents). These results correspond to a certain extent with those of Scwienbacher (2002), 13% of the European venture capitalists stated 'no particular preference' and 12% 'other exit routes'. However, it is still notable that so many entrepreneurs do not have a clear picture of their exit, especially when considering that the exit is an important part of a VC company's business model. This might be an indication of a latent problem in the VC/entrepreneurial relationship, that is, entrepreneurs might not realize that entering the relationship with a venture capitalist implies that it is more or less inevitable that on exit the entrepreneur will lose some or all of his or her control over the venture. In the next section, an analysis of the impact of the organizational form of the VC company on exit strategies is presented.

10.4.2 *Is the venture capitalist's organizational form related to its exit strategy?*

To examine whether exit strategy is associated with type of VC organization, the variables 'Exit strategy' and 'Venture Capital Organization' were cross-tabulated and the chi-square statistic was computed. The results are summarized in Table 10.3.

The value of the chi-square statistic is 12.723 with 6 degrees of freedom, and is significant at the 5% level. The contingency coefficient, which measures the strength of

Table 10.2 Descriptive data of the sample

VC organization	Venture capital firms		Portfolio firms	
	#	%	#	%
Captive	7	10%	15	10%
Independent	54	77%	103	68%
Public Sector	9	13%	34	22%
Sum	70	100%	152	100%

Table 10.3 Cross-tabulation of exit strategy versus venture capital organization (VCOrg)

			Venture capital organization			Total
			Independent	Public sector	Captive	
Exit strategy	IPO	Observed %	67	19	14	100
		Expected %	68	22	10	100
		% Within VCOrg	28	24	40	28
	Trade sale	Observed %	79	14	7	100
		Expected %	68	22	10	100
		% Within VCOrg	45	24	27	38
	Buy-back	Observed %	50	50	0	100
		Expected %	68	22	10	100
		% Within VCOrg	6	18	0	8
	Unclear	Observed %	56	31	13	100
		Expected %	68	22	10	100
		% Within VCOrg	21	35	33	26
Total		% Within Exit strategy	68	22	10	100
		% Within VCOrg	100	100	100	100

association, has a value of 0.278 and is also significant at the 5% level. Thus, there is a statistically significant association between the entrepreneurs' exit strategy and type of venture capitalist's organization. Compared with the null hypothesis of no association,

- public sector VC organizations have fewer trade sale strategies and have more buy-backs and unclear exit strategies;
- independent VC organizations have more trade sale strategies, fewer buy-backs and fewer unclear strategies;
- type of VC organization does not affect the IPO strategies;
- because of the small number of firms backed by captive venture capitalists it is not possible to draw any clear conclusions about their strategies.

Overall, the findings indicate that entrepreneurs entering a relationship with a public sector venture capitalist differ in their exit intentions. We also show that public sector VC organizations tend to choose exit strategies where the entrepreneur can keep a higher degree of control after the exit to a greater extent than do private VC organizations. This is especially pronounced in the case of buy-backs, where the ownership of the firm returns to the entrepreneur.

Public sector VC organizations have a notably higher number of entrepreneurs who are unsure of their exit strategies (35% of entrepreneurs backed by public sector venture capitalists versus 21% of entrepreneurs backed by independent venture capitalists). This might imply that public sector venture capitalists do not highlight exit issues as much as the independent venture capitalists do.

As mentioned above, there might be factors other than the organizational form that affects exit strategies. Investment duration, type of business, or the firm's stage of development have, for instance, been suggested to have an effect on choice of exit. Several of these factors have been controlled for in the selection of the sample (for instance that all entrepreneurs have approximately the same investment time). To control for, and to check if, the entrepreneurial firms' stage of development can explain some of the results, a separate test was performed. One rationale for this is that Swedish public sector VC organizations promote themselves by stating that they invest slightly earlier than independent venture capitalists. There were no insignificant associations between firm stage of development, VC organization and exit strategy ($\chi^2 = 3.6$, $p = 0.9$). Thus, the firms' stage of development cannot explain the link between VC organization and the entrepreneur's exit strategy.

10.4.3 Does exit strategy affect the exit-directed activities?

Next, the relationship between preferred exit strategy and exit activity is analyzed. As Relander et al. (1994) proposed, exit activities may vary from active to reactive strategies. With active exit activity, the exit strategy is known, constantly borne in mind, and becomes a guide for how the firm is managed. Reactive exit-directed activities are more about catching opportunities when they occur.

To examine whether the intensity of exit-directed activities was influenced by the chosen exit strategy and VC organization, a two-way full-factorial ANOVA was used. The data meet the assumption of equal variances ($p = 0.28$). The results are summarized in Table 10.4. While the direct effect of venture capitalists' organizational structure is insignificant, both the direct effect of exit strategy ($p = 0.00$) and the interaction effect ($p = 0.039$) are significant. Thus, the intensity of exit-directed activities varies depending on (1) the chosen exit strategy and (2) from which type of VC organization a firm is exiting.

Examination of contrasts, presented in Table 10.5, revealed the following pattern: firms exiting through trade sale exhibit significantly higher intensity of exit-directed activities than all other exit strategies. The intensity of exit-directed activities, arranged in descending order, is as follows: trade sale, IPO, buy-back and unclear.

The explanatory power of the interaction effect between exit strategy and type of VC organization is lower (partial $\eta^2 = 0.080$) than that of exit strategy (partial $\eta^2 = 0.170$), but significant (plots of estimated marginal means are available from the author upon request). Firms exiting via trade sale and IPO from public VC exhibit higher intensity of activities compared with firms exiting via the same strategies from independent

Table 10.4 4×3 factorial ANOVA[a] dependent variable: intensity of exit-directed activities

Source	F	Sig.	Partial η^2
Corrected model	7.365	0.000	0.346
Intercept	772.586	0.000	0.848
Exit Strategy	9.491	0.000	0.170
VC Organization	0.337	0.715	0.005
Exit Strategy × VC Organization	2.418	0.039	0.080

[a] Four exit strategies: trade sale, IPO, buy-back, unclear; three VC organizational forms: public, independent, captive.

Table 10.5 Examination of contrasts

Simple contrast	Dependent variable: intensity of exit-directed activity	
	Mean Difference	Significance
IPO – Trade	−1.43	0.046
Buy-back – Trade	−2.455	0.018
Unclear – Trade	−3.806	0.000

VC organizations. This effect is more pronounced for trade sales, and only marginally noticeable for IPOs. The pattern is reversed when it comes to buy-backs and unclear strategies: firms exiting via these strategies from independent venture capitalists show higher intensity of exit-directed activities than firms exiting from public venture capitalists. Because there are only a few firms backed by captive VC organizations, they are not discussed here.

10.5 Conclusion

The first aim of this study was to examine the relation between exit strategies and venture capitalists' organizational form. The relation to and dependence on fund providers are the major motives for why organizational form could affect the venture capitalists' behavior in general and exit behavior in particular. Private independent VC organizations need to produce exits that give them a high reputation and a track record when collecting new funds in the future. Captive venture capitalists do not have to raise capital from third parties but might, on the other hand, need to consider their parent companies' objectives when acting on the VC market. Finally, public sector VC organizations are limited by statutory constraints, public demands, and might lack appropriate incentive structures. The findings indicate that the organizational form of the venture capitalist (especially when comparing private independent VC organizations with public sector venture capitalists) affects exit strategies and activities. Entrepreneurs backed by public sector VC organizations tend to have fewer trade sale exit strategies and more buy-back strategies. Furthermore, the proportion of unclear exit strategy was significantly higher among the entrepreneurs financed by the public sector venture capitalists.

The second aim of this study was to examine whether the intensity of exit-directed activities varies depending on the exit strategy and the venture capitalist's organizational form. One finding was that there is a significant difference in the intensity of exit-directed activities between different exit strategies. This difference shows up especially strongly when comparing IPO and trade sale exit strategies. A trade sale exit strategy is found to be associated with significantly more activity and is integrated into the firm's overall strategy. On the opposite side is the buy-back strategy that seems to be handled more on an ad-hoc basis. There was no direct relationship between the intensity of exit-directed activities and organization form. However, firms exiting via trade sale and IPO from public VC organizations were found to exhibit higher intensity of activities compared with firms exiting via the same strategies from independent venture capitalists.

Acknowledgments

The author would like to thank Barbara Cornelius for helpful contributions to the chapter and Vladimir Vanyushyn for his statistical expertise and comments. Opinions (and the potential errors) expressed in this chapter are, of course, those of the author alone. This chapter is also a part of Anders Isaksson's PhD dissertation (2006).

References

Ayayi, A. (2004). Public Policy and Venture Capital: The Canadian Labor-Sponsored Venture Capital Funds. *Journal of Small Business Management*, 42(3):335.

Barry, C.B., Muscarella, C., Peavy, J.W. and Vetsuypens, M. (1990). The Role of VCs in The Creation Of Public Companies. *Journal of Financial Economics*, 27(2):447–471.

Bienz, C. (2005). A Pecking Order of Venture Capital Exits – What Determines the Optimal Exit Channel for Venture Capital Backed Firms? Working paper. Center for Financial Studies and Goethe University, Frankfurt.

Black, B.S. and Gilson, R.J. (1998). Venture Capital and the Structure of Capital Markets: Banks Versus Stock Markets. *Journal of Financial Economics*, 47(3):243–277.

Brav, A. and Gompers, P.A. (1997). Myth or Reality? The Long-Run Underperformance of Initial Public Offerings: Evidence from Venture and Nonventure Capital-Backed Companies. *Journal of Finance*, 52(5):1791–1821.

Bygrave, W.D., Hay, M.G. and Peeters, J.B. (1994). *Realizing Investment Value*. London: Pitman Publishing.

Cumming, D.J. (2002). Contract and Exits in Venture Capital Finance. Working Paper, University of Alberta School of Business.

Cumming, D.J. and MacIntosh, J.G. (2001). Venture Capital Investment Duration in Canada and the United States. *Journal of Multinational Financial Management*, 11(4–5):445–463.

Cumming, D. and MacIntosh, J.G. (2002). Venture Capital Exits in Canada and the United States. Working Paper. University of Alberta and University of Toronto.

Cumming, D. and MacIntosh, J.G. (2003). A Cross-country Comparison of Full and Partial Venture Capital Exits. *Journal of Banking and Finance*, 27(3):511–549.

Cumming, D., Fleming, G. and Schwienbacher, A. (2006). Legality and Venture Capital Exits. *Journal of Corporate Finance*, 12(2):214–245.

Duhachek, A., Coughlan, A.T. and Iacobucci, D. (2005). Results of the Standard Error of the Coefficient Alpha Index of Reliability. *Marketing Science*, 24(2):294–301.

European Private Equity and Venture Capital Association (2004). *EVCA Yearbook 2004*. Brussels: EVCA.

Gompers, P.A. (1995). Optimal Investment, Monitoring, and the Staging of Venture Capital. *Journal of Finance*, 50(5):1461–1490.

Isaksson, A. (1998). Venture Capital Exit Behaviour in Sweden. Paper presented at the 10th Nordic Conference on Small Business Research, Växjö University, 14–16 June 1998.

Isaksson, A. (2006). The Venture Capital Process. PhD dissertation, Umeå School of Business.

Isaksson, A., Cornelius, B., Landström, H. and Junghagen, S. (2004). Institutional Theory and Contracting in Venture Capital: The Swedish Experience. *Venture Capital*, 6(1):47–71.

Jeng, L.A. and Wells, P.C. (2000). The Determinants of Venture Capital Funding: Evidence Across Countries. *Journal of Corporate Finance*, 6(3):241–289.

Kaplan, S.N. and Strömberg, P. (2003). Financial Contracting Theory Meets the Real World: An Empirical Analysis of Venture Capital Contracts. *Review of Economic Studies*, 70(2):281–315.

Megginson, W. and Weiss, K. (1991). Venture Capitalist Certification in Initial Public Offerings. *Journal of Finance*, 46(3):879–903.

Neus, W. and Walz, U. (2005). Exit Timing of Venture Capitalists in the Course of an Initial Public Offering. *Journal of Financial Intermediation*, 14(2):253–277.

Nunally, J.C. (1978). *Psychometric Theory*. 2nd edition. New York: McGraw-Hill.

NUTEK (2006). *Riskkapitalbolagens aktiviteter: Fjärde kvartalet 2005* (The Venture Capital Companies Activities: Fourth Quarter 2005). Stockholm: NUTEK (Swedish Agency for Economic and Regional Growth) and SVCA.

Petty, J.W., Bygrave, W.D. and Shulman, J.M. (1992). Harvesting the Entrepreneurial Venture: A Time for Creating Value. *Journal of Applied Corporate Finance*, 7(1):48–58.

Relander, K., Syrjänen, A.P. and Miettinen, S. (1994). Analysis of the Trade Sale as a Venture Capital Exit Route. In Bygrave, W.D., Hay, M.G. and Peeters, J.B. (eds) *Realizing Investment Value*. London: Pittman Publishing, 132–196.

Ruhnka, J.C., Feldman, H.D. and Dean, T.J. (1992). The 'Living Dead' Phenomenon in Venture Capital Investments. *Journal of Business Venturing*, 7(2):137–155.

Sahlman, W.A. (1990). The Structure and Governance of Venture Capital Organizations. *Journal of Financial Economics*, 27(2):473–524.

Schwienbacher, A. (2002). *An Empirical Analysis of Venture Capital Exits in Europe and in the United States*. Memo April 2002, University of California at Berkeley, Berkeley CA.

Smith, D.G. (2001). Control Over Exit in Venture Capital Relationship. Paper presented to the Annual Meeting of European Financial Management Association, Lugano, Switzerland, June.

Swedish Private Equity and Venture Capital Association (2006). *SVCA Medlemsmatrikel* (Swedish Private Equity & Venture Capital Association's Member Register). Stockholm: SVCA.

Van Osnabrugge, M. and Robinson, R.J. (2001). The Influence of a Venture Capitalist's Source of Funds. *Venture Capital*, 3(1):25–39.

Wang, C.K. and Sim, V.Y.L. (2001). Exit Strategies of Venture Capital-backed Companies in Singapore. *Venture Capital*, 3(4):337–359.

Wright, M. and Robbie, K. (1996). Venture Capitalists, Unquoted Equity Investment Appraisal and the Role of Accounting Information. *Accounting & Business Research*, 26(2):153–168.

11 Private equity fund managers do not overvalue their company investments

Tom Weidig, Andreas Kemmerer, Tadeusz Lutoborski, and Mark Wahrenburg

Abstract

We study the valuation behavior of private equity fund managers using a European private equity fund investor's database. We not only have complete cash-flow information from all 2500 indirect company investments of their funds, but also all of its 15 000 valuations by the fund managers. Our overall conclusion is that private equity fund managers do not overvalue. They value conservatively in line with valuation guidelines. The average observed valuation of the company investments is close to at-cost value over the first two years of investment life. Over the following years, the valuation reflects a fairer value and is strongly influenced by the valuation year. Interestingly, the average valuation declines. We believe this effect is due to the early write-off of bad investments combined with the inability to recognize or write-up top performing investments. We also look at the difference between the last valuation and the exit price to see whether the fund manager under- or overvalues. Unlike previous research, we find no evidence that the last valuation before the exit overvalues the investment. In fact, the largest underestimation comes from exceptionally well-performing company investments. Moreover, we find little evidence that factors such as fund manager's experience, market segment, or fund size strongly influence the valuation behavior.

11.1 Introduction

Private equity funds invest in privately held companies whose shares are not traded on a stock exchange. No market price exists, and the fund managers estimate the value or exit price of their investments using established valuation guidelines. Partial exits or third-party transactions provide useful yardsticks for valuation. The valuation of company investments is also important for the managers to have a target in mind for their negotiations on an exit price.

The situation is even more difficult for the fund investors because of the information gap and potential conflict of interest with respect to their fund manager. They do not have direct access to the portfolio companies; they need to rely on the fund managers to value the portfolio companies for them, based on accepted valuation guidelines, and report these valuations. Fund managers provide disclosure through reports and informal communication, such as conference calls and board meetings. The reports are typically quarterly or half-yearly (see Kemmerer and Weidig, 2005). Moreover, fund investors need information on the value of the underlying portfolio companies not only after exit but throughout the life of the fund for the purpose of portfolio-, risk-, and liquidity management. For example, a pension fund might have a legal obligation to report the value of its investments to its pension fund contributors. Or, a portfolio manager needs to know the exposure of the portfolio of fund investments, possibly as an input to a cash-flow forecasting model, in order to plan liquidity reserves or future commitments to new funds. Therefore, understanding the quality of the fund manager's valuation is of particular importance in the private equity fund industry.

In this chapter, we deal with the quality of valuation reported on the portfolio companies during the first five years (or 20 quarters) of a fund's life. We first review the literature on valuation and discuss the currently accepted valuation guidelines. Second, we describe the data sample, which offers an unbiased view of the European market. Third, we present our empirical findings on the average valuation with respect to the quarters since investment, and the deviation of the exit price from the last valuation by the fund managers.

11.2 Valuation guidelines

National associations have set up valuation standards[1]. The valuation standards are not legally binding; most fund investors require them from the fund managers and managers generally accept them. The guidelines state that the methodology shall be disclosed and consistently applied over the fund's life, and a review should be conducted by outsiders, such as auditors.

The valuation method distinguishes between quoted and non-quoted companies. Quoted companies in the portfolio are valued at the stock price minus a discount for illiquidity (up to 20%) and lock-up period (not less than 25%). For non-quoted companies, two approaches – a conservative or a fair market value approach – are possible. For the conservative approach, all unquoted investments should be at cost unless there has been a new financing round, a partial sale, or a write-down. A new financing round or partial sale should be 'a material investment or sale by or to an independent third party at arm's length,' where a material share is typically more than 5% of the shares. Write-downs are in multiples of 25% for material events.

For the fair market value approach, it is the price an independent buyer is expected to pay on the valuation day. Such value can be determined by comparing similar companies or by using a valuation methodology. The EVCA suggests several methods. Fund investors make sure that the guidelines are rigorously followed and sometimes they discuss the reported valuations with fund management. They also compare the valuations of the companies invested in by two or more of their funds.

11.3 Literature review

Cumming and Walz (2004) is probably the most notable empirical study to date, with cash-flow information on 221 funds invested in 5040 portfolio companies, spanning 32 years from 1971 to 2003 and 39 countries from North and South America, Europe, and Asia. However, they do not have the quarterly valuations of the company investments

[1] See Grabenwarter and Weidig (2005) for more details.

by the fund manager, but only the valuation or the resulting interim Internal Rate of Return (IRR) at the end of the data period: it would be very interesting to track actual ultimate performance to reported performance as at today. This would allow us to look into the overvaluation issue more deeply by not only comparing predicted with reported valuation but by looking at the actual developments of the reported valuation. Given the structure of our dataset, as it stands now, this is [currently] not possible.

11.3.1 Macroeconomic effects on valuation

Gompers and Lerner (2000) analyze the relationship between valuation of portfolio companies and the availability of capital for private equity. They propose the 'money chasing deals argument': a greater offer of capital, that is higher growth rates in investment level, has a significant impact on the price of company investments. And, such an increase in capital can not be linked to an increase in investment opportunity because the greater amount of capital increases the fight for the best investment opportunities, which leads to an increase in the price. Thus, some capital must go to mediocre investments. Also, the number of weak fund managers increases because of a lack of experienced ones. These factors contribute towards lower performance.

Cumming and Walz (2004) state that company investments are less likely to be overvalued during recession. Fund managers seem to write-down their investments faster and the domiciliation of the fund influences its valuation behavior. This is also related to the legal environment within which the funds operate.

11.3.2 Fund characteristics

Several studies look at the influence of experience on the success of company investments. Cumming and Walz (2004) claim that new fund managers overvalue more than experienced managers. Welpe (2004) found similar results. But analysis by Blotevogel (2005) of the European Investment Fund database, a European fund investor, claims higher valuation for experienced managers. This could be due to better performance rather than overvaluation. For example, Kaplan and Schoar (2003) write that actual performance correlates positively with experience.

Other factors are also said to influence valuation behavior. Cumming and Walz (2004) claim that valuation behavior is related to various factors. First, large funds value their investments higher. However, larger funds are more likely to be managed by experienced fund managers. Second, they state that syndicated investments are less overvalued. However, syndicated investments are also more likely to be of high quality, because more funds are invested. The risk of such projects is also typically lower. Third, they find that early stage investments are overvalued. Venture capital investments are more risky, and a valuation proof is difficult. Moreover, the information asymmetry is bigger as the companies act in very specialized markets. Finally, they state that investments in industries with a high market-to-book ratio are overvalued. The market-to-book ratio measures the ratio between the asset value of a company and its valuation on the stock exchange. Such industries include the technology sector, because a company's immaterial value such as know-how, patents, and human capital has a greater impact than material value such as machines and real estate. Venture capital has similar features. The immaterial value is hard to value, especially because of the high information asymmetry. A longer holdings period means that the fund manager gets to know the company better to judge its value. Cumming and MacIntosh (2003) look at partial disinvestments in the U.S. and Canada, and find that partial exits are relatively rare.

11.3.3 Critical review

Previous studies link valuation behavior to the economic environment and fund characteristics, such as region, first-time funds, or sector. Such studies are difficult to get right. First, the data sample needs to be unbiased and large. A dataset coming from a large fund investor and not from the portfolio companies themselves is probably the best assurance of a relatively unbiased sample at company level. Collected company data from data providers such as Venture Economics may suffer from survivorship or other biases. Second, every study uses a different sample covering a different market and time period, which may naturally lead to inconsistent findings. Also, the private equity market has been evolving rapidly in the 1990s, and is very different from during the 1980s and earlier. Therefore, datasets dating back more than ten years are interesting in the sense that they include boom and bust periods, but will not reflect the current market well. Third, disentangling valuation from performance is not easy as valuation is influenced by performance. For example, if one subsample has a higher valuation, two interpretations are possible: the realizable value (due to the market or fund manager) is higher or the manager overestimates the value. Fourth, many independent variables are inter-related, which makes statistical analysis more difficult and therefore vulnerable to subtle biases. For example, a larger fund has more experienced fund managers, which may indirectly influence the valuation accuracy. Fifth, most studies compare two subsamples using a t-test, and look at the p-value to determine whether the two samples come from the same distribution. However, the effect size[2] (also known as Cohen's d) and not the p-value is the most appropriate measure. It states by how much the average of both samples differs considering statistical fluctuation. For example, a t-test with a low p-value might conclude that two subsamples are statistically different, but if their averages differ by only 0.1%, this is a negligible effect (and might even be due to some subtle bias or a few outliers in one subsample). Therefore, we only talk about a relationship with an independent variable if the effect size is larger than 0.2.

11.4 Data sample

We are grateful to have had access to the database of a European private equity fund investor who invests into early stage VC, but also in lower mid-market funds across European countries. The database includes the reports sent by the fund managers and the cash flows from and to the fund. Information on fund characteristics was available either electronically or in paper form.[3] Information on fund level consists of the fund net asset value plus the date of the report, experience (that is, first time fund or not), stage

[2] The effect size is widely used in medical science but not so in social science. For more information see Cohen (1988).

[3] Moreover, one of us had regular contact with the professionals from back office.

(venture capital, mid-market), geographic, focus (regional, technology), and fund size. A fund report also includes information on the individual portfolio companies. Information on the company includes stage, vintage year, industrial sector, country, and type of investment. Most relevant to this chapter, the valuations of the company investment, amounts of purchase, partial or total sales, and write-downs, and the corresponding dates are reported. All cash amounts are linked to a currency: Euro, British Pound, Danish Krone or Swedish Kronas.

Our sample is unique in that we have the quarterly valuations of the company investments as reported by the fund managers, which allow us to get a closer look at valuation behavior. Moreover, all funds must report on all their companies, which is very different to the databases of a data provider such as Venture Economics, which relies on voluntary data reporting. Moreover, we have access to all information available to the fund investor, unlike the database of Venture Economics where only anonymous data is available. Thus, any remaining bias of the sample can only be the result of atypical investment behavior of the fund investor with respect to the general market. Looking at EVCA data, we estimate that our investor invests in about 15% of all funds in a given year, on average. Thus, we believe that our fund investor's investment behavior is a good representation of the European private equity industry.

However, the average fund age is about four years nine months, and most funds are still active and not completely liquidated. As we are not looking at the performance of these funds but solely at the reporting behavior of the fund managers during the investment period, we do not need the funds to be liquidated. However, we are aware that the sample largely captures the period 1999–2004 when the industry has shown a dramatic increase followed by a considerable consolidation. On the other hand, historical data before the 1990s are likely to represent a very different private equity industry.

To summarize, we consider the database to be an unbiased in-depth view of fund managers' behavior for the years after 1997.

11.5 Empirical findings

The first investment in a company took place in 1994. Our last data update is from end of April, 2005. As there is a time gap between reports' closing date and delivery, we only consider data until 31 December 2004. We disregard those funds that do not have the typical fund structure, such as mezzanine funds and atypical buy-out funds. Second, we eliminate all funds that have not yet had a draw-down. We distinguish VC funds and mid-market funds. Furthermore, we exclude all non-equity investments such as loans, debts, convertible loans, subordinated loans, or loan notes. We also exclude all transactions for which we were not totally confident of the equity nature. The cash amounts are converted into Euro amounts using the day exchange rate. Exchange rates were taken from the free public database of Oanda Corporation.[4]

Finally, we have data from around 200 funds, 1800 company investments, approximately 5000 transactions, and more than 11 000 valuations. A transaction can be a

[4] The database is available under http://www.oanda.com.

company investment, an (partial or full) exit, or a write-off without sales revenues. Companies were valued up to 26 times. The average number of valuations per company is 6.2.

One-third of the company investments are fully exited. The rest are still held by the fund, and possibly partially exited. Only 29% of all company investments were completely sold in the first disinvestment round. The typical (median) amount invested in a fund is €23.1 million, and €2.2 million in a single company. The average amount invested in a fund is €13.3 million, and €1.3 million. There is a significant difference between median (typical) and medium (average) value. This is characteristic of many aspects in the private equity industry, because there are many outliers.

We find that only 30% were completely divested in one transaction, which is in contradiction to the findings of Cumming and MacIntosh (2003) who suggest, using a Canadian sample, that partial exits are rare.

11.5.1 Average and median valuation over fund life

We first investigate the ratio of reported value for exited and non-exited company investments to invested amount as a function of investment duration. Figure 11.1 shows that the median is one until quartile seven, and then declines. The situation is less pronounced for the mean value. One possible explanation is that the valuation is at cost in the first years according to standard practice, and then the fund managers shift to fair-value with write-downs or new information coming from third-party transactions. Interestingly, the median valuation decreases considerably more than the average. This is mostly due to bad investments being written-down or written-off, the sold investments being of better value than the remaining company investments. The difference

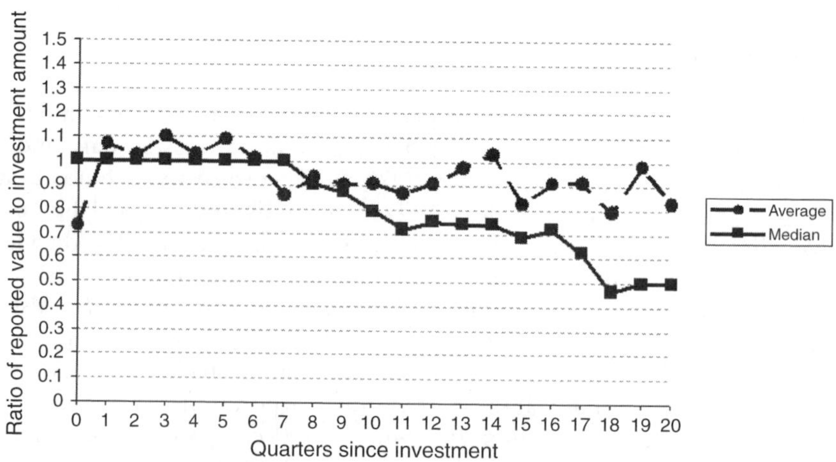

Figure 11.1 Decline of valuation after two years. The ratio of reported value to investment amount by quarters since first investment is shown. The company valuations and investment amounts are gathered from funds' reports. The average and median are calculated for the period from 1998 to 2004

between average and median is typical of private equity numbers. A few well-performing companies more than compensate for weak performance of the majority of (or typical) companies.

11.5.2 Difference between last valuation and exit price

We use the following measure to determine the accuracy of the fund manager's valuation by comparing the last valuation before the exit with the actual exit price:

$$\text{Difference} = \frac{\text{Valuation} - \text{Exit Price}}{\text{Investment Amount}} \tag{11.1}$$

We scale the difference by the investment amount to be able to compare between different company valuations. It is also possible to divide by valuation. The advantage is that the underlying performance does not influence the scaling, but other issues arise such as how to treat valuations that are set to zero for accounting reasons but are not yet exited. In any case, a positive value indicates that the fund manager has overvalued the company investment before the sale. A negative value shows an undervaluation. The duration between the last valuation date and the exit date is typically less than three months and randomly distributed within the three months.

The average difference is −0.23, and the median difference is 0.00. Fund managers therefore undervalue their investments by an average amount of 23% of the invested capital. However, when we plotted valuation difference against time interval between last valuation date and exit date, we did not find a trend of decreasing valuation accuracy with increasing time interval.

Figure 11.2 shows that there are far more extreme undervaluations, which causes the average difference to be negative. We hypothesize that two things prevent managers from overvaluing: the conservative valuation rules are slow to catch significant value gains, and the inability to predict an exceptional performing company. The median amount is zero, which indicates that in the majority of sales (that is typical sales) the valuation is close to the sales price. It is also possible that the sales price could already be known at that time. However, when we plotted valuation difference against time interval between last valuation date and exit date, we did not find a trend of decreasing valuation accuracy with increasing time interval.

Next we investigate whether valuation difference depends on investment duration. The pattern of undervaluation is consistent across all quarters since investment (see Figure 11.3). The median is close to zero, and the average fluctuates below the zero line. The average undervaluation is most apparent during the boom year 2000 (see Figure 11.4). We only show the years from 2000 to 2004, because earlier years had fewer than 20 data points. The fund managers undervalued their investment for each year, and especially in the boom year 2000 with an undervaluation of 140%. We also looked at various subsamples over the exit year, and found the strongest effect for VC companies, and non-first-time funds in the year 2000. We conclude that the undervaluation is mainly the result of exceptionally well-performing companies in 2000. The valuation practice is not able to capture these investments because of the constraints imposed by the valuation and reporting guidelines. This fits well with the fact that such investments occur most

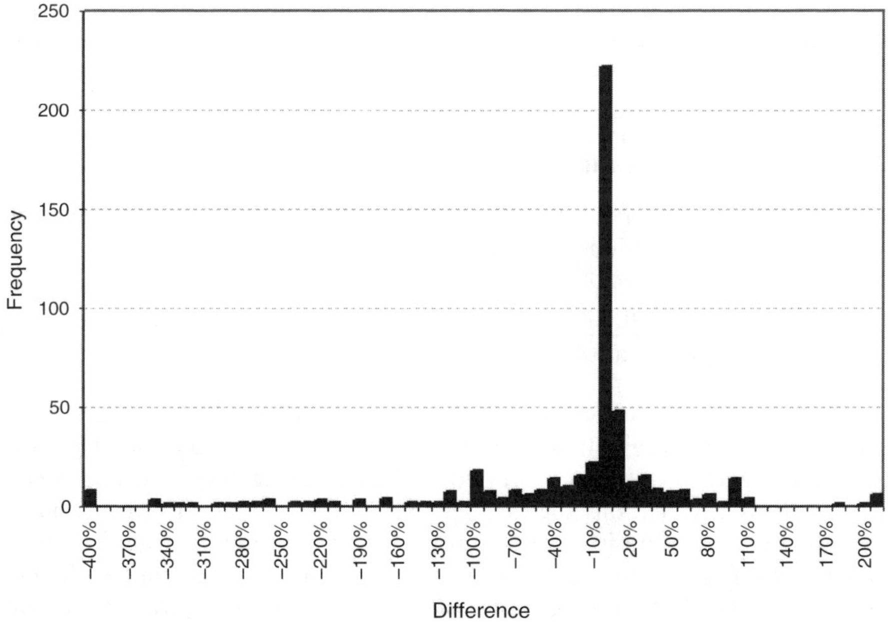

Figure 11.2 Distribution of valuation differences. The frequencies of each interval for the period from 1998 to 2004 are shown. The invervals refer to the average differences between last valuations of the company to exit price, shown as a percentage of the investment amount. The company valuations, exit prices, and investment amounts are gathered from funds' reports

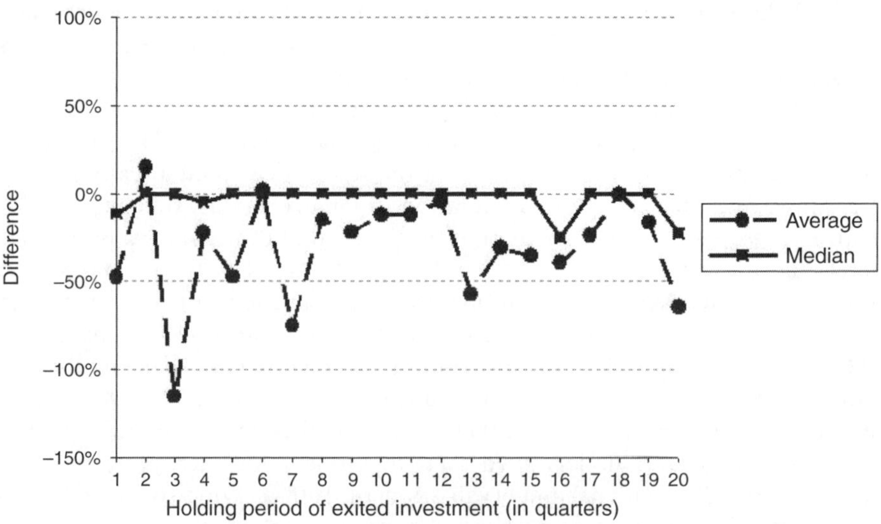

Figure 11.3 Undervaluation for all periods until exit. The difference between last valuation and exit price is shown as a percentage of investment amount by quarters since first investment. The company valuations, exit prices and investment amounts are gathered from funds' reports. The average and median are calculated for the period from 1998 to 2004

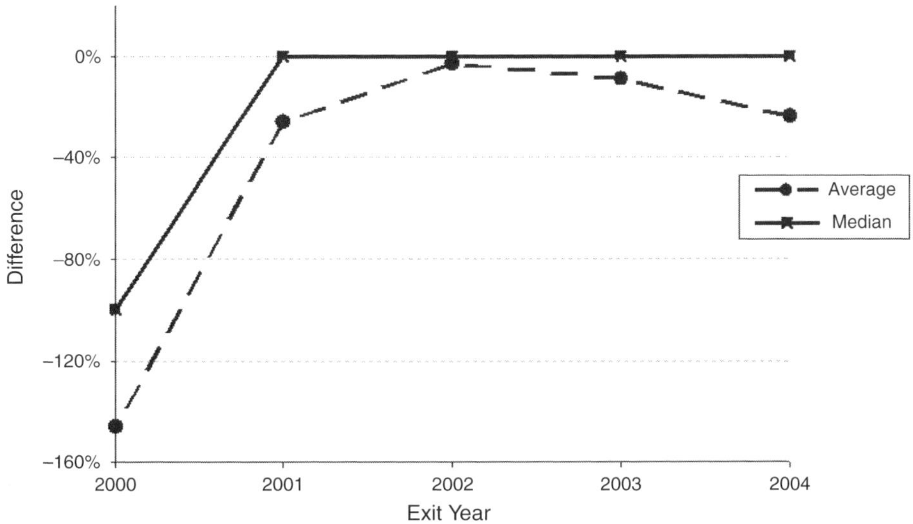

Figure 11.4 Highest undervaluation at exit in boom year 2000. The average difference between last valuation and exit price is shown as a percentage of investment amount by exit year. The company valuations, exit prices, and investment amounts are gathered from funds' reports

often in a boom year (here 2000), and for the VC segment. And at least in our sample non-first-time funds have more such investments.

A comparison between subsamples with respect to segment, experience, fund size, and technology shows that they are statistically significantly different (see Table A11.1 in the Appendix). However, the effect size (Cohen's *d*) is very small. The only substantial effect is on nature of disinvestment. Fund managers undervalue the companies to a lesser extent if they sell their complete company investment. The average difference for total exits is −0.16 compared with −0.46 for partial exits. We are not sure why this is the case. To summarize, we cannot confirm the findings of other researchers, namely Cumming and Walz (2004). We can only claim a strong influence from total or partial exit on valuation behavior. We believe that the methods and data used by Cumming and Walz do not allow for great accuracy. First, they use the IRR, which includes aspects of timing and amount. Second, they calibrate the unrealized IRR (which includes past cash flows and the valuation) with an estimation of realized IRR and not the actual exit. Third, they did not compute effect size, and cannot therefore distinguish between a strong or weak effect by an independent variable.

In order to analyze the dispersion, we also look at the absolute difference between last valuation and exit price. The average absolute difference is 0.59, and 0.12 for the median. The fund managers get their valuation wrong by 59% of the invested capital. However, most data points are close to zero, which indicates that the typical valuation before sale is quite accurate. In Figure 11.5 there is a secondary peak at 100%, which is due to complete write-offs of at-cost-held company investments. It is less clear why there should be a peak at −1. Again correlation analysis shows little effect on the valuation behavior from other factors, except whether there is a complete disinvestment or a partial one.

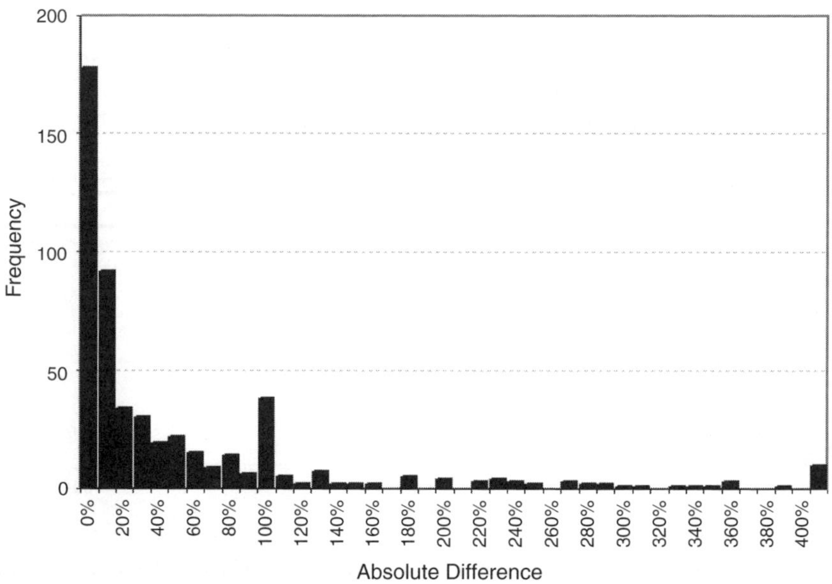

Figure 11.5 Distribution of absolute valuation differences. The frequencies of each interval for the period from 1998 to 2004 are shown. The intervals refer to the absolute average difference between last valuation and exit price shown as a percentage of investment amount. The company valuations, exit prices, and investment amounts are gathered from funds' reports

11.6 Conclusion

Our findings indicate that the valuations of private equity fund managers on average underestimate the exit price. Such undervaluation seems to be due to the conservative valuation guidelines and the inability of managers to account for exceptionally well-performing company investments. Unlike other studies, we find little evidence that factors such as experience, market segment, or fund size significantly influence the valuation behavior. There are statistically significant differences, but the size of the difference (effect size) is almost always negligible. The only exceptions are partial exits: the fund manager values a company more accurately before a total exit than before a partial exit.

Acknowledgments

We would like to thank the fund investor for access to their database and their professionals for answering our queries. The fund investor would like to remain anonymous, and we have ensured that no confidential information is contained in this chapter, based on feedback from them. Tom Weidig was responsible for the editorial part and involved at the analysis and discussion level. Andreas Kemmerer had the initial idea, access to the data, and contact with the fund investor. Mark Wahrenburg gave support, input, and feedback. He and Andreas Kemmerer supervised Tadeusz Lutoborski who filtered and analyzed the data for his Diploma thesis.

References

Blotevogel, R. (2005). A Principle-Agent Approach to Understanding the Net Asset Value in VC. Bachelor Thesis, University of Birmingham, AL.

Cohen, J. (1988). *Statistical Power Analysis for the Behavioural Sciences*. Mahwah NJ: Lawrence Erlbaum Associates.

Cumming, D.J. and MacIntosh, J.G.(2003). A Cross-Country Comparison of Full and Partial Venture Capital Exits. *Journal of Banking and Finance*, 27(3):511–548.

Cumming, D.J. and Walz, U. (2004). Private Equity Returns and Disclosure Around the World. EFA 2004 Maastricht Meetings Paper No. 4233 (28 March 2004). Available at SSRN: http://ssrn.com/abstract=514105

Gompers, P.A. and Lerner, J. (2000). Money Chasing Deals? The Impact of Fund Inflows on the Valuation of Private Equity Investments. *Journal of Financial Economics*, 55(2):281–325.

Grabenwarter, U. and Weidig, T. (2005). *Exposed to the J-Curve: Understanding and Managing Private Equity Fund Investments*. London: Euromoney Books.

Kaplan, S.N. and Schoar, A. (2003). Private Equity Returns: Persistence and Capital Flows. Working Paper, University of Chicago, Chicago.

Kemmerer, A. and Weidig, T. (2005). Reporting Value to the Private Equity Fund Investor. Available at SSRN: http://ssrn.com/abstract=762305.

Welpe, I. (2004). *Venture-Capital-Geber und Ihre Portfoliounternehmen: Erfolgsfaktoren der Kooperationen*. Wiesbaden: Gabler Edition Wissenschaft.

Appendix

Table A11.1 Comparison between subsamples

	Percent	Min	Max	Median	Average	Standard deviation	Correlation (Spearman)	K-S test[a]	Difference test[b]	Effect size[c]	Percent change[d]
Sum	100%	−9.35	5.95	0.00	−0.27	1.16		0.000			
Exit year											
till 1998	3%	−1.00	0.00	0.00	−0.30	0.43	−0.062	0.000	0.000′**		
1999	2%	−5.74	0.00	−1.00	−1.41	1.96	−0.124**	0.001			
2000	7%	−9.35	0.54	−1.00	−1.46	2.05	−0.241**	0.000			
2001	15%	−5.45	4.58	0.00	−0.26	1.32	0.014	0.000			
2002	20%	−3.37	2.32	0.00	−0.03	0.76	0.132**	0.000			
2003	25%	−3.49	5.95	0.00	−0.09	0.82	0.048	0.000			
2004	28%	−8.23	2.30	0.00	−0.24	1.07	0.23	0.000			
Investment year											
until 1998	24%	−5.74	1.71	0.00	−0.40	1.02	−0.102*	0.000	0.072′		
1999	20%	−9.35	4.58	0.00	−0.40	1.50	−0.044	0.000			
2000	31%	−8.23	3.89	0.00	−0.28	1.13	0.024	0.000			
2001	12%	−3.57	5.95	0.00	−0.02	1.05	0.069	0.000			
2002	9%	−6.01	1.01	0.00	−0.10	1.03	0.057	0.000			
2003	3%	−0.47	1.00	0.00	0.03	0.29	0.045	0.001			
2004	1%	0.00	2.30	0.00	0.77	1.33	0.057				
First time fund?											
Yes	78%	−9.35	5.95	0.00	−0.27	1.16	−0.004	0.000	0.929″	0.01	−5
No	22%	−7.00	4.58	0.00	−0.28	1.21					

Large fund?											
Yes	56%	−9.35	5.95	0.00	−0.30	1.25	−0.034	0.000	0.440″	0.05	24
No	44%	−8.23	3.89	0.00	−0.24	1.05					
Venture capital?											
Yes	62%	−9.35	5.95	0.00	−0.26	1.18	0.011	0.000	0.797″	0.04	−14
No	38%	−8.23	3.89	0.00	−0.30	1.14					
Technology?											
Yes	64%	−9.35	5.95	0.00	−0.25	1.23	0.037	0.000	0.395″	0.05	−18
No	36%	−8.23	1.71	0.00	−0.31	1.05					
Total exit?											
Yes	63%	−9.35	5.95	0.00	−0.16	1.15	0.200**	0.000	0.000″**	0.27	−66
No	37%	−7.00	4.58	−0.03	−0.46	1.17					

Descriptive statistics, correlations, difference tests, and effect size test for the analysed variable are presented. The analysed variable is calculated as the difference between last valuation and exit price shown as a percentage of investment amount. The company valuations, exit prices and investment amount are gathered from funds' reports. A single (double) asterisk indicates that the number is statistically significant on the 5% (1%) level.

[a] The K-S test determines whether two datasets differ significantly.

[b] The difference test tests the hypothesis that several means are equal.

[c] The effect size (Cohen's *d*) shows how large the difference is. A Cohen's *d* between −0.15 and +0.15 signals a negligible effect, a Cohen's *d* between | 0.15 | and | 0.40 | signals a small effect and a Cohen's *d* larger than | 0.40 | and less than | 0.75 | signals a medium effect.

[d] The difference between two averages shown as a percentage.

12 A search model of venture capital, entrepreneurship, and unemployment

Robin Boadway, Oana Secrieru, and Marianne Vigneault

Abstract

In this chapter, we develop a search model of venture capital in which the number of successful matches of entrepreneurs and venture capitalists at any moment in time is a function of the number of entrepreneurs searching for funds, the number of venture capitalists searching for entrepreneurs, and the number of vacancies posted by each venture capitalist. We show that, in the market equilibrium, the level of advice offered by VC companies is inefficiently low compared with the social optimum. Furthermore, the number of vacancies, the level of employment, and the number of potential entrepreneurs are generally either too low or too high relative to their socially optimal level. Policy to achieve the social optimum consists of a capital gains subsidy, an employment tax or subsidy, and an investment tax or subsidy.

12.1 Introduction

Venture capitalists specialize in screening and monitoring projects in particular industries, and in financing small entrepreneurs in those industries. Venture capitalists also offer valuable advice to these small and young firms, which helps them to overcome difficulties arising from their lack of business experience, and enhances their ability to turn a good idea into a profitable enterprise. The specialized screening and monitoring abilities of VC companies makes them informed investors and enables them to reduce the agency costs between entrepreneurs and outside investors (Casamatta, 2002; Amit et al., 1998; Admati and Pfleiderer, 1994; Chan, 1983). Moreover, the presence of venture capitalists in the market increases welfare by helping entrepreneurs to offer high-return projects (Chan, 1983). Indeed, the existing evidence suggests that firms backed by venture capitalists are more innovative, speed up their time to market, and grow faster than their industry counterparts (Hirukawa and Ueda, 2003; Keuschnigg, 2002; Hellmann and Puri, 2000; Kortum and Lerner, 2000; OECD, 1996).

The evidence also shows that a large VC firm can receive up to 1000 investment proposals each year, but it finances only about a dozen of them (Sahlman, 1990). This indicates that experienced VC is scarce, possibly because of the slow entry of experienced venture capitalists. We assume in our model that VC is in limited supply. Therefore, an entrepreneur who has a business idea but no funds may or may not find a venture capitalist that can screen and invest in the project. To capture this idea, we employ a simple stylized search model of VC where the number of successful matches of entrepreneurs and venture capitalists at any moment in time is a function of the number of entrepreneurs searching for funds, the number of VC firms searching for entrepreneurs, and the number of vacancies posted by each venture capitalist.[1] Our model is a static analogue to the usual dynamic search model, which simplifies the analysis considerably without sacrificing the basic insight of search models.[2] We use our model to examine the implications of imperfect matching for the level of employment and the level of frictional unemployment. These are important issues in the debate on the role of government's involvement in providing incentives for entrepreneurial activity. The rationale for government intervention is that entrepreneurship has been identified as a key component in an economy's ability to grow and alleviate high unemployment.

Our study extends the literature on entrepreneurship in three ways. First, it includes search unemployment. Second, it explicitly models the occupational choice of individuals to become workers or entrepreneurs. Third, our model explicitly incorporates the role of venture capitalists as informed investors who have superior knowledge of a particular industry and have superior screening skills. These qualities provide an important motivation for potential entrepreneurs to engage a venture capitalist as a means of screening their projects. Optimal policy in our model involves correcting for inefficiencies created by entrepreneurs' employment decisions, VC companies' decisions in screening projects and advising entrepreneurs, and the occupational choices of individuals to become workers or entrepreneurs.

The remainder of the chapter is organized as follows. Section 12.2 sets up the model and examines the various decisions made by entrepreneurs and venture capitalists. The social optimum is then examined in Section 12.3, and is followed in Section 12.4 by an analysis of the government policies that can achieve it. Section 12.5 offers concluding comments.

12.2 The model

The economy comprises F venture capitalists and I individuals. Both F and I are fixed, and I is a large number. Individuals can become entrepreneurs, workers, or unemployed. Entrepreneurs have no initial wealth; if they become entrepreneurs, they need external financing to start a project. The project requires an initial investment, k. A venture capitalist provides the initial investment and business advice in exchange for a share, α, of the new business' profits. As workers, individuals are identical, but if an individual becomes an entrepreneur, then the individual is one of two types, 1 or 2, that differs according to the project's probability of success. There is a fixed proportion, z, of type 2 individuals. Projects undertaken by type 1 entrepreneurs are assumed, for simplicity, to have zero probability of success. The probability of success of a type 2's project, p, depends on the managerial advice provided by the venture capitalist, a; that is, $p = p(a)$, and is increasing and concave. Advice is critical for the success of the project, and thus $p(0) = 0$. If successful, the entrepreneur of type 2 employs labor according to the production technology, $f(l)$, with $f'(\cdot) \geq 0$ and $f''(\cdot) < 0$, and workers are paid the wage w.

[1] For example, see Pissarides (2000) for the standard labor market search model. Inderst and Muller (2004), Michelacci and Suarez (2002), and Keuschnigg (2002) also employ a search model of VC, although their focus is different from ours.

[2] See Johnson and Layard (1986) for the static search model. Boadway et al. (2004) have shown that the static model is analogous to the steady-state version of the dynamic model.

For simplicity, projects that are unsuccessful produce no output, and their workers receive no wages.

An important assumption of the model is that individuals do not know their type prior to making their occupational choice. This assumption captures the notion that the VC company has superior knowledge of the industry, and thus the entrepreneur engages a venture capitalist to screen a project in order to determine whether it is worthwhile. In this setting, we denote by P the number of the I individuals who decide to become potential entrepreneurs. VC financing is scarce, and so not all potential entrepreneurs are 'matched' with a venture capitalist. We denote by v the 'vacancy' rate of financiers. Creating a vacancy is costly because it entails the screening of potential entrepreneurs. The screening process is assumed to be perfect, and so only potential entrepreneurs of type 2 are taken on by the venture capitalist. Costly screening thus creates frictions in the VC market, and these frictions are captured by a matching function, $x(P, vF)$, which is increasing, concave, continuously differentiable in both arguments, and homogeneous of degree one (i.e. constant returns to scale). The matching function gives the number of matches that result per unit time.

The probability that a vacancy is matched with a potential entrepreneur is:

$$\frac{x(P, vF)}{vF} = x\left(\frac{P}{vF}, 1\right) \equiv q(\theta), \tag{12.1}$$

where

$$\theta = P/vF \tag{12.2}$$

is a measure of the scarcity of VC. Similarly, the probability that a potential entrepreneur is matched with a vacancy is:

$$\frac{x(P, vF)}{vF} = \frac{vF}{P}x\left(\frac{P}{vF}, 1\right) = \frac{1}{\theta}q(\theta). \tag{12.3}$$

We denote the elasticity of $q(\theta)$ by $\eta(\theta)$. By the properties of the matching function, $q'(\theta) \geq 0$ and $0 < \eta(\theta) < 1$.

The venture capitalist incurs three separate costs. The first is the cost of creating a vacancy, δ, associated with the screening of projects, and is increasing and strictly convex in the number of vacancies that are successfully matched and screened; that is, $\delta'(q(\theta)v) > 0$ and $\delta''(\cdot) > 0$. The venture capitalist also incurs a cost when advising a type 2 entrepreneur. A linear advice cost function, ga, is assumed for simplicity. The final cost incurred by the venture capitalist is the financing cost of the initial investment, k, at the exogenous interest rate, r.

In the market equilibrium, the sequence of events is as follows:

- Stage 1: Occupational choice – individuals choose whether to become potential entrepreneurs or workers.
- Stage 2: Matching and screening – venture capitalists choose the number of vacancies. Venture capitalists and potential entrepreneurs are matched according to a matching function and screening takes place. Potential entrepreneurs who do not find a match and those who do find a match, but are screened to be of type 1, become unemployed.

- Stage 3: Bargaining – following a successful match and screening, the venture capitalists and the entrepreneurs bargain over the division of profits.
- Stage 4: Choice of advice – the venture capitalists choose the level of managerial advice.
- Stage 5: Hiring – the success of the projects is revealed and entrepreneurs hire labor.

The equilibrium concept we use for solving this game is that of subgame perfection. Therefore, we begin by first solving for stage 5.

12.2.1 Stage 5: the entrepreneur's choice of labor

Recall that only type 2 entrepreneurs have survived the screening process in the final stage of the game. We assume that if entrepreneurs are not successful, they become unemployed and receive zero revenues. In this case, their workers are laid off and receive no pay. At this stage, a, α, w, v, and θ have been determined in previous stages. A representative entrepreneur of type 2 chooses labor to maximize expected profits. Recall that the project is successful with probability p and the entrepreneur obtains a share $(1-\alpha)$ of profits. With probability $(1-p)$ the project fails and the entrepreneur receives zero revenues.[3] The entrepreneur's problem in selecting labor is to:

$$\max_{l}(1-\alpha)p(a)[f(l)-wl]. \tag{12.4}$$

The solution to the entrepreneur's problem solves the first-order condition:

$$f'(l)=w \tag{12.5}$$

That is, workers are paid the marginal product of labor. Condition (12.5) determines $l(w)$, with $(\partial l/\partial w)<0$, as expected. Substituting $l(w)$ into the entrepreneur's objective function defines the profit function, $\pi^{\mathrm{E}}(a, w, \alpha)$.

12.2.2 Stage 4: the venture capitalist's choice of advice

At this stage, the venture capitalist chooses the amount of advice, a, for each of the entrepreneurs in their portfolio so as to maximize profits, taking α, w, v, and θ as given. Given the homogeneity of type 2 entrepreneurs, we know that the equilibrium involves the symmetric treatment of all entrepreneurs taken on by the VC firm. Furthermore, the assumption of a linear advice cost function implies that we can examine the venture capitalist's choice of advice for a representative type 2 entrepreneur. The venture capitalist's problem is therefore to:

$$\max_{a}\alpha p(a)(f(l)-wl)-(1+r)k-ga-\delta(q(\theta)v). \tag{12.6}$$

The first-order condition,

$$\alpha p'(a)(f(l)-wl)-g=0 \tag{12.7}$$

[3] Allowing individuals to receive an exogenous outside income in the event of failure does not alter our results. Consequently, to simplify the notation, we assume that individuals earn zero income if entrepreneurs are unsuccessful.

determines the optimal advice function, $a(\alpha, w)$. The second-order condition for a maximum

$$D = \alpha p''(a)(f(l) - wl) < 0 \tag{12.8}$$

is satisfied. Substituting $a(\alpha, w)$ into the venture capitalist's objective function defines the profit function, $\pi^{V}(a, w, v, k, \theta)$ for a representative project. Total differentiation of (12.7) gives:

$$\frac{\partial a}{\partial \alpha} = -\frac{p'(f(l) - wl)}{D} > 0; \tag{12.9}$$

$$\frac{\partial a}{\partial w} = \frac{\alpha p' l}{D} < 0. \tag{12.10}$$

Thus, as one would expect, a higher share of profits provides the venture capitalist with incentives to supply more advice, and an increase in the wage rate reduces the VC companies' payoff and, thus, their incentive to supply advice.

12.2.3 Stage 3: Nash bargaining

At this stage, the venture capitalist bargains individually with each entrepreneur, given w, v, and θ. The venture capitalist and the entrepreneur anticipate $a(\alpha, w)$ and $l(w)$ determined at stages 4 and 5, respectively. The Nash bargaining problem is:

$$\max_{\alpha} [\pi^{E}]^{\beta}[\pi^{V} - k]^{1-\beta}, \tag{12.11}$$

where π^{E} is determined in stage 5 and π^{V} is determined in stage 4. The entrepreneurs' bargaining power is denoted by $\beta \in (0, 1)$. The threat point for the entrepreneur is zero because the entrepreneur obtains zero profits in the event that bargaining with the venture capitalist is unsuccessful. The threat point for the VC firm is the initial investment, k, because they get to keep the initial investment in the event that bargaining with the entrepreneur is unsuccessful.

The optimal equity share, $\alpha(w, v, \theta)$, solves the following first-order condition:[4]

$$\pi^{E} = \beta\Phi + \beta[\pi^{V} - k](1 - \alpha)\frac{(p')^2}{\alpha p''}, \tag{12.12}$$

where $\Phi \equiv \pi^{E} + \pi^{V} - k$ is the total surplus to be divided between the entrepreneur and the venture capitalist. The second term in (12.12) is negative by the properties of the probability function $p(a)$, which gives rise to the following proposition:

Proposition 1: In equilibrium, the entrepreneur obtains a share of the surplus that is smaller than their bargaining power, β.

[4] The proof is provided in the Appendix.

The reasoning for proposition 1 is straightforward. From (12.9), providing the venture capitalist with a larger share of the surplus induces an increase in the venture capitalist's provision of advice, which benefits both the venture capitalist and the entrepreneur. Thus, the entrepreneur is willing to accept a smaller share of the surplus, because doing so increases the expected size of the surplus.

12.2.4 Stage 2: choice of vacancies

The venture capitalist chooses the number of vacancies so as to maximize expected profits, taking as given θ and w and anticipating $a(\alpha, w)$, $l(w)$, and $\alpha(w, v, \theta)$, which are determined at the later stages. The venture capitalist's problem is to:

$$\max_{v} q(\theta)v(1-z)[\alpha p(a)(f(l)-wl)-ga-(1+r)k]-\delta(q(\theta)v). \qquad (12.13)$$

The optimal number of vacancies, $v(w, \theta)$, solves the first-order condition:

$$(1-z)[\alpha p(a)(f(l)-wl)-ga-(1+r)k]+v(1-z)p(a)(f(l)-wl)\frac{\partial \alpha}{\partial v}-\delta'=0. \qquad (12.14)$$

12.2.5 Stage 1: occupational choice

Individuals choose whether to become workers or entrepreneurs by comparing the expected payoffs in each situation. In doing so, individuals anticipate $l(w)$, $a(\alpha, w)$, $\alpha(w, v, \theta)$, and $v(w, \theta)$, determined at later stages. An individual who decides to become a worker obtains wages, w, with probability p. An individual who decides to become an entrepreneur obtains profits, π^E, provided that the individual obtains a match with a venture capitalist and is screened to be of type 2. In equilibrium, an individual is indifferent between becoming a worker or an entrepreneur. This implies that the following occupational-choice equilibrium condition must hold:

$$pw=\frac{1}{\theta}q(\theta)(1-z)\pi^E. \qquad (12.15)$$

Equation (12.15) determines the wage rate, $w(\theta)$, which can be either increasing or decreasing in θ.

12.2.6 The market equilibrium

Solving stages 1 through 5 backwards provides the recursive solution for the market equilibrium values of l, a, α, v, and w as functions of θ. If we denote by E the total number of entrepreneurs, E must be equal to the number of venture capitalists multiplied by the number of vacancies screened and filled by each venture capitalist:

$$E=(1-z)q(\theta)Fv. \qquad (12.16)$$

Furthermore, equilibrium in the labor market requires that individuals become either entrepreneurs or workers:

$$P+lE=I. \qquad (12.17)$$

Equations (12.16) and (12.17) and the definition of θ given in (12.2) determine the market equilibrium values for θ, E, and P.

12.2.7 Unemployment

We denote by $\hat{U}$ the number of ex-ante unemployed. We define ex-ante unemployment as the level of unemployment before it becomes known which entrepreneurs' projects are successful. Ex-ante unemployment therefore results only from matching frictions in the market for VC. Since the total number of potential entrepreneurs, P, is equal to the total number of entrepreneurs, E, plus the number of unemployed, $\hat{U}$, it follows that

$$\hat{U} = P - E. \tag{12.18}$$

Ex-post unemployment, on the other hand, also includes workers and entrepreneurs who become unemployed because of the failure of entrepreneurs' projects. If we denote ex-post unemployment by $\bar{U}$, the number of ex-post unemployed is given by:

$$\bar{U} = \hat{U} + (1-p)(1+l)E. \tag{12.19}$$

12.3 The social optimum

Since all agents are risk-neutral and care only about expected income, we can abstract from redistributive motives and treat aggregate output or GDP as an index of social welfare. GDP is given by:

$$Y = F\{(1-z)q(\theta)v[p(a)f(l) - ga - (1+r)k] - \delta(q(\theta)v)\}. \tag{12.20}$$

The social optimum is said to be constrained Pareto efficient when l, a, and v maximize GDP subject to (12.16), (12.17), and (12.2). From (12.17), the optimal choices of l and v determine the optimal division of individuals between entrepreneurs and workers. That is, (12.17) determines the optimal number of potential entrepreneurs, P.

For the social optimum, equations (12.16), (12.17), and (12.2) can be solved for the scarcity of venture capital function, $\theta(l, v)$, the properties of which are:

$$\frac{\partial\theta}{\partial l} = -\frac{E}{\Delta} < 0, \tag{12.21}$$

$$\frac{\partial\theta}{\partial v} = -F\frac{\theta + (1-z)q(\theta)l}{\Delta} < 0, \tag{12.22}$$

where $\Delta = Fv\{1 + l(1-z)q'(\theta)] > 0$. Equation (12.21) shows that an increase in the number of workers, l, by reducing the number of potential entrepreneurs makes VC less scarce. Equation (12.22) shows the effect of an increase in the number of vacancies on θ. An increase in v increases the fraction of entrepreneurs who fail each period, and decreases the number of potential entrepreneurs who find a match each period. VC becomes less scarce as a result.

The planner's problem can be treated as an unconstrained one by using the function $\theta(l, v)$ obtained above from (12.16), (12.17), and (12.2). For this problem, the first-order conditions for the social optimum are:

$$\frac{\partial Y}{\partial l} = F\left\{(1-z)q(\theta)vpf'(l) + [\Psi(1-z) - \delta']vq'\frac{\partial\theta}{\partial l}\right\} = 0, \tag{12.23}$$

$$\frac{\partial Y}{\partial a} = F(1-z)qv[p'f(l) - g] = 0, \tag{12.24}$$

$$\frac{\partial Y}{\partial v} = F\left\{(1-z)q\Psi - \delta' q + [\Psi(1-z) - \delta']vq'\frac{\partial\theta}{\partial v}\right\} = 0, \tag{12.25}$$

where $\Psi = p(a)f(l) - ga - (1+r)k$. These first-order conditions determine the socially optimal values l^*, a^*, and v^*. Then, from (12.16) and (12.17), we obtain the optimal number of potential entrepreneurs P^*, and, from (12.18) and (12.19), we obtain the optimal levels of ex-ante and ex-post unemployment.

A comparison of the first-order conditions for the social optimum with those of the no-intervention or laissez-faire market equilibrium given in (12.5), (12.7), and (12.14) gives rise to the following proposition:

Proposition 2: Employment, advice, the number of vacancies, the supply of entrepreneurship, and unemployment in the laissez-faire market equilibrium are inefficient.

To see this, we evaluate the derivatives of GDP with respect to l, a, and v given in (12.23), (12.24), and (12.25) at the laissez-faire market equilibrium. Doing so gives:

$$\frac{\partial Y}{\partial l}\bigg|_{\text{mkt}} = F\left\{(1-z)qvw + (\Psi(1-z) - \delta')\, vq'\frac{\partial\theta}{\partial l}\right\} \gtreqless 0, \tag{12.26}$$

$$\frac{\partial Y}{\partial a}\bigg|_{\text{mkt}} = F(1-z)qv[(1-\alpha)p'f + \alpha p'wl] > 0, \tag{12.27}$$

$$\frac{\partial Y}{\partial v}\bigg|_{\text{mkt}} = F\left\{q(1-z)\left((1-\alpha)pf + \alpha pwl - vp(f - wl)\frac{\partial\alpha}{\partial v}\right)\right.$$
$$\left. + (\Psi(1-z) - \delta')\, vq'\frac{\partial\theta}{\partial v}\right\} \gtreqless 0. \tag{12.28}$$

Equation (12.26) reflects the effect of an increase in l, starting from the market equilibrium, on social welfare. Beginning with the market's selection of employment, entrepreneurs choose labor to maximize their own profits, taking the wage as a cost and ignoring the effects of their choice of employment on workers' welfare and total expected output via the cost of additional vacancies of venture capitalists. The first effect is positive; that is, an increase in the level of employment increases workers' welfare and total output. The latter effect is a matching externality, in that an increase in employment, by reducing the number of potential entrepreneurs, decreases the scarcity of VC. In equilibrium, the venture capitalists respond by increasing vacancies. The second term in (12.26) is, thus, negative. The total effect of an increase in l on social welfare is, as a consequence, ambiguous. If the effect of an increase in l on workers' welfare dominates the matching externality effect, the right-hand side of (12.26) is positive. That is, an increase in l increases welfare and the employment level is inefficiently low compared with the social optimum. The reverse is true if the matching externality effect dominates. The employment level is, thus, inefficiently low or high, depending on which effect dominates.

Equation (12.27) shows the effect of an increase in the level of advice, starting from the market equilibrium, on social welfare. The venture capitalists' choice of advice considers only their own share of profits, which includes labor costs, and is thus inefficiently low compared with the social optimum. An increase in the level of advice above the market equilibrium increases welfare.

Equation (12.28) reflects the effect of an increase in the number of vacancies, starting from the market equilibrium, on social welfare. The venture capitalists select the number of vacancies by taking into account the effect of v on their own profits and ignoring the effect on the entrepreneurs' share of profits and on the cost of additional vacancies of all venture capitalists. The latter is a matching externality, in that an increase in v increases vacancies by (i) increasing the flow out of entrepreneurship, and (ii) decreasing the scarcity of VC.

Given that l and v are inefficient in the market equilibrium, so too are $P(= I - lE)$ and $E = (1 - z)q(\theta)Fv$. In particular, the number of potential and actual entrepreneurs may be inefficiently low or high, depending on the magnitudes of the various externalities described above. Similarly, given that l, E, and P are inefficient in the market equilibrium, the levels of ex-ante and ex-post unemployment defined in (12.18) and (12.19) are also inefficient. Thus, unemployment also may be too high or too low in the market equilibrium, compared with the social optimum.

12.4 Optimal policy

The social optimum can be achieved in the decentralized market setting if the government has at its disposal an appropriate set of policy instruments. The set we consider comprises an employment tax, τ, levied on entrepreneurs, a capital gains tax, t, levied on venture capitalists, and an investment tax, σ, levied on venture capitalists. An optimal policy must be such that the first-order conditions for l, a, and v for the market are equivalent to the first-order conditions for the social optimum given by (12.23), (12.24), and (12.25). Note that for l, a, and v to be chosen optimally, the tax rates must be chosen such that the Nash bargaining solution determines the 'optimal' division of profits and the occupational choice condition determines the 'optimal' wage rate; that is, the wage at which the optimal number of individuals choose to enter the entrepreneurship lottery.

With the set of policy instruments defined above, entrepreneurs' profits are written as:

$$(1 - \alpha)p(a)[f(l) - (w + \tau)l]. \tag{12.29}$$

Similarly, a venture capitalist's expected profits before screening has taken place can be written as:

$$q(\theta)(1 - z)\{(1 - t)[\alpha p(a)(f(l) - wl) - (1 + r + \sigma)k] - ga\}\,\delta(q(\theta)v). \tag{12.30}$$

With the inclusion of taxes, the market first-order conditions for the selection of l, a, and v are given by:

$$f'(l) = w + \tau, \tag{12.31}$$

$$(1-t)\alpha p'(f(l) - wl) - g = 0, \tag{12.32}$$

$$q(\theta)(1-z)(1-t)[\alpha p(a)(f(l) - wl) - (1+r+\sigma)k] + q(\theta)v(1-z)p(a)(f(l) - wl)\frac{\partial \alpha}{\partial v} - \delta' q(\theta) = 0. \tag{12.33}$$

A comparison of the first-order conditions (12.23), (12.24), and (12.25) with (12.31), (12.32), and (12.33) yields the results for optimal policy described in Sections 12.4.1–12.4.3.

12.4.1 Employment taxes

Proposition 3: The optimal employment tax is given by:

$$\tau^* = \{[1-(1-z)q(\theta^*)v^*p(a^*)]f'(l^*) - w^*\} + (\Psi(1-z) - \delta'(q(\theta^*)v^*))\, v^* q'(\theta^*)\frac{\partial \theta}{\partial l} \gtrless 0. \tag{12.34}$$

Intuitively, the employment tax is chosen so as to internalize the externalities caused by the entrepreneurs choosing the employment level without taking into account the effect of their choice on the total expected output and the cost of additional vacancies of venture capitalists. The first term in (12.34) is of ambiguous sign and the second term is positive according to (12.21). Since the expression on the right-hand side of (12.34) is of ambiguous sign, it follows that the government can tax or subsidize employment to achieve the social optimum. The government chooses to tax/subsidize employment such that the optimal tax/subsidy closes the gap between the employment level chosen by the entrepreneur and the socially optimal employment level:

$$\tau^* = \frac{\partial \pi^E}{\partial l}\Big|_{\tau=0} - \frac{\partial Y}{\partial l}. \tag{12.35}$$

12.4.2 Capital gains taxes

Proposition 4: The optimal capital gains tax is negative and given by:

$$t^* = 1 - \frac{f(l^*)}{\alpha^*(f(l^*) - w^* l^*)} < 0. \tag{12.36}$$

The intuition for Proposition 4 is straightforward. In the market equilibrium, venture capitalists provide a level of advice that is too low compared with the social optimum. In order to induce a higher level of advice, it is optimal for the government to subsidize capital gains. It is straightforward to show that the optimal capital gains subsidy closes the gap between the level of advice chosen by the venture capitalist and the socially optimal level of advice:

$$t^* = \frac{1}{\alpha p'(a)(f - wl)} \left\{ \frac{\partial \pi^V}{\partial a}\Big|_{t=0} - \frac{\partial Y}{\partial a} \right\}. \tag{12.37}$$

12.4.3 Investment taxes

Proposition 5: The optimal investment tax is:

$$\begin{aligned}\sigma^* = &\frac{1}{q(\theta^*)k}\Bigg\{q(\theta^*)\alpha^* p(a^*)(f(l^*) - w^* l^*) \\ &+ \frac{1}{(1-t^*)}(1-z)(\Psi - \delta'(q(\theta^*)v^*)v^* q'(\theta^*))\frac{\partial \theta}{\partial v} - \frac{q(\theta^*)p(a^*)f(l^*)}{(1-t^*)} \\ &+ \frac{q(\theta^*)t^*(1+r)k}{(1-t^*)} + q(\theta^*)v^* p(a^*)(f(l^*) - w^* l^*)\frac{\partial \alpha}{\partial v}\Bigg\} \gtreqless 0.\end{aligned} \tag{12.38}$$

As expected, the optimal investment tax can be negative or positive. The government chooses the optimal investment tax in order for venture capitalists to internalize the externalities that arise from their choice of vacancies. Thus, the optimal investment tax closes the gap between the number of vacancies chosen by the market and the socially optimal one:

$$\sigma^* = \frac{1}{kq(\theta^*)(1-z)(1-t^*)} \left\{ \frac{\partial \pi^V}{\partial v}\Big|_{\sigma=0} - \frac{\partial Y}{\partial v} \right\}. \tag{12.39}$$

From our discussion in the previous section, the optimal tax rates correct for the fact that both entrepreneurs and venture capitalists (i) do not take into account their choices on expected total output, (ii) include the wage as a cost, and (iii) do not take into account the matching externalities. We showed in the previous section that the level of advice in the market equilibrium is too low relative to the social optimum. Optimal policy therefore involves a capital gains subsidy (i.e. $t^* < 0$). The signs of the optimal employment tax and investment tax depend on the relative strengths of these three factors. Thus, it may be optimal to tax or subsidize employment and investment.

The set of three policy instruments we considered are sufficient to restore the inefficiencies arising in the market equilibrium. With the employment tax, capital gains tax, and the investment tax chosen optimally, the levels of employment, advice, and the number of vacancies become efficient. As a result, the number of entrepreneurs and potential entrepreneurs, and the levels of ex-ante and ex-post unemployment, are all efficient.

12.5 Conclusion

We have employed a search model of VC finance to examine venture capitalists' incentives to screen entrepreneurs' projects and to advise entrepreneurs. We have also examined individuals' occupational choice decisions and the implications of imperfect matching for the level of employment and the level of frictional unemployment. Our analysis has shown that, in the market equilibrium, the level of advice provided by the venture capitalist is inefficiently low compared with the social optimum because the venture capitalist considers only their own share of profits when selecting their level of advice. At the same time, the VC organization's portfolio size is inefficient from a social viewpoint because the venture capitalist ignores the additional effort cost on the part of entrepreneurs and on the cost of additional vacancies of all venture capitalists (i.e. the matching externality). These two effects work in opposite directions, and thus the size of the portfolio in the market equilibrium can be inefficiently low or high. We have also found that entrepreneurs' employment of labor can also be inefficiently low or high in the market equilibrium because entrepreneurs maximize their own profits without taking into account the effects of their choices on expected aggregate output and the cost of additional vacancies of all venture capitalists. This further implies that the number of potential entrepreneurs and the level of unemployment are inefficient. We have determined that an optimal policy to achieve the social optimum consists of: (i) a negative capital gains tax to achieve the socially optimal level of advice, (ii) an employment tax (or subsidy) on entrepreneurs to achieve the socially optimal level of employment, and (iii) an investment tax (or subsidy) to achieve the socially optimal number of vacancies. The optimal employment and investment taxes (or subsidies) ensure that the number of potential entrepreneurs, ex-ante and ex-post unemployment, are restored to their efficient levels.

An interesting extension of our model would be to allow for more than one type of entrepreneur to be taken on by the venture capitalist, which could result in shifts in the types of entrepreneurs that would receive VC financing in response to changes in the government's policy instruments. A further extension would be to allow entrepreneurs access to both VC and bank financing. In such a setting, it may be possible for banks to free-ride on screening undertaken by venture capitalists and offer entrepreneurs better financing terms that might entice them away from a VC organization. Incorporating both VC and bank financing into our model could also help identify factors that make VC financing more attractive than bank financing.

References

Admati, A.R. and Pfleiderer, P. (1994). Robust Financial Contracting and the Role of Venture Capitalists. *Journal of Finance*, 49(2):371–402.

Amit, R., Brander, J. and Zott, C. (1998). Why Do Venture Capital Firms Exist? Theory and Canadian Evidence. *Journal of Business Venturing*, 13(6):441–466.

Boadway, R., Cuff, K. and Marceau, N. (2004). Agglomeration Effects and the Competition for Firms. *International Tax and Public Finance*, 11(5):623–645.

Casamatta, C. (2002). *Financing and Advising: Optimal Financial Contracts with Venture Capitalists*. Centre for Economic Policy Research Discussion Paper, No. 3475. London.

Chan, Y.S. (1983). On the Positive Role of Financial Intermediation in Allocation of Venture Capital in a Market with Imperfect Information. *Journal of Finance*, 38(5):1543–1568.

Hellmann, T. and Puri, M. (2000). The Interaction Between Product Market and the Financing Strategy: The Role of Venture Capital. *Review of Financial Studies*, 13(4):959–984.
Hirukawa, M. and Ueda, M. (2003). *Venture Capital and Productivity*. Unpublished Working Paper. University of Wisconsin-Madison.
Inderst, R. and Muller, H. (2004). The Effect of Capital Market Characteristics on the Value of Start-Up Firms. *Journal of Financial Economics*, 72(2):319–356.
Johnson, G. and Layard, P. (1986). The Natural Rate of Unemployment: Explanation and Policy. In Ashenfelter, O.C. and Levard, R.G. (eds), *Handbook of Labor Economics, Vol. II*. Amsterdam: Elsevier, 921–999.
Keuschnigg, C. (2002). *Venture Capital Backed Growth*. University of St. Gallen, Discussion Paper No. 2002–04. St. Gallen, Switzerland.
Kortum, S. and Lerner, J. (2000). Assessing the Contribution of Venture Capital to Innovation. *RAND Journal of Economics*, 31(4):674–692.
Michelacci, C. and Suarez, J. (2002). *Business Creation and the Stock Market*. CEPR, Discussion Paper No. 3513. London.
Organization for Economic Cooperation and Development (1996). *Venture Capital and Innovation*. OCDE/GD(96)168. Paris.
Pissarides, C. (2000). *Equilibrium Unemployment Theory*. Cambridge MA and London: MIT Press.
Sahlman, W.A. (1990). The Structure and Governance of Venture-Capital Organization. *Journal of Financial Economics*, 27(2):473–521.

Appendix: Proof of equation (12.12)

The Nash bargaining problem is:

$$\max_{\alpha}[\pi^E]^{\beta}[\pi^V - k]^{1-\beta}, \tag{A12.1}$$

where

$$\pi^E = (1-\alpha)p(a)(f(l) - wl), \tag{A12.2}$$

$$\pi^V = \alpha p(a)(f(l) - wl) - (1+r)k - ga - \delta(q(\theta)v), \tag{A12.3}$$

The first-order condition is:

$$\beta[\pi^E]^{\beta-1}[\pi^V - k]^{1-\beta}\frac{d\pi^E}{d\alpha} + (1-\beta)[\pi^E]^{\beta}[\pi^V - k]^{-\beta}\frac{d\pi^V}{d\alpha} = 0, \tag{A12.4}$$

with

$$\frac{d\pi^E}{d\alpha} = \frac{\partial\pi^E}{\partial\alpha} + \frac{\partial\pi^E}{\partial a}\frac{\partial a}{\partial\alpha} = -p(a)(f(l) - wl)\left[1 + (1-\alpha)(f(l) - wl)\frac{(p')^2}{D}\right], \tag{A12.5}$$

and

$$\frac{d\pi^V}{d\alpha} = \frac{\partial\pi^V}{\partial\alpha} + \frac{\partial\pi^V}{\partial a}\frac{\partial a}{\partial\alpha} = p(a)(f(l) - wl). \tag{A12.6}$$

Gathering like terms, the first-order condition can be written as (12.12).

Part Three

Financing and Contracting

13 Capital structure in new technology-based firms: Venture capital-backed versus non-venture capital-backed firms in the Irish software sector

Teresa Hogan and Elaine Hutson

Abstract

We address the venture capital financing issue from the firm's perspective, using survey data for 110 new technology-based firms (NTBFs) in the indigenous Irish software sector. External finance for the sample firms largely comprises private equity, most of which is VC. Half of our sample firms – 49% – are venture capital-backed, and VC comprises 65% of their total financing requirement. For the remaining firms that do not have VC backing, more than two-thirds of their finance is sourced internally. Using the pecking order hypothesis as a theoretical framework, we examine several measures of founders' perceptions of information asymmetry, such as the extent to which they believe banks and venture capital providers understand their business.

13.1 Introduction

It is well understood by policymakers around the world that new technology-based firms (NTBFs) that develop technologically sophisticated products and services are important vehicles for innovation, and make a disproportionate contribution to economic growth and employment. Europe has lagged behind the U.S. in the development and growth of technology firms, and a common explanation for this is that the market for private equity – in particular venture capital – is not as well developed as it is in the U.S. (European Network for SME Research (ENSR), 2002; European Commission, 2001, 1999). Recent interest by policymakers, however, has not been matched by academic research on financing, particularly from the demand side. This is a serious shortcoming because NTBF owner-managers' financing decisions are not well understood. There is little comprehensive research on the capital structure of NTBFs, and we know virtually nothing about owner-managers' perceptions of the various potential providers of finance. If this is the case, how can we be sure that supply constraints explain the low levels of VC finance in Europe, rather than demand-side factors?

The Irish software sector provides an excellent laboratory for examining the financing decisions of NTBFs. Unlike many other European countries, Ireland has a well-developed

VC market, as venture capitalists from around the world followed the computer and biotechnology industries to Ireland during the 1990s. Most VC goes to the burgeoning indigenous software sector.[1] Using survey data, we examine the financing of 110 privately held indigenous software companies, half of which (54) are VC-backed. We address two questions. First, how different is the capital structure of VC-backed firms from non-VC-backed firms? In answering this question, we are able to get some idea of how the start-ups and the more established NTBFs that are not VC-backed finance their operations.

After presenting summary data for the sample – age and size (by number of employees and turnover) – we present and discuss the sources of finance for the 96 firms that provided detailed information on financing. VC-backed firms tend to be younger and larger than their non-VC-backed counterparts. There is a substantial difference in the capital structures of the two cohorts that extends beyond the simple VC-backed versus non-VC-backed dichotomy. Non-VC-backed firms, for example, make more use of consulting revenues and government grants to fund their operations.

In the second part of our chapter, we examine the survey responses to several questions and statements posed to firm founders relating to their attitudes to information asymmetries in bank and VC markets. It is well understood that bank lending to small and medium-sized firms (SMEs), and in particular NTBFs, is associated with information asymmetries that give rise to adverse selection and moral hazard (Stiglitz and Weiss, 1981). We find that VC-backed firm founders perceive greater information asymmetries in bank markets and lesser asymmetries in VC markets than their non-VC-backed counterparts.

13.2 Theoretical background and testable implications

Two main theories explain the broad and diverse range of observed capital structures. The static trade-off hypothesis suggests that there is an 'optimal' capital structure for each firm, which trades off the tax benefits of debt against the increasing likelihood of financial distress as leverage rises. The pecking order hypothesis (POH) of Myers (1984) and Myers and Majluf (1984) posits that as a result of information asymmetries between firms and providers of finance, internal sources are preferred over external, debt is the preferred source of outside finance, and equity is issued only as a last resort. In this paper we use the POH as a framework for examining NTBF financing decisions.

At the heart of the POH is the asymmetry of information between the company's management and 'uninformed' outside investors. This asymmetry implies that a new issue of equity signals overvaluation, and the POH predicts that in order to avoid this adverse signaling problem managers will finance projects from retained earnings where possible. Debt is the preferred outside source of finance because it is less sensitive to adverse signals.

While there has been mixed evidence on whether it holds in listed firms, most studies of small privately held firms provide strong support for the POH (Berggren et al., 2000; Cosh and Hughes, 1994). The rationale for this pattern of financing, however, cannot be the same for SMEs as it is for large firms. The information asymmetries discussed in Myers (1984) and Myers and Majluf (1984) arise from the separation of ownership and

[1] Irish-based manufacturers produce over 40% of all packaged software and 60% of all business software sold in Europe. Software contributes €13 billion annually to Irish GDP, of which €1.5 billion is attributable to the emerging cluster of indigenous software firms (National Informatics Directorate, 2004).

control, and this is not a feature of most small businesses. Stanworth and Gray (1991) explain the preference for internal sources of finance in SMEs by pointing out that small firm debt markets suffer from information asymmetries that give rise to moral hazard and adverse selection. Since the repayments on debt financing are fixed, debt holders face an asymmetric payoff. They do not participate in the additional returns generated if the firm is successful, but they share in the losses if the firm fails. As the owner-manager is the beneficiary if the firm is successful, SME borrowers have an incentive to 'gamble with the bank's money' and pursue high-risk projects. Adverse selection arises if debt providers such as banks have difficulties in discriminating between 'good' and 'bad' investment projects, resulting in financing constraints for all small business. Several studies have confirmed that adverse selection is a serious issue for SMEs (Michaelas et al., 1999; Berger and Udell, 1998; Chittenden et al., 1996; Binks and Ennew, 1994).

13.2.1 Information asymmetries in NTBFs

For NTBFs, as for SMEs generally, internal funds are the preferred financing source (Lindholm-Dahlstrand and Cetindamar, 2000; Bank of England, 1996; Roberts, 1991, 1990). There is some evidence, however, that NTBFs are less likely to issue debt than other small businesses, and therefore do not fit the standard pecking order. Hyytinen and Pajarinen (2002) find a negative relation between high technology and debt in Swedish SMEs, and U.S. and U.K. evidence on NTBFs is that debt is not the preferred source of outside funding at start-up (Moore, 1994; Brewer and Genay, 1994; Roberts, 1991, 1990) and on a continuing basis (Roberts, 1991, 1990; Oakey, 1984).

The main theoretical explanations for NTBFs' preference for equity over debt relate to asymmetry issues. NTBFs face worse information asymmetries in debt markets than the general population of SMEs (European Commission, 2003; Berger and Udell, 1998; Bank of England, 2001, 1996). High-technology investment projects are associated with greater 'technology uncertainty' than other SMEs; that is, banks do not understand high-technology businesses (European Commission, 2001; Bank of England, 1996; Deakins and Hussain, 1993; Oakey, 1984). For this reason, banks tend to avoid lending to NTBFs. Moral hazard is also a potentially serious problem in NTBFs, because monitoring research and development activity is particularly difficult for outsiders (Jordan et al., 1998).

Theory and evidence from studies of venture capitalists demonstrate that they are best equipped to overcome these information asymmetry and moral hazard problems (Gompers and Lerner, 2003; Amit et al., 1998). Their ongoing relationship with the firm allows venture capitalists to closely monitor and advise managers and, by ensuring that the owner-managers' interests are aligned with their own (Sahlman, 1990), reduce moral hazard. Information asymmetries are less likely because VC firms usually have in-depth knowledge of markets and technologies in specific fields (Norton and Tenenbaum, 1993; Ruhnka and Young, 1991; Gupta and Sapienza, 1991).

The POH gives rise to the following predictions for NTBFs. First, NTBFs perceive greater information asymmetries in debt markets than in VC markets. Second, VC-backed firms perceive greater information asymmetries in debt markets and lesser asymmetries in VC markets than their non-VC-backed counterparts. We address these issues by asking founders to respond to a series of statements relating to their perceptions of information asymmetries in bank and VC markets.

13.3 Survey and sample characteristics

The software sector is subdivided into 'products' and 'services'. Software services include consulting, implementation, support services, operations management, and training. Software product companies are those that are primarily involved in the development and commercialization of their own products, and these are the focus of our study. At the end of 2001 there were 257 indigenous software product SMEs in Ireland. The survey design is based on self-administered questionnaires using the tailored design method (Dillman, 1976, 2000). The number of valid returns was 117, giving an impressive response rate of just under 46%.[2]

Most respondents describe their position as founder and CEO (54%) or founder, technical director, and CEO (28%). The remaining 18% hold other key positions in the company. A total of 7% describe their roles as founder and technical director, 6% claim to be founder and sales/marketing director, and 2% are founder and chief operations officer. 'Other' includes two founders who are chairpersons and two founders who describe their role as joint CEO.

The number of VC-backed and non-VC-backed firms in the study is similar: 56 of the 110 firms (51%) for which survey data are available had not received VC backing, and 54 (49%) were funded by venture capitalists.[3] Of these 110 firms, 96 (41 VC-backed and 55 non-VC-backed firms) provided a detailed breakdown of current sources of finance.

Table 13.1 summarizes the age of the sample firms. Panel A shows that the youngest firm is less than 1 year old, and the oldest is 27 years. The average age is under 6 years (5.8 years), and the median is 4 years. The VC-backed firms are younger than the non-VC-backed; the mean age of the former was 4.8 years (median 3.5) at the time of the survey, and the latter group were on average 6.7 years old (median 5). The table also reports the number of firms in four age categories (Panel B). As seen in column [6], 60% of firms in the sample are less than 5 years established, and 81% are less than 10 years old. A total of 21 firms (almost 19%) are over 10 years old. Comparing the two groups, there are a higher proportion of non-VC-backed firms in both the youngest and oldest age categories. Ten (17.9%) of the non-VC-backed firms are less than 2 years old compared with five (9.3%) of the VC-backed firms. A total of 17 (30.4%) of the non-VC-backed firms are at least 10 years old compared with four (7.4%) of the VC-backed firms. It is possible that the younger firms have not yet sought the support of venture capitalists but, for the older firms, the likelihood is that they are not interested in being VC-backed.

Table 13.2 summarizes the data on firm size. Two measures of size are provided: employment and sales. Panel A shows employment data for 108 firms that provided information for 2002. Total employment in the full sample is 2609, or an average of 26 employees per firm (median 12.5). The VC-backed firms employ over twice as many people as the non-VC-backed firms; the former employ a total of 1755 people, giving an average of 32.5 employees per firm, and the latter a total of 854 people, which is 16 employees per firm.

Turnover figures for 2001 are presented in Panel B of Table 13.2. Most respondent firms are relatively small when size is measured by sales. Almost one-third turned over less

[2] Response rates of 10% and less are commonly reported in small business mail surveys (Curran and Blackburn, 2001).

[3] Seven firms were excluded on the basis that they provided insufficient information on whether or not they had received VC funding.

Table 13.1 Company age structure

Panel A: Age (years)

	Venture capital-backed ($n = 54$)	Non-venture capital-backed ($n = 56$)	Total ($n = 110$)
Mean	4.8	6.7	5.8
Median	3.5	5	4
Min	1	0	0
Max	19	27	27

Panel B: Number of firms in each age category

	[1] Number of firms	[2] Proportion of sample	[3] Number of firms	[4] Proportion of sample	[5] Number of firms	[6] Proportion of sample
<2 years old	5	9.3%	10	17.9%	15	13.6%
2–4 years	31	57.4%	20	35.7%	51	46.4%
5–9 years	14	25.9%	9	16.1%	23	20.9%
10+ years	4	7.4%	17	30.4%	21	19.1%

Table 13.2 Company size

Panel A: Employment

	Venture capital-backed ($n = 54$)	Non-venture capital-backed ($n = 56$)	Total ($n = 110$)
Total	1755.0	854.0	2609.0
Mean	32.5	15.8	24.1
Median	20.5	8.5	13.5
Min	0.0	0.0	0.0
Max	200.0	140.0	200.0

Panel B: Turnover

	Number	%	Number	%	Number	%
Pre-revenue	12	23.1	9	16.1	21	19.4
<€127 000	1	1.9	12	21.4	13	12.0
€127 000 – €634 999	15	28.8	11	19.7	26	24.1
€635 000 – €1 269 999	7	13.5	10	17.9	17	15.7
€1 270 000 – €3 809 999	11	21.2	11	19.6	22	20.4
€3 810 000+	6	11.5	3	5.4	9	8.3
	52		56		108	

Turnover figures were requested in Irish punts, as Euro notes and coins were not introduced until 2002, but we report our findings in Euro only.

than €127 000, and 55.5% had sales less than €635 000. Twenty-nine percent of firms had a turnover of greater than €1 270 000, and only 8% had a turnover of greater than €3 810 000. There is little difference between the two groups except that the VC-backed firms have a higher proportion of firms recording both no turnover and turnover of more than €3 810 000.

13.4 Capital structure

Table 13.3 provides summary capital structure information at each stage for the 96 firms in the sample that provided detailed funding information. Because of the well-known difficulty of inducing owner-managers to reveal financial data, this information was requested in percentage form. Panel A presents the average figures for the sample overall; Panel B provides a breakdown for the non-VC-backed firms, and Panel C provides details for the VC-backed firms. Columns [3] to [6] present the proportion of total financing obtained from internal sources, including personal savings [3], consulting revenues [4], and retained profits [5]; column [6] presents the total from internal sources. Columns [7] to [11] provide information on external sources, including bank loans [7], venture capital [8], private/angel capital [9], and government grants [10]; column [11] presents the total external financing. Rows [A] to [D] delineate the results for the four age bands representing different stages in the life cycle of the software product firm: start-up (less than 2 years), commercialization (2–4 years), growth (5–9 years) and maturity (more than 10 years).

The average figures for the full sample show a 50/50 divide between internal and external sources of finance. A mere 4% of finance is provided by banks, and the remaining outside finance (46%) is private equity and government grants. As we argue in a prior paper (Hogan and Hutson, 2005), while our findings appear to be evidence against the POH, they are consistent with the spirit of Myers' (1984) and Myers and Majluf's (1984) theory, because they suggest that firms prefer sources of finance associated with the lowest level of information asymmetry. For NTBFs, this is venture capital.

The average figures for the full sample mask the substantial difference between the capital structures of VC-backed and non-VC-backed firms. In contrast to the 50/50 split between internal and external funding for the sample overall, Panel B shows that non-VC-backed firms are much more dependent on internal sources than their VC-backed counterparts in Panel C. On average, the non-VC-backed firms finance 72% of their capital requirement from internal sources of funds, compared with 20% for VC-backed-firms. Venture capital, as expected, is clearly the key difference between the two groups, accounting for 65% of all funding for the VC-backed subsample. The financing hierarchy for the non-VC-backed group is similar to the sample overall – internal, outside equity, and then debt. For the VC-backed firms, the pecking order is different again – outside equity comprises the vast majority of financing, followed by internal finance, and then debt.

Interesting patterns emerge when the two subsamples are aged. Internal finance remains the dominant source of finance for the non-VC-backed firms irrespective of age, with retained profits taking over from savings in the growth and maturity phases. The exception to the absolute dominance of internal sources of finance occurs for firms 2 to 4 years old, when considerable resources must be mobilized for the commercialization effort as start-up funds and savings have run down and sales have not yet taken off. Only half of

Table 13.3 Sources of finance in different age categories

	Number of firms	Internal sources of financing%				External sources of financing %				
		Savings [3]	Consulting revenues [4]	Retained profits [5]	Total internal [6]	Bank loans [7]	Venture capital [8]	Private investors [9]	Govt grants [10]	Total external [11]
Panel A: Full sample										
[A] Start-up (<2 years)	12	43.0	27.0	2.5	**72.5**	0.0	13.0	10.0	4.5	27.5
[B] Commercialization (2–4 years)	46	10.0	13.5	8.5	**32.0**	3.0	38.0	18.5	8.5	68.0
[C] Growth (5–9 years)	20	9.5	28.0	18.0	**55.5**	6.5	28.0	3.0	7.0	44.5
[D] Maturity 10+ years	18	10.0	20.0	46.0	**76.0**	5.0	11.0	5.0	3.0	24.0
All firms	**96**	**14.0**	**19.0**	**17.0**	**50.0**	**4.0**	**28.0**	**11.0**	**7.0**	**50.0**
Panel B: Non-venture capital-backed firms										
[A] Start-up (<2 years)	10	51.5	32.5	3.0	**87.0**	0.0	0.0	9.5	3.5	13.0
[B] Commercialization (2–4 years)	20	20.0	17.5	12.5	**50.0**	6.5	0.0	31.5	12.0	50
[C] Growth (5–9 years)	10	9.5	36.0	35.5	**81.0**	8.0	0.0	2.5	8.5	19.0
[D] Maturity 10+ years	15	12.0	23.5	50.0	**85.5**	5.0	0.0	5.5	4.0	14.5
All firms	**55**	**21.5**	**25.0**	**25.5**	**72.0**	**5.0**	**0.0**	**16.0**	**7.0**	**28.0**
Panel C: Venture capital-backed firms										
[A] Start-up (<2 years)	2	0.0	0.0	0.0	**0.0**	0.0	78.5	13	8.5	100.0
[B] Commercialization (2–4 years)	26	2.5	10.0	5.0	**17.5**	1.0	67.5	8.0	6.0	82.5
[C] Growth (5–9 years)	10	9.5	19.0	1.0	**29.5**	5.0	56.0	4.0	5.5	70.5
[D] Maturity 10+ years	3	0	0.0	26.5	**26.5**	8.5	65.0	0.0	0	73.5
All firms	**41**	**4.0**	**11.0**	**5.0**	**20.0**	**2.5**	**65.0**	**7.0**	**5.5**	**80.0**

the financing requirement for non-VC-backed firms is provided by internal sources, and money from private investors (32%) and government grants (12%) take up the slack.

Retained profits are essentially absent for the VC-backed firms except for those greater than 10 years old, whereas amongst the growth and maturity phase firms, retained profits comprise a very high proportion of financing for the non-VC-backed group (36% and 50%, respectively). Another major difference between the two groups is the near-absence of savings for the VC-backed cohort, and the presence of savings as a source of finance even amongst the older non-VC-backed group.

As we discussed in Hogan and Hutson (2005), we have found that consulting revenues are an important source of funds for software firms, and the ability of these software product firms to earn money from consulting work gives them considerable financial flexibility. Comparing the two subsamples, it is clear that consulting revenues are much more important for the non-VC-backed firms (25% overall versus 11% for the VC-backed subsample). Consulting revenues appear to play a very critical part in financing on an ongoing basis when venture capital is absent.

13.5 Founders' perceptions of information asymmetries

Table 13.4 reports the founders' perceptions on a number of issues relating to information asymmetries. Panel A relates to banks and Panel B to venture capitalists. In each case the response for the full sample is presented, followed by the findings for the founders of VC-backed and non-VC-backed firms.

If bank managers are unable to assess the technological basis for investment proposals, then information asymmetries will be severe and adverse selection will restrict the flow of debt funds to the technology sector. Overall, the extent to which founders perceive that banks understand their business shows strong evidence of severe information asymmetries in the market for bank finance in that only 9% of founders believe that banks understand their business (row [1]), while 57% of founders do not agree with this statement. This is consistent with findings from the Bank of England (1996), that few NTBF firms believed that banks understood their products or markets.

Comparing the two subgroups, it is clear that the founders of VC-backed firms perceive even greater information asymmetries in bank markets than their counterparts in non-VC-backed firms. Only 4% of founders of VC-backed firms believe that banks understand their business, compared with 14% of founders of non-VC-backed firms, and the difference in founders' perceptions on this issue is significant using a chi-square test (p-value = 0.06).

Corroborating the findings in relation to perceptions of bank understanding, row [2] shows that only 17% of founders believe that banks are willing to provide long-term loans to their companies. This falls to 7% for VC-backed firms, while 25% of non-VC-backed firms believe that banks are prepared to lend to them, and this difference is highly significant (p-value = 0.00). A similar pattern arises in our findings on at-call lending (row [3]). The response overall shows that founders believe banks are willing to provide them with overdraft facilities, and this makes sense because at-call lending is seen as less risky than long-term loans from the bank's point of view. As with their perceptions on long-term loans, the founders of VC-backed firms have a much more negative attitude to banks' willingness to provide overdrafts than non-VC-backed firms, with 43% of the

Table 13.4 Founders' perceptions of bank and venture capital finance

	(a) Disagree (%)	(b) Neither agree nor disagree (%)	(c) Agree (%)
Panel A: Banks			
[1] Banks understand my business (*n* = *110*)	**57.3**	**33.6**	**9.1**
Venture capital-backed ($n = 54$)	66.7	29.6	3.7
Non-venture capital-backed ($n = 56$)	48.2	37.5	14.3
Chi-square *p*-value: .063			
[2] Banks are willing to provide a long-term loan to my company (*n* = *108*)	**54.6**	**28.7**	**16.7**
Venture capital-backed ($n = 54$)	74.1	18.5	7.4
Non-venture capital-backed ($n = 56$)	35.2	38.9	25.9
Chi-square *p*-value: .000			
[3] Banks are willing to provide overdraft facilities to my company (*n* = *108*)	**34.3**	**12.0**	**53.7**
Venture capital-backed ($n = 54$)	42.6	13.0	44.4
Non-venture capital-backed ($n = 56$)	25.9	11.1	63.0
Chi-square *p*-value: .136			
[4] Banks lend money to companies with cash/fixed assets (*n* = *105*)	**4.8%**	**18.1%**	**77.1%**
Venture capital-backed ($n = 51$)	3.9%	15.7%	80.4%
Non-venture capital-backed ($n = 56$)	5.6%	20.4%	74.1%
Chi-square *p*-value: .741			
Panel B: Venture capitalists			
[5] Venture capitalists understand my business (*n* = *109*)	**21.1%**	**31.2%**	**47.7%**
Venture capital-backed ($n = 54$)	22.2%	22.2%	55.6%
Non-venture capital-backed ($n = 55$)	20.0%	40.0%	40.0%
Chi-square *p*-value: .122			
[6] Venture capitalists invest in companies with cash/fixed assets (*n* = *103*)	**49.5%**	**33.0%**	**17.5%**
Venture capital-backed ($n = 49$)	67.3%	20.4%	12.2%
Non-venture capital-backed ($n = 54$)	33.3%	44.4%	22.2%
Chi-square *p*-value: .003			

former believing that banks are unwilling to provide overdraft facilities compared with 26% for the latter.

Myers (1977) predicts that firms whose assets are dominated by intangibles (such as growth opportunities and research and development assets) would find it difficult to get bank finance. NTBFs, particularly software firms, are typical examples of such firms. Our findings suggest that founders are aware of this issue, as row [4] shows that almost 77% believe that banks lend money to companies with fixed assets and/or cash. On this issue there is little difference between the two subgroups.

The founders of software product companies in Ireland appear to have a more positive perception of venture capital, as shown in Panel B of Table 13.4. Whereas only a small minority of founders (9%) believe that banks understand their businesses, row [5] shows that 48% of founders believe that venture capitalists understand their businesses, and only 20% do not believe this to be the case. Respondent founders appear to hold this view irrespective of whether or not their firms are VC-backed, and the difference in responses between the two groups on this issue is not significant.

Row [6] shows that, unlike for banks, founders believe the presence of fixed assets is not a prerequisite for venture capitalist involvement. Only a small minority of founders (17.5%) believe that venture capitalists invest in firms with fixed assets, and the majority disagreed with the statement. Interestingly, the founders of non-VC-backed firms are more likely to perceive that venture capitalists invest in firms with fixed assets. Only 12% of VC-backed firm founders believe that venture capitalists invest in firms with fixed assets, and 67% disagreed with the statement, while the corresponding figures for non-VC-backed firms are 22% and 35%, respectively. The perceptions of non-VC-backed firm founders regarding VC providers preferring to back firms with cash or fixed assets, and their lower positive response to the statement 'venture capitalists understand my business', show that there are perceived information asymmetries in the VC market for many firm founders.

NTBF owner-managers clearly do not perceive asymmetries in VC markets to the same extent that they perceive asymmetries in the bank–client relationship. Founders of VC-backed firms perceive even greater information asymmetries in debt markets than their counterparts in non-VC-backed firms. While both groups have a more positive perception of venture capitalist's ability to understand their activities relative to banks, the founders of firms without VC backing have more negative perceptions of venture capitalists than VC-backed firm founders, and more positive attitudes to banks.

Our findings on perceptions regarding asymmetries go some way to explaining why some firms do not seek venture capital; or alternatively for some firms in the non-VC-backed cohort, it may be the result of applying for VC backing and being rejected.

13.6 Conclusion

New technology-based firms are a potential source of innovation and wealth creation in Europe, which makes them of particular interest to governments and policy makers. This chapter has demonstrated that NTBFs have a capital structure that is untypical of SMEs in general. They have a higher proportion of private equity in their capital structure than SMEs, and very low levels of debt. However, NTBFs themselves are not a homogeneous group, and we have highlighted marked differences in the capital structures of VC-backed and non-VC-backed firms in the Irish software sector. Our findings for VC-backed firms are of particular interest, because the hierarchy of financing is so different from the predictions of the pecking order hypothesis – outside equity completely dominates these firms' capital structures. Internal finance is unimportant except for the older firms that use some retained earnings, and debt is essentially irrelevant.

Our findings confirm that venture capital does overcome perceived information asymmetries in debt markets. This is not, however, overwhelmingly the case, and the fact that there are exceptions to this finding shows that VC is not universally the preferred source of finance for NTBFs, and they are not always able to overcome the substantial informational asymmetries that characterize NTBF capital markets. Nonetheless, the promotion of a buoyant VC market is an important policy objective in the EU, and it is clear from our study that many NTBF founders would benefit from and support such a policy.

References

Amit, R., Brander, J. and Zott, C. (1998). Why Do Venture Capital Firms Exist? Theory and Canadian Evidence. *Journal of Business Venturing*, 13:441–446.

Bank of England (1996). *The Financing of Technology-Based Small Firms*. London.

Bank of England (2001). *Financing of Technology-Based Small Firms*. London.

Berger, A.N. and Udell, G.F. (1998). The Economics of Small Business Finance: The Role of Private Equity and Debt Markets in the Finance Growth Cycle. *Journal of Banking and Finance*, 22(6–8):613–673.

Berggren, B., Olofsson, C. and Silver, L. (2000). Control Aversion and the Search for External Financing in Swedish SMEs. *Small Business Economics*, 15(3):233–242.

Binks, M. and Ennew, C. (1994). The Provision of Finance to Small Businesses: Does the Banking Relationship Constrain Performance? *Journal of Small Business Finance*, 4(1):57–73.

Brewer, E. and Genay, H. (1994). Funding Small Business Through the SBIC Program. *Federal Reserve Bank of Chicago Economic Perspectives*, 18:22–34.

Chittenden, F., Hall, G. and Hutchinson, P. (1996). Small Firm Growth, Access to Capital Markets and Financial Structure: Review of Issues and an Empirical Investigation. *Small Business Economics*, 8(1):59–67.

Cosh, A. and Hughes, A. (1994). Size, Financial Structure and Profitability: U.K. Companies in the 1980s. In Hughes, A. and Storey, D.J. (eds), *Finance and the Small Firm*. London: Routledge, 19–63.

Curran, J. and Blackburn, R.A. (2001). *Researching the Small Enterprise*. London: Sage.

Deakins, D. and Hussain, G. (1993). Overcoming the Adverse Selection Problem: Evidence and Policy Implications from a Study of Bank Managers on the Importance of Different Criteria Used in Making a Lending Decision. In Chittenden, F., Robertson, M. and Watkins, D. (eds), *Small Firms: Recession and Recovery*. London: Paul Chapman.

Dillman, D. (1976). *Mail and Telephone Surveys*. New York: John Wiley.

Dillman, D. (2000). *Mail and Internet Surveys*. 2nd edition. New York: John Wiley and Sons.

European Commission (1999). *Risk Capital Markets: A Key to Job Creation in Europe, from Fragmentation to Integration*. Report prepared by Delphine Sallard, Directorate General II, Economic and Financial Affairs, Euro Papers no. 32.

European Commission (2001). *Innovation Management: Building Competitive Skills in SMEs*. Innovation Papers, No. 8, Luxembourg: Office for Official Publications of the European Communities.

European Commission (2003). *Green Paper on Entrepreneurship in Europe*. Luxembourg: Office for Official Publications of the European Communities.

European Network for SME Research (ENSR) (2002). *Observatory of European SMEs, 2002: High-Tech SMEs in Europe*. Report No. 6. Prepared for Enterprise Directorate-General by KPMG Special Services and EIM Business and Policy Research in the

Netherlands in co-operation with the ENSR and Infomart. Luxembourg: Office for Official Publications of the European Communities.

Gompers, P. and Lerner, J. (2003). Equity Financing. In Acs, Z.J. and Audretsch, D.B. (eds), *Handbook of Entrepreneurship Research*. Dordrecht: Kluwer Academic Publishers, 267–298.

Gupta, A.K. and Sapienza, J.J. (1991). Determinants of Venture Capital Firms' Preferences in Terms of Industry and Geographical Scope of Their Investment. *Journal of Business Venturing*, 7(5):347–362.

Hogan, T. and Hutson, E. (2005). Capital Structure in New Technology-Based Firms: Evidence from the Irish Software Sector. *Global Finance Journal*, 15(3):369–387.

Hyytinen, A. and Pajarinen, M. (2002). *Financing of Technology Intensive Small Business: Some Evidence from the ICT industry*. Helsinki: The Research Institute of the Finnish Economy Discussion Paper No. 813.

Jordan, J., Lowe, J. and Taylor, P. (1998). Strategy and Financial Policy in U.K. Small Firms. *Journal of Business Finance and Accounting*, 25(1 & 2):1–27.

Lindholm-Dahlstrand, A. and Cetindamar, A. (2000). The Dynamics of Innovation Financing in Sweden. *Venture Capital*, 2(3):203–221.

Michaelas, N., Chittenden, F. and Poutziouris, P. (1999). Financial Policy and Capital Structure Choice in UK SMEs: Empirical Evidence from Company Panel Data. *Small Business Economics*, 12(2):113–130.

Moore, B. (1994). Financial Constraints to the Growth and Development of Small High Technology Firms. In Hughes, A. and Storey, D.J. (eds), *Finance and the Small Firm*. London: Routledge, 112–144.

Myers, S.C. (1977). Determinants of Corporate Borrowing. *Journal of Financial Economics*, 5(2):147–175.

Myers, S.C. (1984). The Capital Structure Puzzle. *Journal of Finance*, 39(3):575–592.

Myers, S.C. and Majluf, N.S. (1984). Corporate Financing and Investment Decisions When Firms have Information That Investors Do Not Have. *Journal of Financial Economics*, 13(2):187–221.

National Informatics Directorate (2004). Software Industry Statistics for 1991–2003. http://www.nsd.ie/htm/ssii/stat.htm

Norton, E. and Tenenbaum, B.H. (1993). Factors Affecting the Structure of Venture Capital Deals. *Journal of Small Business Management*, 30(1):20–30.

Oakey, R.P. (1984). *High Technology Small Firms*. London: Frances Pinter.

Roberts, E.B. (1990). Initial Capital for New Technological Enterprise. *IEEE Transactions on Engineering Management*, 37(2):81–93.

Roberts, E.B. (1991). *Entrepreneurs in High Technology; Lessons from MIT and Beyond*. Oxford University Press.

Ruhnka, J.C. and Young, J.E. (1991). Some Hypotheses About Risk in Venture Capital Investing. *Journal of Business Venturing*, 6(2):115–133.

Sahlman, W.A. (1990). The Structure and Governance of Venture Capital Organisations. *Journal of Financial Economics*, 27(2):473–521.

Stanworth, J. and Gray, C. (1991). *Bolton Twenty Years On: The Small Firm in the 1990s*. London: Chapman, on behalf of the Small Business Research Trust.

Stiglitz, J.E. and Weiss, A. (1981). Credit Rationing in Markets with Imperfect Information. *American Economic Review*, 71(3):383–410.

14 German business ventures – entrepreneurs, success factors, and financing

Ann-Kristin Achleitner, Christoph Kaserer, Niklas Wagner, Angela Poech, and Martin Brixner

Abstract

During recent years, German business ventures have used venture capital financing to a steadily increasing extent. Yet, relatively little research has been conducted on the relationship between venture companies and VC investors in Germany. In particular, the initial process that gives rise to VC investments is, for the most part, not covered. Furthermore, little evidence is available on the acquisition, the use of, and the benefit of VC financing. Based on an unparalleled survey among more than 300 German business ventures, this chapter addresses central questions from the investors' as well as the business ventures' perspectives. We study the relationship between the entrepreneurs' characteristics, the ventures' characteristics, and the ventures' success. Our results indicate that the degree of innovation of the venture is a key determinant of success. A look at the personal background of the entrepreneurs reveals that they are in their late 30s, on average, and have reasonable professional experience. Interestingly, financial intermediaries, including banks as well as consultants, so far do not seem to play a major role in the matching of VC demand and supply in Germany.

14.1 Introduction

Over recent years, German business ventures have increasingly made use of VC financing. Yet relatively little research has been conducted on the relationship between venture companies and VC investors in Germany. In particular, the initial process during which VC investments arise is relatively little covered. Furthermore, little evidence is available on the acquisition, the use of, and the benefit of VC financing. Previous evidence of entrepreneurial activity is therefore rather exceptional. Storey (1994) gives an early European overview, while in recent years the Global Entrepreneurship Monitor (GEM; Lückgen and Sternberg, 2005; Bergmann et al., 2004) has offered in-depth information on entrepreneurial activities for more than 30 countries. We find the GEM country reports on Germany for the years 2003 and 2004 very helpful for an overview of German entrepreneurial activity. Lehnert (2004) offers the KfW-Gründungsmonitor, an annual publication on company foundations in Germany, which provides interesting findings on German entrepreneurs. Previous studies that focus on German business ventures, such as Werner (2000) and Kulicke (1993), were based on relatively small samples: Werner empirically examines 221 ventures, Kulicke uses a sample of 93 ventures. Other studies that draw on a richer sample, for instance Brüderl et al. (1996), focus on a particular region or industry.

This chapter aims at providing broader and more conclusive empirical evidence on business ventures in Germany. In 2004, we succeeded in setting up an unparalleled survey among more than 300 German business ventures, which addressed central questions on financial aspects from both the investors' as well as the ventures' perspective. The results are presented in this chapter, which is structured as follows. In the second section we describe the questionnaire design and illustrate the sample composition. In addition, we give the methods of data analysis used. The results of our analysis are presented in the third section. In a first step, we depict the main characteristics of the entrepreneurs in our sample. In a second step, we examine the business ventures. In a third, we link the presented characteristics with entrepreneurial success. To do so, we first describe which criteria indicating success we use. Subsequently, we take a closer look at the relationship between the venture company and the venture capital investor. In the conclusion we highlight the key findings and their implications.

14.2 Research set-up

14.2.1 Questionnaire design

The questionnaire is a key element of our study, which was conducted in 2004. It was a joint project of the Center for Entrepreneurial and Financial Studies (CEFS) at Munich University of Technology (Technische Universität München, TUM) and the StartUp-Initiative.[1] The questionnaire consists of two parts; the first to collect information on the basic venture and entrepreneur characteristics, the second focuses on financial aspects. Most questions offer multiple choice answer options. A corresponding online questionnaire was used to address the survey's target audience. The questionnaire was online from 3 March 2004 to 9 April 2004.

14.2.2 Sample composition

The questionnaire collected information on business ventures with considerable growth and earnings potential and a sound business plan. The top 500 business ventures according to the StartUp business plan competition for each year from 1997 to 2004 were invited to participate, as we found this group to reflect the target group very well.[2] Overall, 473 business ventures participated in the survey. However, we had to exclude 148 questionnaires from our dataset as key information was missing. One questionnaire had to

[1] As one of its main activities the StartUp-Initiative carries out a nationwide business plan competition on an annual basis. The StartUp-Initiative is a cooperation of *Stern* (weekly German news journal), Sparkassen (German savings banks), McKinsey & Company Inc. (international consultancy) and ZDF (nationwide German TV station under public law). It was founded in 1997.

[2] As with any selection this induces various biases. Nevertheless we decided to limit our selection to the top 500 ventures to make sure that only high-potential ventures enter our sample. The top 500 ventures represent on average roughly the best 50% that participate in the StartUp business plan competition. Business ventures that did not participate were barred from the survey. With regard to the standing of the competition in Germany we believe that no significant bias resulted from this procedure.

be excluded because of obviously misleading specifications. Thus, the survey yielded a dataset comprising specifications for 324 high-potential business ventures. A look at the sample composition with regard to different criteria showed that the sample contained companies of all types; we believe that the sample reflects the overall composition of German business ventures well. However, this impression cannot be verified by statistical means, as far too little consistent and reliable information is available on the whole of German business ventures. The following tables indicate how the sample is made up in terms of company age (Table 14.1), business model (Table 14.2), and industry classification (Table 14.3).

Table 14.1 Sample composition by company age

Company age	#	%
<1 year	106	32.7%
1 to 3 years	102	31.5%
3 to 5 years	83	25.6%
5 to 10 years	33	10.2%
>10 years	0	0%
n.s.	0	0%
Total	324	100%

Table 14.2 Sample composition by business model

Business model	#	%
Manufacturing	112	34.6%
Commerce	60	18.5%
Services	149	46.0%
n.s.	3	0.9%
Total	324	100%

n.s., not stated.

Table 14.3 Sample composition by industry classification

Industry	#	%	Industry	#	%
Services	136	41.9%	Medical engineering	10	3.1%
Software/IT	31	9.6%	Telecommunication	8	2.5%
Biotechnology	22	6.8%	Environmental engineering	5	1.5%
Consumer goods	19	5.9%	Measurement and control technology	5	1.5%
Handicraft	14	4.3%	Other industries	64	19.8%
E-commerce/Internet	10	3.1%			
Total				324	100%

14.2.3 Data analysis

In a first step the data are assessed with basic descriptive statistics, such as mean, median, and variance. In a second step OLS regressions are used to show interrelations within our dataset. The coefficients are t-tested if they differ significantly from zero. For dependent variables, which are dichotomies, logistic regressions are used. Mostly, criteria that are used as indicators for business venture success are taken as dependent variables, and business venture characteristics and characteristics of the entrepreneur served as independent variables. Wherever the findings of a regression are discussed in this chapter we include a table summarizing its statistical results. For complementary information on regressions, for example the underlying calculus and assumptions, we recommend Backhaus et al. (2003) and Moser and Schmid (2003).

14.3 Results

14.3.1 Characteristics of the entrepreneurs

The entrepreneurs behind German business ventures differ considerably in their professional and academic background. On average the entrepreneurs were in their late 30s (mean 37.6 years old) when they launched their venture. This is in line with other studies on entrepreneurial activity in Germany, for example the GEM country report on Germany for 2003 (Bergmann et al., 2004).

With increasing professional experience and seniority the ability to launch a business is greatly increased. However, the willingness to take on risks decreases with increasing age, inter alia because of increased family obligations and decreasing stamina. Werner (2000) demonstrates how these effects work in an opposing manner in such a way that makes the launch of a venture most likely in the late 30s. The entrepreneur's age at launch of venture did not vary considerably over different industries.[3] At the time of foundation the entrepreneurs had more than ten years of professional experience, in general.[4] More than 70% of the entrepreneurs hold a university degree. Graduates in engineering, business sciences, and natural sciences make up more than two-thirds of this group. Overall, roughly one-fifth hold a doctoral degree. We find that the majority of entrepreneurs worked as white-collar employees prior to the launch of their venture; 26.8% in an executive position, 28.6% in a non-executive position. Compared with their share in the working population in Germany, it shows that white-collar employees in executive positions are inclined to launch their own business. One-fifth of the entrepreneurs were self-employed in the run-up. These numbers are comparable with the information found on entrepreneurs

[3] The highest average age was found for business ventures that focus on environmental engineering (39.2 years). Ventures in the fields of measurement and controlling technology, telecommunications and E-commerce/internet show a relatively low average age (34.2, 34.4, and 35.0 years, respectively).

[4] Professional experience was not specifically asked for in the questionnaire. The majority of entrepreneurs hold a university degree. If one makes the assumption that they began their studies at the age of 21 they typically graduated at the age of 27. Thus they had 11.6 years after graduation to gain professional experience before they launched their business venture. Neither professional activities during their course of study, nor periods of unemployment, nor entrepreneurs without such an academic background are taken into consideration for this estimation. Thus, it has to be seen as a rough approximation in the absence of better information. For additional information on student characteristics and study patterns see OECD (2004).

in similar studies, for example Brüderl et al. (1996). Less than one-tenth (9.4%) are unemployed.[5] Table 14.4 summarizes the findings for the academic background,[6] Table 14.5 presents those for the professional occupation prior to the launch of the venture.

14.3.2 Characteristics of the German business ventures

Nearly half (152; 46.9%) of the polled business ventures were founded by a single person, roughly one-third (110; 34.0%) by a team of two entrepreneurs. Approximately

Table 14.4 Academic background of the entrepreneurs

Highest achieved degree	%
Secondary school	7.3%
High school	5.6%
Apprenticeship (mercantile)	8.7%
Apprenticeship (technical)	7.3%
Natural sciences	13.4%
Engineering science	19.8%
Medical science	3.0%
Law	2.0%
Business sciences	16.5%
Humanities	5.0%
Other studies/sciences	11.2%
Total	100%
Complementary doctoral degree	19.1%

Table 14.5 Precedent professional occupation

Precedent professional occupation	%
Pupil/Apprentice	3.0%
Student	5.6%
Public official	2.3%
White-collar employee, non-exec.	28.6%
White-collar employee, executive	26.8%
Self-employed	20.8%
Unemployed	9.4%
Other occupations	3.1%
Total	100%

[5] A closer look at the business ventures started out of unemployment revealed that they created far below average revenue and less employment than the other business ventures in this sample. However, some of these companies might enable the founder to make a living and thus offer an alternative to unemployment. The data collection for this study is not geared to collect a dataset that would allow valid conclusions to be drawn on businesses that were founded out of an unemployment situation in general.

[6] Because of the differences in academic systems we found it of little use to include the German degrees that were originally asked for. Instead we included what we consider to be the best matching equivalent degree in an Anglo-Saxon academic system.

Table 14.6 Overview of sample composition

	Turnover 2003 in €000	Job creation in positions of full-time employment	Degree of innovation individual estimation, from 1 (low) to 5 (high)
Overall	755	7.3	3.7
By business model			
Manufacturing	385	5.9	4.1
Commerce	1688	17.1	3.4
Services	626	4.7	3.5
By company age			
<1 year	97	1.8	3.7
1 to 3 years	231	3.0	3.6
3 to 5 years	679	9.5	3.7
5 to 10 years	4154	29.7	3.6

one-fifth (62; 19.1%) of the business ventures are launched by a team of three or more entrepreneurs. On average two (1.92) entrepreneurs joined forces to start their venture.[7]

Not surprisingly, we find that the sample is very heterogeneous in terms of average annual revenue, job creation, and degree of innovation.[8] Table 14.6 summarizes these results. Commercial business models require a high level of turnover to operate since the achievable profit margins are usually relatively modest. The average revenue by business model seems to be inversely proportional to the achievable profit margin in this field. Revenue increases steadily over time, the huge gap between the average turnover for companies between 3–5 years and 5–10 years is mainly due to a handful of very successful companies older than 5 years that are included in the sample. The same holds true for job creation. Interestingly, the perceived degree of innovation does not vary over age of business[9] but over business model. The degree of innovation seems to play a crucial role for manufacturing business ventures.

[7] The numbers vary by industry. Business ventures that focus on medical engineering or biotechnology are launched by bigger teams (2.5 entrepreneurs on average), smaller team sizes are found in services, handicraft, and consumer goods (1.62, 1.57, and 1.32 on average, respectively). For some industries only a small subsample is available so caution is advised in the interpretation. The initial outlay to start a business venture varies with the industry and it seems to fit that the smallest team sizes are found in industries such as services or handicraft that require relatively modest initial outlay.

[8] The degree of innovation of the business venture was asked for directly in the survey. It was indicated on a scale from 1 to 5 and reflects the subjective impression of the entrepreneur. This impression is subject to various distortions, yet we believe that this is the best way to determine the degree of innovation. Other proxies for the degree of innovation, such as the number of patents filed, are likely not to favour one industry over another. In addition, the quality of these alternative proxies is variable.

[9] Possibly, the degree of innovation is truly invariant over company age. However, comparisons of that kind suffer inevitably from a survivorship-bias. It may also be that the perceived degree of innovation is invariant as different counteracting effects, which may be linked to the survivorship-bias, offset.

14.3.3 Success factors for German business ventures

Business ventures are likely to run losses in the first years and may use more cash than they generate. This holds true for promising and less promising business ventures alike. As a result many indicators for success that are widely used in corporate finance are unable to tell successful and unsuccessful ventures apart. In this contribution, we use three indicators for business venture success, which account for business venture characteristics. We study the growth in revenue and in (full-time) employment from 2003 to 2004.[10] In addition, we examine whether or not a business venture has reached break-even up to the time of questioning.[11] These characteristics were also used in previous studies on the success of venture, for example Werner (2000) and Wanzenböck (1998).

We examine to what extent characteristics of the entrepreneur are suitable to explain venture success. We included the following characteristics in our regressions on the success indicators: age, gender, previous experience in a management position, previous self-employment, and academic background (degree in natural sciences/engineering, degree in business sciences, other university degree, and doctoral degree).[12] Table 14.7 gives the results.

Overall, we obtain fairly low R^2 and F-values. We will not elaborate on the results from the regressions on growth in revenues and growth in employment because of the extremely low explanatory power. The regression on break-even has a much higher degree of explanation. (Pseudo-)R^2 of this degree of distinctiveness are not uncommon for this type of study (see, for instance, Werner, 2000). We do not find a significant relationship between age, gender, previous experience in a managing position, previous self-employment, and the success indicators. Yet there is evidence that a strong academic background has a positive impact on the ventures' success. The findings are most meaningful with respect to attainment of break-even. In spite of the low explanatory power of the regressions we maintain that the academic background of the entrepreneurs seems to play a crucial role in the venture's success.

As we try subsequently to explain business venture success directly from venture characteristics, we obtain results with similar explanatory power. Examples are given in Table 14.8, which summarizes the findings of three regressions. Break-even, growth in revenue, and growth in employment are explained by the business model, the number of founders, the number of full-time employees in 2003, and the degree of innovation.

Focusing on the significant coefficients, we find that the number of founders impacts negatively on the attainment of break-even. Perhaps entrepreneurs are more likely to join forces when they are to launch a business venture with high initial outlay or this is due to the remuneration, which is paid to the founders, being the company's management. The number of employees in 2003 barely influences the growth in revenues. The degree of innovation is the only venture characteristic that shows a significant impact on two success indicators. The higher the degree of innovation the less likely it is that the business venture has already reached break-even. In various industries, such as biotechnology or medical engineering, highly innovative companies have considerable initial outlay and do

[10] For 2003 actual numbers were available, whereas numbers for 2004 are estimates from the entrepreneurs.

[11] As the indicator for break-even is a dichotomy, logistic regressions are applied when break-even was used as dependent variable in a regression.

[12] If a venture is founded by more than one entrepreneur it was sufficient if a criterion was met by at least one of the group.

Table 14.7 Business venture success and characteristics of the entrepreneur

	Break-even	Growth in revenues	Growth in employment
Age of entrepreneurs at founding (average in years)	0.018 (0.867)	0.015 (0.434)	−0.003 (−0.288)
Participation of female entrepreneurs (1 = yes; 0 = no)	−0.011 (0.001)	−0.022 (−0.038)	−0.110 (−0.769)
Experience in a management position (1 = yes; 0 = no)	−0.333 (1.086)	−0.486 (−0.937)	0.119 (0.915)
Previous self-employment (1 = yes; 0 = no)	0.217 (0.400)	−0.178 (−0.291)	−0.088 (−0.596)
Degree in natural sciences/engineering (1 = yes; 0 = no)	0.935* (7.700)	0.007 (0.012)	0.120 (0.827)
Degree in business sciences (1 = yes; 0 = no)	0.988** (7.820)	0.326 (0.528)	0.296** (2.009)
Other university degree (1 = yes; 0 = no)	0.870 (5.759)	0.843 (1.374)	−0.071 (−0.475)
Doctoral degree (1 = yes; 0 = no)	0.230 (5.248)	0.009 (0.014)	0.123 (0.799)
R^2	0.141(a)	−0.029(b)	0.01(b)
F-value	—	0.365	1.238

[a] Pseudo-R^2.
[b] Adjusted R^2.
* Significant at a 10% level of significance; ** significant at a 5% level of significance.
t-values (respectively Wald-values) included in parentheses.

not generate substantial revenues for the first years. However, being highly innovative they do have ample growth potential, so our finding for the importance of the degree of innovation on the growth of revenues seems perspicuous. With regard to the moderate R^2 and fairly low F-values these regressions can only serve as a first indication. We find the relationship between degree of innovation and business venture success the most promising.

In a next step we examine how our indicators of venture success vary with the degree of innovation. In addition, we study the average revenue and the average number of full-time employees in 2003. The results are summarized in Figures 14.1 to 14.5.

As depicted in Figure 14.1 the average revenue in 2003 increases with the degree of innovation. As stated earlier, it may take longer for highly innovative companies to generate substantial earnings, but they show considerable growth potential. The relation illustrated in Figure 14.1 provides evidence that highly innovative companies manage to tap their earnings potential. We do not have information on how many highly innovative companies perished over time, so we cannot adjust for a survivorship bias, which might boost the average revenue of the remaining ventures. Interestingly, even though highly innovative ventures operate on far higher levels of revenue they do not fall short with

Table 14.8 Business venture success and venture characteristics

	Break-even	Growth in revenues	Growth in employment
Business model – Dummy 1 (1 = Manufacturing)	0.138 (0.168)	−0.755 (−1.243)	0.193 (1.374)
Business model – Dummy 2 (1 = Commerce)	−0.321 (0.679)	0.323 (0.477)	−0.087 (−0.526)
Founded by a team of entrepreneurs (1 = yes; 0 = no)	−0.242 (0.406)	−0.134 (−0.182)	0.109 (0.742)
Number of founders	−0.336** (4.500)	0.106 (0.306)	−0.037 (−0.819)
Number of full-time employees in 2003	0.020 (1.740)	−0.049* (−1.699)	−0.005 (−1.073)
Degree of innovation (1 = very low; 5 = very high)	−0.283* (6.216)	0.517** (1.893)	0.068 (1.063)
R^2	0.099(a)	0.008(b)	0.011(b)
F-value	—	1.216	1.341

Business model of reference: services.
[a] Pseudo-R^2.
[b] Adjusted R^2.
* Significant at a 10% level of significance; ** significant at a 5% level of significance.
t-values (respectively Wald-values) included in parentheses.

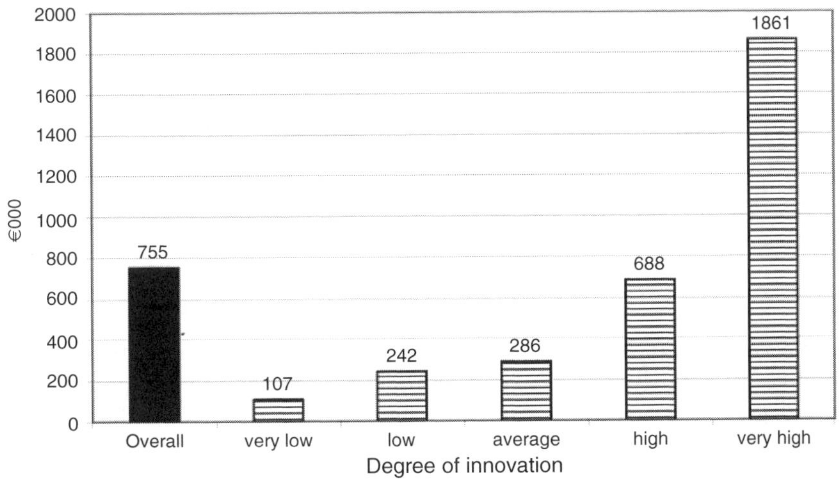

Figure 14.1 Average revenue in 2003

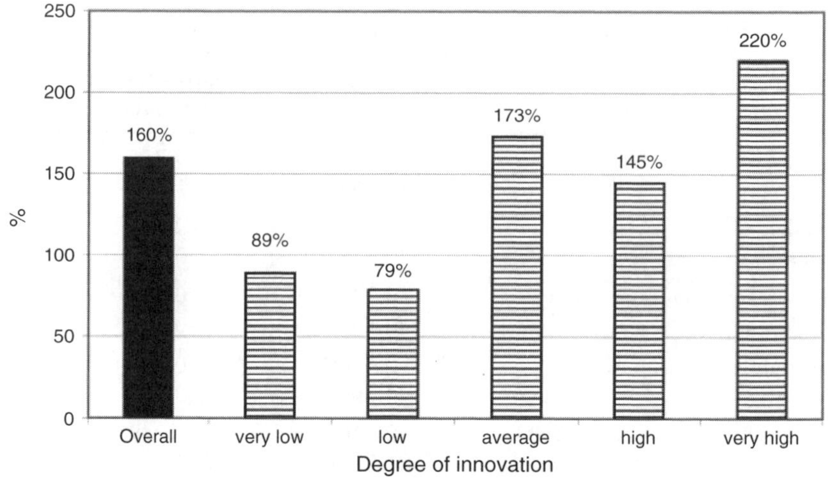

Figure 14.2 Average growth in revenue from 2003 to 2004

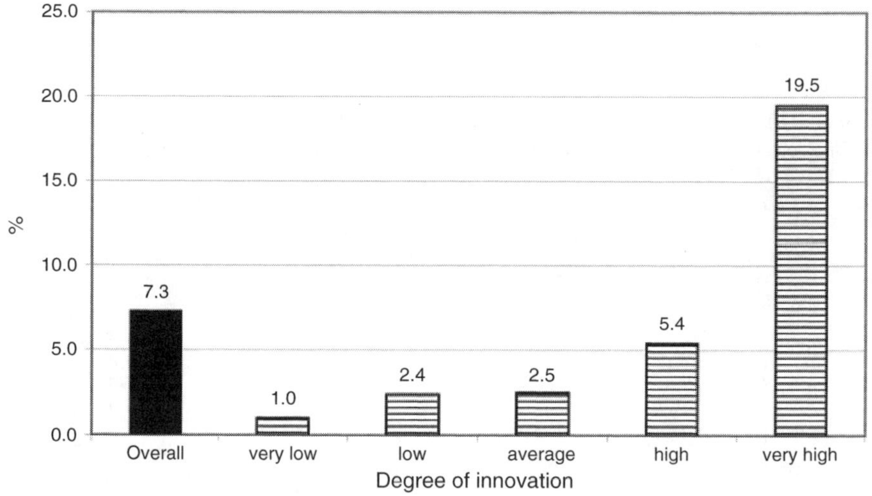

Figure 14.3 Average number of full-time employees

regard to expected earnings growth, as shown in Figure 14.2. The overall level of expected growth in revenue is fairly high (79% of annual growth being the minimum for ventures with a low degree of innovation). This may be due to the fact that the sample is made up from only the most promising ventures from the StartUp business plan competition. However, the fact that 2004 numbers are expected numbers, which certainly reflect up to a point the entrepreneur's desired revenue development, also does have an effect. For the number of full-time employments, which are illustrated in Figure 14.3, we find a very similar pattern to the average revenue. In total, business ventures have an extensive

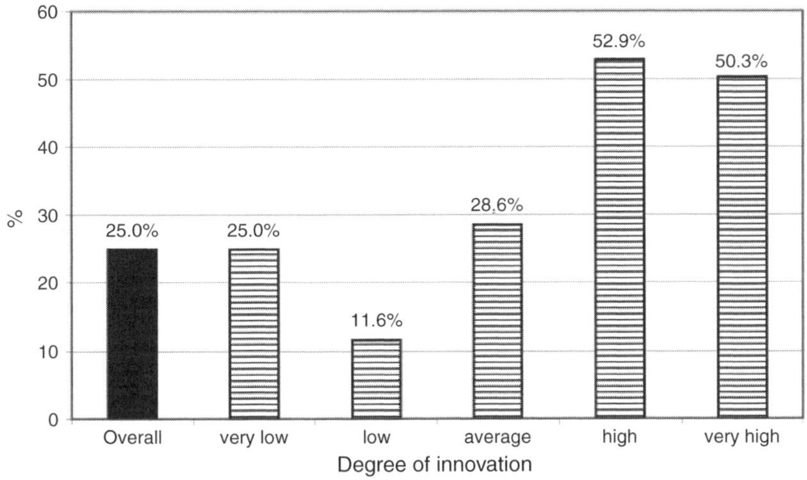

Figure 14.4 Average growth in full-time employment from 2003 to 2004

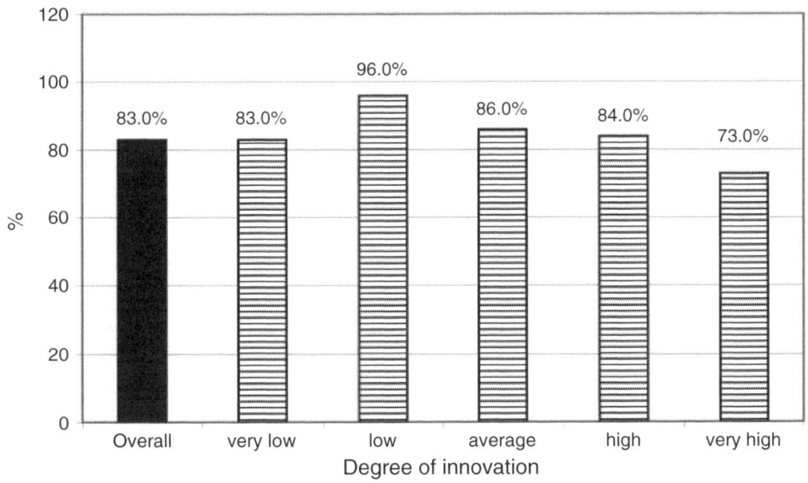

Figure 14.5 Attainment of break-even in 2003

employment effect.[13] It stands to reason that highly innovative ventures require, to some extent, a highly skilled workforce. Again, as the sample only includes ventures that have not perished it becomes evident that innovative ventures have funds to remunerate their skilled workforce over time. The pattern found in the expected growth of full-time employment, Figure 14.4, resembles the pattern found in the expected growth of revenues, though the growth in full-time employment is at a considerably lower overall level. Surprisingly, ventures with a very low degree of innovation expect a fairly high

[13] Achleitner and Klöckner (2005) examined the employment effect of ventures with VC funding. They included both the number of jobs created and the quality of the employment in their analysis.

increase in full-time employment. It has to be borne in mind that some of this growth takes place in ventures with a very small workforce, so the percentage increase is high. The chance that a venture has reached break-even does not vary to the same extent with the degree of innovation as with the other aspects. It is likely that ventures that are successful enough to survive have managed to break even.

We maintain that the academic background of the entrepreneurs and the degree of innovation have the most impact on the venture's success. It stands to reason that the academic background of the entrepreneurs influences the degree of innovation of the venture they launch. Thus, we decided to test whether a stronger academic background leads to a higher degree of innovation. In addition, we examined which other factors drive the degree of innovation. The results are summarized in Table 14.9. The regression on the degree of innovation uses only the entrepreneur's characteristics as independent variables. Regressions have shown that the venture's characteristics contribute very little to the explanation of the degree of innovation.

In comparison with the regressions on the success indicators presented in Tables 14.7 and 14.8, the regression on the degree of innovations shows fairly high explanatory power. Again, the age of the entrepreneur is not significant. It seems that age is more a

Table 14.9 Determinants of the degree of innovation

	Degree of innovation
Age of entrepreneurs at founding (average in years)	−0.005 (−0.710)
Participation of female entrepreneurs (1 = yes; 0 = no)	−0.320*** (−2.985)
Experience in a managing position (1 = yes; 0 = no)	0.084 (0.794)
Previous self-employment (1 = yes; 0 = no)	0.319*** (2.784)
Degree in natural sciences/engineering (1 = yes; 0 = no)	0.121 (1.077)
Degree in business/economics (1 = yes; 0 = no)	0.190 (1.568)
Other university degree (1 = yes; 0 = no)	0.207* (1.812)
Doctoral degree (1 = yes; 0 = no)	0.412*** (3.249)
R^2	0.09(a)
F-value	5.598

[a] Pseudo-R^2.
* Significant at a 10% level of significance; *** significant at a 1% level of significance.
t-values included in parentheses.

determinant of the likelihood that a person will start his own venture than of the venture's degree of innovation.

We find in our sample that ventures launched by or with the participation of a female entrepreneur show a lower degree of innovation. To some extent this is due to the fact that female entrepreneurs are less active in manufacturing ventures that represent those with the highest degree of innovation by business model (see Table 14.2). In Germany there is a substantial difference in the course of study selected by male and female students. The Statistische Bundesamt (2003) offers detailed information in its annual report on these differences. A look at the academic background of the entrepreneurs in this field reveals that they often hold degrees in subjects in which women are relatively under-represented. We believe that gender itself does not determine the degree of innovation, but it does influence the choice of a subject major. Regressions that use either gender or the various university degrees as independents support this reasoning. As we asked for the degree of innovation directly, differences reported may also result from differences in the way entrepreneurs assess themselves. There is evidence that women are more conservative when they have to give an estimate of their venture's degree of innovation (see Bergmann et al., 2004), which also contributes to the lower degree of innovation seen for ventures with female participation.

We find that the resulting academic background determines to some extent the degree of innovation. All university degrees have a positive impact on the degree of innovation, yet they could not be proven to be significant (with the exception of the category 'Other degrees').

Entrepreneurs who hold a doctoral degree tend to start more innovative business ventures. Again, up to a point this may be explained by the peculiarities of the German academic system. In natural sciences it is fairly common to complement the first university degree with a doctoral degree. Entrepreneurs with a natural science background are most often active in ventures that pursue innovative business ideas.

It is interesting to compare the importance of experience in a management position with the importance of previous self-employment. Experience in a management position does not seem to add to the degree of innovation. Previously self-employed founders tend to start more innovative ventures; perhaps they better understand the importance of differentiating one's business from that of competitors.

We find in our sample that highly innovative ventures are the most successful. Figures 14.1 to 14.5 illustrated impressively the role of the degree of innovation. However, the degree of innovation is not estimated easily; potential VC investors may find it difficult to assess this with the information that is available to them. Based on our findings we propose that special attention should be paid to an entrepreneur's solid academic background. We do not find age and gender to be important. We obtained mixed results for previous professional experience. Having given some guidance on how to identify potentially successful ventures we now turn to financing opportunities for young business ventures in Germany. We focus on external equity financing and highlight the role of VC financing.

14.3.4 Venture capital financing for German business ventures

In our sample, 243 ventures received funding through some type of external equity. Within this group, 28 ventures obtained funding from business angels, private venture

Table 14.10 Relationship between VC funding and business development

	With VC funding	W/o VC funding
Revenue in 2003 in €000	2353.3	316.2
Full-time employees	9.7	4.8

capitalists or corporate venture capitalists. These ventures differ in many aspects from those without VC financing. Table 14.10 gives an overview of the revenue achieved and the number of full-time employees in 2003 for both groups.

It is evident that ventures with VC financing dwarf ventures without such funding. However, we cannot conclude from our dataset whether VC funding stimulated growth to that extent or whether VC was only provided to companies that had already grown to a certain size. Probably both apply and each amplifies the other. Our dataset indicates that the search for investors to provide external equity is time-consuming for German ventures. On average, ventures with VC funding needed 39 weeks to find an investor. Compared with the average of 14 weeks for the 243 ventures that received any kind of external equity, it becomes obvious that ventures that plan to draw on VC are well advised to allow extra time. VC investors examine potential investment opportunities carefully; this process may also account for some of the differences in the averages. Figures 14.6 and 14.7 illustrate the degree of satisfaction from the investees' perspective. We found that ventures with VC financing spend on average 3 hours per week (13.25 h/month) in direct contact with their main investor. From the investees' perspective this seems to be about the right amount of time, as Figure 14.6 illustrates. Moreover, the investees are convinced that they benefit from the contact with their main investor (Figure 14.7).

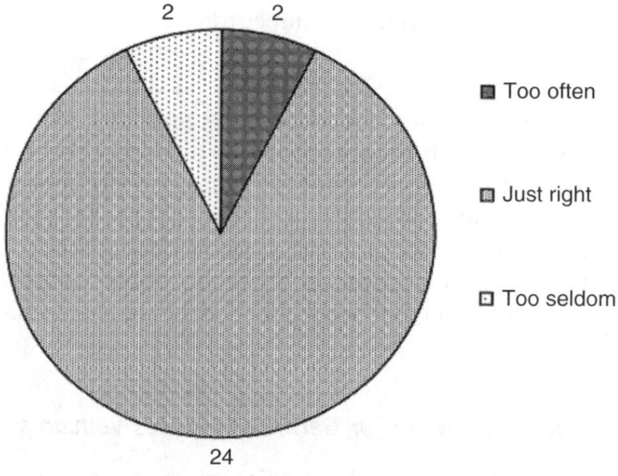

Figure 14.6 Investee's judgment on the contact frequency with the main investor ($n = 28$)

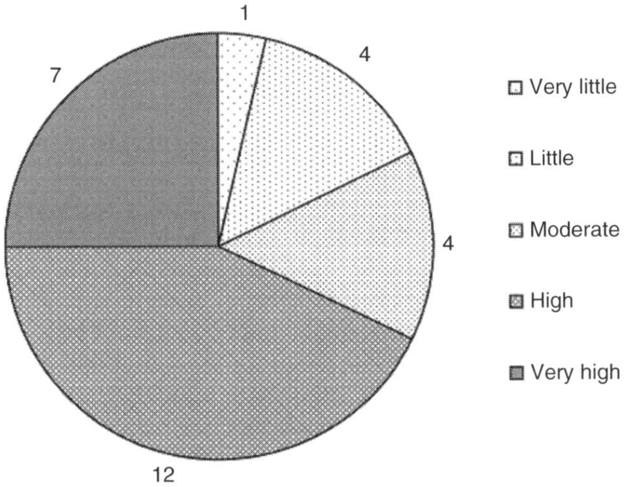

Figure 14.7 Perceived benefit from the contact with the main investor ($n = 28$)

For VC, the right investor and right investee do not often get together. This is partly due to the idiosyncrasies of VC financing and partly because there is simply a lack of information on the market participants.

In such a situation it would be desirable if intermediaries, such as tax accountants or lawyers, facilitated the match of offer and demand for VC. Our data show that these intermediaries fail to take this role. For 227 ventures from our sample we have information on who supported the investee in his search for external equity investors. Figure 14.8 summarizes this information.

Entrepreneurs looking for external equity financing mainly relied on their own research to find a suitable investor. In this classification, we also take into consideration funds

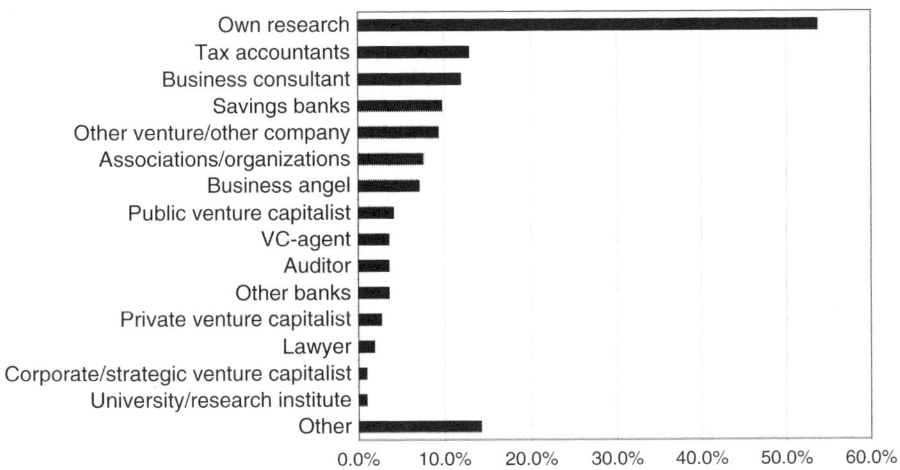

Figure 14.8 Facilitators in the search for an external equity investor

provided through friends and family. Typically these investors are approached without the help of an intermediary. The predominance of own efforts to some extent is due to the fact that in our sample ventures, friends and family often act as investors. However, we see the importance of own research also as a sign for the undeveloped role of intermediaries in the German market. When we look at intermediaries only tax accountants and business consultants seem to play a notable role.

It is interesting to see that savings banks take such a prominent role. This can be explained to some extent by their endeavor to offer comprehensive financing within the Sparkasse finance group.[14]

Recommendations from other ventures or other companies are noteworthy. It is interesting to see that agents that focus on venture capital are distant from mainstream suggestions and therefore the influence of universities and research institutes can be neglected in this case. As VC investors we believe that it would be helpful for tax accountants and business consultants to get in touch with business ventures in Germany. As most entrepreneurs still have to rely mainly on their own research, a certain degree of visibility in the German market is also needed. All other potential facilitators should also question whether their current efforts to promote external equity financing for German business ventures are sufficient. As we point out in Section 14.3, the entrepreneurs behind the most promising ventures are often university degree holders so it would be preferable if universities and research institutes decided to get more involved.

14.4 Conclusion

We have derived findings on the success factors for German business ventures and addressed important financial aspects for such ventures with recourse to a more substantial sample than in previous studies. The sample we use is limited neither to certain industries nor to particular regions. We consider this study as a contribution to narrow the research gap for German VC financing.

We conclude that the degree of innovation is crucial for the success of a business venture. Characteristics of the entrepreneur or characteristics of the business venture itself that foster the degree of innovation add to the venture's success. Characteristics that reduce the degree of innovation reduce its success. We find that the entrepreneurs' academic background is certainly one of the key elements that drive the degree of innovation. We conclude that certain fields of study, such as natural sciences and business sciences, are associated with a favorable business development in general. Potential entrepreneurs should ensure that they have a solid academic background. People with such backgrounds should be encouraged to think about launching their own business venture. In this regard it is comforting to know that our study did not show a relationship between the age of the founders and the ventures' success. On average, we find the entrepreneurs to be in their late 30s when they start their ventures. However, it has to be borne in mind that market timing is always important and that a window of opportunity will close over time. The more innovative ventures in our sample manage to generate considerable revenues. They also create substantial employment opportunities.

[14] It has to be borne in mind that the sample was built on a database from a business plan competition, in which the Sparkasse finance group takes a leading role.

For venture capitalists we recommend paying special attention to the degree of innovation of a venture they assess and – as it is easier to observe – the academic background of the entrepreneurs. They also have to bear in mind that intermediaries play a minor role in the matching of supply and demand for VC in Germany; only tax accountants and business consultants seem to be moderately active in this field. The majority of Germany business ventures have to be self-reliant when looking for potential equity investors. Thus, venture capitalists interested in the German market are well advised to be visible in that market and to be approachable. The German Equity Forum as well as the G-Forum, which take place on an annual basis, offer excellent opportunities for venture capitalists to get in touch with German business ventures. We found evidence that once the initial hindrances are overcome the entrepreneurs are positive about the relationship with their main investor. Most of the entrepreneurs in our sample have the impression that they benefit from contact with their main investor and that such contact is not too time-consuming. Yet we lack information on the degree of satisfaction of VC investors who fund German ventures. Certainly, the performance of such an investment must be considered. We believe that future research is needed on the actual performance of VC investments in Germany.

Of course, we would have liked the characteristics of the entrepreneurs and the characteristics of the business venture to explain the ventures' success more distinctively. Future research could try other characteristics or success indicators. Yet we are convinced that the same characteristics and success indicators could yield a more satisfactory degree of explanation in a modified research set-up. This research set-up should account for interrelations between and within venture and entrepreneur characteristics and the resulting collinearity issues. We strongly encourage future researchers to opt for statistical means and not to choose a purely qualitative approach. We are convinced that the field of VC financing is a very challenging one in which interdisciplinary teams will obtain the best results, and that it is a very rewarding field with high economic importance.

References

Achleitner, A.-K. and Klöckner, O. (2005). *Employment Contribution of Private Equity and Venture Capital in Europe*. European Private Equity and Venture Capital Association (EVCA) Research Report, Brussels.

Backhaus, K., Erichson, B., Plinke, W. and Weiber, R. (2003). *Multivariante Analysemethoden: Eine anwendungsorientierte Einführung*. 10th edition. Berlin: Springer.

Bergmann, R., Lückgen, I. and Sternberg, H. (2004). *GEM-Länderbericht Deutschland 2003*. Cologne: Wirtschafts- und Sozialgeographisches Institut.

Brüderl, J., Preisendörfer, P. and Ziegler, R. (1996). *Der Erfolg neugegründeter Betriebe*. Berlin: Duncker & Humblot.

Kulicke, M. (1993). *Chancen und Risiken junger Technologieunternehmen. Schriftenreihe des Frauenhofer-Instituts für Systemtechnik und Innovationsforschung (ISI)*. Heidelberg: Physica-Verlag.

Lehnert, N. (2004). *KfW-Gründungsmonitor 2004*. Annual publication of the KfW Banking Group, Frankfurt am Main.

Lückgen, I. and Sternberg, H. (2005). *GEM-Länderbericht Deutschland 2004*. Cologne: Wirtschafts- und Sozialgeographisches Institut.

Moser, K. and Schmid, F. (2003). *Beschreibende Statistik und Wirtschaftsstatistik*. Berlin: Springer.

Organization for Economic Cooperation and Development (2004). *Education at a Glance: OECD Indicators*. Paris: OECD.

Statistisches Bundesamt (2003). *Datenreport 2002*. 2nd edition. Bonn: Bundeszentrale für politische Bildung.

Storey, D.J. (1994). *Understanding the Small Business Sector*. London: Routledge.

Wanzenböck, H. (1998). *Überleben und Wachstum junger Unternehmen*. Vienna: Springer.

Werner, H. (2000). *Junge Technologieunternehmen. Entwicklungsverläufe und Erfolgsfaktoren*. Wiesbaden: Deutscher Universitäts-Verlag.

15 Financing practices in the German venture capital industry: An empirical study

Andreas Bascha and Uwe Walz

Abstract

This chapter investigates the various agency theoretical approaches to explain the use of different financial securities in VC finance, and compares them with survey data on the German VC market. Our empirical results suggest that the use of convertible securities, relative to other instruments, is generally influenced by the anticipated severity of agency problems. In contrast to traditional debt–equity mixes, the additional features of convertible securities such as state-contingent payoff functions (milestones) and the de-coupling of the payoff from the control problem seem to be much more suitable to address the control and incentive problems at the exit stage. Another important finding indicates that the use of a debt-like financing instrument that is very specific to the German market, the so-called silent partnership, can be explained by return requirements and the anticipated proportion of buy-backs, underlining the special role of public–private partnership agencies in Germany.

15.1 Introduction

Recently, the important role of venture capital organizations in providing financing for young and fast-growing firms has spread to most countries in Continental Europe. This is also because it has become widely accepted, among academics as well as politicians, that venture capital is playing an important role in the development of the overall economy.[1] The growing degree of acceptance of and the growth of VC can also be observed in Germany where, over the last decade, the VC industry has abandoned its niche existence.[2]

According to the U.S. role model the typical venture capitalist is characterized by a number of attributes.[3] Most importantly venture capitalists furnish companies with active capital, also called smart money, by getting directly involved in the management of portfolio firms. Further, they are mostly organized as closed-end funds, and want to invest for a limited period of time with the possibility of an attractive exit channel (in order to improve their re-funding ability). Portfolio firms are mostly provided with capital in a staged manner over various financing rounds, and the use of financing instruments

[1] Kortum and Lerner (2000), for instance, show that in the U.S. much of the growth in patenting appears to have been spurred by the activities of venture capitalists.

[2] See Spotorno (2004) and Glen (2002).

[3] See Sahlman (1990) for an almost classical overview.

ranges from traditional debt and equity to convertible securities such as convertible debt and convertible preferred shares.

A growing body of literature, both theoretical and empirical, has evolved over the past two decades and looks into the details and mechanisms of the North-American VC industry.[4] Very few empirical studies exist to date for the German VC industry, where appropriate data are almost entirely absent.[5]

Against this background our study aims, with the collection of proper data, at shedding further light on the specific aspects of the German VC market. This study is focused particularly on the financial relationship between the venture capitalists and their portfolio firms, with respect to the use of various financial instruments such as debt, equity, and convertible securities. Various agency theoretical approaches that explain the use of different financial securities in VC finance are investigated with respect to empirically testable hypotheses and then tested with our survey data.

Our results are threefold. First, it appears that the use of convertible securities relative to other feasible financing instruments is, for the most part, determined by proxy variables indicating the severity of agency problems. Second, regarding the importance of convertible securities relative to traditional debt–equity financing, our results are broadly in line with theoretical explanations arguing that the additional features of convertible securities such as state contingent payoff functions (milestones) and the de-coupling of the payoff from the control problem are much more suitable to address the control and incentive problems at the exit stage. The third important finding indicates that the use of a debt-like financing instrument that is very specific to the German market, the so-called silent partnership, can be explained by the special role played by public–private partnership agencies in Germany.

The chapter is organized as follows. In the next section we briefly investigate the theoretical literature on the use of different financial instruments in VC contracts in order to identify empirically testable hypotheses. In Section 15.3 our dataset is discussed. Section 15.4 presents a descriptive analysis of our data. In Section 15.5 we try to identify the factors determining the choice of different financial instruments in the German VC industry. In Section 15.6 we provide a brief summary.

15.2 Theoretical background

With perfect capital markets, that is with the absence of information costs, bankruptcy costs, and taxes, the famous irrelevance result of Modigliani and Miller (1958) holds. Financial structure does not have any impact on firm and investment value. In reality the assumptions of Modigliani and Miller are, however, often violated in a number of ways. Particularly in high-tech start-ups informational asymmetries and bankruptcy costs play an important role. Therefore, on the one hand, the possibility of raising external capital may be precluded entirely,[6] and on the other, the financial structure can be used

[4] For an overview see Gompers and Lerner (1999). For empirical studies on the structure of VC contracts, see Kaplan and Stromberg (2003, 2004) as well as Lerner and Schoar (2006).

[5] See, for example, Mayer et al. (2005), Schefczyk (2004), Audretsch and Lehmann (2002), Kuemmerle (2001), or Lessat (1999).

[6] See, for example, Greenwald et al. (1984).

to improve the value of firms and investment projects.[7] Financial economists have argued that specialized intermediaries, such as venture capitalists, can address these imperfections better than others.

Venture capitalists have developed special mechanisms to overcome the various agency problems between investors, fund managers, and entrepreneurs. The most common ones are financial covenants in partnership agreements (Feinendegen et al., 2003), screening mechanisms (Chan, 1983), control rights (Hellmann, 1998; Chan et al., 1990), and staging of the investment (Bergemann and Hege, 1998).

Regarding financial structure the most remarkable feature in the North American VC industry is the broad reliance on convertible securities. Various empirical studies have shown that the percentage of VC deals using some sort of convertible securities ranges from 20.9% to 94.5%, depending on the analyzed dataset.[8] These observations have led researchers to think about potential determinants of financial structure in VC contracts, especially the additional value of convertible securities.

Compared with traditional financial instruments such as loans, bonds, and equity, convertible securities exhibit significantly different structures and economic effects. Convertible securities are a mixture of debt and equity and a call option. This implies that, in contrast to debt and equity financing, the control and state contingent payoff mechanism associated with convertible securities gives room for much more flexibility.

Starting from a set of comparable assumptions, existing theoretical research on the design of VC contracts is based on different aspects of agency theory. These studies can be separated into two broad categories. On the one hand, these models look into the design of optimal incentives during the implementation of the project. On the other, there are models that focus on the fact that venture capitalists typically invest in their portfolio companies only for a limited period of time. Therefore, conflicts of interest may arise between the two parties over when and how the venture capitalist's exit should take place.

The main idea behind all these theoretical analyses is that in young and fast-growing firms a multiple of moral hazard problems (and sometimes adverse selection problems, too) exist at the same time, and in a variety of forms. These extended moral hazard problems are arguably the reasons for the observed complexity of contracts and the use of highly flexible instruments such as convertible securities.

The first class of models focuses on incentive problems during the implementation period of the portfolio firm's project. Typically, venture capitalists are actively involved in the management of the portfolio firm. Hence, a two-sided moral hazard problem may arise in the sense that the entrepreneur, as well as the venture capitalist, has to be induced to put in optimal effort. Because of the disutility of effort the entrepreneur as well as the venture capitalist may not undertake first-best actions in order to enhance the probability of success of the project. Repullo and Suarez (2004) as well as Casamatta (2003) have shown that such double moral hazard problems can be better addressed by convertible securities than by equity finance. The basic intuition is that on the one hand, because of the fixed repayment part of the convertible security, the entrepreneur has an incentive to reach, via his own effort, payoffs above the fixed repayment level. On the other hand, because of the conversion option, the venture capitalist has a more

[7] See, for example, Myers and Majluf (1984).
[8] See, for example, Cumming (2005), Kaplan and Stromberg (2004), Trester (1998).

pronounced incentive to put in effort with convertibles than with equity finance. The superiority of convertible securities is especially justified because the fiercer the effort problem, the higher the desired return of the venture capitalist relative to the return of the entire project. That is, we should expect a heavier reliance on convertible securities, first when venture capitalists and entrepreneurs are reaching for high goals (such as an IPO), second when the management resources of the venture capitalist are scarce (for example, a high number of portfolio firms), and third when venture capitalists have a high hurdle rate.

Another potential incentive problem during the implementation period is so-called window dressing. When capital contributions are staged, entrepreneurs have an incentive to create potentially unjustified positive signals about the probability of success of their project in order to achieve the next financing round. Cornelli and Oved (1997) have shown that if the difference in returns across possible states is very large, convertible securities prove to be superior to debt–equity contracts. This is due to the fact that the entrepreneur, by manipulating signals, runs the risk that the venture capitalist will exercise his conversion option, thus allowing him to buy underpriced equity when the development of the firm is most favorable. Consequently, we expect a more frequent use of convertible securities if capital contributions are staged, for example in start-ups, and if firm value differs significantly between the anticipated outcomes, for example IPOs against trade sales or buy-backs.

The second class of models deals with potential agency conflicts at the exit stage. From the outset of the project to the exit stage the crucial problem is in an inability to write a fully state-contingent contract, if there are different options about how and when the venture capitalist reacquires the liquidity of his investment and under what circumstances the entrepreneur loses or retains control over his firm.[9] Berglöf (1994), Bascha (2001), Bascha and Walz (2001), as well as Hellmann (2006) have highlighted the problem of an efficient choice between different exit channels. Whereas Hellmann (2006) focuses on a double moral hazard problem, the other models introduce the idea that both contracting parties associate non-monetary benefits or losses with different exit options. On the one hand there is the entrepreneur valuing positively his independence after the venture capitalist's exit. On the other hand there is the venture capitalist benefiting from a stronger reputation effect when a firm successfully goes public than with other exit options.[10] As individual effort choices influence the probabilities of different outcomes, there might be external effects to the non-monetary utilities associated with these outcomes. In contrast to traditional financing instruments such as debt and equity, convertible securities provide additional flexibility to align incentives and provide an efficient governance structure. Therefore, we would expect more convertible securities to be used if venture capitalists take into account the possibility of an IPO as a viable exit channel.

To sum up, the common features of all these models are that convertible securities should be used more often the more pronounced the incentive problems are. For example, if the parties aim at high goals such as IPOs, management resources of the venture capitalist are scarce and the higher are monetary return requirements.

[9] Many of the models of ownership (Hart and Moore, 1990; Grossman and Hart, 1986) and financing choice (Hart and Moore, 1998) depend on this assumption of incomplete contracting.

[10] See, for example, Black and Gilson (1999) or Gompers and Lerner (1999).

15.3 The data

We conducted a full survey by sending a questionnaire to all regular members of the German Venture Capital Association (BVK), ending with an effective participation rate of 49.6%. Rather than asking for data on the individual investments of the VC firm, our questions targeted aggregate financial behavior of the venture capital firms.

We distinguish two sets of questions. First, we are interested in some general characteristics such as age and number of portfolio firms, type of fund organization used (closed funds), the venture capitalists' required return relative to market average (subjective appraisal), and percentages of the venture capitalists' investments in different types of portfolio firms (start-up or expansion phase). Second, we ask for the relative frequencies of the various financial instruments in the investments as well as for the relative importance of various expected exit channels.

We complete our dataset by collecting general data for all non-responding VC firms via the internet, relying on the company information given on the webpage of the BVK and the respective firms. There we look for the NUMBER of financed portfolio firms, the AGE of the venture capitalist and his status (whether there was an influence of PUBLIC authorities or not). With these data we are able to test for selection bias in our sample by running a binary probit estimation for RESPONSE, which takes the value 1 if a response occurred and 0 otherwise (Table 15.1).

The status variable PUBLIC is significant only at the 5% level and seems to be small. Hence, we consider a possible selection bias in our data to be a minor problem.

Table 15.1 Binary probit estimation for selection bias. Dependent variable RESPONSE

Explanatory variable	Estimated coefficient	*p*-Value
CONST	0.611769	0.0116
PUBLIC	0.738647	0.0300
AGE	0.001171	0.5905
NUMBER	−0.014514	0.1672

Number of observations: 87, McFadden $R^2 = 0.1$.

15.4 Descriptive analysis

The first of our main objectives is to describe the financial behavior of VC firms in the German private equity market. Therefore, we focus on the use of different financial instruments. Against this background, it is crucial to consider specific aspects of German commercial law. While portfolio firms organized as public corporations can rely on equity and convertible securities,[11] the law entails a special treatment for portfolio firms organized as private limited companies. While they are not allowed to use convertible debt,[12] they can make use of equity-type instruments (partnership interests). Other specific

[11] See §§192 ff Aktien Gesetz (German Stock Companies Act).
[12] See §§238 HGB (German Commercial Code).

financial instruments allowed, such as participating certificates, do not fall into one of our broad categories. In our questionnaire, these instruments are included in the category 'other financial instruments'. Silent partnerships, a specific German debt-like financing instrument, loans, and proprietors' loans are independent of the legal form. We constructed the following categories and asked for their relative frequencies in the contracts.

As can be seen from Table 15.2, the instrument of silent partnerships is the most widely used in the German VC industry, followed by pure equity finance, debt–equity mix, and convertibles. Overall we obtain a relation of equity to non-equity and other financing instruments of about 51% to 49%. The financial instruments used by the majority of firms are pure equity (70%) and silent partnerships (63%). Looking at the detail, we find that there is always a large number of VC firms who do not use the respective financial instrument at all. As can be seen from Figure 15.1 this is especially true for the case of convertible securities (57.41%) and debt–equity mixes (66.67%), where even the majority of firms do not apply them. Thus, our findings are comparable with those of Cumming (2005), where it is shown for the Canadian VC market that a variety of securities are used, and convertibles were not the most frequent.

Table 15.2 Financial instruments used (percent)

	Equity only	Debt–equity mix	Convertible securities	Silent partnerships	Silent partnerships and debt	Other financial instruments
Mean	26.6	14.4	10.6	33.1	5.6	10.7
Median	20	0	0	15	0	0
Max	100	100	90	100	88	90
Min	0	0	0	0	0	0

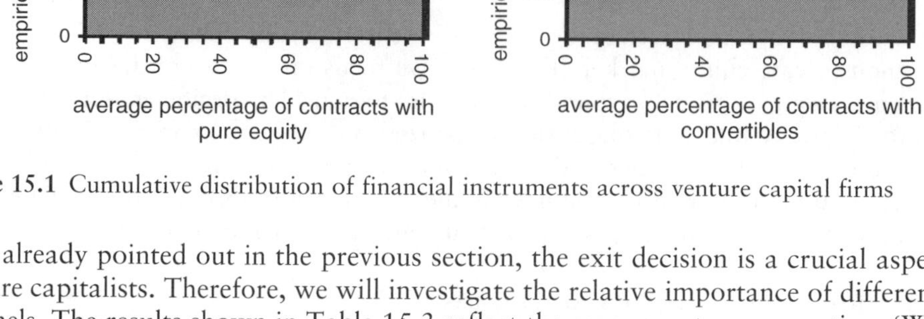

Figure 15.1 Cumulative distribution of financial instruments across venture capital firms

As already pointed out in the previous section, the exit decision is a crucial aspect for venture capitalists. Therefore, we will investigate the relative importance of different exit channels. The results shown in Table 15.3 reflect the responses to our question: 'What is

Table 15.3 Expected exit channels (in percentage points)

	IPO	Trade sale	Buy-back	Liquidation	Other
Mean	27.89	25.23	24.78	9.64	12.4
Max	70	100	100	70	100
Min	0	0	0	0	0

the expected frequency of an IPO, trade sale, buy-back, liquidation, or other alternative as an exit channel from your portfolio companies?'

Obviously venture capitalists like to see a high frequency of exits realized through IPOs and trade sales. On the other hand, there is also a significant frequency of anticipated buy-backs. This might be due to the fact that German entrepreneurs are said to have a strong preference for control over their firms and hence tend to favor a buy-back in order to remain independent. The important point we want to stress here is that at the contracting stage parties are relying mostly on their expectations in order to structure their financial relationship.

From our theoretical considerations it follows that the degree of uncertainty and risk involved might be crucial. Therefore, the stage of investment is potentially decisive for the financial structure.

We asked for the percentage of portfolio firms in the start-up or expansion phase. It turns out that the average of portfolio firms in the start-up stage is 36.9%, whereas it is 59.8% for the expansion period.[13] As mentioned above, we collected some general data, reflecting age and status of the venture capitalist as well as the number of firms in their portfolios. We aimed to capture an important feature of the German market regarding the status of the venture capitalist. Using the membership list of the BVK we characterize a venture capitalist as being PUBLIC if the ownership structure indicates that there might be an influence of public authorities either directly or indirectly.[14] We otherwise define the respective venture capitalist as being private. In the first case we set the PUBLIC variable equal to 1 and in the second case equal to 0. We thus find 43% of venture capitalists to be public. This corresponds well with the findings of Schefczyk (2004) who shows that 38% of all VC firms were either public co-investment companies, investment companies for medium-sized firms (Mittelständische Beteiligungsgesellschaften), or saving/regional banks (Sparkassen, Landesbanken).

The data on the variable AGE reflect the fact that German VC firms are rather young (50% of the firms have been established in the last decade). Few old firms exist and the mean age is 14.4 years, which mirrors the youth of the German private equity market.[15] Figure 15.2 additionally shows the size profile of the venture capitalist's portfolios. This distribution is highly skewed because only a few venture capitalists manage a large number

[13] The remaining part (the two figures do not add up to 100%) is in other phases of the investment cycle, for example seed, turnaround and buy-out stages.

[14] Banks or finance institutions mainly controlled by public authorities are very often interested in the promotion of regional business structures and employment.

[15] With respect to the characterization of very old firms care is needed. First, there are some international players that have been engaged in the German market for a typically much shorter time. Second, some firms have been active in another industry before entering the VC business.

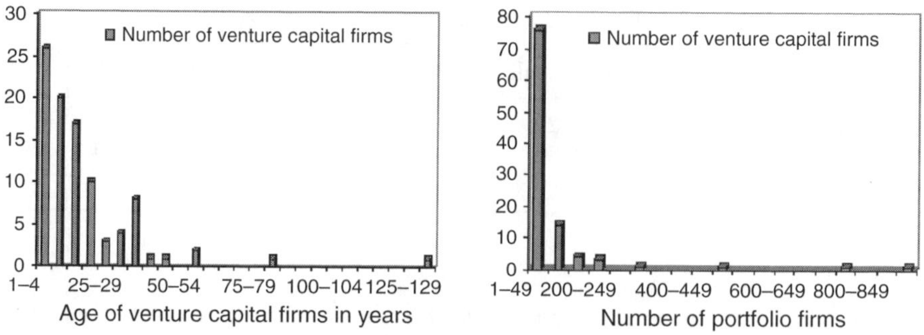

Figure 15.2 Age of venture capitalists and number of firms in their portfolio

of portfolio firms. Eleven venture capitalists have invested in 100 or more portfolio companies, of which eight are public and three private. This highlights once again the important role of public companies in the German market.

15.5 Does theory match with practice?

In this section we turn to our second goal, namely the analysis of the financial contract design between investors, venture capitalists, and portfolio firms.

Our theoretical discussion showed the exit problem to be a decisive factor in the design of the financial structure. This exit problem is aggravated if the VC firm itself is financed via a closed-end fund. The relevant information is the binary variable CLOSED, equal to 1 if the form of closed-end funds is used and 0 otherwise. From an economic point of view, closed-end funds can reduce the agency problems between the VC firm and the investor. For example, venture capitalists do not want to terminate their investments in poorly performing firms at due time because of the associated loss of reputation. Therefore, one would expect this organizational form to be most common with private and young VC firms, where agency problems and (marginal) reputation effects are potentially the highest. This is confirmed by the data. The results of the binary probit estimation reported in Table 15.4 reveal that PUBLIC and AGE have a negative and significant impact on the use of closed-end funds.

Table 15.4 Binary probit estimation for the use of closed-end funds. Dependent variable CLOSED

Explanatory variable	Estimated coefficient	*p*-Value
CONST	0.525984	0.3042
PUBLIC	−1.361245	0.0031
AGE	−0.060653	0.0560
STARTUP	0.004033	0.5447
NUMBER	−0.001159	0.6881

Number of observations: 57, McFadden $R^2 = 0.28$.

Turning to the financial contract design between venture capitalist and portfolio firms, we have already seen in the descriptive analysis that there is always a significant number of VC firms in our sample that do not use the respective financial instrument. Therefore for the majority of our estimations we use the censored regression model (Tobit).[16]

In the set of explanatory variables we include IPO (+), TRADE SALE (+, −), BUY-BACK (−), EXPANSION (+, −), CLOSED (+), RETHIGH (+), RETMEAN (+, −), with the signs in parentheses representing our expectations of the variables' influence on the perceived extent of agency problems. As one can see, we thereby break down the RETURN variable into separate binary variables RETHIGH, RETMEAN, RETLOW, which take the value of 1 if the answer in the questionnaire occurred in the respective category and 0 otherwise.[17] We take AGE and NUMBER as additional control variables. Hence, we choose to disregard LIQUIDATION, STARTUP, RETLOW, and PUBLIC as explanatory variables. This is because the LIQUIDATION, STARTUP, and RETLOW are residual variables for the exit, stage, and return questions. With regard to PUBLIC there is a high correlation with RETURN. Hence, only one of them should be included in the same set of explanatory variables. The first step is a Tobit estimation for the dependent variable CS, which denotes the frequency of convertible securities in percentage points given as an average over all contracts of a single venture capitalist (Table 15.5).

Table 15.5 Tobit estimation on the use of convertible securities. Dependent variable CS

Explanatory variable	Estimated coefficient	*p*-Value
CONST	−22.00753	0.1953
IPO	0.470047	0.0089
TRADE SALE	−0.389272	0.0897
BUY-BACK	−0.165778	0.4800
EXPANSION	−0.073275	0.5527
CLOSED	7.966538	0.3489
RETHIGH	46.74868	0.0015
RETMEAN	22.52156	0.0451
AGE	1.104376	0.0182
NUMBER	−0.149694	0.2541

Number of observations: 47, adjusted $R^2 = 0.51$.

All significant agency variables can be interpreted in line with theoretical considerations. Most importantly the higher the expected amount of IPOs, the more pressing is the exit problem and the higher the effort required from both agents. This effect is also very robust against the variation of the assumed underlying distribution function. In a regression that controls for robust standard errors and covariance (Huber/White) IPO is the only

[16] See, for example, Amemiya (1985: chapter 10). From a statistical point of view this makes the usual linear regression model inappropriate. Economically one can think of the Tobit model as a model that explains a certain threshold effect. In our context this means that there might be different levels of agency problems such that venture capitalists switch from traditional financing instruments such as debt and equity to more sophisticated ones.

[17] This avoids the problematic interpretation of an ordinal explanatory variable on the right-hand side. See Greene (1993), for the problem of threshold effects in this context.

variable that remains significant at the 5% level. The negative influence of TRADE SALE is only significant at the 10% level. This finding could be interpreted as slight evidence for the argument that the expected frequency of IPOs and trade sales has different effects on the anticipated severity of agency problems, calling for a more or less extensive use of convertible securities. We will investigate this argument in the next estimation on the relation between convertible securities and debt–equity financing in greater detail.

Further, it turns out that VC firms with high return claims use convertible securities, with their flexible incentive and control mechanisms, significantly more often. This result favors on the one hand the double moral hazard models and indicates on the other that public–private partnership agencies face less pressure to solve agency problems because of their moderate return requirements. We regard this as a major explanation for the quantitatively lower importance of convertibles in Germany.

The last significant variable, AGE, can also be interpreted in the light of the special structure of the German VC market. As a matter of fact, older venture capitalists have more experience with this special kind of financial instrument. Additionally, the international players on the German market are not only much older than original German VC firms but also much more familiar with convertibles.

For the most part the theoretical models explain the superiority of convertible securities over traditional financing instruments such as debt–equity mixes as a benchmark case. Though debt–equity mixes show flexibility in payoff structures, and include the possibility of a control change in poor states, the additional features of convertible securities, such as state contingent payoff functions (milestones) and the de-coupling of the payoff from the control problem, are much more suited to deal with the complexity of agency problems in VC finance. For example, the conversion option can either widen the spread in payoffs leading to improved incentives or transfer control rights even in good states. Both effects are not available under debt–equity mixes. However, since these instruments are quite closely inter-related, it is sensible to compare them with each other and to analyze the features that make one or the other more attractive. For that reason we compute the difference between the two variables, convertible securities (CS) and debt–equity mixes (DE) and call this new variable CSDE. As this new variable ranges from −100% to +100%, the problem with a large number of zero observations at the sides of the distribution is avoided. Hence, we are able to perform an ordinary-least-squares regression (Table 15.6).

The only two significant variables are IPO (5% level) and TRADE SALE (1% level). This supports the theoretical hypothesis that it is mainly the anticipated agency problems associated with IPOs that drive the decision to use convertible securities instead of traditional debt–equity mixes, as argued by Bascha (2001), Bascha and Walz (2001) and Hellmann (2006). The negative sign of the variable TRADE SALE is consistent with the explanation offered by Berglöf (1994), since in this model the use of convertibles is not really necessary if the venture capitalist sells together with the entrepreneur in a trade sale.

Next, we take a closer look at the two remaining categories in VC finance, equity and silent partnerships. As outlined in the previous section, these instruments are used by the majority of venture capitalists. For both variables we run the same Tobit estimation as for CS above.

There are no significant variables other than RETMEAN, indicating that the use of equity finance alone is not influenced by our proxies for the severity of agency problems (Table 15.7). Further, the significance of RETMEAN supports the interpretation that pure equity finance is the most suitable instrument for the financing of average portfolio

Table 15.6 Ordinary-least-squares estimation for the difference between convertibles and debt–equity mix. Dependent variable CSDE

Explanatory variable	Estimated coefficient	*p*-Value
CONST	0.360767	0.9816
IPO	0.463478	0.0473
TRADE SALE	−1.012117	0.0014
BUY-BACK	0.007762	0.9672
EXPANSION	−0.059985	0.7017
CLOSED	−10.88889	0.3440
RETHIGH	18.04575	0.3267
RETMEAN	14.45264	0.2575
AGE	0.695995	0.1972
NUMBER	−0.022024	0.5275

Number of included observations: 47, adjusted $R^2 = 0.24$.

Table 15.7 Tobit estimation for the percentage of equity used. Dependent variable EQUITY

Explanatory variable	Estimated coefficient	*p*-Value
CONST	−12.17049	0.4800
IPO	0.260096	0.2522
TRADE SALE	0.070897	0.8129
BUY-BACK	−0.184656	0.4135
EXPANSION	0.192387	0.2330
CLOSED	−3.035397	0.7889
RETHIGH	17.14406	0.3557
RETMEAN	40.36616	0.0018
AGE	−0.419376	0.4653
NUMBER	−0.039564	0.5291

Number of observations: 47, adjusted $R^2 = 0.22$.

firms showing a normal degree of agency problems. Using equity finance the venture capitalist both becomes a residual claimant to the returns of the project, which enhances his incentive to put effort into the project, and also receives control and information rights in order to monitor the firm. Together with the results above, this confirms the view that the incentive properties and the complexity of the chosen financial structure vary positively with the anticipated degree of incentive and control problems faced by the contracting parties.

This relates also to the following results in Table 15.8. There, we aggregate silent partnerships and debt to form the variable SILENTDEBT. According to the theory of traditional moral hazard, the use of silent partnerships and debt should be most prominent if it suffices to provide the (risk-neutral) entrepreneur with the right incentives (Harris and Raviv, 1979). That is for the venture capitalist, for a low degree of control and monitoring problems, and a minor importance of the exit problem. For example, if the

Table 15.8 Tobit estimation on the use of silent partnerships and debt. Dependent variable SILENTDEBT

Explanatory variable	Estimated coefficient	p-Value
CONST	76.84001	0.0000
IPO	−0.595809	0.0162
TRADE SALE	−0.122496	0.6757
BUY-BACK	0.355371	0.0247
EXPANSION	−0.046739	0.7552
CLOSED	−41.16246	0.0010
RETHIGH	−62.61049	0.0038
RETMEAN	−38.29968	0.0006
AGE	−0.024771	0.9576
NUMBER	0.010978	0.7034

Number of observations: 47, adjusted $R^2 = 0.70$.

venture capitalist does not aim at an IPO, he is not refinanced by a closed-end fund and his return requirement is below market average. Additionally, entrepreneurs who aim at a buy-back and are reluctant to share control over their firm prefer debt-like financing instruments. Also, with debt finance venture capitalists get a sufficiently hard claim in order to enforce their payoff rights in the case of a buy-back.

All significant effects are completely in line with theory. Most notably, we find a significant and negative effect for initial public offerings and a positive effect for the buy-back alternative as exit channels on the choice of debt-like financing instruments by German venture capitalists. Together with the negative effects of CLOSED, RETHIGH, and RETMEAN, respectively, it becomes quite obvious that silent partnerships and debt financing are most often used if the venture capitalist does not care much about the incentive and control aspects of the exit problem and does not aim exclusively at maximizing the returns from investments. In this context one could argue that public–private partnership agencies are traditionally supporting the financing of start-ups and medium-sized firms by publicly guaranteed loans in order to promote regional development. As they do not face the same extent of agency problems as private venture capitalists, they are more likely to use rather low-powered incentive-compatible financing instruments such as debt and silent partnerships.

15.6 Conclusion

In this chapter, we have investigated various agency theoretical approaches to explain the design of financial contracts in VC finance and compared them with survey data on the German VC market. One of our empirical results suggests that private and young venture capitalists refund themselves significantly more often by means of closed-end funds. This indicates that there may be a significant difference between private venture capitalists and public–private partnership agencies in the perceived extent of agency problems.

Our results are broadly in line with the theoretical hypotheses derived in the literature regarding the determinants of the chosen financial structure. We find that in cases when venture capitalists expect a high frequency of initial public offerings as the exit channel they are more inclined to use the more complex and flexible financial securities, especially convertible securities. Higher return claims and the use of closed-end funds also make the use of these instruments more likely. In contrast with traditional debt–equity mixes, the additional features of convertible securities, such as state contingent payoff functions (milestones) and the de-coupling of the payoff from the control problem, seem to be much more suitable to address the control and incentive problems at the exit stage. Another important finding indicates that the use of debt-like financing instruments can be explained by low return requirements and the anticipated proportion of buy-backs, underlining the special role of public–private partnership agencies in Germany.

Acknowledgment

Andreas Bascha works for the German Central Bank (Deutsche Bundesbank) which, as a matter of policy, disclaims any responsibility for any publication or statements by any of their employees. The views expressed herein are those of the authors alone and do not necessarily reflect the view of Deutsche Bundesbank.

References

Ameniya, T. (1985). *Advanced Econometrics*. Oxford: Blackwell.

Audretsch, D.B. and Lehmann, E. (2002). *Debt or Equity? The Role of Venture Capital in Financing the New Economy in Germany*. CEPR Discussion Paper Series, No. 3656. London: Centre for Economic Policy Research.

Bascha, A. (2001). *Hybride Beteiligungsformen bei Venture Capital: Finanzierung und Corporate Governance in jungen Unternehmen*. Wiesbaden: DUV.

Bascha, A. and Walz, U. (2001). Convertible Securities and Optimal Exit Decisions in Venture Capital Finance. *Journal of Corporate Finance*, 7(3):285–306.

Bergemann, D. and Hege, U. (1998). Dynamic Venture Capital Financing, Learning and Moral Hazard. *Journal of Banking and Finance*, 22(6–8):703–735.

Berglöf, E. (1994). A Control Theory of Venture Capital Finance. *Journal of Law, Economics and Organisation*, 10(2):247–267.

Black, B.S. and Gilson, R.J. (1999). Venture Capital and the Structure of Capital Markets: Banks Versus Stock Markets. *Journal of Financial Economics*, 47(3):243–277.

Casamatta, C. (2003). Financing and Advising: Optimal Financial Contracts with Venture Capitalists. *Journal of Finance*, 58(5):2059–2085.

Chan, Y. (1983). On the Positive Role of Financial Intermediation in Allocation of Venture Capital in a Market with Imperfect Information. *Journal of Finance*, 38(5):1543–1568.

Chan, Y., Siegel, D.R. and Thakor, A.V. (1990). Learning, Corporate Control and Performance Requirements in Venture Capital Contracts. *International Economic Review*, 31(2):365–381.

Cornelli, F. and Oved, Y. (1997). *Stage Financing and the Role of Convertible Debt*. CEPR Discussion Paper Series, No. 1735. London: Centre for Economic Policy Research.

Cumming, D.J. (2005). Capital Structure in Venture Finance. *Journal of Corporate Finance*, 11(3):550–585.

Feinendegen, S., Schmidt, D. and Wahrenburg, M. (2003). Die Vertragsbeziehungen zwischen Investoren und europäischen Venture Capital Fonds: Eine empirische Untersuchung und Klassifizierung unterschiedlicher Vertragsmuster. *Zeitschrift für Betriebswirtschaft*, 73(11):1167–1195.

Glen, J. (2002). The European Venture Capital Market. In Greenwood, R.P. (ed.), *Handbook of Financial Planning and Control*. Aldershot: Gower, 325–336.

Gompers, P.A. and Lerner, J. (1999). *The Venture Capital Cycle*. Cambridge MA: MIT Press.

Greene, W.H. (1993). *Econometric Analysis*. New York: Prentice Hall.

Greenwald, B.C., Stiglitz, J.E. and Weiss, A. (1984). Information Imperfections in the Capital Market and Macroeconomic Fluctuations. *American Economic Review, Papers and Proceedings*, 74:194–199.

Grossman, S. and Hart, O.D. (1986). The Costs and Benefits of Ownership: A Theory of Vertical and Lateral Integration. *Journal of Political Economy*, 94(4):691–719.

Harris, M. and Raviv, A. (1979). Optimal Incentive Contracts with Imperfect Information. *Journal of Economic Theory*, 20(2):231–259.

Hart, O.D. and Moore, J. (1990). Property Rights and the Nature of the Firm. *Journal of Political Economy*, 98(6):1119–1158.

Hart, O.D. and Moore, J. (1998). Default and Renegotiation: A Dynamic Model of Debt. *Quarterly Journal of Economics*, 113(1):1–41.

Hellmann, T.F. (1998). The Allocation of Control Rights in Venture Capital Contracts. *RAND Journal of Economics*, 29(1):57–76.

Hellmann, T.F. (2006). IPOs, Acquisitions and the Use of Convertible Securities in Venture Capital. *The Journal of Financial Economics* Forthcoming.

Kaplan, S.N. and Stromberg, P. (2003). Financial Contracting Theory Meets the Real World: An Empirical Analysis of Venture Capital Contracts. *Review of Economic Studies*, 70(2):281–316.

Kaplan, S. and Stromberg, P. (2004). Characteristics, Contracts, and Actions: Evidence from Venture Capital Analyses. *The Journal of Finance*, 59(5):2177–2210.

Kortum, S. and Lerner, J. (2000). Assessing the Contribution of Venture Capital to Innovation. *RAND Journal of Economics*, 31(4):674–692.

Kuemmerle, W. (2001). Comparing Catalysts of Change. Evolution and Institutional Differences in the Venture Capital Industries in the U.S., Japan and Germany. In Burgelman, R.A. and Chesbrough, H. (eds), *Comparative Studies of Technological Evolution*. Research on Technological Innovation, Management and Policy, Vol. 7. Amsterdam: Elsevier, 227–261.

Lerner, J. and Schoar, A. (2006). Transaction Structures in the Developing World: Evidence from Private Equity. *Journal of Finance* Forthcoming.

Lessat, V. (1999). *Beteiligungskapital und technologierorientierte Unternehmensgründungen: Markt – Finanzierungen – Rahmenbedingungen*. Wiesbaden: Gabler.

Mayer, C., Schoors, K. and Yafeh, Y. (2005). Sources of Funds and Investment Activities of Venture Capital Funds: Evidence from Germany, Israel, Japan and the United Kingdom. *Journal of Corporate Finance*, 11(3):586–608.

Myers, S.C. and Majluf, N.S. (1984). Corporate Financing and Investment Decisions when Firms Have Information That Investors Do Not Have. *Journal of Financial Economics*, 13(2):187–221.

Modigliani, F. and Miller, M. (1958). The Cost of Capital, Corporation Finance and the Theory of Investment. *American Economic Review*, 48(3):261–297.

Repullo, R. and Suarez, J. (2004). Venture Capital Finance: A Security Design Approach. *Review of Finance*, 8(1):75–108.

Sahlman, W.A. (1990). The Structure and Governance of Venture Capital Organizations. *Journal of Financial Economics*, 27(2):473–521.

Schefczyk, M. (2004). *Erfolgsstrategien Deutscher Venture Capital Gesellschaften.* Stuttgart: Schäfer-Pöschel.

Spotorno, L. (2004). The Venture Capital Industry in Europe: Trends and Figures. In Caselli, S. and Gatti, S. (eds), *Venture Capital: A Euro-System Approach*. Heidelberg: Springer, 285–315.

Trester, J.J. (1998). Venture Capital Contracting Under Asymmetric Information. *Journal of Banking and Finance*, 22(6–8):675–699.

16 Covenants in venture capital contracts: Theory and empirical evidence from the German capital market

Ron C. Antonczyk, Wolfgang Breuer, and Klaus Mark

Abstract

Young innovative firms operate in high-tech branches and their value is mainly determined by specific, non-transferable knowledge controlled by the entrepreneur and other important employees. We discuss which specific forms of agency problems and hold-up conflicts arise from this particular situation. Moreover, we show that typical characteristics of venture capital contracts, such as stage financing and vesting provisions, are utilized to mitigate these problems in certain ways that could not be accomplished by simple capital structure optimization or the sole establishment of monetary incentive contracts. Using a hand-collected sample of contracts from the German VC market, we analyze whether there is empirical evidence for our hypotheses of the relevance of particular covenants in VC contracts. We compare our results with those of other empirical papers in the same spirit, such as Kaplan and Strömberg (2003) and Gompers and Lerner (2004).

16.1 Introduction

Young innovative firms operate in high-tech branches and their value is mainly determined by specific, non-transferable knowledge controlled by the entrepreneur and other important employees. We discuss which specific forms of agency problems and hold-up conflicts arise from this particular situation. Moreover, we show that typical characteristics of VC contracts are utilized to mitigate these problems in certain ways that could not be accomplished by simple capital structure optimization or the sole establishment of monetary incentive contracts. Using a hand-collected sample of contracts from the German VC market, we analyze whether there is empirical evidence for our hypotheses of the relevance of particular covenants in VC contracts. We compare our results with those of other empirical papers in the same spirit, such as Kaplan and Strömberg (2003).

16.2 Venture capital, agency problems, and hold-up

The relationship between an entrepreneur and his or her venture capitalist(s) is burdened by agency conflicts (hidden information and hidden action) and hold-up problems (Gompers and Lerner, 2004; Kaplan and Strömberg, 2001). In contrast to other financing relationships between the management of a firm and outside investors, conflict intensity may be especially high in VC financing. This is due to the fact that factors causing these conflicts are more severe in the environment of firms operating in high-tech industries and developing innovative products. Table 16.1 provides an overview of the factors that intensify agency conflicts and hold-up problems in the relationship between the entrepreneur and the venture capitalist as well as contractual provisions to reduce these problems.

The factors listed on the left-hand side of Table 16.1 lead to several serious conflicts between the parties involved. First, the entrepreneur's preferences concerning project decisions and the allocation of his or her work time among different projects as a result of (1) (Table 16.1) cause hidden action conflicts between the entrepreneur and the venture

Table 16.1 Specific factors that cause agency and hold-up problems in venture capital financing and contractual provisions to mitigate these conflicts

Factors causing severe agency and hold-up problems	Contractual provisions to mitigate agency and hold-up problems
1) The entrepreneur views himself more as an engineer or a scientist than as a manager and reaps benefits from being self-employed. 2) Lack of a track record. 3) High volatility of market environment and high complexity of production process. 4) Relatively small probability of success. 5) Lack of physical assets that could be used as collateral and importance of specific human capital. 6) Lack of precise indicators for economic success. 7) Interdependent principal–agent relationships between the entrepreneur and the venture capitalist, since the latter typically consults the growth company.	*Hidden action* a) The entrepreneur receives a substantial part of the equity of the portfolio firm. b) Debt should not be a major financing source. c) The venture capitalists receive additional information and control rights. d) The entrepreneur's wage and shareholding is made dependent on the earnings situation of the portfolio firm; separation of cash-flow rights and voting rights. e) Stage financing. f) Anti-dilution provisions concerning the shareholding of the venture capitalist. *Hidden information* Basically the same provisions as used to mitigate hidden action problems; offered as a menu of contracts to induce a self-selection process. *Hold-up* a) Competition clauses. b) Vesting provisions. c) Prohibition of sale of entrepreneur's shares. d) The venture capitalists receive additional control rights.

capitalist. As a consequence of factor (3) there is a substantial informational asymmetry between the entrepreneur and outside investors, which enables the entrepreneur to pursue such opportunistic behavior. Furthermore, because of factors (2) and (4), it is very difficult to mitigate moral hazard problems with reputation effects.

The lack of reputation effects and the private non-pecuniary benefit the entrepreneur reaps from being a self-employed executive may cause incentives for window dressing in order to delay necessary restructuring that, in many cases, would involve a management change or the liquidation of the project (Cornelli and Yosha, 2003). Moreover, in a volatile environment, in combination with limited wealth of the entrepreneur, a capital structure that leaves the entrepreneur as a substantial residual claimant on the margin also intensifies risk-shifting incentives (Mark, 2005: 142). Because of factors (5), (6), and (7), it is difficult to create traditional incentive schemes (such as performance-sensitive income streams or the utilization of collaterals) conventionally used to mitigate agency conflicts (Bester and Hellwig, 1989; Williamson, 1988; Harris and Raviv, 1979; Jensen and Meckling, 1976).

Factors (2), (3), (4), (5), and (6) are also accountable for intensive hidden information problems in VC financing. The lack of a track record and large informational asymmetries make it difficult for venture capitalists to select the most talented entrepreneurs and those business models with substantial growth opportunities. In addition, there are considerable difficulties in creating efficient signaling devices (Leland and Pyle, 1977) in VC environments. Since the probability of success is quite low anyway, reputation effects that would worsen the entrepreneur's chances of raising capital in the future in case he or she has been proven to be incapable of running the growth company do not establish substantial signaling costs for the entrepreneur. Furthermore, the simultaneous appearance of hidden information problems and hidden action problems makes it difficult or even counter-productive to create signaling devices by making the entrepreneur's income stream highly dependent upon profits. Particularly, extremely performance-sensitive contract designs used to select managers with high capabilities may, at the same time, attract gamblers.

Finally, VC financing will often be burdened by hold-up problems (Hart and Moore, 1994). Because of the high volatility of the environment of growth firms, contracts will likely prove to be incomplete during the progress of the financing relationship, allowing the parties to enforce renegotiation of the financing conditions. The respective conflicts are usually severe in VC financing since the contracting parties carry out highly specific investments. If the portfolio firm fails, literally all invested venture capital will be lost. On the other hand, the entrepreneur also typically invests a substantial amount of money (at least in proportion to his or her wealth), which to some degree prevents the entrepreneur from detrimental behavior. The larger part of VC investment, however, is used to build up the entrepreneur's (specific) human capital, which will not be sunk entirely if the entrepreneur is able to apply it somewhere else. Therefore, in unforeseen contingencies the entrepreneur often will possess more negotiating power if the venture capitalist is not able to prevent him or her from using his or her human capital outside the portfolio firm and thus stealing the core competencies of the firm (Rajan and Zingales, 2001; Zingales, 2000). Regarding the complexity of innovation processes, such stealing is usually not verifiable in a court. Venture capitalists also have to worry about key employees leaving the firm in the wake of the entrepreneur's exit. Furthermore, venture capitalists face the problem that key employees might leave the firm if their expectations about the existence of a basis for a successful future in the growth firm change. Thus, in designing VC contracts and interacting with the portfolio firms' representatives during the financing relationship, venture capitalists have to account for the large fraction of organizational capital in growth firms that can be interpreted as a network of interacting human capital and cannot be rebuilt easily.

16.3 Incentive instruments in venture capital financing relationships

Because of the problems outlined in the preceding section, the entrepreneur should receive a substantial part of the firm's equity to make his or her personal wealth dependent on firm value. However, it follows from (6) that there will be serious problems regarding the assessment of the value of the portfolio company. According to factor (7), one has to consider that the venture capitalist also should receive a substantial part of the firm's equity. Of course, making the investor residual claimant leads to a dilution of the entrepreneur's incentives. Moreover, pure debt financing typically proves not to be a good alternative either, because of factors (3) and (5) (risk-shifting incentives and no collateral). Notwithstanding these problems, regarding that venture capitalists have a long-term investment horizon and regarding their intensive involvement in the affairs of their portfolio companies, one might argue that the venture capitalist should be able to restructure the firm and to correct the entrepreneur's mistakes after the firm goes into bankruptcy. As a debt holder, the venture capitalist could rely on the monetary incentive effects of debt as long as the portfolio firm is solvent. When the firm becomes insolvent because of poor management decisions, the venture capitalist can still restructure. In most circumstances, however, (pure) debt financing will prove to be an inferior strategy in VC finance: the lack of a track record and the importance of the organizational capital lead to extraordinarily high costs of financial distress. Therefore, restructuring clearly has to start before the growth firm has to file for insolvency. Even if the venture capitalist as a debt holder had the necessary control rights in the form of credit covenants to change corporate policy in time, debt financing would not be favorable, since in order to use such control rights effectively the venture capitalist needs comprehensive knowledge about the innovation project, which is expensive to acquire. In most cases, interest rates will not be high enough to cover costs of gathering enough information because of legal or economic restrictions (for example, as a consequence of potential risk-shifting problems). As a result, pure debt is not a suitable VC financing instrument and venture capitalists almost always have an equity stake to participate without limitations in the growth opportunities of their portfolio firms (Mark, 2005: 156). Simple equity or debt financing will thus hardly be sufficient to mitigate incentive problems on the entrepreneur's side, creating a need for additional covenants.

To begin with, hidden action problems are typically somewhat reduced by information and control rights held by the venture capitalist. For example, the venture capitalist receives veto rights for important transactions or the right to appoint members of the supervisory board independently of his or her shareholding. Considering the fact that VC contracts usually establish a long-term financing relationship, it is plausible that the venture capitalist learns about the entrepreneur's management capabilities and the earnings potential of the portfolio firm as the relationship progresses. This should enable the venture capitalist to gradually adjust incentive instruments such as performance-sensitive payments as time elapses. Furthermore, it seems useful to construct some incentive instruments that are conditional on the entrepreneur's success in meeting milestones, which are explicitly written into the VC contract. This is exactly the intuition for stage financing, a common practice in VC finance (Bergemann and Hege, 1998; Sahlman, 1990). In addition, stage financing establishes limits concerning the financial facilities at the entrepreneur's disposal. A similar incentive device is established by variable allocation of the shares of the portfolio firm, which awards the entrepreneur if he or she fulfils the milestones contractually agreed upon. Stage financing may also be important as a device for the venture capitalist to operate on a reduced level of financial risk. Stage financing is often combined with anti-dilution rights that protect the venture capitalist from losses in future financing rounds.

Instruments to mitigate hidden action problems can also be used to reduce hidden information problems. For this purpose, the instruments mentioned above have to be structured as a menu of different VC contracts that are offered to the entrepreneur at the beginning of the financing relationship. The choice among the admissible contracts establishes a self-selection device for the entrepreneur. Through his or her decision, the entrepreneur reveals some of his or her private information. But, as discussed above, in VC financing we would expect to find combinations of hidden information and hidden action problems. Therefore, performance-sensitive provisions used as a signaling device should be complemented by measures to mitigate resulting risk-shifting incentives in order to deter gambling. Such measures would be control rights, for example.

Hold-up conflicts will be reduced if the termination of the financing relationship between the entrepreneur and the venture capitalist is expensive from the entrepreneur's point of view. To reach this, VC contracts very often encompass competition clauses, prohibition of sale provisions, and vesting provisions. Competition clauses prohibit the entrepreneur from working for another company in the industry for a certain period of time after the termination of his or her employment for the portfolio firm. A prohibition of sale provision forbids the entrepreneur to sell his or her shares unless the venture capitalist agrees. Through vesting provisions, the entrepreneur's shareholding increases over time. If the entrepreneur quits his or her job against the interests of the venture capitalist, the entrepreneur will lose the right to gain additional shares that would otherwise be given to him or her in the future.

16.4 Empirical data

The data employed in this chapter consist of 51 VC investments and were provided by three venture capitalists. The 51 datasets consist of business plans, investment proposals, financing contracts, and financial statements of the portfolio firms covering several years. The data entail only investments in German young innovative firms as well as first round investments and were supplemented by general information about the venture capitalists. Contracts were written between January 1998 and May 2004. Though information was provided by only three venture capitalists, a sample selection bias can be neglected insofar as in 14 cases the venture capitalists acted only as co-investors. In these cases, another venture capitalist analyzed the growth companies and designed the contract. Therefore, we have reached a satisfying sample as, altogether, 14 different venture capitalists acted as lead investors. In addition, characteristics of the dataset prove to be similar to the corresponding results of other empirical studies analyzing the German VC market (additional information is available from the authors upon request).

16.4.1 Funding vehicles

As predicted, in the dataset we have no pure debt financing. Moreover, German venture capitalists often use combinations of different financing vehicles (in 51% of all cases). Furthermore, dormant holdings, financing vehicles with a long tradition in Germany, are widely used (in 41.1% of all cases); Bascha and Walz (2002) and Schefczyk (2004) have similar results for the occurrence of that financial instrument. Dormant holdings can effectively range from being almost debt up to almost equity, depending on how the contracting parties agree upon the allocation of cash flows and control rights. Therefore, it is difficult to draw conclusions concerning the incentive effects that are induced by the use of such financing vehicles without taking a closer look at corresponding contractual rules. On the one hand, all dormant holdings we found excluded participation of the dormant partner in losses of the portfolio company. In addition, they did not entail a participation of the dormant partner in hidden reserves and carried an average fixed interest rate of 7.9%. Another debt-like feature of dormant holdings is the obligation of repayment after a certain period of time (on average 5.7 years in our sample). The dormant holdings also certificate prior claims compared with the other shareholders. Finally, dormant holdings lack several typical shareholders' rights (in particular, voting rights).

On the other hand, in 85.5% of the observed cases, dormant holdings were provided with subordination clauses compared with debt holders in order to avoid immediate insolvency, since most assets of growth companies cannot be accounted for as such according to accounting principles. In our sample, the lack of shareholders' rights is compensated by a broad range of veto rights concerning corporate policy. In addition to the fixed interest payments, 95% of the dormant holdings certificate a participation in corporate net income, which can amount to 50%. The average participation was 16.8%. In 52.6% of the cases, the net income participation was fixed to a percentage of the dormant holding's nominal value and cumulative. That is, missed participations of dormant partners in years with negative earnings have to be paid with seniority, as soon as the growth company returns to a positive net income.

Our data suggest that convertibles are less common in Germany than in the U.S. The analysis of the VC contracts – especially those parts governing the relationship between dormant partners and the firm – demonstrates, however, that dormant holdings can create payment and control structures quite similar to those of convertibles. For example, in 15% of the cases the contracts contain clauses that the dormant holding would automatically convert into ordinary shares without any further payments by the venture capitalist if certain milestones were met. Moreover, when in our sample dormant holdings were combined with common shares, on average 81.9% of the funds flowed to the portfolio firms established a dormant holding, while only 18.1% of the funds were given for ordinary shares. As a result, venture capitalists possess a debt-like claim if the portfolio firm exhibits a poor performance. If, instead, the portfolio firm is a high flyer, the venture capitalists' claims owing to their dormant holding will be easily repaid and their ordinary shareholding implies an unlimited participation in the increase in the firm's value. Thus, the payment structure is conditional upon the economic development of the portfolio firm and this flexibility gain can be used to optimize incentives for both the entrepreneur and the venture capitalist (Schmidt, 2003).

Regarding the inferiority of pure debt or pure equity financing in VC financing mentioned above, convertibles – as well as combinations of equity, dormant holdings, and information and control rights for the venture capitalist – give the venture capitalist to some extent the opportunity for a simultaneous use of the advantages of the specific incentive effects of equity and debt. The debt-like claim forces the entrepreneur to account for certain thresholds, as he or she is confronted with fixed payment obligations, and therefore can be used to mitigate some agency conflicts. In addition, an incentive effect of debt highlighted by Allen and Gale (1988) can be induced: When the portfolio firm proves to be only mediocre (so-called living dead), conflicts between the entrepreneur and the venture capitalist stemming from costly state verification can be mitigated, because the entrepreneur faces fixed amounts of interest and repayment. On the other hand, as an equity holder, the venture capitalist fully profits from the growth options of the firm, so the small number of high flyers can be sufficient to cover the control costs borne by venture capitalists. In addition, venture capitalists have in most cases sufficient control rights (and information) to enforce major changes within the management if earnings worsen, but before the portfolio firm has to file for insolvency, which would serve as a bad signal and lead to high costs of financial distress.

16.4.2 Special clauses in venture capital contracts

Venture capital contracts typically comprise a series of covenants which reduce agency and hold-up problems that cannot be mitigated by simple capital structure optimization (Mark, 2005: 214). Table 16.2 shows the relative frequencies of such clauses in our

Table 16.2 Venture capital covenants and relative frequencies

Covenant	Relative frequencies in own sample	Relative frequencies in Kaplan and Strömberg (2003)
Venture capitalist's information rights	100%	—
Competition clauses	100%	70%
Venture capitalist's veto rights for important business activities	96%	—
Right of first refusal	87%	—
Tag-along right	59%	—
Drag-along right	53%	—
Prohibition of sale of entrepreneur's shares	51%	—
Liquidation preferences	47%	100%
Ex ante stage financing	43%	15%
Anti-dilution	41%	95%
Time vesting	29%	41%
Control switch	20%	18%
Variability of the entrepreneur's stake	16%	53%
Redemption right	2%	79%

dataset and compares them with frequencies in the study of Kaplan and Strömberg (2003) about the VC market in the U.S.

Competition clauses and special information rights for the venture capitalist are always included in the contract. Rights for the venture capitalist to prohibit certain business transactions are also almost always utilized. These provisions also show a high level of standardization. In addition, rights governing the selling process of shares are relatively often included in contracts. Rights of first refusal and prohibition of sale provisions prevent the entrepreneur from selling his or her shares to outside investors against the will of the venture capitalist. Time vesting provisions (as well as prohibition of sale provisions) are used to bind the entrepreneur to some extent to the portfolio company, since leaving the firm leads to high expenses. If the venture capitalist and the entrepreneur have different preferences concerning a trade sale transaction, the venture capitalist can use drag-along rights to force the entrepreneur to sell his or her shares. Tag-along rights, in contrast, enable the venture capitalist to participate in the gains of a trade sale transaction initiated by the entrepreneur.

Ex-ante stage financing is incorporated in 43% of the contracts. That is, the venture capitalist releases additional funds only if the entrepreneur meets certain milestones (Kaplan and Strömberg, 2004). Whereas in the U.S. nearly all VC contracts include liquidation preferences and anti-dilution rights, these agreements are present only in 47% and 41%, respectively, of the contracts we analyzed. All anti-dilution provisions in our dataset are full ratchet. That is, if in future financing rounds shares will be issued at prices lower than the current share price, the venture capitalist receives additional shares in order to retain his or her current stake. In the U.S., in contrast, we often find average prices concerning issued shares in new financing rounds (Kaplan and Strömberg, 2003). Liquidation preferences in our dataset (as common in the U.S.) not only give the venture capitalist seniority of claims if the portfolio company is liquidated, but also guarantee a prior claim if a minimum firm value cannot be reached in a trade sale or an IPO. In 71% of the cases, the liquidation preference guarantees a payment that is higher than the original VC investment.

In 20% of the contracts there is a control switch provision: If milestones are not met or earnings deteriorate, the venture capitalist has the right to change the management, appoint additional board members, or buy additional shares at face value until the voting majority is reached. While in the U.S. redemption rights are included quite regularly in VC contracts, they are very seldom found in Germany. Redemption rights give the venture capitalist the right to demand that the portfolio firm redeems the venture capitalist's shares, mostly at nominal value plus interest, as contracted. Also, provisions that give the entrepreneur additional shares if certain milestones are met are not as common in Germany as in the U.S. (according to our data, however, stock option plans are involved in 55% of the contracts and in 63% the management receives variable wages).

For a proper assessment of the relative frequencies shown in Table 16.2, the intensive use of dormant holdings in Germany has to be taken into account. As mentioned above, various incentive effects being established by clauses not common in Germany can be reproduced by dormant holdings – in particular if they are combined with regular shareholding by the venture capitalist. Our view is confirmed by the fact that the frequencies of clauses, which can be rebuilt by dormant holdings, rise sharply when the analysis is restricted to cases with venture capitalists buying ordinary shares only.

16.5 Contract design and characteristics of portfolio firms

As a further step, we now want to analyze whether or not characteristics of portfolio firms that can be interpreted as indicators for the existence of certain incentive conflicts and the use of special contract clauses discussed in the last section are related. Naturally, we cannot examine clauses that are included in (nearly) all contracts or are (almost) never agreed upon. That excludes competition clauses, information, and veto rights, and rights of first refusal as well as redemption rights. Furthermore, we focus on those clauses that we expect to vary with firm characteristics. Several rights concerning the process of share sales (tag-along, drag-along) are not expected to be essentially influenced by our indicators.

Following the approach of similar empirical work by Gompers (1995), Kaplan and Strömberg (2003), Gompers and Lerner (2004) for the U.S., and Cumming (2005) for Canada but focusing on the German VC market, we use firm characteristics as predictors that are publicly observable, such as, for example, the age of the portfolio firm and the affiliation to a certain industry. These characteristics are taken as indicators for the severance of certain conflicts that should correlate with a more frequent use of appropriate contract clauses. The following binary indicators were extracted from the dataset: whether a firm already had positive revenues at the date of VC investment (EARLYSTAGE = 0) or not (EARLYSTAGE = 1), whether a firm operates in a high-tech industry (HIGHTECH = 1) or not (HIGHTECH = 0), and whether it is the first time a firm receives VC funding (1st ROUND = 1) or not (1st ROUND = 0). The predictors do not correlate significantly with each other.

The variables EARLYSTAGE and HIGHTECH should be positively correlated with nearly all factors causing the severity of incentive conflicts, which were discussed in Section 16.2. In high-tech industries the probability that the entrepreneur follows an objective function driven mainly by technical interests should be higher. Firms without positive revenues and operating in high-tech industries are supposed to face higher external risks. So one would expect that these variables are suitable indicators for a lower probability of success of the growth company. In addition, affiliation to high-tech industries should be an adequate indicator for a substantial lack of physical assets and dependence upon the human capital of the entrepreneur and key employees. Firms without positive revenues can hardly have current success indicators or track records. The importance of the entrepreneur's human capital, however, is not expected to be positively related to the variable EARLYSTAGE. To summarize, HIGHTECH should be positively correlated with severe hidden information and hidden action conflicts as well as with hold-up problems, whereas EARLYSTAGE is only expected to be an indicator for agency conflicts.

The variable 1st ROUND can be interpreted as an indicator for the venture capitalist's knowledge concerning the quality of the innovation project and the entrepreneur's management abilities. However, there should be little correlation between this variable and other firm characteristics. As a result, 1st ROUND is more directly related to the venture capitalist's information at the time of entering the financing relationship and thus expected to be predictive for hidden information problems only. Table 16.3 gives an overview of the predictors of incentive conflicts and corresponding contractual provisions that reduce these conflicts.

Table 16.3 Predictors, incentive conflicts, and contractual provisions

Predictor	Incentive conflicts	Contractual provisions
HIGHTECH	– Hidden information – Hidden action – Hold-up	*Hidden information and hidden action*: • Fraction of firm equity held by the entrepreneur (EQUITYEN) • Variability of the entrepreneurs' stake (VARSTAKE) • Instruments inducing incentive structures similar to debt financing (DEBTINCENT) • Liquidation preference (LIQPRE)
EARLYSTAGE	– Hidden information – Hidden action	• Anti-dilution rights (ANTIDILUT) • Entrepreneur's wage exhibits variable components (WAGEVAR) • Ex-ante stage financing (MILESTONE) • Fraction of members of the supervisory board named by the venture capitalist (BOARDVC)
1st ROUND	– Hidden information	*Hold-up*: • BOARDVC • Time vesting (VESTING) • Prohibition of sale of entrepreneur's shares (PROSALE) • Control switch (CONTROLSW)

A set of ordinary-least-squares (OLS) and logistic (log) regressions has been performed relating the three indicators to the contractual provisions. Only EQUITYEN and BOARDVC are (approximately) interval-scaled and thus can be analyzed using OLS regressions. All other variables are binary and indicate whether the corresponding provision is present or not and therefore logistic regression analysis seems appropriate. If a provision is present, the corresponding variable takes the value of 1, and 0 otherwise. Table 16.4 summarizes the results of the regressions. For the logistic regressions, the effect coefficients are shown, hence coefficients smaller than 1 lower the probability that the provision is agreed upon and coefficients larger than 1 raise that probability.

Out of the six regressions in the first part of Table 16.4, four are globally significant and explain between 18.6% and 38.7% of the variation of the dependent variables. Only the use of liquidation preferences (LIQPRE) and anti-dilution rights (ANTIDILUT) cannot be explained by one of the exogenous variables. The fraction of equity held by the entrepreneur (EQUITYEN) is higher if the firm receives VC funding for the first time. This could be explained by a decline in informational asymmetry once the financing relationship is established and the venture capitalist begins his or her regular monitoring. A distorting influence, however, may result from the fact that the allocation of the firm's equity might largely be determined by the relationship between the firm value and the amount of funding provided by the venture capitalist. Therefore, the equity stake of the entrepreneur could also decline in later financing rounds simply because the venture capitalist claims additional shares for additional funding. This hypothesis could

Table 16.4 Ordinary-least-squares (OLS) and logistic (log) regressions of various venture capital contractual provisions on various independent variables for 51 investments by 3 (14 lead) venture capitalists

	EQUITYEN (OLS)	VARSTAKE (log)	DEBTINCENT (log)	LIQPRE[a] (log)	ANTIDILUT[a] (log)	WAGEVAR (log)
Constant	**0.408*** **	**0.125***	0.808	2.282	0.547	**0.075***
HIGHTECH	0.014	**9.558***	**0.065****	1.078	6.007	**7.440***
EARLYSTAGE	−0.074	1.741	1.634	0.704	1.916	**5.334***
1st ROUND	**0.267*****	0.263	**15.000****	0.967	0.284	2.715
(Adj./Pseudo-) R^2	0.269	0.186	0.369	0.009	0.136	0.387
F-/Likelihood-Ratio-Statistic	**6.317*****	**6.918***	**16.505*****	0.165	2.652	**8.985****

	MILESTONE (log)	BOARDVC (OLS (1))	BOARDVC (OLS (2))	VESTING (log)	PROSALE (log)	CONTROLSW (log)
Constant	0.437	**0.485*****	**6.865*****	**0.182****	2.250	**0.083****
HIGHTECH	0.583	0.088	0.063	1.571	0.356	4.000
EARLYSTAGE	**5.097****	0.041	–	–	–	–
1st ROUND	2.434	**−0.213*****	–	–	–	–
(Adj./Pseudo-) R^2	0.246	0.254	0.034	0.009	0.064	0.064
F-/Likelihood-Ratio Statistic	**9.433****	**4.401****	0.004	0.288	2.398	1.761

Asterisks indicate statistical significance at the *** 1%, ** 5%, and * 10% levels. All significant results are printed in bold.

[a] Only cases in which equity was used exclusively were analyzed since debt-like financing vehicles make the provision redundant.

be supported by the fact that neither EARLYSTAGE nor HIGHTECH are significantly correlated with EQUITYEN.

If the portfolio firm operates in a high-tech industry, we find agreements on variable stakes (VARSTAKE) for the entrepreneur more often. This corresponds to the general prediction of agency theory that high informational asymmetry between the entrepreneur and the venture capitalists (as in high-tech industries) should lead to the use of highly intensive monetary incentive instruments for the entrepreneur. EARLYSTAGE and 1st ROUND may show no significant influence, because there may be no indicators of economic success to make the incentive instrument dependent upon – either because no revenues have been generated yet or simply because the venture capitalist knows too little about the growth company at this point in time. The use of financing instruments that induce debt-like incentive structures (DEBTINCENT) is positively related to the variable 1st ROUND. This highlights the signaling function of debt-like payment structures (Ross, 1977). Interestingly, we find that in high-tech firms debt-like instruments are less frequently used. This could result from the lack of valuable collaterals and the higher uncertainty concerning the market development in such firms, which would enforce risk-shifting incentives. There is a statistically significant positive relationship between the use of variable wage components for the entrepreneur (WAGEVAR) and the variables HIGHTECH and EARLYSTAGE, while the variable 1st ROUND has no statistically significant influence. Thus, variable wage components may be primarily used to mitigate hidden action rather than hidden information problems. Furthermore, 1st ROUND already is strongly affiliated with the use of debt-like instruments and therefore the entrepreneur in many cases already is residual claimant (of course, the same argument applies to the relation between 1st ROUND and VARSTAKE).

In the second part of Table 16.4, only the regressions concerning MILESTONE and BOARDVC (OLS (1)) have a significant *F*- or likelihood-ratio-statistic, respectively, and a value for the coefficient of determination that is greater than 0.1. None of the regressions intended to show the relationship between hold-up problems and provisions (which should have been indicated by HIGHTECH only) seem to support our predictions. Just like EQUITYEN, BOARDVC seems to be mainly driven by the allocation of shares and not by agency or hold-up problems. As theory predicts, when investing in pre-revenue firms, venture capitalists prefer (ex-ante) stage financing (MILESTONE). The non-existence of a significant relationship between HIGHTECH and MILESTONE as well as between HIGHTECH and CONTROLSW might be explained by the fact that stage financing and control switch provisions are substitutes concerning the allocation of power, thus reducing the separate predictive power of HIGHTECH for both variables. Both instruments transfer to some degree residual control rights from the entrepreneur to the venture capitalist. Control switch, however, is a somewhat gentler instrument, since the entrepreneur usually retains his or her job in the portfolio firm after the venture capitalist has taken over control.

Whereas Kaplan and Strömberg (2004) find that vesting provisions (VESTING) are more often employed in firms from industries with generally high levels of R&D expenditures (which should be an indicator comparable with HIGHTECH), we do not receive corresponding results. This may be caused by multiple incentive effects for the entrepreneur when vesting provisions are employed. It has been argued that vesting provisions reduce hold-up risks from the venture capitalist's point of view as they make leaving the growth company costly for the entrepreneur. However, vesting provisions can have negative incentive effects in moderate slumps. Comparably to the incentive effect of stage financing, vesting provisions cause massive risk-shifting and window dressing incentives for the entrepreneur because he or she faces strictly negative consequences (that is, being fired and losing all shares simultaneously). Such unfavorable side effects should particularly be avoided if the human capital of the entrepreneur and other key employees is very important to the firm. As a result, these negative side effects may have led to our empirical outcome that there is no significant relationship between HIGHTECH and the use of vesting provisions. Generally, non-significant regressions related to hold-up problems may be explained by the fact that HIGHTECH, on the one hand, does indicate hold-up conflicts and therefore the need for the venture capitalist to bind the entrepreneur to the portfolio firm and to be in control of the portfolio firm. But on the other hand, HIGHTECH might either indicate situations where gentle or hard measures are needed. Thus, the predictive power of HIGHTECH might be split among control switch, stage financing, vesting, prohibition of sale, and venture capitalists' board membership, rendering regression results insignificant.

Kaplan and Strömberg (2003) find that intensive monetary incentives are more often used in firms where venture capitalists are in a strong control position. They argue that this way the venture capitalist can use his or her power to avoid risk shifting while benefiting from intensive monetary incentives for the entrepreneur. We have similar results insofar as in portfolio firms that are pre-revenue (EARLYSTAGE) we more often find instruments that transfer control to the venture capitalist, such as stage financing (MILESTONE), as well as performance-sensitive compensation (WAGEVAR).

Non-significance of coefficients may also be explained by either costly contracting or problems of using indirect indicators. Contracting leads to expenses, for example analyzing likely agency and hold-up conflicts, bargaining between the parties, and writing and enforcing the contract. If such costs are higher than the costs of continued agency and hold-up problems, using standardized contracts may be favorable. Using indirect indicators such as firm characteristics may not measure those risk factors that are actually relevant from the venture capitalist's point of view. Also, various firm characteristics can have several implications concerning incentive conflicts which imply different contractual measures (Kaplan and Strömberg, 2004). Therefore, variables such as HIGHTECH are somewhat imprecise indicators.

16.6 Conclusion

The financing relationship between venture capitalists and entrepreneurs is burdened by severe agency and hold-up problems because of the special characteristics of growth companies. We examined 51 VC contracts of the German VC market in order to identify differences and similarities to the U.S. VC market. By employing OLS and logistic regressions, we further analyzed whether or not the use of certain contractual provisions can be explained by agency theory or hold-up conflicts. As a proxy for the factors in the environment of innovative firms that lead to certain conflict patterns we used firm characteristics such as the affiliation to a high-tech industry or the existence of positive revenues of the growth company at the time of funding. Most of the resulting significant relations between indicators and contractual provisions can be explained by agency or hold-up theories, while insignificant coefficients might stem from substitution effects or complementary effects among provisions, costly contracting, or the application of indirect indicators.

References

Allen, F. and Gale, D. (1988). Optimal Security Design. *Review of Financial Studies*, 1(39):229–263.

Bascha, A. and Walz, U. (2002). Financing Practices in the German Venture Capital Industry: An Empirical Assessment. CFS Working Paper, 2002/08.

Bergemann, D. and Hege, U. (1998). Dynamic Venture Capital Financing. *Journal of Banking and Finance*, 22(3):703–735.

Bester, H. and Hellwig, M. (1989). Moral Hazard and Equilibrium Credit Rationing: An Overview of the Issues. In Bamberg, G. and Spremann, K. (eds), *Agency Theory, Information, and Incentives*. Berlin: Springer, 135–166.

Cornelli, F. and Yosha, O. (2003). Stage Financing and the Role of Convertible Securities. *Review of Economic Studies*, 70(1):1–32.

Cumming, D. (2005). Capital Structure in Venture Finance. *Journal of Corporate Finance*, 11(3):550–585.

Gompers, P.A. (1995). Optimal Investment, Monitoring, and the Staging of Venture Capital. *Journal of Finance*, 50(5):1461–1489.

Gompers, P.A. and Lerner, J. (2004). *The Venture Capital Cycle*. 2nd edition. Cambridge MA: MIT Press.

Harris, M. and Raviv, A. (1979). Optimal Incentive Contracts with Imperfect Information. *Journal of Economic Theory*, 20(2):231–259.

Hart, O.D. and Moore, J. (1994). A Theory of Debt Based on the Inalienability of Human Capital. *Quarterly Journal of Economics*, 109(4):841–879.

Jensen, M.C. and Meckling, W.H. (1976). Theory of the Firm: Managerial Behavior, Agency Costs and Ownership Structure. *Journal of Financial Economics*, 3(4):305–360.

Kaplan, S.N. and Strömberg, P. (2001). Venture Capitalists as Principals: Contracting, Screening, and Monitoring. *American Economic Review*, 91(2):426–430.

Kaplan, S.N. and Strömberg, P. (2003). Financial Contracting Meets the Real World: An Empirical Analysis of Venture Capital Contracts. *Review of Economic Studies*, 70(2):281–315.

Kaplan, S.N. and Strömberg, P. (2004). Characteristics, Contracts and Actions: Evidence from Venture Capitalist Analyses. *Journal of Finance*, 59(5):2177–2210.

Leland, H.E. and Pyle, D.H. (1977). Informational Asymmetries, Financial Structure and Financial Information. *Journal of Finance*, 23(2):371–387.

Mark, K. (2005). *Venture Capital und die Governance-Struktur innovativer Unternehmen*. Aachen: Shaker.

Rajan, R.G. and Zingales, L. (2001). The Firm as a Dedicated Hierarchy: A Theory of the Origins and Growth of Firms. *Quarterly Journal of Economics*, 116(3):805–851.

Ross, S.A. (1977). The Determination of Financial Structure: The Incentive-Signalling Approach. *Bell Journal of Economics*, 8(1):23–40.

Sahlman, W. (1990). The Structure and Governance of Venture-Capital Organizations. *Journal of Financial Economics*, 27(2):473–521.
Schefczyk, M. (2004). *Erfolgsstrategien deutscher Venture Capital-Gesellschaften*. 3rd edition. Stuttgart: Schäffer-Poeschel.
Schmidt, K.M. (2003). Convertible Securities and Venture Capital Finance. *Journal of Finance*, 58(3):1139–1166.
Williamson, O.E. (1988). Corporate Finance and Corporate Governance. *Journal of Finance*, 43(3):567–591.
Zingales, L. (2000). In Search of New Foundations. *Journal of Finance*, 55(3):1623–1653.

17 Supply and demand of venture capital for biotech firms: The case of the Belgian regions of Wallonia and Brussels

Véronique Bastin, Georges Hübner, Pierre-Armand Michel, and Mélanie Servais

Abstract

Venture capital (VC) represents a critical resource of funds for life sciences companies, as their activities have a remote payback and require substantial equity investments. This chapter reviews the major financing issues according to bio-entrepreneurs and professional investors. On the basis of interviews of samples of biotechnology companies and investors in the Belgian regions of Wallonia and Brussels, we analyze the qualitative issues underlying financing decisions along a structured framework. Bio-entrepreneurs seem generally aware of the environment and VC firms' investment criteria, but diverge on four specific dimensions: managerial qualities, contents of the business plan, risk and return requirements, and external growth. This chapter provides guidelines to improve common understanding along these lines.

17.1 Introduction

The Lisbon agenda, adopted in March 2000, was set in order to lead the EU to have the most competitive economy in 2010. Thanks to the knowledge-based source of value creation of the life sciences sector, and because of the increasing needs for therapeutic products and services of an ageing population, many member countries or regions, such as the Walloon and Brussels regions of Belgium studied in this chapter, have identified the industry of biotechnologies[1] as one of their focal points of development.

Consequently, and in spite of the delay observed in the milestones of the Lisbon agenda, the biotechnology industry is currently experiencing a major expansion in Europe. According to the European private equity survey conducted by the European Venture Capital Association (2003), the biotechnology industry attracted €1.1 billion in 2002 compared with €0.8 billion in 2001, representing its highest annual figure to date.

Yet, as most are still young, biotech firms have been faced with major challenges since the collapse of the financial bubble on technology firms; most notably the search for

[1] Biotechnology includes 'any technique that uses living organisms, or parts of such organisms, to make or modify products, to improve plants or animals, or to develop microorganisms for specific use' (Arojärvi, 2001).

funds in order to develop their activities beyond the seed investment stage. Complex regulations, long drug development times (Robbins-Roth, 2001), uncertainties over likely costs of R&D (Bank of England, 2001; U'Prichard and Pullan, 1997), importance of the intellectual property rights, and distant horizon of positive cash flows are all factors that contribute to biotechnologies being perceived as one of the riskiest industries in the modern economy (Senker, 1998).

As a result, managers of these companies have to face the challenge of attracting and retaining investors particularly in the first development stages. Any drug development activity requires investors' commitment to support the project for almost a decade before the company knows whether the new drug will ever generate profits. Failing to get sufficient financing at any stage may eventually cause the firm to collapse. The financial community considers such companies as being highly risky and perceives the assessment of their technology as complex and uncertain. These mixed feelings represent major hindrances for the obtaining of equity capital as well as bank debt (Moore, 1994). Moreover, Lockett et al. (2002) and Murray and Lott (1995) document a bias against investment in European high-technology companies, especially at the seed and start-up levels.

But the potential shortage for the biotechnology industry goes beyond the equity funding gap – namely the market failure in the sufficient provision of external private equity for firms that are at the early stage of growth – that has been already identified in the literature (Mason and Harrison, 2003; Harding, 1999; Murray and Marriott, 1998; Murray, 1994). The potential mismatch between the demand for funds by biotechnology firms and the supply of funds by venture capitalists (VCs) is likely to result in a globally insufficient funding for the future development of the life sciences sector, as shown by Bergeron et al. (2002) for Canada and Bastin et al. (2005) for Wallonia and Brussels.

Thus, many viable companies could be impeded by an increasing scarcity of financial resources and a rising suspicion of generalist investors. Managers of biotechnology firms are faced with the challenge of identifying all available financing possibilities and accurately assessing and conveying their financial needs. This task is especially difficult for biotech SMEs managed by scientists, generally lacking time and personal interest for these activities.

To bring a solution to this mismatch, it is crucial to gain some insights into the sources of misunderstanding between entrepreneurs and financiers. So far, the literature has extensively described the financing difficulties for such R&D companies (Hall, 2002; Lockett et al., 2002; Haar, 2001) and the criteria that VC organizations used to choose which firms to fund (Hall and Hofer, 1993; MacMillan et al., 1987, 1985; Tyebjee and Bruno, 1984). However, to our knowledge, no author has yet studied how these VC organizations' investment criteria can be sources of financing issues or difficulties for biotechnology firms. A fortiori, the extent to which the source of misunderstandings with demanders of VC may impact on the likelihood of finalizing the deal has not yet been systematically assessed.

The primary objective of this study is to analyze the major qualitative dimensions that can be sources of financing issues and difficulties according to the biotech entrepreneurs and to investors in such companies, and to match the points of view of the demanders and suppliers of capital. The output of this analysis consists in the mapping of the relative level of mutual understanding between these economic agents for different characteristics of the negotiation terms. From the examination of the similarities, differences, or divergences of their opinions, we then identify the key dimensions that are responsible for the mismatch between the expectations of the entrepreneurs and the different kinds of venture capitalists.

These dimensions are retrieved from qualitative material gathered from field interviews. Nevertheless, to preserve a sufficient degree of comparability between both groups of actors, we restrict the study to a limited geographical area, namely the regions of Wallonia and Brussels in Belgium. The research methodology has been designed so as to obtain a high degree of homogeneity between material collected from entrepreneurs and investors.

This study contributes to giving a better view of the qualitative issues underlying financing decisions to the public authorities, companies, and investors, which will in turn allow them to make accurate decisions and to correct their present attitudes and judgments in the light of communication shifts arising during the negotiation process. The subjacent goal of the chapter is to work out guidelines to improve the competitiveness and the profitability of SMEs in the biotechnology industry.

The chapter is structured as follows. We first give a brief profile of the Walloon and Brussels biotechnology sector before detailing concisely the VC trends in Belgium in Section 17. In Section 17.4, we describe the methodology used for the interview, the sample of Walloon and Brussels biotech firms and the suppliers of funds, and the dimensions studied in the empirical survey. Then, in Section 17.5, we analyze the interviews collected from the different actors before confronting the diverse opinions of entrepreneurs and investors, and formulate a critical analysis of the financing issues and difficulties that will provide some lessons for the future.

17.2 Context

17.2.1 Biotech in Wallonia and Brussels

Belgium has an excellent reputation for developing advanced technologies, especially in life sciences. The Belgian biotech environment comprises universities, research centers, and several science parks attracting major international investments from biopharmaceutical and agro-food companies.

In 2002, the Belgian life sciences market numbered 157 companies, including 97 firms in Wallonia and Brussels. A total of 80% of these companies were small and medium-sized firms, reaching only 20% of the total biotech revenue. The larger contribution in the Walloon biotech turnover comes from global leaders, which stimulate the biotechnology field in the region. The healthcare and services subsectors represent more than 80% of the activities in Wallonia in terms of revenue. This latter subsegment requires large amounts of long-term VC but has a greater added value. However, the majority of the Walloon biotech SMEs belong to the diagnostics and research biologicals subsectors, in spite of their wish to develop therapeutic products. The reason is probably a perceived lack of funds required for therapeutics activities (Bastin et al., 2005).

17.3 Venture capital in Belgium

In Belgium, the amounts of funds raised and invested decreased in 2002. To some extent, the phenomenon is due to the drop in valuations in the public markets (European Venture

Table 17.1 Evolution of Belgian venture capital and private equity investments in biotechnology and in high technology 1997–2002 (€ million)

Investments	1997	1998	1999	2000	2001	2002
Biotechnology	24.9	8.1	49.8	47.4	65.3	54.8
High technology	134.3	170.1	395.3	399.7	142.1	128.5
Total	179.9	260.6	673.4	564.8	409.6	360.0
% of biotechnology in total investments	13.9	3.1	7.4	8.4	15.9	15.2

Source: European Venture Capital Association (2003).

Capital Association, 2003). Indeed, tough times in public markets have caused problems for both privately held businesses and their investors. In 2002, funds raised (€125 million) were 81% lower than in 2001 (€650 million), partly because of the decline in capital gains generated by exits. Table 17.1 details the main investment figures for the biotechnology sector over the last six years before the interviews took place.

With €360 million in 2002, the total amounts invested in private equity have significantly decreased compared with the €409 million figure in 2001. Meanwhile, the proportion of high-technology investments in total investments has increased by 1%. Looking at the biotechnology industry, we observe a small decrease in investments. However, the percentage of biotechnology in the total investment (15.2%) remains high compared with the European situation (4%).

17.4 Methodology

The objective of comparing the dimensions considered by entrepreneurs and venture capitalists when they meet each other for a financing round involves working with essentially qualitative opinions. Yet, for their meeting, they must display a reasonable degree of homogeneity. The methodological choices adopted in this study were driven by this key consideration.

17.4.1 Semi-structured interviews

To obtain our dataset, a series of interviews with biotech entrepreneurs and investors in Wallonia and Brussels were carried out in order to gather opinions concerning the financing issues and difficulties in the biotechnology sector. We used a framework of semi-directed interviews that lasted between 1 h and 1.5 h. In such semi-structured interviews, a list of themes is covered, although these may vary from one interview to another (Saunders et al., 1997). This means that we can omit or add some questions in particular interviews, given the company-specific context. Indeed, the same sets of financing dimensions were tackled during these interviews but we never asked defined and clear questions. In this way, we introduced the different dimensions in the discussion and the interviewees gave us their opinions on the financing issues or difficulties linked to the subject. All the data gathered during the interviews were recorded on tapes.

The questionnaires feature a common part for both groups, and a distinctive part for each subsample. The first part of the questionnaire aims at gathering company-specific information (general description of the company, operational and financial information) while the second part collects the opinion of both biotech entrepreneurs and investors regarding several dimensions as potential sources of financing issues or difficulties. The particular questionnaire design, with a common set of questions for homogeneous indicators, enables us to avoid any potential bias related to the wording of each particular question, as they are expressed in a similar fashion.

17.4.2 The sample

A sample of 20 biotech entrepreneurs were interviewed between October 2002 and February 2003 in the Wallonia/Brussels region. The questionnaire had been pre-tested on three biotechnology entrepreneurs (included in the final sample) and adapted. The sample was built so that all biotechnology subsectors in the region of Wallonia–Brussels could be suitably represented. Table 17.2 presents the sampling distribution of the biotechnology companies according to their subsector of activities.

The adopted classification is the one proposed by the OECD and the Belgian Bio-industries Association (BBA). In order to avoid any bias in the representativeness of the sample, we apply a weight of $1/n$ for any n-activities company.[2] Table 17.3, Panels A and B, details the distribution of our sample according to the size (approximated by the number of employees) and the age (stage of development) of the sample companies.

In a similar fashion, 24 investors were interviewed, three of whom pre-tested the questionnaire. Twelve come from the Walloon Region, nine from Brussels, two from the

Table 17.2 Distribution of the biotech firms sample in Wallonia and Brussels per sector of activities

Sector	Sample*	Percentage of sample	Population**	Percentage of the population
Bio-pharmaceutical	7.83	39%	43	44%
Services and technology platforms	5.67	28%	23	24%
Bio-agriculture	3.67	18%	17	18%
Bio-environment	2.33	12%	11	11%
Other	0.5	3%	3	3%
TOTAL	20	100%	97	100%

* Firms are classified according to the interviewees' responses (multiple responses were allowed).
** Firms are classified according to the Belgian Bioindustries Association biotechnology classification as of September 2002 (http://www.bba-bio.be).

[2] With this calculation method, the 'bio-pharma' activity, for example, is present within 7.68 companies (four mono-activity companies + five two-activity companies with a weight of 0.5 + one three-activity company with a weight of 0.33) out of the 20, representing 39% of the sample.

Table 17.3 Employees and development stage of the biotech companies belonging to the sample

Categories	Number in the sample	% of sample
Panel A: Number of employees		
<5	2	10%
Between 5 and 20	7	35%
Between 20 and 100	7	35%
>100	4	20%
TOTAL	20	100%
Panel B: Development stage		
Start-up <2 years	6	30%
SME >3 years	4	20%
Last stage of development	1	5%
Profitability stage	7	35%
Other	2	10%
TOTAL	20	100%

Table 17.4 Distribution of the investors sample in Wallonia and Brussels per category of venture capitalists

Sector	Sample	Percentage of the sample	Population	Percentage of the population
Private VCs	11	46%	50	46.3%
Public VCs	6	25%	36	33.4%
State-owned	2	8%	5	4.6%
Business angels	2	8%	5	4.6%
Bank VCs	3	13%	12	11.1%
TOTAL	24	100%	108	100%

Table 17.5 Specialization of the sample of investors in biotechnologies and new technologies

Investors	Number specialized in biotech	Number specialized in new tech	Number generalist
Bank VCs	0	0	3
Private VCs	3	2	6
Public VCs	0	2	4
Business angels	0	0	2
State-owned	0	0	2
TOTAL	3	4	17

Flemish region, and one from France. They were all selected on the basis of the inclusion of biotechnology companies in their portfolio or their involvement in the Wallonia/Brussels region. All types of private equity investors were met: business angels networks, private venture capitalists, private equity departments of banks, public VC organizations and state-owned granting organizations. Table 17.4 details the distribution of the types of interviewed suppliers of funds. Table 17.5 states the number of investors specialized in biotechnology, new technology, or generalist. We notice that very few Belgian venture capitalists are specialized in biotechnology.

17.5 Literature: relevant dimensions

The advantage of semi-structured interviews is that interviewees (investors and entrepreneurs) can freely express their opinion on the proposed themes. The literature on biotechnology characteristics and VC investments enables us to bring out seven major dimensions that can be elicited as sources of financing difficulties or issues. Before analyzing the results of the interview process, we propose a discussion of the common conception of the relevance and key features of these criteria.

17.5.1 Scientific and management quality

Given the uncertainties encountered by high-technology companies such as biotechnologies, venture capitalists spend a great deal of time and effort seeking signals of a start-up quality (Hall and Hofer, 1993). The due diligence process made by VC firms examines both intangible (quality of leadership, competitive positioning, corporate culture, intellectual property rights . . .) as well as tangible assets (cash, technology, market share . . .) of the company (Harvey and Lush, 1995).

Several studies of VC investment criteria (MacMillan et al., 1987, 1985; Tyebjee and Bruno, 1984) produce some general findings indicating that the characteristics of the entrepreneur are of utmost importance. According to Zacharakis and Meyer (2000), some of the most important selection criteria are top management experience and skills. Many investors interviewed by Muzyka et al. (1996) prefer to select an opportunity that offers a good management team and reasonable financial and product-market characteristics, even if the opportunity does not meet the overall fund and deal requirements.

Leytes (2002) mentions the personality of the entrepreneur as one of the paramount ingredients examined by venture capitalists involved in investments in biotechnology companies. Indeed, for many investors, one of the main reasons of financing failure is the lack of credibility of the management (Mason and Harrison, 2002). However, Zucker et al. (1998) also underline the importance of having skilled scientists in a biotechnology company. In other words, competent managers and researchers are both necessary to support the technology development (Amburgey et al., 1996).

17.5.2 Economic and regulatory environment

In times of uncertainty about valuations, high-risk industries such as biotechnologies are disproportionately penalized on financial markets as investors want stability and security (Crocker, 2003). Therefore, since 2000, biotechnologies have experienced many difficulties in raising public funds and their market valuations have steadily declined. However, under these unfavorable circumstances, the shortage of capital can be partly offset by specialized funds, whose sensitivity to temporary negative shocks is alleviated by their longer investment horizon; by government agencies, filling their stabilizing role through making up for equity gaps (Manigart et al., 2002); or by alliances with larger companies (Lerner et al., 2003). This may partly explain why the share of European VC in the biotech sectors has held up well compared with other sectors. One reason is the set-up of many biotech companies in the late 1990s (Crocker, 2003).

Investors in the biotechnology industry also have to take into account their dynamic environment and the importance of regulations (Senker, 1998, Prevezer et al., 1998) because the restrictive legal rules governing the industry today may have evolved within a ten-year period. For example, in the bio-pharmaceutical subsector, the regulatory climate dictates the process for developing a new drug, making the development time longer and the expenses higher (for the FDA, McClellan (2003) estimates these development costs at more than US$800 million and DiMasi et al. (2003) estimate them at US$802 million). While the latter authors estimate that average time from the start of clinical testing to marketing approval for a representative drug is 90.3 months or 7.5 years, the FDA 2003 performance report (McClellan, 2003) advocates that development time can, in many cases, exceed a decade. The uncertainty concerning this legal framework represents one of the main problems for the biotechnology industry (Senker, 1998).

17.5.3 Competitive environment and the pipeline of products

Muzyka et al. (1996) underline the importance of the strategy-market criteria for VC investment decisions. The ease of market entry, the ability to create post-entry barriers, the sustained share competitive position, the nature and degree of competition, the uniqueness of the product and technology, and the market size: these all represent important investment decision criteria.

Deeds et al. (1999) claim that rapid development of new products is a key factor of success for high-technology firms because a new products portfolio increases the likelihood of survival and improves external visibility and legitimacy. Moreover, the dynamic of the competitive environment of biotechnology companies (changing technologies and intense global competition) requires that the companies develop a steady stream of innovative products.

17.5.4 Intellectual property rights and information disclosure

According to Lerner (1994), biotechnology firms displaying good intellectual property protection are more likely to obtain VC financing. Indeed, patents seem to be crucial to the high-risk/return structure of the biotechnology companies (Carbone, 2003). Patents obtained for newly developed products give a temporary monopoly situation to the holder. Without this protection, any competitor could easily take the innovative idea and develop cheaper drugs because of the low R&D expenses he would have (Hübner et al., 2003). In other words, patent protection is a kind of winner-takes-it-all race.

A patent gives the inventor a temporary monopoly that allows her to practice high prices for the patented product and thus improve the benefit flows. By signaling innovative capabilities, patents help start-ups to acquire additional resources and increase the likelihood that they will obtain financing (Lerner, 1994; Kenney, 1986). According to Lockett et al. (2002), one of the main reasons for rejecting technology projects concerns the lack of intellectual property protection.

Moreover, the disclosure of sensitive information to potential investors regarding the products in research and development and/or the technology appears to be a difficulty in the financing process (Bergeron et al., 2002). Information asymmetries between a developing firm and potential financiers can lead to a situation where only poor quality products become available on the market (Haar, 2001). Indeed, investors will not invest in a project for which they have insufficient information to value it correctly, uncertainty being greater for high-technology companies than for others.

17.5.5 Business plan

A realistic business plan that includes credible assumptions and sufficient information can also affect the investment decision (Mason and Harrison, 2002). Indeed, information asymmetries can lead to a misevaluation of the company's potential economic growth.

17.5.6 Perceptions of risk and return and valuation problems

High business risk in VC investments mean that a higher return is required (Manigart et al., 2002). Indeed, many venture capitalists are unwilling to invest in new technology companies because of perceived high risks and low returns (Mason and Harrison, 2002). Lockett et al. (2002) also highlight that VC investors are more disposed to impose higher expected rates of return on new high-technology-based firms, regardless of their degree of specialization in high-tech investments.

In Europe, investors seem to show some aversion for risky investment. The VC industry here is less likely to fund high-technology companies such as biotechnologies than in the U.S. (Manigart and Struyf, 1997). Consequently, the risky nature of a project is one of the main reasons of financing failure on the investor's side.

Valuation of start-up new technology-based firms represent an acute issue for generalist VC firms. Indeed, technology-based start-ups have few collateralizable assets, while they often rely on the potential subsequent economic value of intangible assets. The presence of patents triggers additional valuation problems for traditionally based valuation methods because cash flows are erratic and often negative in the early years (Lockett et al., 2002).

Thus, the highly uncertain environment of biotechnology companies makes the valuation relatively complex and the discounted cash-flow methods are insufficient. According to Remer et al. (2001), 'European biotechnology investors and managers revealed an adverse attitude towards risks and an admitted lack of capability to deal with the uncertainties in most investment opportunities.'

17.5.7 Alliances, mergers, and acquisitions

According to Senker (1998), an interesting feature of the biotechnology industry is the enormous expansion in strategic alliances between large and small companies. Many of these alliances specifically relate to exchanges of technology, or to joint R&D projects, as firms attempt to develop and expand their technological expertise. Alliances provide myriads of advantages associated with the direct and indirect access to complementary resources (Chung et al., 2000). Alliances may also confer an aura of legitimacy (Baum and Oliver, 1991) that facilitates the search for funds. Therefore, alliances give a positive signal to the potential investors as it suggests that the company has earned encouraging evaluations from specialized actors (Baum and Silverman, 2004). Moreover, Baum et al. (2000) establish a positive relationship between the alliances of young biotechnology firms with other organizations, and their performance growth.

All these dimensions were thoroughly discussed with both the investors and biotech entrepreneurs during the interviews.

17.6 Empirical material

This section describes the key qualitative findings obtained from the survey, along with the seven dimensions identified above, by comparing answers provided by the sample of entrepreneurs with those given by the venture capitalists.

Table 17.6 reports the number of biotech and VC respondents who expressed an opinion regarding the various topics that emerged from the literature review and that interviewees considered as relevant for the understanding of the financing issues in biotechnology.

Given that the interviewing methodology does not systematically address all topics in detail, we do not view the percentage of respondents who stated an opinion for each topic as a relevant criterion for assessing their importance. Rather, the intensity of the expressed opinion and the consistency (or divergence) of the different responses provides a better indicator of the acuteness of the issue and the strength of the result.

17.6.1 Scientific and management quality

Scientific and technological quality

In Wallonia and Brussels, scientific and technological quality is often quoted as an important aspect when discussing team qualification, know-how, competitive advantage, etc. with investors. Discussions on the scientific aspect differ depending on the degree of sophistication of the investor. According to several 'bio-pharmaceutical' interviewees, investors specialized in life sciences pay a great deal of attention to science quality and speak the same language as biotech entrepreneurs. However, generalist investors who have difficulties in understanding the business, call for outside experts to assess the project. 'The challenge of the technology and biotech is to make its business understandable. We must find the right balance between the customer approach, the field, what is understandable and the technological aspect' (quote by a venture capitalist).

Some investors mention that the scientific quality in Wallonia and Brussels is excellent but underline that the technology has to be adequately protected. Inherent in this field, the use of patents is considered as the sole serious tool that reassures the investor regarding the protection of intellectual property.

Management quality

According to some entrepreneurs surveyed, investors attach a great deal of importance to the following trio: the scientist, the sales officer, and the financier. Above all, investors search for a charismatic balanced team with complementary profiles and experiences.

Table 17.6 Summary of the perceptions of bio-entrepreneurs and investors

Topic	Biotech companies		Venture capitalists	
	Yes	No	Yes	No
1. Scientific and management quality				
1.1. Scientific quality				
Important but not understood by generalist investors	4			
Essential but not a problem in Wallonia			2	
1.2. Management quality				
Essential, search for complementary profiles			3	
A manager should be assigned to the scientist			6	
Difficult for scientists to have all competences	8			
2. Economic and competitive environment				
2.1. Economic environment				
Skepticism and caution from investors	5		8	1
Importance of skepticism depends on the type of investors	3		1	
Impact on the capacity to start a major investment	4			
Impact on the customers' financing	2			
Investors consider biotech as market niches	3		2	
2.2. Regulatory environment				
Obstacle but not an investment barrier	11	3	6	3
3. Competition				
3.1. Competitive environment				
Project innovative and unique	6		11	
No competition is a negative signal for investors	4		4	3
3.2. Pipeline of products				
Reduce product risk of failure	7		5	
Concentrate on the core business	4	4	5	3
4. IP rights				
4.1. Intellectual property				
Crucial for investors	17	1	17	
Entry barrier	6		3	
Lack of resources to manage the follow-ups	7		2	
4.2. Information disclosure				
Reluctance to give info to specialized investors	7	10	3	5

(*Continued*)

Table 17.6 Continued

Topic	Biotech companies		Venture capitalists	
	Yes	No	Yes	No
5. Business plan				
Lack of strategy and focus			3	
Inadequacy asked/required funds	5	3	8	2
Difficult to predict the market	5			
6. Risk/return perception				
6.1. Rate of return				
Lack of economic knowledge by the scientists			3	2
Scientists' unawareness of risk/return trade-off			4	2
Investors requirement not compatible with biotech	6	2		
Difference in perception => barrier to financing	5	2		
6.2. Risk				
Investors unaware from the ≠ segments risk levels	3			
Investors too risk averse	5			
Development time underestimated by investors	5	1		
Managers are too optimistic			5	
Risk underestimated by scientists			4	
6.3. Valuation problems				
Lack of competence of investors and scientists	5			
Potential issue during negotiations	4	4	7	0
Lack of objective criteria for valuation			2	
7. Alliances/M&A				
7.1. Strategic alliances				
Make the financing research easier	18	1		
Partnership with international groups is positive			12	0
7.2. Mergers and acquisitions				
Reluctance from entrepreneurs	5	7	3	1
Good possibility to exit			5	

'A good manager must have a global view of his business, meticulousness, and anticipation capacities.'

The project instigator is often a pure scientist without managerial knowledge: 'Founders are often academics. For them the economic world is relatively abstract; they do not notice all the implications it has' (quote by a venture capitalist). Investors consider, however, that it is not relevant to turn a scientist into a manager at all costs. Many biotechnology entrepreneurs are consistent in their opinion as they believe that it is difficult for a scientist to possess all competences. This is why a professional manager is frequently assigned to the scientist. 'The lab researcher will have many difficulties to prove that he has a complete panel of competences. That is why a business developer is often assigned to him' (quote by a venture capitalist). However, experienced life sciences managers seem to be a rare resource in Wallonia and Brussels.

Public and private incubators appear to be necessary for both groups not only because of the services they bring but also because of the synergies they create between companies. Incubators often introduce a skilled intermediary who has to harmonize the investor/entrepreneur relationship.

17.6.2 Environment

Economic environment

Since the start of the stock market crash in mid-2000, investors have expressed increasing suspicion towards biotechnology. Actually, both investors and biotech entrepreneurs recognize that: 'at the time, we observed a kind of frigidity from the investors' (quote by an entrepreneur). Indeed, the economic situation pertaining to the end of 2002 moderated the investors' enthusiasm for high-technology firms.

In Wallonia and Brussels, most biotechnology firms do not seem to be directly affected by the unfavorable economic situation, investors considering these companies to be particular market niches. 'The biotech amalgam could have raised doubts from the investors in the current economic environment. However, venture capitalists considered our business as a special market niche' (quote by an entrepreneur).

Two major impacts of the financial markets' performance have been well underlined by some bio-entrepreneurs interviewed: 'An impact on the capacity to start a major investment because of the difficulty to raise venture funds'; 'An impact on the customer company which may have financing difficulties in such an economic situation. This in turn leads to higher credit risk for their Walloon suppliers.'

Regulatory environment

The most important source of regulatory constraints for biotechnology companies directly or indirectly results from the fact that new drugs to be introduced on the U.S. market, by far the largest market for therapeutic products, must be approved by the FDA. This approval process slows down the commercialization and the benefits.

The impact of regulations on investment decisions varies from one subsector to another. In the bio-pharmaceutical segment, for example, the regulatory constraints are more demanding and influence product development time and failure risk. Regulation shifts constitute a relatively high risk for investors. Recent regulations, notably the new

European directive for diagnostic activities,[3] slow down the product commercialization process and delay the company's profitability phase. A typical complaint heard from biotech managers is: 'Because of this new regulation, 50% of our research capacity must be employed for administrative tasks' (quote by an entrepreneur).

Regulatory constraints remain an important difficulty especially for university spin-off companies. Academic researchers do not master environmental and regulatory constraints and have, for this reason, difficulties in convincing suppliers of funds.

Yet, if the regulatory environment represents a negative point in an investment dossier, it does not constitute a barrier in itself. Product development time and failure risk in the validation process will be integrated in the project valuation. In other words, investors take into account these difficulties and give a lower price at entry: 'If the returns come later, we will only value at 60 instead of 100.'

17.6.3 Competition

Competitive environment

The competitive environment of biotechnology firms is also an important factor for investors when deciding which companies to fund. A venture capitalist states: 'We always try to find companies for which competition is relatively restricted.'

However, even if it is clear that excessive competition can be harmful to the firm's development, most entrepreneurs are aware of the positive effects of healthy competition. First, a competitive environment is a vehicle of change that spurs innovation. Second, the lack of reputation and/or track record of an activity can be as problematic for the search for funds as an environment that is too competitive. Indeed, when the activity is yet undeveloped, biotech entrepreneurs have to demonstrate the interest of the project to investors. A scientist explains: 'We have to be the first to develop the drug but have also to be able to prove to the investors that we have a potential market for our product.'

Moreover, absence of competitors could be a sign of market deficiency and lead to reluctance to invest in such projects. VC firms view big pharmaceutical competitors less as a potential threat than as a very serious possibility to exit, especially at times when the possibility for an IPO is severely restricted.

However, competitive environment can constitute an impediment to the capacity to obtain funds when it becomes too complicated to identify competitive advantages and unique developments. Most biotech entrepreneurs interviewed underline that 'competition is not a major financing difficulty when the firm is in a specialized sector and the intellectual property is well protected'.

Pipeline of products

According to many biotech companies, strong competition in the sector and the risk of product failure constrain the firms to own products in different development stages. In such a competitive environment, the race for new products crucially depends on the time dimension.

[3] Directive 98/79/CE of the European Parliament and the Council of 27 October 1998 on in vitro diagnostic and medical device.

Nevertheless, we observe two contradictory aspects regarding the size of the pipeline. On the one hand, a large pipeline of products reduces failure risk through diversification and, on the other hand, the company must concentrate on its core business and not spread its effort in additional activities. Investors attempt to find a balance between these two contradictory motivations, especially according to the product development time and investment portfolio. 'It is clear that we (investors) prefer the perspective of a pipeline with products at different maturity stages but it is not always the case' (quote by a venture capitalist).

As claimed by investors, for start-up companies, quality and uniqueness prevail over quantity. 'Entrepreneurs are interested in many things, they want to learn everything and will be lost in thought... we must stop them.' Suppliers specialized in life sciences and owning a diversified biotech portfolio are not concerned about investing in a one-product firm, provided they know the life cycle well. Conversely, generalist investors confer a large importance to the length of the product pipeline because they are more risk averse and search different opportunities of development in a company.

17.6.4 Intellectual property rights

Intellectual property

Intellectual property is considered a valuable asset since it ensures an exclusive know-how to create new products and protect investments. Patents confer a monopoly to the innovator and raise entry barriers. A good intellectual property protection is a sine qua non investment condition for most investors and many of them examine in detail the patents portfolio before giving funds. In other words, 'no protection, no money' is the motto of VC firms in this particular industry.

However, it is necessary to bear in mind that patents may also constitute a serious burden, especially for small companies, since existing protection may restrict creativity and product development. Other investors underline that patents must not be an obsession. A firm could hold originality – a specific know-how – without specifically having to protect it.

In the regions under study, the main perceived difficulty regarding intellectual property protection is the lack of firms' resources to construct a patent portfolio and the difficulty on managing the patent follow-up. 'Small structures as ours are not able to enter in the patent game... not either to bring a legal action against a company.' As a consequence, Walloon and Brussels biotech companies feel that they cannot take advantage from their patent valuation potential often enough.

Information disclosure

In high-technology sectors such as biotechnology, entrepreneurs fear industrial espionage. Although there is less danger of espionage with investors than with partners as part of strategic alliances, bio-managers are reluctant to disclose sensitive information. This leads to a disruption in the negotiation process, as investors need the maximum information to value the project properly. An investor explains: 'I think that the scientist must be aware that he has to disclose a minimum of information to sell his project... we cannot buy a cat in a bag.' In practice, confidentiality clauses are used to solve the potential problem of information disclosure between investors and managers but interviewees mostly view mutual trust as a key factor of success instead.

17.6.5 Business plan

The business plan is a fundamental factor when trying to convince suppliers of funds, since it has to prove the value-added of the project. Two major difficulties are highlighted by the investors. First, they identify a lack of focus and strategy. Investors embrace too large a span of activities in their business plan and too seldom surround a clear target. Moreover, entrepreneurs give too many technical and scientific explanations instead of commercial strategy. This observation underlines again the differences in language between the scientific and the business worlds. As an entrepreneur says: 'Most of the words in the business plan were introduced by us (entrepreneurs) for the first time.' Second, investors regret the lack of realism and a discrepancy between funds asked by entrepreneurs and funds required to develop the company. Entrepreneurs are often too optimistic in that they underestimate the funds required to finance the growth and development of the activities. This lack of realism regarding the future funding requirements typically leads to self-financing strategies that mean a suboptimal corporate development. In particular, they often underestimate overheads, marketing, and patent costs. 'It would be a pity if the company misses a project because a researcher has underestimated something he does not understand' (quote by a venture capitalist).

Some bio-entrepreneurs underline the complexity of assessing and predicting such a dynamic market as biotechnology: 'One of our main difficulties is to assess the market for our product as biotechnology is quite uncertain.'

Scientists' lack of experience in writing a good business plan can be partially offset by the extensive use of technology-transfer offices in universities, or by recourse to external consultants. However, many biotech companies estimate that non specialized consultants do not understand the technology and restrict themselves to their own knowledge of finance.

17.6.6 Differences in perceptions of risk and return

Rate of return

Although the notion of risk and return is crucial for investors, it does not seem to be well understood by many scientific entrepreneurs. Divergences of language and mutual misunderstanding between investors and biotech companies lead to different perceptions in risk, in sector predictability, in product development time and in risk of product failure. 'When we discuss with bankers, we come up against a wall of incomprehension' (quote by an entrepreneur). According to many investors, fund-seekers do not think about return; they only see the needed money to finance development and growth without taking into account risk and economic reality. 'The entrepreneurs are always in love with their project.'

However, most experienced managers consider that this return requirement from the investors is consistent with the risk they take. 'When you invest in biotech it is high risk. High risk, high return.' This difference of perception regarding required return and consequently valuation clearly represents a barrier to financing.

Predictability and risk

The biotechnology sector is considered as particularly risky and the ability to keep up with technological innovation is an important component thereof. According to entrepreneurs, 'investors are too risk averse and are not aware of the difference in risk between the biotechnology sub-sectors. For instance, the diagnostic segment which is a quite traditional industry (except for R&D activities) is less risky than the therapeutics.' Another scientist also underlines, 'I would say that in the biotechnology industry we have a panel of different risks which have to be funded.' However, the perception of the risks in the biotechnology sector seems to depend on the investor's knowledge of the sector.

Product-failure risk and development time represent major issues for investors, who consider that these issues require appropriate planning and that managers tend to underestimate them. Biotech entrepreneurs feel that they themselves represent a key asset to ensure success and that they are more competent to assess the riskiness of the project.

Valuation

Most interviewees consider that company valuation represents a major issue during the negotiation. Indeed, it is often complex to define and quantify the project market potential because of the high level of innovation in biotechnology. Many misevaluations on the part of the investors result from a poor presentation of the business plan. 'If investors feel you want to sell a Lada and that they do not want to pay for a Mercedes, it is your fault.'

A variety of valuation methods are used by investors (discounted cash-flow, real options, ratio methods, benchmarking) and depend on the experience in biotechnology and their financial background. All these valuation methods aim at establishing the fair value of the future potential of the market, of the patents, of the acquisitions, and in general of all sources of economic value-added of the corporate activities.

To reduce their risk, investors tend to use milestones whose principle is to release capital stage by stage as some predefined criteria are fulfilled. Another justification of the milestones process is 'to avoid that the managers live in artificial comfort (if they receive all the capital in one go) and reduce their focus and motivation'.

In practice, the staging of financing generates some problems. First, it makes the negotiations more complex and second it requires a decision at each financing stage. If the intermediate objectives are not achieved, investors with short-term vision are tempted not to release the predicted amount while in the long term it would be profitable to continue the financing. On the other hand, short-term maximization of utility by managers may lead to fulfillment of the formal milestone requirement at any price, even if this would result in a milking of the firm's assets. This danger is present especially for qualitative milestones such as the achievement of strategic alliances with larger companies.

17.6.7 Alliances/mergers and acquisitions

Strategic alliances

According to the managers, such alliances help in the search for funds. The suppliers of funds appreciate strategic alliances with international pharmaceutical groups for many reasons. First, such alliances represent a proof of credibility and quality for the company.

As explained by many investors, alliances with a well-known group have a due diligence value. 'For services companies, deals with Merck or Pfizer are quality guarantees. Moreover, such alliances give more value to the business plan of the small biotechnology company.' Second, partnerships provide experience and expertise to the young biotech company. Some entrepreneurs mention that 'alliances allow us to have faster intellectual property and to shorten the delay for discovering new drugs because of the know-how of the partner.' Third, as mentioned by a venture capitalist, 'companies learn to respect severe deadlines because powerful partners use milestones'. Fourth, alliances with a 'big' (bio)pharma enable access to markets that could not be reached without. Finally, investors view such alliances as an additional way to exit. 'When the alliance has to end by a takeover, there is already a likely buyer.'

However, both groups of investors and biotech entrepreneurs recognize the existence of some negative aspects of alliances. In particular, the risk of industrial espionage represents a difficulty when partnering with other companies. A scientist explicitly states that 'disclosing our intellectual property to the partner can be dangerous'.

17.6.8 Mergers and acquisitions

Investors always wish to speak with the bio-entrepreneurs about the possibilities for exit. Therefore the mergers and acquisitions (M&A) dimension is crucial for them, especially when the IPO possibilities are weak. 'It is important for investors to know if there are exit potentials, if we can be repurchased by others' (quote by an entrepreneur). The biotech managers must be willing to discuss the potential repurchase of their company with the investors. In practice, it seems that discussing M&A generates a reaction of fear and pessimism on the part of the entrepreneurs, more especially among scientists. Indeed, they act as if they want to keep their project for themselves and are very reluctant to speak about M&A because of the loss of responsibility and control when they are acquired by a large international group. An investor says 'It is not easy to make them understand this dimension. For the scientists, their discoveries are their toys and they are very selfish.' Stock options are often used as compensation for this loss of control.

17.7 Analysis of perceptions

From the results of the previous section and the numbers displayed in Table 17.6, we can perform a more thorough analysis in two areas. First, the matching of answers provided by managers of biotech companies and by venture capitalists provides material enabling us to investigate the dimensions of accordance or discordance between these groups and their underlying reasons. Second, we can further analyze the sources of disagreements within each group by looking at the distributions of opinions between subgroups of managers or investors.

17.7.1 Analysis between groups

We identify five different interpretations of the comparisons between answers provided by bio-entrepreneurs and investors: criteria of agreement, criteria of disagreement, misunderstandings, mixed feelings, and disjoint criteria.

Criteria of agreement

For several criteria, there is an objective convergence of opinions between entrepreneurs and venture capitalists. These are related to the scientific and management quality, economic environment, the role of innovation and of the product pipeline in the competitive analysis, strategic alliances and, above all, the role of intellectual property. These criteria mostly relate to the environment and to the intrinsic quality of the scientific or industrial project rather than to strategic, managerial, or financial arguments.

The strongest concordance of opinions concerns the analysis of intellectual property. Although not everyone is convinced of the economic relevance of such protection, almost all interviewees – from both sides – claim that companies are forced to display a significant intellectual property protection to get external funding. The wide support for such a Machiavellian view suggests that patents primarily work as a signal on the biotechnology market in Wallonia and Brussels.

Sometimes, the same kind of opinion is justified with a different kind of analysis by the interviewees. This problem of communication is typically encountered for scientific quality, management quality, and the role of strategic alliances. For the criterion of scientific quality in Wallonia and Brussels, there seems to be a consensus view that it is important and sufficient but not always adequately understood by the other group. Thus, both entrepreneurs and investors share the same view but sometimes believe that they are alone in that view. The divergence seems to be only a matter of communication. Similarly, the feeling that it is necessary to associate professional managers to the scientist is shared by both groups, but through different analyses: it is a natural association for investors, while it is just seen as the outcome of the difficulty of turning a scientist into a manager for the entrepreneurs. Lastly, the justification of the importance of strategic alliances is put forward differently by both groups: it is mostly viewed as a helping device for the research into additional funds for managers, while investors perceive them more like an external validation of the relevance and quality of the business model. Although perceptions of these biotechnology-specific criteria seem to differ, they yield converging outcomes regarding their importance and the extent to which they are met by the companies in Wallonia and Brussels.

Criteria of disagreement

Managers of biotechnology companies and investors diverge in their analysis in two families of criteria: business plan and finance.

Discrepancies are observable at the level of the business plan. When they express an opinion, investors consider that bio-entrepreneurs do not embrace a strategic vision of their activity. Such a view is not at all accepted by the managers, who consider that the very high unpredictability of their markets precludes them from adopting a sharp strategic commitment at the level of the business plan.

The disagreement is strongest for criteria that relate to the risk and return analysis. A majority of investors tend to believe that scientists are unaware of the risk–return trade-off, but this opinion is not shared by everyone. We observe a more radical standpoint by the entrepreneurs, who often claim that investors require a return that is too high and too quick with respect to the specificities of the sector. The clearest opposition is related to the perception of risk. Investors clearly consider that entrepreneurs are too optimistic, while managers of biotech companies blame the VC industry for not accounting for their potential and not giving them the time necessary to prove it. To some extent, the discrepancy between their opinions is less about the intrinsic riskiness of the investment than about its expected payback period.

The conflict between scientists and suppliers of funds on the valuation criterion is perceptible: they have consistently different opinions about the value and the potential of the company. In fact, many investors declare their lack of objective criteria in this field. By contrast, several managers of biotechnology companies claim that nobody, including investors, is able to correctly value biotechnology companies.

Mixed feelings

For some criteria, opposite opinions are observed within a single group. In general, when a divergence of opinion appears within one group, it also appears within the other group. This is the case for the pipeline of products (should one concentrate on core activities?), information disclosure (are managers reluctant?), funding requirements (do entrepreneurs ask enough?), and mergers and acquisitions (are managers reluctant?).

These criteria, where mixed feelings are observed, belong to two categories: strategic choices and attitudes of managers. As disagreements appear in both groups, this suggests that personal experiences, rather than a consensus view of the sector, primarily drives the standpoint adopted by each individual. This should probably be related to the perception of success or failure of the investment relationship between these two parties.

More surprising though is the difference in the perception of the potential trouble caused by valuation issues during negotiations. Venture capitalists agree that valuation can create a problem that endangers the deal. This view is not shared by all managers, which could signal that some managers are more interested in the possibility of developing their activity than in the ex-ante valuation of the fruits of this development.

Disjoint criteria

A few criteria are only quoted by one family of interviewees. For the biotech companies, these criteria are the limitations induced by economic environment. Managers display a certain degree of moroseness from the side of the entrepreneurs, who seem to feel that the potential of their industry is not properly recognized and is likely to be hindered by outsiders.

Such a vision is not shared at all by investors. They mostly cite the entrepreneurs' lack of economic focus, especially regarding the projections at or beyond their economic horizon. Symptomatic of this analysis is the quote by several investors that M&As should be mostly considered as a good possibility for exit, a dimension that is not spontaneously present in the mind of those entrepreneurs interviewed.

17.7.2 Analysis within groups

Sources of discordance

Table 17.7 divides the interviewees by the category of biotechnology companies and investors to which they belong. We report only the results for the criteria showing some disagreement within groups.

Table 17.7 Details of differences of perceptions within bio-entrepreneurs and investors

	Biotech companies				Venture capitalists							
	Biopharma, services		Bioagro, bio-environment, others		Private VCs		Public VCs		Bank VCs		Business angels	
	Yes	No	Yes	No	Yes	No	Yes	No	Yes	No	Yes	No
2.2. Regulatory environment: Obstacle but not an investment barrier	7	2	4	1	5			2	1			1
3.2. Pipeline of products: Concentrate on the core business	2	4	2		1		1	2	2		1	1
4.2. Information disclosure: Reluctance to give information	5	6	2	4	2	3		1		2	1	
5. Business plan: Inadequacy asked/required funds	3	2	2	1	2	1	2	1	2		2	
6.3. Valuation problems: Potential issue during negotiations	3	3	1	1	4				2		1	
7.2. Mergers and acquisitions: Reluctance from entrepreneurs	3	4	2	3	1	1	2					

Only the first three lines provide additional information compared with Table 17.6. The business plan, valuation, and M&A criteria display evenly spread opinions. Thus, the disagreements observed for the criteria cannot be attributed to any particular category of companies or investors.

The opinions expressed about the constraints created by the regulatory environment are contrasted within the sample of investors. Private VC firms and Private Equity funds (bank VC firms), which belong to most international and specialized categories of investors, do not express any serious concern. The public venture capitalists and one business angel appear to be much more skeptical concerning the seriousness of hindrances created by the regulatory environment. Thus, this external constraint is given more weight by more local players.

The willingness to have a wide portfolio of products (second line of Table 17.7) appears to be much stronger within the therapeutic-based companies. Given the intrinsic danger and uncertainty of their business, they prefer to diversify their activities. Again, public venture capitalists and business angels are slightly more supportive of this view.

Finally, and not surprisingly, managers of biopharmaceutical companies are more reluctant than others to disclose information to their investors. This reluctance is understandable given the crucial role of IP in the therapeutic business. Only some private VC firms and one business angel perceive this reluctance. The degree of specialization of the former and the networking activities of the latter are likely to explain this feeling.

Specialized versus generalist investors

Throughout the interviewing process, opinions varied according to whether they would be applicable to specialized or generalist investors. They would not easily fit in a table, but a discussion of them is definitely worthwhile.

The influence of the economic environment on the investor's decision varies according to the investor's level of specialization in biotechnology. Generalist investors are more sensitive to the economic climate for two main reasons. First, because of their lack of scientific expertise, they consider biotechnology as extremely risky and are reluctant to invest in biotech projects. Second, long development time and high capital needs in biotechnology do not really match the strategy of suppliers of funds in a tough economic period, where shorter payback periods are particularly sought.

For regulatory constraints, again one must clearly distinguish between generalist and specialized investors. Indeed, specialized investors understand the sector and its legal aspects, and consider them as fundamental parameters in the financing decision. 'If you understand the biotechnology industry well, you can live with a more distant outlook.'

The problem of information disclosure also appears to be dealt with differently between investors. Generalist investors usually do not understand the technical details in depth and the risk of information disclosure is limited unless they employ a biotechnology expert to evaluate the project. 'This is not a problem because generalist investors will not ask extremely technical questions on the product . . . we speak from the market, the different applications.' On the other hand, the risk is more significant when negotiating with specialized biotechnology funds who are in contact with competitors and are able to understand the project in detail: 'The disclosure of information can represent a danger when we deal with specialized investors who are also in contact with a competitor.'

For risk and return also, a distinction between generalist and specialized investors has to be made. As several biotechnologists mentioned in the interviews: 'Investors' required rate of return and payback horizon are not always compatible with biotechnology activities.' Indeed, generalist investors have short- to mid-term returns expectations that are incompatible with the reality of the industry, which is characterized by long development time, heavy regulations, and a huge requirement for funds. In connexion with this dimension, assessing the value of biotech firms is done with little scientific-based negotiation except for specialized investors. The latter have a greater ability to understand the sector and use more sophisticated valuation methods.

17.8 Conclusion

Matching the two perceptions shows divergences of opinion for many particular aspects. In general, we observe that entrepreneurs are aware of the environment and investment criteria. However, key differences are mostly observed along four dimensions: required qualities (both scientific and managerial), content of the business plan, risk and return requirements, and external growth via alliances and M&As. Only the last three produce opposing conclusions and thus are likely to cause conflict between managers and investors in the funding process. They touch upon strategic and financial matters.

A limited understanding of the biotech sector in Wallonia/Brussels and, more generally, in Europe represents a fundamental problem. Because of the complexity and the high level of innovation in biotechnology, non-specialized suppliers of funds have difficulty in correctly understanding this sector. Some generalist investors do not invest because they have no knowledge about biotech activities. On the other hand, scientific entrepreneurs lack the management experience and stature to attract international funds. In general, the research world is not on the economic world's wavelength. Because of the difference in language between scientists and financiers, discussions are often misunderstood.

Specialized investors are not totally satisfied by the current situation either. They consider in general that the companies have to be proactive. Firms must also understand that investors plan short- or medium-term exit possibilities. They also have to show their willingness to collaborate with investors.

According to these findings, we attempt to formulate some policy recommendations in the sector.

The first observation concerns the difference in language between bio-entrepreneurs and suppliers of funds. According to entrepreneurs, few investors are specialized in biotechnology. As a consequence, investors display large technical and scientific knowledge deficiencies that make valuation very difficult. One solution to this problem could be an increasing intervention of biotechnology-specialized funds led by experienced industry stakeholders. On the other hand, bio-entrepreneurs and especially scientists also have significant knowledge deficiencies in many managerial aspects. In our opinion, specific support structures could improve the congruence between two naturally divergent concerns: the suppliers of funds are more concerned about value creation whereas companies are concerned about technological aspects. Indeed, observations tend to show the importance of emphasizing the efforts made for the development of incubation and development centers for biotechnology companies. Moreover, education programs for scientists focused on managerial matters, such as the preparation of business plans, should be more developed.

A second dimension concerns many bio-entrepreneurs' lack of realism regarding the potential growth of their firm. Indeed we observe that many biotech managers are not (or do not want to be) aware of the development potential and the demands of external financing. They confine themselves to a self-financing strategy that will be severely constraining in the long run. A consequence of this is a mismatch between the company's real needs and its external demand for funds.

Moreover, we often observe a suboptimal corporate development. This finding is confirmed by the relatively high weighting of the diagnostics subsegment, the emphasis on product development in the short term and the recourse to self-financing to develop new products. Indeed, we believe that the industrial structure – featuring many diagnostic activities – is the result of capital rationing that restricts the migration of competences towards the therapeutic segment. This latter subsegment requires huge amounts of long-term VC but has a greater added value. The VC industry could respond to this type of concern by becoming less generous in the number of investments but investing more in each one that it does invest in. This requires larger investable amounts per fund and, probably more importantly, slightly more downstream financing. Too many projects are funded extremely early in their life cycle, based on sound scientific premises but without an actual proof of concept at the industrial level.

Finally, we underline the necessity for scientists in Wallonia and Brussels to develop an entrepreneurship culture. Indeed, scientists in these regions do not have the same entrepreneurial spirit as their North American colleagues, particularly for cultural reasons (no social reward to business success, large social penalty for bankruptcies, no prestige perceived from leaving the field of pure science) that are beyond the scope of this chapter. A radical shift of mentality is not likely in the short term but it must be a long-term objective, pursued at the level of the society as a whole, starting with the educational model.

Acknowledgments

The authors would like to thank Michel Bergeron, Tom Göbels, Renaud Martin, Muriel Toussirot, Michaël Haguinet, and Dominique Schmetz for their help in field research and analysis. This research has been carried out under the auspices of the National Funds for Collective Research (FRFC) of Belgium. Field research has been partly financed by the Programme '4 × 4 pour Entreprendre' of the Walloon Region of Belgium. Georges Hübner thanks Deloitte (Luxembourg) and the Luxembourg School of Finance, University of Luxembourg, for financial support. All errors are ours.

References

Amburgey, T.L., Dacin, T. and Singh, J.V. (1996). Learning Races, Patent Races, and Capital Races: Strategic Interaction and Embeddedness within Organizational Fields. In Baum, J.A.C. and Dutton, J.E. (eds), *The Embeddedness of Strategy: Advances in Strategic Management*. Greenwich: JAI Press, 303–322.

Arojärvi, O. (2001). How to Value Biotechnology Firms: A Study of Current Approaches and Key Value Drivers. Working Paper, Helsinki School of Economics and Business Administration, Helsinki, Finland.

Bank of England (2001). *Financing of Technology-Based Small Firms*. http://www.bankofengland.co.uk/publications/financeforsmallfirms/hightech2001.pdf.

Bastin, V., Bergeron, M.Y., Hübner, G., Michel, P.A. and Servais, M. (2005). Venture Capital Financing in Biotechnologies: A Prospective Assessment. Working Paper, HEC-Management School, University of Liège, Liège, Belgium.

Baum, J.A.C. and Oliver, C. (1991). Institutional Linkages and Organizational Mortality. *Administrative Science Quarterly*, 36(2):187–218.

Baum, J.A.C. and Silverman, B.S. (2004). Picking Winners or Building Them? Alliance, Intellectual, and Human Capital as Selection Criteria in Venture Financing and Performance of Biotechnology Startups. *Journal of Business Venturing*, 19(3):411–436.

Baum, J.A.C., Calabrese, T. and Silverman, B.R. (2000). Don't Go it Alone: Alliance Network Composition and Start-up Performance in Canadian Biotechnology. *Strategic Management Journal*, 21(3):267–294.

Bergeron, M.Y., Kryzanowski, L. and Zorgati, S. (2002). Financing Related Issues and Difficulties of Canadian Biotechnology Companies: Analysis from the Viewpoint of Suppliers and Evaluation of Adequacy of Capital Supply and Demand. Working Paper, Chair in Management of Bio-industries, University of Quebec at Montreal, Montreal, Canada.

Carbone, J. (2003). Ethics, Patents and the Sustainability of the Biotech Business Model. *International Review of Law, Computers and Technology*, 17(2):203–218.

Chung, S., Singh, H. and Lee, K. (2000). Complementarity, Status Similarity and Social Capital as Drivers of Alliance Formation. *Strategic Management Journal*, 21(1):1–22.

Crocker, G. (2003). *Endurance: The European Biotechnology Report 2003*. Cambridge: Ernst & Young.

Deeds, D.L., DeCarolis, D. and Coombs, J. (1999). Dynamic Capabilities and New Product Development in High Technology Ventures: An Empirical Analysis of New Biotechnology Firms. *Journal of Business Venturing*, 15(3):211–229.

DiMasi, J.A., Hansen, R.W. and Grabowski, H.G. (2003). The Price of Innovation: New Estimates of Drug Development Costs. *Journal of Health Economics*, 22(2):151–185.

European Venture Capital Association (2003). *Annual Survey of Pan-European Private Equity and Venture Capital Activity. EVCA Yearbook 2003*. EVCA.

Haar, B. (2001). Venture Capital Funding for Biotech Pharmaceutical Companies in an Integrated Financial Services Market: Regulatory Diversity Within the EC. *European Business Organization Law Review*, 2:585–602.

Hall, B.H. (2002). The Financing of Research and Development. *Oxford Review of Economic Policy*, 18(1):35–51.

Hall, J. and Hofer, C.W. (1993). Venture Capitalists' Decision Criteria in New Venture Evaluation. *Journal of Business Venturing*, 8(1):25–42.

Harding, R. (1999). *Venture Capital and Regional Development*. London: Institute for Public Policy Research.

Harvey, M.G. and Lush, R.F. (1995). Expanding the Scope of Due Diligence. *Journal of Business Venturing*, 10(1):5–21.

Hübner, G., Michel, P.A. and Servais, M. (2003). *Valeur et Risque des Brevets pour Les Biotechnologies*. Brussels: Larcier.

Kenney, M. (1986). *Biotechnology: The University-Industry Complex*. New Haven CT: Yale University Press.

Lerner, J. (1994). Venture Capitalists and the Decision to go Public. *Journal of Financial Economics*, 35(3):293–316.

Lerner, J., Shane, H. and Tsai, A. (2003). Do Equity Financing Cycles Matter? Evidence from Biotechnology Alliances. *Journal of Financial Economics*, 67(3):411–446.

Leytes, L.J. (2002). Raising Venture Capital in the Biopharma Industry. *Drug Discovery Today*, 7(22):1125–1127.

Lockett, A., Murray G. and Wright, M. (2002). Do U.K. Venture Capitalists Still Have a Bias Against Investment in New Technology Firms. *Research Policy*, 31(6):1009–1030.

MacMillan, I.C., Siegel, R. and Subba Narasimha, P.N. (1985). Criteria Used by Venture Capitalists to Evaluate New Venture Proposals. *Journal of Business Venturing*, 1(1):119–128.

MacMillan, I.C., Zenman, L. and Subba Narasimha, P.N. (1987). Criteria Distinguishing Successful Ventures in the Venture Screening Process. *Journal of Business Venturing*, 2(2):123–138.

Manigart, S. and Struyf, C. (1997). Financing High Technology Startups in Belgium, An Explorative Study. *Small Business Economics*, 9(2):125–135.

Manigart, S., de Waele, K., Wright, M., Robbie, K., Desbrières, Ph., Sapienza, H.J. and Beekman, A. (2002). Determinants of Required Return in Venture Capital Investments: A Five Country Study. *Journal of Business Venturing*, 17(4): 291–312.

Mason, C.M. and Harrison, R.T. (2002). Barriers to Investment in the Informal Venture Capital Sector. *Entrepreneurship and Regional Development*, 14(3):271–287.

Mason, C.M. and Harrison, R.T. (2003). Closing the Regional Equity Gap? A Critique of the Department of Trade and Industry's Regional Venture Capital Funds Initiative. *Regional Studies*, 37(8):855–868.

McClellan, M.B. (2003). *2003 Performance Report to the President and the Congress*. Food and Drug Administration, United States.

Moore, B. (1994). Financial Constraints to the Growth and Development of Small High-Technology Firms. In Hughes, A. and Storey, D.J. (eds), *Finance and the Small Firm*. London: Routledge, 112–144.

Murray, G.C. (1994). The Second 'Equity Gap': Exit Problems for Seed and Early Stage Venture Capitalists and their Investee Companies. *International Small Business Journal*, 12(4):59–76.

Murray, G.C. and Lott, J. (1995). Have UK Venture Capital Firms a Bias Against Investment in New Technology-based Firms? *Research Policy*, 24(2):283–299.

Murray, G.C. and Marriott, R. (1998). Why has the Investment Performance of Technology-Specialist, European Venture Capital Funds Been so Poor? *Research Policy*, 24(2):283–299.

Muzyka, D., Birley, S. and Leleux, B. (1996). Trade-offs in the Investment Decisions of European Venture Capitalists. *Journal of Business Venturing*, 11(4):273–287.

Prevezer, M., Stiut, D. and Swann, G.M. (1998). *The Dynamics of Industrial Clustering: International Comparisons in Computing and Biotechnology*. Oxford: Oxford University Press.

Remer, S., Ang, S. and Baden-Fuller, C. (2001). Dealing with Uncertainties in the Biotechnology Industry: The Use of Real Options Reasoning. *Journal of Commercial Biotechnology*, 8(2):95–105.

Robbins-Roth, C. (2001). *From Alchemy to IPO: the Business of Biotechnology*. Cambridge: Perseus Publishing.

Saunders, M., Lewis, P. and Thornhill, A. (1997). *Research Methods for Business Students*. London: Pitman.

Senker, J. (1998). *Biotechnology and Competitive Advantage: Europe*. Cheltenham: Elgar.

Tyebjee, T.T. and Bruno, A.V. (1984). A Model of Venture Capitalist Investment Activity. *Management Science*, 30(9):1051–1066.

U'Prichard, D.C. and Pullan, L.M. (1997). The Future of Drug Industry Research and the Zeneca Response. *Research Technology Management*, 40(6):35–39.

Zacharakis, A.L. and Meyer, G.D. (2000). The Potential of Actuarial Decision Models: Can They Improve the Venture Capital Investment Decision? *Journal of Business Venturing*, 15(4):323–346.

Zucker, L.G., Darby, M.R. and Brewer, M.B. (1998). Intellectual Human Capital and the Birth of U.S. Biotechnology Enterprises. *American Economic Review*, 88(1): 290–306.

Part Four

Performance

18 Simple and cross-efficiency of European venture capital firms using data envelopment analysis

Greg N. Gregoriou, Maher Kooli, Philipp Krohmer, and Rainer Lauterbach

Abstract

We apply data envelopment analysis (DEA) and use the basic and cross-efficiency models to evaluate the performance of European venture capital firms. With the ever-increasing number of VC firms, DEA can be used as an alternative appraisal method for ranking their efficiency. We rank VC firms by efficiency score and compare the results among European countries where VC firms are popular.

18.1 Introduction

According to the European Venture Capital Association (EVCA/Thomson Venture Economics/PricewaterhouseCoopers, 2006), European VC funds invested €11.4 billion in 6576 portfolio firms in 2005, more than a 10% increase from 2004 (€10.3 billion in 8044 firms) and a 36% increase from 2003 (€8.4 billion in 8398 firms). In Europe, VC funds obtain the predominant share of their funding from banks, pension funds, insurance companies, fund of funds, and corporate investors. Over the last 26 years since 1980, at 31 December 2005, European VC funds had generated cumulative returns since inception of pooled Internal Rate of Return (IRR) 5.6% per annum (p.a.) and a top quarter IRR of 23.9% p.a. net to investors after management fees and carried interest (EVCA/Thomson Venture Economics/PricewaterhouseCoopers, 2006). These figures indicate that performance of VC investments varies widely, and investors have to focus on the best-performing VC firms to outperform investments in other asset classes. The main objective of our study is to evaluate the performance of European VC firms using data envelopment analysis (DEA). To the best of our knowledge, this is the first study that uses this approach in the VC context.

DEA is a non-parametric technique that measures the relative efficiency of decision-making units (VC firms in our case) on the basis of observed data, and produces an efficiency score as a single number between 0 and 1.00.[1] Its main benefit is that it identifies

[1] An efficiency score of 1.00 refers to an efficient VC firm (or best-performing firm that lies on the frontier), whereas a score of less than 1.00 signifies the firm is inefficient.

the best-performing VC firm and determines the relative efficiencies of a set of similar VC firms. DEA was initially developed by Charnes et al.(1978). It was later adapted by Banker et al. (1984), who improved the Farrell (1957) technical measure of efficiency from a single-input, single-output process to a multiple-input, multiple-output process. The Charnes et al. (1978) and Banker et al. (1984) models are the basic DEA models and were originally developed for non-profit organizations. Later we discuss an alternative DEA model: the cross-efficiency DEA model.

The power of DEA lies in its ability to deal with several inputs and outputs while not imposing a precise relation between input and output variables. An institutional investor first selects a VC fund manager and commits a certain equity amount to the VC fund. The VC fund manager selects VC firms and invests capital into these firms with the aim of maximizing returns and minimizing risks. Depending on the performance of the VC portfolio firms, the VC fund at the end of the investment period can return capital to the institutional investor. DEA is able to take the performance measured on the VC firm level as output variables and VC fund manager variables as input variables, as VC fund managers influence the selection of, and provide added value to, VC firms. The single measure of performance takes into account the multiple measurements of inputs and outputs to evaluate a VC firm's efficiency level because the VC firms themselves are used as the benchmarks. We find that many VC firms are inefficient when evaluated by basic DEA models. Having an alternative performance measure such as DEA is important because it enables investors potentially to pinpoint the reasons behind a VC firm's poor performance. Once the weaknesses are recognized, an investor can learn and adjust his selection in the future to reach a perfect efficiency score in future investments by comparing a VC firm with poor performance to VC firms having achieved an efficiency score of 1.00.

For institutional investors considering using VC firms as alternative investment vehicles, it is critical that a performance measure provides not only a precise appraisal of the VC firm's performance, but also an idea of the quality of the VC fund management with respect to certain criteria (variables such as inputs and outputs). Using DEA could present investors with a useful tool for ranking VC firms, not by historical returns but by peer group appraisal, and shed some insight into the efficiency and inefficiency of VC firms.

While the benefit of DEA is relevant to all VC markets, it is of special interest to the VC industry in Europe because of the homogeneity within each country. Several studies have emphasized the specific features of the European VC industry and the varying nature of national VC industries within different European countries as well as the differences between the European and the U.S. VC industries.[2]

This chapter is organized as follows. In Section 18.2 we reflect on the relevant literature on the VC industry. In Section 18.3 we discuss the different DEA methodologies. Section 18.4 contains a description of the data. Section 18.5 contains a discussion of the empirical results and, finally, the last section summarizes our conclusions.

18.2 Background

In contrast to public equity or fixed income, the success of an investment in a VC firm does not depend only on the optimal investment selection, but also on the active involvement

[2] For instance, Bottazzi et al. (2004) study the volatility and longer-term facts of the European VC industry.

of the VC fund manager in the development of the portfolio firm. Chan (1983) confirms the positive role of VC funds as financial intermediaries. A theoretical model explaining why VC funds are value-enhancing is provided by Casamata (2003). Empirical support of the investor's value-added role is given by Lerner (1995), as well as MacMillan et al. (1989). The development of portfolio firms can be improved by the investor's action as confirmed by Hellmann and Puri (2002), Kaplan and Stroemberg (2000), and Hege et al. (2003). Lerner (1995) examines the representation of investors on the boards of private firms in their portfolios and demonstrates the importance of such representations around the time of chief executive officer (CEO) turnover. These findings demonstrate the importance of VC fund management resources for the performance of the portfolio firm.

We analyze the spread of VC fund management as input variable in our analysis. As VC fund managers do not invest once in a company, but rather do so several times, their resources are relevant over the total post-investment period. VC fund managers apply special financing methods such as staging, which is the stepwise allocation of capital instead of a single up-front investment. According to Sahlman (1990) and Gompers (1995), staging through financing rounds can be used by the investor to mitigate information asymmetries, to reduce agency problems and to control the progress of the firm. Positive influence of staging on performance is examined by Wang and Zhou (2004), Cuny and Talmor (2003), Hsu (2002), as well as Neher (1999).

We focus our study on the European VC industry. Studies that focus on the relevance of location and its relationship to legal regulations, macroeconomic conditions, or investment pattern include Bottazzi et al. (2005), Keuschnigg (2004), Cumming (2002), Jeng and Wells (2000), and others. Analyses of the varying levels of development, investment rates, and decision-making qualities between the VC markets of different European countries are provided by Desai et al. (2003), Amason et al. (1994), Robbie et al. (1992), Birley (1989), Manigart (1994), as well as Birley and Muzyka (1996).

We consider fund size as a relevant input factor for our DEA model. Previous empirical studies have confirmed the importance of fund and portfolio size on performance, such as those by Cumming (2003), Gottschalg et al. (2003), as well as Lerner and Schoar (2002). Furthermore, as input factor we look at the level of committed capital on the overall market at the initial investment of a fund into a company as an input variable. The theory of Inderst and Mueller (2003) and the findings of Gompers and Lerner (2000) highlight that growing inflows of capital into venture funds increase the valuation of these funds' new investments and enhance the relation between changes in valuations and the ultimate success of the firms. Furthermore, Gompers (1995) argues that growth of the investment pool may measure entry by inexperienced investors. These new entrants may overinvest and may not monitor companies as effectively as experienced investors. As in the case of free cash-flow agency costs, the increase in investment is excessive and would have a negative impact on performance. Bottazi et al. (2004) focus their study specifically on the volatility and long-term aspects of the European VC industry.

We select the return on investment based on actual cash flows as output variable. The specific return and risk characteristics of European Private Equity funds have been empirically analyzed on the basis of cash flows by Diller and Kaserer (2004). However, they do not provide analyses on the differences of performance between various European countries, as offered within this study.

A comparison of the determinants of VC performance in Europe versus the U.S. is carried out by Hege et al. (2003). Their study on performance does not explain differences of VC performance between various European countries, which our analyses do. They base their performance measurement on a hand-collected questionnaire dataset, supplemented by valuation data (not cash-flow data) from Venture Economics. For the hand-collected questionnaire dataset, they apply the same grid used by Gompers (1995), which considers IPO related success measures that are difficult to interpret. The IRR figures in Hege et al. (2003) are subject to measurement error because IRR measurements based on Venture Economics data alone may lead to milestone bias, which can materially affect researchers' estimates of returns and valuation patterns over time. Venture Economics only provides dates of financing rounds, not the exact date of cash injections. The exact date of cash injections often differs from the date of the financing round because rounds are often broken up into several cash injections, referred to as milestone rounds. This weakness has been identified in Kaplan et al. (2002), who stress the impossibility of accurately measuring milestone-round information using Venture Economics data alone.

Unlike these previous studies, our dataset provides information for each cash injection or milestone round within specific financing rounds. This enables exact IRR performance measurement.

18.3 Methodology

DEA has many advantages over traditional parametric techniques such as regression. Regression analysis approximates the efficiency of VC firms under investigation relative to the average performance. In contrast to regression methods, DEA focuses on the individual quarterly observations of VC funds and optimizes the performance measure of each portfolio VC firm of each VC fund. However, proper care must be used in determining the input and output variables. The basis of regression analysis focuses on central tendencies, whereas DEA focuses on extreme observations. Traditional regression analysis specifies linear equations that are assumed to adequately describe each VC firm under examination. In contrast, DEA examines each VC firm uniquely by generating individual relative efficiency scores in comparison with the entire sample under investigation. Furthermore, the benefit of DEA over regression methods is that it does not require prior hypotheses about the specific form of the production function. Instead, DEA creates a best practices frontier solely on the basis of observed quarterly values, making model mis-specification impossible. Mis-specification is a frequent problem in regression analysis and one that can yield incorrect conclusions. Furthermore, DEA avoids the problems traditionally associated with regression-based models that require random assumptions about the exact relationships between input and output variables (Darling et al., 2004).

In its most elementary form DEA uses inputs and outputs to calculate an efficiency score that provides the relative efficiency of a VC firm when compared with its peers. The first step in DEA is to produce an efficient frontier using Pareto optimality.[3] DEA then calculates the efficiency score of each Decision Making Unit (DMU) relative to the best practices/efficient frontier. In this study, the DMUs are VC firms. As the return to the institutional investor depends ultimately on the performance of the individual VC firm, we define the performance of the VC firm as output variables and define as input

[3] Pareto optimality means the best that can be attained without putting any group at a disadvantage. In other words, a group of firms becomes better off if an individual firm becomes better off and none become worse off.

variables characteristics of the VC fund manager responsible for the VC firm portfolio selection.

The efficiency frontier consists of the 'best-performing' VC firms, for example the most efficient at transforming the inputs into outputs (Charnes et al., 1981). A VC firm not on the frontier would have an efficiency score less than 1.00 and would be labeled inefficient. Similarly, a VC firm with an efficiency score of 0.85 is merely 85% as efficient as the top-performing VC firm. A best-performance frontier charts the maximum or minimum level of output (input) produced for any assumed level of input (output), where outputs represent the degree to which the VC firm's goal has been achieved.

18.3.1 Basic efficiency

The main distinction between the two basic DEA models is that the Banker et al. (1984) model uses varying investment returns to scale to examine the relative efficiency of VC firms, while the Charnes et al. (1978) model uses constant investment returns to scale. To obtain robust results, it is customary that a proper working sample should be in the order of three times the number of VC firms as the number of input and output variables (Charnes et al., 1981). In addition, DEA uses a comparative measure of relative performance.

We adapt the notation from Adler et al. (2002) for the basic and cross-efficiency models. By comparing n VC firms with s outputs, denoted by y_{rk} in Equation (18.1), where $r = 1, \ldots, s$, and m inputs denoted by x_{ik}, $i = 1, \ldots, m$, the efficiency measure for fund k is:

$$h_k = Max \frac{\sum_{r=1}^{s} u_r y_{rk}}{\sum_{i=1}^{m} v_i x_{ik}}, \tag{18.1}$$

where the maximization is done on the weights u_r and v_i, which are all constrained to be positive. An additional set of constraints requires that the same weights, when applied to all VC firms, do not allow any VC firm with an efficiency score greater than 100% and are displayed in the following set of constraints:

$$\frac{\sum_{r=1}^{s} u_r y_{rj}}{\sum_{i=1}^{m} v_i x_{ij}} \leq 1 \text{ for } j = 1, \ldots, n$$

The efficiency score falls between 0 and 1.00, with VC firm k regarded as efficient upon receiving an efficiency score of 1.00. Therefore,each VC firm selects weights to maximize its own efficiency with respect to the constraints present (see Equation (18.2)).

$$h_k = Max \sum_{r=1}^{s} u_r y_{rk} + c_k$$

constraint:

$$\sum_{i=1}^{m} v_i x_{ij} - \sum_{r=1}^{s} u_r y_{rj} - c_k \geq 0 \text{ for } j = 1, \ldots n, \tag{18.2}$$

$$\sum_{i=1}^{m} v_i x_{ik} = 1,$$

$$u_r \geq 0 \text{ for } r = 1, \ldots, s,$$

$$v_i \geq 0 \text{ for } i = 1, \ldots, m.$$

An extra constant variable, denoted by c_k, is added in the Banker et al. (1984) model to allow variable returns to scale between inputs and outputs. A VC firm is considered scale efficient if the level of its operation is optimal. If the scale efficiency is reduced or increased, the efficiency will weaken. A VC firm is considered technically efficient if it is able to maximize each of its outputs per unit of input, thus signifying the efficiency of the conversion process of the variables. Technical efficiency is calculated using the Banker et al. (1984) model in this chapter.

In a production frontier, constant returns to scale imply that if there is an increase in the inputs of a VC firm it will consequently result in a proportional increase to its outputs. In other words, a linear relationship would be present between inputs and outputs. If a VC firm were to increase its inputs by 5%, thereby producing a similar increase in outputs, the VC firm would be operating at constant returns to scale. This implies that irrespective of the scale at which the VC firm operates, its efficiency will stay the same.

On the other hand, if an increase in the inputs of a VC firm does not induce a proportional transformation in its outputs, then the VC firm will display variable returns to scale, implying that as the VC firm alters its level of operations its efficiency can increase or decrease. Therefore, since VC firms can vary their leverage as well as level of operations at different times to magnify returns, we employ the Banker et al. (1984) model (varying returns to scale).

18.3.2 Cross-efficiency

The cross-efficiency model was first seen in Sexton et al. (1986). It establishes the ranking procedure and computes the efficiency score of each VC firm n times using optimal weights measured by the linear programs. A cross-evaluation matrix consists of rows and columns ($j \times k$), each equal to the number of VC firms in the analysis. The efficiency of VC firm j is computed with the optimal weights for VC firm k. The higher the values in column k, the more likely that VC firm k is efficient using superior operating techniques. Therefore calculating the mean of each column will provide the peer appraisal score of each VC firm. The cross-efficiency method is superior to the basic efficiency method because the former uses internally generated weights as opposed to forcing predetermined weights.

The cross-evaluation model used here is represented by Equation (18.3):

$$h_{kj} = \frac{\sum_{r=1}^{s} u_{rk} y_{rj}}{\sum_{i=1}^{m} v_{ik} x_{ij}}, \quad k = 1, \ldots, n, j = 1, \ldots, n. \tag{18.3}$$

where h_{kj} is the score of VC firm j cross-evaluated by the weight of VC firm k. In the cross-evaluation matrix, all VC firms are bounded by $0 \leq h_{kj} \leq 1$, and the VC firms in the diagonal, h_{kk}, depict the basic DEA efficiency score, $h_{kk} = 1$ for efficient VC firms and $h_{kk} < 1$ for inefficient VC firms. The equations show that the problem is generated n times in trying to distinguish the relative efficiency scores of all VC firms.

DEA papers have been published in many sectors, and use of the method has often resulted in technical and efficiency improvements. DEA has also been used recently to evaluate the performance of mutual funds, hedge funds, funds of hedge funds, and commodity trading advisors (CTAs) and determine the most efficient funds (Gregoriou et al., 2005a, 2005b; Gregoriou, 2003; Basso and Funari, 2001; Sedzro and Sardano, 2000; Morey and Morey, 1999; Bowlin, 1998; McMullen and Strong, 1997).

Because the Banker et al. (1984) model relaxes the convexity constraints that exist in the Charnes et al. (1978) model, it permits the measurement of the efficiency of VC firms on a variable returns to scale postulated between the inputs and outputs. For example, as noted, if an increase in the VC firm's input does not generate a relative change in its outputs, the VC firm displays variable returns to scale, implying that as a VC firm alters the level of its day-to-day activities its efficiency could increase or decrease.

As we noted earlier, cross-evaluation is superior to either basic DEA method because (1) efficiency is still measured relative to the VC firm with the highest efficiency score, but (2) having more than one combination of weights of a VC firm that maximizes its own efficiency adds an extra dimension of flexibility. The main idea of DEA is that it is flexible and can be extended to other VC firms to evaluate their individual performance. VC firms with high average efficiency from a cross-efficiency matrix can be considered as a good example for inefficient VC firms to improve their methods.

The inputs and outputs must correspond to the activities of a VC firm in order for the analysis to make sense. We use five variables, three for inputs and two for outputs, since a larger number might clutter the analysis. Three times the variables will result in having sufficient observations (degrees of freedom) to get a good evaluation. Having a great number of variables could result in an overlap of measuring inputs and outputs, thereby producing some problems in interpreting the results. If too many variables are used in the analysis many VC firms could be rated efficient.

In this study we use the variable returns to scale model (Banker et al., 1984) as we find no support for any type of proportional relationship between inputs and outputs. We adopt the input minimization mode whereby the aim of VC is to provide absolute returns irrespective of market conditions.

- The inputs are: (I-1) number of funds divided by the number of general partners (I-2) Fund size and (I-3) Committed capital.
- The outputs are (O-1) Internal rate of return and (O-2) Multiple of cost.

We briefly describe the variables:

- (I-1) As first input variable, we select the number of different funds a VC fund management firm currently has under management, divided by the number of general partners of the VC fund management firm. The smaller the figure, the less the distribution of resources and the more management resources can be focused on a single fund.

- (I-2) At the fund level, we test for the impact of VC fund size on the investment return of the VC portfolio firm. Several empirical studies have confirmed the importance of the fund size on success (Cumming, 2003; Gottschalg et al., 2003). While most studies argue that performance decreases with increasing portfolio size as there is less monitoring and value-added assistance, empirical counterevidence can be found.
- (I-3) As third input variable, we consider the influence of the level of committed capital on the overall market (in US$ millions, at June 2005) at the date of the initial investment of a VC fund into a VC portfolio firm. The inflation adjustment is based on Consumer Price Index (CPI) data for all urban households and all items obtained from the U.S. Department of Labor (http://www.bls.gov).
- (O-1) As the first output variable, we take the calculation of the internal rate of return (IRR) per annum, which is based on the exact cash flows from the VC fund to the VC portfolio firm. As the DEA does not work with negative values or with zero, we add a constant to each observation to make all data positive.
- (O-2) As second output variable, we consider the multiple of cost, which is the total distributed capital from a VC firm back to the VC fund, divided by the total amount invested into the VC firm. In contrast to the IRR per annum, this multiple figure does not reflect time-adjusted return; rather it provides an absolute return figure. As the DEA does not work with negative values or with zero, we also add a constant to each observation to render the data positive.

18.4 Data

The unique dataset we use for this project originates from the database of CEPRES, The Center of Private Equity Research.[4] As of January 2006, the dataset provides detailed information on 171 Private Equity and VC fund managers, 427 PE and VC funds, and their 9950 investments in 8063 different portfolio firms. These investments include more than 27 000 cash injections spanning a period of 34 years (1971–2005) and cover 50 countries in North and South America, Europe, and Asia. For reasons of confidentiality, names of fund managers, funds, and portfolio firms are not disclosed. Although the database is completely anonymous, it provides us with high-quality in-depth data. Previous studies based on CEPRES data include Cumming and Walz (2004) and Krohmer and Lauterbach (2005).

The dataset is extraordinary with respect to the level of detail provided. Our data consist of information about the investment manager, the fund, and the portfolio firms. Together with detailed transaction specific data, the dataset also provides exact monthly cash flows between the portfolio firm and the fund. The cash flows are reported as gross figures, and thus are not biased by any externalities such as management fees and carried interest. Therefore, our cash-flow-based IRR calculations are extremely precise.

The dataset contains information on VC, PE buy-out, and mezzanine funds. As we analyze the efficiency of European VC firms, we exclude in the first step all buy-out and mezzanine funds and investments where the development stage was not disclosed by the fund. In the second step, we delete all non-European funds. Furthermore, as we want to include only unbiased returns as output in our model, the calculation of the returns

[4] Web site: http://www.cepres.de

must be based on objective values. Therefore, we include only partially and fully realized investments; in the case of partially realized investments the IRR is calculated by taking the net asset value (NAV) at the valuation date as the last cash flow paid back to the investor. Hence, we eliminate all unrealized investments, leaving all fully and partially realized investments in the data sample.

The resulting dataset comprises 857 European VC firms belonging to 53 VC fund managers and their 95 funds spanning a period of 21 years (1983–2004), 90% of the investments were made in the years 1991 to 2001. The geographical spread covers 22 European countries. For the analysis, we cluster the observations in five main country-groups: UK (179 observations), France (204), Germany (163), Scandinavia (142), and other European (169). The remaining investments of the group 'Other European' were pursued in 15 countries: Austria, Belgium, Czech Republic, Greece, Hungary, Iceland, Ireland, Italy, Luxemburg, Netherlands, Poland, Portugal, Romania, Spain, and Switzerland. The proportion of the sample regarding regions and countries has similarity to the respective sizes of the European VC markets. The distribution over time of the investments in VC firms in our sample is in line with the market evolution in terms of committed capital on the overall VC market, as shown in Figures 18.1 and 18.2. The VC industry has gone through several fundraising cycles during the last twenty years. After a period of low fundraising at the end of the 1980s and the beginning of the 1990s, Figure 18.1 shows a steady growth of inflows to new funds during the 1990s, reaching its peak in 1999. The burst of the so-called 'internet bubble' led to a dramatic decrease of capital committed to venture funds at the beginning of this century. The number of investments by year illustrated in Figure 18.2 shows a similar shape, although slightly shifted by one year.

Table 18.1 provides descriptive analyses on the two output variables. Panel A summarizes the IRR and Panel B the multiple of cost figures for the entire VC sample. Besides

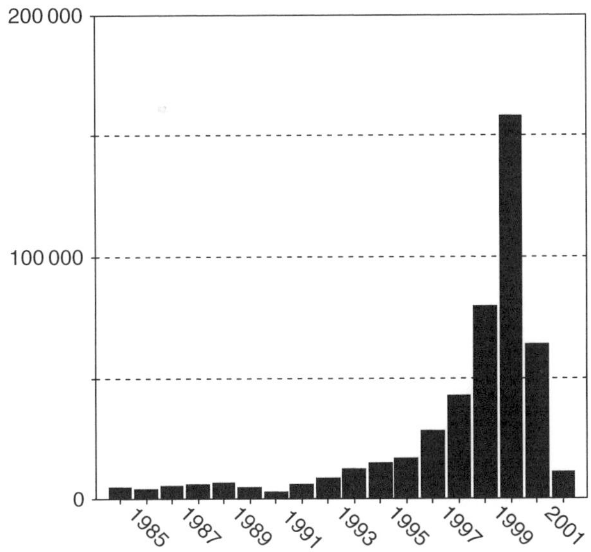

Figure 18.1 Committed capital on the overall venture capital market by fundraising year (US$ millions, June 2005)

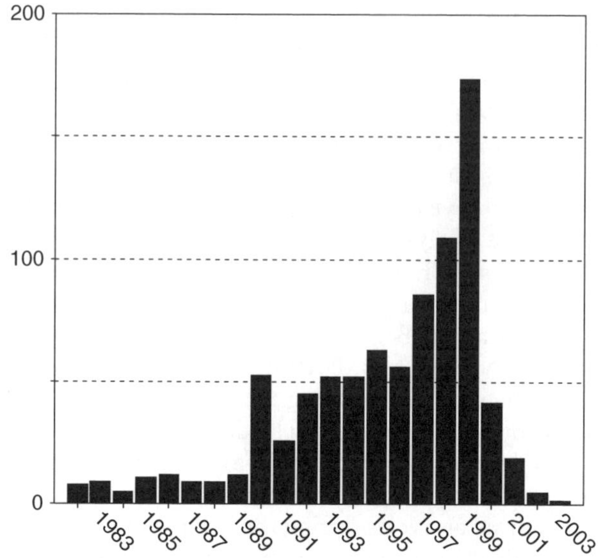

Figure 18.2 Number of venture capital firms by investment year (sample of 859 firms)

Table 18.1 Descriptive analyses of the output variables. The internal rate of return (IRR) and the multiple of cost figures for the entire VC sample used for the following analysis (857 European VC firms) are summarized. The performance calculations are based on exact monthly cash-flow streams between the fund and the entrepreneurial firm. Panel A shows the IRR statistics (as well as mean, median, and standard deviations, it also shows the percentile characteristics in the left column). Country-clusters are considered to analyze structural differences (the investments of the group 'Other European' were pursued in 15 countries: Austria, Belgium, Czech Republic, Greece, Hungary, Iceland, Ireland, Italy, Luxemburg, Netherlands, Poland, Portugal, Romania, Spain, and Switzerland). Panel B shows the results for the multiple of cost

Panel A: Internal Rate of Return (IRR)

All VC Investments			
	Percentiles	N	829
1%	−1.00	Mean	0.14
5%	−1.00	Mode	−1.00
10%	−1.00	Minimum	−1.00
25%	−1.00	Maximum	42.14
50%	−0.02	Median	−0.02
75%	0.27	Std. Deviation	2.43
90%	0.84	Variance	5.90
95%	1.83	Skewness	10.58
99%	9.64	Kurtosis	149.28

Table 18.1 Continued

Panel A: Internal Rate of Return (IRR)

Statistics	N	% of total N	Mean	Median	Std. dev.	Minimum	Maximum
All VC investments	829	100.00%	0.14	−0.02	2.43	−1.00	42.14
UK	175	21.10%	0.19	−0.13	3.37	−1.00	42.14
France	200	24.10%	0.11	0.02	1.19	−1.00	10.53
Germany	153	18.50%	0.60	−0.09	3.81	−1.00	30.58
Scandinavia	136	16.40%	−0.04	0.01	1.05	−1.00	6.73
Other European	165	19.90%	−0.16	−0.09	1.15	−1.00	10.03

Panel B: Multiple of Cost

All VC investments			
	Percentiles	N	857
1%	0.00	Mean	3.69
5%	0.00	Mode	0.00
10%	0.00	Minimum	0.00
25%	0.00	Maximum	1087.50
50%	0.89	Median	0.89
75%	2.13	Std. Deviation	38.43
90%	4.73	Variance	1476.79
95%	8.46	Skewness	26.60
99%	26.44	Kurtosis	743.26

Panel B: Multiple of Cost

Statistics	N	% of total N	Mean	Median	Std. dev.	Minimum	Maximum
All VC investments	857	100.00%	3.69	0.89	38.43	0.00	1087.50
UK	179	20.90%	9.43	0.63	83.15	0.00	1087.50
France	204	23.80%	2.41	1.05	5.08	0.00	39.13
Germany	163	19.00%	2.82	0.55	10.54	0.00	118.90
Scandinavia	142	16.60%	2.03	1.00	3.21	0.00	23.38
Other European	169	19.70%	1.40	0.57	2.52	0.00	18.60

mean, median, and standard deviations, the percentile characteristics are also shown in the left column. Skewness and kurtosis reveal non-normal distributions for both the IRR and the multiple. Because of the high fraction of total losses (IRR of −100%, multiple of 0) the distributions are strongly positive skewed. Venture capital investments are typically investments in young innovative companies, characterized by substantial informational asymmetries and uncertainty. The high risk and return potential of VC investments is depicted by a high number of write-offs on the one hand, and extraordinary returns of the top performing companies on the other (maximum IRR of 4214%, maximum multiple of 1087.5). As mentioned above, DEA focuses on extreme observations (whereas the basis of regression analysis focuses on central tendencies) and is therefore of special interest to the VC industry. Country-clusters are considered for the analyses of structural differences. In

Table 18.2 Descriptive analyses of the fund-related input variables, the number of funds divided by the number of general partners and the fund size for the entire VC sample used for the following analysis (857 European VC firms) are provided. The fund size is in US$ millions, June 2005. The inflation adjustment is based on Consumer Price Index (CPI) data for all urban households and all items. Data are derived from the records of the U.S. Department of Labor (http://www.bls.gov). Additionally, all statistics are provided for the five country-clusters, UK, France, Germany, Scandinavia, and 'Other European'

Number of funds/Number of general partners

Statistics	Mean	Median	Std. dev.	Minimum	Maximum
All VC investments	1.21	0.67	1.20	0.14	4.00
UK	1.90	1.00	1.51	0.14	4.00
France	0.74	0.67	0.52	0.29	4.00
Germany	1.60	0.78	1.45	0.25	4.00
Scandinavia	0.56	0.50	0.29	0.33	2.00
Other European	1.09	0.67	0.91	0.25	4.00

Fund size (in real 06/2005$mil)

Statistics	Mean	Median	Std. dev.	Minimum	Maximum
All VC investments	416.78	153.00	799.86	2.47	5966.26
UK	741.56	333.11	1153.44	6.42	5966.26
France	214.34	29.91	350.12	3.51	2737.81
Germany	427.70	119.17	760.33	3.51	4322.25
Scandinavia	181.25	146.95	443.45	2.47	2737.81
Other European	505.65	216.25	875.02	2.47	4863.15

terms of mean IRR, Germany is the best-performing European country, but also has the highest standard deviation of all. In terms of median IRR, France is the leading region. In difference to the IRR p.a., the multiple figure does not reflect time-adjusted return and the U.K. clearly outperforms the other countries in terms of mean multiple.

Table 18.2 provides descriptive analyses on the input variables. Country comparisons on the number of funds divided by the number of general partners as well as on the fund size are shown. Funds from the U.K. appear to have the highest mean fund size and the highest fund to general partner ratio. The low mean IRR of the U.K. funds supports the argument that increasing portfolio size leads to less monitoring and value-added assistance and thus to lower performance. Contrary to this, Scandinavian funds are the smallest and have the smallest fund to general partner ratio, but do not show the highest mean performance. The strong differences in the portfolio size between the European countries also reflect the differences in stage of development and size of the VC markets.

18.5 Empirical results

An efficiency score of 1.00 signifies that a VC firm is efficient and that no other VC firm has produced better outputs with the inputs used. It does not imply that all VC firms with a score of 1.00 provide the same return during the examination period, however, only that the return is at the maximum of the incurred risk. The efficiency score is not absolute. A VC firm with an efficiency score of 1.00 returning 20% is considered more risky than a VC firm with a score of 1.00 returning 15%. When institutional investors choose a VC fund manager to commit capital to, they can consider how efficient the VC firm investments have been of this fund manager in previous funds. Every VC firm with an efficiency score of 1.00 can be considered as one of the best.

Basic efficiency is not sufficiently complete to assess the performance appraisal of VC firms, because cross-efficiency goes beyond self-appraisal to peer appraisal. VC firms with an efficiency score of 1.00 in the basic model drop in value when the average cross-efficiency measure is used. However, the cross-efficiency scores represent the peer appraisal of each VC firm, thus revealing a VC firm's all-around performance in all areas.

Table 18.3 ranks the order of efficient and non-efficient VC firms for each of the countries examined during the 1983 to 2004 period. We find that a handful of VC firms are efficient but a great majority are deemed inefficient according to the inputs and outputs used. A VC firm that is inefficient (score less than 1.0) such as FJ (Table 18.3: U.K.) with a score of 0.79119, is only 79.119% as efficient as the most efficient VC firms in the analysis. As a result we find a low number of efficient VC firms in each country, which could be the result of the different varying economic conditions present in each country, such as differing GDP or inflation. To properly assess the performance of VC firms, the time series of each VC firm classification must be long enough to include at least one extreme negative market event.

Of the two VC firms classified as efficient by the cross-efficiency scores in Table 18.3, NK and SO attain the highest cross-efficiency scores of 1.00. In other words, peer group analysis has evaluated them as the best all-round VC firms in this category, with a score of 1.00. For the cross-efficiency model, the higher the number the more the VC firm is considered as having done well with per inputs and outputs used. A firm with the highest cross-efficiency score has achieved the highest average relative to its peers. In other words, the VC firm has performed well in all areas.[5]

In Table 18.3 (other countries) we find that the following VC firms, QJ and SJ (Belgium), RK (Netherlands), TS (Switzerland), WL (Denmark), (XY) Portugal, DDW (Spain), are efficient. The rankings of both basic and cross-efficiency models show a significant and positive relationship (Table 18.4). In terms of comparing the validity of both basic and cross-efficiency models we find no negative correlations to support the claim that the observed relationship between the basic and cross-efficiency rankings is not attributed to chance. If it were, we would expect half the significant correlations to be positive and half to be negative.

Table 18.5 presents summary statistics for each country, by breaking down the number of inefficient firms according to incremental levels. The mean basic efficiency scores are highest for VC firms in the Scandinavian countries (Table 18.5, Panel D) and the lowest for Germany (Table 18.5, Panel C). However, the volatility of the efficiency scores for VC firms in Germany is also the lowest. When examining the mean cross-efficiency

[5] The Babe Ruth analogy is a classic example. Babe Ruth was a great home-run hitter and, in terms of basic efficiency (basic DEA model), he would have achieved a score of 100. However, if he was compared with other players on the team he may not have been an all-round player, thus making his cross-efficiency score low compared with a good all-round player (Anderson, 2004).

Table 18.3 Number of efficient and non-efficient VC firms, 1983–2004. The basic and cross-efficiency scores of the 25 randomly selected VC firms in the various countries investigated are reported. A score of 1.0 indicates VC firms are efficient and <1.0 inefficient

	U.K.			France			Germany			Scandinavia			Other	
VC firm	Basic efficiency score	Cross-efficiency score	VC firm	Basic efficiency score	Cross-efficiency score	VC firm	Basic efficiency score	Cross-efficiency score	VC firm	Basic efficiency score	Cross-efficiency score	VC firm	Basic efficiency score	Cross-efficiency score
NK	1.00000	100	CB	1.00000	71.47	CE	1.00000	72.07	Y	1.00000	50.19	QJ	1.00000	70.94
TL	1.00000	32.73	SY	1.00000	51.41	DN	1.00000	96.87	AR	1.00000	61.15	RK	1.00000	81.88
FFR	1.00000	81.65	TJ	1.00000	70.05	SO	1.00000	100	BT	1.00000	97.46	SJ	1.00000	83.46
FJ	0.79119	49.15	TK	1.00000	99.63	CD	0.76830	58.97	BF	0.91063	46.25	TS	1.00000	94.32
CCB	0.67980	20.78	SN	0.69471	37.16	CJ	0.51734	40.08	FFD	0.88548	69.21	WL	1.00000	87.89
FFW	0.55560	43.93	SD	0.59498	32.56	RZ	0.42034	32.88	F	0.81585	41.6	XY	1.00000	75.29
VH	0.45242	33.8	SU	0.57957	28.18	SR	0.41868	27.68	AH	0.80624	43.82	DDW	1.00000	65.07
EEL	0.41327	26.48	RN	0.55402	25.93	NY	0.31782	18.53	AB	0.64942	37.87	VT	0.88877	71.35
EES	0.39948	26.88	SZ	0.55233	28.04	NB	0.23570	16.59	AD	0.62017	35.31	BBP	0.80933	66.06
EEY	0.39948	24.45	SX	0.48365	19.5	ME	0.21444	6.86	U	0.61926	39.2	BBQ	0.77640	64.26
FFG	0.37293	31.26	RV	0.46727	26.4	CX	0.21076	15.42	BY	0.59495	28.08	EEF	0.75028	47.07
FFK	0.34735	29.46	VR	0.46119	19.35	RF	0.20340	16.1	P	0.56156	37.61	YK	0.69450	52.9
EEK	0.31984	20.57	SP	0.44424	25.97	CQ	0.18694	13.74	AO	0.53365	31.86	XI	0.69299	46.75
D	0.31215	21.77	ST	0.43267	23.19	RG	0.15537	9.68	W	0.52486	36.27	QU	0.67774	61.2
OA	0.31087	12.2	SM	0.39704	22.54	BBV	0.13202	9.99	M	0.51330	32.38	VM	0.63490	51.98
EEN	0.28022	17.98	YV	0.35313	24.44	CF	0.12310	8.95	AU	0.50791	30.62	QR	0.62200	50.53
IM	0.27597	24.81	SA	0.33656	18.77	CO	0.10781	7.88	AL	0.50654	31.35	IH	0.58719	48.37
FFI	0.26828	22.96	XD	0.31516	12.91	SB	0.10593	7.85	N	0.49375	31.96	BBO	0.58696	47.34
FFH	0.24984	20.92	SL	0.28960	16.78	MI	0.09490	6.7	BA	0.48943	29.44	ZL	0.58288	34.17
DDU	0.24183	16.85	RY	0.28035	16.46	CI	0.09459	6.92	O	0.47508	30.69	QY	0.55083	41.28
EEB	0.24156	16.03	IU	0.27034	17.63	CW	0.09248	6.46	AX	0.46181	29.47	IO	0.53968	46.44
IG	0.23749	20.98	IR	0.27032	17.57	MC	0.08792	2.72	AF	0.45937	29.01	EEQ	0.53400	35.17
EEE	0.23189	15.47	TC	0.26129	18.31	YX	0.08500	5.39	BN	0.43728	26.09	CP	0.52525	45.35
IN	0.22705	19.77	SE	0.24209	14.2	CC	0.08003	5.85	BH	0.42011	26.53	VN	0.52396	42.39
NG	0.22667	7.66	ZT	0.24099	16.86	RQ	0.07584	5.99	V	0.41844	28.29	EEW	0.51829	26.94

Table 18.4 Basic and cross-efficiency models (Spearman rank correlation). The strength and significance level of both DEA models are reported

	Basic efficiency vs. Cross-efficiency models
U.K.	0.815** (<0.0001)
France	0.922** (<0.0001)
Germany	0.815** (<0.0001)
Scandinavia	0.905** (<0.0001)
Other	0.925** (<0.0001)

Table 18.5 Frequency distributions of efficiency scores for U.K., France, Germany, Scandinavia and Other Countries for entire sample. The number of efficient and inefficient VC firms produced by the basic and cross-efficiency models is reported. Scores are subdivided in increments to better identify the number of inefficient VC firms in each country

Efficiency range	Basic efficiency	Cross-efficiency
Panel A. United Kingdom		
<0.3	141	149
0.3– < 0.4	7	3
0.4– < 0.5	2	2
0.5– < 0.6	1	0
0.6– < 0.7	1	0
0.7– < 0.8	1	0
0.8– < 0.9	0	1
0.9– < 1.0	0	0
1.0	3	1
Sum	156	156
Mean	0.1189	8.5205
Standard deviation	0.18025	13.06887
Min	0.00001	0.17
Max	1.00000	100
Panel B. France		
<0.3	161	173
0.3– < 0.4	4	2
0.4– < 0.5	5	0
0.5– < 0.6	4	1
0.6– < 0.7	1	0
0.7– < 0.8	0	2
0.8– < 0.9	0	0
0.9– < 1.0	0	1
1.0	4	0
Sum	179	179
Mean	0.1457	9.6496
Standard deviation	0.18016	12.01646
Min	0.00001	0.14
Max	1.00000	99.63

(Continued)

Table 18.5 Continued

Efficiency range	Basic efficiency	Cross-efficiency
Panel C. Germany		
<0.3	129	129
0.3– < 0.4	1	1
0.4– < 0.5	2	1
0.5– < 0.6	1	1
0.6– < 0.7	0	0
0.7– < 0.8	1	1
0.8– < 0.9	0	0
0.9– < 1.0	0	1
1.0	3	1
Sum	137	137
Mean	0.0738	5.5511
Standard deviation	0.17203	14.79048
Min	0.00001	0.03
Max	1.00000	100
Panel D. Scandinavia		
<0.3	63	82
0.3– < 0.4	11	11
0.4– < 0.5	9	3
0.5– < 0.6	7	1
0.6– < 0.7	3	2
0.7– < 0.8	0	0
0.8– < 0.9	3	0
0.9– < 1.0	1	1
1.0	3	0
Sum	100	100
Mean	0.2618	16.4670
Standard deviation	0.25674	16.83787
Min	0.010	0.26
Max	1.00000	97.46
Panel E. Other countries		
<0.3	71	79
0.3– < 0.4	6	7
0.4– < 0.5	5	8
0.5– < 0.6	10	3
0.6– < 0.7	5	4
0.7– < 0.8	2	3
0.8– < 0.9	2	3
0.9– < 1.0	0	1
1.0	7	0
Sum	108	108
Mean	0.2521	19.5019
Standard deviation	0.30806	24.32788
Min	0.01	1.06
Max	1.00000	94.32

and volatility scores the rank order is identical to the basic efficiency model. The rank order confirms that both basic and cross-efficiency models can be used as alternative performance appraisal measures when examining VC firms.

18.6 Conclusion

Data envelopment analysis can be used as an alternative selection tool to assist pension funds, institutional investors, and high net-worth individuals in selecting efficient VC firms. We believe DEA to be a complement to traditional measures and can present a more complete picture of VC performance appraisal by providing reliable results.

Having a high cross-efficient VC firm is highly desirable. We hope this research contributes to the advancement in the VC literature and in the field of entrepreneurship. As the DEA method slowly becomes accepted and used by more academics, money managers, and institutional investors, its functional ability will improve the process of selecting efficient and high-performing VC firms.

Future research using other DEA models could examine other aspects of VC firms. It would also be interesting to measure the efficiency of various VC firms using other variables from other database vendors.

References

Adler, N., Friedman, L. and Stern, Z.S. (2002). Review of Ranking Methods in the Data Envelopment Analysis Context. *European Journal of Operational Research*, 140(2):249–265.

Amason, A.C., Manigart, S. and Sapienza, H.J. (1994). The Level and Nature of Venture Capitalists' Involvement in their Portfolio Companies: A Study on Three European Countries. *Managerial Finance*, 20(1):3–17.

Anderson, T.R. (2004). Benchmarking in Sports: Bonds or Ruth: Determining the Most Dominant Baseball Player using DEA. In Cooper, W.W., Seiford, L.M. and Zhu, J. (eds), *Handbook on Data Envelopment Analysis*. New York: Springer, Chapter 15.

Banker, R.D., Charnes, A. and Cooper, W.W. (1984). Some Models for Estimating Technical and Scale Inefficiencies in Data Envelopment Analysis. *Management Science*, 30(9):1078–1092.

Basso, A. and Funari, S. (2001). A Data Envelopment Analysis Approach to Measure the Mutual Fund Performance. *European Journal of Operational Research*, 135(3): 477–492.

Birley, S. (1989). Small and Medium-Sized Enterprises – Is There a European Dimension? *European Business Journal*, 1(4):19–26.

Birley, S. and Muzyka, D. (1996). Trade-Offs in the Investment Decisions of European Venture Capitalists. *Journal of Business Venturing*, 11(4):273–288.

Bottazzi, L., Da Rin, M. and Hellmann, T. (2004). The Changing Face of the European Venture Capital Industry: Facts and Analysis. *Journal of Private Equity*, 7(1):26–53.

Bottazzi, L., Da Rin, M. and Hellmann, T. (2005). *What Role of Legal Systems in Financial Intermediation? Theory and Evidence*. American Finance Association – Sixty Fifth Annual Meeting, 7–9 January, Philadelphia.

Bowlin, W.F. (1998). Measuring Performance: An Introduction to Data Envelopment Analysis. *Journal of Cost Analysis*, 3:3–28.

Casamata, C. (2003). Financing and Advising: Optimal Financial Contracts with Venture Capitalists. *The Journal of Finance*, 58(5):2059–2086.

Chan, Y.S. (1983). On the Positive Role of Financial Intermediation in Allocation of Venture Capital in a Market with Imperfect Information. *Journal of Finance*, 38(5):1543–1569.

Charnes, A., Cooper, W.W. and Rhodes, E. (1978). Measuring the Efficiency of Decision-Making Units. *European Journal of Operational Research*, 2(6):29–444.

Charnes, A., Cooper, W.W. and Rhodes, E. (1981). Evaluating Program and Managerial Efficiency: An Application of Data Envelopment Analysis to Program Follow Through. *Management Science*, 27(6):668–697.

Cumming, D.J. (2002). Contracts and Exits in Venture Capital Finance. American Finance Association Annual Conference, 3–5 January, Washington DC.

Cumming, D. (2003). The Determinants of Venture Capital Portfolio Size: Empirical Evidence. Working Paper, University of Alberta, Canada.

Cumming, D. and Walz, U. (2004). Private Equity Returns and Disclosure Around the World. Working Paper, Goethe University, Frankfurt, Germany.

Cuny, C.J. and Talmor, E. (2003). *The Staging of Venture Capital Financing: Milestones vs. Rounds*. Texas A&M University, London Business School.

Darling, G., Mukherjee, K. and Wilkens, K. (2004). CTA Performance Evaluation with Data Envelopment Analysis. In Gregoriou, G.N., Karavas, V.N., Lhabitant, F-S. and Rouah, F. (eds), *Commodity Trading Advisors: Risk, Performance Analysis, and Selection*. Hoboken NJ: John Wiley and Sons, Inc.

Desai, M., Gompers, P. and Lerner, J. (2003). Institutions, Capital Constraints and Entrepreneurial Firm Dynamics: Evidence from Europe. Working Paper, Harvard University, Cambridge, MA.

Diller, C. and Kaserer, C. (2004). European Private Equity Funds – A Cash Flow Based Performance Analysis. Working Paper, Center for Entrepreneurial and Financial Studies, Munich, Germany.

European Venture Capital Association/Thomson Venture Economics/Pricewaterhouse Coopers (2006). http://www.evca.com.

Farrell, M.J. (1957). The Measurement of Productive Efficiency. *Journal of the Operational and Research Society*, A20, 253–281.

Gompers, P. (1995). Optimal Investing, Monitoring, and the Staging of Venture Capital. *Journal of Finance*, 50(5):1461–1491.

Gompers, P.A. and Lerner, J. (2000). Money Chasing Deals? The Impact of Fund Inflows on Private Equity Valutions. *Journal of Financial Economics*, 55(2):281–324.

Gottschalg, O., Phalippou, L. and Zollo, M. (2003). Performance of Private Equity Funds: Another Puzzle? Working Paper, INSEAD, Fontainebleau, France.

Gregoriou, G.N. (2003). Performance Evaluation of Hedge Funds Using Data Envelopment Analysis. *Journal of Wealth Management*, 5(4):88–95.

Gregoriou, G.N., Sedzro, K. and Zhu, J. (2005a). Hedge Fund Performance Appraisal Using Data Envelopment Analysis. *European Journal of Operational Research*, 164(2):555–571

Gregoriou, G.N., Rouah, F., Satchell, S.E. and Diz, F. (2005b). Simple and Cross-Efficiency of CTAs Using Data Envelopment Analysis. *European Journal of Finance*, 11(2):54–70.

Hege, U., Palomino, F. and Schwienbacher, A. (2003). Determinants of Venture Capital Performance: Europe and the United States. Working Paper, University of Amsterdam.

Hellmann, T. and Puri, M. (2002). Venture Capital and the Professionalization of Start-Up Firms: Empirical Evidence. *The Journal of Finance*, 571(1):169–197.

Hsu, Y.W. (2002). *Staging of Venture Capital Investment: Real Option Analysis*. Taiwan: National Taiwan University.

Inderst, R. and Mueller, H.M. (2003). The Effect of Capital Market Characteristics on the Value of Start-Up Firms. *Journal of Financial Economics*, 72(2):319–356.

Jeng, L. and Wells, P. (2000). The Determinants of Venture Capital Funding: Evidence Across Countries. *Journal of Corporate Finance*, 6(3):241–289.

Kaplan, S.N. and Strömberg, P. (2000). How do Venture Capitalists Choose Investments? Working Paper, University of Chicago, Chicago IL.

Kaplan, S.N., Sensoy, B.A. and Strömberg, P. (2002). *How Well do Venture Capital Databases Reflect Actual Investments?* Chicago IL: University of Chicago Graduate School of Business.

Keuschnigg, C. (2004). Venture Capital Backed Growth. *Journal of Economic Growth*, 9(2):239–261.

Krohmer, P. and Lauterbach, R. (2005). Private Equity Post-Investment Phases – The Bright and Dark Side of Staging. Working Paper, Goethe University, Frankfurt, Germany.

Lerner, J. (1995). Venture Capitalists and the Oversight of Private Firms. *Journal of Finance*, 50(1):301–319.

Lerner, J. and Schoar, A.M. (2002). The Illiquidity Puzzle: Theory and Evidence from Private Equity. NOM Working Paper, MIT and Harvard University, Cambridge MA.

MacMillan, I.C., Kulow, D.M. and Khoylian, R. (1989). Venture Capitalists' Involvement in Their Investments: Extent and Performance. *Journal of Business Venturing*, 4(2):27–48.

Manigart, S. (1994). The Founding Rate of Venture Capital Firms in Three European Countries. *Journal of Business Venturing*, 9(6):525–542.

McMullen, P. and Strong, R. (1997). Selection of Mutual Funds Using Data Envelopment Analysis. *Journal of Business and Economic Studies*, 4:1–14.

Morey, M.R. and Morey, R.C. (1999). Mutual Fund Performance Appraisals: A Multi-Horizon Perspective with Endogenous Benchmarking. *Omega*, 27(2):241–258.

Neher, D.V. (1999). Staged Financing: An Agency Perspective. *The Review of Economic Studies*, 66(2):255–274.

Robbie, K., Thompson, S. and Wright, S. (1992). Venture Capital and Management-led, Leveraged Buy-Outs: A European Perspective. *Journal of Business Venturing*, 7(1):47–118.

Sahlman, W.A. (1990). The Structure and Governance of Venture-Capital Organizations. *Journal of Financial Economics*, 27(2):473–522.

Sedzro, K.T. and Sardano, D. (2000). Mutual Fund Performance Evaluation Using Data Envelopment Analysis. In Dahiya, S.B. (ed.), *The Current State of Business Disciplines*. Rohtak, India: Spellbound Publications Pvt. Ltd, 1125–1144.

Sexton, T.R., Silkman, R.H. and Hogan, A. (1986). Data Envelopment Analysis: Critique and Extensions. In Silkman, R.H. (ed.), *Measuring Efficiency and Assessment of Data Envelopment Analysis*. New Directions of Program Evaluation Publication No. 32. San Francisco CA: Jossey-Bass Publishers.

Vassiloglou, M. and Giokas, D. (1990). A Study of Relative Efficiency of Bank Branches: An Application of Data Envelopment Analysis. *Journal of the Operations Research Society*, 47(3):591–597.

Wang, S. and Zhou, H. (2004). Staged Financing in Venture Capital: Moral Hazard and Risks. *Journal of Corporate Finance*, 10(4):131–155.

19 Agency theory and management buy-out: The role of venture capitalists

Hans Bruining and Arthur Herst

Abstract

In this chapter we demonstrate how the agency theory can be used to prevent a development of divergent interests between the management team and investors after a management buy-out (MBO). Agency costs are caused by increased costs of monitoring by the investor to overcome the problems of self-interest, risk aversion, goal conflict, and information asymmetry. The focus is on divestment MBOs from foreign or local parent companies, of which the majority of the equity after the MBO is owned by venture capitalist. First we position the agency theory along with other popular management theories. Next we go into its history, background, key concepts, and criticism. Then we shift our attention to the MBO and present information on the annual number and value of MBOs in several European countries. We focus on the agency costs of equity and debt by analyzing the monitoring role of venture capitalists, the goal congruence between the new shareholders, the financial unification, and the repayment of debt.

19.1 Introduction

In the agency theory the unit of analysis is the contractual and cooperative relationship between principal and agent. The essence of this relationship is the delegation of decision-making authority and responsibility to the agent by the principal. The agent makes decisions and engages in activities on behalf of the principal, for which the principal rewards the agent. After having delegated decision-making authority and responsibility to the agent, the principal is not a priori sure that the agent will serve the principal's interests. This phenomenon is called the agency problem. In an attempt to solve this problem, the principal uses control measures or coordination mechanisms in order to stimulate the agent to make decisions and to engage in activities that are in the interest of the principal. But these measures involve costs, the so-called agency costs.

A management buy-out or MBO is a transaction in which one or more members of the incumbent top management team acquire all or a part of the shares of their firm, which the parent company wants to divest because of financial, strategic, and/or other reasons. They do this by taking a substantial equity stake in the eyes of the investors (having previously held none or very little) in order to continue to run the company independently for their own account and risk (Robbie and Wright, 1996; Bruining, 1992). If a wider (second and third) tier of managers participates in the transaction the term MBO is still used, even if employees are involved. But if employees acquire the majority or even

100% of the firm's equity and realize the transaction, an employee buy-out is involved. If financing the transaction involves a large amount of debt, and the buy-out initiative is taken by an external shareholder, this transaction is labeled leveraged buy-out. From a management motivational point of view there are no fundamental differences between an MBO, an employee buy-out, and a leveraged buy-out. Both management and/or employees (often together with external investors) have to invest substantial amounts of effort, time, and money, and accept additional responsibilities. First of all they have to make the interest payments and repay the debt (Jensen, 1993; Thompson and Wright, 1991) thereby lowering financial leverage, and second, they have to do their utmost to improve existing market opportunities and/or to identify and develop new market opportunities in order to increase shareholder value (Bruining and Wright, 2002).

In this chapter we aim to answer the question whether the agency theory can be used as a framework to explain the positive effects of changes in the relationships between participants on the agency costs and the economic performance of firms that became independent after an MBO. First we position the agency theory along with other popular management theories. Next we go into its history, background, key concepts, and criticism. Then we shift our attention to the MBO and compare it with other types of buy-outs, such as the employee buy-out and the leveraged buy-out. We present information on the development of the numbers and values of buy-outs in Central Europe (CE) and the United Kingdom (U.K.), and focus on a special type of MBO: the divestment buy-out, in which venture capitalists acquire the majority of the shares. In order to answer the central question of this chapter we base ourselves on this buy-out type and analyze the agency relationships between the buy-out managers and the (new) investors: both the equity investors and the debt investors.

19.2 Agency theory

19.2.1 Positioning the agency theory

Eisenhardt (1989) argues that the agency theory is a useful addition to organizational theory. The agency theory sketches interesting ideas concerning risk, outcome uncertainty, incentives, and information systems that are novel contributions to organizational thinking. Moreover, the agency theory is supported by empirical evidence especially when coupled with complementary theoretical perspectives such as the resource-based view (Barney, 1991). The positive agency theory can be regarded as enriching economics by offering a more complete view of organizations as vehicles for coordination (Jensen, 1983). Furthermore, agency theory shares perspectives with political models of organizations in that it assumes the pursuit of self-interest at the individual level and goal conflicts at the organizational level. However, its mechanism for the solution of goal conflicts is different: co-alignment of incentives in the former versus bargaining and negotiation in the latter. Information processing, another perspective of the agency theory, is shared with the contingency theory. Both theories assume that individuals are bounded rationally and that information is asymmetrically distributed throughout the organization. But the most obvious link is with the management control and accounting literature. This literature presents means/ends relationships as programmable tasks and defines crystallized goals as measurable outcomes. Instead of outcome uncertainty this literature highlights diagnostic control systems to manage behavior, thus aiming at outcome control. Another link can be seen between agency theory and entrepreneurship in established firms. From an agency perspective it is essential to define in an entrepreneurial context who is the principal and who is the agent, in order to provide the set of incentives for engaging in entrepreneurship. Balancing rewards and risks for key personnel in organizations can promote internal corporate entrepreneurship, the process by which firms notice opportunities and act to create additional value. Companies that face strategic uncertainties challenge personal and organizational flexibility and adaptability (Jones and Butler, 1992).

Not surprisingly, agency theory has also much in common with the transaction cost economics perspective. They share the same assumptions of self-interest, information asymmetry, goal conflict, and bounded rationality and have the same view on building efficient organizational structures of control relationships and governance mechanisms. However, the agency theory sees the organization as a nexus of contracts and assumes that organizations must be efficient, whereas the transaction cost economics perspective offers an alternative form of contracting to the organization: the market and hybrid contracting (Speklé, 2001).

19.2.2 Agency theory: history, background, and founding fathers

Alchian and Demsetz (1972) characterize the essence of the classical firm as a contractual structure. In their eyes the employer or firm owner is continually involved in renegotiating the contract terms in such a way that they are acceptable to him as well as the employees or input owners. The firm owner is a specialist who will monitor the members of his team and manage the use of their cooperative inputs. According to the authors the firm is a contractual structure where several input owners cooperate and where one party is common to all contracts with the input owners. This party, the owner of the firm, has the right to renegotiate any input owner's contract independently of the contracts with other input owners, holds the residual claim, and has the right to sell his contractual residual status (Alchian and Demsetz, 1972).

Jensen and Meckling (1976) extend this analysis by focusing on the costs of the agency relationship. The principal's monitoring of the behavior and performance of the agent involves monitoring costs. In some cases it may be in the agent's best interest to signal to the principal that he will not deviate too much from the behavior preferred by the principal; then bonding costs are involved. Jensen and Meckling argue that these monitoring and bonding costs cannot guarantee that the agent will take optimal decisions from the principal's point of view. There may be a residual loss defined as the monetary equivalent of the reduction in welfare experienced by the principal due to divergence. Agency costs, then, are the sum of monitoring costs by the principal, bonding costs by the agent, and the residual loss. Jensen and Meckling reason that this general framework is applicable to agency problems in all kinds of organizations and in all cooperative efforts.

Fama (1980) also extends the conceptual framework. He is not only interested in the contractual relationships but also in other forms of disciplining mechanisms that constrain an agent's opportunities to deviate from, what the principal would consider, optimal behavior. These other mechanisms are based on the operation of either markets or information systems. In addition to executive employment, compensation, and financial contracts, there are the market for end-products, the market for corporate control, the external and internal labor market for managers, and internal (accounting) and external (financial analysts, press) monitoring systems. To what extent these mechanisms operate in practice and their degree of effectiveness is, of course, an empirical issue.

19.2.3 Agency theory: key concepts

In the agency theory the unit of analysis is the (contractual) relationship between principal and agent. The essence of the relationship is the delegation of decision-making authority and responsibility to the agent by the principal. Delegating can affect the principal's reputation, measured by the creation of economic value of the unit for which the principal is responsible, whether the principal is a parent organization, an investor, or the top manager. The agent makes decisions and carries out activities on behalf of the principal, for which the principal rewards him.

According to the agency theory the firm is structured by contracts between principals and agents at different levels in the firm. We use the positive form of the agency theory to identify situations where conflicting interests between principal and agent can occur and discuss governance mechanisms to control the effects of self-interested behavior of the agent. Therefore our focus is on the organizational aspects of the agency relations (Jensen, 1983) and not on the specification of the most efficient reward model to optimize principal–agent contracts. This belongs to the field of the mathematical principal–agent theory.

If the principal delegates decision-making authority and responsibility to the agent, he/she is not a priori sure that the agent will carry out the activities and will make the decisions that maximize the principal's interests. This phenomenon is called the agency problem. Because the principal cannot monitor all the decisions and other activities of his agent and because uncontrollable factors can influence the agent's performance, it is difficult for the principal to determine to what extent the results depend on the capability, effort, and devotion of his agent. This applies whether the parent company, an investor, or the top manager is acting as the principal.

As a consequence of this information asymmetry the agent has the opportunity for shirking behavior. Formulated in another way, the agent has the opportunity to pursue his own interests, thereby harming the interests of the principal. Examples are selecting loss-making investment projects or excessive consumption of perquisites such as expensive automobiles, big board rooms, and excessive personnel. By these actions the agent is able to achieve more power and status but, meanwhile, the value of the firm, which belongs to the principal (i.e. the owner of the firm), is reduced.

According to the agency theory the principal and the agent may have conflicting interests and one of them possibly manipulates a risk they share. This phenomenon is generally referred to as moral hazard. Moral hazard can be present any time parties come into agreement with one another. Each party in a contract may have the opportunity to gain from acting contrary to the principles laid out by the agreement. Because of moral hazard the principal may not be able to distinguish between genuine risks, which the agent cannot possibly control, and failures to take the best possible action that could avoid the dangerous event (Kaplan, 1982).

According to Jones and Butler (1992), agency problems may arise if the entrepreneurial function of the principal is separated from the management function of the agent. The agency problem may become more severe as a result of differences in risk attitudes between principal and agent. Agency theory postulates that the agent is more risk averse than the principal because, when taking over the uncertainty of entrepreneurial activities from the principal, the agent is rewarded with a salary for assuming standard risks. Therefore, the agent has less incentive to start highly uncertain activities. This misalignment of interests between principals-entrepreneurs and agents-managers is worsened by the fact that the agent realizes that, if one or more of these highly uncertain activities fail, his chances of getting a suitable function elsewhere will be reduced. Below we discuss the measures the theory recommends in order to govern the agency relationships efficiently.

19.2.4 Agency theory: control measures

To protect himself against the risk of moral hazard and other opportunistic behavior of the agent, the principal is interested in control measures or coordination mechanisms to stimulate the agent to make decisions that are in the interest of the principal. Jensen and Meckling (1976) distinguish four kinds of control measures:

1. *The contract*: if the firm operates in a highly uncertain environment, the formulation of the contract between principal and agent contract will be less explicit.
2. *Monitoring mechanisms*: these mechanisms include measuring the agent's efforts by means of budget reports, review sessions, instructions, operating rules, and so on. Monitoring by the principal stimulates the agent to observe the directives of his contract with the principal. When the principal strongly depends on the agent, the principal will monitor the agent's behavior more intensively (Noorderhaven, 1992).
3. *Bonding mechanisms*: involve the agent's supplementary signals that he will not deviate too much from the behavior preferred by the principal. The intensity of the use of bonding is closely linked with the extent to which the agent is dependent on the principal.
4. *A reward system*: this system should be related to the agent's performance, and includes the sharing of risks and incentives between the principal and the agent.

These control measures are intended to reduce the divergence of interests between the principal and the agent. In addition to rewarding the agent for his performance, agency costs are incurred. We can distinguish contracting costs, monitoring costs, and bonding costs. In spite of these measures differences may remain between the decisions made by the agent and the decisions the principal would make. Then a residual (cash-flow) loss is involved.

According to Jensen and Meckling, a distinction can be made between agency costs of equity and agency costs of debt. Also, van de Poel (1986) as well as Douma and Schreuder (1991) argue there are also agency costs resulting from the relationship between management and employees: the agency costs of managing employees.

19.2.5 Agency theory and decision making

Besides control measures, Fama and Jensen (1983) argue that the agency problem can also be reduced by partitioning the decision-making process into the following stages:

1. *Initiation*: the generation of proposals for resource utilization;
2. *Ratification*: the decision which proposals to implement;

3. *Implementation*: the execution of ratified decisions;
4. *Monitoring*: the measurement of the performance of the agent and the pay-out of rewards.

Stages 1 and 3 are labeled 'decision management' and are delegated to the agent. Stages 2 and 4 belong to the domain of the principal and are labeled 'decision control'. Looking at delegation this way, we can consider it as a process controlled by using a system of checks and balances. The role of hierarchy is used to discipline behavior in order to reduce the risk of the agent making suboptimal decisions. This partitioning of the decision-making process creates an organizationally well-defined environment for analyzing incentive, monitoring, and bonding relationships.

Without a context of application it is hard to judge whether the agency theory will produce credible analyses, valid explanations, and solutions to reduce the probability of conflicts between principal and agent. Therefore, in Section 19.3 we introduce the MBO as a context to analyze agency relationships.

19.2.6 Agency theory: criticism

Organizational theory has three tasks, to explain: (1) why we observe organizations at all, (2) how organizations transform, and (3) how organizations function (Schreuder, 1983). Many authors (see for a review Eisenhardt, 1989) agree that organizations may be the most efficient governance structure to manage bounded rationality and to protect transactions against opportunism or suboptimal behavior of the agent. The strongest contribution of the agency theory, however, is made with regard to the information variable that had been largely neglected before. One of the assumptions of the economic model of perfect competition is the existence of perfect information to all market parties concerned. Information is usually assumed to be sufficient, costless, and evenly distributed. The agency theory recognizes that economic actors may sometimes find it advantageous to manipulate the informational variable rather than other variables. Therefore the theory focuses on characteristics with great explanatory power as risk attitudes of the principal and the agent, incentives and the possibilities to observe effort and outcome uncertainty. However, other authors consider the concept of suboptimal behavior of the agent questionable. For example, when reviewing the agency theory, Perrow (1986) points out that shirking is not the exclusive right of the agent. The possibility that the principal lies to the agent about levels or threats of lost business is ignored or swept aside by arguing that the firm will protect its reputation. In his view the agency theory appears to be basically incapable of keeping an eye on both parties of the contract.

19.3 Management buy-out

19.3.1 Definition

A management buy-out or MBO is a transaction in which one or more members of the incumbent top management team acquire all or a part of the shares of their firm which the parent company wants to sell because of financial, strategic, and/or other reasons, by taking a substantial equity stake in the eyes of the investors (having previously held none or very little) in order to continue to run the company independently for their own account and risk (Robbie and Wright, 1996; Bruining, 1992).

If a wider (second and third) tier of managers participates in the transaction the term MBO is still used, even if employees are involved. But if employees acquire the majority, or even 100%, of the firm's equity and realize the transaction, an employee buy-out is involved. If financing the transaction involves a large amount of debt, this transaction is labeled a leveraged buy-out. Statistics show that most MBOs and employee buy-outs increase the financial leverage substantially after the buy-out transaction.

From a motivational point of view there are no differences between an MBO, an employee buy-out, or a leveraged buy-out. Both management and/or employees (often together with external debt investors) have to invest substantial amounts of effort, time, and money and take on additional responsibilities. First of all they have to make the interest payments and repay the debt (Jensen, 1993; Thompson and Wright, 1991), and second they have to do their utmost in order to identify and develop market opportunities (Bruining and Wright, 2002).

In our opinion it is not necessary that the buy-out management team has voting control; that is, control based on a majority of the equity stake. Most important is that the buy-out team has management control. This means that the management team is able to control the company because of its specific knowledge of the industry and the company, and because of its proven managerial skills and experience in the company.

It is important that the management equity stake in terms of the amount of personal wealth is significant, because this is a first-class incentive for the management team to do its utmost after the MBO (Bruining, 1992).

19.3.2 Numbers and values

In the European Management Buy-Out Review (2006) of the Centre for Management Buy-Out Research (CMBOR) a comprehensive analysis is given of developments in buy-out markets in Continental Europe (CE) and the U.K. In the CMBOR statistics the MBOs and management buy-ins, where outside managers buy companies, are added up. In terms of deal numbers, management buy-ins have been increasing in popularity in CE since 1995 and in 2005 they reached 411, a new record. The number of MBOs, where inside managers buy companies, fell in 2005 for the third consecutive year to 283. In 2005 management buy-ins provided nearly 60% of the total number of deals in CE. In the U.K., management buy-ins were much less numerous, accounting for only 36% of the total number of deals (Table 19.1).

The value of buy-outs and buy-ins is measured by the (private) equity and debt supply to these firms. As can be seen in Tables 19.1 and 19.2, the U.K. had the largest buy-out market by number as well as value in 2005 and has been the leading market across Europe for many years: in 2005 there were 663 buy-outs totaling €35 092 million. The CE market ended 2005 with a record €88 740 million. France, Italy, the Netherlands, Spain, Sweden, Denmark, Belgium, and Finland all ended 2005 well ahead of their previous record values (Centre for Management Buy-Out Research, 2006: 9).

As has been the case for the last 10 years, divestment of subsidiaries by a foreign or local parent company remains the most common MBO source in CE with 40% of the total of deals. Sale of family or private firms provides the second most common source, with 33% of all deals. Manufacturing was the most active sector in 2005 with 244 deals,

Table 19.1 Number of buy-outs/buy-ins in CE and the U.K.

Country name	1996	1997	1998	1999	2000	2001	2002	2003	2004	2005
Austria	6	7	5	4	13	7	18	12	14	9
Belgium	11	10	19	16	18	25	24	20	36	27
Denmark	14	16	13	18	18	12	18	12	14	30
Finland	25	32	16	19	15	23	29	28	27	32
France	115	138	154	148	131	126	124	143	157	220
Germany	73	99	80	51	67	91	106	105	110	113
Ireland	9	9	15	9	12	16	20	14	10	6
Italy	24	25	32	42	29	17	38	44	43	44
Netherlands	56	61	75	66	79	60	62	74	72	80
Norway	7	6	4	8	7	9	12	16	13	15
Portugal	5	3	5	6	5	1	6	5	3	5
Spain	13	23	38	30	28	36	42	52	33	49
Sweden	16	20	23	33	25	49	25	24	38	39
Switzerland	53	65	51	56	54	50	36	30	28	25
Total (CE)	**427**	**514**	**530**	**506**	**501**	**522**	**560**	**579**	**598**	**694**
MBO	364	436	377	333	332	335	349	332	295	283
Total U.K.	**646**	**709**	**690**	**655**	**618**	**642**	**636**	**710**	**699**	**663**
MBO	439	462	474	465	447	459	482	530	483	427
Total (CE + U.K.)	**1073**	**1223**	**1220**	**1161**	**1119**	**1164**	**1196**	**1289**	**1297**	**1357**

Source: Centre for Management Buy-Out Research (2006)/Barclays Private Equity/Deloitte (adapted).

Table 19.2 Value of buy-outs/buy-ins in CE and the U.K. (€ million)

Country name	1996	1997	1998	1999	2000	2001	2002	2003	2004	2005
Austria	72	128	95	680	734	47	154	303	88	28
Belgium	147	414	820	2595	337	1744	517	1448	2266	4053
Denmark	411	263	267	2165	1313	500	1391	848	260	7460
Finland	724	440	560	1085	675	1047	480	1039	977	2044
France	2189	5275	6317	8387	6503	6387	15 557	8772	11 489	20 454
Germany	1704	3538	5295	4660	15 084	7523	8143	11 908	17 915	11 449
Ireland	116	119	252	1475	259	5021	4930	747	970	770
Italy	1146	3121	673	2756	2550	1002	3428	7773	3013	17 507
Netherlands	1001	1059	3528	2906	1856	4433	1870	4958	7612	10 256
Norway	315	180	22	225	1004	1370	142	308	455	426
Portugal	158	64	83	206	83	2	26	54	8	76
Spain	227	374	859	1715	941	1528	2069	934	2274	9385
Sweden	700	1375	928	2926	3169	3005	1116	2226	1698	4771
Switzerland	1316	2426	1347	1013	1772	715	2766	864	1570	61
Total (CE)	**10 226**	**18 776**	**21 046**	**32 794**	**36 280**	**34 324**	**42 589**	**42 182**	**50 595**	**88 740**
U.K.	**12 555**	**17 114**	**23 270**	**26 862**	**38 349**	**31 343**	**24 842**	**23 559**	**30 140**	**35 092**
Total (CE + U.K.)	**22 781**	**35 890**	**44 316**	**59 656**	**74 629**	**65 667**	**67 431**	**65 741**	**80 735**	**123 832**

Source: Centre for Management Buy-Out Research (2006)/Barclays Private Equity/Deloitte.

followed by the Technology, Media, and Telecommunications sector with 74, Business and Support Systems with 64, Food and Drinks with 49, and retail with 43. However, if we look at the market sectors in terms of value (€million) then Technology, Media, and Telecommunications ranks first, followed by Manufacturing, Business and Support Systems, Leisure and Retail (Centre for Management Buy-Out Research, 2006: 37).

For our purpose we study the most common MBO type: the divestment of a division from a parent company. This MBO represents a situation in which an existing firm makes a fresh new start, liberated from the parent company to which it belonged. Some managers characterize an MBO as an earthquake in their life and the life of the firm. Referring to our definition of an MBO, we must stress its significance for the manager: he is taking part in the equity of the MBO firm and becomes one of its owners. Our own research (Bruining et al., 2004, 1998; Bruining, 1992) shows that cutting ties with the parent company implies an overwhelming amount of work. After the MBO many changes can take place in products, prices, distribution methods, promotion, service strategy, etc. Also new contracts have to be arranged with employees, suppliers, and other participants, and revisions of policies and business plans have to be formulated. In several cases new pension plans or even new administrative systems must be introduced, business staff units must be reorganized, etc. The new owners of the firm do their utmost to make the MBO a success. They make a renewed appeal to the effort, devotion, and participation of their financial backers, employees, and others. In general, all these activities and changes in exploitation of the firm have a positive impact on the economic performance after the MBO.

This improvement is extensively documented in buy-out literature (Harris et al., 2005; Bruining et al., 1998; Robbie and Wright, 1996; Zahra, 1995; Phan and Hill, 1995; Bruining, 1992; Kaplan, 1989; Wright and Coyne, 1985). In our opinion the improved economic performance after the MBO is caused by partly solving the agency problem. We argue that, since the agency problem may arise if the entrepreneurial function of the principal is separated from the management function of the agent, an MBO can be a solution for this problem. In the next section this will be explained.

19.4 Agency theory and management buy-out

19.4.1 Involving venture capitalists

First of all, without venture capitalists with extensive MBO experience, it is nearly impossible for managers to realize an MBO. Venture capitalists accomplish many crucial tasks such as advising on matters determining the buy-out price, negotiating with the parent company, estimating the correct moment for informing employees, clients and suppliers, etc. Venture capitalists also assist in raising the necessary capital to finance the buy-out. Besides, they are adequately equipped to take care of the important monitoring function: supervising the buy-out managers on behalf of the equity and debt investors. Venture capitalists are motivated to perform the monitoring function in a correct and efficient way. If this were not the case, the equity and debt investors may lose their confidence and the venture capitalists may get a bad reputation, resulting in an inability to arrange new buy-outs in the future. Moreover, because of the venture capitalists' experience with previous buy-outs, they are able to monitor management in a relatively inexpensive way.

Therefore, involving venture capitalists results in lower agency costs of equity and in lower agency costs of debt, and in an improved economic performance.

19.4.2 Managers become shareholders

In the second place, by participating in the equity of the MBO, managers show that they have confidence in its success. In other words, by supplying a part of the equity required to realize the divestment buy-out and to buy the firm from the present owner (the parent company) the management team of the subsidiary signals its high expectations concerning the future of the firm. If this team participates in the equity of the firm it manages, the agency costs of equity will decrease since the probability of conflicts between buy-out managers and equity investors will be reduced. This is because, by becoming shareholders in the firm they manage, the buy-out managers will be less inclined to pursue their own objectives such as maximizing their own salaries or excessive consumption of perquisites (for example, an expensive office and a company jet). This would reduce the firm's profits to which they, as equity investors, are entitled. Because of management's stake in the firm's equity, the interests of buy-out managers and external equity investors will converge. Thus, managing the firm in a more efficient way will increase its profits for the external equity investors as well as for the internal equity investors (or buy-out managers), bringing an improved economic performance. If employees participate in the firm's equity similar effects may result.

Managers-shareholders do not benefit by conflicts between equity investors and debt investors. This is because these conflicts would result in increasing the agency costs of debt, and therefore in decreasing the firm's profits to which they are entitled as equity investors. Besides, the venture capitalists involved in the buy-out transaction would not allow actions or activities bringing about an increase in the agency costs of debt. Indeed, as we argued above, involving venture capitalists results in lowering not only the agency costs of equity but also in lowering the agency costs of debt, and thus in an improved economic performance.

19.4.3 Financial unification

Third, financial unification may cause the probability of conflicts between shareholders and bondholders, and thus the agency costs of debt such as monitoring and bonding costs, to decrease. As early as 1988 Copeland and Weston explain that financial unification or strip financing is involved when investors buy the different types of securities a firm has issued. So bondholders also become shareholders and shareholders also become bondholders. Because of this financial unification, the interests of shareholders and bondholders tend to run parallel, resulting in a decrease in the agency costs of debt.

Involving venture capitalists may also lead to financial unification. Above we discussed the role of these MBO specialists, who perform several functions such as monitoring the buy-out managers on behalf of the equity and debt investors. Thus, venture capitalists are representatives of all categories of investors, whether they provide the firm with debt or with equity. It would not be wise for venture capitalists to evoke conflicts between these investor categories, for instance by persuading management to accept risky investment projects in order to favor the equity investors, shareholders while harming the debt investors. Harming the bondholders in this way will result in their refusal to supply these

Table 19.3 MBO and agency costs of equity and debt

Measures	Agency costs of equity	Agency costs of debt
involving venture capitalists	decrease	decrease
managers become shareholders	decrease	decrease
financial unification	no effect	decrease
rapid repayment of debt	no effect	decrease
effect on agency costs:	decrease	decrease
effect on total agency costs:	decrease	

specialists with funds to finance future buy-outs. That is why it is essential for venture capitalists to look after the shareholders' as well as the bondholders' interests.

19.4.4 Rapid repayment of debt

In the fourth place, if a large amount of debt is utilized to finance a buy-out, in other words if a leveraged buy-out is involved, managers and venture capitalists will endeavor to repay the debt as soon as possible to obtain a financial risk profile similar to the industry. This way the agency costs of debt will soon decline, and the firm's economic performance will improve in a couple of years after the buy-out.

Table 19.3 summarizes the above results: after a divestment buy-out the agency costs of equity and the agency costs of debt will decrease. This way the firm's economic performance will improve.

19.5 Conclusion

In this chapter we have shown how agency theory can be used as a framework to explain the positive effects of regulated relationships between venture capitalists and buy-out managers on the economic performance of firms that became independent after a management buy-out (MBO). We presented control measures or coordination mechanisms that limit conflict between managers and stockholders, and optimize the firm's efficiency: monitoring the board of directors by venture capitalists, the partitioning of the decision-making process into a number of stages, the stimulation of the incumbent management by taking part in the firms' equity, the financial unification between equity and debt holders and servicing debt. These mechanisms motivate managers to look for efficiencies to protect the firm against the downside risks as well as for new market opportunities to use the firms' upside potential. Examples are efficiencies in investment programs, in cutting overhead cost, and in disposal of assets. The mechanisms reduce the agency problem by stimulating the agent to make decisions that are in the interest of the principal and result in an improvement of economic performance after the MBO. In our opinion the improved economic performance after the MBO is caused by partly solving the agency problem.

References

Alchian, A.A. and Demsetz, H. (1972). Production, Information Costs, and Economic Organization. *American Economic Review*, 62(5):777–795.

Barney, J. (1991). Firm Resources and Sustained Competitive Advantage. *Journal of Management*, 17(1):99–120.

Bruining, J. (1992). Performance Improvement after Management Buy-Out. Unpublished PhD Thesis, Erasmus University, Rotterdam, the Netherlands.

Bruining, J. and Wright, M. (2002). Entrepreneurial Orientation in Management Buy-Outs and the Contribution of Venture Capital. *Venture Capital*, 4(2):1–22.

Bruining, J., Bonnet, M.P.B. and Herst, A.C.C. (1998). *Financial Leverage and its Implications for Business Management*. Rotterdam: Institute for Business Economic Studies.

Bruining, J., Bonnet, M.P.B. and Wright, M. (2004). Management Control Systems and Strategy Change in Buy-Outs. *Management Accounting Research*, 15(2):155–177.

Centre for Management Buy-Out Research (2006). *European Management Buy-Outs, January–December 2005*. Nottingham University Business School.

Douma, S. and Schreuder, H. (1991). *Economic Approaches to Organizations*. New York: Prentice Hall International Ltd.

Eisenhardt, K.M. (1989). Agency Theory: An Assessment and Review. *Academy of Management Review*, 14(1):57–74.

Fama, E. (1980). Agency Problems and the Theory of the Firm. *Journal of Political Economy*, 88(2):288–307.

Fama, E.F. and Jensen, M.C. (1983). Separation of Ownership and Control. *Journal of Law and Economics*, 26(4):301–325.

Harris, R., Siegel, D.S. and Wright, D. (2005). Assessing the Impact of Management Buyouts on Economic Efficiency: Plant-Level Evidence from the United Kingdom. *The Review of Economics and Statistics*, 87(1):148–153.

Jensen, M.C. (1983). Organization Theory and Methodology. *The Accounting Review*, 8(2):319–337.

Jensen, M.C. (1993). The Modern Industrial Revolution: Exit and the Failure of Internal Control Systems. *Journal of Finance*, 48(7):831–880.

Jensen, M.C. and Meckling, W.H. (1976). Theory of the Firm: Managerial Behavior, Agency Costs and Ownership Structure. *Journal of Financial Economics*, 3(4):305–360.

Jones, G.R. and Butler J.E. (1992). Managing Internal Entrepreneurship: An Agency Theory Perspective. *Journal of Management*, 18(4):733–749.

Kaplan, S.N. (1989). The Effects of Management Buy-Outs on Operating Performance and Value. *Journal of Financial Economics*, 24(2):217–254.

Kaplan, R.S. (1982). *Advanced Management Accounting*. Englewood Cliffs NJ: Prentice-Hall.

Noorderhaven, N.G. (1992). The Problem of Contract Enforcement in Economic Organization Theory. *Organization Studies*, 2(1):229–243.

Perrow, Ch. (1986). *Complex Organizations: A Critical Essay*. New York: Random House, Inc.

Phan, P. and Hill, C. (1995). Organizational Restructuring and Economic Performance in Leveraged Buy-Outs: An Ex Post Study. *Academy of Management Journal*, 38(30):704–739.

Robbie, K. and Wright, M. (1996). *Management Buy-Ins: Entrepreneurship, Restructuring and Active Investors*. Manchester: Manchester University Press.

Schreuder, H. (1983). *Economic Theories of Organization: An Overview and Assessment of Some Recent Developments*. Research Memorandum of the Free University of Amsterdam, RM 1983-11.

Speklé, R.F. (2001). *Beyond Generics: A Closer Look at Hybrid and Hierarchical Governance*. Rotterdam: Erasmus Research Institute of Management, Ph.D. series Research in Management 8.

Thompson, R.S. and Wright, M. (1991). *UK Management Buy-Outs: Debt, Equity and Agency Cost Implications*. Nottingham: Centre for Management Buy-Out Research.

van de Poel, J.H.R. (1986). *Judgement and Control; Individual and Organizational Aspects of Performance Evaluation*. Groningen: Wolters-Noordhoff.

Wright, M. and Coyne, J. (1985). *Management Buy-Outs*. London: Croom Helm.

Zahra, S.A. (1995). Corporate Entrepreneurship and Financial Performance: The Case of Management Leveraged Buy-Outs. *Journal of Business Venturing*, 10(3):225–247.

20 Does the value of venture capital vary over the investee life cycle? Evidence from Irish investees

Nancy Huyghebaert and Sheila O'Donohoe

Abstract

Venture capital plays a catalytic role in the entrepreneurial process, which is vital for competitive vibrancy, economic growth, and job creation. This is particularly true in the Irish context, where venture capital, while still in its infancy, is more comparable to the U.S. and U.K. rather than Continental Europe. This chapter investigates investee perceptions on the nature and quality of VC involvement in Ireland and examines their relation with the investees' assessment of VC value. Overall, we document a life cycle in VC activities. Furthermore, the frequency and type of VC–investee interactions that influence the investees' perceived contribution of VC to performance also differ over the investee life cycle.

20.1 Introduction

Entrepreneurship is important as it contributes to competitive vibrancy, economic growth, and job creation. This is particularly true in Ireland, where the 1990s proved to be the golden years, known as the Celtic tiger era. Over the past decade, the population has grown by 12.5%, from 3.56 million in 1995 to just over 4.01 million in 2004, the second highest rate of increase in the EU. Most of this increase was due to inward migration (Global Entrepreneurship Monitor, 2004). During the same period, the number of new enterprises grew dramatically, with Ireland recording the highest business birth rate in the EU.[1] Also, the number of applications made to the European Patent Office by Irish firms surged from just 22 per million of citizens in 1994 to 83.6 in 2004. In line with the above figures, real GDP grew by 41% over 1996–2004, while full-time employment rose by 38%. Whilst foreign-owned enterprises accounted for much of this, the indigenous sector was still responsible for 34% of the rise in employment (Forfas, 2005).

To finance entrepreneurship, venture capital plays an important role. Indeed, VC is an intermediate external source of funding (mostly equity), typically used for projects with promising but largely unproven business ideas that require relatively long payback periods and are associated with high risk. These projects are hard to finance by means of bank loans as they have unstable cash flows, few collateralizable assets, and activities that

[1] Yet, the European Network for Social and Economic Research (ENSR, 2002) survey concludes that Ireland still has a substantially lower number of businesses less than five years old (as only 14% of Irish businesses are under this age) compared with an average of 21% within the EU.

are expected to undergo radical restructuring and growth. Venture capital contributions have been astounding in terms of number of new companies created and the industries generated. One of the most famous examples is the creation of Apple Computers through the investment by Arthur Rock in 1975. During that year, Rock invested US$1.5 million into the start-up of Apple, which offered consumers a larger choice at lower prices. This spurred demand in the economy for computers while creating jobs in a new industry. When the company floated on the stock exchange three years later, it was valued at US$100 million (Bygrave and Timmons, 1992).

In Ireland, venture capitalists also have played a key role in financing entrepreneurship. Recent examples of Irish companies that used VC and floated successfully are Iona Technology (on NASDAQ in 1997) and Clearstream Technology (on AIM in 2004). Yet, VC is still a relatively new source of financing as the majority of Irish VC investors were only founded in the mid-1990s (Mulcahy, 2005). Figure 20.1 shows that funds raised by Irish venture capitalists have grown steadily from only €9 million in 1996 to a maximum of €228 million in 2000. In 2002, funds raised were only marginally down on the previous year, indicating that the Irish VC market outperformed the rest of Europe, where funds raised dropped by an estimated 47%.

However, this constancy was only temporary, as in 2003 and 2004 the amount of VC raised fell significantly. Overall, VC represented 0.18% of Irish GDP in 2003, compared with 0.55% in the U.S., 0.85% in the U.K. and 0.20% in Continental Europe. During the period 1996–2002, up to 50% of Irish VC was directed towards early-stage ventures, in comparison with only 20% on average for the EU.[2] In addition, venture capitalists in Ireland invest more in high-tech ventures (48% in 1996 and 88% in 2002), compared with a European average of 17% in 1996 and 40% in 2002. Even though there is a trend away from seed and start-up financing in most recent years, the Irish figures are still far above Continental European numbers. EVCA (2005), for example, reports that early-stage ventures account for only 7% of investments in 2004 while replacement and buy-out financing represent 70%.

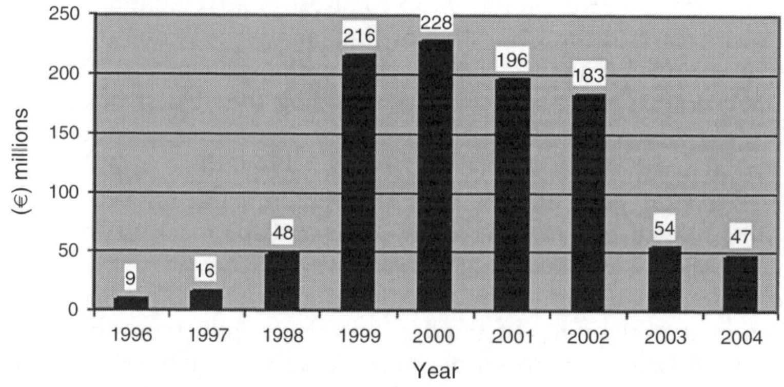

Figure 20.1 Venture capital funds raised in Ireland 1996–2004

[2] Several reasons have been posited to explain why VC participation in early-stage financing differs across countries (Modigliani and Perotti, 2000; Black and Gilson, 1998; Sahlman, 1990), but these are beyond the scope of our study.

This chapter contributes to the literature by gauging investee perceptions on the nature and quality of VC involvement. Hereby, we first examine whether investees report different VC activities depending on the stage in their life cycle, i.e. early-stage versus later-stage. Given that early-stage investments are relatively important in Ireland compared with Continental Europe, the country likely offers an appropriate context for such a study. In addition, we investigate how the frequency and type of venture capitalist–investee interactions influence the investees' perceived contribution of venture capitalists to performance. By contrast, much of the research to date has focused on the decisions and actions of venture capitalists by surveying VC investors. Specifically, the literature on VC until now largely has examined how venture capitalists monitor portfolio firms, typical VC exit strategies and the returns realized by VC companies. Overall, venture capitalists invest for a specific length of time, normally five to seven years. So, they sacrifice short-term liquidity in the hope of significant capital gains at the end of the investment. To reduce risk, they usually provide long-term financing in stages, whereby each stage is linked to the attainment of specific goals. Besides financing, venture capitalists may also create firm value by the advice and services they provide to portfolio firms.

To examine investee perceptions on the nature and quality of VC, a postal questionnaire was sent out to 199 owners/CFOs of Irish companies that received VC during the period 1996–1999, which resulted in a sample of 59 investee companies. Of the respondents, 61% are in an early-stage (seed or start-up) at the time of VC entry. Also, portfolio firms are characterized by their small size and the high-tech nature of their product/service, which generally is considered to enjoy demonstrated market acceptance. We find that venture capitalists use a combination of board representation, face-to-face communication, and telephone calls to interact with investees. They most often contact each other six to ten times per annum and communicate for three to four hours on average. Meeting times are largely spent discussing cash flow, strategy, and market issues. Overall, venture capitalists are highly valued by Irish investees, especially for their funding and managerial support. Little support is found for the VC networking role. More important, this study is the first to demonstrate that early-stage recipients of VC on average perceive more and different benefits from VC involvement compared with later-stage investees. Specifically, up to 60% of early-stage firms rate the contribution of VC to performance as significant, compared to just 41% of later-stage firms. Early-stage firms' perceived benefits of VC are largely confined to the provision of additional equity and monitoring of financial performance. Later-stage recipients also consider venture capitalists to be effective monitors, but additionally they see a role for the VC as a sounding board and mentor, its help in forming/managing the board and implementing strategy. Finally, we show that investees deem the contribution of venture capitalists to performance as significantly larger when VC firms are effectively involved in raising additional equity, helping form and manage the board, improving strategy implementation and acting as a confident/mentor. Spending significant time on raising additional equity and evaluating acquisitions has a positive influence only for early-stage investees whereas effective monitoring of financial and operating performance, instilling greater cost control/discipline and increased vision are considered to contribute to performance only by later-stage investees.

The remainder of this chapter is organized as follows. Section 20.2 provides an overview of the relevant literature and develops our hypotheses. Section 20.3 presents our sample. Next, Sections 20.4, 20.5, and 20.6 document our findings, whereas the final section concludes this chapter.

20.2 Literature review and development of hypotheses

Equity is likely to be an attractive financing source to entrepreneurial ventures for the following reasons. First, equity allows for a better risk-sharing with external financiers. By contrast, debt entails periodic fixed interest payments and capital installments so that the value of the entrepreneur's equity becomes much more volatile. Second, equity offers more flexibility in generating a return for investors, which is especially valuable when internal cash-flow generation is insecure. Early-stage ventures for which initial cash flows are highly uncertain or even negative in the first few years may therefore dislike the fixed payment obligations of debt, especially since control will be turned to creditors following default. Moreover, entrepreneurial firms that need to finance their growth are likely to consume a lot of resources so that debt, with its regular payment obligations, again is not a suitable financing source.

However, with a substantial number of lemons in the market, equity is likely to engender greater adverse selection problems than debt financing. The reason is that low-quality entrepreneurs, when raising financing, take into account that investors that provide equity find it much more difficult to liquidate their venture after having learned of its (low) quality. If private benefits of control are sufficiently large, these entrepreneurs may prefer to continue the firm, to the detriment of external shareholders. Also, they may engage in activities that raise their returns/benefits but harm other shareholders. By contrast, creditors can force a firm into liquidation once it defaults on its debt obligations. As high-quality entrepreneurs find it less costly to promise returns in low-output states, adverse selection and moral hazard problems can be reduced by writing financial contracts that have firms paying out as much as possible in low-output states, i.e. debt (Hart and Moore, 1989; Narayanan, 1988). Alternatively, these problems can also be curbed by the inclusion of restrictive covenants in financial contracts, by requiring board representation, etc. Then, investors – even when providing equity – can force an earlier transfer of control. The literature has shown that venture capitalists indeed include specific contractual features to reduce information and incentive problems, as we argue below.

Venture capital is a form of intermediated, private equity: venture capitalists accept funds from other investors, which they re-invest in high-risk firms with a high growth potential, often in high-tech industries.[3,4] For these firms, bank loans – although also intermediated finance – are less appropriate, as explained above. To deal with adverse selection problems, venture capitalists spend considerable effort in evaluating prospective

[3] The modern theory of financial intermediation ascribes the existence of financial intermediaries to delegated monitoring on behalf of investors (Diamond, 1984). In order to keep the firm from engaging in exploitive activities, the intermediary monitors the firm over the course of the relationship to assess compliance and financial condition and exerts control through directly participating in managerial decision making or renegotiating waivers on covenants. As there are scale economies in information production, intermediated financing prevents many investors collecting the same information and thus allows a saving on monitoring costs.

[4] In the U.S., 80% of VC flows through independent limited partnerships where the VC fund's managers serve as general partners and investors as limited partners, while most of the remaining 20% is provided by subsidiaries of financial institutions (Berger and Udell, 1998). Pension funds are the largest contributor of funds to limited partnerships, leaving behind (which have an equally important stake) banks and insurance companies on the one hand and private individuals on the other. In Continental Europe, bank subsidiaries are by far the largest contributor of funds, followed by pension funds. In Ireland, banks are the largest providers of VC, accounting for 20% on average; government agencies represent around 17% (Mulcahy, 2005).

clients[5] and they develop expertise through specialization by industry and investee stage of development (Dahlstrand and Cetindamar, 2000). In addition, Gompers (1995) finds evidence that venture capitalists stage their investments. The shorter the duration of an individual round of financing, the more frequently the venture capitalist monitors the entrepreneur's performance and progress, and the greater the need to gather information. Gompers studies the beneficial effects of staging on moral hazard problems. Yet, staging may also reduce the incentives of lemons to apply for VC, as they anticipate that their firm will be liquidated as soon as its quality becomes known by the venture capitalist.

In addition to adverse selection, agency problems of equity are likely to be a serious concern for venture capitalists, which usually assume a significant stake in portfolio firms. Moreover, when venture capitalists take on a preferred equity stake, the equity of entrepreneurs becomes junior to that of VC firms and their payoff becomes largely comparable with that of highly levered equity, even when the firm has no debt outstanding. So, entrepreneurs may expend insufficient effort, exhibit expense preference behavior, or invest suboptimally. Again, venture capitalists include specific features in their contracts to deal with potential agency problems. These include monitoring of portfolio firms (Gompers, 1995; Gorman and Sahlman, 1989), staging of investments to ensure optimal exercise of investment options and maintaining the option to periodically abandon projects (Admati and Pfleiderer, 1994; Sahlman, 1990), structuring entrepreneurial compensation schemes and imposing restrictive covenants (Lerner, 1995), forming the top management team (Kaplan and Strömberg, 2003), allocating voting rights and securing a large board representation (e.g. Kaplan and Strömberg, 2003; Fenn et al., 1997; Lerner, 1995).[6] The literature thus has shown that venture capitalists play an active role beyond merely providing funding, often participating in strategic issues, for instance by assisting portfolio firms in forming strategic alliances, and even occasionally in operational decision making. Such an involvement generally means a close collaboration with the firm's owners/managers. Not surprisingly, VC-backed firms on average have demonstrated revenue growth that is more than double the rate of non-VC-backed firms (EVCA, 1998). There is also evidence that VC-backed IPOs do not suffer from the long-run underperformance reported for IPOs in general (Brav and Gompers, 1997; Brophy and Verga, 1988).

This study contributes to the literature by arguing that the involvement of venture capitalists is likely to differ across the company's stage of development or at least that the various VC activities will be valued differently by investees over their life cycle. Churchill and Lewis (1983), for example, argue that a firm's needs, objectives, and management styles vary across the life cycle. First, companies that are in an early-stage (seed or start-up) typically have few tangible assets that can be pledged as collateral for bank loans, whereas internal cash flows are low and uncertain. Not surprisingly, banks generally are unwilling to lend at this stage and financially constrained entrepreneurs are expected to

[5] In line with this, Sahlman (1990) documents that on average only 10% of appeals for funds get approved.

[6] It is often argued that entrepreneurs may be reluctant to raise equity when any form of (even expensive) debt is available, as debt allows them to keep ownership and control (Jordan et al., 1998; Cressy and Olofsson, 1997; Chittenden et al., 1996). Yet, by raising equity from professional VC investors whose intentions are to ultimately sell their stake, entrepreneurs may be able to re-acquire control over time (Black and Gilson, 1998). On the one hand, if entrepreneurs are able to buy out the venture capitalist in an MBO, for instance by leveraging their company, they can re-acquire full control. This alternative might not be feasible for rapidly growing companies that still consume a lot of cash and for whom high leverage therefore is inappropriate. On the other hand, if their firm becomes listed, distributing shares among a wide investor base may ensure that entrepreneurs have de facto control over their firm.

highly value the financing provided by VC firms. Also, as start-ups operate in new markets and/or introduce new products or technologies, and as they have no established track record, venture capitalist advice and monitoring likely have a large impact on firm value, which will be treasured by VC recipients. In fact, the willingness of a VC organization to finance the company may add to the firm's credibility in dealing with other stakeholders, whereas the network of the venture capitalist may also help to provide contacts with potential customers and suppliers. The venture capitalist's focus on performance and help in making strategic decisions may further boost firm value. Overall, we expect a close collaboration between early-stage investees and their venture capitalist, with a lot of frequent and direct communication. During these contacts strategy, market, and product issues likely are important topics because of relatively high environmental uncertainty.

Once companies have gained further experience and their product has demonstrated market acceptance, their risk tends to lessen as cash flows become more stable and assets become more tangible. Also, information production becomes more constant. Berger and Udell (1998), for example, show this progression in a linear fashion across firm size and age. As a result, firms gain access to other financing sources, such as bank loans, and become less dependent on VC financing. Yet, VC may still allow the firm to grow at a faster rate as internal cash flows can be more easily re-invested (higher retained earnings possible). For these firms, the VC is also less likely to add value on a strategic level, as the firm has already proven its valuable business concept. Also, the fact that the company receives financing after screening is less likely to give a strong quality signal as there are few lemons left at this stage of the life cycle. Yet, the venture capitalist may support the building of the company's internal organization, help to better plan company growth, assist in professionalizing the firm's management and board, and instill greater control over the firm's expenses.

20.3 Sample selection

The population of interest is any Irish firm that received VC between 1996 and 1999. The original sample was compiled from a list of investees received from Enterprise Ireland, a government organization that seeks to bridge the equity gap for SMEs and that entered the Irish VC market as a limited partner in 1995. Additional data were gathered from press releases by independent venture capitalists. The time frame was chosen to provide a sufficiently large sample and enable investees to reflect on the venture capitalist's role in their firm. We identified a total of 199 portfolio firms, to which a questionnaire was sent out by regular mail. The questions in the survey are based on the studies of Sapienza (1992), Sapienza et al. (1996) and Mason and Harrison (1996). The postal questionnaires were administered between September and December 2004. A reminder letter and follow-up calls resulted in 59 companies responding to the questionnaire, representing a 29.65% response rate. Of the respondents, 61% are located in the Dublin area while overall 79% of sample firms are clustered around cities. This urban concentration has also been documented for the U.S. and the U.K. (Mulcahy, 2005).

Table 20.1 shows that in 12% of the cases, Irish venture capitalists entered during the seed stage. More important, nearly 50% of VC deals in our sample concern start-up companies. In addition, up to 29% of respondents reported that VC was received during the expansion phase, whereas buy-outs represent only 10% of the sample. In line with the above figures, the vast majority of funding (53%) was directed towards companies with 10–49 employees, suggesting that VC in Ireland is largely invested in small enterprises.

Table 20.2 also shows that there is very little investment in companies with less than 10 and more than 250 employees. These two categories are generally associated with seed and replacement capital, respectively. Overall, these percentages are consistent with those reported by the Irish Venture Capital Association (IVCA, 2002), suggesting that there is no response bias in our sample. Just over 22% of sample firms were in business for more than ten years. These figures contrast with the ENSR (2002) survey findings, which reveal that 68% of Irish SMEs are more than ten years old (EU average of 60%).

When respondents are classified according to industry, the three main sectors are computer software, manufacturing, and medical instruments/devices. Table 20.3 demonstrates

Table 20.1 Classification of investees by stage of development at which venture capital was received

Company stage	Percentage of respondents
Seed	12
Start-up	49
Expansion	29
Replacement/buy-out	10

Table 20.2 Classification of investees by firm size

Firm size	Percentage of respondents
Micro (0–9)	6
Small (10–49)	53
Medium (50–249)	35
Large (>250)	6

Table 20.3 Classification of investees by industry

Industry	Percentage of respondents
Computer software	35
Manufacturing	11
Medical instruments/devices	9
Communications/media	6
Computer hardware	4
Electronics	2
Telecommunications	2
Other*	31

* Other includes pharmaceutical development, electronic transaction provider, chemical/pharmaceutical, telematics, business services, car rental, distributor of security products, linen rental, engineering, life science services, IT consultancy, vision inspection systems, and healthcare.

Table 20.4 Classification of investees by product/service characteristics

Product/service characteristic	Percentage of respondents
The product/service enjoys demonstrated market acceptance	69
The product/service has been developed to a functioning prototype	13
The product/service may be described as high-tech	41
The product/service is proprietary or can be otherwise protected	17

that computer-related investments (software and hardware) represent the largest industry, i.e. 39%. The industries in our sample are all represented in accordance with investment rates recorded by both Enterprise Ireland (2002) and the IVCA (2002), suggesting again that our sample does not suffer from a response bias. Further analysis of industry across firm size (not reported) reveals that all VC investment in electronics is concentrated in micro-enterprises. Similarly, all VC investment in telecommunications and computer hardware is in small enterprises. The vast majority of investees in computer software, manufacturing, and medical instruments/devices are part of the small-firm subsample. The remaining 40% of medical instruments/devices VC and almost 30% of computer software VC are invested in medium-sized enterprises. Up to 67% of VC funding in communications/media is invested in medium-sized enterprises. Finally, the large-firm subsample is made up of only manufacturing and other industries.

The majority of respondents (69%) believed that their product/service already enjoyed demonstrated market acceptance at the time of VC entry, while only 13% of investees confirmed that their product/service had been developed to a functioning prototype only (see Table 20.4). The latter is consistent with our earlier finding that only 12% of investees are in a seed development stage. A total of 41% described their product/service as high-tech, but only 17% of investees enjoyed some protection for it. Further analysis (not reported) reveals that all micro- and small enterprises in the sample believed their product/service to be high-tech while only 31% of medium-sized enterprises considered this to be true.

20.4 Venture capitalist involvement in investee firms

In this section, we first discuss the nature and quality of VC involvement in portfolio firms on a general level. Hereby, we pay special attention to the question whether investee companies perceive venture capitalists to play a role beyond that of traditional financial intermediaries. Also, we examine whether VC activities vary over the investee life cycle, in particular whether these differ between early-stage (seed or start-up) and later-stage (expansion or buy-out) firms.[7]

[7] As our sample is not large enough, we are not able to differentiate between these four stages of development.

Table 20.5 shows that 48% of respondents communicate with their VC provider through a variety of methods, including board representation, face-to-face communication, and telephone calls. Board representation and face-to-face communication, on their own, account for 29% and 19%, respectively. Venture capitalists thus use direct communication with portfolio firms. The combination of various methods is prevalent among both age groups, but marginally more with later-stage investees. While we find no difference in terms of board representation, face-to-face communication is somewhat more popular among investees that received VC at an early-stage in their life cycle. This result is consistent with Sapienza et al. (1996) who find greater face-to-face interaction for early-stage ventures in Europe and the U.S.

Most often (42%), Irish investees have formal communications with their venture capitalist between six and ten times per annum (Table 20.6). Overall, formal communications between 1 and 15 times per year account for 86% of the responses in our survey. So, Irish venture capitalists visit their investees fewer times per annum than their U.S. counterparts, but do more so than their U.K. counterparts (Sweeting and Wong, 1997; Gorman and Sahlman, 1989). Some early-stage respondents are somewhat more closely monitored by their VC provider, with 30% having between 11 and 15 meetings per year. Yet, 22% of early-stage investees communicate only one to five times per annum with their venture capitalist. Finally, later-stage recipients mainly interact six to ten times per year.

Table 20.7 demonstrates that the average meeting time for the majority of investees (52%) is three to four hours in duration. For 43% of companies, meetings last for between one and two hours, while only 5% state that their meetings last more than five hours. Later stage recipients of VC have somewhat longer meetings with their venture capitalist, which may be related to the fact that they generally meet on fewer occasions, as depicted in Table 20.6.

Table 20.5 Nature of venture capitalist–investee communications

Method of communication	Percentage of respondents	Early-stage (%)	Late-stage (%)
Combination	48	39	54
Board representation	29	35	33
Face-to-face	19	22	13
Over the phone	4	4	0

Table 20.6 Frequency of venture capitalist–investee communications

No. of times per annum VC communicates with investee	Percentage of respondents	Early-stage (%)	Late-stage (%)
1–5 times	18	22	17
6–10 times	42	35	46
11–15 times	26	30	22
16–20 times	4	4	4
>20 times	10	9	11

Table 20.7 Duration of venture capitalist–investee communications

Length of meeting time with venture capitalist	% of respondents	Early-stage (%)	Late-stage (%)
1–2 hours	43	46	38
3–4 hours	52	50	54
>5 hours	5	4	8

Table 20.8 Topics discussed during venture capitalist–investee meetings

Topic of discussion	Majority of time spent (%)	Some time spent (%)	Little time spent (%)	Least time spent (%)
Cash-flow issues	41	45	12	2
Early-stage	50	40	10	0
Later-stage	33	57	10	0
Strategy issues	38	49	11	2
Early-stage	53	39	4	4
Later-stage	30	50	20	0
Market issues	32	36	22	10
Early-stage	35	29	19	17
Later-stage	33	33	29	5
Capital expenditures	11	30	23	36
Early-stage	13	44	6	37
Later-stage	33	33	29	5
Product/service issues	8	37	43	12
Early-stage	5	35	55	5
Later-stage	10	45	30	15
Asset sales	3	13	10	74
Early-stage	7	13	7	73
Later-stage	0	11	11	88
Human resource issues	2	26	30	42
Early-stage	0	32	26	42
Later-stage	33	57	10	0

Of the topics discussed during these meetings, Table 20.8 reports that cash flow, strategy, and market issues are major themes. So, Irish venture capitalists are mainly involved at a strategic level within their portfolio firms rather than becoming engaged in investees' day-to-day operations (see also MacMillan et al., 1989, for the U.S.). This result is in accordance with the VC relationship investor view held by Fried and Hisrich (1995) and Hellmann and Puri (2002). We also find differences in the issues discussed during meetings across the investee life cycle. For early-stage firms, cash flow and strategy issues occupy over half of meeting times on average, whereas these issues are less important for later-stage recipients. In both subsamples, one-third of firms spend a majority of time discussing market issues.

Yet, there is a substantial fraction of early-stage firms that devote no time to such issues. Compared with early-stage firms, later-stage firms tend to allocate more time to discussing capital expenditures, product/service, and human resource issues. For some early-stage VC recipients, asset sales become an issue during meetings.

Next, respondents were asked to rank the significance of the venture capitalist's impact in 19 different activities as identified from the literature (see above). For this purpose, a five-item Likert scale was used, ranging from no significance to very significant. The top seven significant activities is reported in Table 20.9. Raising additional equity dominates the list, followed by board formation/management, evaluation of acquisitions, cost control/discipline, cost/profit awareness, acting as a confidant/mentor, and increased vision. By contrast, venture capitalist involvement in marketing and networking is of little or no significance (not reported). These results support prior conclusions that VC firms are capable of adding value mostly in the area of finance (Sapienza et al., 1996; Rosenstein et al., 1993).

Sapienza et al. (1996), for example, compare the value added of a variety of VC roles across four countries from the venture capitalist's point of view. They find that the role of financier and financial-related advice are rated highest, whereas networking roles are considered only of limited importance.[8] Interestingly, our research further documents that early-stage recipients assign greater significance to the venture capitalist's help in raising additional equity whereas VC firm's efforts in instilling greater cost discipline/profit

Table 20.9 Significance of venture capital activities

Venture capitalist activity	Very significant/ significant (%)	Somewhat significant (%)	Little/no significance (%)
Raising additional equity finance	46	30	24
Early-stage	50	32	18
Later-stage	35	24	41
Helping form and manage the board	29	38	33
Early-stage	27	41	32
Later-stage	33	22	45
Helping evaluate acquisitions	29	16	55
Early-stage	30	13	57
Later-stage	28	18	54
Greater cost control/discipline	28	28	44
Early-stage	27	18	55
Later-stage	35	29	36
Greater cost/profit awareness	25	38	37
Early-stage	14	36	50
Later-stage	39	39	22

[8] By contrast, MacMillan et al. (1989) find that venture capitalists in the U.S. rate their activities at a strategic or top-management level as being their most important contribution. Also, Sapienza and Timmons (1989) demonstrate that networking capabilities are rated highest among VC non-financial activities in the U.S. Overall, these results may suggest that venture capitalists and investees value the role of venture capitalists rather differently and further research is required on this topic.

awareness are rated more significant by later-stage investees. In addition, we find that some later-stage investees benefit from the venture capitalist's help in forming/managing the board, even though some other firms found this role of no/little significance.

Finally, respondents were asked to rate the effectiveness of VC firm involvement in 21 different activities, which contain those on the previous list.[9] Table 20.10 demonstrates that in contrast to previous answers, the venture capitalist roles perceived as being most effective are dominated by managerial functions, while obtaining equity is ranked only fourth. The monitoring of financial and operating performance is deemed particularly effective by later-stage firms, as is the role of the venture capitalist as a sounding board and confidant/mentor, its assistance in establishing and managing the board, and its help in improving strategy implementation. Yet, a large proportion (47%) of later-stage investees considered the venture capitalist's help in implementing strategy as having little/no effect. The two key areas where early-stage firms rank venture capitalists as highly effective are in securing equity financing and monitoring financial performance. In sum, most of the roles that are rated as being both significant and effective take place at the strategic level, with very little intervention at the operational level.

Table 20.10 Effectiveness of venture capitalist activities

Venture capitalist activity	Very effective (%)	Somewhat effective (%)	Little/no effect (%)
Monitoring financial performance	58	31	11
Early-stage	46	41	13
Later-stage	67	28	5
Monitoring operational performance	47	36	17
Early-stage	32	41	27
Later-stage	61	35	4
Serving as a sounding board	41	35	24
Early-stage	39	44	17
Later-stage	50	17	33
Obtaining sources of equity	40	20	40
Early-stage	46	23	31
Later-stage	28	22	50
Helping form and manage the board	36	31	33
Early-stage	32	36	32
Later-stage	44	17	39
Improved strategy implementation	30	30	40
Early-stage	18	41	41
Later-stage	47	6	47
As a confidant/mentor	28	23	49
Early-stage	24	24	52
Later-stage	35	29	36

[9] *Effectiveness* was meant to capture the investee's perceptions on whether VC financing, monitoring, and professionalization of the firm had the desired result. It differs from *significance*, which is classified as *importance* in the study of Sapienza et al. (1996), as this variable only measures the time devoted to particular roles/tasks.

20.5 Valuation of venture capitalists by investees

To date, the value added by venture capitalists has largely been measured by: (a) comparing the early stock returns of VC-backed versus non-VC-backed IPOs (Brav and Gompers, 1997; Brophy and Verga, 1988) and (b) gauging venture capitalists' opinion of where they felt value was added to the organization (Sapienza et al., 1996; MacMillan et al., 1989). This study adopts a different approach by asking investee firms to rate company performance before and after VC firm's involvement and to rank the venture capitalist's overall contribution to their performance. No study to date has surveyed the perceptions of portfolio companies. Furthermore, as the vast majority of Irish firms that received VC over the last few years have not floated on the Irish or any other stock exchange, the first method is not suitable in our study.

Table 20.11 indicates that 39% of respondents believed that their company performed above industry average after VC firm involvement, compared with only 15% before. Furthermore, the number of firms performing at and below industry average decreased also during the time of venture capitalist involvement. When the sample is split into those that received funding at an early versus late stage, we find that especially early-stage companies operating at industry average demonstrate improved performance. So, venture capitalists are highly able in helping springboard early-stage firms to commanding positions in their respective industries. Later-stage firms also benefit from VC firm involvement, particularly those operating below industry average: 30% say they were below the industry average pre-VC investment compared with only 8% afterwards.

Overall, 83% of investees considered the intervention of the venture capitalist to be at least somewhat significant, with 7% rating the intervention as extremely significant (Table 20.12). Whilst more firms at an early-stage found the contribution of the VC firm to performance as significant or extremely significant (51% and 9%, compared with 35% and 6% for later-stage investees), more firms at this early-stage found it to be of little or no significance in contrast with those at a later-stage, i.e. 22% versus 13%. These results indicate that VC investment is much more beneficial for some firms than for others, especially in the early stage.

Table 20.11 Company performance before and after venture capitalist involvement

Company performance	Pre-VC involvement (%)	Post-VC involvement (%)	Difference (%)
Above industry average	15	39	+24
Early-stage	14	41	+27
Later-stage	15	37	+22
At industry average	62	54	−8
Early-stage	68	45	−23
Later-stage	55	55	0
Below industry average	23	7	−16
Early-stage	18	14	−4
Later-stage	30	8	−22

Table 20.12 Overall contribution of the venture capitalist

Perception of overall contribution	Percentage of respondents	Early-stage (%)	Later-stage (%)
Extremely significant	7	9	6
Significant	38	51	35
Somewhat significant	38	18	46
Little significance	9	13	7
Insignificant	8	9	6

20.6 Relation between venture capitalist involvement and their perceived contribution to performance

In this section, we examine whether there is a significant relation between the frequency and type of venture capitalist–investee interactions and the perceived contribution of the venture capitalist to firm performance. For this purpose, we applied a one-way analysis of variance (ANOVA) procedure. According to Diamantopoulos and Schlegelmilch (2000), one-way ANOVA gives reasonably good results even when the sample size is small and variables are not normally distributed. In addition, we used a chi-square test to examine the relation between VC firm involvement and performance contribution.[10] The latter test – which requires fewer degrees of freedom – was also applied in the subsamples of early- and late-stage firms, respectively. Table 20.13 reports all results. As indicated by the *F*-values associated with the ANOVA analyses, 10 out of the 20 variables that capture the frequency and type of VC involvement are statistically significant in the full sample; these are also significant under the chi-square test, where three additional variables become statistically significant.

The contribution of venture capitalists to performance on average is deemed greater (and significantly so) the longer the duration of communications between the VC firm and its portfolio firm, when venture capitalists are considered significant for raising additional equity, helping form/manage the investee board, evaluating acquisitions, instilling greater cost control/discipline, acting as a confidant/mentor, and increasing investee vision. Furthermore, the contribution of venture capitalists to performance is deemed larger when they are viewed by investees as effective for their monitoring of financial performance, as a sounding board, as a source of equity, helping form/manage the board, improving strategy implementation, and as a confidant/mentor. In addition to financing the portfolio firm, these roles again are primarily at a strategic management level. Table 20.13 also reveals some important differences between early- and later-stage investees regarding the relation between VC firm involvement and venture capitalist's contribution to performance. Spending significant time on raising additional equity and evaluating acquisitions has a positive influence only for early-stage investees, whereas effective monitoring of financial and operating performance, instilling greater cost control/discipline, and increasing

[10] For the purpose of the ANOVA analysis, contribution is ranked on a five-item Likert scale, with 1 = no significance and 5 = extremely significant; in the chi-square test, it is rated as 1 = very significant/significant and 0 = otherwise. As some cells have a count less than five, we selected an exact significance test (Fisher's exact test) for the Pearson's chi-square test.

Table 20.13 Perceived contribution of the venture capitalist to investee performance: determinants and differences across the investee life cycle

Variables	Mean contribution	One-way ANOVA in full sample		Chi-square test in full sample		Chi-square test in subsample of early-stage		Chi-square test in subsample of later-stage	
		F-value	*p*-value	χ-value	*p*-value	χ-value	*p*-value	χ-value	*p*-value
Nature of communications:									
Combination used	3.409								
No combination used	3.240	0.958	1.000	0.371	0.692	1.260	0.818	0.398	0.670
Frequency of communication:									
<11 times p.a.	3.368								
≥11 times p.a.	3.285	2.809	0.189	0.248	0.781	1.457	0.676	0.875	0.397
Duration of communications:									
<3 hours	2.947								
≥3 hours	3.555	2.728	0.338	2.607*	0.085	3.449	0.245	0.000	1.000
Majority of time spent at meetings:									
Cash-flow issues	3.176								
Non-cash-flow issues	3.416	1.258	0.576	0.304	0.739	0.579	0.782	1.974	0.489
Majority of time spent at meetings:									
Strategy issues	3.444								
Non-strategy issues	3.280	1.407	0.638	0.178	0.837	0.516	0.767	0.875	1.000
Majority of time spent at meetings:									
Market issues	3.571								
Non-market issues	3.214	3.065	0.246	0.564	0.573	0.649	0.866	3.859	0.159
Raising additional equity:									
Very significant/significant	3.761								
Somewhat/little/no significance	2.954	3.183	0.200	3.845**	0.029	8.077**	0.016	2.950	0.381

(*Continued*)

Table 20.13 Continued

Variables	Mean contribution	One-way ANOVA in full sample		Chi-square test in full sample		Chi-square test in subsample of early-stage		Chi-square test in subsample of later-stage	
		F-value	*p*-value	χ-value	*p*-value	χ-value	*p*-value	χ-value	*p*-value
Helping form and manage board:									
Very significant/significant	4.076								
Somewhat/little/no significance	3.000	12.075***	0.001	6.630***	0.003	9.281***	0.003	5.931**	0.046
Helping evaluate acquisitions:									
Very significant/significant	4.090								
Somewhat/little/no significance	3.033	9.764***	0.007	3.499**	0.023	7.256**	0.032	4.326	0.204
Greater cost control/discipline:									
Very significant/significant	4.000								
Somewhat/little/no significance	3.060	7.561*	0.051	4.426**	0.018	2.991	0.302	7.183**	0.017
Greater cost/profit awareness:									
Very significant/significant	3.416								
Somewhat/little/no significance	3.272	0.615	0.803	0.251	0.779	1.526	0.807	1.436	0.796
Increased vision:									
Very significant/significant	2.913								
Somewhat/little/no significance	1.840	5.415*	0.024	5.056*	0.025	1.852	0.174	3.697*	0.080
Act as a confidant/mentor:									
Very significant/significant	2.912								
Somewhat/little/no significance	1.750	6.900**	0.012	6.261**	0.012	2.739	0.183	3.790*	0.090
Monitoring financial performance:									
Very effective	3.730								
Somewhat/little/no effect	2.736	5.300*	0.051	6.726***	0.003	2.573	0.417	7.875***	0.008
Monitoring operating performance:									
Very effective	3.619								
Somewhat/little/no effect	3.041	2.111	0.417	2.064	0.139	1.691	0.700	4.936*	0.067

Serving as a sounding board:									
Very effective	3.789								
Somewhat/little/no effect	3.000	3.427	0.154	3.786**	0.030	4.063	0.109	1.532	0.802
Obtaining sources of equity:									
Very effective	4.000								
Somewhat/little/no effect	2.851	12.754***	0.000	9.636***	0.000	6.908**	0.025	6.298**	0.027
Helping form and manage board:									
Very effective	4.000								
Somewhat/little/no effect	2.931	13.446***	0.000	7.476***	0.002	10.919***	0.002	5.688**	0.045
Improved strategy implementation:									
Very effective	4.000								
Somewhat/little/no effect	3.032	7.742**	0.014	4.897**	0.012	5.304*	0.085	8.115**	0.013
As a confident/mentor:									
Very effective	4.000								
Somewhat/little/no effect	3.096	10.048***	0.003	3.879**	0.028	5.830**	0.034	6.290*	0.061

*** significant at the 1% level; ** significant at the 5% level; * significant at the 10% level.

vision are deemed to contribute to performance only for later-stage investees. Overall, these results are largely consistent with those presented in Table 20.10. They confirm our hypotheses that investee perceptions on the contribution of venture capitalists in sourcing fresh equity, in determining the firm's strategy, in monitoring performance, and professionalizing portfolio firms differ across the investee life cycle and play a unique role in determining their general concept of the value added by VC firms.

20.7 Conclusion

This research has probed the value-adding capabilities of Irish venture capitalists from the investees' perspective. Our results show that while financing is highly important, Irish VC firms play a role beyond that of traditional financial intermediaries. Specifically, we find evidence that they add value at a strategic management level, which is in accordance with the relationship investor view held by Fried and Hisrich (1995) and Hellmann and Puri (2002). Interestingly, we document that some VC firms' activities are significantly more valued by early-stage than by later-stage firms, and vice versa. On the one hand, early-stage firms' benefits of VC are largely confined to the provision of additional equity and monitoring of financial performance, whereas on average they attach less importance to the non-financial activities. Later-stage recipients also consider venture capitalists to be effective monitors, but they further see a role for the VC firm as a sounding board and mentor, for giving help in forming/managing the board and in implementing strategy. Furthermore, we document that the nature, frequency, and length of communication differ depending upon the investee stage of development.

So, our results suggest that there is a life cycle in VC activities, which is consistent with earlier findings of Grant (1996), Ruhnka and Young (1991), and Dahlstrand and Cetindamar (2000), among others, that venture capitalists specialize in industries and firm development stage. Actually, our study provides an additional economic rationale for this by pointing out the contribution to investee value rather than stressing the scale economies of specialization in reducing adverse selection and moral hazard problems. Indeed, we document a relation between the frequency and type of venture capitalist–investee interactions and the perceived contribution of venture capitalists to performance. Overall, VC firms are deemed to contribute significantly by providing finance, monitoring, professionalizing investee boards and strategies, and acting as a confidant/mentor. Yet, these perceptions again differ across the investee life cycle, with early-stage firms valuing more the financing role and later-stage firms stressing somewhat more their monitoring. While our study offers some new insights on the value of VC, a major caveat, however, is that our sample is too small to conduct extensive multivariate research on this topic. Another avenue for future research that results from our study is to simultaneously question venture capitalists and investees on the contribution of VC organizations in portfolio firms, as our results suggest that perceptions may differ across investors and beneficiaries.

Acknowledgments

The authors are very grateful to Damian Rossiter for his work in collecting the data. In addition, they acknowledge financial support from Technological Sector Strand 1.

References

Admati, A.R. and Pfleiderer, P. (1994). Robust Financial Contracting and the Role for Venture Capitalists. *Journal of Finance*, 49(2):371–402.
Berger, A.N. and Udell, G.F. (1998). The Economics of Small Business Finance: The Roles of Private Equity and Debt Markets in the Financial Growth Cycle. *Journal of Banking & Finance*, 22(6–8):613–673.
Black, B.S. and Gilson, G.D. (1998). Venture Capital and the Structure of Capital Markets: Banks versus Stock Markets. *Journal of Financial Economics*, 47(3):243–277.
Brav, A. and Gompers, P. (1997). Myth or Reality? The Long Run Underperformance of Initial Public Offerings: Evidence from Venture and Non-Venture Capital-Backed Companies. *Journal of Finance*, 52(5):1791–1821.
Brophy, D.J. and Verga, J.A. (1988). More than Money? The Influence of Venture Capitalists on Initial Public Offerings. Paper presented at the Babson Entrepreneurship Conference, 5–7 May, Calgary.
Bygrave, W. and Timmons, J.A. (1992). *Venture Capital at the Crossroads*. Boston MA: Harvard Business School Press.
Chittenden, F., Hall, H. and Hutchinson, P. (1996). Small Firm Growth, Access to Capital Markets and Financial Structure: Review of Issues and Empirical Investigation. *Small Business Economics*, 8(1):59–67.
Churchill, N. and Lewis, V. (1983). The Five Stages of Small Business Growth. *Harvard Business Review*, 61(3):30–50.
Cressy, R. and Olofsson, C. (1997). The Financial Conditions for Swedish SMEs: Survey and Research Agenda. *Small Business Economics*, 9(2):197–194.
Dahlstrand, A.L. and Cetindamar, D. (2000). The Dynamics of Innovation Financing in Sweden. *Venture Capital*, 2(3):203–221.
Diamond, D.W. (1984). Financial Intermediation and Delegated Monitoring. *Review of Economic Studies*, 51(3):393–414.
Diamantopoulos, A. and Schlegelmilch, B.B. (2000). *Taking the Fear Out of Data Analysis: A Step-by-Step Approach*. Dryden Press.
Enterprise Ireland (2002). *Seed and Venture Capital Reports 1994–2001*. Dublin: Enterprise Ireland.
European Network for Social and Economic Research (ENSR) (2002). *The European Social Research Enterprise Survey 2002 in the European Commission (2002), The Observatory of European SMEs*. (CD-Rom).
European Venture Capital Association (EVCA) (1998, 2005). *EVCA Annual Yearbook*. Brussels: EVCA.
Fenn, G.W., Liang, N. and Prowse, S. (1997). The Private Equity Market: An Overview. *Financial Markets, Institutions and Instruments*, 6(4):1–105.
Forfas (2005). *Annual Employment Survey 2004*. Dublin: Forfas.
Fried, V.H. and Hisrich, R.D. (1995). The Venture Capitalist: A Relationship Investor. *California Management Review*, 37(2):101–113.
Global Entrepreneurship Monitor (GEM) (2004). *Executive Report*. Joint publication with Ewing Marion Kauffman Foundation, Babson College and London Business School.
Gompers, P.A. (1995). Optimal Investment, Monitoring, and the Staging of Venture Capital. *Journal of Finance*, 50(5):1461–1491.

Gorman, M. and Sahlman, W. (1989). What Do Venture Capitalists Do? *Journal of Business Venturing*, 4(4):231–248.

Grant, R.M. (1996). Towards a Knowledge-Based Theory of the Firm. *Strategic Management Journal*, 17(2):109–122.

Hart, O. and Moore, J.H. (1989). Default and Renegotiation: A Dynamic Model of Debt. *The Quarterly Journal of Economics*, 113(1):1–41.

Hellmann, T. and Puri, M. (2002). Venture Capital and the Professionalisation of Start-Up Firms. *Journal of Finance*, 57(1):169–197.

Irish Venture Capital Association (IVCA) (2002). *Report on Venture Capital Investment Activity*. Dublin: Matheson Ormsby Prentice.

Jordan, J., Lowe, J. and Taylor P. (1998). Strategy and Financial Policy in UK Small Firms. *Journal of Business Finance and Accounting*, 25(1):1–27.

Kaplan, S. and Strömberg, P. (2003). Financial Contracting Theory Meets the Real World: An Empirical Analysis of Venture Capital Contracts. *Review of Economic Studies*, 70(2):281–315.

Lerner, J. (1995). Venture Capitalists and the Oversight of Private Firms. *Journal of Finance*, 50(1):301–318.

MacMillan, I.C., Kulow, D.M. and Khoylian, R. (1989). Venture Capitalists' Involvement in their Investments: Extent and Performance. *Journal of Business Venturing*, 4(1):27–47.

Mason, C.M. and Harrison, R.T. (1996). Informal Venture Capital: A Study of the Investment Process, the Post-Investment Experience and Investment Performance. *Entrepreneurship and Regional Development*, 8(1):105–125.

Modigliani, F. and Perotti, E.C. (2000). Legal Enforcement and Investor Protection. *International Review of Finance*, 1(2):81–96.

Mulcahy, D. (2005). *Angels and IPOs: Policies for Sustainable Equity Financing of Irish Small Businesses*. Dublin: The Policy Institute, Trinity College Dublin.

Narayanan, M.P. (1988). Debt versus Equity under Asymmetric Information. *Journal of Financial and Quantitative Analysis*, 23(1):39–51.

Rosenstein, J.B., Bygrave, A.V. and Taylor, N.T. (1993). The CEO, Venture Capitalists and the Board. *Journal of Business Venturing*, 8(1):99–113.

Ruhnka, J.C. and Young, J.E. (1991). Some Hypotheses about Risk in Venture Capital Investing. *Journal of Business Venturing*, 6(2):115–133.

Sahlman, W.A. (1990). The Structure and Governance of Venture Capital Organizations. *Journal of Financial Economics*, 27(2):473–524.

Sapienza, H.J. (1992). When Do Venture Capitalists Add Value? *Journal of Business Venturing*, 7(1):9–28.

Sapienza, H.J. and Timmons, J.A. (1989). Launching and Building Entrepreneurial Companies: Do Venture Capitalists Add Value? In Brockhaus, R.H., Sr (ed.), *Frontiers of Entrepreneurship Research*. Wellesley MA: Babson College.

Sapienza, H.J., Manigart, S. and Vermeir, W. (1996). Venture Capitalist Governance and Value Added in Four Countries. *Journal of Business Venturing*, 11(6):439–469.

Sweeting, R.C. and Wong, C.F. (1997). A UK Hands-Off Venture Capital Firm and Handling of Post Investment. *Journal of Management Studies*, 34(1):126–152.

21 German banks as venture capitalists

Tereza Tykvova

Abstract

This chapter analyzes whether, in Germany, venture capital funds owned by banks behave differently from independent venture capitalists when taking their portfolio companies public. The results suggest that banks are more risk averse and, via their VC subsidiaries, they tend to build relationships with potential credit customers. Moreover, the findings of this chapter are consistent with the conjecture that independent VC funds are more intensively involved in the management of their portfolio companies than bank-based funds. However, I cannot confirm that independent funds, in general, grandstand more than bank-based funds.

21.1 Introduction

The typical picture of venture capital firms is that they operate via closed-end funds, collecting money from institutional investors such as pension funds or insurance companies (Barry, 1994). Such funds must typically fulfill a long list of covenants (Gompers and Lerner, 1996), but, beyond this, in their decision-making they are independent from their capital providers. However, besides such 'independent' funds, alternative organizational forms also exist. Those are funds that belong to industrial companies, to banks, or to government (so-called captive funds). In some countries, independent funds by far dominate the market; in other countries other structures play an important role. The analysis of this chapter deals with the German market, where banks traditionally play an important role in many financial markets' segments. Also in the VC market, banks with their own VC funds are important players, possessing a large market share. As these funds have other governance structures, know-how, and objectives than independent funds, I conjecture that there should be differences in the investment patterns between these two types of funds.

First, bank-based and independent venture capitalists typically have differing governance structures. Managers of bank-based venture capitalists act as employees of the mother company rather than as partners of an independent VC fund. Generally, bank-based venture capitalists employ lower-powered incentive structures than independent venture capitalists. Empirical evidence for the German market can be found in Weber and Dierkes (2002). Higher-powered incentive structures may lead managers of independent funds to more excessive risk taking.

Second, bank-based and independent venture capitalists are supposed to aim at differing objectives. According to Hellmann et al. (2003), banks offer VC to companies in order to gain customers for their core business, namely credit provision. Compared with that, independent VC funds are primarily interested in profit maximization from their current activities. If they do not earn enough money for their investors, they will experience difficulties when raising further funds. Gompers (1996, 1993) argues that independent VC funds take their portfolio companies public early in order to impress the investors and be able to raise capital for future funds (grandstanding). Barry (1994) concludes that captive VC funds do not have incentives to grandstand.

Third, bank-based and independent venture capitalists may offer their portfolio companies differing levels of management support. Independent funds typically act as active investors with a deep involvement in the company's management (see for example Barry, 1994; Amit et al., 1998). Bank-based venture capitalists usually employ more passive strategies (see for example Gompers and Lerner, 2001a, 2001b, 1999). There are obviously several reasons for such differences. Both aspects mentioned above, namely higher-powered incentive structures and the need to convince investors, induce managers of independent funds to carry out more intensive monitoring and support activities for their portfolio companies.

All these issues make investigating the differences between bank-based and independent funds worthwhile. In this chapter, I evaluate possible consequences of the aspects discussed above on the duration of VC financing before the company is taken public and on the venture capitalists' retention rate beyond the initial public offering (IPO). Concretely, I conjecture that the less intensive monitoring and support of their portfolio companies, on the one hand, and the aim of maximizing the pool of potential customers on the other, result in quicker and more intensive exits (i.e. a shorter financing period and a lower retention rate) of bank-based venture capitalists compared with independent VC funds. Another argument for shorter financing periods of bank-based funds is that, for reasons discussed at the beginning of this section, the managers of these funds are more risk averse than their colleagues from independent funds. Therefore, they are expected to prefer later stage deals that are closer to IPO. Contrary to this conjecture, the grandstanding hypothesis suggests that independent VC funds should exit more quickly.

The rest of the chapter is organized as follows. The following section gives a short overview of the German VC market. The third section discusses briefly the duration of the venture capitalists' financing and their post-IPO retention rate. In the fourth section the hypotheses are developed. Then, in the fifth section, the dataset is described and some summary statistics are given. The sixth section is devoted to the multivariate analyses of the duration of VC financing and the venture capitalists' retention rate. The last section states the conclusions.

21.2 Venture capital in Germany

Until the 1990s the VC industry in Germany was rather small. This changed quite drastically in the 1990s. The first push came through reunification, leading to the establishment of the VC market, especially in East Germany. These operations were clearly driven by subsidies and dominated by quasi-public agencies (Mittelständische Beteiligungsgesellschaften). The second push was paralleled by the establishment of the Neuer Markt, a stock market segment for young innovative firms, in 1997. This platform provided a viable new exit channel for venture capitalists.

Traditionally, the German financial system is dominated by banks. In the 1990s nearly all large (and several small) players in the German banking industry established their own VC subsidiaries. In contrast to many other countries, bank-based VC funds have a considerable market share in Germany. As they differ in their governance structures, incentives, and aims from independent funds, which are organized as limited partnerships, they may also differ in their strategies and play differing roles in their portfolio companies.

Many German banks are public or quasi-public (Sparkassen and Landesbanken). As a result of overall economic policy, there is a large proportion of VC organizations that are basically owned by these (quasi-)public banks. The main objective of these VC firms is, in most cases, not to maximize returns but rather to promote local firms. In any case, their concentration on profit maximization is much less pronounced than is the case with VC funds of private banks. As VC funds of (quasi-)public banks have, to a certain extent, differing aims and corporate governance structures than those of private banks, a distinct evaluation of these two groups seems appropriate. Thus, I carry out the analyses for the sample of all bank-based VC funds and, additionally, only for the subsample of funds owned by private banks. However, the results do not differ much. One reason is that the group of funds owned by public banks is rather small in my dataset.

Whereas bank-based venture capitalists active in Germany are mostly affiliated in the domestic market, the sample of independent VC funds is dominated by venture capitalists from abroad. These are usually closed-end funds, in which the investment managers own a (small) part of the fund (typically 1%), but their share on profit, so-called carried interest, is much larger (typically 20%).

21.3 Duration of the venture capital financing and the venture capitalists' retention rate

For several reasons, I conjecture that there should be differences in the investment patterns of independent and bank-based VC funds. They are evaluated through two aspects of the financiers' involvement: (i) the length of the venture capitalists' participation before the company is taken public and (ii) the venture capitalists' retention rate beyond the IPO.

Concerning the duration of the VC financing, Gompers (1993) formulates the grandstanding hypothesis: the reason some venture capitalists take their portfolio companies public too early (after short financing periods) is that these VC firms want to increase their reputation in order to be able to attract capital for new funds. In his model, successful IPOs increase the venture capitalists' reputation because they serve as a quality signal for (potential) fund investors. In an empirical investigation, Gompers (1996) shows that grandstanding is common in the U.S. VC market.

Tykvová (2003) argues that the venture capitalist's non-monetary contribution (advice and monitoring) is decisive for the timing of the IPO. She shows in a theoretical model that those venture capitalists who are able to add more value via their management support, take public their portfolio companies later compared with those who contribute less. The reason is that the companies can profit from the input of skilled venture capitalists, whose management contribution increases the firm value. Thus, waiting is profitable for highly skilled venture capitalists as they can achieve higher prices for their portfolio companies when they take them public later.

Venture capitalists usually exit only partially at the IPO and retain part of their shares beyond the IPO (Lin and Smith, 1998; Megginson and Weiss, 1991; Barry et al., 1990). Thus, after the IPO, venture capitalists may further serve as advisors and monitors of their portfolio companies.

21.4 Hypotheses

Which differences should be expected between bank-based and independent VC funds with respect to the duration of financing before IPO and the venture capitalists' retention rates? I formulate the hypotheses on the basis of the following aspects: differing value-added through management support, differing governance structures, and differing aims between these two types of funds.

Bank-based and independent VC funds may generate differing value-added for their portfolio companies. Compared with banks, which typically employ passive portfolio management strategies, independent VC funds tend to have a more pronounced role in corporate governance and monitoring of the companies they finance (Gompers and Lerner, 2001a, 2001b, 1999). In order to optimize the benefits from their contribution, independent VC funds should therefore finance their portfolio companies for longer time periods, whereas bank-based VC funds are expected to act as bridge investors. Moreover, as independent funds can add larger value, not only before but also after the IPO, I further conjecture that they want to retain a larger fraction of their shares beyond the IPO in order not to lose their influence on the company's management.

One of the reasons why a lower value-added and, thus, shorter financing periods and lower retention rates are expected with bank-based VC funds, is the differing governance structure of these funds. Their managers act as employees of the mother company rather than as partners of an independent venture capitalist. Typically, their remuneration is less incentive-based. Moreover, independent venture capitalists must raise funds for their business from capital markets. So, they are more dependent on success of their current fund than bank-based VC funds who typically receive capital from their parent company. All these issues lead to the conclusion that partners of independent VC funds exert more effort and, thus, create higher value.

Independent and bank-based VC funds may have differing aims. Hellmann et al. (2003) formulate the relationship hypothesis. They state that banks provide companies with venture capital in order to get access to potential customers. If this is true, bank-based VC funds should provide less capital for shorter time periods in order to maximize the pool of potential customers. So, shorter financing periods with bank-based funds are expected. Moreover, after the IPO, these funds should considerably reduce participation in their companies in order to free capital for deals with new companies (potential future credit customers). Hence, more extensive selling at the IPO with bank-based VC funds is expected.

Another argument for shorter holding periods of bank-based funds is risk aversion. I conjecture that bank-based funds, which on general are more risk averse than independent funds, invest in later stage companies that are closer to IPO.

Grandstanding should be more pronounced with independent VC funds. These venture capitalists strongly care about their reputation because they have to collect money from independent investors. Thus, the managers of these funds feel increased pressure to carry out an exit. As a result, contrary to what is stated above, shorter financing periods with independent VC funds are expected.

The hypotheses are summarized in Table A21.1. I conclude that bank-based VC funds have lower retention rates. Concerning the duration of the pre-IPO VC financing, the impact of bank-based venture capitalists remains unclear. I have two contradictory hypotheses: a shorter versus a longer holding period of bank-based venture capitalists.

Table 21.1 Hypotheses: bank-based versus independent venture capital funds

Bank-based VCs have ...	due to
... lower retention rates after IPO	value added, governance, relationship
... shorter holding periods prior to IPO	value added, governance, relationship, risk aversion
... longer holding periods prior to IPO	grandstanding

21.5 Data

The analysis of this chapter is based on a unique hand-collected database of IPOs on Germany's Neuer Markt. This market segment was founded in March 1997, as a platform for IPOs of young innovative companies, and closed in June 2003. The advantage of using this dataset is that, from the listing prospectuses of the companies on the Neuer Markt, one can obtain detailed information on the ownership structure and its development. Such detailed information is not available in listing prospectuses of companies from other market segments. Alternative data sources such as the databases of the shareholder structure of German companies (for example, Markus Databank or Hoppenstedt Aktienführer) have many gaps and enormous time lags. Lastly, there were few venture-backed IPOs in other periods and in other market segments, another reason for dealing with companies from the Neuer Markt.

The Appendix comprises the variables used in this study and their descriptions. All financial data before 1999 were converted into Euros. Only 'real' IPOs are considered. Thus, firms that were listed on another exchange when going public on the Neuer Markt were excluded. The data were obtained from several sources:

- German Stock Exchange (date of IPO, market value, classification of the industry, shareholder structure immediately after IPO, data on designated sponsors, and lead underwriters),
- listing prospectuses (shareholder structure before IPO, duration of the VC financing before IPO, the firm's age and book value, bookbuilding span, names of the designated sponsors and lead underwriters, duration of the lock-up period),
- directories of German, European, and U.S. VC associations (affiliation, type of venture capitalist),
- web pages of VC firms (affiliation, type of venture capitalist).

There were 327 IPOs on the Neuer Markt, 179 of them were venture-backed. (I use the term venture capital to describe private equity investing in start-up, seed, expansion, and later stage firms. Moreover, management buy-outs and buy-ins are included. Thus, the terminology of this chapter adopts the term venture capital (VC) to refer to both 'venture capital' and 'private equity', as usually used in the European context.) The VC fund that held the largest share of the equity prior to the IPO was labeled the lead VC fund. There were 86 companies backed by independent and 72 companies backed by bank-based lead VC funds. Twenty companies were backed by a corporate lead venture capitalist and for

Table 21.2 Summary statistics

	Independent banks	Indep	Banks	*t-test (vs. indep)*	Private banks	*t-test (vs. indep)*
MV (mil. euro)	284.6	313.0	250.7	0.2737	265.3	0.4500
BTM	0.0257	0.0218	0.0303	0.0725*	0.0298	0.1156 (*)
AGE (years)	11.9	10.8	13.1	0.1946	12.9	0.2739
DURATION (years)	1.5	1.8	1.0	0.0065***	1.1	0.0218**
RETALL (%)	75.5	83.9	65.4	0.0000***	65.2	0.0000***
POSTIPOALL (%)	17.7	21.0	13.6	0.0016***	14.5	0.0120**
RETSINGLE (%)	80.1	84.2	73.2	0.0002***	71.5	0.0001***

*, **, and *** point to significance at the 10%, 5%, and 1% levels, respectively.
(*) indicates significance at the 15% level.

one company I was not able to find out the names of the venture capitalists. From the 72 IPOs backed by bank-based lead VC funds, 15 were backed by a lead venture capitalist owned by a public bank. In many companies there were multiple VC funds. In all 179 venture-backed IPOs, participation of an independent venture capitalist can be found 243 times and participation of a bank-based one 143 times, from which 42 cases are venture capitalists of public banks.

Table 21.2 offers summary statistics of the main variables for the whole sample and for the subsamples. It further includes tests on whether there are differences between the IPOs backed by independent and bank-based VC funds (separately for the group of all banks and the group of private banks only). Firms backed by independent venture capitalists are larger, but the difference in market values (€313.0 million versus €250.7–265.3 million) is not significant. Independent venture capitalists tend to back growth firms (= lower book-to-market ratio). Moreover, these firms are more than two years younger when they go public than firms backed by bank-based venture capitalists (not significant).

Large and significant differences in the duration of pre-IPO VC financing and the venture capitalists' involvement after the IPO between the two types of VC funds can be found. With an independent lead venture capitalist, companies obtain VC for a longer period (1.8 years) than with a bank-based lead VC fund (1.0–1.1 years). Venture capitalists sell only a part of their holdings at the IPO and maintain a considerable impact in their portfolio companies. Within the subsample of firms backed by independent funds as lead venture capitalists, the group of VC firms retains nearly 84% of its pre-IPO holdings on average, whereas it is approximately 65% within the subsample of firms financed by bank-based funds as lead venture capitalists. The post-IPO share of venture capitalists in the company under an independent lead fund is 21.0%, under a bank-based fund only 13.6%, respectively 14.5% if VC funds owned by public banks are excluded. If we look at the retention rate of each single venture capitalist in all companies on the Neuer Markt, we also find enormous and significant differences. It reaches 84.2% for independent venture capitalists on average and only 71.5% or 73.2% for bank-based VC firms, depending on whether funds owned by public banks are considered or not.

21.6 Multivariate analyses

21.6.1 Duration

In this section, using multivariate analysis, I test whether bank-based VC funds have longer or shorter financing periods than independent funds before they take their portfolio companies public. The relationship hypothesis implies that bank-based VC funds exit their portfolio companies faster than independent venture capitalists. The reason is that the former want to free funds for financing of further companies, as their aim is to maximize the pool of potential credit customers. Moreover, such behavior is also consistent with the value-added hypothesis, stating that independent funds create larger value via their management support and, thus, finance their companies for longer time periods in order to attain more attractive valuations. Furthermore, the risk aversion hypothesis leads to the same outcome. Contrary to this, the grandstanding hypothesis would imply longer pre-IPO holdings of bank-based VC funds as independent venture capitalists experience a strong pressure to exit.

To deal with this problem, I conduct a hazard rate analysis to model the duration between the first venture capitalist's equity holdings and the IPO, employing two commonly used parametric models (Weibull and exponential) and one semi-parametric model (Cox proportional hazard model). The duration of the VC financing is regressed on the venture capitalists' type dummy (INDEP), industry dummies, the start-up dummy, and the company's book-to-market ratio. If the estimated coefficients, which are given in Table 21.3, are positive, then this variable increases the hazard ratio, and vice versa. Using the three models mentioned above, columns 2–4 comprise estimations within the entire sample. In columns 5–7, the same three hazard rate models are used, but VC funds of public banks are not included in the analysis.

All six models deliver similar outcomes and provide evidence for the differing behavior of bank-based and independent VC funds with respect to the duration of pre-IPO VC financing. The results are consistent with the relationship, the value-added, and the risk aversion hypotheses. The coefficient on the dummy variable INDEP is always negative and significant at the 1% level. Thus, because of the differences in the venture capitalists'

Table 21.3 Hazard rate models – length of the pre-IPO venture capital financing. Dependent variable: DURATION

	Whole sample			Public banks excluded		
	Weibull	Exponential	Cox	Weibull	Exponential	Cox
INDEP	−0.66***	−0.57***	−0.65***	−0.65***	−0.56***	−0.64***
MEDIA[a]	1.28***	1.16***	1.23***	1.53***	1.36***	1.48***
START-UP	−0.53**	−0.48**	−0.51**	−0.51**	−0.46*	−0.47*
BTM	−6.62**	−6.01*	−6.91**	−5.90*	−5.28	−6.36*
p-value	0.0000	0.0000	0.0000	0.0000	0.0000	0.0000
Number obs.	134	134	134	123	123	123

[a] Other industry dummies are not significant.

*, **, and *** point to significance at the 10%, 5%, and 1% levels, respectively.

aims and managerial contribution, independent venture capitalists finance their portfolio firms for significantly longer periods than bank-based VC funds before they take them public. This contradicts the grandstanding hypothesis.

Further, companies that belong to the sector of Media and Entertainment are financed for significantly shorter periods. Other industry dummies, which are not significant, are not depicted in the table. The investment in a start-up company leads to a longer financing period. Moreover, growth stocks are taken public faster.

21.6.2 Retention rate

Venture capitalists maintain their investment following the IPO. In this section, the extent of their exit in the course of the IPO at the level of the firm and the VC level is modeled. The determinants of the fraction of shares retained by the venture capitalists after the IPO are explored. At the firm level, the pre-IPO holdings of the group of venture capitalists are taken as a benchmark. The fraction retained lies between 0% (when all venture capitalists sell their complete shareholdings at the IPO) and 100% (when none of the venture capitalists sells any shares). At the VC fund level, the fraction of retained shares for each single venture capitalist is estimated.

Because the dependent variable is limited (it is placed between 0 and 100), Tobit regressions are used. Besides the venture capitalists' characteristics and involvement, the impact of the market, company, and other market participants' characteristics on the retention rate are analyzed. The relationship hypothesis implies that bank-based venture capitalists are short-term investors, who typically provide the company with funds for an IPO and who dispose of a large fraction of their holdings directly at the IPO. Another reason for a lower post-IPO retention rate by bank-based venture capitalists is that independent VC funds are able to provide better management support, and, therefore, aim at longer relationships during which they increase the firm value and, thus, their future revenues.

Table 21.4 provides the results from Tobit regressions for the determinants of the fraction of old shares retained by all venture capitalists (columns 2 and 4) and by single venture capitalists (columns 3 and 5) following the IPO (i) for the whole sample (columns 2 and 3) and (ii) excluding funds owned by public banks (columns 4 and 5). The slopes for the dummy variable INDEP are in italics. For all other variables, only coefficients (but not slopes) from Tobit regressions are depicted.

The expected differences between independent and bank-based venture capitalists are confirmed. The results comply with the relationship and the value-added hypothesis. If the lead venture capitalist is independent, the fraction sold by the group of venture capitalists is significantly lower compared with bank-based lead VC funds. Significant differences can be found also at the level of single venture capitalists. The results indicate that an independent lead fund increases the retention rate of the group of venture capitalists by approximately 13–14 percentage points. The positive impact of fund independence on the retention rate for a single independent venture capitalist reaches 5–8 percentage points. All these results are significant at the 1% level.

Concerning other variables, the coefficients on the duration of the lock-up period by the lead VC firm, the reputation of designated sponsors and lead underwriters, as well as the hot issue dummy, are significantly different from zero. The positive sign on the hot issue dummy and the negative sign on the reputation of designated sponsors (lower

Table 21.4 Tobit models – fraction retained by the venture capitalists beyond the IPO

	Dependent variable			
	RETALL	RETSINGLE	RETALL	RETSINGLE
	Whole sample		Public banks excluded	
	VCs' characteristics and involvement			
INDEP	17.71***	13.43***	19.38***	15.43***
slope	*12.94****	*7.83****	*14.41****	*5.37****
LOCKDUR	2.31***	2.45***	2.25**	2.24***
DURATION	1.10		1.08	
PREIPOALL	−0.17		−0.15	
PREIPOSINGLE		−0.22		−0.18
	Market and company characteristics			
HOTISSUE	14.13**	19.70***	12.77*	15.60**
BTM	−105.6	−83.8	−111.6	−58.3
MV	17.76	−0.01	18.73*	−0.01
AGE	−0.09	−0.44	−0.06	−0.46
BOOKSPAN	71.58	29.47	36.83	19.90
	Other market participants			
DSREP	−3.46***	−3.87***	−3.48***	−4.19***
UNDREP	1.20	4.16***	1.62	5.04***
p-value	0.0000	0.0000	0.0000	0.0000
Number obs.	130	358	120	319

*, **, and *** point to significance at the 10%, 5%, and 1% levels, respectively.

rank = better reputation) are consistent with the following conjecture: when venture capitalists expect rising share prices (in hot issue markets) and high liquidity (having designated sponsors with a high reputation), they retain a larger fraction of their old shares. Moreover, the results of the Tobit analysis indicate that high-quality underwriters (lower rank = better reputation) certify the companies and allow the venture capitalists to sell a significantly larger fraction already at the IPO.

21.7 Conclusion

The analysis of this chapter highlights clear differences in the way bank-based and independent funds act as VC providers in Germany. Compared with independent funds, bank-based funds take their portfolio companies public faster and they sell a larger fraction of their old shares already at the IPO. These findings are consistent with the value-added, the relationship, and the risk aversion hypotheses. On the contrary, I do not find support for the conjecture that independent funds grandstand more than bank-based funds.

References

Amit, R., Brander, J. and Zott, C. (1998). Why do Venture Capital Firms Exist? Theory and Canadian Evidence. *Journal of Business Venturing*, 13(6):441–466.

Barry, C.B. (1994). New Directions in Research on Venture Capital Finance. *Financial Management*, 23(3):3–15.

Barry, C.B., Muscarella, C.J., Peavy, J.W., III and Vetsuypens, M.R. (1990). The Role of Venture Capital in the Creation of Public Companies. *Journal of Financial Economics*, 27(1):447–471.

Gompers, P.A. (1993). The Theory, Structure, and Performance of Venture Capital. PhD. Thesis, Harvard University, Chapter IV.

Gompers, P.A. (1996). Grandstanding in the Venture Capital Industry. *Journal of Financial Economics*, 42(1):133–156.

Gompers, P.A. and Lerner, J. (1996). The Use of Covenants. *Journal of Law and Economics*, 34(2):463–498.

Gompers, P.A. and Lerner, J. (1999). *The Venture Capital Cycle*. Cambridge MA: MIT Press.

Gompers, P.A. and Lerner, J. (2001a). The Venture Capital Revolution. *Journal of Economic Perspectives*, 15(2):145–168.

Gompers, P.A. and Lerner, J. (2001b). *The Money of Invention: How Venture Capital Creates New Wealth*. Boston MA: Harvard Business School Press.

Hellmann, T., Lindsey, L. and Puri, M. (2003). Building Relationships Early: Banks in Venture Capital. Working Paper, Stanford University.

Lin, T.H. and Smith, R.L. (1998). Insider Reputation and Selling Decisions: The Unwinding of Venture Capital Investments During Equity IPOs. *Journal of Corporate Finance*, 4(3):241–263.

Megginson, W.L. and Weiss, K.A. (1991). Venture Capitalist Certification in Initial Public Offerings. *Journal of Finance*, 46(3):879–903.

Tykvová, T. (2003). Venture-Backed IPOs: Investment Duration and Lock-Up by Venture Capitalists. *Finance Letters*, 1(2):61–65.

Weber, C. and Dierkes, M. (2002). *Risikokapitalgeber in Deutschland; Strukturmerkmale, Entscheidungskriterien, Selbstverständnis*. Berlin: Edition Sigma.

Appendix

Table A21.1 Variable definitions

Variable	Description
AGE	Age of the company at IPO (years)
BOOKSPAN	Width of the bookbuilding span; upper value minus lower value divided by the middle value
BTM	Book-to-market ratio
DSREP	Rank of the designated sponsor[a] with the lowest rank[b], the value is between 1 and 10 (deciles); 1 is the best rank
DURATION	Duration of the venture capital financing prior to the IPO (years)
HOTISSUE	Dummy variable: one, if the firm went public during the hot issue period (between March 1, 1999 and November 30, 2000), zero otherwise
INDEP	Dummy variable: one, if the lead VC is independent, zero otherwise
LOCK-DUR	Duration of the lock-up period of the lead VC (months)[c]
MEDIA	Dummy variable: one, if the firm belongs to Media & Entertainment industry, zero otherwise
MV	Market value at the IPO (mil. euro)
POSTIPOALL	VCs' share (= all VCs) after the IPO (in %)
PREIPOALL	VCs' share (= all VCs) before the IPO (in %)
PREIPOSINGLE	VCs' share (= all VCs) before the IPO (in %)
RETALL	Fraction retained by the VCs (= all VCs) after the IPO (in %); the pre-IPO share of this VC is labeled as 100%
RETSINGLE	Fraction retained by the single VC after the IPO (in %); the pre-IPO share of this VC is labeled as 100%
START-UP	Dummy variable: one, if the venture capital financing begins in the start-up or seed-phase (up to two years since the setting up of the company), zero otherwise
UNDREP	Rank of the lead underwriter[d] with the lowest rank, the value is between 1 and 10 (deciles); 1 is the best rank

[a] Each share on the Neuer Markt had to have at least two designated sponsors. Their main task was to provide liquidity for the trading of this security.
[b] The ranks are based equally on the number of their mandates on the Neuer Markt and on their rating by the German Stock Exchange in the preceding period (= quarter).
[c] As prescribed by the Rules and Regulations Neuer Markt, old investors are not allowed to sell their retained shares during the period of 6 months beyond the IPO. They, however, often commit themselves to holding their shares for periods longer than this requirement.
[d] The rank depends on his activities as the lead underwriter (the number of new issues on the Neuer Markt and their volume in the previous year).

22 Long-run venture-backed IPO performance analysis of Italian family-owned firms: What role do closed-end funds play?

Stefano Caselli and Stefano Gatti

Abstract

This chapter examines the long-run stock market performance of Italian initial public offerings between 1990 and 2005. We distinguish between family and non-family business IPOs using the power subscale F-PEC. Buy-and-hold abnormal returns are calculated in order to determine abnormal returns. Our results show that three years after going public, investors, on average, realized abnormal returns of −38.7% for Italian IPOs. However, non-family IPOs performed insignificantly better. Regression analysis shows that for the whole sample there is a positive size effect. In family-owned businesses, strong family involvement has a positive impact on long-run stock market performance, whereas the age of the firm has a negative influence. Specific attention is given in this chapter to the role played by closed-end funds. The presence of an institutional investor increases the abnormal return after three years for the whole sample. But, when a family-owned business has a closed-end fund in its shareholders group, this fact has a positive impact on long-run stock market performance: the highest performances for the whole sample are found in this group of firms.

22.1 Introduction

The aim of this chapter is to analyze medium to long-run performance of family and non-family firms that were listed on the Italian stock exchange, the Borsa Italiana, from 1990 to 2005.

The notion of a family-owned firm, as intended in the present empirical study, is based on a dual premise: the level of ownership, and the participation and involvement in management and control of the firm. Regarding the former, family-controlled firms are defined as those in which the founding family (also in terms of family relationship between partners) holds a sizable number of shares. As for the latter, the weight of the family in management and supervisory bodies was taken into consideration. This made it possible to do away with so-called 'entrepreneurial ventures' that have an ownership structure and managerial system very similar to family businesses. However, such ventures are much younger in age, have a less complex system of relationships, set objectives that are not wholly comparable, and operate in sectors and markets with a focus on new technologies (Marchisio and Ravasi, 2000).

The family business phenomenon is absolutely essential for economic development in general, and represents the main form of business in all advanced economic systems. For instance, according to Klein (2000), in Germany 60% of companies are family-controlled; these businesses secure 58% of all employment and generate 55% of the nation's GDP. Soria (2002) examines the same phenomenon in Spain and presents even more significant data. This country, in fact, has over 1.5 million family-owned firms, which account for around 60–65% of the GDP and provide jobs for more than 80% of the work force. Moving on to an investigation of the American or Italian context, the situation is nearly analogous (Colli, 2003; Colli et al., 2003; Yanagisako, 2002).

Despite the key role that family businesses play in terms of offering employment and producing wealth for the society as a whole, little attention has been paid to these enterprises by European economists. They have neglected to investigate the distinctive attributes of this success and have examined the features that distinguish family-owned firms from other kinds of businesses much too superficially. This chapter explores the valuation of family businesses by stock markets in the three years following the initial public offering in Italy, and follows studies on German and Spanish markets by Jaskiewicz et al. (2005).

In terms of the specific issue of IPOs, this chapter will offer a more in-depth look at a factor that is rarely mentioned in the literature, that is, similarities and differences between family and non-family businesses. For example, a characteristic trait of the former compared with the latter is the question (which has yet to be answered) relating to succession (Sharma et al., 2003), which is the number one cause of death for these firms. In fact, in Spain and Germany more than 85% of family-owned firms do not survive to the third generation. In Italy, on the contrary, the situation is somewhat better (Colli et al., 2003), both as a result of greater emotional involvement of family members and the smaller number of cases (on average, in Italy this type of firm is younger). In this kind of operational context, an IPO can be a tactic for solving the succession problem for family businesses, diversifying wealth and financing future growth of the company at the same time (Mazzola and Marchisio, 2003). This issue will be addressed later in this chapter, along with further implications of an IPO on management and expected behavior of family firms.

A study of IPOs among family businesses is also important from the perspective of individual investors. This is due to the discernible differences between IPO performance of these companies and that of similar operations undertaken by normal firms, which could give rise to very different trading and portfolio management strategies. In this sense, the present study can provide interesting ideas for asset management, or may prove an appropriate source of information for creating protection mechanisms for portfolio positions.

From an empirical standpoint, the relationship between IPOs and investment performance in the sphere of family-owned firms is quite unique. Indeed, investigations conducted to date bring inconsistencies to light. On one hand, some test results show significant underperformance of IPOs of family businesses, compared with non-family firms or other benchmark indices (Ehrhardt and Novack, 2003; Aussenegg, 1997). On the other hand, a vast bibliography attests to better long-run performance for listed family firms with respect to others (Villalonga and Amit, 2004; Anderson and Reeb, 2003).

From an institutional standpoint, unlike in other studies (Caselli et al., 2006; Caselli, 2005), here family businesses are not taken as one large set. In fact, the assumption in this chapter is that it is only logical to acknowledge the existence of variables linked to ownership and involvement in decision making that can impact IPO performance. To provide the most objective meaning to the concept of family firm, in this study, first the F-PEC approach (Astrachan et al., 2002) is used to measure the level of influence of the family in question in running the business. Then the relationship between this influence and overall market evaluation is determined.

The reasons for the choice of the time horizon, from 1990 to 2005, were primarily structural. First of all, during that time there was a sizeable increase and then a sudden drop in the number of IPOs. Second, the time frame in question provides an excellent example of the application of economic and financial integration policies resulting from the creation of the European Union.[1] Van der Elst (2000) points out that growth in European stock markets in the 1990s was essentially driven by the entrance of new businesses, a phenomenon especially apparent in Germany, France, and Spain.

Moreover, in these countries, evaluations of listed firms peaked during the year 2000. In terms of liquidity and trading volumes the Italian market has greatly improved, but is not among the frontrunners such as the U.K.,[2] France, Germany, and Spain.[3]

The AIdAF (Italian family business association) and the Borsa Italiana have shown special interest in promoting research on this issue, and have offered their know-how as well as access to their databanks. This has led to the decision to analyze the performance of Italian IPOs in an attempt to understand the reasons behind such operations and factors that can give rise to repercussions on performance. In other words, this study does not focus solely on performance, but also seeks to identify causes or contingent situations that have brought about end results.

The research method applied in this context is the same as that of Jaskiewicz et al. (2005). Assuming that the situation in Italy is comparable with that in other countries, or more specifically with the rest of the continent (La Porta et al., 1997), it is reasonable to suppose a priori that the findings of this empirical testing would be consistent with previous results. In other words, lacking other specific factors, it is only natural to assume that IPOs of family-run businesses typically perform worse than the overall market in Italy. This is true even though a priori one cannot claim that the underlying causes are the same as those in Germany, Spain, or the U.S.

This chapter is structured as follows: the next section summarizes the main results and the more interesting hypotheses gleaned from a comprehensive analysis of all existing empirical studies on IPOs and performance. The third section details the method utilized for compiling the sample and outlines the process that was implemented to obtain results. The following two sections provide data derived from applying the model of analysis, and an interpretation of these data. An outline is also given of the process used to come to an understanding of the reasons behind performance. In the final section, the key findings on the Italian financial system are summarized.

[1] The EU's interaction led to the creation of a single economic market in 1992 and paved the way for the introduction of the Euro as a common currency in 1999 for 12 member states. EU members on the continent have comparable bank-oriented financial systems, which typically feel little influence from stock markets. This is due to a high concentration of lending institutions as well as a pervasive influence of the banking sector in the governance of listed firms, resulting from shareholding by banks in these businesses.

[2] The U.K., though part of the European arena, differs greatly in terms of corporate governance because this country uses markedly different systems from those found in Continental Europe (Allen and Gale, 2000).

[3] For information on the situation in Germany and Spain, see Jaskievicz et al. (2005).

22.2 Literature and hypotheses

The aim of this section is to present the main results of empirical research on IPO performance, with particular reference to family businesses. In addition, the hypotheses to be empirically tested are illustrated. It must first be stressed, however, that because of the lack of any extensive bibliography on this issue, general conclusions and/or findings regarding foreign markets serve as guidelines for developing hypotheses regarding the Italian system.

The literature recognizes the existence of various interpretative models to explain the reasons why family firms go public. Beyond obvious strategic reasons (Maherault, 2004), there exists a role for transforming the function of the firm within its network of relationships (Anderson et al., 2005). Ritter (1991, 1984) proposes the theory of Hot Issue Markets as an explanatory model. The basic interpretation of this research is quite simple; it relates the decision to opt for listing on the regulated market with the level of share prices, holding that the IPO option is primarily an opportunistic move by firms with an eye to profiting from a bull run. According to Ritter (1991, 1984), IPOs occur more frequently when the stock market is on the rise, because when investors are optimistic they are willing to pay higher prices to buy stocks.

Beyond strategic and opportunistic motivations, Marchisio and Ravasi (2000) and Langemann (2000) also cite financial and institutional reasons prompting the decision to go public. The former arise out of the desire to gain stronger bargaining power in all relationships, to have greater chances for financing, and to enhance the possibilities for management to participate in corporate performance through appropriate incentive plans. The latter, instead, relate to the higher level of managerial complexity in terms of handling succession and shoring up the process of managerial professionalization.

Moreover, apart from the realities of businesses, the decision to go public, and the venture capital raised on the markets as a result, can be driven by other more generic reasons, such as the desire to boost growth rates or the need to reduce the debt–equity ratio.

In terms of ownership, examining the pros and cons of going public is strategically important to pinpoint the variables that investors take into account in weighing the characteristics of operations undertaken by firms, and to reduce informational asymmetries typical of IPOs. In fact, with IPOs, potential financial backers cannot know a priori whether the actual allotment of resources will coincide with what was promised at the outset. When investors know more about initiatives that take place on regulated markets, they can assess operations more accurately; consequently, they normally have a greater tendency to invest heavily (Leland and Pyle, 1977).

Once a firm is listed, the literature recognizes two performance phenomena that are critical both for longstanding shareholders in family firms, as well as newcomers in VC: (1) in the short run, an IPO is typically and notably underpriced, which converts into a considerably high return during the first day of listing (Kuklinski, 2003, who offers a broad, in-depth analysis of existing literature; Ritter, 1984; Ibbotson, 1975); (2) in the medium to long run, which is normally from three to five years, return on an IPO is lower than overall stock market performance (Jaskiewicz et al., 2005; Ritter, 1991).

The key results of this negative performance are illustrated in Table 22.1, which recaps research conducted in Europe and the U.S. In addition to returns, time horizons and

Table 22.1 Empirical research on IPOs in Europe

Country	Authors	Time horizon	Sample size	Sampling time	Abnormal return (%)
Austria	Aussenegg (1997)	1984–1996	51	60	−74%
Denmark	Jakobsen and Sorensen (2001)	1984–1992	76	60	−30.4%
Finland	Keloharju (1993)	1984–1989	79	36	−21.1%
France	Leleux and Muzyka (1997)	1987–1991	79	36	−30.3%
France	Derrien and Womack (2003)	1992–1998	264	24	−6.3%
Germany	Schlag and Wodrich (2000)	1884–1914	163	60	−7.8%
Germany	Schmidt (1988)	1984–1985	32	12	−10.2%
Germany	Uhlir (1989)	1977–1986	70	15	−11.9%
Germany	Wittleder (1989)	1961–1987	67	12	−4%
Germany	Ehrhardt (1997)	1960–1990	160	36	−5.2%
Germany	Hansson and Ljungqvist (1992)	1978–1991	162	20	−1.9%
Germany	Ljungqvist (1997)	1970–1993	145	36	−12.1%
Germany	Jaskiewicz, Gonzalez, Menendez and Schiereck (2005)	1990–2000	153	36	−32.8%
Italy	Giudici and Paleari (1999)	1985–1995	84	36	−2.6%
Poland	Aussenegg (1997)	1991–1996	57	36	20.1%
Portugal	Almeida and Duque (2000)	1992–1998	21	12	−13.8%
Spain	Alvarez and Gonzalez (2005)	1987–1997	37	36	−27.8%
Spain	Jaskiewicz, Gonzalez, Menendez and Schiereck (2005)	1990–2000	43	36	−36.7%
Sweden	Loughran, Ritter and Rydqvist (1994)	1980–1990	162	36	1.2%
Switzerland	Kunz and Aggarwal (1994)	1983–1989	34	36	−6.1%
Switzerland	Drobetz and Kammermann (2002)	1983–2000	120	14	−6.8%
Turkey	Kiymaz (1998)	1990–1995	138	36	44.1%
Great Britain	Levis (1993)	1980–1988	712	36	−8.1%

(*Continued*)

Table 22.1 Continued

Country	Authors	Time horizon	Sample size	Sampling time	Abnormal return (%)
Great Britain	Leleux and Muzyka (1997)	1987–1991	220	36	–19.2%
Great Britain	Espenlaub, Gregory and Tonks (2000)	1985–1992	588	60	–21.3%
Great Britain	Brown (1999)	1990–1995	232	36	–20.1%
Great Britain	Kurshed, Mudambi and Goergen (1999)	1991–1995	240	36	–17.8%
USA	Simon (1989)	1934–1940	20	60	6.2%
USA	Stigler (1964)	1949–1955	46	60	–25.1%
USA	Reilly (1973)	1963–1965	115	36	–20.7%
USA	McDonald and Fisher (2003)	1969–1969	142	12	–18.1%
USA	Gompers and Lerner (2003)	1935–1972	3661	60	–34.8%
USA	Ritter (1991)	1975–1984	1526	36	–29.1%
USA	Aggarwal and Rivoli (1990)	1977–1987	1598	12	–13.7%
USA	Loughran (1993)	1967–1987	3656	72	–33.3%
USA	Cusatis, Miles and Woolridge (1993)	1965–1988	146	36	33.6%
USA	Loughran and Ritter (1995)	1970–1990	4753	60	–30%
USA	Brav et al. (2000)	1975–1992	4662	60	–38.6%
USA	Ritter and Welch (2002)	1980–2000	6169	36	–23.4%

Source: Jaskiewicz et al. (2005).

sample sizes are also given to allow a fairer and more homogeneous comparison.[4] These studies show that for different samples, time horizons, sampling times, and countries, IPO performance is very well defined and that underperformance with respect to a chosen benchmark is an extensive phenomenon. It must be stressed, however, that the methodology used in each study may significantly affect results. From a geographical perspective, it can also be said that not all European countries are sufficiently covered. For instance,

[4] Barber and Lyon (1997) show that differences in methodologies utilized can greatly impact and modify abnormal return calculations. Consequently, the level of comparability of results is extremely limited. Quite probably, older studies yield less significant results because of the use of less sophisticated models. This naturally increases as the number of empirical studies rises.

there are several studies on the German market but, to the best of our knowledge, this is only the second study on the situation in Italy.

Admittedly, most of the literature concurs on the validity of both of the explanatory theories outlined above. In this chapter, however, as Jaskiewicz et al. (2005) propose, only the second conclusion is investigated with regard to Italy, though in greater depth. This hypothesis is explored and tested by taking into consideration the effect of the presence or absence of closed-end funds in the shareholders' group.

After framing the issue in general terms, various hypotheses can now be detailed that on the one hand relate to general notions concerning IPOs, while on the other they are drawn from distinctive traits of family firms.

The development of these hypotheses follows a common theme. The primary aim is to ascertain whether findings regarding IPOs in general can also be applied to operations undertaken by family businesses. Second, tests focus on understanding whether conclusions drawn regarding family businesses are also applicable in the Italian context. Specifically, the first three hypotheses refer to IPOs as a whole, the last two arise from evidence gleaned specifically from the sphere of family businesses.

22.2.1 The existence of a 'window of opportunity' (hot issue markets)

According to this approach, companies should go public when stock exchange listings are on the rise, so as to exploit a higher evaluation. In fact, realizing that market investors tend to trust optimistic forecasts on future results, companies could find it economically convenient to take advantage of this collective euphoria. In other words, optimism that typifies investor behavior translates into high market demand for shares in IPOs. This being the case, even immature companies, or businesses with performance that cannot easily be sustained, can present themselves to investors and sell their stock at high prices. From an empirical point of view (Ritter, 1991), firms that go public during periods of overoptimism often show considerably poorer performance in the years that follow, compared with companies that choose other times. Moreover, this propensity is much more pronounced among small companies with accelerated growth rates.

H1: For a family business, long-run underperformance, if it occurs, is more pronounced in the years following a high number of IPOs.

22.2.2 Market over-reaction

According to this line of reasoning, medium to long-run underperformance of IPOs represents a natural correction of the high yield captured on the first day of listing (i.e. Theory 2 is a consequence of Theory 1). In fact, De Bondt and Thaler (1987) and Ritter (1991) find evidence of analogous performance, in particular for smaller businesses and for those that succumb to significant underpricing.

H2: Underperformance, if it occurs, is greater for IPOs of family businesses with low capitalization.

22.2.3 The small firm effect

Brav and Gompers (1997) and Brav et al. (2000) point out that negative performance for IPOs can be linked to the broader issue of performance of SME stocks, which typically have low market value and/or a low debt–equity ratio. The distinguishing feature of each, in fact, is marked underperformance. As IPOs of family businesses normally involve smaller sums than IPOs of non-family firms (Maherault, 2004; Astrachan and McConaughy, 2001; Capaldo and Raffa, 1999), this may be a factor that explains why the former have worse performance than the latter.

H3: Underperformance, if it occurs, is greater for IPOs of family-owned SMEs.

Though several empirical studies have been conducted on IPO performance in Europe and the U.S., literature that focuses on family firms is rare. In addition, no source offers an adequate comparison of different situations in various geographical areas. Table 22.2 summarizes the major studies on family-owned firms, but results cannot be measured against one another because different methodologies and definitions were used. However, despite the lack of comparability, it can be stated that these IPOs underperform to a significant degree with respect to the market and IPOs of other companies. For this reason, beyond general motivations such as the small firm effect or market over-reaction, at least two more specific explanations can be recognized.

22.2.4 Blockholder control

Some time ago, Berle and Means (1932) addressed the issue of the relationship between performance and control. Later, several authors sought to ascertain the significance of this link without ever arriving at a definitive conclusion. On one hand, according to the

Table 22.2 Studies on IPOs of family-owned firms

Country	Authors	Time horizon	Sample number	Sampling time	Abnormal return (%)
Austria	Aussenegg (1997)	1984–1996	31	60	−118.6%
Germany	Ehrhardt and Novak (2003)	1970–1991	105	36	−8.1%
Germany	Lowinski and Schiereck (2003)	1991–1998	64	36	−59.2%
Germany	Kuklinski, Lowinski, Schiereck and Jaskiewicz (2003)	1977–1998	146	60	−43.4%
Italy	Mazzola and Marchisio (2003)	1995–2000	37	36	−31.7%
Germany	Jaskewicz, Gonzalez, Menendez and Schiereck (2005)	1990–2000	153	36	−32.8%
Spain	Jaskewicz, Gonzalez, Menendez and Schiereck (2005)	1990–2000	43	36	−36.7%

Source: Jaskiewicz et al. (2005).

tenets of the convergence of interest hypothesis proposed by Jensen and Meckling (1976), a strong concentration of ownership can align the interests of partners and management, which would ensure lower agency costs and fewer informational asymmetries. On the other hand, a high concentration of power and/or ownership increases the risk that the people in such positions could create entrenchments or defensive barriers, which would make external control practically impossible. In this respect, therefore, a high concentration of ownership or power corresponds to a potentially negative situation (Morck et al., 1988).

Since empirical studies provide no precise guidelines, in this chapter the control factor is examined utilizing the F-PEC technique, as well as the variable of ownership share. According to this model, to analyze the commitment of the family within their business, in addition to the family's shareholdings, one must also consider the presence of family members on the Board of Directors and in management, along with their roles in control functions. The next section details how this model was constructed and applied. Nevertheless, since it is not possible to know the impact on performance of ownership share a priori, two hypotheses are put forth here in this regard:

> H4a: Medium to long-run underperformance, if it occurs, is greater in family businesses in which the theory of convergent interests is respected.
> H4b: Medium to long-run underperformance, if it occurs, is greater in family businesses where family involvement is strong.

22.2.5 Business age

According to Ward (2001) and Maug (2001), the main goal of IPOs for family firms is to find a viable solution for problems linked to succession. For this reason, relatively speaking such operations are undertaken later in their life cycle, i.e. when these firms are already mature. Anderson and Reeb (2003) also assert and prove that the business age variable is a key factor to consider in analyzing performance.

Within the framework of this study, one could logically expect the age of a family firm to have a negative impact on performance, because problems relating to succession may be more pressing.

> H5: Medium to long-run underperformance, if it occurs, is greater for older family firms.

22.3 Data sample and methodology

The hypotheses put forth in the previous section were tested on a dataset of Italian IPOs dating from 1990 to 2005. Beginning with the total number of IPOs that took place during this time period, and utilizing the Borsa Italiana sector classification,[5] operations undertaken by certain enterprises were excluded: banks and/or financial institutions, foreign firms, companies for which complete datasets were unavailable,[6] and businesses listed on high-growth markets. Also, through the use of data provided by AIFI (the

[5] http://www.borsaitalia.it
[6] Specifically, Datastream databanks were used to gather information.

Italian private equity and venture capital association) and AIdAF, all companies could be categorized as family-owned and non, and venture-backed and non.

From 1 January 1990 to 31 December 2005 there were 189 IPOs in Italy, but the entire sample could not be used for the present study. A total of 38 IPOs were from the financial sector, 2 were foreign firms, 45 took place in high-growth sectors, and 6 showed discontinuity in terms of prices or other data that made analysis impossible. After dealing with various difficulties, the final sample consisted of 102 firms, 73 of which were family-owned. As far as the presence of VC investors, 34 of the total 102 firms and 21 of the 73 family businesses met this condition.[7]

In order to define family-owned firms, as mentioned above a special technique was used to clarify the role that families actually play in running such businesses. Specifically, to ascertain family influence, three factors were taken into account: ownership share, the presence of family members on the Board of Directors or in managerial roles, and the presence of family members on the Board of Auditors or in supervisory bodies.[8] Direct or indirect participation of more than 25% of total shareholders' equity (EQfam/EQtotal) was the minimum for defining the set of potential family firms.

Then, activities undertaken by family members within the companies in question were examined, making reference to corporate organizational charts, members of the Boards of Directors, or other managerial or supervisory bodies. Specifically, administrative influence was measured by comparing the number of family members (BoDfam) to the overall number of board members (BoDtotal), while supervisory board influence was calculated as the number of family members (SBfam) compared with the total number of members on this committee (SBtotal).

As proposed by Klein (2000) as well as Astrachan et al. (2002), in this chapter, too, we define family businesses (FB) as those that respect the following relationship:

$$FB \cong \frac{EQfam}{EQtotal} + \frac{BoDfam}{BoDtotal} + \frac{SBfam}{SBtotal} > 1 \qquad (22.1)$$

At a mathematical and statistical level, this refers to the F-PEC power subscale. The main advantage of this approach is the use of a continuous scale with its three subscales: power, experience, and culture. These subscales integrate most of the existing variables used for the definition of family businesses in the literature. Consequently, this approach can be interpreted on the one hand as a tool that can provide a map for objectively defining the concept of family-owned firms (Handler, 1989) and on the other, it may be seen as an objective, transparent approach that can produce comparable results even when applied in different geographical contexts (Jaskiewicz et al., 2005).

After having applied Equation (22.1) to each of the 102 IPOs, the number of family businesses that went public in Italy during the time period in question could be calculated. As Klein (2000) suggests, all companies with an FB score lower than 0.5 were excluded because they could not be defined as family businesses. Also eliminated from the group

[7] The small number of venture-backed companies may be attributed to at least two factors. First, private equity in Italy gained ground only in the second half of the 1990s. Second, the private equity and venture capital association (AIFI) began systematically gathering data on venture-backed operations only in 1995. See Caselli et al. (2006).

[8] On the importance and interpretation of decision making and supervisory bodies in family businesses, see Schulze et al. (2001), Zahra and Pearce (1989), Fama and Jensen (1983).

of family firms were those with an FB from 0.5 to 1, because in these cases the presence of family members, though significant, did not have a major impact on managerial traits. Only companies with an FB score of 1 or more were considered family businesses, and when this figure was greater than 1.5, the firm in question was defined as strongly family-oriented.

Of the whole sample of firms that went public in Italy from 1990 to 2005, 73 met the prerequisites of family businesses, that is, 72% of the total. These data are not comparable with the findings of Jaskiewicz et al. (2005), since their research sample also included firms with an FB > 0.5, while in the present study the minimum limit was set at 1. Nonetheless, Italy proves to have a higher number of family businesses than Germany or Spain. If the 0.5 minimum had been applied in the present study, more than 93% of the total number of companies in the sample would have been part of the family category.

The data in Table 22.3 illustrate that, on average, equity held by the family (EQfam) is exceptionally high. This fact alone explains nearly half the FB score for over half of the sample. In terms of corporate control, it can be stated that Italian family businesses tend to take power and make their influence felt, especially by holding sizeable blocks of shares in the company.

Once the two sets of businesses were identified, performance had to be calculated at the time of listing. Specifically, the concept of performance is the change in the company's market valuation measured by its daily stock price over a period of 36 months in comparison with the benchmark return. To eliminate any problem arising from the interpretation of the concept of performance, buy-and-hold abnormal returns (BHAR) were used instead of cumulative abnormal returns (CARs). The three main reasons for this choice were: (1) to preclude any estimation error that commonly results from CAR analysis, as Barber and Lyon (1997) point out; (2) to provide a performance estimate that can be derived from a portfolio actually held by an investor; (3) to be able to carry out periodic rebalancing, i.e. to make performance comparable with reference to different time horizons.

For all 102 companies that make up the initial sample, BHARs were calculated and compiled on a monthly basis over a time horizon of 36 months starting at time of listing, and adjusted for the expected benchmark performance. In analytical terms, the following equation was used:

$$BHAR = \frac{1}{N}\sum_{i=1}^{N}\left[\prod_{t=ti}(1+Rit)-1\right]-\left[\prod_{t=ti}(1+E(Rit))-1\right] \tag{22.2}$$

Table 22.3 F-PEC scores for family firms

F-PEC	Italy
Mean	1.46
Median	1.31
Standard deviation	0.61
EQfam <25%	0 firms
26% < EQfam <50%	11 firms
51% < EQfam <75%	24 firms
EQfam >75%	38 firms

where Ret is the return on stock *i* in month *t* net of the effect of dividends, new issues, split downs, and splits. *N* is the number of shares, *T* is the number of months (in this case, 36), *ti* is the date of the closing price on the first day of trading and *E(Rit)* is the benchmark return.

It is clear from Equation (22.2) that all IPOs have the same weight; in other words, an equally weighted system was adopted that assumes, at a portfolio level, an equal investment in all stock regardless of the size of the operation or of the company. The most obvious result of this method of calculation is that the weight of small issuances is much greater than it would be if criteria capable of weighting each issuance for its actual market value were used. As far as holding shares in portfolio, the underlying hypothesis assumes a holding period of 36 months and, in the case of delisting, a holding period equal to time on the market.

Another very interesting matter to consider when implementing the methodology is the choice of benchmark. Barber and Lyon (1997), Engel and Keilbach (2005, 2002) and Caselli et al. (2006) propose approaches based on a comparison of like pairs of companies. In the present study, this would mean a comparison between family and non-family businesses that differ solely in terms of family participation in ownership and/or decision making and family involvement in the management and control of the business.

Nonetheless, because of the limited size of the Italian market, a similar approach would not be applicable in every case, especially considering how significant the phenomenon of family companies has become. From a wholly practical viewpoint, adopting such a specific approach would mean comparing family-centered and somewhat less family-centered firms. For this reason, the Mibtel index, which is calculated on a daily basis by the Borsa Italiana, was used as benchmark. The performance of this index was calculated in the same way and with the same frequency as for individual shares of IPOs.

In order to corroborate the findings of Brav and Gompers (1997) and Brav et al. (2000), which show that underperformance occurs most frequently among SMEs, Equation (22.2) was also applied with reference to another market index capable of summarizing the overall performance of SMEs: the MSCI Small Cap in Euro.

Lastly, once BHAR was obtained, a distinction was also made between companies that had a VC investor in the shareholders' group from those that had no institutional investors. The aim was to simplify the analysis of the role of VC investors in market valuations.

22.4 Empirical results

Table 22.4 shows results on BHAR scores of the Italian IPOs in the sample. Positive (negative) values indicate higher (lower) performance of listed firms compared with the benchmarks.

Overall, it is clear that IPOs do underperform to a statistically significant degree, both in light of the country-based index (Mibtel), as well as the size-based index (MSCI Mid Cap).

Specifically, findings show the existence of an average negative abnormal return of 38.7% compared with the MSCI Mid Cap Index. This means that on average an IPO investment generates a loss of nearly 40% in the first three years. Family businesses show even worse results, as underperformance hits 42.5% when measured against the

Table 22.4 BHAR three years after the IPO

	Average	%BHAR < 0
	Sample total = 102 companies	
BHAR – Mibtel	−37.1%***	72%
BHAR – MSCI Mid Cap	−38.7%***	75%
	Family businesses = 73 companies	
BHAR – Mibtel	−40.7%***	81%
BHAR – MSCI Mid Cap	−42.5%***	84%
	Non-family businesses = 29 companies	
BHAR – Mibtel	−28.0%**	49%
BHAR – MSCI Mid Cap	−29.1%**	52%

***, ** Statistically significant at the 1%, 5%, and 10% levels, respectively.

same index. Considering only the national context (i.e. using Mibtel performance as the benchmark) results improve slightly but confirm the hypothesis of negative returns in the medium to long-run. In addition, these findings are also confirmed by other indicators, such as the percentage of negative BHARs within different groups in the study. The largest figures are found among family businesses.

At this point our aim was to verify the role played by VC investors, applying Equation (22.2) to more specific categories than simply family and non-family businesses. Findings are given in Table 22.5.

Data on the Italian market show the significant presence of venture backing within the shareholders group at the time of the IPO as guarantor of performance that is, on average, better than quotations. In fact, venture-backed businesses in general achieve much better results: the level of underperformance runs only from 4.7% to 6.2%, depending on the

Table 22.5 BHAR three years after the IPO, and contribution of venture capital investors

	Number of businesses	BHAR – Mibtel	BHAR – MSCI Mid Cap
Total sample	102	−37.1%	−38.7%
Family businesses	73	−40.7%	−42.5%
Non-family businesses	29	−28.0%	−29.1%
Venture-backed businesses	34	−4.7%	−6.2%
Non-venture-backed businesses	68	−53.3%	−55.0%
Venture-backed family businesses	21	+0.2%	−1.1%
Non-venture-backed family businesses	52	−57.2%	−59.2%
Venture-backed Non-family businesses	13	−12.7%	−14.3%
Non-venture-backed Non-family businesses	16	−40.4%	−41.1%

benchmark used. This is much lower than the overall average, and also lower than the figure for companies without venture backing.

The type of company that apparently benefits the most from a closed-end fund in its shareholders group is the family-owned firm, because data show either minimal underperformance (−1.2% measured against the MSCI Mid Cap Index) or in some cases even slight overperformance (+0.2% compared with the Mibtel). Moreover, these results are statistically significant compared with the scores for the group taken as a whole. At the same time, it can be stated that closed-end funds tend to work better in a family rather than a non-family context. However, this conclusion calls for further study, because in this chapter venture-backed family businesses are only those that can orchestrate relationships with the financial world in a most advantageous way.

As shown in Table 22.3, of the several companies included in this empirical study, management is not in the hands of members of the founding family but rather they participate by means of the share equity in their possession.

22.5 Explanations of IPO underperformance

In order to identify phenomena that can impact the results of an IPO, an econometric model was developed based on a linear regression between BHAR calculated with reference to the Mibtel and some explanatory variables for the different hypotheses described in Section 22.2, which are briefly outlined below:

1. YEAR – YEAR: the hot issue market was measured with a dummy variable equaling 1 if the company went public in a year when IPOs in Italy were highly concentrated (in 1991, from 1997 to 2000, and in 2003); otherwise it equaled 0 and had no influence for the purposes of the model.
2. MV: initial underpricing (Hypothesis 2) can be seen as a determinant of the price correction that is seen in the years following the IPO. This trend is more obvious for companies with low capitalization. In order to insert this element into the model, a dummy variable equal to 1 was used if the market value of the firm at the end of the first day of trading was in the lowest quintile of capitalization; if not, it was 0.
3. SIZE: the small-firm effect is taken into consideration by means of the natural logarithm of turnover at the end of the year in which the IPO took place.
4. %OWN: the impact of the ownership structure is estimated by the percentage of possible votes in assembly held by key shareholders. If this variable is positive, it signifies that the presence of a leading shareholder reduces agency costs and informational asymmetries (Hypothesis 4a), while a negative value demonstrates that management and ownership may be entrenched behind shareholding in the business (Hypothesis 4b).
5. F-PEC: with reference to the ownership structure, another variable incorporated in the econometric model is the F-PEC score. The hypothesis to be tested refers to whether the level of control, ownership, and management can influence medium to long-run performance. Clearly, when the F-PEC score is taken into consideration, the percentage of votes is of no importance, and vice versa.
6. AGE: the impact of the age of the business is quantified with a dummy variable equal to 1 if the firm is over 20 years old, and 0 if it is not. During empirical testing, other

numbers were also assigned, such as 25, 40, or 50, but no significant differences arose that would warrant these changes in the context of the present study.

Consequently, the final model (22.3) is as follows:

$$BHAR\,(Mibtel) = a_i + b_1{}^{*}Year_i + b_2{}^{*}MV_i + b_3{}^{*}size_i + b_4{}^{*}\%own_i + b_5{}^{*}F - PEC_i + b_6{}^{*}age + e_i \quad (22.3)$$

Table 22.6 shows the scores of the explanatory variables in the model when applied only to family businesses in the sample. Moreover, we opted not to make a distinction between venture-backed and non-venture-backed family businesses because the small sample size would have invalidated the quality of the findings. Regression 1 differs from Regression 2 because of the variable utilized to define the impact of the presence of the family on medium to long-term performance.

The only variables that can provide a significant explanation for performance of returns on Italian IPOs are the size and age of the firm. Specifically, we can assert that the larger the firm, the better the performance. Older firms, on the contrary, have poorer results, most likely because the problem of succession becomes more pressing. From this analysis, Hypotheses 3 and 5 prove to be valid in the national context and in the time frame in question. Worthy of note is the fact that despite a substantial difference in returns for family as opposed to non-family businesses, the presence of a blockholder does not impact performance. Consequently, both Hypotheses 4a and 4b must be rejected, likewise Hypotheses 1 and 2, which do not reach statistically significant levels.

In order to further test the relationship between performance and family participation in a business, Model (22.3) was applied first to family businesses in which the F-PEC falls between 1 and 1.5, and then to those with a score over 1.5. Results are summarized in Table 22.7.

Firm size and age are still explanatory variables, and their significance is very similar to what was seen above. Similarly, not even through further testing can Hypotheses 1 and 2 be accepted. Nonetheless, in terms of the relationship between performance and weight of core owners in the business, a statistically significant figure emerges that is positive when

Table 22.6 Explanatory variables of underperformance in the sample of family-owned businesses

Variables (73 firms)	Regression 1	Regression 2
Constant (a_i)	−0.547*	−0.524**
YEAR	−0.193	−0.204
MV	0.005	0.006
SIZE	0.158***	0.153***
%OWN	0.004	
F-PEC		−0.008
AGE	−0.511***	−0.509***

***, **, * Statistically significant at the 1%, 5%, or 10% level, respectively.

Table 22.7 Explanatory variables of underperformance as a function of F-PEC score

Variables (73 firms)	1 < F-PEC < 1.5 (33 firms)	F-PEC > 1.5 (40 firms)
Constant (a_i)	−0.791**	−0.782**
YEAR	−0.114	−0.106
MV	0.008	0.006
SIZE	0.173***	0.165***
F-PEC	0.185	0.222*
AGE	−0.544***	−0.536***

***, **, * Statistically significant at the 1%, 5%, or 10% level, respectively.

the F-PEC score is higher than 1.5. In fact, if the family is very active in the company, medium to long-term performance tends to be better, while when family influence is less intense (1 < F-PEC < 1.5) this relationship is not clear.

From these findings one can deduce that strong involvement by the owner family has a positive impact on performance, but this participation must not be limited to simply an equity stake. Since significant results were achieved only with F-PEC scores higher than 1.5, one can assert that shareholding is necessary, but alone it is not enough to impact company performance. In addition, the more the family is involved in the firm, the greater its impact on performance.[9] Consequently, the theory of convergent interest proposed by Jensen and Meckling (1976) is supported by empirical evidence, and Hypothesis 4a is proven to be true. Naturally, Hypothesis 4b must be rejected.

After having identified and analyzed the role of explanatory variables for family business performance, this study moved on to verify the feasibility of applying these conclusions to non-family firms as well. However, in order to frame the question in these terms, Model (22.3) was modified and broadened with the aim of taking into account various kinds of businesses and the correlations between different explanatory variables.

In analytical terms, the evolution described above yielded Equation (22.4):

$$BHAR\,(Mibtel) = a_i + \sum_{i=1}^{n} b_i{}^* X_i + c_i{}^* FAMILY + \sum d_i{}^* FAMILY^* X_i + e_i \tag{22.4}$$

where X_i are previously utilized variables.[10] (Again, this is an evolution of the model.) FAMILY is a dummy variable (equaling 1 if the firm is family-owned and 0 if it is not), while X_i^*FAMILY are the interaction terms of the variable FAMILY with MARKET VALUE, OWNERSHIP, AGE, and SIZE. From a financial viewpoint, in this way one can see whether some factors are more important for family or non-family businesses. Table 22.8 shows the outcome of applying Equation (22.4).

Both for family and non-family firms, empirical data confirm the small size effect (Hypothesis 3). Larger firms, on average, perform better than smaller companies, regardless of their classification or their core shareholder structure.

[9] These findings are in line with results gathered by Jaskiewicz et al. (2005) regarding the situation in Germany and Spain.

[10] Since the F-PEC score is not calculated for non-family firms, in Model (22.4) it does not appear among the explanatory variables (i.e. the X_i's).

Table 22.8 Explanatory variables for underperformance for the entire sample

Variables (102 firms)	Regression 3
Constant (a_i)	−1.105***
YEAR	−0.194
MV	0.236
SIZE	0.153***
%OWN	−0.002
AGE	0.188
FAMILY	0.346
FAMILY*MV	−0.118
FAMILY*SIZE	0.005
FAMILY*%OWN	0.003
FAMILY*AGE	−0.706***

***, **, * Statistically significant at the 1%, 5%, and 10% level, respectively.

Contrary to findings reported up to this point, from calculations with Model (22.4), the variable AGE is not statistically significant and is positive, while the interaction term FAMILY*AGE is negative and is statistically significant. The sum of these two figures is the overall effect of age on performance for family-owned firms, while for non-family businesses only AGE should be considered in the relationship between age and results, because in this case FAMILY*AGE is 0. (In fact, FAMILY equals 1 only if the firm is family-owned.) What emerges from all this is that for family-owned firms, age has a negative impact (0.188–0.706 = −0.518) approximately equal to the result from Model (22.3), while for non-family businesses the effect of age is not statistically significant. Once again, the fact that age negatively influences performance for family-owned firms is confirmed, quite probably because of problems associated with succession.

22.6 Conclusion

In this empirical study, IPO performances of family and non-family businesses that were listed on the Borsa Italiana from 1990 to 2005 were analyzed. To break down the sample and accurately identify those firms that could be grouped in the family category, the F-PEC score was calculated, as Astrachan et al. (2002) suggest. Specifically, firms with an F-PEC score above 1 were considered family businesses. In addition, with data provided by AIFI, firms that were backed by closed-end VC at the time of their IPO were distinguished from those that had no institutional investor among their shareholders.

As regards measuring IPO performance, a method was utilized that reflects a buy-and-hold investment strategy with a holding period of 36 months from the first day of listing. Findings from this study show the following:

- All IPOs performed much worse than the market as a whole, regardless of the benchmark used.
- Family businesses performed worse than non-family businesses, though the difference was not significant.

- Venture-backed firms had substantially better results than companies without closed-end venture backing.
- The type of firm that reaped the greatest benefit from having closed-end funds in its shareholders group was the family business; in some cases, in fact, its performance even exceeded that of the benchmark.

As possible explanations for underperformance in the medium to long-run with respect to stock market performance overall, the following factors were identified: size, age, and the influence of the owner family. Aspects such as a hot issue market, market over-reaction, or participation in share capital did not significantly impact IPO performance.

Brav and Gompers (1997) and Brav et al. (2000) prove that smaller firms have worse performance than larger firms. Conclusions drawn in this study are in line with the findings of these American authors. In some ways, the present results tend to support theirs because, beyond demonstrating lower performance of IPOs of family-owned firms versus others, for the entire sample a size effect was noted whose effect was independent of the presence of the family.

Underperformance among IPOs of family businesses is also related to the age of the firm: the older the company, the lower its performance, as the problem of succession becomes urgent. Moreover, the effect of this aspect is felt regardless of the level of family involvement. On the other hand, as far as non-family businesses are concerned, no significant relationship appears to exist between age and underperformance (see also Mazzola and Marchisio, 2003).

The degree of involvement of the owner family (i.e. total shareholding) in terms of decision making and control mechanisms has a positive impact on the firm's IPO performance. In this sense, the theory of convergent interest proposed by Jensen and Meckling (1976) is fully supported by data on Italian family businesses. At the same time, there is no link between equity held by the family and performance of the firm. These findings show that the influence and contribution of family members within the firm are seen in a positive light by the market only if they are involved in management, and not simply in VC financing. As Leland and Pyle (1977) also found, the degree of involvement in corporate management and control in Italy is interpreted as a positive sign by the market because of the enhanced quality of the firm as a whole.

References

Aggarwal, R. and Rivoli, P. (1990). Fads in the Initial Public Offering Market? *Financial Management*, 19:45–57.

Almeida, J. and Duque, J. (2000). Ownership Structure and Initial Public Offerings in Small Economies – The Case of Portugal. Mimeo, Lisbon University of Technology, Lisbon.

Allen, F. and Gale, D. (2000). *Comparing Financial Systems*. London: MIT Press.

Alvarez, S. and Gonzalez, V.M. (2005). Signalling and the Long-Run Performance of Spanish Initial Public Offerings (IPOs). *Journal of Business, Finance, and Accounting*, 32(1–2):323–348.

Anderson, A.R., Jack, S.L. and Drakopoulou Dodd, S. (2005). The Role of Family Members in Entrepreneurial Networks: Beyond the Boundaries of Family Firm. *Family Business Review*, 18(2): 135–154.

Anderson, R. and Reeb, D. (2003). Founding Family Ownership and Firm Performance: Evidence from the S&P500. *Journal of Finance*, 58(3):1301–1328.

Astrachan, J.H. and McConaughy, D.L. (2001). Venture Capitalist and Closely-Held IPOs: Lessons for Family Controlled Firms. *Family Business Review*, 14(4):295–312.

Astrachan, J.H., Klein, S.B. and Smyrnios, K.X. (2002). The F-PEC Scale of Family Influence: A Proposal for Solving the Family Business Definition Problem. *Family Business Review*, 15(1):45–58.

Aussenegg, W. (1997). Die Performance Österreichischer Initial Public Offerings. *Finanzmarkt und Portfolio Management*, 11(4):413–431.

Barber, B. and Lyon, J. (1997). Detecting Long-Run Abnormal Stock Returns: The Empirical Power and Specification of Test Statistics. *Journal of Financial Economics*, 43(1):341–372.

Berle, A. and Means, G. (1932). *The Modern Corporation and Private Property*. New York: Harcourt, Brace & World.

Brav, A. and Gompers, P. (1997). Myth or Reality? The Long-Run Underperformance of Initial Public Offerings: Evidence from Venture and Non-Venture Capital Backed Companies. *Journal of Finance*, 52:1791–1821.

Brav, A., Geczy, C. and Gompers, P. (2000). Is the Abnormal Return Following Equity Issuance Anomalous? *Journal of Financial Economics*, 56:206–249.

Brown, E. (1999). Long-Run Performance Analysis of a New Sample of UK IPOs. Mimeo, University of Edinburgh, Edinburgh.

Capaldo, G. and Raffa, M. (1999). Growth, Organization and Management of Family Firms in Italy: Critical Aspects and Research Areas. Université de Bordeaux Working Paper Series.

Caselli, S. (2005). Competitive Models of Corporate Banking within the Italian Banking System. *Small Business*, 1:143–167.

Caselli, S., Gatti, S. and Perrini, F. (2006). Are Venture Capitalists a Catalyst for Innovation or Do They Simply Exploit it? Working Paper, Bocconi University, Milan.

Colli, A. (2003). The History of Family Business, 1850–2000. Working Paper, Bocconi University, Milan.

Colli, A., Perez, P.F. and Rose, M.B. (2003). National Determinants of Family Firm Development? Family Firms in Britain, Spain and Italy in the Nineteenth and Twentieth Centuries. *Enterprise and Society*, 4(1):28–64.

Cusatis, P., Miles, J. and Woolridge, J. (1993). Restructurings Through Spin-Offs: The Stock Market Evidence. *Journal of Financial Economics*, 33:293–311.

De Bondt, W. and Thaler, R. (1987). Does the Stock Market Overreact? *Journal of Finance*, 40(2):793–805.

Derrien, F. and Womack, K. (2003). Auctions vs. Bookbuilding and the Control of Underpricing in Hot IPO Markets. *Review of Financial Studies*, 16:31–61.

Drobetz, W. and Kammermann, M. (2002). Performance of Initial Public Offerings: The Evidence for Switzerland. Mimeo, University of Basel and University of St. Gallen, Switzerland.

Ehrhardt, O. (1997). *Boerseneinfuehrungen von Aktien am Deutschen Kapitalmarkt*. Wiesbaden, Germany.

Ehrhardt, O. and Novack, E. (2003). The Effect of IPOs on German Family-Owned Firms: Governance Changes, Ownership Structure and Performance. *Journal of Small Business Management*, 41(2):222–232.

Engel, D. and Keilbach, M. (2002). Firm Level Implications of Early Stage Venture Capital Investments. An Empirical Investigation. ZEW Discussion Paper 02–82. Wien.

Engel, D. and Keilbach, M. (2005). Firm Level Implications of Early Stage Venture Capital Investments. An Empirical Investigation. ZEW Discussion Paper on Entrepreneurship Growth and Public Policy 22-05. Wien.

Espenlaub, S., Gregory, A. and Tonks, I. (2000). Reassessing the Long-Term Underperformance of UK Initial Public Offerings. *European Financial Management*, 6:319–342.

Fama, E. and Jensen, M.C. (1983). Separation of Ownership and Control. *Journal of Law and Economics*, 26(2):301–325.

Giudici, G. and Paleari, S. (1999). Underpricing, Price Stabilization and Long-Run Performance in Initial Public Offering: A Study on the Italian Stock Market Between 1985 and 1998. Mimeo, Politecnico di Milano, Milan.

Gompers, P. and Lerner, J. (2003). The Really Long-Run Performance of Initial Public Offerings: The Pre-NASDAQ Evidence. *Journal of Finance*, 58(4):1355–1392.

Handler, W. (1989). Methodological Issues and Considerations in Studying Family Businesses. *Family Business Review*, 2(3):257–276.

Hansson, B. and Ljungqvist, A.P. (1992). Mispricing of Initial Public Offerings – Evidence from Germany. Working Paper, University of Lund.

Ibbotson, R. (1975). Price Performance of Common Stock New Issues. *Journal of Financial Economics*, 2(1):235–272.

Jakobsen, J. and Sorensen, O. (2001). Decomposing and Testing Long-Run Returns: An Application on Danish IPOs. *European Financial Management*, 7:393–417.

Jaskiewicz, P., Gonzalez, V.M., Menendez, S. and Schiereck, D. (2005). Long-Run IPO Performance Analysis of German and Spanish Family-Owned Businesses. *Family Business Review*, 18(3):179–202.

Jensen, M. and Meckling, W. (1976). Theory of the Firm: Managerial Behaviour, Agency Costs and Ownership Structure. *Journal of Financial Economics*, 3(2):305–360.

Keloharju, M. (1993). The Winner's Curse, Legal Liability, and the Long-Run Performance of Initial Public Offerings in Finland. *Journal of Financial Economics*, 34:251–277.

Kiymaz, H. (1998). Turkish IPO Pricing in the Short and Long-Run. Mimeo, Bilkent University, Bilkent.

Klein, S. (2000). *Familienunternehmen-Theoretische und Empirische Grundlagen*. Wiesbaden: University of Wiesbaden.

Kuklinski, J. (2003). *Short and Long-Run Performance of Initial Public Offerings in the German Stock Market: The Family Business Experience 1977 to 1988*. University of Witten, Herdecke Germany.

Kuklinski, J., Lowinski, F., Schiereck, D. and Jaskiewicz, P. (2003). The Performance of Family-Owned Companies at the German Stock Market. Working Paper, European Business School, Oestrich-Winkel.

Kunz, R. and Aggarwal, R. (1994).Why Initial Public Offerings are Underpriced: Evidence from Switzerland. *Journal of Banking and Finance*, 18:705–723.

Kurshed, A., Mudambi, R. and Goergen, M. (1999). On the Long-Run Performance of IPOs. Working Paper, Case Western Reserve University, Tunis.

Langemann, A. (2000). *Ökonomische Vorteile Eines Börsenganges*. University of Frankfurt am Main, Germany.
La Porta, R., Lopez-De-Silvanes, F., Shleifer, A. and Vishny, R.W. (1997). Legal Determinants of External Finance. *Journal of Finance*, 52(3):1131–1150.
Leland, H. and Pyle, D. (1977). Informational Asymmetries, Financial Structure and Financial Intermediation. *Journal of Finance*, 32(2):371–387.
Leleux, B. and Muzyka, D. (1997). European IPO Markets: The Post-Issue Performance Imperative. *Entrepreneurship Theory & Practice*, 21:111–118.
Levis, M. (1993). The Long-Run Performance of Initial Public Offerings: The U.K. Experience 1980–1988. *Financial Management*, 22:28–41.
Ljungqvist, A. (1997). Pricing Initial Public Offerings: Further Evidence from Germany. *European Economic Review*, 41(7):1309–1320.
Loughran, T. (1993). NYSE vs. NASDAQ Returns: Market Microstructure or the Poor Performance of Initial Public Offerings. *Journal of Financial Economics*, 33:241–260.
Loughran, T. and Ritter, J. (1995). The New Issues Puzzle. *Journal of Finance*, 50(1):23–51.
Loughran, T., Ritter, J. and Rydqvist, K. (1994). Initial Public Offerings: International Insights. *Pacific-Basin Finance Journal*, 2:165–199.
Lowinski, F. and Schiereck, D. (2003). Familienunternehmen als Underperformer? Zur langfristigen Renditeentwicklung Boersennotierter Familienunternehmen. In Lange, K. and Schiereck, D. (eds), *Nachfolgefragen bei Familienunternehmen: Unternehmenskauf und Private Equity als Alternative zur Boerse*. Heidelberg: Finanz Colloquium Heidelberg.
Maherault, L. (2004). Is There Any Specific Equity Route for Small and Medium-Sized Family Businesses? The French Experience. *Family Business Review*, 17(3):221–235.
Marchisio, G. and Ravasi, D. (2000). Family Firms and the Decision to go Public: A Study of Italian IPOs. Working Paper, Bocconi University, Milan.
Maug, E. (2001). Ownership Structure and the Life-Cycle of the Firm: A Theory of the Decision to go Public. *European Finance Review*, 5(3):167–200.
Mazzola, P. and Marchisio, G. (2003). The Strategic Role of Going Public in Family Businesses' Long-Lasting Growth: A Study of Italian IPOs. Working Paper, Bocconi University, Milan.
McDonald, J. and Fisher, A. (1972). New Issue Stock Price Behaviour. *Journal of Finance*, 27:92–102.
Morck, R., Shleifer, A. and Vishny, R. (1988). Management Ownership and Market Valuation: An Empirical Analysis. *Journal of Financial Economics*, 20(3):293–315.
Reilly, F. (1973). Further Evidence on Short-Run Results for New Issues Investors. *Journal of Financial and Quantitative Analysis*, 8:83–90.
Ritter, J. (1984). The 'Hot Issue' Market of 1980. *Journal of Business*, 57(1):215–240.
Ritter, J. (1991). The Long-Run Performance of Initial Public Offerings. *Journal of Finance*, 46(1):3–28.
Ritter, J. and Welch, I. (2002). A Review of IPO Activity, Pricing, and Allocations. *Journal of Finance*, 57:1795–1828.
Schlag, C. and Wodrich, A. (2000). Has There Always Been Underpricing and Long-Run Underperformance? IPOs in Germany Before World War I. Mimeo, University of Frankfurt, Frankfurt.
Schmidt, R. (1988). Underpricing bei Deutschen Erstemissionen 1984/85. *Zeitschrift fuer Betriebswirtschaft*, 58:1193–1203.

Schulze, W.S., Lubatkin, M.H., Dino, R.N. and Buchholtz, A.K. (2001). Agency Relationships in Family Firms: Theory and Evidence. *Organization Science*, 12(3):99–116.

Sharma, P., Chrisman, J.J. and Chua, J. (2003). Succession Planning as Planned Behavior: Some Empirical Results. *Family Business Review*, 16(1):1–15.

Simon, C. (1989). The Effect of the 1933 Securities Act on Investor Information and the Performance of New Issues. *American Economic Review*, 79:295–318.

Soria, F. (2002). *Los Principales Retos de la Empresa Familiar en el Siglo XXI. Fusiones y Adquisiciones.* Capital & Corporate, Octubre, University of Mexico City.

Stigler, G. (1964). Public Regulation of the Security Markets. *Journal of Business*, 37:117–142.

Uhlir, H. (1989). Der Gang an die Boerse und das Underpricing-Phaenomen. *Zeitschrift fuer Bankrecht und Bankwirtschaft*, 1:2–16.

Van Der Elst, C. (2000). The Equity Markets, Ownership Structures and Control: Towards an International Harmonisation? FLI – Financial Law Institute Working Paper 2000-04, Louvain.

Villalonga, B. and Amit, R.H. (2004). *How do Family Ownership, Control and Management Affect Firm Value?* EFA 2004 Maastricht Meeting, Paper No. 3620, Stockolm.

Ward, J.L. (2001). Developing Effective Ownership in the Family-Controlled Business. *Director's Monthly*, 25(7):1–9.

Wittleder, C. (1989). *Going public: Die Publikumsoeffnung Deutscher Aktiengesellschaften.* Koeln: Institut fuer Wirtschaftspolitik.

Yanagisako, S.J. (2002). *Producing Culture and Capital: Family Firms in Italy.* Princeton NJ: Princeton University Press.

Zahra, S.A. and Pearce, J.A., II (1989). Boards of Directors and Corporate Financial Performance: A Review and Integrative Model. *Journal of Management*, 15(2):118–145.

23 Securitization and venture capital fundraising

Paul U. Ali

Abstract

Dedicated venture capital and private equity funds are an important source of finance for venture capital projects. In common with the VC projects in which they invest, these funds typically finance their investments through the issuance of equity interests, whether as common or preferred stock, trust units, or interests in limited partnerships. This chapter explores a new financing mechanism for venture capital and private equity funds, namely securitization. This development is yet another incident of the seeming rush to convergence of the equity-based market for managed funds and the debt-based securitization market. The chapter explains the legal structure of securitizations of venture capital and private equity funds. It also highlights the key legal issues arising out of the use of securitization to finance VC and private equity investments.

23.1 Introduction

Dedicated venture capital and private equity funds are the principal means by which early stage and expansion stage VC projects are financed in Europe. These funds are, however, no different to actively managed mutual funds that invest in listed equities, in that they too are, in essence, specialist management vehicles that invest the pooled contributions of their investors. The investors in European venture capital and private equity funds have, to date, been primarily banks and institutional investors based in the U.K., Sweden, and the Netherlands.

According to the EVCA (2006), approximately €72 billion was raised in the 2005 calendar year by European VC and private equity funds. Over two-thirds of the funds raised were sourced from banks (18%) and institutional investors (academic endowments, funds of funds, insurance companies, and pension funds) (52%). Only a minority of funds was sourced from the capital markets (1%).

That last figure is ripe for increase, given the increasing convergence in Europe of the private equity and securitization markets. This chapter presents an overview of the legal structure of private equity securitizations, which provide an obvious template for a capital markets mechanism for financing European VC funds.

23.2 European private equity securitizations

The use of securitization to finance private equity funds was pioneered by two Swiss private equity management firms: the Partners Group, which closed the Princess and Pearl securitizations in 1999 and 2000, respectively; and Capital Dynamics, which closed the Prime Edge and Pine Street securitizations in 2001 and 2002, respectively (Koenig, 2005). Most recently, SVG Capital, a fund of funds listed on the London Stock Exchange, closed the second of its Diamond private equity securitizations in January 2006 (Fitch Ratings, 2005).

These securitizations have each involved the issue to investors in the capital markets of mainly debt securities backed by interests in a diversified portfolio of equity interests. Equity interests in private equity funds have dominated these securitized portfolios, although the issuers have the ability, as in the case of the first Diamond private equity securitization that SVG Capital closed in September 2004, to include limited investments in VC funds in their portfolios (Moody's Investors Service, 2004; Standard & Poor's, 2004).

The structures employed in the securitization of these equity interests in VC and private equity funds are a modified version of the structures that are now routinely used by commercial banks in Europe to securitize their corporate loan books (Ali, 2005). The securities issued in these structures are familiar to investors in the European capital markets and, consequently, securitization offers an efficient means for European VC funds to source additional funds from the European capital markets.

23.3 Generic Collateralized Private Equity Obligations structure

The structures employed in the securitization of private equity funds are collectively known as Collateralized Private Equity Obligations (CPOs), signifying their evolution out of the Collateralized Debt Obligations (CDOs) used in the securitization of corporate loans by banks. The CPO structure, in common with CDOs and other cash securitizations, revolves around an orphan entity that holds equity interests in private equity funds and issues securities that are serviced out of the cash flows generated by those interests.

The entity itself will normally be structured as a limited liability company or a trust, but whatever the legal form of the entity, it is necessary to ensure that it is independent of the sponsor of the transaction (which is usually a manager of a fund of funds that invests in private equity funds) and that any transfers of interests in private equity funds from the sponsor to the orphan entity is on commercially defensible terms. This is to ensure that the corporate veil between the orphan entity and the sponsor remains intact so that there is no consolidation of the orphan entity's assets (and liabilities) with those of the sponsor. It also ensures that assets transferred from the sponsor to the orphan entity cannot be reclaimed by the creditors of the sponsor, by unwinding any such transfer as a fraudulent conveyance or voidable preference, on the sponsor's insolvency.

The exposure to the underlying private equity funds can be achieved by the orphan entity investing directly in a diversified portfolio of private equity funds. It is, however, far more common for the exposure to be achieved through an intermediated fund of funds (one managed by the sponsor of the CPO). The proceeds raised by the orphan entity from the issue of securities are exchanged for equity interests in the fund of funds that, in turn, uses the proceeds received by it to make direct investments in a range of private equity funds.

The same result can be achieved by substituting a total return swap for the fund of funds. Under this swap, the orphan entity receives, in exchange for the remittance of the proceeds from the issuance of securities, variable amounts linked to the performance of a notional portfolio of equity interests in private equity funds. Total return swaps are more likely to be found in privately placed, unrated CPOs. Rated CPOs, in contrast, invariably employ a fund of funds to achieve the necessary exposure.

The securities issued by the orphan entity to the investors are predominantly in the form of debt instruments (with the possible exception of the junior-most tranche) and are serviced out of the cash flows generated by the secondary sale or, more commonly, the redemption of the equity interests held by the orphan entity in the fund of funds. The redemptions are, in turn, financed by the fund of funds selling or redeeming the equity interests held in the underlying private equity funds. On maturity, the securities issued by the orphan entity will similarly be redeemed for cash out of the proceeds of the interests held by it in the fund of funds.

These securities are limited recourse securities, in common with the securities issued in all other securitizations. Consequently, investors are entitled only to receive their pro-rata share of the proceeds generated on the maturity of the securities from the orphan entity's realization of its interests in the fund of funds. The orphan entity is therefore not liable to the investors for any shortfall on the principal amount following its distribution of the proceeds of realization.

Also in common with other securitizations, the securities issued in a CPO will be credit-tranched. Credit-tranching involves the combination of one or more security interests with a priority agreement to effect the division of the securities into differentially rated tranches. The higher-rated or more senior tranches of securities are accorded seniority or preference in terms of their claims against the orphan entity for payment of principal and interest. The lower-rated or mezzanine and junior tranches therefore insulate the senior tranches against loss. Consequently, the coupon payable on a particular tranche of securities varies inversely with the relative ranking of that tranche.

23.4 Investors in CPOs

CPOs, while employing CDO technology, differ from the majority of CDOs in one important respect. The latter are predominantly used by commercial banks to manage their balance sheets and capital adequacy requirements. The securitization of corporate loans, which is effected by a sale of those loans to an orphan entity, removes those loans from the balance sheet of the transferor bank and also allows that bank to release the risk capital held by it against the loans. In contrast, CPOs are not motivated by balance sheet and capital adequacy concerns. Instead, CPOs are employed as distribution platforms for the underlying private equity funds (in the same way that funds of funds are used to distribute interests in private equity funds) and as a source of finance for those funds.

In addition, the return characteristics of the CPO differ markedly to the return characteristics of the majority of CDOs. Where a CDO has been established for balance sheet or capital adequacy purposes, the portfolio of corporate loans held by the orphan entity remains generally static (subject to the replacement of loans that no longer satisfy the portfolio criteria or the replenishment of loans that have been paid down). The return to the investors reflects principal and interest payments received by the orphan entity as the loans are paid down. The orphan entity and hence the investors are thus in an analogous position to a lender of the loans.

The orphan entity and the investors in a CPO are, on the other hand, in an analogous position to an actively managed mutual fund and its investors, respectively. The portfolio of equity interests held by the orphan entity is a dynamic portfolio, with the securities issued by the entity serviced out of the cash flows generated from the active trading of the equity interests, that is the capital gains (or losses) realized by the orphan entity on its investments in the underlying private equity funds via an intermediated fund of funds.

The returns received by the investors in a CPO are also transformed from those received by the orphan entity on the underlying private equity funds. In a balance sheet-driven CDO, both the orphan entity and the investors receive returns on debt (principal and interest on the underlying loans for the former, and principal and interest on the securities issued by the orphan entity for the latter). The orphan entity in a CPO, however, receives equity-based returns on the private equity funds (being the variable capital return received from the realization of its interests in the intermediated fund of funds) but pays returns on debt to the investors (again, principal and interest on the securities issued by it). Capital losses on the orphan entity's holding of private equity funds will be reflected in reduced principal payments to the investors (in the same way that the loss of principal attributable to borrower default or insolvency will be passed on to investors in CDOs) but capital gains made by the orphan entity will, in general, only partially be passed on to the investors through their use to finance the enhanced coupons payable on the securities issued by the orphan entity. The balance of the capital gains will ordinarily be remitted to the manager of the orphan entity's portfolio (in the form of performance fees) but may, in some structures, be shared with the junior-most tranche of securities issued by the orphan entity (where such a tranche is issued, it will often be held by the manager or interests associated with the manager). That tranche of securities, unlike the other, more senior, tranches, is more properly characterized as a hybrid, rather than debt.

23.5 Funds of private equity funds

The insertion of a fund of funds between the issuer in a CPO and the underlying private equity funds has two important benefits for investors (Ali, 2005). First, the investors can, through the fund of funds, obtain exposure to private equity funds that are rarely traded, closed to new investors, have relatively high minimum investment thresholds, or have relatively high outstanding commitment requirements. Second, funds of funds may offer liquidity advantages by providing an alternative means for investor exit.

These advantages, however, do not come free of certain drawbacks of which investors must be aware (Ali, 2004). Funds of funds are relatively expensive, as investors in a CPO will find that the returns on the underlying private equity funds will be depleted by the fees levied by the managers of those funds and also the manager of the fund of funds (and these fees will be in addition to the fees payable to the manager of the CPO) (Brown et al., 2002).

In addition, the increased liquidity offered by the fund of funds may prove to be a drag on returns (as the fund of funds must maintain a cash buffer to provide greater liquidity than the underlying private equity funds) or illusory (as rather than redeeming interests directly in the underlying private equity funds, the orphan entity, when it seeks to realize its investment, will in fact be redeeming fractional interests in the interests in the underlying private equity funds) (Ali et al., 2003). The assertion of enhanced liquidity is also questionable. In practice, the secondary market for the underlying interests in private equity funds is largely illiquid, with sales often being made under pressure and thus at deep discounts (Fitch Ratings, 2006).

Investors may, moreover, find that the diversification benefits of the fund of funds have been overstated. The fund of funds may be overdiversified by being spread across too many private equity funds. This may result in the dilution of the contribution of individual private equity funds to the return generated by the fund of funds (Lhabitant and De Piante Vicin, 2004). There is also the risk of duplication of investment positions within the fund of funds, leading to the greater correlation of returns generated by the individual constituents of the securitized portfolio (Lhabitant, 2002). Both these results have been demonstrated in the case of funds of hedge funds.

23.6 Conclusion

Securitization offers European VC funds an efficient and familiar means to increase the share of funds sourced from the capital markets. It is efficient because the base technology – Collateralized Debt Obligations – has already been successfully employed in the European capital markets to finance private equity funds; it is familiar because investors in the European capital markets understand and are comfortable within the base technology. Moreover, the portfolios of private equity funds that have been securitized to date have included limited investments in VC funds. Accordingly, it is only a relatively small step to securitize a portfolio of predominantly equity interests in VC funds.

Having said that, there are two key points that prospective investors in a securitization of VC funds need to be aware of. First, the returns delivered to them will, as a general rule, be debt-based, in contrast to the equity-based returns they would have received had they invested directly in private equity funds or indirectly in such funds via a fund of funds. Second, the use of an intermediated fund of funds in the securitization means that the investors will encounter the same issues as if they had invested directly in a fund of funds, rather than indirectly via a securitization vehicle.

References

Ali, P.U. (2004). Funds of Hedge Funds and Fiduciary Investors. *Australian Business Law Review*, 32(7):362–366.

Ali, P.U. (2005). Applying Securitization Technology to Hedge Funds. In Gregoriou, G.N., Hubner, G., Papageorgiou, N. and Rouah, F. (eds), *Hedge Funds: Insights in Performance Measurement, Risk Analysis, and Portfolio Allocation*. Hoboken NJ: John Wiley & Sons, Inc.

Ali, P.U., Stapledon, G. and Gold, M. (2003). *Corporate Governance and Investment Fiduciaries*. Rozelle, New South Wales: Lawbook Company.

Brown, S.J., Goetzmann, W.N. and Liang, B. (2002). Fees on Fees in Funds of Funds. Working Paper, Yale International Center for Finance, New Haven CT.

European Private Equity and Venture Capital Association (EVCA) (2006). *Annual Survey 2005* (June).

Fitch Ratings (2005). *SVG Diamond Private Equity II plc*. Credit Products Presale Report (22 December).

Fitch Ratings (2006). *Going Public with Private Equity CFOs*. Credit Products Criteria Report (6 February).

Koenig, O. (2005). Securitisation of Private Equity. In de Vries Robbe, J.J. and Ali, P.U. (eds), *Securitisation of Derivatives and Alternative Asset Classes*. The Hague: Kluwer Law International.

Lhabitant, F.S. (2002). *Hedge Funds: Myths and Limits*. Chichester: John Wiley & Sons, Inc.

Lhabitant, F.S. and De Piante Vicin, M.L. (2004). Finding the Sweet Spot of Hedge Fund Diversification. Working Paper, EDHEC Risk and Asset Management Research Center, Nice, France.

Moody's Investors Service (2004). *SVG Diamond Private Equity plc*. International Structured Finance Pre-Sale Report (19 July).

Standard & Poor's (2004). *Diamond Private Equity plc*. Credit Ratings – Presale Credit Reports (9 August).

24 Total loss risk in European versus U.S.-based venture capital investments

Dieter G. Kaiser, Rainer Lauterbach, and Denis Schweizer

Abstract

The highest risk in venture capital and private equity investments is the total loss of the capital invested in one deal. This chapter is the first to provide evidence that there are systematic differences regarding the total loss risk for European and U.S.-American venture capital (VC) and private equity investments. In this study we measure the risk of total losses for a set of investments twofold: (1) the probability of one failure to the total number of investments in a given fund portfolio, and (2) the fraction of capital lost in one failure to the total capital injected in all deals of a fund portfolio, which we define as the total-loss–capital ratio. We use a unique dataset and analyze 1011 matched private equity and VC investments in Europe and the U.S. during the period of 1979 through 2003 in regards to total losses.

24.1 Introduction

Research on specifics of VC financing in Europe has concentrated foremost on legal and regulatory aspects (Bottazzi and Da Rin, 2004; Desai et al., 2003; Muzyka and Birley, 1996) as well as on return characteristics (Diller and Kaserer, 2004: Hege and Palomino, 2003). While previous studies have confirmed several differences in VC and private equity financing between Europe and the U.S. (Schmidt and Wahrenburg, 2004; Schwienbacher, 2002), the aspect of risk differences has not been yet analyzed in detail. As the highest risk in VC and private equity investments is the total loss of the capital invested in one deal, we focus on the empirical analyses of this ultimate risk. In this study we measure the risk of total losses for a set of investments twofold: (1) the probability of one failure to the total number of investments in a fund portfolio, and (2) the fraction of capital lost in one failure to the total capital injected in all deals of a fund portfolio, which we define as the total-loss–capital ratio. We use a unique dataset by merging the Venture Economics and CEPRES databases and analyze 1011 matched private equity and VC investments in Europe and in the U.S. during the period of March 1979 through November 2003, in regards to total losses. In each total loss, the complete capital invested in this stake is lost. To assess the risk of total losses, fund managers usually do not work with quantitative risk models, but apply heuristics based on their investment experience for the selection and monitoring of their portfolio companies (Gompers et al., 2005). To share risks, fund managers syndicate their investments according to Wilson (1968) as well as Lockett and Wright (2001). Venture capitalists have developed special instruments such as staging to mitigate the specific risks inherent in young firms and high technology, as confirmed by Gompers (1995) and Sahlmann (1990). Therefore, we analyze this dataset to test three hypotheses in detail concentrating on the following aspects: (1) investment experience of the fund management, (2) syndication of a stake with other investors, and (3) the focus of the investor on venture capital. After analyzing the total dataset for these hypotheses, we investigate the commonalities as well as differences in regards to total losses for U.S.- versus European-based deals.

Our results show that more experienced European investment firms prefer a lower probability of failure at the expense of a higher total-loss–capital ratio. We conclude that based on cultural differences the more experienced European firms seem to be more focused on the avoidance of a failure than on the amount of capital lost.

This chapter is structured as follows: in Section 24.2 the hypotheses are developed. The dataset is introduced in Section 24.3. In Section 24.4 we develop a model regarding the statistical significance of total losses. The results of the econometric analyses are thereupon presented and interpreted in Section 24.5. Finally, the conclusion follows.

24.2 Determinants of total losses of pre-market equity capital stakes

Equity capital stakes of publicly listed companies have been analyzed with a variety of risk models that are not optimal when applied to private companies. Common risk measurements of listed companies such as volatility, lower partial moments, and value-at-risk are based on daily measurable stock prices. These risk measurements are not suited for stakes of private companies, because they are long term, not easy to convert into liquid assets, and their rating is carried out in longer intervals through the investment of a new investor. Because the changes in value are not transparent and are not measurable on a daily basis they are subject to a certain subjective evaluation and the computed volatility can be underestimated (smoothing). In addition, there is the inefficiency of the markets, the long transaction times and the high transaction costs. The risk of private equity capital stakes is thus more difficult to quantify. To give consideration to the inherent properties of private equity and VC investments, new risk measurements and their determinants need to be analyzed.

For risk analysis we use two types of measurement. The first is the probability of total loss, which we define as the ratio of investments ending with a write-off to the total number of investments in a sample. In our analyses we take all investments of a private equity or VC fund as the sample. This probability is similar to the drop-out rate in loan financing, where the fact of a total loss is considered regardless of the capital lost per write-off.

$$Probability\ of\ total\ loss = \frac{\sum investments\ ending\ as\ write\text{-}off\ [number]}{\sum all\ investments\ of\ a\ sample\ [number]}$$

Second, to capture the capital lost per failure, we introduce the following asymmetric risk measurement: the total-loss–capital ratio. We define a consistent risk measurement for various magnitudes of funds by setting the lost capital per written-off investment in relation to the total capital that the fund has invested in all deals up to that observation moment. To standardize the values each financing is adjusted for inflation with the U.S. consumer price index and subsequently computed on the basis of 2003 real U.S. dollars. As a dependent variable for our analysis the total-loss–capital ratio per stake results from this as follows:

$$\text{Total Loss Capital Ratio per Stake} = \frac{\sum \text{Payment in lost Portfolio Management Company}_{Fund(i)}[\$]}{\sum \text{Payment in all Portfolio Management Companies}_{Fund(i)}[\$]}$$

As financial intermediaries, fund managers make an active selection and weighting decision that should optimize the risk–return profile of the fund. While for an investor in a fund the whole fund return is relevant, this return is earned only through each particular deal investment decision of the fund management. We thus analyze factors that are relevant for the particular investment decisions.

The total-loss–capital ratio of private equity capital stakes depends on many factors that cannot be extensively analyzed in the context of this confined survey. Earlier work, for example from Amit and Thornhill (2003), shows that company-specific factors, such as a lack of entrepreneurship or adjustment difficulties to changing market challenges, can be the cause of company failures. When analyzing stake losses, we do not concentrate on factors that are company-specific but deliberately focus on factors that are specific for financial intermediaries. Through those surveys, present work about total losses can be complemented. In this chapter we focus on three relevant questions: (1) a particular fund manager makes his stake decisions subjectively on the basis of heuristics and experience. Our first question is thus about the effect of the investment experience of the fund manager on the total-loss–capital ratio. (2) Stake decisions are not made independently of particular funds but, in the case of syndicated stakes, also collectively and parallel to several funds. According to the theory of Wilson (1968), in the case of syndication, a group of decision makers take a collective risk (decision making under uncertainty) and share the collective profit. Through syndication, the investors aim at risk sharing that, in the case of the highest risk, the total loss, has a special weight. Within the consortium each individual investor can decide which stake ratio the particular stake has concerning his fund. Because of the above-mentioned relevance of syndication for each investor we focus in our second question on the role of syndication concerning total losses. (3) Venture capital is generally exposed to higher risk because of the early phase risks and technology risks of young and innovative companies. The professional practice with these higher risks of loss forces VC funds to the application of instruments that control the magnitude of the particular total losses as strictly as possible in order to improve overall the limit of the lost capital for the fund. Because of the generally higher risk of this kind of investment, limitations of particular total losses are necessary so that the total loss of the fund does not become disproportionately high. Our third question thus concentrates on the special characteristics of VC funds concerning total losses.

24.2.1 Investment experience of the fund management

Institutionalized investors of private equity capital are usually venture capital and private equity companies that, through funds, take stakes in portfolio companies with marked-off capital amounts and maturities. As professional financial intermediaries these funds represent the interests of their investors relating to the portfolio companies. One of those interests is the aim to achieve a maximal profit at minimal risk. Compared with the debt capital offering of banks, it would seem consequential if those funds developed and applied systematic models for estimating the risk of equity capital stakes. In practice, however, those funds usually do not use standardized risk models but rather heuristics and personal evaluations, which are largely based on the experience and the know-how of the fund manager. There are different reasons for this. On the one hand, relevant qualitative factors are in part difficult to transfer to quantitative models. Examples are the performance of the executives of a portfolio company or the competitiveness of newly developed products and services. On the other hand, the relevant risk factors and their evaluation in various industries, markets, and business stages can vary greatly. There exists, for example, a clear difference between the risk of getting a new drug through long-lasting and costly admission procedures and the risk of bringing a new software for mobile communication devices to market when the target market has not yet developed. In a growth scenario with a build-up of a new sales and distribution branch, other risk factors are relevant compared with consolidating a firm. One could basically say: the more expertise and knowledge the fund manager has in the particular case, the better the risk–profit evaluation. With every stake the fund manager holds, his expertise and knowledge increase. Thus, with increasing investment experience of the fund manager, his selection expertise for evaluating total losses and also his skill of constructive influence on the portfolio company in order to avoid total losses increases. From this conclusion, the first question for the empirical analysis can be deduced:

> Question 1: Can the increasing investment experience of a fund manager reduce the default risk of an equity capital stake?

With each fund that the fund manager has managed up to the time of the respective equity capital stake, his investment experience has increased. We thus measure the experience with the variable 'number of funds of the fund manager'. Furthermore, we assume that the fund management teams stay relatively constant across the various funds.

24.2.2 Syndication

A syndication occurs if more than one investor has stakes in an equity stake. Various articles explore the reason for syndication. Wilson (1968) develops the theory that investors use syndication to reduce and share risk. Admati and Pfleiderer (1994) explain in a theoretical model that VC investors syndicate their stakes in particular in the late financing rounds in order to hold their share in a company constant. Lerner (1994) claims, with the help of empirical surveys, that experienced investors in particular use syndication to gain information before acquiring company stakes. Amit et al. (2002) build upon this survey and explain, with their empirical surveys, that investors do not syndicate so much to optimize their stake selection but mainly to add value to the consortium through the additional knowledge, contacts, and experience of the other investors. Lockett and Wright (2001) examine reasons for syndication on the basis of 60 companies and find risk sharing and risk reduction as the main reason. Lockett and Wright's survey (2003) confirms that investors use syndication on the one hand for resource-based risk reduction and, on the other, for a wider diversification and spreading of the financing risk to several investors (risk sharing). Company stakes that require particular high sums of invested capital can involve particularly high risks, which a single investor might not want to take on completely. Thus, among other reasons, investors syndicate in order to use the chances collectively and, at the same time, share the risk. Since present surveys agree that syndication is used for sharing and reducing of stake risks, and that a total loss is the highest risk of a stake, we analyze whether syndication is especially observable in the case of total losses. From this we deduce the second question of our empirical analysis:

> Question 2: Do fund managers syndicate in particular in the case of risky stakes?

24.2.3 Investment focus on venture capital

Companies in early stages of development and in the technology sector have a particularly high default risk. This is a specialist field of fund managers who focus on offering venture capital. They generally have special knowledge of technology markets and a sound understanding for the business models of young and innovative companies. On the one hand, VC fund managers can better evaluate the risk with their special knowledge and experience and they can support the companies in their development. On the other hand, they generally do not offer the investment capital in one single advance payment but invest the capital step by step in partial payments depending on the development of the company. This gradual financing is called staging and can reduce the financing risk systematically. Sahlman (1990) characterized staging as an effective instrument for controlling company stakes. Staging can alleviate information asymmetries and agency conflicts. Gompers (1995) claims that the main advantage of staging is that at each partial payment the fund manager has the option to abort the project. Venture capital funds, compared with private equity funds, apply staging mainly to limit the loss of the particular stake in time in the case of a negative development. We thus have the third question:

> Question 3: Is the share of a total loss in the total capital invested smaller for venture capital funds than for funds with other investment focuses?

24.3 Data description

For generating the dataset, the contents of the Venture Economics databank was compared with the information from the CEPRES databank in November 2003, and the information about equity capital stakes that are available in both databanks were merged. The dataset is described in detail by Krohmer and Lauterbach (2005). While the data from Venture Economics are solely based on information that has been voluntarily provided by the fund companies, the CEPRES databank contains information that has been partially verified by certified accountants in the context of a due diligence audit. By merging the information of congruent stakes, the validity of the information increases. Both databanks, independently of each other, contain extensive details on equity capital financing, but measure partly different characteristics of each financing: Venture Economics, for example, contains information for assessing financing rounds of portfolio companies, which does not exist in CEPRES. CEPRES, on the other hand, provides information about the precise cash flows for each investment, which is missing in Venture Economics. By merging the information of each financing that coincide in both databanks, over 150 original variables from both databanks can be additionally analyzed for each financing. Accordingly, a very detailed analysis is possible for the intersection of both datasets. At the time of merging, the substantially larger databank, Venture Economics, contained over 220 000 finance cases.

Each of those has been compared with the entries of the CEPRES databank that were available at that time: 5308 investments in 4476 companies, which were conducted by 229 private equity and venture capital funds from 74 different investment management firms.

The complete merged dataset contains 1747 investments for which the following four criteria are congruently available in both databanks: (i) the name of the investment management firm, (ii) the name of the fund, (iii) the name of the portfolio company in which the fund invested, and (iv) the date at which the investment was conducted. All unrealized investments were removed from this dataset since this survey concentrates on the characteristics of total losses compared with other realized and only partially realized stakes.

After this data reduction the dataset contains 1011 different investments from 136 different venture capital and private equity funds that are applied from 23 investment management companies. A total of 169 of those investments have been total losses. This corresponds to a proportion of 16.7% of all observed stakes.

The dataset can be considered representative because, with respect to the distribution of important aspects, it matches the total market for private equity and VC stakes. The frequency distribution of the timing for the beginning and the end of the investments corresponds with the market development for the observed period. The country-specific frequency distribution of the stakes is comparable with the magnitude of the regional private equity and VC markets: most of the investments (854) were made in the U.S. The rest are divided between 21 countries in Europe, Asia, and Latin America. In Europe, the U.K. is represented with 110 investments, followed by Germany with 51, and France with 43. The industry sectors in Europe are portioned out as follows: information technology (22.22%), healthcare and life science (14.96%), consumer discretionary (11.97%), industrial production (10.26%), internet and media (9.40%), telecommunication (6.84%), financial services (2.99%), materials (2.14%), services (1.71%), and others (17.52%). In comparison with Europe, the industry sectors in the U.S. are portioned out as follows: information technology (24.55%), healthcare and life science (18.78%), internet and media (11.04%), industrial production (10.54%), consumer discretionary (8.90%), telecommunication (7.08%), financial services (1.98%), materials (1.98%), services (0.82%), and others (14.33%). Overall, 454 investments are attributed to the high-tech sector.

Following the analysis of the total loss risk subject to the impact of manager experience, the sector of the investment, as well as the age of the investment, it is important to compare the distinctive differences and mutual features between the U.S. and Europe (see Table 24.1).

European investment managers seem to be more risk averse and seemingly try to minimize the number of losses. Nevertheless, in the case of a loss, European managers seem to be more strongly affected by total loss risk than their American colleagues. This risk aversion and tendency to minimize the number of failures seem to be typical European characteristics since, independent of the sector, the investment stage, and the age, the loss probability of European managers is lower than that of the American peer group. One possible reason for these differing regional approaches might be that the fundraising process is more successful in Europe if the manager has had fewer losses previously. In the U.S. the reverse seems to be the case.

Following the argument above, Europeans are more risk averse than Americans. Considering the total loss ratio it seems that the European strategy is more beneficial in cases

Table 24.1 Descriptive statistics

Dataset description	US			Europe		
	No. of observations	Total loss		No. of observations	Total loss	
		Probability of	Capital ratio		Probability of	Capital ratio
Sector						
Non high-tech	279	8.96%	3.18%	124	5.79%	3.69%
High-tech	328	22.09%	2.66%	110	17.27%	2.37%
Stage						
Early	153	31.37%	2.36%	73	26.03%	2.41%
Expansion	141	7.09%	3.24%	34	8.82%	6.73%
Later	89	8.99%	4.28%	94	3.19%	0.82%
Turnaround	17	11.76%	6.44%	3	0.00%	0.00%
Age						
<1 year	125	15.20%	2.67%	44	15.91%	1.75%
1 to 5 years	217	21.66%	2.57%	309	20.39%	3.20%
<5 to 20 years	177	12.99%	3.55%	196	12.76%	3.42%
<20 years and older	103	1.94%	2.86%	97	1.03%	2.86%

of high risk. The total-loss–capital ratio shows heterogeneous results, therefore it is hard to tell which strategy is more successful considering the total loss – the American or the European one.

24.4 Description of the model

For the statistical examination of the three questions, linear regression analysis is used to analyze the linear dependency between the endogenous variable and the exogenous variables. In order to conduct a reasonable classification of the variables into exogenous and endogenous, a theoretical foundation of the direction of effect has to be worked out in advance, which was discussed in detail in Section 24.2. Accordingly, syndication, the number of the fund manager's managed funds to date, and the classification into VC fund and non-VC fund as exogenous variables affect the endogenous total-loss–capital ratio. The two exogenous variables, syndication and classification of the fund, are dummy variables and have a value of 1 if the criterion is satisfied and a value of 0 if it is not. In applying the method of ordinary least squares, the parameters of the following equation can be estimated in order to prove statistically if the exogenous variables have an effect, how large the effect is, and in which direction the effect goes.

$$Y_i = \beta_0 + \beta_1 \cdot X_{i1} + \beta_2 \cdot X_{i2} + \beta_3 \cdot X_{i3} + \varepsilon_i.$$

In the equation above, Y_i denotes the endogenous variable total-loss–capital ratio, β_0 is the constant, X_1, X_2, X_3 are the exogenous variables with β_1, β_2, β_3 as the

Table 24.2 Regression results of the model test when observing total losses

Variable	Coefficients	Standard error	*t*-statistic	Probability
Constant	0.055256	0.015420	3.583423	0.0005
Number of funds of the fund manager	−0.002337	0.001333	−1.752922	0.0824
VC fund [Y/N]	−0.032374	0.014695	−2.203126	0.0297
Syndication [Y/N]	0.018198	0.005648	3.221744	0.0017
Adjusted R^2	0.232758	Prob (*F*-statistic)		0.0000

corresponding parameters that have to be estimated. ε is called the error term and contains the unexplained component of the regression. In order to have a reasonable interpretation of the regression results, the fundamental assumptions of regression analysis have to be tested. The usual procedures and tests for multicollinearity and autocorrelation do not support the existence of either one, and thus a violation of the regression assumptions, which is hardly unexpected since the exogenous variables have been selected carefully and only cross-sectional data have been used. In contrast, the null hypothesis of homoskedasticity when applying the White heteroskedasticity test and taking the cross-product into account, has to be rejected at the 5% significance level. For this reason, the covariance matrix of the parameters taking heteroskedasticity into account has been estimated consistently after the procedure of White (1980). The regression results can be seen in Table 24.2.

The *F*-statistic tests for the combined significance of the considered exogenous variables on the dependent variable. On the basis of the *F*-distribution, the probability of error for the *F*-value being different from 0 can be determined. If the probability is smaller than the given significance level we refer to this as a significant effect concerning the significance level. In this case, the combined effect of the exogenous parameters on the total regression are significant at the 1% level. After testing for the combined significance of the exogenous variables, the exogenous variables are tested individually for their significance.

24.5 Results

Based on the model developed in the previous section, we test the statistical significance regarding total losses by the use of regression analysis. The regression results can be found in Table 24.2.

Table 24.2 shows that the exogenous variable ‘number of funds of the fund manager’ is significant at the 10% level by taking White’s adjusted covariance matrix into account. The more funds a fund manager has managed so far, the lower the total-loss–capital ratio. Thus, the first question has a positive answer for the whole dataset: that managers reduce the loss per total loss with increasing investment experience. When we look at the regional results (see Table 24.3) we find a very interesting pattern. While the probability of total loss for U.S.-based funds, at 20.5%, is higher for managers that previously managed at least two funds (while 2 is the median for our dataset) than the probability of total loss measured for less experienced managers (11.5%), our findings for European-based funds are diametrically opposed. When we look at the total-loss–capital ratio, we observe

Table 24.3 The impact of manager experience on total losses

No. of previous funds of investment firm at time of investment				No. of observations	Total-loss–capital ratio					Probability of total loss
					Mean	Median	95% percentile	75% percentile	25% percentile	
US										
No. of previous funds ≥ 2	No	Total loss (Y/N)?	No	269	5.60%	4.75%	12.98%	7.01%	2.96%	
			Yes	35	5.04%	3.73%	14.73%	6.50%	2.87%	11.50%
	Yes	Total loss (Y/N)?	No	388	3.63%	2.89%	9.77%	5.11%	1.31%	
			Yes	100	2.85%	1.85%	8.13%	3.90%	0.57%	20.50%
Europe										
No. of previous funds ≥ 2	No	Total loss (Y/N)?	No	54	3.54%	1.28%	17.76%	4.06%	0.82%	
			Yes	22	2.70%	1.56%	6.66%	3.70%	1.05%	28.90%
	Yes	Total loss (Y/N)?	No	77	7.65%	5.75%	18.22%	10.06%	3.09%	
			Yes	11	5.29%	3.66%	16.24%	9.37%	1.85%	12.5%

lower mean results for experienced fund managers in the U.S. and higher mean results for European managers. The pattern changes again when we look at less experienced fund managers. In this case, managers from the U.S. have a higher mean total-loss–capital ratio of 5.04% than European funds at 2.70%. So, in aggregate, we show for U.S.-based funds that the probability of a total loss is higher in the U.S. with experienced managers but, at the same time, the total-loss–capital ratio is lower with experienced funds when compared with less-experienced U.S. funds. Our results for European managers show that the probability of a total loss is lower in Europe with experienced managers but, at the same time, the total-loss–capital ratio is higher with experienced funds in contrast to less-experienced European funds.

These results could be explained by cultural, legal, and regulatory differences between Europe and the U.S. Desai et al. (2003) find that institutional factors induce capital constraints with impact on entry and on the ability of firms to transition and grow, particularly in lesser-developed markets. In Europe, the risk awareness of investors and managers is widespread and therefore one could argue that U.S.-based funds would be willing to take more risk. Also the European VC industry is not as developed as in the U.S., so it is possible that, because the number of previous funds in our dataset is measured by the number of funds of the investment firms and not the manager, in the U.S. more new funds are issued by more experienced managers who previously worked for other investment firms. To further investigate the possibility that U.S.-based investment firms are willing to take more risk, we investigate the two sectors in private equity investments that are considered to be the most risky and that are dominated by U.S.-based private equity firms: high-tech (see Table 24.4) and early stage (see Table 24.5). Our results show that, within these two sectors, the total-loss–capital ratios and the probabilities of total losses are higher in the U.S. than in Europe.

The variable 'syndication' is significant at the 1% level (see Table 24.2). The result gives a positive answer to the second question, in the sense that syndication is conducted in particular in the case of a higher total-loss–capital ratio. We do not interpret this regression result to mean that syndication is the cause of a higher total-loss–capital ratio (causality), but that investors syndicate particularly in the case when stakes contain higher profit chances and, at the same time, a higher risk of default. According to the present work, syndication is used to share the risk among investors and, simultaneously, enable a participation in the higher profit chances. For a better interpretation of the regression results on syndication we introduce a comparison between stakes with, and stakes without, syndication in Table 24.6. As can be seen, a syndicated stake has a higher risk of default for U.S. (16.9%) and European (19.1%) investments compared with non-syndicated investments (13.1% and 7.2%, respectively). This risk of default is not necessarily increased through syndication (causality). Rather, syndication is conducted in the case of a higher risk of default. This supports the idea that in the case of a higher risk, syndication is applied for risk sharing. Apart from the risk of default, the magnitude of the total loss concerning the fund volume can be a risk measure. In a comparison of the average capital share of a stake in the fund investment volume with and without syndication, this share is almost equal in the case of continuation of the company and clearly different in the case of a total loss. The total-loss–capital ratio is considerably higher with syndication in both the U.S. (3.21%) and Europe (2.45%) than without (2.01% and 1.56%, respectively), but the magnitude is much higher in the U.S. than in Europe; this also supports the hypothesis on the risk awareness of European investors.

Table 24.4 High-tech investments and total losses

High-tech				No. of observations	Total-loss–capital ratio					Probability of total loss
					Mean	Median	95% percentile	75% percentile	25% percentile	
US										
High-tech (Y/N)?	No	Total loss (Y/N)?	No	254	5.48%	4.91%	12.99%	7.06%	2.64%	
			Yes	25	3.18%	2.86%	9.44%	4.41%	0.91%	8.96%
	Yes	Total loss (Y/N)?	No	254	3.77%	3.04%	9.71%	5.21%	1.31%	
			Yes	72	2.66%	1.95%	6.81%	3.75%	0.90%	22.09%
Europe										
High-tech (Y/N)?	No	Total loss (Y/N)?	No	114	4.92%	3.12%	17.08%	6.26%	1.66%	
			Yes	7	3.69%	0.61%	13.37%	3.96%	0.48%	5.79%
	Yes	Total loss (Y/N)?	No	91	2.91%	2.00%	7.21%	4.31%	1.07%	
			Yes	19	2.37%	2.24%	4.53%	3.73%	0.88%	17.27%

Table 24.5 Early stage investments and total losses

Early stage				No. of observations	Total-loss–capital ratio					Probability of total loss
					Mean	Median	95% percentile	75% percentile	25% percentile	
US										
Early stage (Y/N)?	No	Total loss (Y/N)?	No	404	5.08%	4.16%	12.24%	6.70%	2.27%	
			Yes	50	3.18%	2.86%	9.06%	3.92%	1.09%	11.01%
	Yes	Total loss (Y/N)?	No	105	2.93%	2.23%	8.02%	3.90%	0.99%	
			Yes	48	2.36%	1.85%	6.05%	3.53%	0.54%	31.37%
Europe										
Early stage (Y/N)?	No	Total loss (Y/N)?	No	158	4.75%	2.64%	15.77%	6.10%	1.20%	
			Yes	7	3.61%	1.27%	12.20%	2.68%	0.97%	4.24%
	Yes	Total loss (Y/N)?	No	54	3.16%	2.34%	6.91%	4.00%	1.27%	
			Yes	19	2.41%	2.05%	5.44%	3.82%	0.68%	26.03%

Table 24.6 The impact of syndication on total losses

Syndication				No. of observations	Total-loss–capital ratio					Probability of total loss
					Mean	Median	95% percentile	75% percentile	25% percentile	
US										
Syndicated (Y/N)?	No	Total loss (Y/N)?	No	245	4.38%	3.58%	12.24%	6.18%	1.21%	
			Yes	37	2.01%	1.01%	12.08%	1.86%	0.32%	13.1%
	Yes	Total loss (Y/N)?	No	138	4.48%	3.77%	11.33%	6.37%	2.38%	
			Yes	28	3.21%	2.59%	9.37%	4.41%	1.14%	16.9%
Europe										
Syndicated (Y/N)?	No	Total loss (Y/N)?	No	142	3.62%	2.13%	10.20%	4.21%	1.09%	
			Yes	11	1.56%	0.84%	6.66%	2.05%	0.43%	7.2%
	Yes	Total loss (Y/N)?	No	38	4.41%	2.40%	15.55%	6.89%	1.37%	
			Yes	9	2.45%	3.28%	4.44%	3.79%	0.75%	19.1%

Table 24.7 Venture capital investments and total losses

VC fund				No. of observations	Total-loss–capital ratio					Probability of total loss
					Mean	Median	95% percentile	75% percentile	25% percentile	
US										
VC fund (Y/N)?	No	Total loss (Y/N)?	No	248	6.39%	5.60%	13.14%	8.24%	3.55%	
			Yes	19	4.70%	3.34%	14.73%	7.68%	2.17%	7.1%
	Yes	Total loss (Y/N)?	No	412	3.26%	2.63%	7.86%	4.50%	1.26%	
			Yes	116	3.21%	2.21%	8.03%	4.31%	0.72%	22.0%
Europe										
VC fund (Y/N)?	No	Total loss (Y/N)?	No	102	6.83%	4.59%	18.22%	9.96%	1.26%	
			Yes	6	6.22%	4.70%	16.24%	10.97%	0.43%	5.6%
	Yes	Total loss (Y/N)?	No	72	2.93%	1.57%	8.35%	4.22%	0.87%	
			Yes	28	2.88%	1.78%	9.37%	3.75%	1.12%	28.0%

For both regions, this confirms that the investor selects syndication not only in the case of a higher risk of default, but that with those stakes, he also takes a larger stake share. From this we can claim that, with those stakes, a higher risk must have been accompanied simultaneously by considerably higher chances of profit. This assumption is supported by the results of Amit et al. (2002), which find syndication particularly with stakes that have a higher expected return.

The exogenous variable 'VC fund' is significant at the 1% level (cf. Table 24.7). Venture capital funds in the U.S. (3.21%) and Europe (2.88%) have a relatively low total-loss–capital ratio per stake compared with other private equity funds (4.70% and 6.22%, respectively). Thus, we have a positive answer for the third question. Venture capital managers operate in a market segment with a higher risk and use instruments such as staging in order to reduce the total-loss–capital ratio per stake. Altogether, the stake risk in the VC segment can be balanced, since the higher risk of default has a reduced total effect on the fund through the relatively smaller total-loss–capital ratio per stake.

For computing the failure probabilities of private equity stakes one cannot use the same variables that are used for credit losses. The choice and weight of the relevant variables for private equity stakes have not yet been decided by theoretical models or empirical surveys. Our results provide three possible variables for models that compute total losses of private equity stakes. More work is needed to identify additional significant variables. If an appropriate number of different variables of sufficient quality are identified, models that are similar to the credit risk models discussed can also be developed for private equity stakes.

24.6 Conclusion

To date, usually no standardized procedures for determining the risk of default have been applied. The transmission of the procedures used by banks for determining credit loss probabilities to the equity capital market is possible only in a limited way. This empirical analysis uses a large dataset to analyze three aspects that play a role in total losses of private equity stakes: (1) private equity and VC companies make their investment decisions mainly on the basis of heuristics and subjective evaluations of the fund management. Furthermore, the investment experience plays an important role in evaluating the risk–return outlook. Our empirical results show that with increasing investment experience of the fund management, the share of a total loss in the fund volume (total-loss–capital ratio) is reduced for European funds but is increased for U.S.-based funds. Therefore, we can argue, more experienced investment firms in the U.S. accept a higher probability of failure for a lower total-loss–capital ratio. In contrast, more experienced European investment firms prefer a lower probability of failure at the expense of a higher total-loss–capital ratio. We conclude that based on cultural differences the more experienced European firms seem to be more focused on the avoidance of a failure than on the amount of lost capital. (2) In the present work, risk sharing as a reason for syndication has been supported by many investors. Our results show a clear relationship between syndication and the higher loss probability as well as the higher total-loss–capital ratio for both U.S.- and European-based funds. From the results, we do not interpret syndication as being a cause for the higher total-loss–capital ratio, but in the case of stakes with particularly high profit and risk chances, the instrument of syndication is more often applied among other reasons for risk reduction. (3) Special risks exist for stakes of young companies in the technology sector. Venture capital funds have specialized in this. These funds can only earn an attractive total return for the fund if they systematically limit the risk of the particular stake as soon as possible. In this, the special know-how and experience of the management, as well as the use of staging, play a role. In staging, the total amount of money is not provided at one time in advance, but is gradually invested in parts, depending on the development of the company. The results of our analysis support the statement that funds with an investment focus on VC ensure that the share of each total loss on the fund volume is relatively small compared with other funds. We did not observe significant differences between European and U.S. funds for the 'VC fund' variable.

This study is the first to provide evidence that there are systematic differences regarding risk for European and U.S.-American VC and private equity investments, measured by the proxy of total losses. Future areas of theoretical and empirical research could include the implications of our findings on the performance or the disposition of resources, and could also include the development of strategies to mitigate the total loss risk, such as disproportionate diversification to hedge against defaults or other methods to limit the operational risks through thorough due diligence processes.

References

Admati, A. and Pfleiderer, P. (1994). Robust Financial Contracting and the Role of Venture Capitalists. *Journal of Finance*, 49(2):371–403.

Amit, R. and Thornhill, S. (2003). Learning about Failure: Bankruptcy, Firm Age and the Resource-based View. *Organization Science*, 14(5):497–509.

Amit, R., Antweiler, W. and Brander, J.A. (2002). Venture-Capital Syndication: Improved Venture Selection vs. the Value Added Hypothesis. *Journal of Economics & Management Strategy*, 11(3):422–452.

Bottazzi, L. and Da Rin, M. (2004). The Changing Face of the European Venture Capital Industry: Facts and Analysis. *Journal of Private Equity*, 8(1):26–53.

Desai, M.A., Gompers, P.A. and Lerner, J. (2003). Institutions, Capital Constraints and Entrepreneurial Firm Dynamics: Evidence from Europe. Harvard NOM Working Paper No. 03–59.

Diller, C. and Kaserer, C. (2004). European Private Equity Funds – A Cash Flow Based Performance Analysis. Center for Entrepreneurial and Financial Studies, München, Working Paper.

Gompers, P.A. (1995). Optimal Investment, Monitoring, and the Staging of Venture Capital. *Journal of Finance*, 50(5):1461–1491.

Gompers, P.A., Kovner, A., Lerner, J. and Scharfstein, D.S. (2005). Venture Capital Investment Cycles: The Impact of Public Markets. NBER Working Paper No. W11385, Cambridge MA.

Hege, U. and Palomino, F. (2003). Determinants of Venture Capital Performance: Europe and the United States. Risk Capital and the Financing of European Innovative Firms Conference No. 1.

Krohmer, P. and Lauterbach, R. (2005). Private Equity Post-Investment Phases – The Bright and Dark Side of Staging. University of Frankfurt, Working Paper, Frankfurt, Germany.

Lerner, J. (1994). The Syndication of Venture Capital Investments. *Financial Management*, 23(3):16–27.

Lockett, A. and Wright, M. (2001). The Syndication of Venture Capital Investments. *Omega International Journal of Management of Science*, 29(5):375–390.

Lockett, A. and Wright, M. (2003). The Structure and Management of Alliances: Syndication in the Venture Capital Industry. *Journal of Management Studies*, 40(8):2073–2104.

Muzyka, D. and Birley, S. (1996). Trade-Offs in the Investment Decisions of European Venture Capitalists. *Journal of Business Venturing*, 11(4):273–288.

Sahlman, W.A. (1990). The Structure and Governance of Venture-Capital Organizations. *Journal of Financial Economics*, 27(2):473–522.

Schmidt, D. and Wahrenburg, M. (2004). Contractual Relations between European VC-Funds and Investors: The Impact of Reputation and Bargaining Power on Contractual Design. University of Frankfurt, Working Paper.

Schwienbacher, A. (2002). An Empirical Analysis of Venture Capital Exits in Europe and in the United States. University of Namur, Working Paper.

White, H. (1980). A Heteroskedasticity-Consistent Covariance Matrix Estimator and a Direct Test for Heteroskedasticity. *Econometrica*, 48(4):817–838.

Wilson, R. (1968). The Theory of Syndicates. *Econometrica*, 36(1):119–132.

Index